Primary Mathematics Today

FOURTH EDITION

Towards the 21st century

Addison Wesley Longman Limited
Edinburgh Gate, Harlow,
Essex, CM20 2JE
and Associated Companies throughout the world.

First published 1970
Second edition 1976
Third edition 1982
Fourth edition 1994
Sixth impression 1997

Set in Times Roman 9 on 11 points

Produced by Longman Singapore Publishers Pte Ltd
Printed in Singapore

ISBN 0 582 08357 5

The publisher's policy is to use paper manufactured from
sustainable forests.

Cover photograph: John Birdsall

PRIMARY MATHEMATICS TODAY

FOURTH EDITION

Towards the 21st century

ELIZABETH WILLIAMS
AND HILARY SHUARD

Revised by Hilary Shuard

PUBLISHER'S NOTE

Hilary Shuard died on Christmas Eve 1992. As the obituary in *Strategies* magazine stated, she was "an outstanding figure in mathematics education over the past few decades." Longman is proud to have worked with her on the four editions of *Primary Mathematics Today* and to dedicate this fourth edition to her memory. We are grateful to Eric Albany for his work on the Appendix, the only part of the book Hilary had not completed.

PREFACE

In recent years, many writing teams have attempted to cover wide ranges of work in modern school mathematics: we have had various series of books from such teams, covering the age range 11–18, together with teachers' guides following work through year by year and topic by topic; we have also had teachers' guides on modern methods in mathematics teaching and some class texts for the age range 5–13. However, very few individual authors, or pairs of authors in collaboration, have attempted the formidable task of covering a wide age range in this way. It is certainly not a task to be set about lightly. Miss Shuard and Mrs Williams are to be congratulated on having tackled it so successfully.

Under one cover we have here a text which brings together, for each stage of development in primary and middle school, both general guidance for the teacher and detailed indications of how to approach the appropriate individual topic in the classroom. If any lecturer, or student in a college of education, or practising teacher in a classroom, is in any doubt about the implications of modernising mathematical work at this level in schools, here is a book to settle his/her doubts. As such, it deserves to become a standard work for all who are concerned to teach mathematics to younger children. It combines in a comprehensive fashion a thoughtfulness about child development with a thorough knowledge of the mathematics needed in this development, together with clear evidence of the authors' knowledge of practical classroom activity in the subject.

W. H. COCKCROFT

University of Hull, 1970

PREFACE TO THE FOURTH EDITION

The task of revising and updating an encyclopedic text such as *Primary Mathematics Today* is a formidable one. It is just over 20 years since it was first published, and the changes over those years in the teaching of mathematics at all levels have been many and varied. The changes we will surely have to face as we move 'towards the 21st century' will no doubt be just as challenging.

Previous new editions have seen the introduction of new material, and the dropping of old, together with appropriate changes of emphasis, all in the light of changing professional thinking about good primary classroom practice. In these respects, the changes in this fourth edition are similar to earlier ones. However, more has had to be done and is to be welcomed: account has been taken of the educational forces now affecting all our work at primary level. The first of these forces, acting indirectly, is the GCSE with its insistence on coursework, and hence on work of an investigational nature; the second, acting directly, is the National Curriculum with its attainment targets and assessment of 7 and 11 year olds.

Finally, consideration of a different but no less important kind is given to the ways in which computers can be used to good effect at this level, in work on databases, on LOGO and turtle geometry, on spreadsheets, and on programming in elementary BASIC.

This edition gives us an opportunity to benefit from Hilary Shuard's present understanding of the links between secondary and primary styles of work, to gain from her inside knowledge of the thinking behind the National Curriculum proposals, and to study in detail her views on how best to incorporate computer-based work into the primary curriculum.

SIR WILFRED COCKCROFT

Warmington, Warwickshire, 1991

CONTENTS

NOTE ON THE STRUCTURE OF THE BOOK

The table below classifies the chapters according to the main themes to which they contribute. The teacher may find it helpful to follow a particular theme, such as the development of the number system, through later chapters. In the early part of the book, odd-numbered chapters often emphasise children's activities, and are followed immediately by chapters which bring out the mathematical structure underlying the activities. Later, children's activities and the ideas on which they are based are so closely interwoven that a separation would be artificial.

Theme	*Chapters*
Children's early mathematical development	1, 2
The number system and number operations	1, 3, 4, 6, 8, 9, 14, 15, 17, 18, 19, 22, 24, 27, 32, 33, 35, 36, 37
Shape and space	1, 5, 10, 12, 23, 25, 34, 35, 36, 38
Quantity and its measurement	7, 16, 26, 29, 30
Probability and handling data	20, 21
The use of mechanisms	13, 31
The use of calculators	9, 17, 19, 27, 33
Computing	11, 28
The unity of mathematical structure	39

INTRODUCTION

The intention of this book is to present a survey of primary school mathematics in the light of the important changes in mathematics, its uses and modes of teaching, which have been taking place in recent years and continue to demand the attention of teachers. The book is not in the first instance a text-book of mathematics for teachers. It is rather a study of primary children learning mathematics in newer ways. We try to show how children can, with the help of a sympathetic and encouraging teacher, take part in a meaningful programme. Some mathematical ideas and procedures which may be new to many teachers are, however, explained alongside those sections of the text where we describe activities through which they may be presented to children.

The major influences making for change have come from many sources but each has played a part in shaping the fuller and more coherent programme which we attempt to set out here. New thinking and new inventions are affecting every aspect of mathematical education. Deeper insight into children's ways of learning is modifying our conception of the means by which the development of their thinking can be stimulated and guided. In the early decades of this century the work of Binet on the psychology of reasoning and his interest in the role that everyday activities can play in its growth became well known. Many teachers began to observe in their own classrooms children's responses to practical situations. Maria Montessori and Margaret Macmillan strengthened the movement through their programmes of free constructive play both with objects in common use and with specially designed materials. In recent decades the influence of Piaget has been strong. His experiments revealed the many misunderstandings and misinterpretations of simple natural phenomena which occur with children who have not had enough experience to bring out the true relationships involved. Of even greater importance is his record of observation of the stages of development of children's thinking and its dependence on the individual's reactions to actual objects and their properties. The art of teaching is being transformed into the art of devising situations in which children will wish to probe, to organise things and ideas encountered in the world, and to make connections between them.

During their explorations children shape their perceptions into clear thoughts; these they can display in pictures, diagrams, models and symbols which will be memorable to themselves and meaningful to others. This is the start of mathematical thinking.

More recently, the idea has clarified that children are not empty vessels which the teacher can fill with mathematical knowledge. Instead, children are, at every level, thinking beings who need to *construct* their own mathematical meanings through reflecting on their experiences, and putting together ideas which they draw from a wide diversity of experience. Thus, each new mathematical idea must develop in children's minds through their own activities, handling objects, comparing measurements or shapes, reflecting on the results of experiments and communicating them to others. Much of children's work will be a co-operative effort. A group of children will often explore freely, with the teacher's guidance, a situation which interests them. Each child needs to take the new knowledge thus gained, see it in relation to other mathematical ideas and thus build up an organised mental structure. Systematisation which has no basis of ideas springing from experience has too often been a feature of mathematical education in the past. Experience which children never build into an inter-related body of ideas would be equally regrettable. In this book we try to show how to form a foundation for coherent mathematical thinking.

In the contemporary scene there are three factors which help children to acquire an understanding and mastery of operations with numbers in decimal notation. First is the introduction of various types of apparatus designed to illustrate numerical notation and procedures. By means of their own experimenting children can learn how a number system is built up, how operations can be carried out on numbers, and what relationships can be discovered among certain sets of numbers. The particular value of material based on the cube is seen in its limitless extension, through cuboids and cubes, which matches the possible continuation of number notation both to the left and to the right. The second factor is the worldwide use of decimal currencies. This provides not only representations of different denominations in the decimal scale of numbers but also an array of activities connected with shopping which demand accurate operations within the decimal system. Thirdly, there is the use of metric units of measure. Although their adoption is not yet universal they are now so familiar in everyday use that they can give children valuable opportunities of mastering decimal fractions.

The two most recent additions to mathematical equipment, and the most dramatic innovations, are the microcomputer and the pocket calculator. Calculators are very cheap and portable, and are now almost universally used, whenever adults need to make calculations beyond the range of their mental skills. Calculator use is now permitted in public examinations, and even at the primary age, many children now have a calculator of their own. Computers have become familiar pieces of equipment in primary classrooms, and many children also have access to a computer at home. As soon as children can count they begin to be interested in what a calculator can do. From quite early days they will check their own answers to simple additions against those of the electronic device and thus build up memorable sequences. There will be similar experiments with the other number operations. The recognition of *which* operation is needed must come from realistic experience of problem situations but much can be learned by realising what the calculator has produced. Its results must fit in with the expectations and estimates that the children have based on their insights into the problem. It must be seen to check; otherwise the procedures must be re-examined. A mistake may have been made in planning the operations which the calculator is to carry out, or the wrong key may have been pressed. Children soon learn from a calculator the effects of each basic operation; they see how numbers can be related; they feel free from the burden of repetitive procedures; they can undertake formidable computations which produce concise and useful results within a few seconds of calculator time. Such a tool must have a considerable effect on school programmes.

It is often thought that the major use of the calculator at the primary stage is as a tool which enables children easily to carry out arithmetic operations using decimal notation. This view underestimates the value of the calculator; children who use calculators learn a great deal about the structure of numbers from the calculator. Certainly, before children can use calculators effectively they must have a limited knowledge of how numbers are written, and of place value notation, so that they

can appreciate the meaning of a digit in different places. As that knowledge grows so will their range of skills with the calculator. They must also have learned the nature of the operation they wish to perform, both in practical terms and in the relationship between the numbers they are handling. For instance, if children are combining two sets of the same kind of objects, or finding the total cost of two purchases, or putting together two quantities of the same material, the numbers may be small enough for them to identify the operation required, carry out the addition mentally, and record the result in symbols. When a wider range of numbers is involved, including decimal fractions, the calculator will give results which can be examined and given an approximate check. Understanding thus grows through the use of the calculator; and the instrument itself stimulates its effective use. Teachers will want children to record the calculator's operations. Three entries can be made: the statement of the required operation, an estimate of the result, and the reading on the calculator.

The influence of the calculator on the teaching of multiplication and division is far-reaching. The numbers that emerge have more digits and written calculations are complicated; this encourages the use of a calculator. At this point children become aware that a calculator does not use the conventional two-number way of writing a common fraction. For example, $\frac{3}{4}$ must be given decimal form; this can be found on the calculator by dividing 3 by 4. In this book we have discussed recent developments in the treatment of decimals and fractions. As the operations required to solve a problem become more complicated it becomes necessary for the children to list each operation in the right order. This scheme will then be carried through and in due course recorded and checked. This is essential since most calculators can exhibit only one number in the display.

The calculator has uses other than computations. It can show the patterns that are made by repeating operations, e.g. adding 2, or multiplying by 10; relations between operations or between certain sets of numbers can be investigated without the burden of repeated written calculations. The calculator can be the instrument of enquiry.

The other numerical electronic device which has become available in schools in the last ten years is the computer. Simple mathematically orientated software has made computers very valuable in the learning of mathematics, even by young children. In Chapter 11 we discuss the use of LOGO, a piece of software which is very attractive to young children. LOGO enables children to use the computer as a drawing tool, thus investigating many aspects of shape, and making procedures which instruct the computer to draw pictures of their own design. Database software is also discussed in this chapter; a database can help children to organise data that they have gathered from surveys, and to look for connections between different items of data. In Chapter 28, more advanced mathematical software, which is suitable for older primary children, is discussed. The types of software considered are spreadsheets, which can be used to simplify tabulation and calculation with numerical data, and the BASIC programming language, which is well adapted to writing simple programs to handle numbers. The rapid growth in the day-to-day use of calculators and computers has now brought them into the environment of the majority of people. Education must therefore provide children with some skill in their use, so that when they become adults they will be able to use this developing technology with knowledge and confidence.

A change which has presented difficulties to some teachers is the broadening of the content of mathematics in the primary school. Some of the material which has been introduced into primary schools was previously taught at the secondary stage, and this material is familiar to primary teachers, although its presentation to younger children is necessarily different. But some ideas now being introduced are unfamiliar in school mathematics. A similar development can be seen in the teaching of science; both subjects have grown and changed tremendously over the years. The first new schemes of secondary school mathematics, such as the first series from the School Mathematics Project, were greatly influenced by developments in mathematicians' understanding of the structure of their subject. More recent schemes have been influenced by the growth of comprehensive secondary education, and the need to make a broad understanding of mathematics available to as many people as possible. The introduction of the Certificate of Secondary Education (CSE), followed by the General Certificate of Secondary Education (GCSE), have had a substantial influence, in particular through the requirement for children to undertake investigative coursework in GCSE. As mathematics has broadened and changed, it has become clear that some of the ideas with which mathematicians work are so fundamental and so simple that children can use them with understanding in their first approaches to shape, number, measures and other aspects of mathematics. Moreover, children understand mathematics better when these fundamental ideas

are used from the beginning. Changes do not then have to be made in the approach at a later stage.

The most recent development in the school mathematics curriculum in England and Wales is the introduction of a National Curriculum for all pupils aged 5 to 16. The National Curriculum is stated in terms of Attainment Targets at ten increasing levels of difficulty. At the ages of 7, 11, 14 and 16, each child is assessed, and assigned a level on each Attainment Target. Thus, each class contains children who are working at different levels, and most children are working at different levels on different Attainment Targets.

In mathematics there are five Attainment Targets. These Attainment Targets ensure that a broad curriculum is attempted, as the targets cover the themes of Number, Algebra, Measures, Shape and Space, and Handling Data. Each theme appears at every level, to ensure that each child's work in mathematics develops continuously. A further theme, which is intended to permeate and influence all the work in mathematics, is that of Using and Applying Mathematics. This theme requires that children should investigate practical problems, problems drawn from the whole curriculum, and real-life problems; children should also undertake investigations within mathematics itself. Within this theme, value is placed on children's planning for a task, on the mathematical thinking which they undertake when carrying out the task, and on their communication of the results in oral, written or visual form.

In most chapters of this book, the last section draws attention, for the use of readers in England and Wales, to the Attainment Targets which are dealt with in that chapter. In these sections, there is less mention of Using and Applying Mathematics than of the content themes. However, it will be apparent to the reader that the book makes it clear that children learn mathematics through using and applying it in practical problems, in real-life situations, and in the practical exploration of mathematical ideas. It would be excessively tedious for the reader if the Attainment Target on Using and Applying Mathematics were quoted in full at the end of every chapter.

The basic mathematical ideas which teachers need to understand are few in number and are easy to grasp in terms of our everyday experience. One basic concept springs from children's ability to recognise and pick out things which are alike or different. When children have made a collection of things which have some common property, such as colour, size, position or purpose, they have had a first experience of the basic concept of a *set*. It will be seen that it is derived from children's capacity to *classify*. Before children learn to count they will meet the notion of *correspondence* when they handle sets of things. For example, if they have a set of spoons and a set of forks it may happen that to each fork there corresponds a spoon and vice versa. The two sets have the same number. Number *operations* are studied very carefully in a modern programme, in order to see the effects of an operation, the conditions under which it can work and the situations in which it proved to be useful.

Another aspect of the material is the study of *change* and *movement*. Change includes the important process of growth and will often be exhibited in graphs. The idea of *invariance*, that is, of a property which is not altered when certain changes are made, is of great importance; for instance, the fact that pouring water from one container to another of different shape does not alter the quantity of water lies at the basis of the measurement of volume. Movement, or change of position, is investigated in connection with the changes, or *transformations*, which certain movements bring about in lines and shapes. Its study is carried further by examining the movements of basic mechanisms, such as the lever and the wheel, and the ways in which they are activated and controlled. Experiments with such mechanisms are practical illustrations of mathematical relationships and are discussed in Chapters 13 and 31.

The book begins with children's first experiences of objects and events, and traces the growth of mathematical ideas in the light of the findings of research on the development of children's thinking. Properties of space become familiar to children at an early age; recognition of shape, relative position and size precedes awareness of number. The experience of handling objects and using them constructively yields mental patterns which are necessary to the mental activity of thinking. Children need to find means of representing such properties as *order, correspondence* and *ratio* if they are to develop the mental imagery on which mathematical growth depends. This representation may be in symbols or number sentences, or by means of tabulations or diagrams, or it may be in words. Children are forming continually, deliberately or spontaneously, images of the objects of their thoughts. These images are a necessary part of the understanding of abstract ideas. It is a remarkable fact that our number system is very clearly represented by points on a line; operations on numbers can be matched by operations on

lengths marked on a line. The use of such a *number line* is fully developed in this book.

The plan of the book is based on the stages of development of children's thinking from their early intuitions to the capacity for handling abstract ideas which is becoming evident at the end of the primary school. The lines of growth are followed through in fields such as spatial properties, number and computation, the measurement of quantity, movement and mechanisms, probability and data handling, and the use of calculators and computers. Although these aspects are often treated in separate chapters in the early part of the book, their inter-connections are constantly stressed so that the unity of mathematics is not lost. For example, spatial apparatus is used to stimulate understanding of shape, size and number. Another link is found in studying movement which is fundamental to operations with numbers, to measuring, to changes of shape and position, and to mechanisms. For older primary children, the aspects have become so closely interwoven that they are often treated as a unity, for instance in the handling of such topics as graphs, ratios and approximations.

Not all children can be expected to cover all the subject-matter that is suggested. The age of transfer from primary to secondary schools is varied and some children are able to follow a fuller programme. In any case, some children need the challenge that some of the more difficult topics offer. Mathematics is a growing body of knowledge which is used extensively and powerfully in the contemporary world. The patterns and structures which are its concern are essential to many adult occupations. Children want to find out about ideas which they can see are important; we should encourage them to use their curiosity and inventiveness to the full.

This new edition has enabled us to include numerous extensions and modifications of the text and the sample scheme. We have made various improvements to the diagrams, usually intended to give clearer clarity. It is our hope that primary school teachers, whether in infant, junior, first or middle schools, will find that this book gives them a confident command of the mathematics it presents and a good stock of realistic suggestions for planning children's effective learning.

The book should also be helpful to students on initial teacher education courses as well as to experienced teachers. Only a minority of primary teachers have had special mathematical training; the language and the ideas presented here have therefore been kept as simple as possible. Over-simplification, however, would carry the risk

that major mathematical points would be missed or
distorted. We are encouraged by the persistence and
imaginative adaptability of teachers who have
worked with us, and who have played a
considerable part in the development of the ideas in
this book, to believe that very many teachers will be
prepared to find a new light and fresh enjoyment in
a renewed study of mathematics.

FIRST DISCOVERIES

1 | *The Child's First Discoveries*

EARLY EXPERIENCES

A child is born into a world of space and time. Events take place in succession, often with a pattern of repetition and routine. People and objects come and go, move and change. Experiences appear to come in isolation, as sensations provoking a physical or emotional response; e.g. a child may *see* a bright light, *hear* a tone of voice, or *feel* the touch of his or her own body. There is little that is obviously mathematical in such experiences but gradually repetition of a sensation brings recognition of the thing repeated, for instance the sight of a feeding cup, or the sound of mother's footsteps. Change, particularly movement, draws attention to the changing object and stimulates awareness of it. For example, the shape of a feeding cup becomes obviously known, and if it is removed the baby's eyes follow its movement. An unfamiliar object, say a cat, is noticed just because it moves, whereas unmoving objects form an undifferentiated background. During the five years before starting school a child has a vast range of experiences building up familiarity with a great variety of things and the ways in which they change. These are sorted out and related to one another. All children have pre-school experiences of this kind and it is out of this body of natural early mathematical activity that the future learning of mathematics must grow.

PERMANENCE

Although children begin early to recognise things, they do not at first realise that things are still in existence when they are not seen. For instance, if a toy is hidden, a child behaves in the early stages as though it had disappeared for ever. In time, through putting things in certain places and finding them again, watching a thing disappear and reappear, or enclosing a toy inside a box, a child learns that things continue to exist when out of sight. This awareness of *conservation*, as it is called, is essential if a child is to realise that a set will still have as many things in it when it is rearranged, or have the same amount of biscuit if it is broken into two or more parts. We deal with this notion of constancy again in later chapters when we consider counting and measuring.

RECOGNITION OF LIKENESSES AND DIFFERENCES

The sorting or classifying of experiences depends on recognising similarities and differences. This is seen clearly in children's awareness of shape. They identify a shape in a very general way, not perceiving minor differences, but rejecting a shape that is substantially different in its general outline. This recognition, though *global*, is definite. A child under 2 years of age will firmly reject a substitute for a favourite Teddy or his/her own spoon or bowl. An adult has similar experience of forming a general impression without registering detail. For instance, in driving through a strange town we may receive a series of unanalysed impressions. On a second visit we have a sense of 'having been here before', yet without recognising particular features. With repeated visits more detail is observed and changes from previous observations will be noticed. A young child first notices large obvious differences such as the general outlines of shape, whether a box

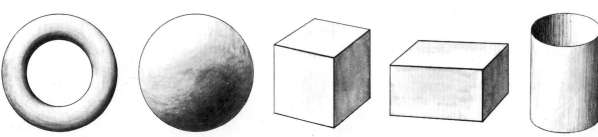

Figure 1 : 1

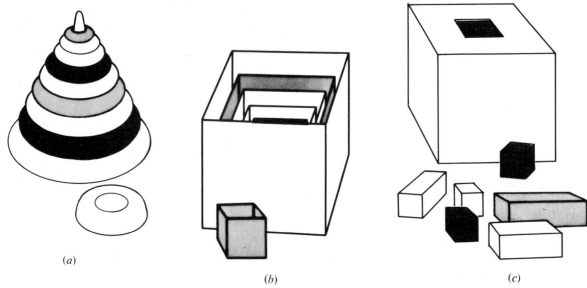

(a)

(b)

(c)

Figure 1 : 2

is open or closed, whether there are any holes or big dents in a surface, or if one dog is considerably larger than another. With more experience finer differences and more detailed likenesses are noticed. It is through handling an object and discovering what can be done with it that a child comes to notice some of its properties. Children soon discriminate between some things that are very similar and recognise certain ways in which they differ: whether they are round or have corners; whether they are big or small, near or far away, and so on. Some of these shapes are shown in Figure 1 : 1.

Differences of shape, size and position become familiar and are more precisely distinguished. Thus we can see that a child's awareness of mathematical properties comes from three types of experience:

i) repetition of experiences of the *same* object or event

ii) the contrast between two *different* things or events

iii) the child's own *manipulation* of things or *observation* of their behaviour.

THE INFLUENCE OF PLAY

Children's voluntary activities are most clearly seen in their play. At first, actions are purely exploratory and manipulative; children discover the things around them, and what they can do with these things, including their own limbs. It is chiefly through movement, sight and touch that discoveries

come at this stage, known as the stage of *sensori-motor* perception. A wide range of toys, differing in colour, size and shape, and providing opportunities for a variety of movements and arrangements, proves invaluable from an early age. Three different types of mathematical toy are shown above to illustrate the kind of shape and the forms of activity which will give important mathematical ideas over a period of several years.

First the *shapes* are distinguished. If an adult selects a ring, or a cube or a box from these three toys children of a year or so will choose a ring, a cube or a box to match the toy which the adult has chosen. Later, children try to reconstruct toys such as (a) or (b) but fail because they cannot yet discriminate between the sizes of the rings or boxes. Before 2 years of age they can put a ring on the mushroom stalk (a), a small box into the larger open box (b) and a cube into the slot in the top of box (c). But only by chance do they choose the right *sizes* to put *two* rings on the mushroom or *two* boxes into the larger one. Further possibilities of experiment with these toys are discussed on page 59.

Realistic toys such as animals, cotton reels, beakers, miniature cars, are a valuable source of mathematical perceptions but it is significant that children enjoy toys like those in Figure 1 : 2 which are constructed entirely on a mathematical pattern. Play with such materials shows that children spontaneously take to the sorting and matching which the toys stimulate. All through the primary school children need to experiment with both kinds of things: the realistic in which mathematics can be discovered, and the structural which make mathematical relations easy to see.

Bodily movements are an equally important source of perceptions. Stretching, turning, balancing, climbing and clapping give notions of position, distance, direction and rhythm, all of which will be developed at a later stage.

THE INFLUENCE OF ENVIRONMENT

Toys are given to children not only for enjoyment but also to provide activities which increase their understanding of the things around them. But the incidents of daily life are at least as stimulating to a growing awareness of how things and people are related to one another and to the child. The variety of what goes on around children is immense; their own actions are nearly as diverse. Children put spoons in cups, see over the table, find that they are growing out of shoes. They turn handles, want more to drink, and so on. They watch the movements of people, cars and wheels, and see how to fit lids on to tins. It is from these experiences with actual things and people that mathematical ideas are developed. In due time an abstract mathematical idea will be distilled from some of them, e.g. the idea of roundness or of one thing fitting on to another. This idea will itself become so real a part of mental life that in its turn it will be related to other ideas and so give rise to new abstractions. This foundation of practical experience is essential to a coherent growth of mathematical insights and is needed as a basis for each extension into a new field of mathematical thinking.

REACTIONS TO ENVIRONMENT

When children encounter new experiences they try to relate them to previous experiences of a similar kind. They recognise some elements which are alike, and often identify the new thing completely with the old. Thus a child who has only known a dog among animals will assume that a new kind of animal is also a dog, although it may be a cat or a deer. This may mean that some aspect of the new object or event is distorted to make it fit into the previous idea. For example, a child who has a doll which will lie in a toy cot will expect that a much larger doll will do the same thing. It is from watching such actions that we can see which ideas have already formed in the child's mind. When children meet discrepancies with what they already know they may simply ignore them, putting the new

thing aside or pretending that it did behave as expected. In such cases children learn nothing new and do not extend the range of their ideas. Alternatively, they may experiment and compare, and thus realise that in some respects there is a difference between the new experience and the old; thus observation enlarges children's fields of understanding. For example, the child whose doll is too long for the cot may try first one doll and then the other and be led to a comparison of lengths. When children accommodate their actions and thinking to the new experiences they change their own patterns of behaviour and modify their earlier concepts.

PERCEPTION AND THE DEVELOPMENT OF LANGUAGE

Young children recognise and differentiate many things before they use any language to name or describe them. As children begin to rely more on perception of things around them, so great a number of impressions come to them that they need to be able to represent them in some way. Just as language develops through the need to talk about the categories of things that are important in everyday life, such as drink, bed, dog, car, so mathematical language is needed to describe the experiences of shape, pattern and relationship that children find in their active play and observation. A child's vocabulary soon includes such words as *more, hole, under, round, flat, out, tall, sharp, fast, gone, throw*. Most of these refer to shape, size, position or movement. The use of these words in conversation with others helps a child to form an idea of a range of objects or situations to which a word applies and to recognise the common elements that belong to them. Words are also an aid in distinguishing the qualities that belong to some objects and not to others. For example, 'car' is at first used for any vehicle or model that has a general shape of bonnet, body and wheels. Later 'lorry' names a special type within the notion of 'car'. As discrimination grows, 'tractor', 'fire engine' etc. are named from their shapes.

Words also help to make relationship clear, e.g. *'inside', 'belongs to', 'more', 'some', 'all'*. As experience increases, the words are used more precisely and show the greater discrimination which a child is using. It can be seen that this recognition of special subdivisions within a whole category is the starting-point for the partitioning of collections of things which leads to the operations of adding and subtracting (*see page 100*). At every stage of mathematical education we find that new discoveries demand the development of a language that gives the neatest expression to the relations and operations that are being considered. The way is then open for further discoveries through the use of the ideas expressed in language.

REPRESENTATION

Language is not the only way in which experiences are represented. Play becomes representational while continuing also to include purely manipulative activities. For example, boxes will serve as garages for toy cars. Children act out, with whatever materials are available, events that have interested them in their surroundings, and they reveal in so doing what it is that has impressed them. They also represent interesting objects by others that are at hand, which have properties that make them suitable symbols; for instance, a child may use a rod as a train. In these procedures children are calling on mental patterns that they have already formed, and are developing them further through their actions. The patterns and form of events and things are taking shape in their minds, as their ability to use representative objects shows. As examples we can quote the child who plays at pouring out spoonfuls of medicine to give to the dolls, matching a spoonful to the dolls in turn; or a child may float a piece of wood for a ship, recognising that wood floats on water. In each case an awareness of a mathematical relationship is shown in the particular representation, but it is clearly without precision.

Further attempts at representation either in play or in drawing, or it may be in imitation, may reveal to the child the shortcomings of the representation and lead to the realisation of details and relations that had previously escaped notice. For instance, the child may observe that trucks must be fastened together if they are to be pulled. Moreover, the

manipulation of symbolic objects, their combination or separation, may be possible when the original objects are too large or inaccessible, as in the case of a child who acts or draws an aircraft landing.

The growth in understanding that comes from devising a way of representing a thing or a situation will be seen in later chapters both in regard to number and to spatial properties. To the teacher a study of children's spontaneous representations reveals the mental structures that they have already formed, the properties of which they are aware and those that have so far not been fully realised. Piaget[1] notes the difficulty a child has in drawing a house or a tree on the side of a hill and shows that at 5 or 6 years of age they will be drawn perpendicular to the slope as in Figure 1 : 3, instead of vertically. This representation shows that the idea of vertical and horizontal has not yet been fully established (*see page 360*).

EARLY SPATIAL CONCEPTS

In the early stages children have no interest in *How much?* or *How many?* Questions of quantity and number do not enter into their play. *'Big'* is used only to distinguish an object from a *'little'* one. A child may miss a *particular* toy, but does not notice if an *unnamed* one, say a brick or car, is missing from several of the same kind. We see that children's first discoveries of a mathematical kind are concerned with space. Notions of quantity and number develop later. Even in children's growing awareness of spatial properties of space and position, they ignore the properties that include some idea of measurement, such as those of lengths of straight lines and the size of angles. These have no place in their thinking although they may move in straight lines and push trucks along straight paths. For example, in making a fenced yard for a set of miniature animals, a child may make opposite sides neither equal nor straight. Children notice what are called *topological* properties first, i.e. those not involving measurement but concerned with such things as the general outline of a shape, whether it is open or closed or has one or more holes in it, the nearness of one thing to another, the position of a thing between two others. Thus, though distance has little meaning for them, they understand what is meant by *'next to'* and *'between'*.

These trends can be observed in children's interest in fitting or pushing things into holes, in

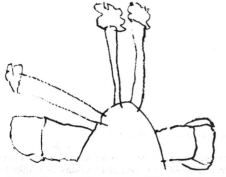

Figure 1 : 3 *Trees and houses on a hill. Age 5 years*

[1]Piaget, J. *The Child's Conception of Space*, page 382.

their arrangement of their toys, and in their interest in their own position relative to members of the family. From these first simple relationships will develop the number and spatial concepts which are fundamental to mathematics.

THE PRELUDE TO NUMBER

The value of the early experience of handling a variety of things and playing with them freely is that children build up many mental pictures and store up memories of patterns of actions. These they can recall and use for identification of similar objects. Recognition comes from recall of touch, sound or movement, and their association with a mental picture of the thing itself. From a wealth of such activities there gradually emerges a notion of a whole *class* of things which are alike in some way and can be distinguished from all others. It starts with recognising that there is *another* thing like the first, and then *another* and *another*, and so on. This is the beginning of true classification and the idea of a *set* or recognisable collection of things.

Another idea, which develops later, is that of an *order* or *sequence*. This may be an order of events, such as putting on one's clothes, or an order of size as in placing dolls or cars in order of size, the largest first. It is important to notice that this making of a sequence begins (as in the making of a set) by taking only two things at first and selecting the 'big one' and placing the 'small one' next to it. Another one of the set is then taken and placed where it will fit in size, first if it is the biggest, last if it is the smallest, or between the other two if it is smaller than one and bigger than the other.[2] It can be seen that this is a complicated judgement to make and few children can deal with more than three things in this way before the age of five.[3] Yet most children will have now developed a clear idea of two—two shoes, two children, two biscuits—and will be able to relate two things in a variety of ways: smaller, nearer, under, etc. But the general idea of a number has yet to be reached.

These two ideas of *set* and *sequence* are fundamental to the understanding of number, time, measurement and many other important mathematical concepts. They may be compared with the two types of pattern found in music and analysed only at a much later age:

i) a chord as a set of notes played together,

ii) a tune as a sequence of notes, and a rhythm as a sequence of time intervals.

The practical experiences of likenesses, differences, regularities and relationships, from which these two basic ideas of a set and a sequence develop, are necessary for their proper growth. At 5 years of age children still need many such experiences. For those whose play activities have hitherto been restricted, a considerable range of manipulative and representative forms of play have to be provided. Before such an abstract and complex idea as number can be formed in children's minds they need to have carried out with concrete materials these operations of sorting, separating, combining and ordering, out of which a number sequence grows.

[2]Cf. the story of the three bears.

[3]Cf. the ordering of sizes possible with the toys shown in Figure 1 : 2(*a*) and (*b*). This can be done by children in a practical experimental way with the rings or cubes.

2 | THE GROWTH OF THINKING: PATTERNS IN THE MIND

THE DAWN OF THINKING

Mathematics is concerned with structures and operations, i.e. with mental images and the ways in which they can be manipulated in the mind. In other words, mathematics depends upon thinking.

New-born children respond to certain physical sensations with physical responses. Thinking comes with the development of the body, with experiences of movement, and with the growing activity of the brain in recording and organising impressions. These impressions may be the result of impacts from outside or of a child's own movements. As soon as they can move and see, children begin to come to terms with their environment. They have to develop awareness of the different kinds of order and relatedness that will help them to recognise, forecast and control both their own actions and the behaviour of things around them. There are three mathematical fields of experience, each having its own characteristic kinds of relationships, which children must become familiar with: the experience of *space*, the experience of *number,* and the experience of *quantity.* These are not entirely separate. Numbers are used in a world of space and can tell us about some of its properties. Certain shapes can be so organised that they illustrate the ways in which numbers are related. Figure 2 : 1 shows two ways of putting 4 cubes together, and the arrangement of 9 triangular tiles in rows holding 1, 3, 5 tiles.

Without number we cannot measure quantity since we must count the measuring units. Yet comparisons of quantity lead to a deeper understanding of numbers as well as revealing some unnoticed properties of space. For instance, measuring a length will show that whole numbers

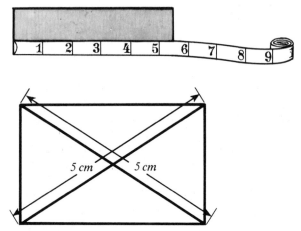

Figure 2 : 2

cannot give us a sufficiently exact answer, and we have to think about fractions. Measuring the lengths of the two diagonals of a rectangle suggests that the diagonals must be equal (Figure 2 : 2).

Mathematical thinking develops through active experience in all three fields. Action and experience necessarily precede thinking. As Piaget says,[1] 'Thought can only replace action on the basis of the data which action itself provides.'

During this century psychologists have made extensive studies of the development of thought in children. In particular Piaget and the investigators who worked with him at his research institute in Geneva spent many years in trying to trace the gradual growth of ideas about numbers, quantity and space, and in studying the ways in which children's thinking changes as they grew older. The

[1] Piaget, J. *The Child's Conception of Space*, page 453.

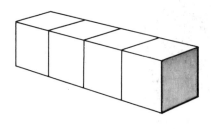
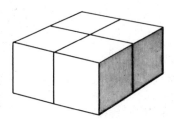
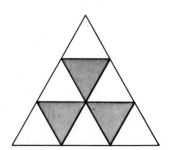

Figure 2 : 1

great majority of children do not think like adults until adolescence. The complex processes of thought are acquired gradually, developing from the extremely simple forms found in the young infant. What the psychologists have observed is of the greatest importance to teachers in planning the experiences they will offer to children. It is these experiences of making discoveries through their own actions and attempting to express what they have discovered which enable children to *think* mathematics instead of merely carrying out operations mechanically and without real understanding. Moreover, familiarity with the characteristic growth of children's thinking helps a teacher to identify the stage which an individual child has reached. Many of the experiments and observations undertaken and analysed by the Geneva School have been repeated in this country and checked by alternative methods. Not all Piaget's findings have been confirmed but a considerable number have been verified and a general pattern of development seems to have been established.

Stages of growth

The following stages of growth have been distinguished, though some writers number them differently and different children learn at different rates.

i) The *period of sensori–motor intelligence,* from birth to about $1\frac{1}{2}/2$ years: when sensations and actions are the important things in children's experience and the means through which they learn.

ii) The *period of preparation for and organisation of concrete operations*
(*a*) from about $1\frac{1}{2}/2$ years to about 4 years: the stage when *representation* becomes possible in the form of language, imaginative play and drawing
(*b*) from about 4 years to about 7 or 8 years: the period of *intuitive thinking* when judgements about size, shape, relationships, etc., are based on children's experiences and their interpretations of their experiences, and are made without reasoning
(*c*) from about 7 or 8 years to 12 years or later: the stage when *logical operations* can be carried out *with concrete materials* or in a particular situation.

iii) *The period of formal operations*: logical operations can now be carried out in the mind without the aid of concrete materials.

These stages are fairly well-marked but the ages differ among children. Their rate of development depends in part on innate ability but there is strong evidence that it is considerably influenced by the kind and range of exploratory and constructional activities that have been open to a child. The transition from one stage to the next is not sudden. A child will show on occasion during stage 1 some of the characteristic thinking of stage 2, and during stage 2 will sometimes operate at the level of stage 1.

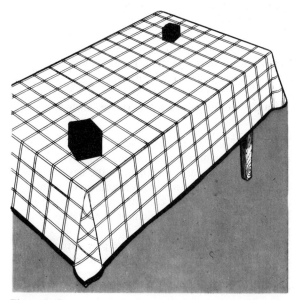

Figure 2 : 3

Figure 2 : 4

Regression to an earlier way of thinking may take place at any age in the face of a completely novel situation or a very difficult problem. We will now examine each of these stages in more detail.

STAGE 1: THE PERIOD OF SENSORI–MOTOR INTELLIGENCE

In this stage children pass from experiencing actions and sensations as unrelated episodes to the co-ordination of the images received and the systematisation of actions. Children discover that things continue to exist even when they cannot see them (*see page 19*). This means that a child has a mental picture and not merely the direct image of an object seen. The establishment of a mental picture of a thing not seen is the prerequisite of thinking. The awareness that things still exist when they are out of sight is then extended. An object may be moved nearer to a child or farther away, or turned in another direction. The object looks different but the child now recognises that it is the same object although its *apparent* size and its *apparent* shape have changed with the shift of position.

The examination of Figures 2 : 3 and 2 : 4 will show how skilled is this recognition of sameness. It seems to develop through handling, say, the brick in Figure 2 : 3 and seeing the different representations of its shape as the hands turn it about. This variety of shapes gives rise to a composite mental picture and from this the brick in any position will be *perceived,* i.e. recognised as a brick when any *particular* visual image of it is presented. Similarly *movement* of an object, or of a child relative to the object, will produce awareness of the constancy of the object in spite of its apparent change of size or shape.

It will be noticed that the things which children are learning to recognise in different positions are all seen in relation to themselves. Although children move objects about they do not yet relate them in their minds to one another. The objects remain independent of one another in their thinking.

The systematising of actions which takes place during this period is particularly important because the organisation of simple movements is the foundation of the mental structures which will develop in subsequent stages. For example, children learn to *reverse actions,* such as picking up and putting down, and this is a preliminary to going back in thought, as when children see that $3 + 2 = 5$ implies that $5 - 2 = 3$. Children also carry out *chains of actions* leading to a satisfactory result; for instance, a child sees a toy on a chair, crawls across the floor and reaches up to take it. This is the forerunner to following out a chain of thought to reach a new understanding or to work out a plan. The two procedures of reversing and forming a chain can then be combined and the whole sequence of actions can be reversed.

Towards the end of this period children begin to make experiments with things. For example, they put one brick on another to see whether it will balance to make a tower. This foreshadows with concrete material the experiment in the mind which adults carry out when faced with a difficult situation, they *think out* or picture what would happen if they took a certain line of action. They may imagine two or more possible courses of action, visualising their results, and then selecting the one which will lead to success. As Piaget says, 'A logic of action precedes a logic of thought.'

Their dependence of the development of thinking on patterns of action continues through Stages 1 and 2. New types of thinking require new action patterns as a necessary preliminary.

STAGE 2(A): THE DEVELOPMENT OF REPRESENTATION

In Stage 2(a) the power of representation emerges. This is probably the most powerful instrument of mathematical thinking, as we shall see when we consider the part played by symbols in later periods. Speech provides the first symbols which come to stand for the composite pictures and the patterns of action which have been developed in the mind during Stage 1. Children can use word symbols to state briefly:

i) a pattern of *action*, e.g. 'I will *fetch* the ball'

ii) a *collection* of things, e.g. *all* the balls

iii) a *connection* between two things, such as a ball *in* the basket.

These symbols can be combined to represent a complex series of actions; a child may say 'I will *fetch all* the balls and put them *in* the basket'. The use of words greatly increases the range of mental activity which children can carry out. They are no longer limited to mental pictures as the tools of thinking.

During this period, imaginative play expresses children's feelings and enables them to represent and act out experiences which have been important to them. Given a set of bricks, for example the colourful and varied shapes included in

Paul (3½ years)

Me on my bike. David (5 years)

Figure 2 : 5

Poleidoblocs,[2] or a supply of boxes, tins and rings, children will make shapes which for *them* represent houses, beds, aeroplanes, bridges or people. Through symbolising the actual things in this way, children extend their power to understand how things behave and how they can be influenced. This kind of play reveals that children are still looking at things in reference to themselves, noticing what they mean to *themselves* and what *they* can do with them.

Drawings can be equally fruitful both in showing us what children have really observed and in stimulating them into further insights. The representations are not photographic but they represent what the child has perceived. They correspond in their structure to the mental pictures the child has formed. Drawings show clearly how egocentric are children's impressions and how limited is their awareness of the connections between the things themselves. For example, in drawings of a man, a child at $3\frac{1}{2}$ years may show a head and a body not connected by a neck, two arms which may be joined to head or body and two legs vaguely attached to the body. A hat will be drawn *above* the head but not *on* the head because the child has not yet seen the relationship of fitting

the hat to part of the head. In drawing a mechanism a child will show all the parts, but they are not connected (Figure 2 : 5).

Children's ideas about many situations are similarly unrelated. For instance, they may hold two contradictory ideas at the same time, believing that a quantity is larger than another in one position and smaller if the position is changed (*see page 76*). As yet, children cannot relate two ideas together either to see that they are not contradictory or to produce a new idea from them.

Representation in speech or drawing permits communication with others and conversation helps children to discover the contradictions and lack of accuracy in their drawings and descriptions (*see page 22*). This is, therefore, a period of considerable growth towards relating mental structure to actual forms and relationships.

STAGE 2(B): THE PERIOD OF INTUITIVE THINKING

The stage from about 4 years to about 7 or 8 years is of particular interest to teachers because for many children it covers the first two or three years at school. In this period children's thinking is dominated by their *perceptions*, i.e. by the

[2]Designed by Dr Margaret Lowenfeld.

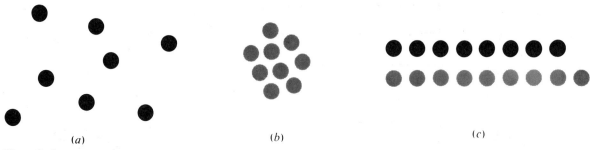

(a)   (b)   (c)

Figure 2 : 6

interpretations they give to their experiences of seeing, hearing, touching, moving, etc. These may be mistaken. As the proverb says, appearances are deceptive, and children may be the more deceived because they tend to identify what they see with similar but not identical things seen before. It is not possible to reverse a perception as one can an action because it depends on earlier experiences as well as on the visual image one is actually seeing. A door standing ajar is seen as such in a flash and a very young child will say 'door' because the visual picture fits into complex the set of images of the objects to which the name *door* is given. The child has not reached this recognition by any *sequence* of actions or thinking which could now be reversed. In order to be further developed a percept must be co-ordinated with another percept; it may then be corrected for inaccuracies.

Children may wrongly say that the beads in Figure 2 : 6(a) are more than those in 2 : 6(b), which are grouped together more closely. If the beads are set out so that each bead in (b) is opposite one bead from (a), it can be seen that one of the sets has more beads than the other (Figure 2 : 6(c)). Children perform such co-ordinations during this period but since perception is not reversible, thinking that depends on perceptions can still be erratic or inconsistent; it can be contradicted by a new perception which is not fully co-ordinated with

it. For example, children at this stage will agree that two squares, one red and one blue, are equal because one fits on the other. The blue one is then cut in half as in Figure 2 : 7(B). A green square is then treated in the same way and its two halves placed end to end as in Figure 2 : 7(C). Children will agree that the two halves in (B) are equal to (A), and agree that the square which made (C) was equal to (A). But they will say that (C) is bigger than (B). Apparently they are judging only by length and not taking into account the change in width. Expressed in symbols they agree that $(A) = (B)$ and $(A) = (C)$ but do not recognise that $(C) = (B)$. They *perceive* that $(C) > (B)$, *mistakenly*.

Thinking which is based on perceptions and not on reasoning is said to be *intuitive*. Since perceptions are mental structures produced by sensations, past as well as present, it is clear that intuitive thinking about a thing or a situation takes place only when there is a direct contact with the object of thought. For instance, towards the end of this period a child will suddenly 'see' intuitively that the square and the 'diamond' in Figure 2 : 8 are identical shapes, one of which has been rotated.

Such an intuitive judgement, based as it is on past actions and perhaps on head movements made by the child at the time, comes often in a flash. Reasons for the judgement cannot be given but clearly the child has built up correspondences, matching sides and corners in an imagined movement. The revelation of the identity of the two shapes is entirely convincing. This kind of intuitive thinking, stimulated by rich experiences of

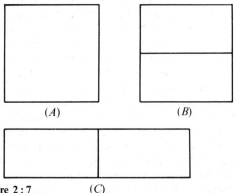

(A)   (B)

(C)

Figure 2 : 7

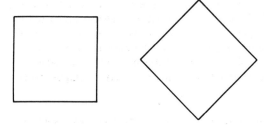

Figure 2 : 8

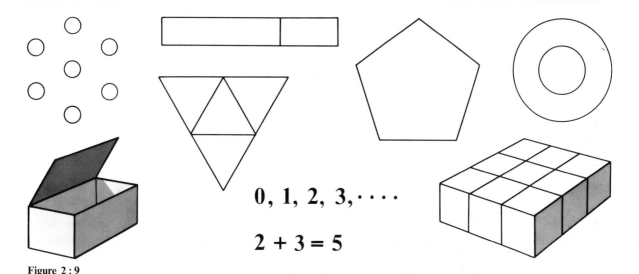

$$0, 1, 2, 3, \cdots$$

$$2 + 3 = 5$$

Figure 2 : 9

manipulating things, continues through the years and applies to increasingly complex situations. It is indeed an essential feature of creative mathematics. Fostered throughout the Primary years it will strengthen and bring inventiveness to the learning of mathematics at the Secondary stage.

STAGE 2(C): THE PERIOD OF CONCRETE OPERATIONS

This is the stage when logical operations can be carried out with concrete materials. Children can now begin to think logically provided their thinking is guided by contact with real things and actual situations. By the age of 7 or 8 their experiences should have been wide enough for their view of the world to be less self-centred; they can now discover and consider relationships between things without reference to their own viewpoint. Their thinking will therefore have a much wider range, and their conclusions will be more general and also more precise. We say that it is a period of *logical operations* with concrete materials; we must consider what we mean by *operations* in this sense and what the word *logical* implies here.

We have seen that mathematics has two aspects: it is concerned with patterns or structures which can be pictured in the mind; it is also concerned with *operations*,[3] i.e. with the mental manipulation of these mental pictures. The mental images are created by many experiences of things, observing them, handling them, constructing imaginatively

with them. Such images are of many kinds: a variety of shapes and constructions, symbols, sequences, symbolic statements. Figure 2 : 9 shows but a few examples of mental images which a child may have, though they may fluctuate and be vaguer than these diagrams suggest.

Activities of many kinds, such as moving bricks and toy cars to make constructions, giving one plate of a set to each of a collection of dolls, cutting squares into triangles, filling a square cavity with small cubes, are the forerunners to carrying out similar actions entirely 'in the imagination', as we say. The mental pictures of the different objects are related to one another or moved about in the mind and the results of such mental movements are seen as mental pictures. These activities of the mind, developed from actual observations and handling of physical objects, are called *operations*. Piaget speaks of operations as internalised actions, a phrase which reminds us that these mental activities can take place when the objects involved are no longer present and the physical actions on which they are based are past. In fact the actions may not be consciously recalled. For example, a child has five cars, and is promised two more. The mental picture of five cars is supplemented with two more. The child visualises the new collection and makes the count of seven (or counts on two beyond five). The result is expressed as 'I shall have seven cars'. The important characteristic of mental operations is their fluidity. In the child's mind, it is possible to go back to the original five cars; mentally, the extra two can be removed, and the child can go back to the starting-point (*see page 164*).

Children can now mentally take to pieces the buildings they have made and build different shapes

[3]An operation also has a structure and can become a mental image and an object of thought.

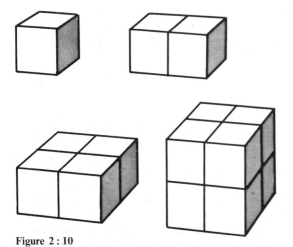

Figure 2 : 10

in their minds; these, too, they can undo. This feature of operations, that the thinker can mentally undo them and go back to the starting-point, is called *reversibility.* Piaget says, 'An operation may be defined as an action which can return to its starting-point, and which can be integrated with other actions also possessing this feature of reversibility.'[4] An example will show how a sequence of actions, each reversible, leads to a sequence of mental operations. A child begins to build with a collection of small cubes using the notion of twos. First, two cubes make a rod or cuboid; two such cuboids go together to make a square-shaped layer; another such layer on top makes a cube. The child can reverse each action, and can even reverse the entire sequence to give the separate cubes as they were to begin with (Figure 2 : 10).

After such experience the child can create the whole procedure mentally, and count to match the number of cubes to each shape in turn, forming mentally the number sequence 1, 2, 4, 8. The important factor here is the practical experience which made possible the mental imagery both of shapes and of the actions.

During the period of concrete operations children master a variety of operations, some of them quite complex. These grow from three simple operations which are fundamental to the process of counting and underlie all mathematical thinking. The sources of these three operations are the following patterns of action:

i) *classification.* Through recognising the likeness of one thing to another and distinguishing it as different from other things, children can form a collection or *class* of things that are alike, say cars, farm animals or cups. They can sort out model farm animals into separate classes: pigs, horses, cows. They are *not* thinking of *how many* in each class but only of where any particular animals belongs;

ii) forming *one-to-one correspondences.* This is the operation of matching each of one kind of thing to each thing of another kind, e.g. one packet of crayons to each child at a table, or one 'cup of tea' to each doll. From these matchings children see the *relationships* 'more than', or 'less than', or 'the same as' ('just as many as');

iii) *seriation* or forming sequences. For example, dolls are arranged in order of height, jugs according to how much they hold, boxes in order of mass. This means that a child is using the *relationship* of more or less for the purpose of putting an object into its proper place in a sequence.

These elementry patterns of action give rise to mental operations. Children become able to sort out in their minds things that they can image, say to distinguish cars from lorries. They can match in their minds the number of spoons to the number of people expected; they can arrange in order the steps needed in making a paper boat, and so on. Children are relating things in their minds, and the relationship is the connection they have perceived between certain things. They are now able to recognise this relationship and use it in their thinking, so that they will match forks to spoons without reference to the people for whom they are required. From the basic operations of classifying, matching and ordering more complex operations are evolved and more complicated relationships are perceived.

The simplest operation which creates more complex relationships is that of putting together or adding. We use the word addition usually to mean putting two numbers or two lengths etc. together. It has a broader meaning which we use here; it signifies putting together two classes, or two sequences, or two relations, and so on, without necessarily involving the numbers or sizes of the things concerned. We will give examples to illustrate this development in a child's powers.

Classification. A child sorts out all the dolls' coats and also sorts out all the dolls' hats. The child combines them into one class called dolls' outdoor clothes. This may be written as coats + hats ↔ outdoor clothes, or in symbols

$$C + H \leftrightarrow O$$

[4] Piaget, J. *The Child's Conception of Space*, page 39.

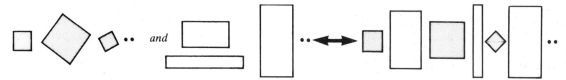

Figure 2 : 11

A child sorts a collection of toy animals into sheep, horses and cows. Then the child sorts another collection into sheep, goats and pigs. If the two classifications are combined, the four classes of horses, cows, goats and pigs still remain, but the two collections of sheep can be put into *one class*, the class of sheep.

(sheep, horses and cows) with (sheep, goats and pigs)

$\leftrightarrow$ (sheep, horses, cows, goats and pigs)

If we write in symbols what has happened to the sheep it is

class S + class S $\leftrightarrow$ class S

This is not a statement about the numbers in each class but states only that two classes of the same class form one class. Through these experiences of combining the classes into which things can be sorted a child gradually builds up more general ideas of classes and will be able to think of *all* the domesticated animals, *all* the wild animals, and finally of *all* the animals in the world. Such a general awareness is shown when a child sees that squares and oblong rectangles make up the whole class of rectangles (Figure 2 : 11).

Correspondences also can be combined. Each doll can be given a cup; a saucer can be placed under each cup. Then a child can see that each doll has been given a saucer and can use this kind of matching as a tool for thinking.

We have seen that *seriation* depends on using the relation 'bigger' (or smaller) to connect each successive pair of things in a sequence. Such *relations* can also be added. If one tin is taller than another, and the second tin is taller than a third, then the child, putting the two relations together, will be able to say that the first tin is taller than the third (Figure 2 : 12).

Two *sequences* can be matched. For example, if toy cars are to be put in garages of different sizes so that the biggest car goes into the biggest garage, and so on; in Stages 2(a) and 2(b) a child may carry this out by trial and error. At stage 2(c) (*see pages 16 – 17*) the child can mentally make two sequences arranged according to size and fit the smallest car to the smallest garage and so in order up to the largest car in the largest garage (Figure 2 : 13). This can be done without actual experiment.

Similarly a child will be able to select suitable cylinders to represent chimneys on models of houses in a sequence of sizes (Figure 2 : 14).

In Chapter 7 we shall see how important this matching of sequences is in dealing with changes which takes place in successive intervals of time.

Two sequences of the same kind can be put together by dovetailing to make a new sequence, as in the discs shown in Figure 2 : 15.

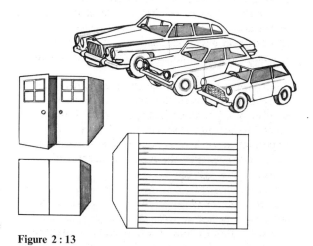

Figure 2 : 13

If h_1 > h_2 and h_2 > h_3 then h_1 > h_3

Figure 2 : 12

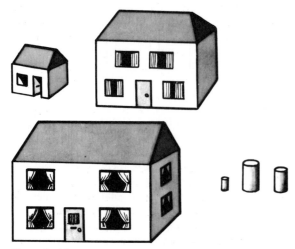

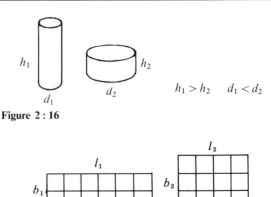

Figure 2 : 16

$h_1 > h_2 \quad d_1 < d_2$

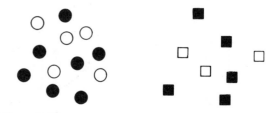

Figure 2 : 14

$b_1 < b_2 \qquad l_1 > l_2$

Figure 2 : 17

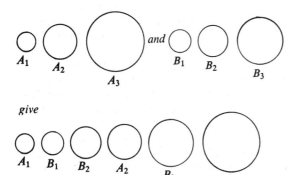

and

give

Figure 2 : 15

Similarly the sequence of odd numbers and the sequence of even numbers can be combined to give the sequence of whole numbers.

$(1, 3, 5, 7 \ldots)$ and $(2, 4, 6, 8 \ldots) \rightarrow$
$(1, 2, 3, 4, 5, 6, 7, 8 \ldots)$

In this instance the reverse operation, i.e.

$(1, 2, 3, 4, 5, 6, 7, 8 \ldots) \rightarrow (1, 3, 5, 7 \ldots)$ and
$(2, 4, 6, 8 \ldots)$

is likely to be discovered first.

A more complex operation arises when two *different* relations have to be taken into account at the same time. For instance, if two glass jars differ in height and also in diameter their capacity can only be compared if both factors are considered. At the stage we are considering, a child cannot yet calculate the volumes but can make an estimated comparison by thinking about the two kinds of measurement, height and diameter (Figure 2 : 16).

If two rectangles are to be compared with regard to their surfaces (areas) both length and breadth must be considered (Figure 2 : 17).

The two relations are said to be *multiplied.* In the case of the rectangle we can see that multiplication

of the numbers of units in the length and breadth would in fact give the area, but by multiplication of relations we mean the wider procedure in which we consider two relations at the same time, whatever kind of connection there may be between them.

An experience in which two relations have to be considered simultaneously is the common one of finding the way home after a journey on a strange road. Two changes are involved. What was behind on the way out is now in front; what was on the right is now on the left. If children who have recently come to a school are asked to draw a plan of the journey home, the difficulties they have in making the changes from their images of the journey to school are quite apparent. Estimations of directions and the positions of landmarks may all be faulty. In the period from 7 to 11 years of age considerable development in dealing with the relations involved can be seen.

An operation which is similar in kind to the one just discussed is that of classifying according to two different qualities, say shape and colour, or age and height. A collection of beads is classified first for shape: round or square (Figure 2 : 18).

In each pile some are black and some are white. They are now sorted according to colour, putting black above and white below (Figure 2 : 19). A pattern at once emerges in which all the round and all the square are separated and also all the white

Figure 2 : 18

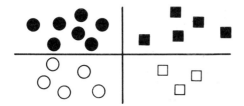

Figure 2 : 19

and all the black are separated. There are now four classes:

black and round; black and square;
white and round; white and square.

They have been formed from two classes different in colour and two classes different in shape. If there had been three different colours and two different shapes the result of carrying out both classifications would have been six classes, as Figure 2 : 20 shows.

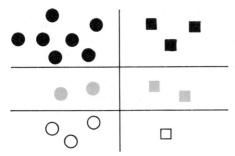

Figure 2 : 20

It is easy to see why this procedure is called the multiplication of classes but it must be remembered that it is the resulting *kinds of classes* that are thought about here rather than the *numbers* produced. Experience of such classifications and attempts to work out the resulting patterns mentally is an interesting and valuable task.

The operations we have been describing were referred to as *logical* operations carried out with concrete material; we said that we would discuss the word *logical* as used here. Logic is the study of the principles of human reasoning. Logical operations are part of this system and so obey the rules of logical thinking. Some of these rules are discussed in Chapter 4. When we apply 'logical' to this stage of children's thinking we mean that the mental operations that they are able to carry out at Stage 2(c) have some of the structures of adult thinking. But whereas adults are able to think and reason without the use of physical aids, or indeed without reference to physical facts, children at the stage of concrete operations require a basis of concrete experience for their mental operations. The reasoning which they can then carry through is in sharp contrast to intuitional judgements. The best justification that a child can give for an intuitional judgement is that, 'you can *see* that it is so'. In reasoning, on the other hand, the operations of comparing, matching, etc., will be carefully used to show the truth of a judgement. At the stage of intuitive thinking, children will say that the diagonals of a rectangle are equal because they *look* equal; later they mentally match the sides and angles of the two diagonal triangles in the rectangle to *reason* that they are equal (Figure 2 : 21).

Operations of the complex character which children from 7 to 11 years carry out are much easier for children who have plenty of opportunities for the constructive play which is characteristic of this age. The requirements of many constructions oblige a child to take a number of factors into account and thus encourage the kind of logical thinking that is necessary in all aspects of mathematics. Towards the end of this period many of the concepts formed should have become sufficiently clear and meaningful for a child to think effectively without contact with actual material and to carry out steps of thinking entirely in terms of concepts, where these have been firmly established.

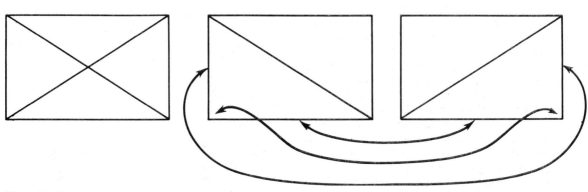

Figure 2 : 21

STAGE 3: THE PERIOD OF FORMAL OPERATIONS

From the age of 11/12 years, some children begin to enter the period of formal operations, when thinking can take place without reference to actual objects or to events in the real world. For other children, this stage is delayed until later, and for all children, their entry into this period is patchy, so that some concrete activities are needed for several years, usually at the introduction of new ideas. In the period of formal operations it is possible, often pleasurable, for young people to invent some hypothesis and work out logical consequences. The construction of logical systems is the method of advanced mathematics and has proved valuable in providing structures which scientists can use. For most pupils in secondary schools logical reasoning will be concerned with the world of number, space, quantity and time, and for such thinking they will need the sure foundation of active manipulation and concrete operations already outlined.

FOSTERING THE GROWTH OF THINKING

In this chapter we have tried to trace the growth of children's power to think mathematically and to carry out the operations which are the fundamental ways of dealing with the numerical, quantitative and spatial properties of the things and events they encounter. The study of this growth is important to the teacher because the chief purpose in teaching mathematics to children must be to foster in them the understanding of relationships and the capacity for sound thinking which a scientific and technological environment requires. To help all children to develop their natural gift for such mental activity a teacher must be able to recognise at any time the kind of thinking that a child's work reveals. Only then can the next steps be planned to encourage further growth. Our knowledge of the stages through which children's thinking passes should convince us of the necessity of allowing them ample opportunities for experimenting and constructing with a wide range of objects and materials, for making their own judgements, for expressing their findings in their own ways, and for thinking through for themselves the way to new discoveries and the solution to problems.

It is evident that the spatial experiences embodied in this chapter not only reveal relationships involving size and position, with their logical implications, but also provide the spatial imagery which will serve to revive the perception of a particular relationship when it is present. They also make children familiar with the names and characteristics of many basic shapes and arrangements which will be of more significance later on.

3 | THE BEGINNING OF COUNTING

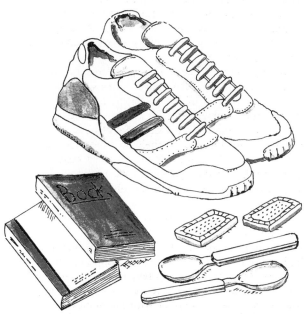

experience: they find that there are *many* objects of the same kind, though they do not yet know *how many*; they also begin to recognise the presence of *two* things, for example two shoes, two spoons, two biscuits (Figure 3 : 1). The first kind of experience depends on a recognition of the likeness of such things as balls or cars or children and on the capacity to distinguish them from other kinds of things, i.e. on the power of classification. The second type of experience appears to be a recognition of the pattern made by two like things, i.e. of the existence of 'one and another'. We must consider how these two simple forms of recognition lead to the ability to count the objects that children can handle or see, and later to recognise the patterns and structures of a system of numbers.

Figure 3 : 1

EXPERIENCES PRELIMINARY TO COUNTING

Children begin to be aware of number as a feature of things in their surroundings through two kinds of

CLASSES AND SETS

By the time that children start school they are able to use many nouns; these show that they have recognised many classes of things that they use, see and play with at home or out of doors. Children

Figure 3 : 2

Figure 3 : 3

may have played at shops, an airport, or a farm, and have deliberately sorted and arranged things of the same kind together. However, children may not yet have classified spontaneously a box of bricks into different shapes or colours; they may not have noticed the different kinds of leaves on plants or the various shapes of tins. Experience of classifying toys, materials, and the collections of interesting things that children and teacher bring to school will be valuable both in stimulating the children's observation and in giving them the basis on which the notion of number will be built. From the earliest days children should meet the word *set* used to mean a collection of any kind of thing that they can recognise as belonging to the set, and to which they can add another of the same kind (if one exists), e.g. a set of shells, a set of toy elephants, the set of acorns or berries brought by the class, the set of empty milk cartons, or a set of packets to put in the class shop, and so on (Figure 3 : 2). There is no thought of *counting* yet, but 'more', 'a few', 'a lot'

will be used in discussing the various sets. More important is the awareness of the connection between the members of a set, the common property which makes it possible to decide whether another object belongs to the set or not. All members are related to one another in the possession of this '*likeness*'. Those objects that are '*not like*' the members in this respect are *outside* the set.

Some of the children's imaginative and constructional activities will strengthen their familiarity with the idea of sets and give them the pleasure of putting sets of things together to make, say, a large picture of a village or farm, or a bright and satisfying pattern of coloured shapes. If a class works in small groups, each group can make a set of a particular animal, building or shape, and then decide where to place their contributions to the scheme the class is carrying out. It is important that children should have this experience of combining sets into a whole as well as finding various sets within a large collection (Figure 3 : 3).

Peter's set

Mary's set

Figure 3 : 4

Birthdays

This month and next month

June   July

Figure 3 : 5

COMPARISON OF SETS

Comparison of collections is the next step towards counting. The companionship of other children in the class, and the awareness that other children nearby are making different things, or have more things on their table, will lead naturally to comparison. Children need to know how to check whether another child's set has more or fewer things in it, or whether there are enough pencils for the children at the table or in the group. Children begin to match the two sets, one thing from the first to one thing from the second. They do this by placing them side be side or close together in some way. The teacher can make similar matchings, drawing simple pictures of things brought by two different sets of children, recording the things in two rows or two columns.

In Figure 3 : 4 we notice that size and shape do not matter but the things in the picture are recognisably shells. One set contains shells that are alike in belonging to Mary. The other set, quite distinct from Mary's set, contains shells that are alike in belonging to Peter. The children can now *see* that Mary's set has more shells and some children may say that it has *one* more than Peter's set.

To ensure that the members of the two sets are placed in positions where the one-to-one matching can be seen, it is useful to have squared paper in 5-cm or 2-cm squares on which pictures or drawings or name-cards of objects can be arranged in rows or columns starting from a common base. For example, children can record those children whose birthdays fall during this month or will fall

next month. Each child places a name-card in the appropriate space in the correct column (Figure 3 : 5).

Or the class may record the children whose names begin with letters B and M (Figure 3 : 6).

Another type of comparison comes from sorting tins brought by the children for their shop, perhaps

Figure 3 : 6

into rounded tins and square tins. Each children can draw or cut out the shape of one tin and fix the picture on a square in the appropriate row (Figure 3 : 7).

When these records have been made, the children then say whether one set contains 'more than', 'less than' or 'as many as' the other set. The relationship of one set to the other has been discovered.

![Figure 3:7]

Figure 3 : 7

THE FIRST NUMBERS

It will be noticed that the use of the word 'one' has been assumed. At this stage it means a single thing and is not yet part of a count. The active life of the classroom will soon lead any children who have not yet recognised *two* to become aware of two things and to discriminate between one and two quite consistently. Statements about the differences between sets should now be freely made and if matching shows the difference in number to be *one* or *two* a sentence should record it in the children's own simple language. Games, rhymes, matching pairs of things, labelling pictures of sets of two things, folding and cutting shapes into halves to make two pieces, finding sets of two to match a given set, all these activities will help to make the names 'one', 'two', and the symbols 1, 2, for these two numbers familiar.

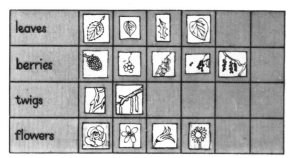

Figure 3 : 8

COMPARISON OF SEVERAL SETS: ORDERING

The comparison of sets of things without counting is now extended to include several collections. For example, different groups of children in the class can each choose something which they could find in the garden or playground. They are asked to bring in a few. They may bring leaves, berries, twigs, flowers. These are recorded after discussion by putting pictures on squared paper as in Figure 3 : 8.

The children find that the berries make the set with most things in it, the twigs the set with fewest things. Between them are the sets of leaves and of flowers. The set of flowers has just as many in it as the set of leaves; they can be matched exactly. There is one more in the set of berries than in the set of leaves. There are two twigs, there are two more flowers than twigs.

Given a heap of mixed shapes, either three-dimensional solid shapes or flat tiles (circles, squares, triangles, etc.), children can sort and make sets of things of the same shape. They can match the sets either by placing them side by side, one-to-one, or by arranging them on squared paper. They can say which shape makes the set with most things in it, which set has the fewest, and whether any sets match exactly. It is now a short step to putting the sets in order. Small sets such as those shown in Figure 3 : 9 are easily ordered. The difference between the sets can now be clearly seen

Figure 3 : 9

on this block graph. Leaves and flowers are obviously matching sets.

An abacus with four or five rods, open at the top, can also be used for sorting and ordering, using beads of different colours or shapes. Figure 3 : 10

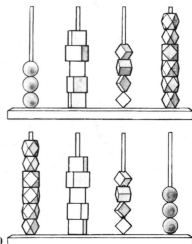

Figure 3 : 10

shows the random order, and then the ordering on another abacus according to which set has most, fewer, etc.

Later on children will use beads to *represent* objects of some other kind, toys perhaps, matching a bead to each toy.

THE EMPTY SET

As children sort a mixture of things into two or more sets they can put them into separate boxes labelled with a suitable picture or word. Some of these classifications can be recorded by the children in drawings; each set can then be enclosed in a ring to show that all the objects in it were put into the same box. See Figure 3 : 11 for a classification of shapes.

The sets can then be matched and ordered. If there are four different kinds of things in a large collection and a small haphazard handful is drawn from it, sorting this handful will sometimes show that one of the four kinds is entirely absent. Of the four boxes into which the separate sets were to be put one box is empty. The word '*empty*' and the phrase '*none at all*' should be used in talking about this situation (Figure 3 : 12).

The box for the squares is empty; it has no squares in it at all. If the sets are ordered as before the set of squares will be the smallest; it has none at all. An empty ring is a good symbol for the

discs

squares

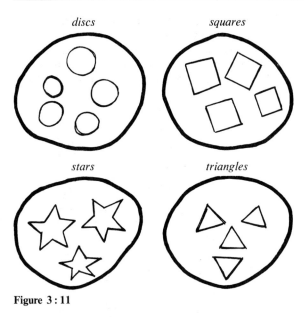

stars

triangles

Figure 3 : 11

Figure 3 : 13

collection was made or what each set contains. For example, a child could make in clay a pig, a cow, a horse and a sheep to be 'the animals on my toy farm'; or might use various tins and boxes and bricks and cotton reels to make an engine; the objects are not alike but the child can say 'these are the things I used for my engine'. In these instances children can define the set although they did not begin with a classifiation. To show that they are thinking of these objects together they can put a ring round them, as in Figure 3 : 13.

Much experience of making and matching sets is needed. Examples can be taken from the life of the classroom. The names of children absent each day are listed. Today's list is compared with yesterday's; are there more, fewer, or just as many as yesterday? Children match milkbottles or plates to the children at one table. A set of spoons is matched to a set of bottles, shown in a picture, as in Figure 3 : 14.

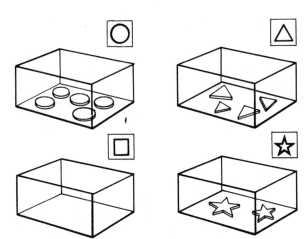

Figure 3 : 12

number of things in 'the empty set'[1] and the children will find it easy after these experiments to write 0 for zero when they want to state the number of things in an empty set.

MAKING SETS

So far, many of the sets which the children have made have been the result of classifying although they have also handled sets of mixed objects during some activities. They can also *make* sets of mixed objects provided that they can say how the

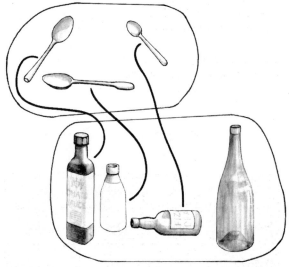

Figure 3 : 14

[1] See Chapter 8 for further discussion of the empty set.

Pictures of sets can be widely used now as material for questions, stories and discussions.

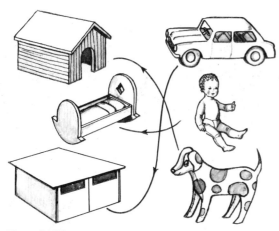

Figure 3 : 15

MATCHING SETS

It will be seen that the matching of sets leads to the idea of number. When two sets can be matched exactly, each member of one set being matched by one member of the other, and no member being left unmatched, the two sets, however different their members, are said to have the same *number*. Any other set which can be matched exactly to them also has the same number. Any set of *two* things matches any other set of *two* things, and children who now know the look of two things will pick out matching sets of two things at sight. Similarly any set of *three* things matches any other set containing three members. Practice in matching such sets will build up the notion of the number three (Figure 3 : 15).

From a number of picture sets a child can pick out the sets that match exactly. We have a special symbol for matching, or *equivalence*; it is a double-headed arrow: 'set A ↔ set B' says 'set A matches set B'. In Figure 3 : 16 set A is not equivalent to set B or to set C, but set B ↔ set C.

Figure 3 : 16

We do not use the equal sign for sets except when the two sets have exactly the same *members*; e.g. {dog, cat, pig} and {cat, pig, dog}. The equal sign is used for the *numbers* of members of equivalent sets, so that we can say that the *number* of set B equals the *number* of set C when set B ↔ set C. Children will not need to use this statement of equality of *numbers* until the notion of number has become well established.

THE IDEA OF INCLUSION

Although children can clearly see that one set has more members than another and can sort and separate one class of things from a mixed collection, they do not easily recognise one special kind as *part* of the whole. To help them to form this concept they need practical experience. Among the mixed toy farm animals in a meadow they can sort the sheep and put them all together in the middle. A fence can be put round them as shown in Figure 3 : 17.

Figure 3 : 17

The idea of *inclusion* is important for understanding both numbers and measuring. It is dealt with more fully in later chapters. Here it is sufficient to notice that children find it difficult to answer the question 'Are there more animals (of all kinds) than there are sheep?', but they see that there are other animals as well as sheep and are therefore beginning to see that sheep form part of the whole set of animals and that animals *include* sheep. Various activities and discussions are required to build up this part-whole or inclusion idea. For example, the family includes the children; the children include 'me', 'my brother', 'my sister'. Poleidoblocs contain a set of pointed shapes (pyramids and cones) which can be placed together among the rest. When children begin to recognise numbers greater than two they must come to realise that a set of three things includes a set of two things, a set of four things includes a set of three things and also includes a set of two things.

DISCOVERING THREE

Through continued handling of sets with more or fewer members, children are growing more aware of the number property of sets, and will soon be ready to count. Meanwhile they will almost certainly have learned to recognise the look of three things, realising that three is one more than two. The visual patterns which a set of three things can make are basically of only two kinds, either a row or a triangle (Figure 3 : 18).

Figure 3 : 18

Figure 3 : 19

DISCOVERING FOUR

Four is easily recognised when a set of four things is in view. Its patterns are simple (Figure 3 : 20).

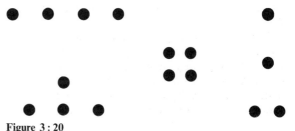

Figure 3 : 20

These patterns show three as one and one and one, and also as two and one (or one and two). The three of a family, 'me' and 'Mum' and 'Dad', is an important grouping with other sets of three. The patterns made by three are easily recognised and recalled and therefore children quickly learn the number name, *three*, and the numeral, *3*. The will used them for all the sets of three things they encounter. A child can now name the order of sets of one, two and three members and the sequence becomes very familiar; it may even suggest to a child that it could be followed further (Figure 3 : 19).

Experimenting with a set of coloured rods such as Cuisenaire may lead to an ordering of the rods according to their length (*see page 54*). This emphasises a sequence which increases by equal steps. Before the number names from one to ten are learned it is well to establish the equivalence of the two-rod to two unit cubes; a set of three cubes can be replaced by the three-rod. Thereafter the sequence may be carried farther, when children are ready.

These patterns are seen as

  i) one and one and one and one

 ii) three and one (or one and three)

iii) two and two

 iv) one and one and two (or two and one and one).

Shapes made with rods, sticks and strips will also illustrate these patterns.

Sets of one, two, three and four members can now be put in order and matched with their numbers, the names and numerals being attached. Any four objects in a set can now be matched with

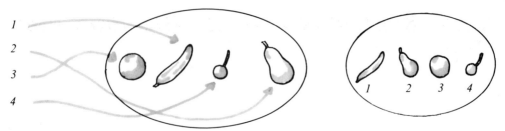

Figure 3 : 21

the four number symbols in whatever order we choose to select them (Figure 3 : 21).

A child frequently meets 'four': four children at a table. 'Mum' and 'Dad' and 'me' and 'my sister', a square made by four equal rods. There are plenty of opportunities for using four both practically and in imaginative play.

MATCHING NUMBER NAMES TO SETS: ORDINAL NUMBERS FIRST TO FOURTH

The order of the first four number names is learned quickly and it is the matching of these names in order to each of four things in turn which probably constitutes a child's first true count. As children count, touching or moving each thing as they say 'one, two, three, four', they are using the idea of order, matching the order of the number names to the order in which the things are touched. If four children are asked to come to the teacher, the order in which they come may lead to using the ordinal numbers *first*, *second*, *third*, *fourth*, linking each to the name of a child. If children at a table are asked to see who can do something very quickly, the ordinal numbers, first, second, etc. will be used as they hurry to finish. At this point they can also learn another ordinal number, *last*. The way in which the counting (cardinal) numbers and the ordering (ordinal) numbers become connected in a child's mind is discussed on pages 92 to 94. At the present stage the children's experience of them is entirely practical. They are learning through this experience the vocabulary of counting and ordering the small sets in which they can recognise the number of members on sight.

LEARNING THE SEQUENCE OF NUMBER NAMES

The social situations in a classroom provide children with many reasons for counting small numbers and also matching larger sets. Some interesting experiences occur when they compare the capacities of jars and jugs by recording cupfuls, or compare the heights of two growing plants seen against squared paper. Such opportunities should be fully used. As is pointed out in Chapter 7, comparisons of quantity extend the notion of number beyond that attached to a set of separate objects. Both kinds of experience should be available to children at this stage. Children appreciate not only the practical use of counting; they also enjoy the patterns and rhythms which reflect the structures of numbers and their sequences.

The number names up to twenty will be learned by most children before they have understood the meaning of a number such as nine or seventeen. The reciting of the *sequence* one, two, three, . . . , nineteen, twenty can establish the pattern of sound-names which will presently need to be used. It is a valuable acquisition as long as the teacher does not assume that because children can repeat the names they know how to use the numbers. The time spent in handling uncounted sets and the first four counting sets gives a foundation of confident understanding which makes for continued interest and rapid learning in later years. It ensures that symbols are always introduced to describe something that a child has made or discovered. These symbols have a meaning and can therefore be used to describe similar situations or to make new discoveries.

The emphasis in this chapter has been on the acquisition of an awareness of the numbers one to four through a great variety of individual and group activities; a teacher will find it useful to record the extent to which each child shows confidence in identifying and naming particular shapes and patterns, such as rectangles, showing columns and rows, closed curves to contain a set, arrangements of discs or tiles to show the properties of numbers and the relationships between their parts.

4 | SETS, RELATIONS AND THE BEGINNING OF STRUCTURE

TYPES OF CLASSIFICATION

Through their sorting and other activities young children are building up mental patterns which are fundamental both for mathematics and for the logical thinking which will develop later. Piaget believes[1] that children's thinking, by the stage of concrete operations, has itself a logical and mathematical structure which becomes more complex in successive stages of development.

If a teacher understands the type of mental structure which children are capable of constructing at a particular stage of development, he or she may be able to provide experience which will enable the children to develop more rapidly and more easily. It is not yet known how far experience planned by the teacher can influence the development of mental structures, nor whether it is necessarily desirable to attempt to force the development. But the parallel study of mathematical structure and of the development of thinking in children must illuminate the teaching of mathematics. If children have not reached a stage when they can handle the logical structure of a topic in mathematics they will not be able to understand it, or to learn it other than by rote. The teacher will find that the three strands:

i) the structure of mathematics,

ii) the analysis of logical thinking,

iii) the psychology of children's mental development,

all throw light on one another, and on the variety of experiences which children need in their mathematics learning.

In Chapter 2 we gave an outline of the stages of children's mental development in the light of the investigations of Piaget and others. We now try to relate that mental development to some of the logical and mathematical structures which children are building up. We also begin to develop a language which can be used to describe these structures.

As they play with different materials, experiment with their surroundings, sort through their toys, talk to their families, and begin to notice similarities and differences, young children are gradually forming in their minds two inter-related systems of classification. One is non-numerical. This will be used to establish patterns and relationships among the objects in the world and provide a framework for the logical thinking which will develop later. The second will lead to numerical experiences.

When children sort through a box of materials and separate out the buttons from the other things in it, they are setting up the (non-numerical) classification of the *class of buttons*. Buttons have certain properties in common which distinguish them from everything else in the world. As children learn to name things correctly and to apply the names with greater discrimination, so their system of classification becomes more organised. The word 'motor car' implies the existence of the *class of motor cars*, but a child will then distinguish the *class of lorries*, the *class of buses*, and the *class of milk vans* from the class of motor cars, so giving the classification a finer structure.

The question 'How many?' is not a question which a child will ask about this general class of motor cars. The only sensible question is 'Is this a car?'; that is, 'Does this particular object belong to the class of motor cars?'

But alongside the developing power of classification comes the idea that some classes or sets[2] contain more or fewer things than others (*see page 54*). The class of dogs cannot be compared numerically with the class of cats, because it is not a *practical* possibility to count all the cats and dogs in the world, although *theoretically* they form a limited set which could be counted. All that a child can do is to decide whether an animal belongs, say, to the class of dogs or the class of cats; but the set of cups on the table can be compared numerically with the set of saucers on the table. When we form the general concept of the class of dogs, we take no account of any characteristic of the animals other than their quality of being dogs. But the objects in

---

[1] See, for instance, Piaget, J. *Logic and Psychology*.

[2] We shall, as far as possible, use the word *class* for a general classification, and *set* when the members are regarded as distinguishable and the set can be compared numerically with other sets.

the set of cups on the table can be distinguished from one another by their position, or by the order in which they are pointed to or thought of, and so the set of cups can be compared quantitatively with other sets.

When we *count*, the members of a set must be put into an order by the very act of counting, but when we *classify*, the members of the class need not be ordered in any way.

When a child first uses the idea, a *set* is a collection of *things*. In everyday language there are many names for sets:

a flock of sheep   a pair of gloves
a class of children[3]   a train set or a tea-set

but when children talk in school about sets of things, they use the word 'set' more and more as the mathematical name for a collection. A set may have many or few members. The set consisting of the staff of a one-teacher school has a single member; the set consisting of all the cars on the roads of the world at the present moment has very many members; and the set consisting of all the points which go to make up a line has infinitely many members.

When defining a set, it is necessary that such a clear description of it be given that the question 'Does any particular object belong to the set?' can always be answered with an unequivocal yes or no. 'The set of boys' needs an upper age limit for complete definition, but the set consisting of 'all the boys in this school' leaves no doubt, for the registers can be consulted.

A set can usually be defined in one of two ways, either by making a list of its members,[4] or by giving some property by which those members can be distinguished.[5] The set, all of whose members have the property of belonging to a particular school, can equally well be defined by giving a list of their names. The set whose members are the odd numbers less than 10 can equally well be described as the set whose members are 1, 3, 5, 7, 9.

As children grow older, they gradually extend and refine their idea of a set. The first sets which children make are sets whose members all have a common property; young children will count the set of cups on the table, but will not yet regard the cup, saucer and plate which they lay for themselves as forming a set. As well as the many sets of objects in the classroom which can be sorted, there are many sets of commercial materials designed for sorting into sets. These have the characteristic that they can be sorted in more than one way, so that they extend children's ideas of classification. For instance, one commercial set of toy animals can be sorted into ducks, rabbits, cats, and so on, and can also be sorted into colours. Alongside the experience of sorting which these materials give, the children are developing the language which describes their actions:

'*all* the *yellow* things go there;
the *pink elephant* goes the other side.'

Another set of useful materials is the Logiblocs; they have four different attributes by which they can be sorted:

i) by *shape*: there are squares, oblongs, circles and triangles,

ii) by *size*: they are either large or small,

iii) by *thickness*: they are either thick or thin.

iv) by *colour*: they are red, blue or yellow.

Materials such as these provide a great variety of types of classification which children can find out how to handle.

Many games can be devised which enable children to manipulate combinations of the basic sets into which the blocks fall. For instance, in the 'one-difference game' a train of blocks is built in which each block must differ in exactly one attribute from its neighbours (Figure 4:1). Similar games, in which two attributes are changed each time, or in which a pattern is copied according to the rules of the game (as in Figure 4:2), provide

---

[3]It is unfortunate the word 'class' is used for a limited set of children who are taught together, when *the class of children* is the general classification for all human beings under a certain age.

[4]Definition *by extension.*

[5]Definition *by intension.* Inhelder and Piaget, in *The Early Growth of Logic in the Child*, describe some difficulties which young children encounter in relating these two methods of classification.

The '*one difference game*'

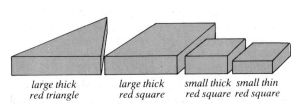

large thick   large thick   small thick   small thin
red triangle   red square   red square   red square

Figure 4 : 1

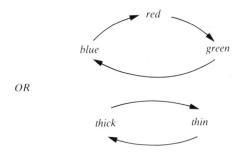

Figure 4 : 2

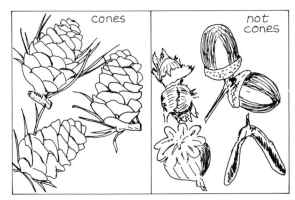

Figure 4 : 4

fruitful sources of logical thinking and of discussion between children, and with the teacher.

These experiences of sorting, reasoning and deduction can be continued for slightly older children by games such as Mastermind (Figure 4:3), in which a child has to copy an unseen pattern of coloured pegs, and is supplied at each move with information about how many colours are right, and how many pegs are in the right place.

© Invicta Plastics Ltd

Figure 4 : 3

THE REPRESENTATION OF SETS

Diagrams can be used to make permanent some of the classifications which young children have done. At a later stage a diagram *represents* the actual objects, and so aids thinking. Children should build up a knowledge of several different ways in which sets can be represented.

When young children sort out all the fir cones from the conkers and acorns, they often push them to opposite ends of the table. This leads to the simplest type of *Carroll diagram*. All the members of the set are put on one side of the line on the diagram (Figure 4 : 4), and all those objects which are not members go on the other side. Lewis Carroll (the author of *Alice in Wonderland*) was the first

mathematician to use these diagrams (which bear his name) systematically as an aid to logical thinking.

A *Venn diagram* is another type of representation which also distinguishes objects which are members of a set from those which are not. Children will put a 'fence' round all the triangles; all the things which are not triangles go outside the fence (Figure 4 : 5).

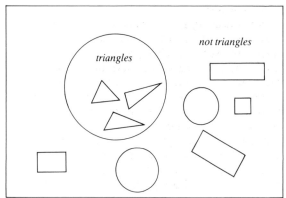

Figure 4 : 5

A *sorting tree* or *decision tree* gives a third representation. This type of representation is very useful for young children; the objects to be sorted can physically be pushed along the tree, and a decision made at the branching point (Figure 4 : 6). Whenever a decision is made about whether an object is to be placed in a set, a child has to answer 'yes' or 'no' to a question such as, 'Is it a triangle?' This is the first introduction to *binary* decisions, which play an important part in logic and computing.

Gradually, children begin to be able to use more than one attribute in their classification. They can make the set of *yellow triangles*, then the set of *big yellow triangles*. These classifications can be

Figure 4 : 6

(a)

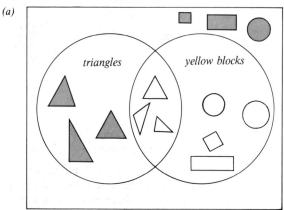

(b)

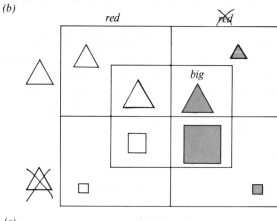

(c)

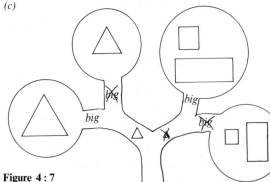

Figure 4 : 7

recorded in Venn diagrams (Figure 4 : 7(*a*)), or in Carroll diagrams (Figure 4 : 7(*b*)), or by pushing blocks along the branches of a tree (Figure 4 : 7(*c*)). The construction of diagrams helps children to make permanent some of the classification they have done, and to talk about what they are doing, so that they build up the language of logical thought:

> 'The big yellow triangle goes here because it is yellow AND it is big',
> 'the big red triangle goes over there because it is big and it is NOT yellow',
> 'this space contains the pieces that are red OR blue'.

Many types of classification can be found in the environment. Figure 4 : 8 shows the method which a class used to show the relationships between various subsets of itself, the girls, the children wearing dark jerseys, and those wearing black wellingtons.[6]

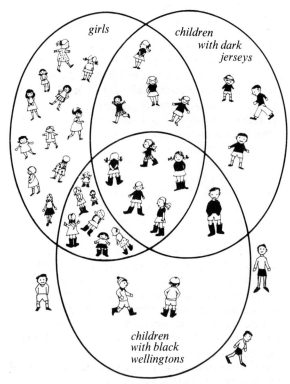

Figure 4 : 8

At first, children will need physically to place the members of a set within the 'fence' which separates

[6]Another way in which classification into subsets can be recorded is shown in Figures 3:7 and 3:8.

the things which belong to the set from those which do not, and then to draw or symbolise them. Later they will come to see the space inside the fence as a symbol for the set, containing as many or as few members as necessary.

Eventually, it is realised that the members of a set need to have no inherent property; all that is necessary is that they should be separated in thought from everything else in the world. An understanding of this point is needed for the understanding of addition, for when children combine two sets, such as a set of red bricks and a set of blue bricks, they can only add if they can see the red and the blue bricks together as one total set which can be counted.

Children also extend their idea of a set by realising that the members of a set need not necessarily be *things*. By the end of their junior school years many children can hold in their minds the ideas of such sets as

the set of multiples of 2
the set of prime numbers
the set of shapes which a child can draw.

All of these are abstract, unlimited sets. The members of a set may themselves be sets. Each class in a school is a set of children, and a head teacher may sometimes think of the school as a set of classes. The conscious organisation of sets into hierarchies in this way is a somewhat sophisticated mental development, but it is inherent in the structure of our number system. A ten is a set of ones; a hundred is a set of tens; and a thousand is a set of hundreds.

It seems likely that the handling of structural apparatus (*see page 96*), where a 'hundred' can be changed for ten 'tens' or for a hundred 'ones', may help children in the hierarchical organisation of sets. For some time, however, children using the apparatus appear to keep in mind only two adjacent types of unit at the same time, changing 'ones' for 'tens', and then to focus on another adjacent pair and change 'tens' for 'hundreds'. The understanding that a thousand is at the same time ten hundreds, a hundred tens and a thousand ones comes fairly late.

It now becomes clear that a set is not the same as its members. A choir is not the same as the individual members of the choir. They have become a unity and can be thought of as a single body. A set of ten things, the object which teachers call 'a ten', is different from ten isolated things. It is because the separate objects can be held in the mind as a unity that they are said to have the structure of a set.

The relationship between a set and its members is very well illustrated by the type of structural apparatus known as Unifix (*see page 95*), which consists of interlocking plastic cubes. A child who makes a set of cubes does not have to hold in mind that the cubes form a set, but can physically lock those cubes together into a unity (Figure 4 : 9) or break the set apart into its elements, thus symbolising the relationship between the set and the members from which it is composed.

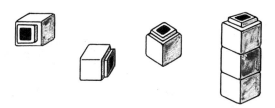

Figure 4 : 9

SUBSETS AND THE INCLUSION RELATION

The set of red triangles is a *subset* of the set of triangles. It goes inside a 'fence' in a Venn diagram, and this fence is inside the fence which separates the triangles from the rest of the Logiblocs (Figure 4 : 10).

When any set is defined, the words 'the set of' will always be needed. It may simplify writing addressed to the teacher if a symbol is used for the words 'the set of'; however, this symbol, which is used in higher mathematics, should not be used with young children, most of whose descriptions of sets will be oral. The symbol is a pair of curly brackets { }, and

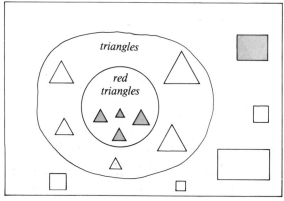

Figure 4 : 10

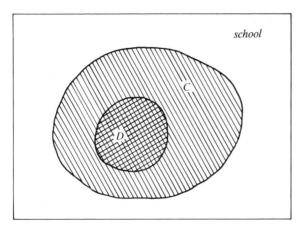

Figure 4 : 11

C = the set of children in Class 1
is abbreviated C = {children in Class 1}

The brackets show that we have in mind *the set of children*, rather than the individual children. The subset of C shown in Figure 4 : 11 can be written

D = {children in Class 1 who stay to school dinner}

It is clear from the diagram that set D is contained in set C; in advanced mathematics this relationship is written $D \subseteq C$, where the symbol $\subseteq$ means 'is contained in'.

To define the relationship more generally, we say that set A is contained or included in set B if every member of set A is also a member of set B (Figure 4 : 12). A is also called a subset of B.

When John eats some of his sweets, the set of sweets he eats is a subset of the set of sweets he had. If

E = {sweets which John has eaten today}
and S = {sweets which John originally had},

then $E \subseteq S$. Of course, John may have eaten all his sweets, but even in that case $E \subseteq S$, as every sweet which John ate is one which he had. But it is now also true that $S \subseteq E$, as every sweet which John had

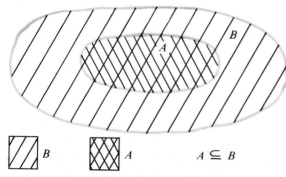

Figure 4 : 12

is one he ate. Then the two sets have exactly the same members, and are equal to each other:

$S = E$ if $S \subseteq E$ and $E \subseteq S$.

This relation between two sets, that one set is contained or included in the other one, is of fundamental importance. A child's set of yellow bricks is contained in the set of bricks of various colours, and the set of children at the working table is contained in the set of children in the class. It is only as children begin to understand the relation of inclusion that they can begin to construct a coherent mental structure for their world. Children can now understand and think with relations like

i) all sheep are animals, but there are animals which are not sheep;
ii) a set of 2 things can be included in a set of 5 things, which leads to $5 = 2 + 3$;
iii) all squares are rectangles, but not all rectangles are squares.

Piaget sees in the mastery of the inclusion relation between sets an essential difference between the pre-operational stage of intuitive thinking and the concrete-operational stage of thinking. Children at the concrete-operational stage can hold in their mind completely the relation between a set and its subsets, and can think reversibly about the relationship, whereas at the previous stage when they fixed attention on a subset they lost contact with the whole set which included it.

The following situation, which illustrates this difficulty, is equivalent to an experiment described by Piaget.[7] Children were shown a collection of brightly coloured green sweets, most of which were wrapped in transparent cellophane, but a few were unwrapped. The conversation given is typical of children of five or six who are at the stage of intuitive thinking:

What colour are the wrapped sweets?—*Green*
What colour are the unwrapped sweets?—*Green*
Are there more green sweets or more wrapped sweets?—*More wrapped*
But aren't these green too? (pointing to the unwrapped sweets)—*Oh yes*
Well then, are there more green sweets or more wrapped sweets?—*More wrapped sweets.*

Children at this stage are not yet able to move backwards and forwards in thought between the set of green sweets and its subset of wrapped sweets. When they think of the wrapped sweets the only other set they can see at the same time is the set of

[7]Piaget, J. *The Child's Conception of Number.*

unwrapped sweets, so it is this set that they compare with the set of wrapped sweets.

A child who has reached the stage of concrete operations reacts to the same situation with complete comprehension, knowing without doubt that there are more green sweets because the unwrapped ones are green too.

The evidence available suggests that 6-year-old children who have been specifically encouraged at school to sort things into sets and to look for relationships between sets appear to be rather more advanced and more confident in their understanding of this and similar situations than those whose mathematical work has been more traditional in character.

PARTITIONING A SET

A particularly important example of the formation of subsets occurs when a set or class is broken up into non-overlapping subsets. The class of children is made up of the class of boys and the class of girls, and these have no members in common. We say that these subclasses form a *partition* of the class of children. The set of books in the classroom library can be partitioned into fiction and non-fiction, but the classes of fiction and picture books do not partition the set of books; they may have some members in common. A partition is a separation of a set into non-overlapping subsets in such a way that every member of the original set belongs to just one of the subsets. In the previous section, the set of sweets was partitioned in two different ways, into wrapped sweets and unwrapped sweets, and into green sweets and non-green sweets. The child could not cope with these two partitionings at the same time.

THE LOGICAL MULTIPLICATION OF CLASSES, AND THE INTERSECTION OF SETS

As children become more skilled in making sets from the things around them, they begin to think of the property defining a set first, and then collect all the objects belonging to that set. They soon begin to do this in more than one way, and to hold two different qualities in mind at the same time, so forming the class of things which belong to *both* of two classes. They can think, when sorting beads, of a class of black beads, or sort according to shape and obtain a class of round beads. *The logical multiplication* of these classes gives the class of round black beads. This process of logical

multiplication gives rise to several classes. If the beads are either black or white, and either round or square, the process of holding in mind both colour and shape at the same time gives rise to four classes: round black beads, round white beads, square black beads and square white beads.

A child who is sorting a limited set of beads may find the device of drawing a fence around those beads which belong to the same set helpful (Figure 4 : 13).

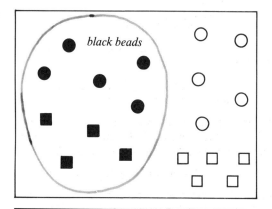

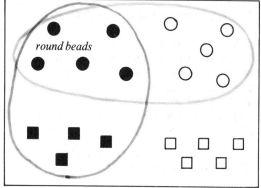

Inside both fences is the set of round, black beads.

Figure 4 : 13

The set of beads which belongs to *both* the black set and the round set is called the *intersection* of the black set and the round set. The symbol ∩ is used in advanced mathematics for intersection so that the intersection of the black and round sets may be written $R \cap B$ (Figure 4 : 14).[8]

[8]'Intersection' is of course merely another name for logical product. The words 'union' and 'intersection' are commonly used by mathematicians, who find it convenient to use terms which do not carry the arithmetical associations from which the words 'sum' and 'product' cannot be divorced.

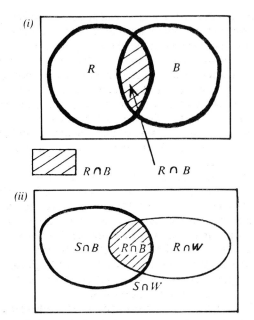

(i)

R   B

$R \cap B$ $R \cap B$

(ii)

$S \cap B$ $R \cap B$ $R \cap W$

$S \cap W$

Figure 4 : 14

For Piaget, reasoning consists of the ability to handle such relationships as these, and he says:

'Just as arithmetical, algebraic or geometrical reasoning consists of combining objects (numbers, signs or figures) by means of the operations of arithmetic, algebra or spatial construction, so in the case of classification, reasoning consists of combining objects by means of operations on classes (logical addition and multiplication, etc.), and in this grouping of objects and classes in hierarchical systems, or separating them one from another.'[9]

The complete set of Logiblocs contains 48 blocks in all, each one of which represents the intersection of four basic sets. Thus the large red triangular block is in the intersection of these four sets:

{large blocks}
{thick blocks}
{red blocks}
{triangular blocks}

Other apparatus can also be used to give similar experiences, and the children themselves can form sets with properties such as

staying to dinner
having a pet
having brothers, sisters, both, or neither
wearing a red jersey, a blue jersey, or neither of these.

[9]Piaget, J. *The Child's Conception of Number*, page 180.

THE LOGICAL ADDITION OF CLASSES, AND THE UNION OF SETS

Another operation with which children come to terms at the stage of concrete operations is that of the *logical addition* of *classes*. If two different classes are combined the result is a new *kind* of class. This method of combination is *logical addition*. For example, the class of *animals* added to the class of *plants* forms the class of *living things*. This is a statement about the *classes* without reference to the *numbers* in the classes. This logical addition is a mental operation on the classes, not on the things themselves. It is also *reversible*; that is, the class of living things with the class of plants excluded is the class of animals. The operation also depends on an understanding of the idea of inclusion, for both the class of animals and the class of plants are included in the class of living things.

Logical addition of classes is independent of number, and is a reversible mental operation which follows earlier experience of classifying sets of objects in this way. For example, the set of triangular Logiblocs can be partitioned into the three subsets of red triangular blocks, blue triangular blocks and yellow triangular blocks, and these can be recombined into the complete set of triangular blocks.

In this case, the subsets do not overlap, but the operation of combining subsets can be performed even if the subsets have some members in common. The operation of combining two sets in this way is called forming the *union of the sets*. For instance, within a school, there will be some children who have cats at home, and some who have dogs.

Let *C* = {children who have cats}
and *D* = {children who have dogs}

Then the *union of set C and set D* is

{children who have cats or dogs at home}

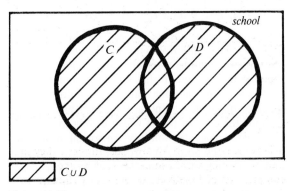

school

C   D

$C \cup D$

Figure 4 : 15

This set is written in advanced mathematics as $C \cup D$, and is illustrated by the Venn diagram shown in Figure 4 : 15.

In general, the union of two sets A and B is the set whose members are members *either* of *A or B* or *both*.

The operation of forming the union of two sets is clearly only another way of stating the operation of the logical addition of classes, and is closely related to the arithmetical operation of adding numbers. It is, however, a more general idea than that of adding numbers. No counting is involved: the actual *sets* are combined rather than the *numbers* of things in them, and indeed the number of things in the union may very well be less than the sum of the numbers of things in the original sets. For instance, some children may have both cats and dogs. If 15 children have cats and 7 have dogs, the number with cats or dogs may be 22, but it may very well be less. If 4 children have both cats and dogs, there will only be 18 in the set of those who have cats or dogs at home.

This type of overlapping classification occurs frequently. The set of children in a class may be divided into three sets:

B = {children with brothers}
S = {children with sisters}
N = {children without brothers or sisters}

The relations between those sets are shown in Figure 4 : 16, and children seem able to handle this classification with confidence at the concrete-operational stage and to realise that the simple addition of numbers is inappropriate to it.

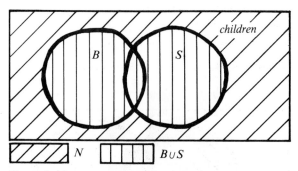

Figure 4 : 16

THE UNIVERSAL SET, AND THE COMPLEMENT OF A SET

Whenever children make any classification, they are always working within some set such as the complete set of Logiblocs, or the set of children in the class. All the classification is done by making

subsets of a particular *universal set.* For instance, we sort out the yellow Logiblocs, taking no notice of any other yellow bricks there may be in the room; or we list the members of the set of children in this school who stay to dinner, taking no notice of all the children in other schools who also stay to dinner. The universal set, for the present, is the set of children in this school. In a Venn or Carroll diagram, the outer frame of the diagram symbolises the universal set, within which the classification takes place.

Within this school, when we list the set of children who stay to dinner, we automatically make another set: the set of children who do *not* stay to dinner. This last set is called the *complement* of the set of children who do stay to dinner. Within a particular universal set, each set has its own complement; within the universal set of Logiblocs, the complement of the set of yellow blocks is the set of blocks which are not yellow.

The symbol $^{\sim}A$ is used in advanced mathematics for the complement of the set A. Young children will not use this symbol; some authors have found crossing out a very effective symbol. Thus ⧄ is the complement of △. In a Carroll diagram, a set and its complement are equally important (Figure 4 : 17(*i*)), but in a Venn diagram, children find it more difficult to see the complement of a set, which lies outside its fence (Figure 4 : 17(*ii*)).

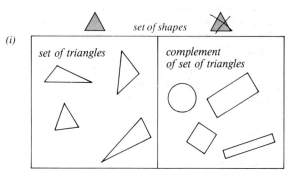

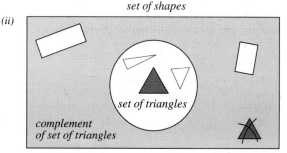

Figure 4 : 17

AND, OR AND NOT

By their work on classifying and forming subsets, children are introduced to the three basic *logical connectives*:

AND, OR and NOT.

These connectives have a fundamental place in all logical thinking, and are also vital to understanding how a computer works. They correspond to the three operations on sets,

intersection, union and *complement*.

The intersection of sets A and B, $A \cap B$, is the set whose members belong to A AND B; the union of sets A and B, $A \cup B$, is the set whose members belong to A OR B (or both); the complement of A, $\tilde{}A$, is the set whose members do NOT belong to A. Thus,

$$A \cap B = A \text{ AND } B,$$
$$A \cup B = A \text{ OR } B,$$
$$\tilde{}A = \text{NOT } A.$$

Children who learn early to classify using AND, OR and NOT have acquired some of the fundamental skills of thinking but they should not be expected to use the formal symbols $\cap$, $\cup$, $\tilde{}$.

RELATIONS BETWEEN SETS

As children become familiar with classification into sets, they see that often the members of two sets are related together. For example, the fact that some children have dogs as pets, some have cats, and some have gerbils, makes a linking process possible between the set of children and the set of animals (Figure 4 : 18). David has a dog and a cat, Elizabeth has a gerbil, Peter has a cat, and nobody has an elephant. The arrows linking the members of the

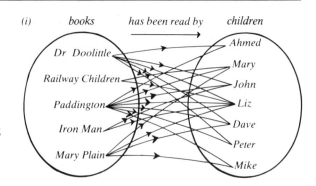

(i)

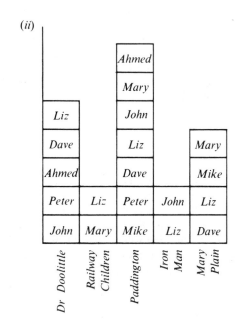

(ii)

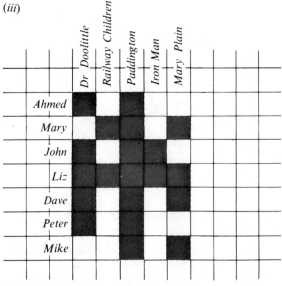

(iii)

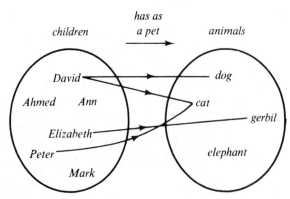

(has as a pet)

Figure 4 : 18

Figure 4 : 19

sets all stand for *has as a pet*. Such a set of links is called a *relation* between the two sets. Children will find very many relations between the sets they make. The set of children is related to the set of months in which they have their birthdays, and to the set of colours of their jerseys, and to the set of foods they may have at teatime, and to many other sets. The set of books in the classroom is related to the set of children by the relation 'has been read by', or to the set of numbers by the relation 'the number of pages in ... is ...'. Children should be encouraged to find such relations between sets, and to record them in some of the ways shown in Figure 4 : 19.

Much work in mathematics depends on the study of relations between sets; counting, in particular, is concerned with a very simple relation between sets, that of *one–one correspondence*. This is discussed on pages 54 and 55.

RELATIONS BETWEEN THE MEMBERS OF A SINGLE SET

The set of children at a table can record their relation to various other sets such as the set of books, but they can also think of themselves as related to each other. For example, they can make a record of the children whom they sit next to. This can be shown in a number of ways (Figure 4 : 20).

The last diagram, in which the set is only shown once, and each member is linked to those members related to it, is probably the clearest. The relation 'is older than' is rather more complicated than 'sits

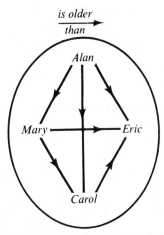

Figure 4 : 21

next to', for if Alan is older than Carol, and Carol is older than Eric, then also Alan is older than Eric (Figure 4 : 21).

In order to find this statement obvious, a child needs to hold the two facts in mind at the same time, and must recognise intuitively that the transitive[10] relation holds. We shall not expect children to be able to do this until the stage of concrete operations, when they will be able to handle with confidence, using concrete materials, combinations of relations such as these.

THE LOGICAL ADDITION AND MULTIPLICATION OF RELATIONS

As they move into the concrete-operational stage of thought, we see that children not only learn, with concrete materials, to handle logical operations on the combination of classes, but also begin to use very similar logical operations on the *relations* between objects belonging to a class. Some further examples of the logical addition and multiplication of relations are now given.

i) *Logical addition of relations*
A relation which children recognise at a very early age is that of 'bigger than' or 'smaller than'. As we have seen (*see page 20*), they use it to arrange things in a sequence, each thing bigger (or smaller) than that which precedes it. Children who have made 'staircases' from bricks or rods of different lengths, such as those found in the Cuisenaire or Stern apparatus (*see plate 1a*), so that each rod in the staircase is longer

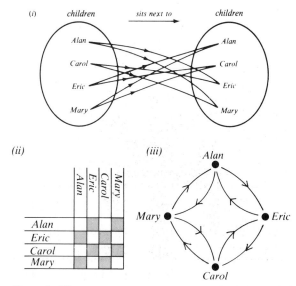

Figure 4 : 20

[10]See page 496.

Figure 4 : 22

than the one before it, will eventually be able mentally to combine all the relations which they can see between neighbouring rods. They will then know, without direct comparison, that because the orange rod is longer than the navy blue rod and the navy blue rod is longer than the brown rod, that it follows that the orange rod is longer than the brown rod, and so on all the way down the staircase. In symbols, if > is used to mean 'is longer than' then children know that

if $O > N$ and $N > Br$, then $O > Br$.

At this stage they are able to *add logically* all the relations between pairs of neighbouring rods (Figure 4 : 22).

    Similarly, a series of several blocks of different weights may now be arranged in order of increasing weight by putting pairs of them in the opposite pans of a balance to find which of the pair is heavier.

ii) *Logical multiplication of relations*
If two *different* relations have to be taken into account at the same time they are said to be multiplied. At the pre-operational stage children are unable to hold in mind more than one relation at a time, so that they are unable to compare, for instance, the capacities of two jugs which differ in width as well as in height. They may indeed think that if the water is poured out of one container into a narrower container (Figure 4 : 23), so that the water level becomes higher, there is now more water. At a later stage they are able to take into account at the same time both the greater height and the smaller base, and so to recognise that the volume is unaltered by the change in its shape. This grasp

of the *logical multiplication of relations* is a characteristic of the concrete-operational stage of thinking.

Figure 4 : 23

ONE–ONE CORRESPONDENCE: THE EMERGENCE OF NUMBER

Alongside the development of the structure of classes, sets and relations, the idea of number is growing in young children's minds. Logically, they must first be able to isolate a set of objects in the mind as an unchanging whole, which is unaffected by any rearrangement of them, before they can understand the property of a set which we call *number*. In practice, the development of the idea of number seems to proceed alongside the development of classification, and to be based both on classification, and on two relations involving sets. These are *one–one correspondences* between the members of two sets, and the *seriation*, or putting into a serial order, of the members of a set.

    Children can set up a one–one correspondence between the members of two sets before they can count. A child who lays a table for a meal will do so without counting by putting a spoon in front of each chair, and so setting up a one–one correspondence between the set of chairs and the set of spoons. Children may be able to give out pencils to the class, and say that there are not enough, long before they can count the children in the class. A one–one correspondence has been set up between the set of children and the set of pencils. The knowledge that two sets have the same number of things in them is more fundamental than knowing what that number is. Two sets *contain the same number of things* or *have the same number* if their members can be put in one–one correspondence with each other. In the same way, '*more*' and '*fewer*' are fundamental ideas which do not involve counting.

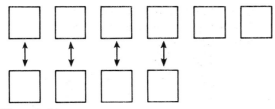

Figure 4 : 24

The sets of bricks in Figure 4 : 24 cannot be put into one–one correspondence. A child who cannot yet count how many there are in each set can decide that the upper set has *more* and the lower set *fewer*.

For children at the stage of intuitive thinking, appearances can interfere with the achievement of one–one correspondence. A game involving the matching of eggs and egg-cups, given by Piaget,[11] shows a stage at which the correspondence between two sets is global and intuitive, rather than one–one. The egg-cups are arranged in a row and the child is asked to take enough eggs for the egg-cups, and to put each egg in front of its cup. These same eggs are then moved closer together, so that they make a shorter line, and the child is asked if there are now enough eggs for the egg-cups. A young child, aged four or five, at the stage of intuitive thinking, will often judge the eggs on overall appearance, not realising the importance of the one–one correspondence between eggs and cups, and will say that there are not now enough eggs.

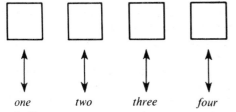

one   *two*   *three*   *four*

Figure 4 : 25

At the next stage, a child has completely grasped that mere changes of position do not alter the number of things in a set, and, with the one–one correspondence in mind, has no doubt that the eggs still match the cups.

When children begin to count, they must learn to say the names of the first members of the number sequence in the correct order. This is not counting, in any real sense of the word, but it gives a permanent, invariable set of sounds which can be put in one–one correspondence with any set of

things the child wishes to count. Counting is pointing to each brick in turn and saying a number name. The child is actually physically setting up a one–one correspondence between the bricks and the sounds at the beginning of the number sequence. (Figure 4 : 25).

The unending sequence of number names is always available for the setting up of a one–one correspondence, but only the beginning of the sequence is ever used in any actual counting operation. As the number names are always used in the same order, the last one which has been named can then be used to describe the whole set of things. So a child says 'four bricks' to describe the fact that there is a one–one correspondence between the set of bricks and the set of words 'one, two, three, four'.

Young children sometimes fail to count correctly because they do not yet understand the importance of an exact one–one correspondence, and are merely imitating an activity which they have seen. They say a number word while making a vague movement with the hand, without making the sound correspond with any object, or else they pass over an object without saying a number word.

ORDERING

The process of counting or pointing to the objects in a set demands the operation of *seriation* or *ordering* of the set. The objects must be pointed to one after the other, that is, in an order. This seriation, which involves the logical addition of relations, is well understood at the concrete-operational stage. The following are some examples of seriations which children at this stage will handle.

i) A set of children may draw round their feet and cut out the resulting footprints. They can now arrange several of these cut-outs on a graph in order of length, and will be able to relate the size of their own feet to those of the other children (Figure 4 : 26).

ii) When children play a game such as skittles and each player has several turns, each child may record the score at each turn by colouring a row of squares on a graph to represent the number scored (Figure 4 : 27). After each turn the children will know who is first, who is second, and so on, by comparing the lengths of their coloured rows, although these are not arranged in order of increasing size.

iii) A record is kept, and a block graph made from the growth in length each week of a young

[11]Piaget, J. *The Child's Conception of Number*, Chapter III.

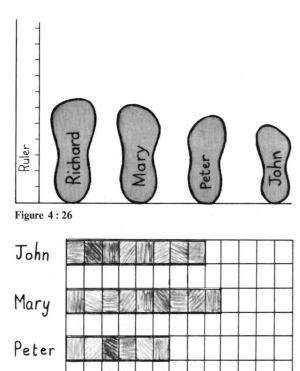

Figure 4 : 26

Figure 4 : 27

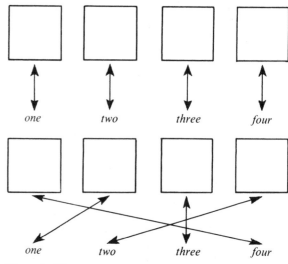

Figure 4 : 29

correspondence with the set of number names always stops at the same word. This realisation, too, can only come from experience and experiment with the rearrangement of sets.

THE GROUPING STRUCTURE OF OPERATIONS

We have tried to show how, as children's understanding increases, they become able to perform mentally certain operations on classes or sets, and on relations, out of which develops an understanding of numbers and operations on them. The structure and behaviour of operations on numbers is the subject-matter of a large part of mathematics, and we shall see later[12] how close is the parallel between the mathematical structure of numbers and the thought-structure which is within children's capacity when they handle real things at the concrete-operational stage. The following five properties are involved in the thought-structure of logical operations which Piaget calls a *grouping*, and which he suggests are characteristic of a child's thinking at the stage of concrete operations.

i) *Composition.* Two mental operations such as classification or relation can be combined, compounded or taken account of at the same time by a process such as logical addition. In the set of living things, $A \cup P = L$ (*see page 50*).

animal, a kitten or hamster, for example. A child at this stage understands the matching of the sequences of weeks and lengths, and can make deductions from the graph (Figure 4 : 28).

In these examples, a correct ordering is inherent in the material which the child is using. But when a set is counted, any ordering will do. The set may be counted in either of the ways shown in Figure 4 : 29, or in several other ways, and the one-one

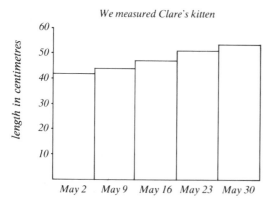

We measured Clare's kitten

Figure 4 : 28

[12]Chapter 39.

ii) *Reversibility.* Combinations are reversible. $A \cup P = L$, for example, can be reversed into *L without P is A.*

iii) *An operation can be cancelled by its opposite.* If a set of red beads is united with a set of blue beads, this operation can be cancelled by removing the red beads. Symbolically, if B is the class of blue beads and R the class of red beads, the effect of the two operations is shown by $(B \cup R)$ *without R is B.*

iv) *The associative law.* The result of combining three classifications does not depend on the order in which the combination is made. For instance, the result of the classification of triangular blocks into red, blue and yellow blocks does not depend on whether the red blocks or the yellow blocks are picked out first. Symbolically

$$R \cup (B \cup Y) = (R \cup B) \cup Y$$

v) *Special identities.*[13] The combination of an operation such as classification with itself adds nothing new to the situation.

The class of boys $\cup$ the class of boys
= the class of boys,

$$B \cup B = B[14]$$

Logical structure and mathematical structure do not develop separately in children's minds, for the two structures are very closely related. Their developing ability to count a set and to arrive at the same number every time helps children to understand the invariant properties of a set or class, and to become aware of its constancy in spite of changes in its appearance. On the other hand, it is only when children understand the invariance of a set that they can count meaningfully, for only a collection which remains constant in number during the counting can be counted.

Needless to say, children are unaware of the structure which thought possesses and of the mathematical patterns toward which they are struggling. Hence, a source of difficulty for the teacher is that children do not know what mental structures are missing when they cannot understand something. It is only by a careful analysis of the thought-process which leads to the development of a mathematical idea that a teacher can provide a progression of suitable experiences through which children will grow mathematically and will be able to handle mentally more complicated structures.

If the framework of mathematical ideas which children develop at this stage is sufficiently coherent and well-understood in concrete situations, they will then more easily be able, at a later stage, to organise abstract thinking, and to build up a logical structure of abstract mathematical ideas on the basis of this concrete experience.

---

[13]For the mathematical use of the word 'identity', which is employed here, see page 237.

[14]This behaviour of logical systems is to be contrasted with the behaviour of numbers in a similar situation. For numbers, $3 + 3 = 6$, but for classes, $B \cup B = B$. Differences are beginning to arise between the structure of numbers and the structure of logical operations.

5 | LEARNING ABOUT SPACE

WHY WE LEARN ABOUT SPACE

The study of the properties of space has several important purposes:

i) It is intended to build up in children's minds, in the course of the primary years, a picture of the spatial structure in which we live, i.e. the universe with the heavenly bodies and the earth seen in relation to one another, and so create some awareness of their relative movements. Children also need to know the shape of our earth and the properties of its surface which have enabled mankind to build roads and navigate ships and aircraft, and represent on maps their positions and routes.

ii) It is equally important for children to know that both living and non-living bodies have characteristic shapes and structures; there are many wonderful examples, such as the bones in the wing of a bird, a spider's web, a snow crystal (Figure 5 : 1).

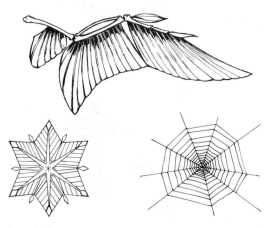

Figure 5 : 1

Adults make complicated structures and mechanisms using similar shapes and forms; these the children can observe and model.

iii) Through their own inventiveness children will learn to appreciate the patterns and forms which people have used for decoration and enjoyment.

iv) Different kinds of manipulations of shapes involve some operations which are common to all kinds of mathematical activity: sorting, combining, partitioning, matching, ordering and the fundamental types of movement.

Practical experience of spatial relationships is one of the foundations on which other mathematical relationships and operations can be built.

THE STARTING-POINT FOR PRIMARY SCHOOL WORK

When children first come to school they have had many experiences which have given them some of the basic concepts of space which are related to shape, position and size. They know that an object remains the same even when a change of position alters its apparent shape and size; but may not identify the representation of a shape drawn in two different positions.

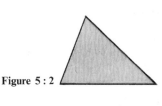

Figure 5 : 2

They see shapes in relation to their own positions and cannot imagine what they will look like to an observer in a different position (*see page 22*). Certain differences of shape and size can be distinguished but discrimination is still very limited and children cannot combine different kinds of relationships or easily fit objects into their place in a sequence. Nor can they measure (*see page 74*). They have developed language and simple representational drawing, but they judge by their perception and do not yet analyse shapes according to the number of their sides or the forms of their corners.

SPATIAL 'PLAY'

Given the new play materials that a school provides, children usually begin spontaneously with

Figure 5 : 3

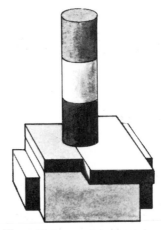

Figure 5 : 4

simple manipulative play to discover what they can do with the things, or they may start with representational play if the things suggest something which interests them. This free play, dependent on the children's own curiosity or impulse, is of great value and should not be curtailed too soon. When fresh material is introduced later on, a period of free experiment with it should be allowed to give children their own insight into some of its properties. Representational play, in which geometrical shapes may represent a garage, a person, an aircraft or a bed, depends very much on likenesses of outline and shape; the representation of a *situation* such as lorries and cars on a road, or dolls at a tea-party, will bring out relative positions, independent of their position in relation to the children. Some toys, such as mosaics and boards with coloured pegs, will stimulate children immediately to make repetitive patterns, often foreshadowing counting in ones, twos, threes, etc. (*see page 205*). Sometimes such pattern-making shows children's awareness of shapes such as squares, rectangles, triangles (Figures 5 : 3 and 5 : 4).

Constructional play is often seen at the age of five, and children will set out to build a bridge from simple unit shapes and make a stable structure out of them. Or a child may build similarly 'my Daddy's office' using a variety of shapes to make a recognisable structure. This power to visualise a construction and select materials to carry it out will grow considerably during the first two years at school and is obviously a means of developing mental pictures to guide a child's purposeful actions.

Free play can be followed by controlled activity with the teacher suggesting ways in which the materials can be used, or setting some

constructional goal before the children. For instance, 'Can you make this pattern?' (Figure 5 : 5), or, 'Can you build a church?' Various forms would be produced but one like Figure 5 : 6 might appear if the children had the pyramid and the triangular prism or wedge to represent the tower and the roof.

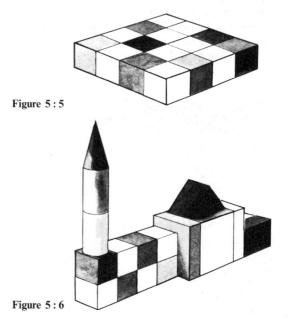

Figure 5 : 5

Figure 5 : 6

SPATIAL MATERIALS AND THEIR USES

A. Three-dimensional objects

It will be noticed that the materials referred to in the preceding section are all three-dimensional things, like those we handle or see in ordinary life. Children sort, match, fit, combine and compare

Figure 5 : 7

Figure 5 : 8

them in the same way as they do the sets of objects which lead to number operations. The significance of three-dimensional material lies in its realism but it also has the advantage of leading children to consider more than one feature at a time. Not only length but breadth and height also must be taken into account; not one face (*see page 286*) but several faces must look right. Thus children are learning to synthesise two or more properties as they fit these shapes together.

The materials to be provided are of two kinds: (1) everyday things in which shape and size are significant and (2) mathematical shapes which have constructional interest in themselves and can also be used for representational building (*see page 98*).

1. *Everyday materials*
Collections of packets for a sweetshop or a supermarket give a wonderful variety of shapes, as shown in Figure 5 : 7.

The properties of these shapes become known through packing them in boxes or arranging a counter display.

Children often use such packets imaginatively to make an engine, aircraft, lorry, a block of flats in the town, or a church or barn in the village (Figure 5 : 9).

Packets of different sizes but of the same shape can be put in order and if filled with small beans or other light small things can also be compared for mass on a simple balance (*see page 77*). Comparing two packets is easy but it is difficult at this age to arrange several in order of mass.

Comparison of the contents of packets of different shapes, some of which are the same size, leads to judgements of *more*, *less*, or the *same* and will lead on to pouring a quantity of water or sand into different containers (some transparent) and thus discovering that the same quantity may occupy different shapes. These activities precede measurement and prepare for more precise experiments in later years (*see page 84*).

Piling packets, or fitting them into boxes in rows and/or layers, gives patterns which illustrate the operations of addition and multiplication, as can be seen in Figure 5 : 8 and 5 : 10.

Figure 5 : 9

Figure 5 : 10

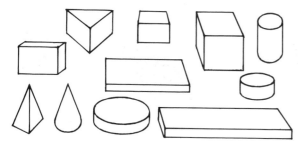

Figure 5 : 11

2. *Mathematically structured shapes*

Mathematical shapes in wood or plastic are available and are designed to show a good range of mathematical properties, and children can use them freely to produce representational constructions. The coloured Poleidoblocs have proved very attractive and stimulating to children. The shapes, colours, precision and weight all contribute to children's satisfaction in using them (Figure 5 : 11).

The cubes and cuboids, their halves and quarters, the cylinders and cones stir the children to make quite complex structures representing what they see around them; for example, Figure 5 : 12 shows the production of a child of five (*see also plate 2*).

Poleidoblocs and Logiblocs include the same shape in different sizes and this leads to pattern-making which illustrates number relations in terms of lengths, surface areas or volumes, but without the child feeling at first the need to measure. Fitting shapes alongside one another gives a comparison of length; putting one block upon another gives a comparison of the areas of their top surfaces; re-assembling the different partitions of a cube shows equality of volume in different shapes.

When children have fitted together such shapes as are shown in Figure 5 : 13, they may say:

i) two blue rods are as long as one green rod;

ii) three blue tiles just cover one yellow tile;

iii) these two halves of a cube are different shapes but each of them is half a cube.

Figure 5 : 12

They should, of course, express these discoveries in their own way. It must be emphasised once more that free imaginative representation must precede the controlled activities which lead to the precise comparisons contained in these statements. The selection of the block (or set of blocks) which is neither too big nor too little but just fits is the necessary preliminary to the procedure of measuring to discover the required size.

Another aspect of fitting which is important mathematically, though it is often neglected, is the making of a hole, cavity or nest into which a certain shape will fit, or alternatively finding the shape (or shapes) needed to fill a given enclosure. In Figure 5 : 14, the same four rods enclose three different holes. Moulds for making jellies or sandcastles show well the relation of shape to hole.

A significant feature of three-dimensional shapes is that they can provide a good model or analogue of our number system. Structural apparatus, such as that provided by Cuisenaire, Dienes, Stern, and others, which is commonly used to enable children to understand number notation and number operations, depends on the way in which cubes and cuboids can be combined. If they all have the same square cross-section they can be placed end to end to form new cuboids. Five cubes placed side by side

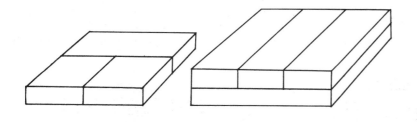

Figure 5 : 13

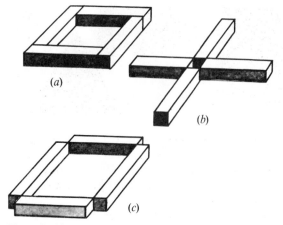

Figure 5 : 16

Figure 5 : 14

form a cuboid or rod whose length is five times that of the cube. If we now make a number system based on five instead of ten we see how the cubes will represent it (Figure 5 : 15).

Now that a large cube has been formed we can continue, making 5 large cubes into one large long cuboid or rod, and 5 of the large rods into one large flat cuboid, and so on without limit. It can be seen that if ten had been chosen as the base number for counting, the shapes made would have been equivalent to 10, 100, 1000, 10 000, etc. cubes, and so would represent the place values of the figures in our decimal number system. This spatial structure is a memorable way of visualising a number notation based on powers of a chosen number, say, 10^1, 10^2, 10^3, 10^4, 10^5, ... It can be built by children in free play before its number significance is realised through counting (*see also Chapter 9*).

An experience which often surprises children at this stage is that the same quantity of material can take different shapes which appear to be unequal. So strongly are they influenced by perception that they will say that they *are* unequal. For instance, children may take a lump of dough, clay, Plasticine or wet sand and roll it into a long thin sausage; they then change its shape and make a short thick sausage. Some children will think the long one bigger, others that the thick one is bigger (Figure 5 : 16).

Only repeated experience and an awareness that length and thickness are both involved will enable children to be certain that the quantity does not change when the shape is altered. Obviously the children should have a good many activities of this kind, e.g. making a ball of clay, and changing it to a flat disc, a ring, a cube, a cone, etc.

B. Two-dimensional materials

Three-dimensional shapes have a particular importance because they correspond to the objects of daily experience. Two-dimensional shapes are either flat patterns as seen on walls or floors, for example, or are representative drawings. It is wise to give ample opportunities for experimenting with solid forms at an early stage, but children's familiarity with pictures in books and their growing pleasure in their own drawings as a means of expression make two-dimensional materials suitable and significant. They have the added advantage that patterns and structures made from them can often be easily drawn by the children or pasted on paper and thus a record of achievements can be made.

Coloured cardboard or plastic tiles in a variety of shapes provide the means for imaginative play. Just as cylinders, cones and pyramids are attractive to children so are circles, semicircles, triangles and rectangles (*see also page 63*) stimulating to the imagination. The square with its useful symmetries is as important as the cube and will be extensively used. Decorative patterns will be made as well as

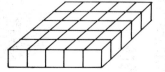

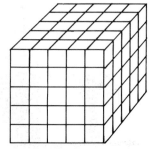

Figure 5 : 15

  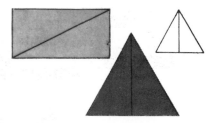

Figure 5 : 17

representations of ships, planes, animals, human figures, etc. The results of such play with tiles are transient but its value lies in the comparative ease with which children can handle the tiles, if they are made of strong card or a non-slip plastic; children thus grow familiar with their shapes. The tiles should have several sizes in each shape, say 2-cm, 4-cm and 5-cm sides or diameters, so that fitting and repetition give coherent forms. Triangles provided should include the equilateral triangle and the diagonal halves of squares and rectangles (Figure 5 : 17).

Circles and semicircles should have diameters corresponding to the sides of the straight-edged shapes.

As dexterity grows children can use gummed coloured paper shapes and stick them on to paper so that all the class can see the designs produced by individuals (*see plates 3 and 4*). Trial efforts using flannelgraph or plastic sheets are a useful preparation for the more permanent stick-on task. If templates are provided, children can cut out fairly accurately geometrical shapes like those in Figure 5 : 18 which are usefully related in size.

The next stage requires more skill. Children can cut out shapes they would like to use to make a class frieze. The whole class will be concerned with placing the shapes to make a 'good' pattern but all the children have to think out the way to cut their own shapes. The shapes need not be confined to those familiar through using tiles, though the tiles

could be used as templates; children can also cut quite freely. In the latter case they often show great originality, cutting out stars, spirals, crescents, etc. about which they will learn more in the future.

Since several identical shapes are usually included in a set given to children, some patterns may give number experience. A simple pattern made from only two different shapes, say squares and triangles, may lead to writing a number sentence about it (Figure 5 : 19). Or if two or more colours of the same shape are used a number statement can be made (Figure 5 : 20), as the child's counting capacity develops.

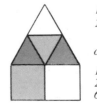

I used 6 tiles
2 squares and 4 triangles

or

I used 6 tiles
2 red 2 blue 2 green
6=2+2+2

Figure 5 : 19

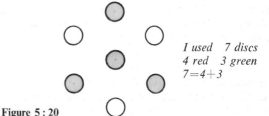

I used 7 discs
4 red 3 green
7=4+3

Figure 5 : 20

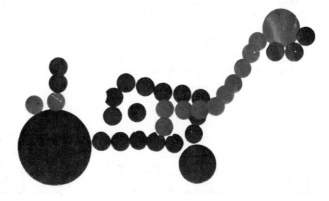

Figure 5 : 18

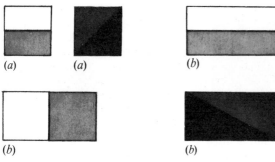

(a)   *(a)*   *(b)*

(b)   *(b)*

Figure 5 : 21

When the children can cut fairly competently they can fold paper shapes into halves, colour the halves differently and cut them out. When different folds are used the halves may have different shapes and the children's own actions in making the halves will help to convince them that these differently shaped halves of the same thing are equal in size. Figure 5 : 21(a) shows two shapes of a half-square. Figure 5 : 21(b) shows three shapes of a half-rectangle.[1] The diagonal halves do not *fold* on to one another so that children may not think they are halves. They need to *cut* them out and then fit one on to another.

It will be seen in Figure 5 : 22 that the diagonal halves of the rectangle can be recombined in several ways.

Older children can experiment to see how many shapes they can make from these two halves. For younger children they afford the opportunity of making a greater variety of patterns. They may notice that the square is a special kind of rectangle and produces only two equal shapes from its triangular halves.

Halves of circles have a special property. When children cut them out they discover that they have the same shape wherever the fold is made. For these experiments each child needs two or three circles of the same size. They can be made by drawing round a suitable round tin lid and cutting out. Plain filter papers as used in science are cheap. The shapes made from these can be coloured and pasted on to paper. Coloured gummed circles are obtainable but they are more expensive. Folding half-circles again into halves will give four pieces or quarters. The notation $\frac{1}{2}$ and $\frac{1}{4}$ is easy to learn; we use $\frac{1}{2}$ when we have cut a shape into *two* equal pieces and $\frac{1}{4}$ when we have cut it into *four* equal pieces. The children will notice that all quarters of circles are the same shape and if any four of them, cut from the same sized circle, are fitted together they can only make a circle. Perhaps some children, experimenting with circles, will make new discoveries; for example, Figure 5 : 23(b) shows that the pattern on the right is the same as the one on the left, but turned round, and they may start a discussion on the rotation of wheels.

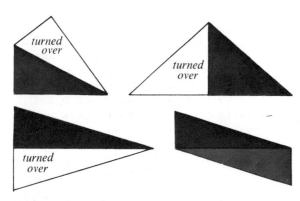

Figure 5 : 22

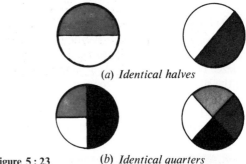

Figure 5 : 23   *(a) Identical halves*   *(b) Identical quarters*

Experiments and puzzles with two-dimensional shapes are a good challenge to inventiveness at about 7 years of age. Some examples can be seen in · Figure 5 : 24.

[1]Children should also have experience of rectangles of other shapes, say 3 cm by 9 cm.

3   *4*   *6*   *9*   *9*   *10*

Figure 5 : 24

Give a child 10 cut-outs of an equilateral triangle. How many different shapes can be made using all of them or some of them? Figure 5 : 24 shows *some* possible shapes.

Given several of each of the shapes shown in Figure 5 : 25 a child can fill the large square in more than one way.

Figure 5 : 26 shows how a child fitted small squares on to a larger square.

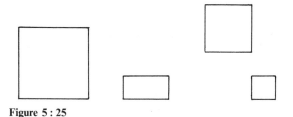

Figure 5 : 25

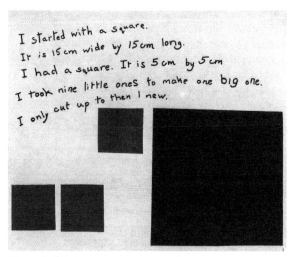

I started with a square.
It is 15 cm wide by 15 cm long.
I had a square. It is 5 cm by 5 cm
I took nine little ones to make one big one.
I only cut up to then I new.

Figure 5 : 26

THE GROWTH OF MATHEMATICAL LANGUAGE

The activities discussed so far in this chapter involve shapes and operations which are generally new to the children. The new concepts which are being acquired must be expressed in some way so that they may be clear in the children's minds and available for use in new thinking. We know that at this age children have a good range of spoken language in which to express their actions, observations and ideas but they have yet to acquire the skills of reading and writing. They have some capacity in drawing of a representational kind though it is independent of measurement and without the accuracy that analysis could give. How then can children register and record the mathematics that they are learning?

Mathematics has three main types of language. It uses the words of common speech and adds to them special words to denote the things it is talking about, the relationships between them and the operations which are performed in mathematics. Children have to learn this special *vocabulary* and it is important that they should begin to do so as soon as they meet mathematical forms and carry out simple operations. Thus we should expect children to use the names of shapes correctly as soon as they can recognise and manipulate them. Triangle, circle, cylinder are no more difficult than aircraft and television; if they have as much meaning for children they will learn them as readily. The written form of such words will constantly be seen and they will form part of the reading vocabulary acquired during the early years.

Before children can read or write (as well as afterwards) they will talk about what they have been making or discovering and this expression will often be the teacher's main guide to a child's range of understanding. Group and class discussions are of the highest importance at the early stages and some of the class talks on daily events and the exhibits on a nature or science table should include references to shape and pattern as well as number. As soon as possible children should be encouraged to write, say, a caption to a diagram or a simple description of what they have done. Both writing and spelling will gradually improve.

The second form of mathematical language is the use of *diagrams*, and in these early years this is a most convicing way of expressing the relationships which children perceive. In this chapter we suggest diagrams of many kinds, made from blocks, tiles or paper cut-outs. Children begin to draw diagrams, too, but while their drawing skill is limited, using squared paper (1-cm or $\frac{1}{2}$-cm for individual use) will help them to draw what they have seen. Accurate drawing on plain paper has to wait until drawing a straight line and measuring have been mastered. Meanwhile, free representative drawing has a valuable place.

The mathematical language which is most abstract is the use of *symbols*: 3, 29, +, =, etc. Because it is abstract, symbolic language normally begins later than the other two forms and is used to express briefly what has already been said in everyday speech and possibly also shown in a diagram. (See Figure 5 : 19). The introduction of a symbol should obviously be made when the idea which it represents is already in the children's minds. For instance, after using tiles of rectangular shape they find other things—door, blackboard, box, book—which have similar shapes, and they learn the name 'rectangle' and perhaps notice its *four* 'square corners'.

The spatial activities described in this chapter lead to all three forms of expression, including the symbols for numbers and operations, but the one that we emphasise here is the correct use of spatial terms.

HORIZONTAL AND VERTICAL

As we have seen, children's exploration of space depends to a great extent on their powers of movement and their observations. They stand and move in an *upright* position normally; usually they see things *balanced* on a *level* base and with a *vertical* axis. Shapes come to be recognised most easily in the position in which they are most frequently seen; if the position is different children will often think they see a different shape.[2] The cube cut diagonally in half provides a good illustration. The 'roof' position is not identified as a half-cube by young children until manipulative experience makes it clear. See Figure 5 : 27.

The notion of *upright* develops from children building brick towers, making fences or trees from twigs, or telephone poles in a model of a street. *Level* is an idea which grows more slowly. Watching a ball or marble rolling down a slope or path leads to a discussion and a model road can be made with slopes as well as level stretches. A simple levelling device is a bottle of water with a small airbubble; alternatively, a cheap spirit level can be provided. It may also be possible for the class to see a builder's level being used in making a wall. Children can now test surfaces inside the school and outside in the playground, as well as in their own constructions, to see whether they are level in any direction.

A plumb bob for testing the upright position is easily made by tying a small heavy bead to a piece of string. Experiments will show that a ball dropped at the top of the line falls down along the line of the string. Older children will learn the words *vertical* and *horizontal*. The making of a simple balance bar, hung on a string loop at the point which allows the bar to rest in the level position, gives useful illustrations of vertical, horizontal, and different slopes. Tin lids supported by strings from the bar enable simple comparisons of weights to be made. See Figure 5 : 28.

 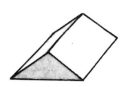

Figure 5 : 27

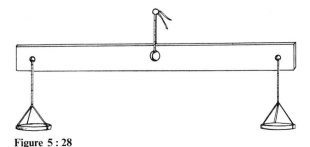

Figure 5 : 28

[2]See Figure 2 : 4 and Figure 5 : 2.

PART 2 | PRACTICAL EXPERIENCE AND EXPLORATION

6 | COUNTING AND RECORDING

LEARNING TO COUNT

The first necessary steps towards understanding numbers have been taken when a child can compare and order sets. Those sets that match, each element of one to an element of the other, have the property of matching. We say they have the same number. If two sets do not match exactly, one set has more things in it than the other. In this case children who have learned the first few numbers will be able to say *how many more* if the difference is within their limited number knowledge, even though they may not yet be able to count the number of things in the sets (Figure 6 : 1).

Several sets can be placed in order of number without counting, if they are compared two at a time. The larger of each pair is placed to the right. A third can be greater than the first and less than the second one considered. It will be placed *between* the other two. In this way a sequence of sets is made, as shown in Figure 6 : 2.

Already, as we have seen in Chapter 3, children who have learned the numbers one to four can identify sets having those numbers. By ordering sets, some with more than four members, and forming a sequence of sets, they can extend their number knowledge. They may know and may be able to say the sequence of number names to twenty or beyond. Now they have to increase their range of experience with sets of objects or their pictures so that they can match the correct number name to sets with five or more members.

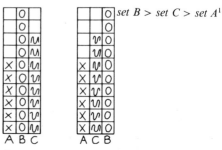

set B > set C > set A[1]

Figure 6 : 2

NUMBERS FROM FIVE TO TEN

i) *Four and one more*

The basic property of the counting numbers is that each of them is one more than the number which precedes it. This fact has already been brought out for the numbers one to four. There are several kinds of experience which will show that putting one more object to a set gives a set which has the next number. A set of four things given one more becomes five: one, two, three, four, five.

We write the number names, or place a card with the correct symbol under the new set. We name the number 'five' and write both the word and the symbol, 5. See Figure 6 : 3.

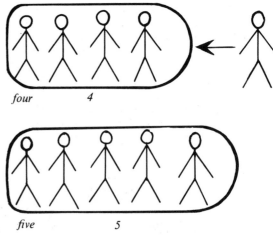

four   4

five   5

Figure 6 : 3

[1] The symbol > means here that one set has more things in it than the other.

Mark's set   *Joan's set*

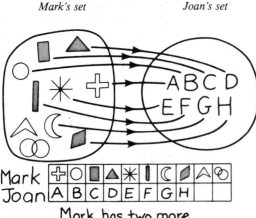

Mark has two more

Figure 6 : 1

ii) *Learning about five*

A set of Cuisenaire or similar rods can be used to make a staircase. One unit cube can be placed above each rod in turn and will thus make a height equal to the next rod. One to four are known; we associate the number five with the next rod. Four and one more is five. We take the five-rod and place unit cubes above it, counting one, two, three, four, five (Figure 6 : 4). Again we write the number name and its symbol: 'five' and 5.

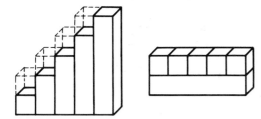

Figure 6 : 4

The number five should now be found in as many activities as possible. Children should think of things that come in fives, making collections with five members and illustrating with pictures: fingers on a hand, petals on some flowers, pence in a fivepence, corners of a square pyramid, panes of glass in some windows, families of five, etc. Given pictures of two, three or four things, children can put more pictures to make sets of five things, e.g. {trumpet, soldier, drum} becomes {trumpet, whistle, soldier, drum, doll}. The recognition of fives in pictures, buying five things at 1 penny each in the class shop (and counting five pennies to pay for them), home play for a family of five (including stories about the family and its needs), letting children take five strides to see who goes farthest – all these are examples of the activities which a teacher can provide. Clapping rhythms in fives helps to bring out the patterns of the ones, twos, or threes which make up sequences of five. 1 . . 2 . . 345 or 12 . . 345 or 12 . . 34 . . 5 are examples of such partitions.

These patterns are seen even more clearly if

children are given five shapes, such as discs, squares, stars, etc., in two or more colours and asked to make patterns. They can draw what they have made and write what they can see (Figure 6 : 5).

Counting backwards as a set of things is dismantled, 5, 4, 3, 2, 1, helps to establish the sequence in the mind, relating each number to the preceding one. Some children, having heard a countdown or waited for a microwave oven to finish, may continue to zero, even if they say 'Blast off' or 'Done'. The name zero and the symbol 0 can be introduced on such an occasion, and the teacher should match it to the fact that after dismantling or putting away we are left with nothing at all.

The ordinal aspect of five must be taught as an extension of first, second, third, fourth, which we dealt with in Chapter 3. If children are arranged in fives for games, races or other activities, they can be called or recorded in order and the *fifth* one identified. This account of learning about five has been given in some detail to show how the ideas of set, sequence, partitioning and order all find a place. The numbers from six to nine will need similar treatment.

iii) *Numbers six to nine*

The names of numbers six to nine and and their symbols will present no difficulty but it has to be remembered that a set with more than five members cannot be recognised on sight without counting. It is thus most important that such sets should be recognised in various patterns. The special characteristics of these numbers should be discovered by children through their own experiments.

The difficulty of recognising the number of a set which has more than five members is met by special features in some types of abacus still in use today. A Russian abacus frequently seen in shops and offices has the 5th and 6th beads on each column coloured differently from the other beads. This arrangement makes it easy to identify 7, 8 and 9, as can be seen in Figure 6 : 6.

Figure 6 : 5

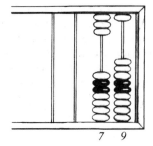

Figure 6 : 6

7 9

The Japanese *soroban* has a separate bead to represent five, so that six is shown by the five-bead and one unit bead (Figure 6 : 7). This reminds us of the Roman use of *vi* for six and *vii* for seven.

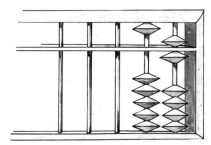

Figure 6 : 7

A set of *six* things makes some interesting patterns and its subsets become very apparent (Figure 6 : 8).

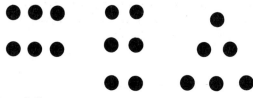

Figure 6 : 8

The children can write what these patterns show, using symbols:

6 = 3 + 3   6 = 2 + 2 + 2   6 = 1 + 2 + 3

It must be emphasised that at this stage we are thinking about the *numbers*, the sets they refer to, the ways of partitioning a set, and the patterns a set can make. We are not yet dealing with the *operations* of adding or substracting numbers; we are comparing, arranging or fitting *things* as a preliminary to operations with *numbers*. We use the symbols to describe what we have discovered about the numbers through such activities.

A six-rod will demonstrate similar patterns to those shown in Figure 6 : 8. A square tray like that provided in Stern apparatus allows the six to be matched by pairs of rods or any other combinations of rods. Each matching can be recorded, e.g. 2 + 2 + 1 + 1 = 6. In play with shapes six appears in the number of faces of the familiar cubes and dice; a six-pointed star can be made from two triangles; six triangles fit together to make a hexagon; some children will be having their sixth birthday at about this time (Figure 6 : 9). Six pennies can be exchanged for 1 fivepence + 1 penny.

Figure 6 : 9

Seven is remembered as the number of days in the week. The names of the days can be written as a set and another set of seven written to match : perhaps the names of the children who are to fill in the weather chart for each day.

Monday	John
Tuesday	Pam
Wednesday	Jean
Thursday	Paul
Friday	Li
Saturday	Alan
Sunday	Saheed

Seven also makes pleasing patterns such as those shown in Figure 6 : 10.

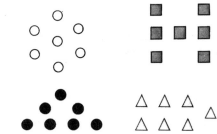

Figure 6 : 10

The important fact about *eight* is that it is four and four. Like six, a set of eight things makes two equal rows. This property can also be seen in the shape made by two squares, as in Figure 6 : 11. It may be compared with the triangles in Figure 6 : 9.

Nine reminds us of six because a set of nine things also makes rows of three. As there are three rows of three they can be arranged as a

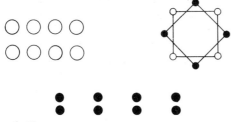

Figure 6 : 11

square. This should be the basic pattern of nine though it will later be known as one less than ten, when the staircase using ten rods is counted down (Figure 6 : 12).

Figure 6 : 12

iv) The number *ten* can be learned at first without reference to the reasons for the special way of writing it. It is represented by the tallest of the set of Cuisenaire or Stern rods and thus has a special place in a child's experience. Ten discs make two rows of five and can also be arranged as a triangle with rows of 1, 2, 3, 4 discs, as Figure 6 : 13 shows.

Figure 6 : 13

Ten quickly becomes familiar through its constant use in money and measuring.

Recording

Before the notation for numbers greater than ten is studied and the special properties of such numbers are discovered, a great deal of counting and recording should be encouraged, with emphasis on numbers up to ten. Children will count and record beyond ten, perhaps up to a hundred, but without knowing the structure of the tens and ones shown in the numerals.

The open abacus is a useful means of keeping a daily record, or the individual scores of a team. Cards at the foot of a column will show the numbers. Comparisons between the various scores

are easily made and thus differences between pairs of numbers become known (*see pages 104–105*).

Daily records of things the children bring or talk about, and counts of things in the classroom, can be listed in numeral form and represented on squared paper. We have seen how comparisons can be made on such a recording without counting the sets. Now the squares show *how many* things in each set and the *numbers* can be written on lines which serve as axes of reference (Figure 6 : 14).

Individual children will keep such records, say of tractors seen, and will show the numbers both as numerals and on a chart. Simple sentences can be written beside the chart.

'I saw seven tractors.'

'David saw nine.'

'David saw two more.'

Attention has been drawn to the numbers whose sets can make two equal rows: 4, 6, 8, 10. They can also be seen as making pairs. Shoes, children, or coloured pencils can be paired. As we count them each number is two more than the one before it (Figure 6 : 15).

These numbers can be shown on squared paper and the steps will be seen to be twos. Going *downstairs* two at a time gives us 10, 8, 6, 4, 2, and then? We see that zero is the starting number. The numeral 0 should be well known now both as the symbol for the number of the empty set and as the beginning from which we measure. Even numbers and their use in doubling and halving seem to form the basis for a good deal of children's mental calculation at a later stage, and it is helpful to emphasise them at this early stage.

Ten as the counting set

We have remarked that sets having the numbers six to ten are difficult to distinguish at a glance. Sets with numbers greater than ten are even more difficult to distinguish, and ten is used as a counting set. When we have one more than ten we keep the one and the ten separated and write one ten and one unit, or say simply 'a ten and a one'. Now we

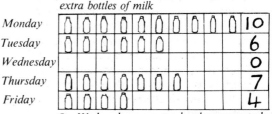

extra bottles of milk

Monday												10
Tuesday												6
Wednesday												0
Thursday												7
Friday												4

On Wednesday no extra bottles were needed. We wrote this as O.

Figure 6 : 14

Figure 6 : 15

can see why eleven is written '11', it means 1 ten and 1 one. The numbers to twenty can be counted now as 1 ten and two, 12; 1 ten and three, 13; and so on, up to 2 tens, twenty.

Besides the usual experiences of putting things together as a packet (or bundle) or *ten* and the extra *ones* when making a count, children will be helped by the use of structural apparatus in which ten is the largest number represented by a rod. Then when the combination of two rods exceeds the length of the ten-rod the extra length required can be made up with unit cubes or a short rod to represent them (Figure 6 : 16).

Figure 6 : 16

On page 103 more detail is given about the use of such apparatus in building up the addition pairs which are equivalent to each of the numbers from eleven to twenty. Here we are chiefly concerned to see how the notation develops an understanding of the structure which the rods disclose.

Most children will not be content to stop at writing 20. They can *say* the number names well beyond twenty and they may well wish to represent them in rods or bundles as well as to use the symbols. It will be noticed that a child can now give meaning to the zeros which occur in writing 10, 20, 30, etc. These numbers can be shown in *tens* without any extra *ones*.

Numbers eleven to twenty

The numbers from ten to twenty are particularly important because they provide the pattern for operations with tens and units in the higher decades. If the combinations and partitions of sets with these numbers are well known, work with larger numbers will develop smoothly. Moreover, the organisation of a set into counting sets and ones is parallel to the use of two kinds of coin, e.g. tenpences and pence, or metric measures such as decimetres and centimetres.

Children need the experience of representing a count of 13 things in several ways, e.g. in a grouping of ten and 3 ones, as a ten-rod and a three-rod, and on a graph as a block of ten squares and three squares (Figure 6 : 17).

The abacus is now used differently. In place of recording various counts on the different rods, we arrange ones on the right-hand rod and let the beads on the next rod represent the counting sets of

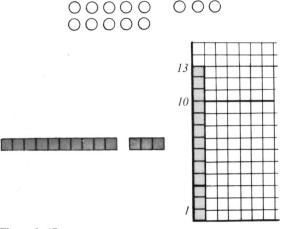

Figure 6 : 17

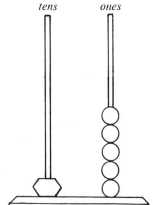

tens   ones

Figure 6 : 18

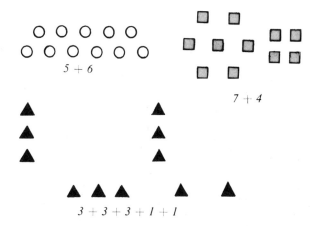

5 + 6

7 + 4

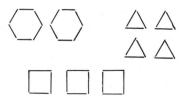

3 + 3 + 3 + 1 + 1

Figure 6 : 19

ten. Clearly this must follow the experience of arranging a number in sets of ten and recognising that these sets must be counted so that the number can be written in symbols or shown on the abacus (Figure 6 : 18).

The activities and explorations suggested for the numbers one to ten must now be extended to these larger numbers so that their special properties become equally well known. We will now look at some of these properties and patterns.

Eleven is not a very interesting number until its multiples are studied. Its behaviour depends chiefly on the way we write it as 1 ten and 1 one. Written in the base of eight as 1 eight and 3 ones it loses even this unique property. Nor does eleven yield any particularly pleasing patterns. A few possibilities are shown in Figure 6 : 19.

Twelve has many attractive and useful features. A set of twelve things will make two rows and so twelve continues the list of numbers that can be counted in twos. A set of twelve things can also be

arranged in threes, fours and sixes, as can be seen in Figure 6 : 20.

These arrangements can also be shown in shapes made with strips or milk-straws (Figure 6 : 21).

Figure 6 : 21

The clock gives interesting experiences of 12, particularly if children fold paper circles to make their own clock faces. Some of the unequal partitions of a set of twelve things are shown in Figure 6 : 22. All such partitions should be found by children, using as many situations as possible.

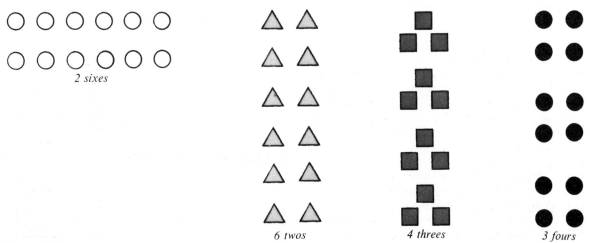

2 sixes

6 twos   4 threes   3 fours

Figure 6 : 20

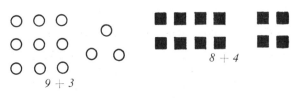

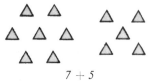

Figure 6 : 22

Thirteen has a bad reputation among the superstitious. In fact, a set of thirteen things cannot make equal rows of any kind and thus 13 is less useful than its neighbour, 12, or even 14. But it can be arranged in some interesting patterns; e.g. it can make two squares by a partition into four and nine. Also, since it splits into six and seven it can make a six-pointed star (Figure 6 : 23).

Figure 6 : 23

Each of the numbers 14, 16, 18, 20 will correspond to sets with 2 equal rows; sets of 15 and 18 make three equal rows. Sets of 17 and 19 do not make equal rows but 17 can be arranged in a pattern of squares and 19 extends the star made with 13. A set of 15 makes a larger triangle of the kind made by 10 (Figure 6 : 24).

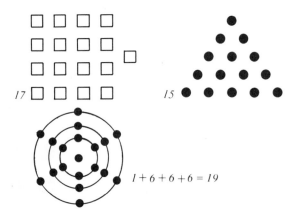

Figure 6 : 24

Given freedom to invent, children will produce a great variety of number patterns, describing them in words and writing something about them in symbols.

RECORDING NUMBER SEQUENCES

As well as recording on squared paper the many counts of sets which give numbers from ten to twenty, children can now represent the sequence of numbers they have found which will correspond to two equal rows: 2, 4, 6, . . . , 16, 18, 20. They can be drawn on $\frac{1}{2}$-cm squared paper and will make a long staircase (Figure 6 : 25).

The numbers which correspond to rows of threes can be similarly represented. The squares may, of course, contain pictures of objects or may be suitably coloured.

Children can read the graphs of 2-row and 3-row numbers both up and down and can discuss the

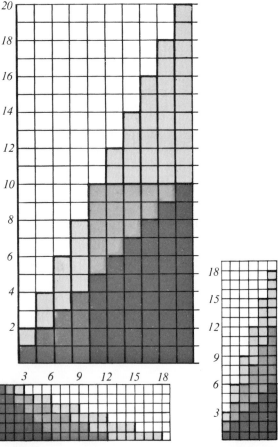

Figure 6 : 25

patterns made by the tops of the columns, the tens, and the individual rows or rods which have their own colours.

It is important that familiarity with the numbers to twenty should be built up not only through the counting of sets of objects, the use of rods and expression on squared paper, as outlined in this chapter. Counting in units of measure, handspans, spoonfuls, footstrips, etc. should go on at the same time, on lines suggested in Chapter 7. Frequent handling of 1-pence and 10-pence coins will further strengthen understanding. It is in these experiences with numbers between 10 and 20 that the foundation of the decimal notation is laid.

Early number in the National Curriculum

As they carry out the activities described in this chapter, children are becoming confident in a National Curriculum Statement of Attainment at Level 1. They should be able to:

- Use number in the context of the classroom and school.

(AT2: Number, Level 1)

The associated statements in the Programme of Study are:

- Count, read, write and order numbers to at least 10.
- Learn that the size of a set is given by the last number in the count.
- Understand the language associated with number, eg 'more', 'fewer', 'the same'.
- Understand conservation of number.
- Make a sensible estimate of a number of objects up to 10.

7 | DISCOVERING QUANTITY: MEASURING

THE IMPORTANCE OF MEASURING

A technological society depends for its efficient running on highly accurate measuring of a wide range of quantities, such as voltages, wind-speeds, tyre pressure, and so on. New discoveries and inventions add new kinds of measuring to the list and often lead to new types of measuring unit.

Measuring can be considered as an extension of the use of number from counting to stating the quantity contained in a continuous whole. Separate objects can be counted and the number in a set of them tells us how many members it contains. Blood counts and Geiger counters remind us of the important of such counting for science and human welfare. But some things are continuous, with no discernible subdivisions; time, for instance, which flows without ceasing (though there is a pattern of days and of seasons); a piece of string (though it has two ends); the mass of a bag of flour. For practical life we must match events to time, decide whether the string is long enough for our purposes, or the quantity of flour sufficient for a recipe. Comparison, fitting, or matching is sometimes necessary and this demands that we should find a way of assessing a quantity.

THE DIFFERENCE BETWEEN NUMBERS AND MEASURES

The distinction between numbers and measures can be clearly seen. Number is a concept which has been set free from the nature or the arrangement of the objects in a particular set. The idea of number develops as the common property of matching sets. The structure of a number such as 12, and number operations such as addition and multiplication are independent of time and place. They do not change however we vary the nature or arrangement of the sets they refer to. We can use them through our mental imagery without in fact relating them to any objects at all.

On the other hand, measures always refer to properties encountered in real situations, whether in the length of an actual path or the pressure of a particular tyre. We find that numbers provide the means for making useful comparisons of such properties, and also that the problems which occur in measuring broaden our conception of the number system, for instance in regard to fractions, decimals, ratio and approximations.

INTUITIVE ASSESSMENT OF QUANTITY

The primitive way of assessing a quantity is based on a visual or manipulative estimate, comparing one whole thing with another or with an image recalled from past experience. People who wish to estimate a long distance will compare it mentally with a distance that they recall, such as the length of a cricket pitch or a familiar path. They may have grown used to carrying 20 kg and will estimate a heavier mass by its feel in comparison with the remembered sensation of carrying a 20-kg mass. In other words, they mentally divide the whole length or mass into parts. Measuring a continuous property depends on this awareness of a whole and its parts.

When children need to compare sizes they also make a judgement 'by eye'. At first they make a direct comparison of two things both within view. Piaget has shown that this intuitive judgement is the earliest step towards measuring. The child has no previous experience on which to base a *mental* comparison. But this intuitive assessment is often faulty. Differences in the position of two equal rods may cause a child to think that one is longer than the other.

At this stage children are not thinking in terms of parts. In Figure 7 : 1(*b*) they do not equate the projecting part of one rod to the projecting part of the other. However, children soon know that the lengths will not be altered by a change of position and they place the rods side by side. They can then

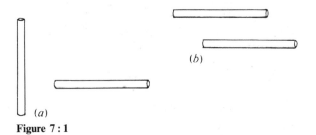

Figure 7 : 1

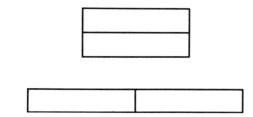

Figure 7 : 2

say whether one rod is longer, shorter, or the same length as the other. Similarly, if two rectangles are placed in the different positions shown in Figure 7 : 2 children will differ in their opinions about the relative sizes of the two resulting shapes. Yet they can reach a judgement by placing one pair of rectangles on the other. In both cases the comparison depends on intution, and experience is needed before the next step can be taken, and the equality of the pairs recognised without experimenting.

THE IDEA OF QUANTITY

The idea of quantity grows slowly from the first intuitive comparisons of *more* or *less* to an understanding of both counting and measuring. Comparing *lengths* or *masses* of objects develops into the complicated process we know as *measuring*; by this we mean finding a suitable unit and using it to enable us *to attach a number to any quantity*. We shall first consider the kinds of experience which foster the ability to deal with quantity in these ways.

CONTRAST AND COMPARISON

Children's first interest in size (of any kind) arises through contrast: big or little, soon or long time, fast or slow (of movement), a little or a lot. Sorting

at this stage means putting all 'big' shapes into one box or pile and putting all the 'little' ones into another. This activity covers many of the things (cars, toys, animals, balls, sticks) with which children play in their first days at school. Such contrasts of size appear in their stories: the great big giant, the tiny little mouse. When children come to school they need many experiences which will stimulate them to take the next step, i.e. to make judgements about a difference between two things which they will describe in words, such as smaller, quicker, more, heavier. They are now comparing two quantities, and seeing a relationship between them. The actions of bringing two things together, pouring from one container into another, cutting up a shape to see whether it will cover another, give them the certainty that the quantities are not altered by these movements; they make these comparisons with confidence (Figure 7 : 3).

Pairs of coloured sticks, rods, nails, ribbons, etc. can be sorted into longer and shorter; the differences between them will be seen with greater discrimination as experience grows. Two shoes, two children, toy cars, dolls, can be placed side by side; their silhouettes can be cut to size and the appropriate label (taller, shorter, longer) attached. Squares or discs can be compared, the smaller square or disc being placed on the larger. Jugs and beakers can be tested to see which holds more, or less, by pouring water or fine grain from one to the other. The children should check that if one holds more the other holds less, and vice versa. In Figure 7 : 4 pictures (*a*) and (*b*) show the experiement of filling the beaker from the larger jug; pictures (*c*) and (*d*) show the partial filling of the jug from the full beaker.

Birthdays give an opportunity for learning 'older' and 'younger' by talking about the child who is 'six today' and another whose birthday has still to come.

A balance bar and a seesaw introduce 'lighter' and 'heavier' when comparing the weights of two

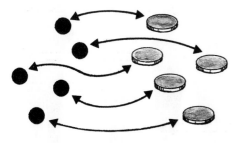

matching two sets

comparing two rods

comparing two masses

Figure 7 : 3

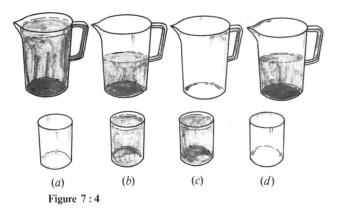

(a)   (b)   (c)   (d)

Figure 7 : 4

children, two sets of conkers, two pet animals, and so on.

All such discoveries through comparing need to be recorded, for example by placing all the longer ones of the couples in a particular box, or by putting an appropriate word or letter on the objects, or by putting drawings or pictures into blanks in given sentences such as the following:

> The (blue) rod is longer than the (red) rod.
> The (flat) tin is heavier than the (tall) tin.
> (Mary) is older than (Paul).

The opposite sentences should also be written; e.g.

> The (red) rod is shorter than the (blue) rod.

These activities do more than prepare children for the idea of measurement; the activities make children more aware of the physical properties of the objects and shapes they are handling. They begin to notice that a doll, for example, has *height* and is not merely *big*. It is a problem to know how to compare two such heights since there is no line along an edge which could be placed beside a corresponding edge. Weight can be felt when children lift heavy things which pull their hands down. They can also *feel* the pressure they must exert at one end of a balance bar to hold steady the mass supported at the other end of the bar. Capacity is seen to be an important property of a cup or bottle but to be independent of shape. It is essential for children to know about these physical properties since the properties decide how the objects possessing them can be used. The act of measuring serves only to help us to use objects efficiently. Without a thorough understanding of the properties, measuring degenerates into recording numbers without knowing the meaning or purpose of what is being done. The importance of the pre-measuring stage cannot be over-stressed.

MATCHING AND ORDERING QUANTITIES

During this period of *qualitative* comparison of such properties as length, capacity or mass, the comparison of sets will be taking place along the lines suggested in Chapter 3. The idea of *number* will be gradually emerging from the processes of matching and ordering sets. The idea of *length* begins to develop when objects are found which can be matched when placed alongside. For example, two or more rods can be fitted against a longer rod, or two bricks can fill the gap left by one brick of larger size (Figure 7 : 5). The *equivalence* of lengths is being established; this is an essential preliminary to measuring with ruler or tape-measure.

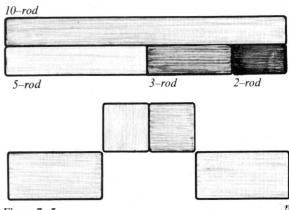

Figure 7 : 5

The next step is to place several lengths in order to form a *sequence*. A few children can be placed in a row and the class invited to put them in order, the tallest (or shortest) first. Silhouettes of a larger

Figure 7 : 6

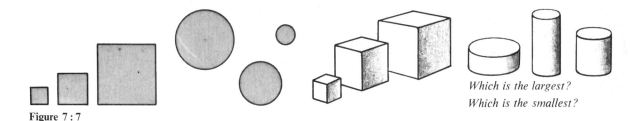

Which is the largest?
Which is the smallest?

Figure 7 : 7

number of children can be drawn and the silhouettes placed in order of height. This brings out the necessity of placing all the feet of the silhouettes on the same 'ground' line so that the tops show the true heights. Sets of rods, pieces of braid, packets, tins, etc. can be placed in order, making a kind of staircase. The 'steps' from one to the next can be discussed. 'Are there any very big steps?' (Figure 7 : 6).

When children are handling solid shapes they will see differences of *surface* as well as of length. For instance, they will have square tiles and discs of varying sizes. These are most easily ordered by placing one upon another. Such objects as cubes and cylinders cannot be reliably compared at this stage unless they are of the same shape, that is unless all their dimensions are in proportion; this is because many children of this age cannot yet take into account two differences, such as height and diameter, at the same time when one must be considered as compensating for the other; for example, the height of one cylinder may be greater than the other but its diameter less. This means that notions of *area* and *volume* cannot be thought about in any general way (Figure 7 : 7).

Capacities are troublesome to order by comparing two quantities at a time but a first step in using a strip for recording can be taken. If a transparent jar has a strip pasted to its side, a child can mark on it the level of water poured from various containers in turn and thus obtain the order of their capacities. A letter or colour symbol will have to be given to each container at this stage (Figure 7 : 8).

The ordering of *masses* is much more difficult than forming a sequence of sets, lengths or capacities, because we cannot measure mass directly but must relate it to *force*. In particular, we connect it with the pull of *gravity*, that is, with *weight*. Even quite young children today are likely to have heard of weightlessness during a journey to the Moon and to have seen pictures of weightless objects floating in a spacecraft. But they know that the *mass* of the sugar (or other material) in the spacecraft is unchanged. It will sweeten just as many cups of tea as when it was on the ground.

To understand that the 'heaviness' of an object is due to a pull, children need experiences of the effect of pulls and pushes. Strong springs, securely fastened to a post or beam, will give opportunities for children to feel for themselves the pull needed to stretch the spring (or the push to compress it). They can compare the pulls of two children by the stretches they cause in the spring. If they compare the sensation of the strong downward pull of a heavy mass in one hand with the weak pull of a

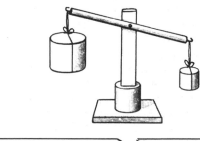

cupful   *bottleful*   *jugful*

Figure 7 : 8

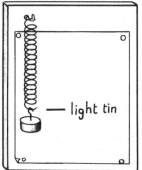

— light tin   — light tin
— heavy tin

Figure 7 : 9

light mass in the other hand, they will experience the same difference as that shown by the stretches each mass will cause when connected to a spring. The mass that feels heavier stretches the spring further than the other. The stretch caused by each mass can be recorded on a strip of paper placed behind the spring (Figure 7 : 9). The stretches caused by several masses could be shown on the strip. Thus the *order* of the masses, from lightest to heaviest, would be represented on the diagram.

Alternatively, two masses can be compared by placing them on a balance bar (Figure 7 : 9). The heavier mass pulls the bar down on the side where it is hung. But such a bar can show the difference between only *two* masses at a time. To arrange three masses in sequence using a balance bar is a very instructive experience since the third mass must be compared with both of the others before its position can be decided. The result can cause a young child some surprise if the size of the objects gives no clue, a small heavy object and a large light one having been included.

In the early stages the ordering of *time* is in effect a sequence of events. 'First we must put away our bricks, then we put on our coats and then we can go out to play.' Such sequences can be recorded in simple *flow charts* made with pictures and sentences. Cards can be used, each card containing a sentence which a child can match to a picture. The cards are then put in sequence as in Figure 7 : 10.

One of the rhythms that we find in everyday life is of special importance for the measuring of time: this is the pendulum. Some children may have seen it swinging in a clock. The teacher can easily set up two or three simple pendulums with strings of

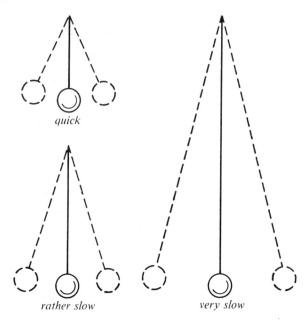

quick

rather slow   very slow

Figure 7 : 11

different lengths which the children can set in motion and observe. They will find that one is slower or faster than another, and will be able to discover that the longer pendulum swings more slowly and the shorter one swings faster (Figure 7 : 11). The pendulums can be placed in order. The next step is to time some of the children's activities by the number of swings of one of the pendulums. The use of a seconds pendulum can follow when minutes and seconds are studied later on. Sandtimers, such as eggtimers, can also be used in time activities.

The *time measurer*, the clock, traditionally had moving hands and the sequence could be seen in the different positions of the hands. This marking of the time of an event by the pattern of the hands is the first step towards the reckoning of the *passing of time* by the *rotation* of the hands. The use of a clock whose hands can be moved to show a sequence of happenings in which the children are interested is a valuable aid. But today digital clocks and watches are increasingly used. This means that children can read the time directly from the clock-face as the number of hours and minutes e.g. 10 : 37, in the same rectangular figures as the calculator uses. Children can watch the changes that occur in the reading as each complete minute or hour is passed. The clock will seem to be *counting* and the children can count with it: 9 : 00, 9 : 01, 9 : 02, 9 : 03, . . . nine o'clock, 1 minute after 9, 2 minutes after 9, . . . 9 : 11, . . . 9 : 59, 10 : 00 . . ., 10

Teacher says time to stop

We put away our bricks

We drink our milk

We go out to play

Teacher says time to come in

We go in to hear a story

Figure 7 : 10

o'clock . . . Children can write the digital figures on squared paper and see their patterns. Soon they are able to read or write these figures as easily as the conventional ones. See Figure 7 : 12.

Money is another very abstract idea. Its use for the exchange of goods can be begun by letting children use one kind of coin for the purchase of things at the class shop. This will be closely related to the beginnings of counting.

Figure 7 : 12

DISCOVERING UNITS OF MEASURE

The ability to count involves realising that the natural numbers increase by unit steps, i.e. two is one more that one, three is one more than two, etc. A similar idea must develop with regard to length, mass and other quantities. It must be possible to think of unit increases. Unit cubes can be placed against a rod, or a series of rods; unit squares can be put alongside strips. A staircase can be formed in which each step is one unit; a number sequence emerges. Simple counts can be made and statements written about the lengths: e.g. 'the rod is as long as five cubes'. This is the first time that a number has been attached to a length and clearly the ability to do this must depend on children's progress with counting. Yet even if this counting of units is correctly done there is no guarantee that children have really grasped that they are finding a measure of length. Nevertheless, they have used the procedure of repeating a unit along a length and this is an essential element in the repetition of a unit in measuring.

Just as any length could be compared with any chosen unit of length, so cotton reels or a similar set of equal masses can be used to balance a mass, such as a toy car. Or a strip of paper, placed beside a spring, can be graduated to show the stretch caused by 1, 2, 3, . . . cotton reels. The toy car can then be hung on the spring and its pull measured by the stretch, shown perhaps as between the 3-reel and the 4-reel marks (Figure 7 : 13).

In all these comparisons and sequences it has been possible to put the objects into a direct physical relationship either in position or through

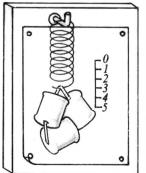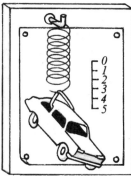

Figure 7 : 13

balancing, etc. A simple count of equivalents or an intuitive judgement is all that has been attempted. True measuring in its fullest sense does not develop until children can compare or order quantities which cannot be brought together.

FINDING A GO-BETWEEN

If two groups of children build towers or make long trains from junk material they may be eager to know which tower is *taller* or which train is *longer*. But the objects cannot be moved. How can they be compared? Direct comparison is impossible. The children should be left to experiment with ways of making a comparison. Piaget has studied children's reactions to this problem.[1] He found that some children will notice the positions of the tops of the objects relative to their own bodies, not taking account of whether the feet are on the same level; others will try to keep one hand at the level of the top of the first object while walking to the second one. Some children will measure in handspans, or use a convenient stick, and so will iterate a unit of their own choice along the objects to be compared. Others will take a long stick or string and mark the ends of the two things; this reveals that the child is thinking of the lengths or heights as parts of, or nested within, the total length of the stick or string – an important idea in connection with a graduated measurer. The crucial feature of this experience is that children must find a go-between, something which can be applied to each object in turn. This opens the way to the general use of a unit of measure, which at this stage will be a matter of personal choice (Figure 7 : 14).

When children have chosen a unit, e.g. a rod, the length of their foot, or the width of the palm, they

[1]Piaget, J. *The Child's Conception of Geometry*, Chapter II.

Figure 7 : 14   Handspan measuring

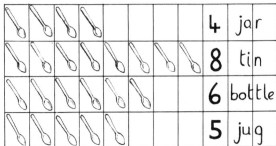

Figure 7 : 16

must repeat the movement of placing it against the object, knowing that the unit is not changed by being moved. To compare the two objects they must now be able to count the number of 'placings' they have made. Once more number and measuring go hand in hand. If the numbers they want for their measures are within their range they can record them in writing. An alternative recording, and one of great value, is to show the measure on a line of paper. If large-square graph paper is used (2-cm or 5-cm) it provides vertical and horizontal guide lines (Figure 7 : 15). The height of a tower can be shown by stepping off the correct number of chosen units up one of the vertical lines; the other towers can be

shown beside it and their comparison discussed. The lengths of the two trains could be drawn in the same way along horizontal lines. Suitable captions will be supplied by the children.

Units of *capacity* are usually the teaspoonfuls or cupfuls of the familiar environment. The comparison of a set of containers will usually be through a count of the units as so many teaspoonfuls, etc. These, too, can be recorded on squared paper. For each spoonful a spoon is drawn in a square along a row or up a column. The various containers can then be seen in terms of their capacity (Figure 7 : 16).

It is less easy for children to find in the classroom things that can be used as units of *mass*. Cotton reels, screws, conkers may be suggested and children soon show that they recognise which of these have a standardised mass and therefore make good units to use with a balance or for graduating a spring scale. A count will be recorded for comparison as before, and a chart on squared paper can also be drawn using picture symbols for the units (Figure 7 : 17).

As many occasions as possible should be found for children to use this new skill of comparing quantities through the measuring unit, encouraging them first to *guess* which of the set is largest, and so on. Such estimating leads children to *think* about the lengths, the feel of the weights, the look of the liquid in the jars, etc. and to realise what quality

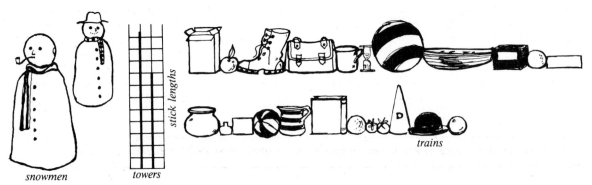

Figure 7 : 15

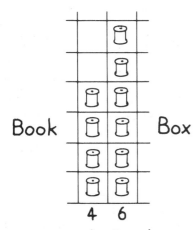

mass in cotton reels

Figure 7 : 17

they are trying to assess. They will look at both top and bottom of a tower, running their eyes up and down; they will not be misled into judging weights by look, nor will they omit to take both width and height into account when comparing surface or volume.

One reason for measuring is that size may change with time. The hamster grows heavier, the plant grows taller: we must measure and record today so that we can compare tomorrow. Recording these changes in size on graph paper is the beginning of a scientific study of growth. In fact, many of the observations of things on the science or nature table can include measures which may be recorded.

GRADUATION AND APPROXIMATE MEASURES

The use of a strip of paper for recording capacities or the stretch of a spring can be most valuably extended at this stage by *graduating* the strip. Once the unit of capacity has been decided upon, a strip can be marked as one spoonful after another is poured into the container. This produces a fairly short number line on which future measures can be read. It can also be used for finding any required quantity, such as three teaspoonfuls of sugar for making a cake in a class project.

A height strip can be used to record the heights of the children, at first without graduation but

merely showing where on the vertical strip each child's head reaches. Usually a good many of the class are near to average height and this crowds the marking about the average point. This will not matter if each child's name is attached to a string and fastened a little way from the strip. This recording will tell us about the children in this class if we can see the markings but the children are not able to *tell* their mothers how tall they are nor compare their heights with those of cousins elsewhere. Even if the strip is then graduated using, say, the length of a stick, it will not do all we want. But children live among people who use standard measures and they hear about centimetres; some child is almost certain to suggest a 'proper' centimetre measure. Most children of this age are familiar with the Cuisenaire number apparatus or similar material based on a 1-centimetre unit. The rods may have been used informally for measuring, taking the edge of the cube or one of the rods as a unit. Now they learn that the edge of the cube is 1 centimetre long and the rods measure 2, 3, 4, . . ., 10 centimetres. A long strip can be graduated in centimetres and then used for measuring the children's heights, etc. This will give occasion for counting up to and beyond 100, so extending the range of numbers the children understand.

The use of a graduated strip, whether for capacity or for length, in improvised or standard units, brings home to children very sharply that the end of the measured quantity is rarely exactly on a mark. The bowl holds *about* 5 cupfuls, or *nearly* 6 cupfuls, or a *little over* 4 cupfuls. This result is, of course, inevitable when we are dealing with a continuous quantity. Since children grow in height continuously, they sometimes find that the top of their head is between two of the fixed marks on the strip. In any case the children see how hard it is to measure accurately and they will be content to give measurement as nearly as possible.

If graduated strips are widely used, e.g. by having one on the edge of a table and one horizontally along a wall, the class will use them freely and talk about what they find. In an effort to state a measure more exactly some children will probably use a *half* to describe the point which seems to be no nearer to 9, say, than to 10. They may say 'a half more than 9' and we should accept this with pleasure and mention it to the other children. See Figure 7 : 18.

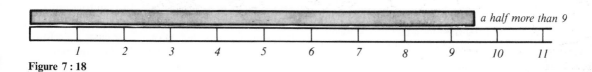

a half more than 9

| 1 | 2 | 3 | 4 | 5 | 6 | 7 | 8 | 9 | 10 | 11 |

Figure 7 : 18

WEIGHING OUT IN CONVENTIONAL UNITS

The metric units of mass are not very convenient for young children with only a limited range of counting. The gram is much too small for them to handle, even if their weighing apparatus were accurate enough to show a difference of 1 gram. On the other hand, the kilogram is too large for most of the objects a young child can handle. The 100-gram mass is the best unit at this stage; it can be treated and counted as 1 unit without connecting it with the kilogram or the gram. It has not been given a popular name but children could call it a hecto, short for hectogram, its metric name which is not used in the International Standard but is available for informal usage.[2] In these early experiences some standard masses should be at hand for children to choose the one suitable for a particular measuring task: kilogram, $\frac{1}{2}$-kilogram, 100-gram and perhaps 10-gram and 20-gram. These standard masses will be used separately and will not be linked until later, unless a child spontaneously experiments and discovers the link between the two

6 hundred grams is too light

7 hundred grams is too heavy

Figure 7 : 19

of them. It is much easier for children at this stage to weigh out a required mass, than it is to find the mass of a parcel. Both kinds of experience are necessary but accurate weighing belongs to a later stage. For shop play we weigh out sweets in packets of 1, 2, 3, . . . 100-grams, and fruit, etc., in $\frac{1}{2}$-kilos or in 100-grams, as in real shops. If no $\frac{1}{2}$-kilo mass is available children may hit on the method of splitting a kilo of sugar into equal shares in the two scale-pans. This shows a considerable understanding of a half, for they know that each half has the same mass. Every opportunity should be taken of letting the children work out such new ideas about quantity and number.

Because of the difficulty of giving a measure a mass precisely, it is useful to state it in a slightly different form from the 'nearly' or 'a little more than' which is a sensible way of describing a length. For mass, which we measure on a balance by finding when the units we are putting on the scale are too many or too few, it is more helpful to say that the weight is *between* 6 hundred grams and 7 hundred grams, or whatever the nearest two numbers may be; 6 hundred grams is too light, 7 hundred grams is too heavy (Figure 7 : 19).

THE NESTING OF QUANTITIES

The process of repeating a unit and making a count produces a pattern which consists of a starting-point and a sequence of equal intervals. This can be seen as a nesting of successive lengths that begin at the same starting-point and have end-points which come ever nearer to the end of the length to be measured (Figure 7 : 20).

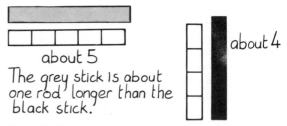

about 5

The grey stick is about one rod longer than the black stick.

about 4

Figure 7 : 20

This pattern is similar to the one made by a count of separate objects. In Figure 7 : 21 the first object counted is named as one. In counting units of a continuous quantity the *first step* from the starting-point is counted as one. It is easy, therefore, to give the starting-point the label 0 and the name *zero*.

---

[2]The use of the notation 100-gram for a unit can be used by children before counting to 100 has been mastered. It can be accepted in the same way as 10p for a tenpence coin or 100 pence for a pound.

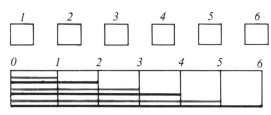

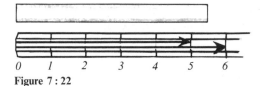

Figure 7 : 21

teacher's feet   *James's feet*

Figure 7 : 23

When a graduated strip such as a ruler or tape-measure is placed against a length, the nesting process shows how measuring may entail fitting the required length *between* two lengths marked on the scale. In Figure 7 : 22 the length to be measured lies between the length of measure 5 and the length of measure 6. The length may be stated as '*nearly* 6 units' or '*a little more than* 5 units'. The three lengths have the same starting-point and the mind can think back to this starting-point and realise that length is a continuous quantity. The end-points of the three lines show the between-ness of the length that has been measured.

Figure 7 : 22

CONVENTIONAL UNITS OF LENGTH

The centimetre has already been introduced to children as a convenient unit for their heights (see page 83). When outdoor lengths are measured children will often use the length of their feet or a footstep. The footstep may vary but the foot provides a fairly stable unit. It has one disadvantage, however. Other children in the class cannot use it; their feet are not usually the same length (see Figure 7 : 23). Consequently they attach a different number to the same quantity. This will inevitably lead to the proposal to use a ruler or a standard unit. Useful as personal and primitive measuring units may be, our children live in a world which constantly uses and talks about measures in a variety of standardised units. We must expect them to know some of these and to want to use them. The essential thing is that they should actually use them at school and learn to know what it is they measure and when it is sensible to use one kind of unit rather than another. Nevertheless, a kind of Robinson Crusoe skill in measuring without sophisticated tools is appreciated.

THE INTRODUCTION OF STANDARD MEASURING UNITS

The advantage of standard units is that they are in common use and have general recognition. They therefore enable us to communicate measurements to others in different times and places. Most children will know the names of such units in daily use as metre, gram, litre, but they may not have realised the quantity which each of them names. Since a unit must be selected for convenient measuring in any particular situation, children should become familiar with the size of each unit as they begin to use it. They need to use and to be given opportunities of choosing a 10-cm rod or a metre-stick, a 100-gram mass or a kilogram, according to the task in hand. But at this first introduction to conventional units they should use one unit only for a particular measurement and state it as a whole number, perhaps making use of a half or a quarter for the extra piece.

Bodily measurements such as the stride, foot or wrist can now be translated into standard units. A group of children can compare their individual measurements. Various classroom and playground measurements may also be found and sent to another class or school for comparison, thus showing the special purpose of standardised units (Figure 7 : 24).

At this stage we can expect children to accept freely the separate units of length, capacity and mass as measures of continuous properties with which they have become familiar. The need to relate the different units which are used for length (or mass or capacity) will not arise until a child

My stride is about as long as 3 rods

Figure 7 : 24

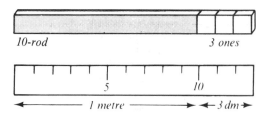

Figure 7 : 25

wants to state a measure more precisely. However, it is possible that a tape-measure which shows both metres and decimetres will be seen, and an informal statement of a length as, say, one metre and three decimetres will be made spontaneously. Such a development corresponds to the experience of putting a ten-rod and a three-rod (or three cubes) on end to show the number 13, i.e. to the use of a counting set of ten. This is the second stage in the representation of number (Figure 7 : 25).

Measuring curved paths and boundaries

Intuitive estimates of length begin with comparisons of objects in which length is an obvious and interesting property, objects which have straight edges against which straight rods or a stretched string can be placed. But if children compare some of the dimensions of their own bodies they will be faced with measuring closed curves such as the distance round the chest, wrist or head. Some of the shapes they handle, particularly cylindrical jars and tins, are circular in cross-section. Some of the paths or drives in the school grounds may be curved. Piaget has demonstrated that young children do not recognise that a zigzag arrangement of sticks has the same length as the sticks placed end to end (Figure 7 : 26). Nor are they convinced that a curved string is just as long as the string stretched straight, provided it is not elastic. Considerable experience of handling string, braid, plastic wire, etc. is needed so that children feel the invariance of the length as the shape is changed.

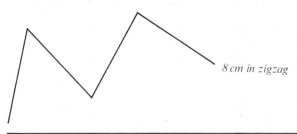

8 cm in zigzag

8 cm in a straight line

Figure 7 : 26

Figure 7 : 27

When this has been established, the use of string (and later of a tape-measure) to decide which is the longer of two paths or boundaries can be fully understood. When children can count units in measuring straight edges, strings on which lengths of curves have been marked can be placed against a graduated strip and the lengths stated in whatever units have been adopted. It helps understanding if the marked strings can be compared directly or their lengths drawn side by side on the floor or blackboard.

A trundle wheel may have been used in free play, but it is now possible for a child to run it along a path or any shape and to count the clicks which mark the revolutions (Figure 7 : 27). A rough comparison of the lengths of two paths can thus be found and recorded. This is an instance of the repetition of the counting unit, in this case the circumference of the wheel; but the successive units *cannot be seen* though they *may be heard* as each click is made. Children may notice the mechanism of the trundle wheel; its axle is fixed to the shaft of the handle and the wheel itself is free to rotate around the axle.

If children are provided with 10-cm rods, metre strings and a trundle wheel, they will be able to choose for themselves an interesting range of measuring both inside the school and in the playground. Their findings should be recorded and then discussed and checked with another group. It is all too easy to let children measure in a haphazard and unfruitful way. It is much better to have some plan, project or question in mind to which measuring will make a contribution.

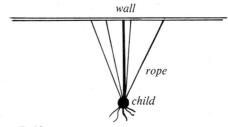

Figure 7 : 29

DISTANCE – AN ABSTRACT PROPERTY

There are two kinds of length which children find difficult to measure: both are in a way invisible. The first is the distance between two unconnected objects; the second is the height of a solid object such as pyramid.

There is a physical edge to a floor and a line of mortar across a wall but there may be no line between one tree and another, or between the starting-point of a jump and its finishing-point. Children have many experiences of holes and gaps and know that they differ in size, but no line is there to be measured. It is interesting that children can walk directly towards people and can visualise the line between them. They can picture the line between two trees, but how can they *measure* it? They must find a go-between. A rod or stick is difficult to iterate in a straight line. A stretched rope is the answer, and it will probably be suggested by children who have already invented ways of comparing inaccessible lengths. Once a rope has been stretched between two points children see that they now have a straight line that can be measured with a metre-rod or metre string (Figure 7 : 28).

If there is open ground between the two trees there is an alternative: a child can take a trundle wheel to one tree and face the other tree. Keeping it steadily in view the child can push the trundle wheel from one tree to the other and record the revolutions made en route. A trundle wheel is not

just a toy; it is a useful tool. For instance, it is used by workers responsible for repairing the main water pipes which lie several metres below streets. With a cyclometer attached, the trundle wheel gives a reading of the surface distance from an access point to the site of a leak located by modern technology. Workers can then dig down confidently to the leak.

Measuring the width of a road or the distance of a child from a wall cannot yet be handled mathematically, but an intuitive procedure, guessing the position of the guide rope, can satisfy children at this stage if it looks right. Figure 7 : 29 illustrates the procedures.

Children see the height of a cone or a pyramid as a property which differs between one cone and another. But how can they say *how* tall it is? One experience that can help is experimenting with bridges. A set of rods, such as the Cuisenaire rods, enable bridges of different heights to be built. The heights can be measured if the supports are upright rods. Then children can find whether a certain cone will pass under the bridge. Is it too tall? Or is there a gap above it when it is pushed through? Children can probably make a bridge which the cone will just pass through, or one which is too tall and one which is too low. They can then make some statement about the height of the cone and perhaps estimate how tall it is (Figure 7 : 30).

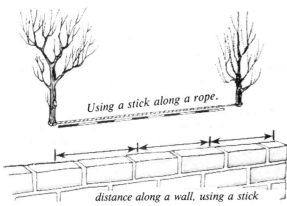

Using a stick along a rope.

distance along a wall, using a stick

Figure 7 : 28

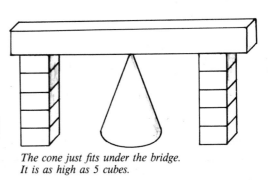

The cone just fits under the bridge. It is as high as 5 cubes.

Figure 7 : 30

UNITS OF CAPACITY

Informal units of capacity are easy to find: cupfuls, juguls, spoonfuls, etc. A group of children can agree to adopt a certain jug as the one they will use as a unit for a variety of comparisons. Pints are still familiar units for measuring milk, drinks and seeds. The metric measure, the litre, is too large for many household purposes and the $\frac{1}{2}$-litre is more frequently used. Fortunately large quantities of water are used in buckets and watering cans, and a litre jug can be used to find how much some vessels of this kind hold, estimating a $\frac{1}{2}$-litre when necessary.

Spoonfuls are used for smaller quantities of such things as salt, vinegar, medicines. But spoons show wide variations in the amount they hold. In cooking and in hospital play, children may suggest the 'medicine spoon' as the standard. The fact that the capacity of the official spoon is 5 millilitres will have no significance at this stage but it will have importance later on when children discover that 1 millilitre has the same volume as 1 cubic centimetre. Meantime children can play with the medicine spoon and use it realistically to graduate bottles or jars and compare the quantities of interesting substances that different vessels contain.

MEASURING TIME

Time, like space, is a condition of our existence and our bodies have a number of time patterns built into them. Rhythm is recognised as the repeat pattern of time and to measure time we must make use of this repetition. The invisible flow of time is a difficult concept for young children but they experience the basic rhythms of day and night, hunger and feeding, breathing and heartbeat.They also get to know the rhythms imposed by our routines of school and family. The clock-face shows some patterns made by the hands which match these routine events. But children have yet to learn how we measure the passage of time, i.e. *duration*. They can see the hands of the clock moving from one hour to the next and associate this movement with the passing from the time of one event to the time of another. The graduation of the clock-face becomes very familiar and we should associate this with the learning of the number circles. The sequence of the hours is then established, but it is the passing of the minutes which gives the more precise idea of measuring time and for this we require an acquaintance with numbers up to sixty. Before this is acquired we can use the knowledge gained of halves and quarters through measuring

length and mass, and folding circles. The telling of time and simple questions about 'How long until?' or 'What will the clock say in half an hour?' can be dealt with if a clock-face can be used. This indicates that children should use actual rotations to enable them to find answers to these questions. They can later count the minutes, stressing the fives and the tens (Figure 7 : 31).

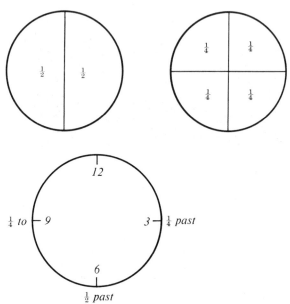

Figure 7 : 31

TIME AND THE CLOCK-FACE

The measurement of time does not usually occur until children realise that intervals of time separate events. If a child's mother goes out, there is an interval of time until her return. A lesson may last from one reading of the clock to another which a child recognises. At this stage, children focus their attention on the movements of the hands and the patterns they make. The minute hand moves through equal distances along the graduated rim of the clock-face. The tip of the hand is marking the equal intervals of time represented by these distances. The units are not yet identified as 5-minute intervals. Each is simply the time taken for the tip of the minute hand to move from one numeral to the next. Children come to realise that this interval is 5 minutes although they cannot yet reckon in fives or recognise the number of minutes past the hour that any particular position shows. For the moment children name the position of the hand by the numeral nearest to its tip.

A digital clock is much easier for children to read than an analogue clock (clock with hands). If a

Figure 7 : 32

grams, and so on. This relationship is of considerable importance and it is worthwhile to encourage children to watch how the hands of a clock move in a pattern and how the figures change on a digital clock.

The measurement of time is the one basic non-metric system. This is partly due to the very ancient tradition of using sixths and twelfths because these were the parts of a circle which were easiest to find, and partly to the ancient belief that there were 360 days in a year. Not many forms of computation are involved in our daily use of time but we need to remember that calculating in hours and minutes is very different from the standard decimal computations with other systems of units of measurement. Children will need help in acquiring the necessary number skills in dealing with timetables and calculating intervals between two points of time.

digital clock can be displayed next to the analogue clock, children will find it easier to link each step of the minute hand with 5 minutes.

The movement of the hour hand is too slow for young children to observe but they see that it has moved when it points to the next numeral. They can therefore recognise the marking of hour intervals by the small hand and can say, for example, that it is just 10 o'clock, nearly or just after 10 o'clock. It can be seen in Figure 7 : 32 that the process of iterating a unit and counting the number of units from a particular starting-point is now being carried out round a circle instead of along a line. It is a peculiarity of the clock-face that the starting-point is labelled 12. This can be explained to the children as marking midday (noon) or midnight. It is the end of one rotation round the clock and the beginning of another. It marks zero as well as twelve.

Telling the time accurately involves the use of two units: hours and minutes. Children have to accept these standardised units as those that we all use. Before they can deal with two units together they will be able to identify the position of the minute hand at the beginning of an hour, and to see that it has returned to this position at the end of an hour, when the small hand again points to a numeral. They thus have two measures of an hour: the complete revolution of the minute hand and the passage of the hour hand from one numeral to the next. Again, comparing a digital clock with the analogue clock makes this easier. This may be the first encounter with the equivalence of measures in two different units. Children will meet similar equivalences when they match metres to cm, kg to

MONEY

To children money has no connection with measuring. It is used only for buying and they pay in coins for what they want, giving the number of coins they are asked for – two pence, four pence, etc. The idea that money measures the exchange value of goods is a very advanced idea. Children only know that a price is attached to goods and they must know what coins to offer. This means that we must treat money differently from the properties of length, mass, etc., which have been discussed earlier in this chapter. Instead of choosing a unit to give us a measure of length by repeating it along a line, we must accept that a number of different coins are already familiar to the children and they must learn the relationships between these standard coins. In length, capacity, mass, etc., we prefer to let the children discover a unit and how it can be used, deferring the use of more than one unit in a single measurement. In money, however, we must take the units as given, and find out how many of one coin are equivalent to another; then a child must learn to match available coins to price.

It is quite obvious that there is a very close connection between the learning of the numbers from one upwards and the handling of coins. The activities at the class shop, which can be controlled by the prices on the goods and the coins made available to the children, must relate to the child's ability to deal with number. For example, the five-pence piece which is exchanged for five pennies *represents* a set of five pennies and can be used instead of five pennies at the shop. Practice in using these equivalents, both at a 'change counter' and in shopping, will greatly help the study of ten. The use of our written ways of showing money belongs to the next stage.

Summary

We have seen how the idea of quantity grows from experiences of the properties of real things and ways of comparing them. Equivalence of a number of small quantities to a larger one must be realised. The need for a unit as an intermediary arises when direct comparison is impossible. Placing quantities in sequence according to size leads on to the repetition or iteration of the unit. This is parallel to the use of the number line to present the sequence of numbers. The continuity of a quantity such as length or capacity means that a precise count of a whole number of units is not generally possible and thus approximate measures and fractional parts have to be used to give a sensible measure. Money is in a different position from the continuous properties we measure and it is well to link it with sets and number. It will be seen that the early stages of learning about measuring are confined to dealing with the growth of understanding through direct experiences with very small numbers. Recording is through diagrams or simple descriptions.

Measures in the National Curriculum

In this chapter we have seen how children gain the knowledge of measures required at Levels 1 and 2 of the National Curriculum. They should be able to:
- Compare and order objects without measuring.
  (AT4: Shape and space, Level 1)
- Recognise the need for standard units of measurement.
  (AT2: Number, Level 2)

The associated statements in the Programme of Study are:
- Compare objects and order objects and events without measuring, using appropriate language.
- Understand the conservation of length, capacity and 'weight'.
- Use coins in simple contexts.
- Use non-standard measures in length, area, capacity, 'weight' and time; compare objects and events and recognise the need for standard units.
- Learn and use the language for common units in length, capacity, 'weight' and time (e.g. m, $\frac{1}{2}$m, l, $\frac{1}{2}$l, kg, $\frac{1}{2}$kg, $\frac{1}{2}$day, hour, half-hour).

8 | THE STRUCTURE OF NUMBER: EARLY STAGES

FROM CONCRETE TO ABSTRACT NUMBER

In Chapter 4 we saw how children form an idea of number from the ideas of a set of things and of the seriation of that set into an order, so that its members can be put into one–one correspondence with the beginning of the sequence of number names. At this stage, number is a very concrete experience to children. They use the word 'three' to describe a set which they have put into one–one correspondence with the set of sounds 'one, two, three'. So 'three' is a descriptive word, an adjective which always describes a set of things. But as children grow older, they must take a further very large step, and detach numbers from the particular sets to which they are attached, arriving at a generalisation.[1] Out of 'three bricks' and 'three apples' must grow the general idea of 'three'. From experiences of counting sets of things such as those shown in Figure 8 : 1, children will come not only to understand 7 apples and 7 animals, but also the number 7. The number 7 becomes detached from apples and animals, and becomes a thing-in-itself, apart from its concrete illustrations. In fact, a number such as 7 changes its function from an adjective to a noun.

What is the noun 'seven'? Has it an independent existence, apart from the examples of seven things with which we surround children? Or is it more like such abstract nouns as 'love' and 'truth', which must be explained by examples and stories, rather than by direct definition? Much mathematical thought is built on the basis of the numbers 'one, two, three, four, . . .', but can 'seven' be defined other than by saying 'here is a set of seven things'? Children can only come to understand the natural numbers through concrete examples of sets of things, but a teacher may wish to examine the nature of the abstraction which children may eventually reach.

It is only within the last century that the definition of number and the foundations of arithmetic have been put on a firm theoretical footing. A method of defining the natural numbers in the abstract, which was given by Bertrand Russell, is interesting because it parallels very closely the stages children pass through in their developing understanding of number.[2]

Russell takes as his starting-point the idea that two sets 'have the same number' if they can be put into one–one correspondence (*see page 30*). This makes it possible to classify all the sets of things that there are or could be. We imagine a collection of boxes into which sets are to be put. All sets which 'have the same number', that is, which can be put into one–one correspondence with one another, go into the same box. For instance, there is a box into which are put all sets which can be put into one–one correspondence with the sound 'one'. In another box is a collection of sets which can be put into one–one correspondence with the set of sounds 'one, two'; in another box a collection of sets which can be put into one–one correspondence with the set of sounds 'one, two, three', and so on.[3] Then corresponding to each box there is a class of sets, and Russell defines the *number* of a set to be *the class of all sets which can be put in one–one correspondence with it. Two is the class of all pairs,*

Figure 8 : 1

[1]This is the first of many generalisations which go into the formation of an adult concept of number.

[2]The most readable account of this which Russell has given is to be found in the *Introduction to Mathematical Philosophy*.

[3]It is helpful to imagine each set of three things being contained in a bag. All these bags can be put into the box labelled 'three'. By this device the identity of each set of three things is not lost.

three the class of all trios, *four* the class of all quartets, and so on. As Russell says:

'. . . there is no doubt about the class of couples: it is indubitable and not difficult to define, whereas the number 2, in any other sense, is a metaphysical entity about which we can never feel sure that it exists, or that we have tracked it down.'

This construction of a class of sets is often seen in infant classrooms, where the teacher uses a row of boxes, each labelled with a number, into which the children put sets. Any couple of things is put into the box labelled 'two', so that children are learning to distinguish couples from other sets; that is, they are forming the idea *of the class of couples*, and are attaching the label 'two' to it. Similarly, the children put any trio they find into the box labelled 'three', and so the idea of the class of sets which have 'threeness' in common is built up. A number is a class of sets which have 'twoness' or 'threeness' or some similar property in common.

It is therefore important that a distinction should be made between the abstract number *three* and any *set of three things*. This distinction is made in advanced mathematics, when a set is distinguished by a pair of curly brackets { }, by putting the letter *n* in front of the brackets to denote the *number of the set*. For example, the number of the set of letters of the alphabet is 26, and so we write

$n\{A, B, C, \ldots, X, Y, Z\} = 26.$

The set itself is not equal to 26; it is the *number* of things in the set which is 26.

THE EMPTY SET AND THE NUMBER ZERO

When children first form sets and begin to operate on them, they always use sets that they have physically made, that is, sets which have some members. But not all sets have members. The set of children in the next room may be empty. When children have spent all their money, their set of pennies is empty. There may be an empty set of pennies even when there is some money left. The state of '*not having any* . . .' always corresponds to the empty set. The empty set is always an abstraction; children have to conceive of the possibility of having a set of objects such as pennies, and then notice that there are not in fact any pennies. At the stage at which a child thinks of a set only as a physical collection of objects, it does not seem likely that the child will be able to understand the possibility of an empty set.

The *number* corresponding to the empty set is *zero*. Using the Russell definition of number, zero is the *class of empty sets*. For children, therefore, zero must make its appearance in connection with what might be there, but is not. There are 3 hamsters and 1 cat, but 0 goldfish. In a game with structural apparatus, there are 3 red rods, but 0 white rods. A child had 5 sweets, but has eaten them all; there are now 0 sweets.

The teacher should distinguish between the *empty set* and the *number zero*, which is the number of the empty set. Zero bears the same relation to the empty set as the number 10 does to the set of a child's toes. The mathematical symbol for the empty set is $\emptyset$, and can be used in contexts in which the number is quite inappropriate. The intersection of the class of boys and the class of girls is empty. Symbolically, $B \cap G = \emptyset$. This statement is a statement not about numbers, but about sets.

At the stage of concrete operations it seems likely that children often use the number zero to indicate the absence of any numbers of things, rather than as a number. It is therefore not a number to them in the same sense that 1,2,3, . . . are numbers. It also has oddities of behaviour, such as the fact that $3 \times 0 = 0$, which seems to set it apart from the other numbers. It is important, however, for the later development of the number system, that children should come to think of zero as a number, rather than as a symbol for the absence of number. The use of number in measuring, where 0 symbolises the starting-point of the ruler, and in graphical work[4] may help to set zero among the other numbers, and so, in particular, to smooth the introduction of positive and negative directed numbers at a later stage.

CARDINAL AND ORDINAL NUMBERS

We have described the genesis in children's thought of the set of numbers

$\{0, 1, 2, 3, \ldots\},$

and we turn now to another aspect of these numbers with which young children have some difficulty at the pre-operational stage. The emphasis, so far, has been on the fact that number is derived from sets of things; that, for instance, all sets of three things can be put in one–one correspondence, and that 'threeness' is common to all such sets.

[4]See, for instance, page 205.

This aspect of number is known as *cardinal number*, and the number three to which it gives rise is the *cardinal number three*, in contrast to another aspect of the number, which leads to the development of the *ordinal number.*

An emphasis on putting things in order (*see page 55*), gives rise to the ordinal numbers. The order may be order of size, among a child's toys or bricks, order of age among the family, or order of time among the habitually recurring events of the day.

When children seriate and count along a row of toy cars (Figure 8 : 2), they are not only setting up a one–one correspondence with the set of number names, but also naming each car by its position in the row. Number two is the *second* in the row, number three the *third*, and so on. When children say 'three', they are not necessarily thinking of the set of three cars that has been counted, but rather that this car is third in the row. They are concerned with the *ordinal number three* or the third position, rather than with the cardinal number three, or the set of three things.

Figure 8 : 2

For the ordinal aspect of number to be present, the things counted must be seen in order. The important feature of a date such as the fourth of January is that it comes after the first, second and third of January, and before the fifth, sixth and later days of the month. The cardinal idea of the set of four days up to and including the 4th January remains in the background.

When one consults page 42 of a book, the numbers are used to show the order of the pages. If the book is opened at page 38, it is too early in the sequence of pages; if at page 45, it is too late. The set of pages 1–42 is a subsidiary idea. But when one says, 'I have read 42 pages of this book', the cardinal idea of the set of pages read is uppermost, and the ordinal idea that the forty-second page has just been read is subsidiary.

For a full appreciation of number, both cardinal and ordinal aspects must be present, but in the early stages of a child's learning they may develop separately, and only come together after considerable experience, as Piaget has shown in some of the experiments which he describes in *The Child's Conception of Number.* Two of his experiments are of particular interest in this context.

In the first experiment,[5] a child is given a set of ten dolls of increasing height. Sets of ten walking sticks of increasing length and ten balls of increasing size are also available. The child is asked to match the dolls and the sticks, or the dolls and the balls, so that each doll can easily find its own stick or ball. This causes considerable difficulty to young children (*see page 39*), but children who are old enough to be able to make the correspondence arrange the dolls and balls in parallel rows of increasing size, so that the one–one correspondence between each doll and its ball is clear. Then the experimenter displaces the balls slightly, so that they are no longer opposite the corresponding dolls, and asks the child to find the ball belonging to a particular doll. The mistakes which some children make in answering this question throw light on the difficulty of coordinating cardinal and ordinal numbers.

One child,[6] for instance, when asked for the ball corresponding to doll number 6, persisted in choosing ball number 5, and when asked why, counted dolls 1 to 5, that is the set of dolls in front

[5]Piaget, J. *The Child's Conception of Number*, Chapter V.
[6]Op. cit., page 110

Figure 8 : 3

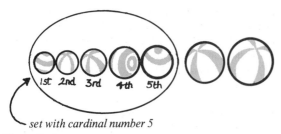

set with cardinal number 5

Figure 8 : 4

of doll 6, and then balls 1 to 5, and pointed to the last ball he had counted, that is to ball 5. Other children made very similar mistakes. A child who was asked for the ball corresponding to doll 5 said, 'There are four in front,' and so pointed to ball 4 (Figure 8 : 3). The child had seen the cardinal number 4, the set of four dolls in front of the fifth, but confused this when counting the balls with the ordinal number 4, and so pointed to the fourth ball.

A child who understood the situation completely pointed correctly to the fifth ball and said, 'I looked to see if there were four' (that is, four in front). To reach complete understanding of the relationship between cardinal and ordinal numbers children have to realise, as they count a row of things, that when they say 'five' they are pointing to the fifth (ordinal) object, and that in doing so they have now counted a set whose cardinal number is 5 (Figure 8 : 4).

The relations between cardinal and ordinal numbers are brought out further by Piaget's next experiment, which also throws light on the concepts involved in the use of structural number apparatus. The experimenter gives a child ten strips of cardboard (Figure 8 : 5), of which the second (*B*) is twice the length of the first (*A*), the next (*C*) three times the length of *A*, and so on. The child puts the cards in order of length and is asked how many cards like *A* could be made from *B*, how many cards like *A* could be made from *C*, and so on. When the child has answered correctly for each successive card, a card such as *F* is taken at random, the staircase remaining in position, and the child is asked how many units it represents. A child who has completely grasped the connection between cardinal and ordinal number will realise at once that the card in the sixth position must be six units long, and so will count along the staircase to find that *F* is the sixth card, and answer that it is six units long. A child who does not yet understand this connection between position and cardinal number will use card *A* with which to measure card *F*, and will find that card *A* must be used six times to cover card *F*. Many children aged 5 and 6 are at one or other of these stages.

In setting up a staircase of strips or rods and counting along it (Figure 8 : 6) children may use a number word such as 'four' in several ways:

i) pointing to the fourth rod, and so using the *ordinal number four*;

ii) pointing to a rod which could be broken up into four unit rods, and so using the rod as a *representation of the cardinal number four*;

iii) pointing to a rod which is four times as long as the first rod, so that the number four indicates a *ratio*, a relationship between lengths;

iv) if children do not think of the rods themselves as representing numbers, they may simply be counting how many rods there are (Figure 8 : 7), and so using the *cardinal number four* in another sense.

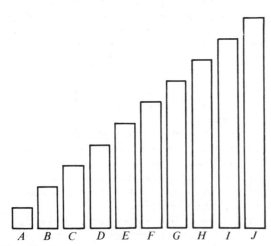

Figure 8 : 5

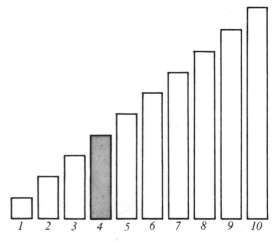

Figure 8 : 6

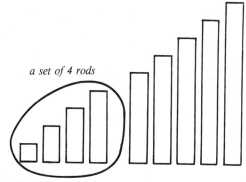

a set of 4 rods

Figure 8 : 7

When children have used structural apparatus, which usually depends on the representation of numbers by lengths, for some time, the different senses in which a word such as 'four' is used come together, so that they use that sense of the number word which is appropriate in any situation.

DIFFERENT TYPES OF STRUCTURAL APPARATUS

The principle of using length to represent number is seen in most of the types of structural number apparatus which are intended to help children to clarify their early ideas of number. A convenient object, which is usually a cube, but may be a cuboid, disc or other shape, is chosen to represent *one unit*. Numbers greater than one are represented by repetition, so that three is represented by a set of three units, usually placed end to end so that the length of the resulting block is three times the length of the original unit. Figure 8 : 8 shows the shape of the unit in some of the common types of structural apparatus.

Number apparatus belongs to one or other to two types, according to whether the units are permanently linked together or not. The Unifix cubes can be linked together by a child to form a rod, as can the Structa cylinders. The Multilink and

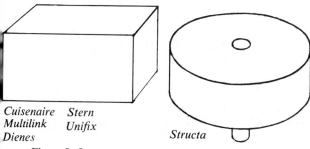

Cuisenaire Stern
Multilink Unifix
Dienes   *Structa*
Figure 8 : 8

Centicube cubes link on all six faces, so that a number can be represented by other shapes as well as by rods. In all these forms of apparatus, children can make their own piece for three units, handle it as a whole, and then break it down into a set of three separate units.

In the second type of apparatus, indivisible pieces represent two units, three units, and so on. The rods representing two units, three units, and so on, in the Dienes and Stern apparatus are marked in unit divisions, so that a child using a three-rod can count and can see that the three-rod is built up from three unit cubes. In the Cuisenaire apparatus, on the other hand, divisions are not marked on the longer rods, but rods of different lengths are systematically dyed in different colours, in order that they may be easily distinguished. Here the emphasis is on length, and so on the *ratio* aspect of number, rather than on breaking a rod down into units. The dark-green Cuisenaire rod is six times the length of the white rod, and children have to measure it with white rods to verify that this is so. Often they will take the white rod to represent one unit, and then the dark-green rod, six times its length, represents six. But the red rod may equally well be taken to represent one unit. The red rod is twice the length of the white rod, and so the dark-green rod is three times the red rod. If the red rod represents one, the dark-green rod will represent three.

Figure 8 : 9 shows representations of the number *three* using some types of structural apparatus. The different types of apparatus all have their value; in general, apparatus such as Unifix or Multilink is very useful when young children are forming number concepts. A cube can be matched to each one of a set of objects; then the cubes can be put together to form a rod, which represents the number of objects (Figure 8 : 10). The intermediate stage, of using a symbolic thing such as a cube to represent each object which is to be counted, is a very important step towards using a number symbol, such as 3, to represent the number of objects in a set. The cubes can be manipulated in ways which represent the manipulation of the objects themselves.

For older children, who have passed through this stage, apparatus such as Cuisenaire or the Dienes Multibase Arithmetic Blocks give a concrete realisation of each whole number, and enable children to study the ways in which the numbers themselves can be combined.

The absence of divisions on the Cuisenaire rods makes them flexible in representing numbers, as soon as children understand that they are

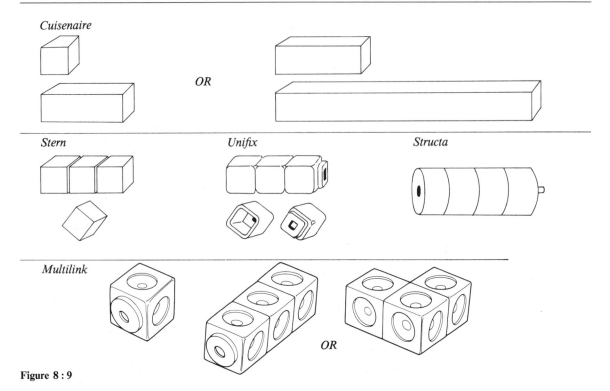

Cuisenaire

OR

Stern   Unifix   Structa

Multilink

OR

Figure 8 : 9

comparing lengths when they give each rod a
number name. If the white rod which is first in the
staircase represents *one*, the subset of the staircase
consisting of the red, crimson, dark-green, brown
and orange rods represents *two*, *four*, *six*, *eight* and
ten (Figure 8 : 11). But if the red rod represents one
unit, the second staircase will be 1, 2, 3, 4, 5, and
the original staircase will be $\frac{1}{2}$, 1, $1\frac{1}{2}$, 2, $2\frac{1}{2}$, 3, $3\frac{1}{2}$, 4,
$4\frac{1}{2}$, 5 (Figure 8 : 12). It is a comparative, or ratio,
idea of number which is developing here.

Many other staircases are of course possible,
using different rods to represent the unit, and so

introducing the representation of different fractions,
e.g. $\frac{2}{3}$, $\frac{3}{5}$. This use of Cuisenaire rods, in which the
size of rod representing one unit is chosen so that
the desired fractions can be studied, is only suitable
for older children.

The Dienes Multibase Arithmetic Blocks differ
from other types of structural apparatus, as they are
intended for the study of the *notation* of numbers.
They are discussed in Chapter 18.

Ancillary pieces of apparatus are obtainable to
match most types of structural apparatus. They are
intended to encourage young children to focus on

tree seeds

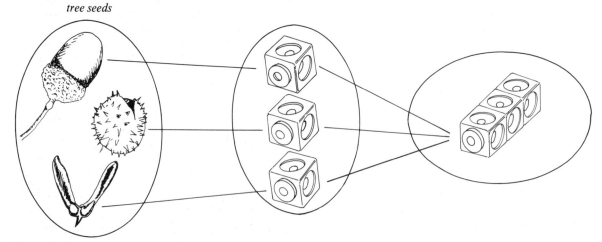

Figure 8 : 10

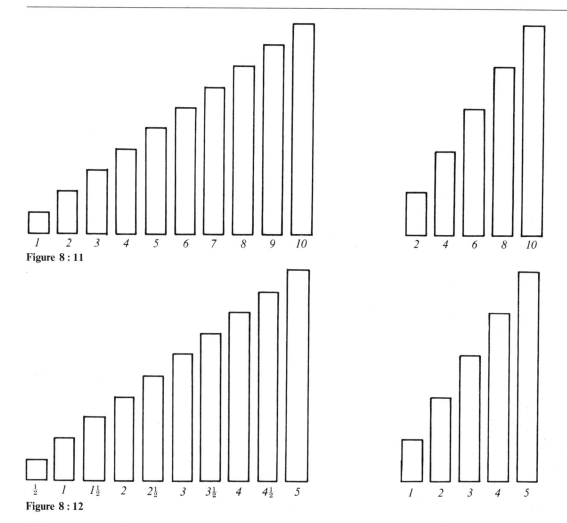

Figure 8 : 11

Figure 8 : 12

different aspects of the concept of number. For example, *counting boards* (Figure 8 : 13(*i*)) encourage the linking of cardinal and ordinal aspects of number, while *pattern boards* (Figure 8 : 13(*ii*)) focus attention on *odd* and *even* numbers.

The use of the lengths of rods to represent numbers also introduces another important representation of numbers, the *number line*. When children make a staircase and compare the lengths of the rods which go up in equal steps, they can record what has been done in a different way as well as drawing the staircase. Figure 8 : 14 shows how a strip of card can be graduated by marking how far each rod reaches along the card. As children do this, they are building up a ruler by a process very similar to that used in graduating a

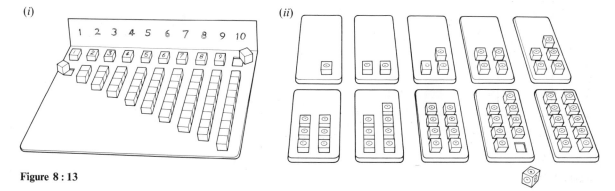

(*i*)   (*ii*)

Figure 8 : 13

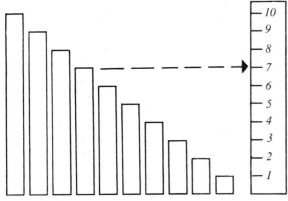

Figure 8 : 14

measuring jar (*see page 79*). They are also taking a first step towards a fundamental mental picture, the number line, in which each number is represented by a length measured from a starting-point or zero.

The *number tracks* designed to fit most forms of structural apparatus form concrete representations of the number line (Figure 8 : 15). Most of these tracks are in sections each of length ten units, and

are of total length one hundred units. The importance of the number line for children's thinking about number cannot be overstated, and it is a most useful experience to fit rods which correspond in number to sets into a number track. Counting, addition, ordering and notation all link together here. Other number lines, which are very easily accessible, are found on rulers and tape-measures.

Figure 8 : 16 shows part of two more number lines, built up from Cuisenaire rods, using first the red rod, and then the orange rod to represent one unit. The teacher will see that all these illustrations are only diagrams of the same number line drawn to different scales, and that the number line has an abstract universal character which is independent of the unit of measurement.

This method of relating decimal and other fractions to their unit, and marking them on the number line, is very important at the stage in middle childhood when children start to read measuring instruments and rulers which are graduated in different ways.

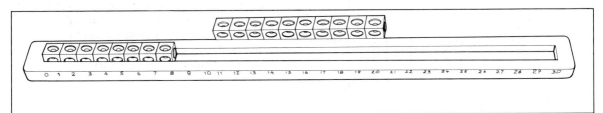

Figure 8 : 15

(a) *The coloured rod is one unit.*

(b) *The coloured rod is one unit.*

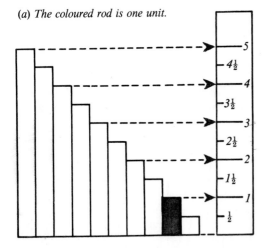

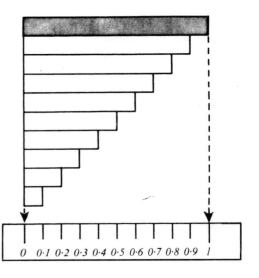

Figure 8 : 16

THE DEVELOPMENT OF CONCEPTS

It will be seen from the analysis of the idea of number in Chapter 4 and this chapter that a mathematical word such as 'three' is used with a variety of different, but closely inter-related, meanings in different contexts. For example, a full appreciation of 'three' involves understanding of its cardinal and ordinal senses, and of the relationships between them, appreciation of the use of 'three' as a ratio, and further extensions of the use of the word as in the contrast between (+ 3) and (− 3), which children will gradually acquire as their understanding of mathematical structure develops. Some of these extensions will be discussed in later chapters. It is helpful for most purposes to use the same word 'three' in all these contexts, as the behaviour of all the different 'threes' is so similar that, when numbers are manipulated, it hardly matters which 'three' we are dealing with. It is most important, however, that children should become aware of as many aspects of number as possible, by meeting numbers in many different situations, as a full appreciation of 'three' only comes when all the senses in which the idea is used are integrated into one whole. When children reach this stage, the ideas of 'a third object', 'a set of three things', 'three times as much', and other ideas which they have attached to the word 'three' are all equally available, and they can move from one to another and choose the one which is most appropriate to any situation.

It is a temptation in the teaching of mathematics to withhold from children some aspects of a concept in the hope of simplifying the idea. This urge to simplify is nearly always mistaken, for children build up concepts by two processes which are known as *assimilation* and *accommodation*. It is easy for children to assimilate new examples to a concept they have formed; new sets of three things are easily assimilated to the cardinal idea of 'three'; but for growth to take place, they need to accommodate their idea of 'three' to take account of the ratio aspect of 'three times as much' as well as the cardinal aspect of 'the set of three things'. Failure to accommodate new aspects will mean that children can only form a concept of numbers which is so limited that it is impossible for them to understand mathematical developments they will meet with later.

The concepts formed at one stage are the building-bricks for the next stage in children's mathematical growth. If they have not had the opportunity to form satisfactory concepts they may be unable to take the next step, or indeed to take a step which may be required several years later, so that mathematical growth is permanently stunted. It is therefore particularly important that children should have a rich variety of mathematical experiences at the stage when early concepts of number and of space are being formed.

9 | ADDITION AND SUBTRACTION

THE DISCOVERY OF ADDITION

While children are finding the patterns they can make with sets of things, they are partitioning these sets into smaller subsets. They will make statements about the numbers of things in the subsets, and these statements can be recorded in addition form (Figure 9 : 1). In this way the idea of addition arises from splitting up or partitioning a set into subsets.

The reverse of this process is that of starting with two separate sets and combining them to make a total set, as in Figure 9 : 2. The number content of this situation will be written $5 + 2 = 7$.

Children need to have experience both of partitioning a set into subsets, and of combining two sets which they have made separately into a total set, and of making number statements in both situations. At first, splitting up a set of seven bricks into two subsets of five bricks and two bricks is a very different action from combining a set of five bricks and a set of two bricks. After some experience, these two actions come together in children's minds, and they realise that $7 = 5 + 2$ and $5 + 2 = 7$ are two statements about the same situation. The actions have become internalised and reversible (*see page 29*); an *operation* has emerged.

Any addition statement such as $5 + 2 = 7$ occurs in a great variety of situations, and can be recorded in several ways. Not ony do children combine sets; they put the 5-rod and the 2-rod of structural apparatus end to end; they put 5 spoonfuls of water into a graduated bottle and then another 2 spoonfuls, and find that the water reaches the 7-spoonful mark; they put out the money that they need to buy something costing 5 pence and something costing 2 pence, and see that there are 7 pence altogether; and so on. Recording on squared

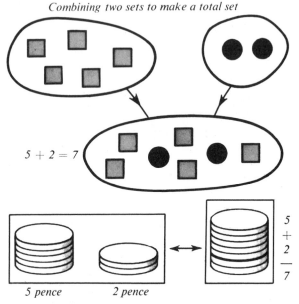

Combining two sets to make a total set

$5 + 2 = 7$

$5 \text{ pence} \qquad 2 \text{ pence}$

$$\begin{array}{r} 5 \\ + 2 \\ \hline 7 \end{array}$$

Figure 9 : 2

paper is often useful, and both horizontal and vertical recording of addition can be used (Figure 9 : 3). Vertical recording leads naturally to the traditional pencil and paper method of addition, while horizontal recording leads to recording the keys pressed when the operation is carried out on a calculator.

Another distinction which children make is that between the actions of adding $5 + 2$ and $2 + 5$. The action of adding 2 bricks to 5 which are already in the number track is very different from the action of adding 5 bricks to 2 which are in the number track. The results of these two actions are, however, the same, so that when the action has become mental children will write either $5 + 2$ or $2 + 5$ for either operation. The order in which the operation is performed has lost its importance, and they now move freely between the two forms.[1]

The teacher will probably notice three stages in children's development as they make and put together sets of five things and two things.

Partitioning a set into subsets

(i)   *(ii)*

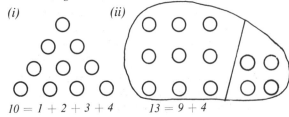

$10 = 1 + 2 + 3 + 4 \qquad 13 = 9 + 4$

Figure 9 : 1

[1] Addition has become commutative (*see page 164*).

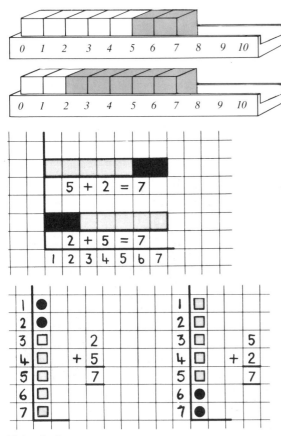

Figure 9 : 3

Figure 9 : 4

It is also easy for children to verify with structural apparatus that $5 + 2 = 2 + 5$, and similar facts. 'Walls' can be built with Cuisenaire rods, or with two colours of Multilink cubes, or the Stern number cases can be used to show this commutative law for addition (Figure 9 : 5).

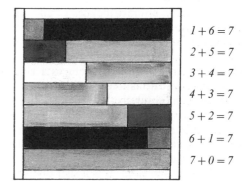

Figure 9 : 5

i) At first they count out a set of five bricks and a set of two bricks. Then they put these sets together and count all the bricks again.

ii) A little later they can remember the idea of the set of five bricks which they have counted while they make a set of two bricks. They therefore only need to count on from five, and count the two bricks as 'six, seven'.

iii) After more experience they remember that a set of five things and a set of two things always makes a set of seven things, so they no longer need to count.

It is important that children should reach the third stage, and should be able to use with understanding and confidence all the addition facts which they will need in later work.

Children will be helped to understand and remember number facts if they use some type of structural apparatus. They quickly come to associate those combinations of rods which together make up a particular longer one (Figure 9 : 4).

More addition situations

Children have to abstract the mathematical operation of addition from all the situations of forming the union of two non-overlapping sets which they meet. They also need to find out that the same numerical relationships turn up when they combine two quantities, or two sums of money. At this stage, they need much experience of situations such as the following:

i) A bar of chocolate can be balanced against five 10-gram masses, and a bag of sweets against four 10-gram masses; if the chocolate and the sweets are put on the balance together, nine 10-gram masses are needed to balance them.

ii) Two rods, one measuring 5 centimetres and the other measuring 4 centimetres, are put end to end. They fit alongside a rod of length 9 centimetres.

iii) At the shop, a pencil costs 5 pence, and a rubber 4 pence. Together they cost 9 pence.

5 pence + 4 pence = 9 pence

The teacher will be able to provide children with many experiences using measures whose numerical content is equivalent to that found in the combination of sets. The teacher should also note that there are situations where two quantities can be combined, but the addition of some of the numbers is inappropriate, such as:

i) mixing a jug of water whose temperature is 20° with a jug of water whose temperature is 30° does not give a temperature of 50°;

ii) playing, on the piano, the second note of a scale together with the third note does not give the fifth note.

From a variety of experiences, children come to learn the different situations in which quantities can be added, and so to abstract the idea of addition from its various concrete embodiments.

It should be emphasised that experience of addition, and discovery of the addition facts, in a variety of different practical situations, is a vital prelude to abstract calculations. At first, recorded calculations should always be the records of practical activities. Only through practical experience can children understand what addition, or any other operation, means. If children do not know what a calculation is for, or what practical situations it might represent, it is a sign that the abstract calculations have outstripped their real comprehension.

FURTHER STEPS IN ADDITION

Through the variety of their practical experiences children become very much at home with the smaller numbers, so that they know immediately that a toy car has two front wheels and two back wheels, making four wheels in all, or that if there is ten pence to spend and four pence is spent, then six pence will remain. This complete familiarity with numbers up to ten will be helped by the use of structural apparatus. Building walls with Cuisenaire rods, Multilink or other structural apparatus, gives a great deal of practice in the analysis of each number up to ten (Figure 9 : 6).

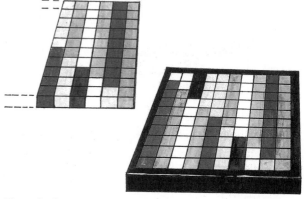

Figure 9 : 6

The analysis of a number can also be recorded, in a more permanent form, on squared paper, using coloured squares or strips of gummed paper (Figure 9 : 7).

It is important that the detailed knowledge of numbers which is obtained by analysing them should not stop at ten, but should gradually be built up during the early school years so that children are very familiar with the numbers up to twenty. This will help them to use numbers easily as they grow older.

We shall see how useful knowledge of the numbers from 11 to 20 is in further addition and

Two ways of recording the analysis of 5

1	+	4	=	5
2	+	3	=	5
3	+	2	=	5
4	+	1	=	5
5	+	0	=	5

1	2	3	4	5
+4	+3	+2	+1	+0
5	5	5	5	5

Figure 9 : 7

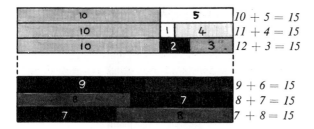

$10 + 5 = 15$
$11 + 4 = 15$
$12 + 3 = 15$

$9 + 6 = 15$
$8 + 7 = 15$
$7 + 8 = 15$

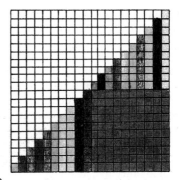

Figure 9 : 9

$9 + 6 = 15$

$13 + 2 = 15$

Figure 9 : 8

very regular, so that once the words twenty, thirty, forty, ... are known, children have little difficulty in extending their counting skills from

twenty one, twenty two, ..., twenty nine,
thirty one, thirty two, ..., thirty nine,
to ninety one, ninety two, ..., ninety nine.

However, some children find it confusing that the number names from eleven to nineteen are irregular, and for a time the teacher may hear children say numbers in the 'teens' as 'onetyfour' instead of 'fourteen'.

in subtraction (*see page 181*). Let us consider 15. Children must first see it as made up of 10 and 5. Here again structural apparatus, whose longest rod is the ten-rod, is useful as children have to make 15 in two parts, as 10 and 5. But they can also make 15 in various other ways, sometimes using two rods, sometimes more. Some of the possibilities are shown in Figure 9 : 8. These are of two types:

i) those which include a ten in one of the numbers:

$13 + 2 = 15,$

ii) those which do not show a ten, such as

$8 + 7 = 15.$

The structure of both types of addition fact should be known by the time children come to do more complicated addition and subtraction.

Work with structural apparatus and graph paper enables children to see the repetition of the pattern of the numbers 1 to 10 in the pattern of the numbers 11 to 20 (Figure 9 : 9). A graph can be continued to show the further repetition of the pattern in higher decades.

By this stage, children's oral counting will be extending considerably beyond twenty. The pattern of the number words, in English, beyond twenty is

How numbers grow

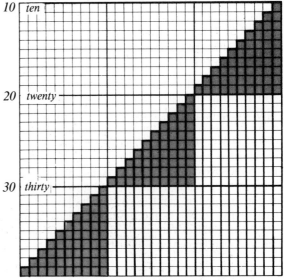

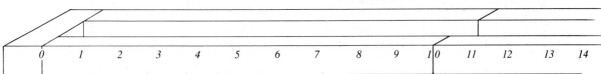

Figure 9 : 10

An extension of the graph of Figure 9 : 9 into higher decades, together with the use of successive pieces of the number track, up to its full length of one hundred, helps to teach the written numbers, and to reinforce the pattern of tens which the number words show (Figure 9 : 10).

Many counting activities, such as recording the number of children present each day, can be based on the number track, and it can also be used to emphasise the building of tens in successive additions. Children very easily see how pushing in a ten, and then another ten, at the beginning of the track converts $3 + 2 = 5$ into $13 + 2 = 15$, $23 + 2 = 25$, and so on (Figure 9 : 11).

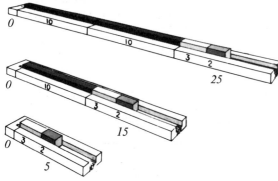

Figure 9 : 11

Another activity which helps this understanding is counting in tens forwards and backwards from any starting number:

> 5, 15, 25, 35, 45, ...
> or   75, 65, 55, 45, 35, 25, 15, 5.

The teacher will see that this process of 'moving up ten' forms the basis for all higher decade addition; children will, however, only be able to make full use of this if they know at sight the sum of any two single digit numbers; that is, if they can immediately and automatically regroup $8 + 7$ as $10 + 5$ or fifteen.[2] The use of structural apparatus helps this regrouping (Figure 9 : 12) and the process of 'moving up ten' can be extended to cover such facts as $18 + 7$, $28 + 7$, and so on. This stage is often left out in children's discovery of number, so that children who know that $8 + 7 = 15$ often do not see

[2] In order to be able to subtract with confidence, they need to regroup 15 as $8 + 7$ (*see page 110*).

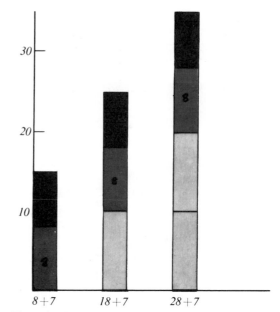

Figure 9 : 12

that $38 + 7$ is related to it, and so count laboriously 7 onwards from 38.

Another piece of apparatus which is useful in the discovery of the behaviour of numbers greater than ten in a slide-rule made from two tape-measures. It is convenient to have one of these fixed to the wall or to a table, the other being movable (Figure 9 : 13). Children who wish to examine $8 + 7$, $18 + 7$, $28 + 7$, and so on measure 7 centimetres on from the 8-centimetre mark, the 18-centimetre mark, and so on. If a tape-measure has markings on both sides, the two ends of it can be used in the same way (Figure 9 : 14). Two rulers marked in centimetres can also be used.

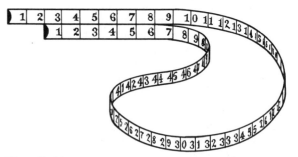

Figure 9 : 14

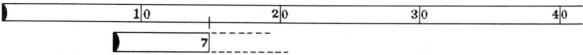

Figure 9 : 13

The slide-rule can also be used to add any two numbers whose sum is less than the length of the tape-measure, although further understanding of this addition will await understanding of the system of notation (*see page 175*). The tape-measure slide-rule is also extremely useful for subtraction (*see page 110*).

THE LANGUAGE OF ADDITION

Children abstract the idea of addition from a great variety of real experience (*see page 100*). If they talk about these experiences, as they should, they will talk about each one in the everyday language appropriate to it. Examples of such language are:

i) 'The chocolate and the sweets *together balance* 90 grams.'

ii) 'I *spent* 6 pence *altogether*.'

iii) 'The box *measures* 22 cm *all the way round*.'

iv) 'When I put another litre of water in the saucepan, *it comes up to* the 3-litre mark.'

It is important that different situations should be described in the language appropriate to each one, but as children realise that the numbers occurring in each situation are combined in the same way, they begin to need signs and language, not only for the numbers, but for the ways in which they are combined. The process of abstraction is helped by the fact that the + and = signs are used in all the contexts in which, for instance, the combination of 5 and 3 is found to be 8. It will also help children if they use the same neutral words, which are not tied to any particular context, when they read the signs. Suitable neutral words for ' + ' and ' = ' are 'plus' and 'equals'.

'Five and three *makes* eight' is not a good way of reading

$$5 + 3 = 8,$$

as children will soon have to learn that

$$5 - 3 = 2$$

is read as 'five take away three *leaves* two'. It is confusing if the sign = is read differently in the two sentences. The more contexts a mathematical word can be used in, the more it helps to direct attention to the mathematical abstraction rather than to the particular context. 'Equals' is a good word, because $5 + 3$ equals 8, and $5 - 3$ equals 2; 'makes' and 'leaves' are less good, because they only apply to addition and subtraction, respectively.

'Add' would be a good reading of the sign ' + ' if it were not grammatically incorrect. Mathematics is a language, and, like English, is written in sentences, each with its verb. The verb in the sentence $5 + 3 = 8$ is 'equals', so it is bad mathematical style also to read ' + ' as a verb. The word 'plus', which is a conjunction, does not suffer from this disadvantage. Children acquire their mathematical style, as they do their English style, from the language which they hear, speak, read and write. It is important that mathematical language should be carefully and accurately used from the beginning, and that children should avoid slang usages in mathematics which they will later have to alter.

However, correct mathematical words are useless if children do not attach the correct meaning to them. Thus, mathematical vocabulary needs to be taught, and should be taught in the context of practical experiences, not merely of sums. For instance,

'You had five pencils and I gave you two more; five *plus* two *equals* seven; now you have seven pencils';

'You had ten pence and you spent three pence; ten *minus* three *equals* seven; you have seven pence left';

'The blocks on the number track say thirteen *plus* two *equals* fifteen.'

TRANSFORMATIONS

When children have made a staircase with structural apparatus, they often add a unit rod to each step of the staircase. This operation transforms the 'one to ten' staircase into a 'two to eleven' staircase. Similarly, the addition of a 2-rod to each step transforms the set of numbers

$$\{1, 2, 3, ..., 10\}$$

into the set of numbers

$$\{3, 4, 5, ..., 12\}$$

and the addition of a 10-rod transforms the set

$$\{1, 2, 3, ..., 10\}$$

into the set

$$\{11, 12, 13, ..., 20\}.$$ See Figure 9 : 15.

We can think of the operation of *adding one*, or *adding seven*, or adding any other number, as an operation which transforms the whole set of numbers. A simple *function machine* (Figure 9 : 16)

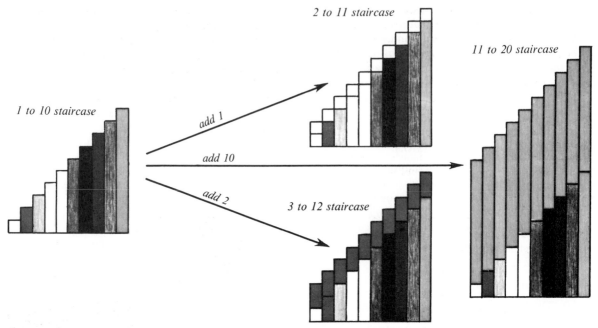

Figure 9 : 15

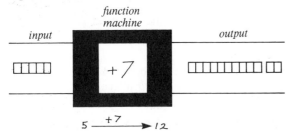

Figure 9 : 16

is a useful way of showing this. The appropriate blocks for the *input* number are pushed along a track, and the machine is operated by a child who performs the + 7 operation before pushing the blocks to the *output*. Children may like to show their skill at adding seven by taking a set of

numbers at random and performing the *transformation* 'add 7' on the whole set by pushing the numbers through the function machine. The results may be recorded as in Figure 9 : 17.

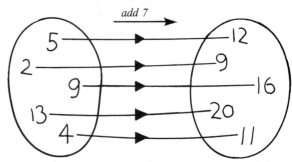

Figure 9 : 17

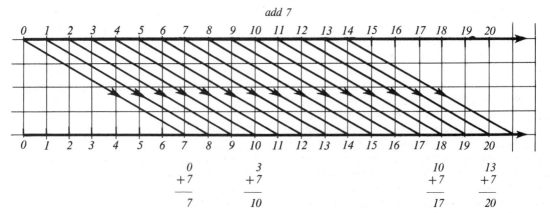

Figure 9 : 18

A more systematic way of showing this transformation is to draw part of the number track or *number line* twice, and to show what happens to each number on it if 7 is added (Figure 9 : 18).

Transformations are also called *mappings*, as each member of a set of numbers is *mapped on to* a member of another set of numbers. A transformation can be illustrated by a relation diagram such as Figure 9 : 17 or 9 : 18, or by a graph (Figure 9 : 19). We see that transformations are relations in which only one arrow leaves each member of the set which is transformed.

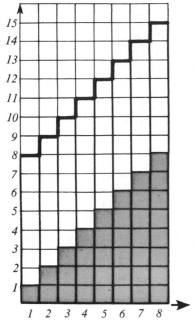

Figure 9 : 19

SUBTRACTION AND ITS RELATION TO ADDITION

When children first meet the idea of subtraction, it does not seem to be related to addition. The children have lost something; they have eaten some sweets or drunk some milk. There were five pence, but four pence have been spent, and only one penny is left. The four pence have permanently and irreversibly gone. Sweets which have been eaten have gone for ever. But if children are to deal mathematically with subtraction situations, this process must become reversible. Before spending money in the shop, children must be encouraged to look at the 4 pence which will be spent, together with the remaining 1 penny, and see that they make 5 pence. Children must be able to separate 5 sweets into 3 to be eaten and 2 to be kept, so that they

can see that the subtraction which will happen is related to addition.

Subtraction is only fully understood when it is seen as an aspect of addition. Figure 9 : 20 shows that 3 sweets out of 5 have been eaten, and illustrates the same experience using structural apparatus. The partitioning of a set of 5 things into two subsets is exactly the same whether it is described by

$$3 + 2 = 5 \quad \text{or} \quad 2 + 3 = 5$$
$$\text{or } 5 - 3 = 2 \quad \text{or} \quad 5 - 2 = 3$$

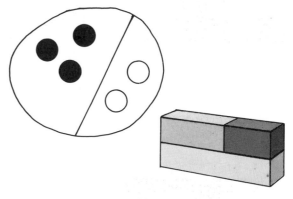

Figure 9 : 20

The physical process of 'taking away' follows the partitioning of the set into its subsets. Children can use the numerical knowledge which they already possess to carry out subtraction if they see its relation to addition, and so they should be encouraged to think of subtraction as a regrouping of a number: '5 – 2 = 3 because 2 + 3 = 5'. The use of structural apparatus, and the discovery of number patterns (see Chapter 6) is helpful here. Each of the diagrams illustrating addition in this chapter also illustrates two related subtractions. For instance, Figure 9 : 11 shows

$$\left.\begin{array}{l} 3 + 2 = 5 \\ 13 + 2 = 15 \\ 23 + 2 = 25 \end{array}\right\} \quad \text{and} \quad \left\{\begin{array}{ll} 5 - 3 = 2, & 5 - 2 = 3 \\ 15 - 13 = 2, & 15 - 2 = 13 \\ 25 - 23 = 2, & 25 - 2 = 23 \end{array}\right.$$

When subtraction is recorded, the notation of an empty box which asks a question is very useful;

$$5 - 3 = \square$$
$$\text{and } 3 + \square = 5$$
$$\text{and } \square + 3 = 5$$

all mean the same thing. Children can write numbers in the box:

$$3 + \boxed{2} = 5,$$

showing that the 2 was the missing number.

THE LANGUAGE OF SUBTRACTION

The language of the practical situations in which children use the idea of subtraction is even more varied than for addition. Some examples follow, with illustrations emphasising the fact that in each case a set is partitioned into two subsets.

i) The children play skittles. A ball *knocks down* 3 of the 9 skittles. Only 6 are *left* standing (Figure 9 : 21).

$6 + 3 = 9$
$3 + 6 = 9$
$9 - 3 = 6$
$9 - 6 = 3$

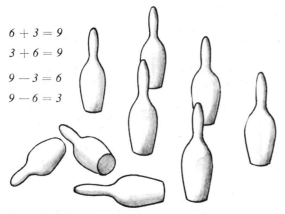

Figure 9 : 21

ii) Peter buys a pencil *costing* 8 pence. He has 2 pence *change* from a tenpenny piece (Figure 9 : 22).

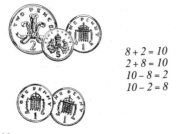

$8 + 2 = 10$
$2 + 8 = 10$
$10 - 8 = 2$
$10 - 2 = 8$

Figure 9 : 22

iii) Sally has 9 pence. Simon has 4 pence. He has 5 pence *less than* Sally (Figure 9 : 23).

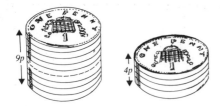

Figure 9 : 23

iv) Robert has 7 marbles. Peter has 4 marbles. Robert has 3 marbles *more* than Peter (Figure 9 : 24).

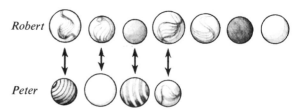

Figure 9 : 24

v) Alan has 8 dominoes. Robert has 5 dominoes. If he takes 3 *more*, they will have *the same* number (Figure 9 : 25).

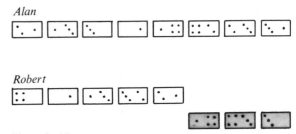

Figure 9 : 25

Children need varied experience to see that in all these situations the idea of splitting a set into subsets is present. In each situation there is a dominant idea:

i) *taking away*, as in 'John has 5 sweets; he eats 2; how many are left?' or

ii) *inverse* or *complementary addition*, as in, 'What must be added to 2 to make 5?' or

iii) *comparison* or *difference,* as in, 'How much more is 5 than 2?'

The teacher must provide a sufficient variety of experiences for children to realise that the numerical content of all the types (i), (ii) and (iii) is the same, and for them to abstract the idea of subtraction, $5 - 2 = 3$, from all three situations. Graphical work can provide a starting-point for many *comparisons* (Figure 9 : 26) and the teacher can take the opportunity of letting the children describe the comparisons in a variety of ways.

Shopping, the numbers of children absent, the number of children who do not drink milk, and various events in the classroom, will provide opportunities for *taking away* and *inverse addition*.

When it embodies so many experiences, how is the sentence '$5 - 2 = 3$' to be read? It should be read as a sentence, so that the most acceptable form of words which is detached from a particular context is 'five *minus* two equals three'. Again, the word 'minus' needs to be taught, and it is a help in

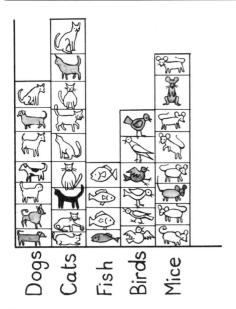

Figure 9 : 26

linking the different subtraction situations together if the vocabulary is taught in all of them. The link with addition can be made at the same time. For instance,

'The ball knocks down 3 of the 9 skittles;
   9 *minus* 3 *equals* 6,
and 6 *plus* 3 *equals* 9';

'Sally has 9 pence, Simon has 4 pence; Sally has 5 pence more;

   9 *minus* 4 *equals* 5,
and 4 *plus* 5 *equals* 9'.

A child should also see and hear 5 – 2 in these ways:

'What must be added to 2 to make 5?'
'How many more is 5 than 2?'
'What is the difference between 5 and 2?'

The link between subtraction and addition is all important and should be emphasised continually.

Even at this early stage, the teacher should bear in mind the fact that children's conception of addition and subtraction will need to change and develop as they grow older. They have to make 'inverse addition' the central idea in the concept of subtraction before they can, later on, make sense of 2 – 5 (*see pages 171–173*). It is not possible to take 5 things from 2 things, and so a concept of subtraction as 'taking away' will be inadequate to meet this new situation. In order for children to accommodate the new idea of subtracting 5 from 2, they must be able to assimilate 2 – 5 to the already

formed idea of 'What must be added to 5 to make 2?', or 5 + □ = 2.

Too much use of the words 'take away', and too great a concentration on 'taking away' situations in subtraction, may hinder or prevent the development of thought which makes understanding of negative numbers possible. The reading of 5 – 2 as '5 minus 2' is a help in making the necessary generalisation.

MORE ABOUT SUBTRACTION: THE SLIDE-RULE

The tape-measure slide-rule can be used for subtraction as well as for addition (Figure 9.27). It will probably be used in two main ways. Children who want to find a number 3 less than 11 will

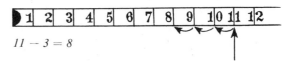

$11 - 3 = 8$

Figure 9 : 27

count back 3 from the 11-unit mark. This starts to build up a concept of subtraction which will be useful later,[3] and will also enable them to subtract accurately using numbers within the range of the tape-measure. If the numbers involved are large, children will find it more convenient to measure backwards, using another tape-measure or the back of the same tape, instead of counting backwards (Figure 9 : 28). At the same time as, or just before, the *tens system of notation* is explored,[4] children may gain useful experience by using the tape-measure slide-rule to find the results of such related additions and subtractions as

2 + 10 =
2 + 20 =   and   12 + 10 =
2 + 30 =   and   12 + 20 =   and   22 + 10 =

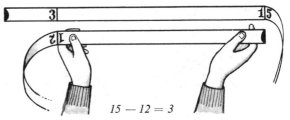

$15 - 12 = 3$

Figure 9 : 28

[3]It is necessary for the understanding of directed numbers (*see page 188*).

[4]See Chapter 15.

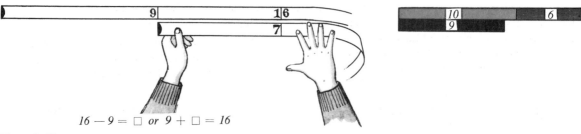

$$16 - 9 = \square \;\; or \;\; 9 + \square = 16$$

Figure 9 : 29

and so on; and in reverse

52 – 10 =
52 – 20 =   and   42 – 10 =
52 – 30 =   and   42 – 20 =   and   32 – 10 =

or 10 + □ = 52
   20 + □ = 52   10 + □ = 42
   30 + □ = 52   20 + □ = 42   10 + □ = 32

and so on. Children should be encouraged to look

for patterns in this type of work, and invent their own patterns. Repeated addition and subtraction of numbers other than 10 on the slide-rule can also be used to give multiplication and division experience (*see page 205*).

The slide-rule can also be used as an aid when subtraction is thought of as inverse addition. Children who want to know 16 – 9 may think of it as, '9 plus what equals 16?' They will then count or measure onwards from the 9-unit mark of the tape-measure until they reach the 16-unit mark (Figure 9 : 29). This use of the slide-rule is exactly parallel to the use of structural apparatus for 16 – 9, when children place a 9-rod alongside rods making up 16, and then find which rod fills the gap.

It is advisable to use both the tape-measure slide-rule and structural apparatus, for each has its advantages. Through repeated use of structural

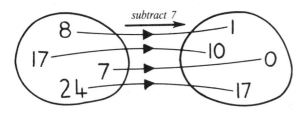

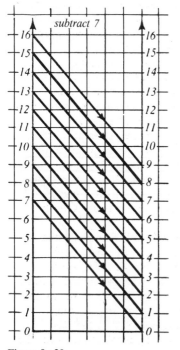

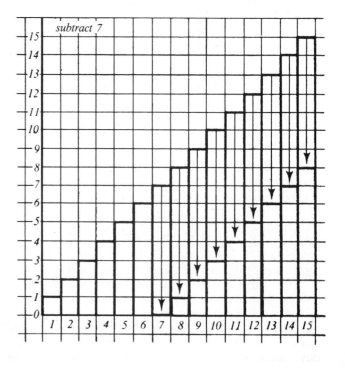

Figure 9 : 30

apparatus children come to remember which rods fit together, and so to remember the addition facts and to associate addition and subtraction with one another. The slide-rule, on the other hand, associates addition and subtraction with movement in a way which will be important for later developments.[5] Children who count or measure onward or back along the tape-measure moves a finger or eye forward or backward along the number line, whereas when they use structural apparatus they estimate what length will fill a gap, without taking account of the direction in which that length is measured.

The use of the tape-measure slide-rule for measuring backwards in subtraction will also help children to see that they can make *subtraction transformations* as well as addition transformations to sets of numbers. Figure 9 : 30 illustrates the transformation 'subtract 7'.

Children will discover that they cannot apply this transformation to the complete set of numbers. Figure 9 : 30 illustrates this difficulty very clearly, showing the attempt to subtract 7 from every member of the set {1, 2, 3, ..., 14, 15}. Children may suggest at this point that more numbers could be put in to show units below the starting-point. Even if this idea does not appear, the graph focuses attention on a problem which is solved later by the introduction of directed numbers.[6]

Alongside children's discovery of the meaning of subtraction, and of its relation to addition, their familiarity with the numbers up to 20 will be developing. The regrouping of 15 as 8 + 7 is often used in a mental addition such as

92 + 15

which can be thought of as

92 + 8 + 7,

or 107. Similarly, the written subtraction method of decomposition

$$\begin{array}{r} 35 \\ -17 \\ \hline \end{array}$$

requires 15 to be regrouped as 7 + 8 to enable the subtraction in the *ones* column to take place. Whether such regroupings are primarily matters of addition or subtraction does not matter. They have a variety of uses, and children at this stage, in their practical activities, should constantly be meeting

[5]See the sections on vectors and directed numbers, pages 165 and 185.

[6]See Chapter 33.

such situations as the following, which involve regrouping.

i) The same distance is measured with rods and with a tape-measure, involving the regrouping of 19 centimetres as 10 centimetres and 9 centimetres.

ii) Two things each costing 9 pence are bought together. The cost is regrouped so that a child can pay with a ten-pence piece and eight pennies.

iii) The shop assistant giving change regroups the money paid, literally or in the imagination, into two parts. Shop assistants often use a 'counting on' or *complementary addition* method in doing this (*see page 107*).

Addition and subtraction which involve numbers greater than 20, sums of money involving more than ten pence, and similar quantities, demand understanding of our system of notation, and will be discussed in Chapter 15. Familiarity with, and regrouping of, numbers up to 20 is a necessary preliminary to this.

INTRODUCTION OF THE ELECTRONIC CALCULATOR

Simple electronic calculators are now so universally available, and universally used by adults, that they need to be taken into account in the teaching of number even to young children. The use of a calculator does not diminish the need for an understanding of how numbers behave, but can be used to enhance children's understanding of number. In the primary school, calculators can most usefully be regarded as forms of structural apparatus, with different properties from other forms of structural apparatus, but equally useful. Number patterns can easily be explored, and relationships found, and because calculators handle large numbers nearly as easily as small ones, patterns can be extended further than would be possible without them.

Calculators also make 'real life' mathematics more accessible. Real life is only rarely limited to numbers under twenty. When calculators are available in the classroom shop, actual prices can be used instead of simplified prices within the range of children's own powers of calculation. Young children can handle the numbers on the class register, and plan the arrangement of chairs for the concert.

Figure 9 : 31

Young children often treat a calculator as if it were a toy, and experiment with it in many different ways. As a result of this individual experimentation, they often find out a great deal about how the number system works. In the classroom, it is sensible to encourage children to use calculators alongside number apparatus. From this they learn that the calculator can do the same operations that they are personally doing with apparatus; thus, they integrate the calculator with the practical experience on which their growing knowledge of numbers is based.

A simple four-function calculator (Figure 9 : 31) can be sensibly used for exploration as soon as a child knows the meanings of the signs +, − and = . A calculator with a *constant* facility is useful at first. This enables the calculator to count by repeatedly adding 1. For instance, the keystrokes $\boxed{0}$ $\boxed{+}$ $\boxed{1}$ $\boxed{=}$ $\boxed{=}$ $\boxed{=}$ will produce the displays 1, 2, 3, ..., at successive pressings of the $\boxed{=}$ key.

Similarly,

$\boxed{8}$ $\boxed{+}$ $\boxed{1}$ $\boxed{=}$ $\boxed{=}$ $\boxed{=}$ $\boxed{=}$

produces the result 12, having added 4 by counting on in ones. The same result is, of course, produced by the keystrokes

$\boxed{8}$ $\boxed{+}$ $\boxed{4}$ $\boxed{=}$

Patterns such as

$$17 + 10 = 17$$
$$27 + 10 = 37$$
$$37 + 10 = 47$$

and so on are very quickly explored, and children can also be asked to find out what to do to make the calculator successively display 17, 27, 37, 47, ... or 97, 77, 57, 37, 17. These activities can also be related to oral counting forwards and backwards in tens, twenties, and so on.

Subtraction is the inverse of addition:

$$27 + 9 = 36 \quad \text{and} \quad 36 - 9 = 27;$$

on the calculator, the keystrokes $\boxed{+}$ $\boxed{9}$ $\boxed{=}$ are undone by the keystrokes $\boxed{-}$ $\boxed{9}$ $\boxed{=}$.

Activities of this type give another way, alongside the structural apparatus, measuring and the host of other activities, through which children can learn about the ways in which numbers behave. Children should be encouraged to predict what number the calculator will show when they have done a calculation. Repeated errors will lead to discussion with the teacher, and to seeing why the child's calculation was in error, with the aid of some type of apparatus, such as Cuisenaire, which does not have the 'black box' quality of a calculator. Indeed, it seems that calculators are more abstract than structural apparatus, but more concrete than pencil-and-paper calculation. Sensibly used, they add much to children's understanding of number.

Early addition and subtraction in the National Curriculum

The early addition and subtraction activities in this Chapter feed into several Attainment Targets. In Attainment Target 1 (Using and applying mathematics) at Level 2, children are expected to:

- Select the materials and the mathematics to use for a practical task.
  EXAMPLE: *Understand that if one child has five pencils and another three pencils, the total number is found by addition.*
  (AT1: Level 2)

Most of the work on addition and subtraction appears in AT2 (Number). Children are expected to be able to:

- Demonstrate that they know and can use number facts, including addition and subtraction.
  (AT2: Level 2)

- solve whole number problems involving addition and subtraction.
  (AT2: Level 2)

The associated statements in the Programme of Study are:

- Know and use addition and subtraction facts up to 10.
  (Level 2)

- Learn and use addition and subtraction facts up to 20 (including zero).
  (Level 2)

- Solve whole-number problems involving addition and subtraction, including money.
  (Level 2)

- Compare two numbers to find the difference.
  (Level 2)

- Use coins in simple contexts.
  (Level 2)

In Attainment Target 3 (Algebra), at Levels 1, 2 and 3, the concentration is on number patterns, including addition and subtraction patterns. Children are expected to be able to:

- Explore number patterns.
  (Level 2)

- Use pattern in number when doing mental calculations.
  (Level 3)

The associated statements in the Programme of Study are:

- Explore and use patterns in addition and subtraction facts to 10.
  (Level 3)

- Develop a variety of strategies to perform mental calculations using number patterns and equivalent forms of two-digit numbers.
  (Level 3)

The beginning of children's later work on algebraic symbolism and algebraic functions has also been described in this chapter, although the word *function* was not used. These ideas are found in Attainment Target 3, in statements in the Programme of Study:

- Understand the use of a symbol to stand for an unknown number.
  (Level 2)

- Deal with inputs to and outputs from simple function machines.
  (Level 3)

The calculator is not mentioned in the National Curriculum until Level 3, where the following statement appears in the Programme of Study:

- Solve problems involving multiplication or division of whole numbers or money, using a calculator where necessary.

However, it is not sensible for children first to meet the calculator as a device for multiplication and division, when it is also able to add and subtract. A more natural introduction to the calculator is for addition and subtraction, where it can be used alongside concrete materials and alongside mental calculation.

10 THE GROWTH OF SPATIAL CONCEPTS

SHAPES AND MOVEMENTS

Space interests children when it contains objects which they can see in relation to one another, or can observe in motion, as they change their position relative to the child or to one another.

Two aspects of space interest children from early days :

i) *Shapes and their properties*
Two questions guide children's investigations in this field. What can be made with shapes of particular kinds and how can a certain shape be made?

ii) *Movements*
These may either change the position of an object or alter the structure of the object itself.

SHAPES AND THEIR PROPERTIES

In Chapters 1 and 5 we have considered a variety of activities which help children to become aware of many shapes and some of their important properties. Now we try to clarify and summarise the ideas that teachers can find revealed in the way children handle shapes. When teachers see the emergence of new concepts they can help to make them more precise if their own understanding is clear.

One of the earliest characteristics which children discern in a shape is whether it is *open* or *closed*. This is an important property of a topological kind, that is, a property which is independent of shape and length. Examples are given in Figure 10 : 1. Children will want to know, 'Can the cow get out of the field, or the fly out of the bottle, or the boy out of the maze?' They also recognise the *closed* curve which encloses a set and later the closed circuit which lights up an electric bulb.

Solid or *hollow*. This seems an easy idea. A solid cube or cylinder is easily distinguished from a hollow one by the difference in weight, if they are made of the same materials, but it is difficult for children to think about the solid shape which forms a cup. Nor can they easily visualise the region within the boundary surfaces of a body such as a cone, and think, for instance, of the height of the vertex above the base. Experience of filling open vessels and weighing their contents hastens the growth of the idea of solidity and of the region within a surface. Immersing bodies in water also gives opportunities for comparison. A solid cube, a closed hollow cube and an open hollow cube all of the same size can be immersed and the effects observed. Without such experiences children cannot

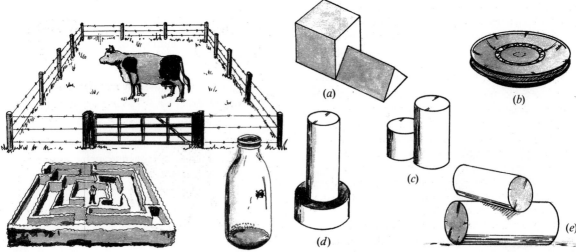

Figure 10 : 1

Figure 10 : 2

(a)

(b)

(c)

(d)

(e)

develop early the concept of a measurable volume for a solid shape as well as for an open container.

It is also stimulating for children to make model cuboids or square pyramids in different ways. A solid version can be modelled in clay or Plasticine, a hollow model can be made from a paper net, and a third variation can be carried out with straws, which show a skeleton of the shape through which the whole of the interior can be seen.

The various parts of the surface of a three-dimensional object may be either *flat* or *curved*. This decides how objects can be fitted one against another. Flat surfaces can be placed together without any gaps. Most curved surfaces cannot be placed in this way. Yet some curved surfaces can be stacked one inside another. Figure 10 : 2 shows the difference.

The straight edge of a ruler will lie anywhere along a flat surface. It will not lie along most curved surfaces, for instance the surface of a sphere, wherever it is placed; but there are some shapes, such as cylinders and cones, on which it is possible to place a ruler to lie along the curved surface in certain positions only (Figure 10 : 2(*c*)).

A flat portion of a surface, such as the circular end of a cylinder or a square which is part of the surface of a cube, is known as a *face*.

A face of a three-dimensional shape can be extended in the imagination in any direction; it can then be seen to be part of a plane: later on children will realise that the points of the face are a subset of the set of points in the plane.

Concave or *convex*. This notion is closely linked with the experience of being inside or outside, but the two ideas must be distinguished. The word *inside* used precisely means within the region enclosed by lines or surfaces. *Outside* means lying beyond the boundary of the region. *Concave* describes a property of a line or surface when it is viewed from a particular standpoint. When we observe, a concave line or surface appears as part of a boundary surface which curves towards us so that we feel ourselves to be inside it. The word *convex* describes the boundary as seen from the other side so that it curves away from the observer. The words concave and convex apply to open as well as to closed figures. A cup illustrates well the concave property when we look at its interior and the convex property when we view its exterior. These properties can be observed and recorded by children when they make various shapes in clay or Plasticine or bend paper to make mobiles.

Among the most fascinating experiences of concavity and convexity are those of the sandcastle and jelly mould type, where a concave surface is filled with moist or plastic material which will set sufficiently to retain its shape when turned out. The concave mould and the convex cast can be compared. A great variety of impressions in Plasticine or wax can be made by children and casts produced from them; leaves, fruits and embossed designs can be used. Two halves of a solid form can be impressed separately, the shapes compared for symmetry, and the two casts subsequently joined to show the whole object, e.g. a puppet head.

The reflections in concave or convex mirrors are fascinating, as are distortions seen in the reflections on the two sides of a brightly polished spoon. A hollow rubber ball with a hole pierced in it can be deformed to make part of its surface concave. Concave surfaces are used as reflectors in torches and electric fires. A radio telescope is a good example of one of the many uses of concave surfaces in modern science and industry. Children can find many others.

The hills and valleys and lakes of a model landscape or island can be seen as convex and concave surfaces. Some interesting questions about measuring depths and heights may arise and lead to enterprising experiments.

To an observer a convex surface seems to fall away from the nearest point whereas the concave surface appears to close in. There are some surfaces which are neither wholly convex nor wholly concave. A pass between two mountains is broadly of this type. It is known as a saddle-back pass because the riding saddle used on horses is of the same shape. Viewed along the length of the horse it is seen to rise towards both the head and the tail. It is concave in this direction. Viewed across the horse it is seen to drop on both sides to the flanks. In this

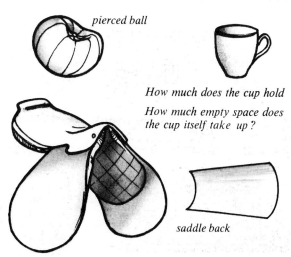

pierced ball

How much does the cup hold

How much empty space does the cup itself take up ?

saddle back

Figure 10 : 3

direction it is convex. See Figure 10 : 3. This is a complex situation which will appeal to many children.

FACES, EDGES AND VERTICES

Children handle many shapes whose edges they recognise as straight or curved. Cups and saucers have *curved edges*; bricks, boxes and packets of cuboid shape have *straight edges*. Balls have *no edges*; many shapes which could be made from a ball of Plasticine have no edges. The *torus* or shape of a tyre inner-tube has a hole through the middle and has no edges. Shapes can be devised which have some straight and some curved edges (Figure 10 : 4).

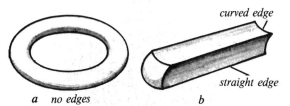

a   no edges   *b*

Figure 10 : 4

Edges are formed where two faces of a three-dimensional shape meet. Thus an *edge* is the set of points common to both faces. If we think of a face as a set of points, an edge is the intersection of the two sets of points which constitute the two faces. The net of a triangular pyramid shows the edges of the base as the straight lines made by folding. The other edges are made when two of the triangular faces are joined (Figure 10 : 5).

It will be seen that each edge is a side of the two faces that intersect. We speak of *edges* of a three-dimensional shape but use *sides* for the lines which enclose a two-dimensional shape. The correct use of these words, for instance the *sides* of a rectangle but the *edges* of a cuboid, makes it easier for children to describe accurately the shapes they make or use.

The importance of edges is brought out when children attempt to make three-dimensional shapes with strips, rods or straws. They quickly find the necessity of giving firmness or rigidity to their constructions by the use of rods additional to those used for the edges. The triangular *pyramid* is *rigid* when made with rods as edges but the triangular *prism* can be *deformed* unless some diagonal rods are inserted in the rectangular faces. See Figure 10 : 6.

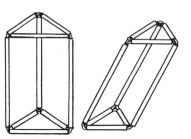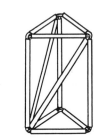

Figure 10 : 6

Children associate the *corners* of everyday objects, such as tables and boxes, with *points* and this is mathematically correct. Two lines which cross have a point in common, the intersection of the two sets of points which constitute the lines. Thus two sides of a flat shape will meet in a point. But the corner of a three-dimensional shape cannot be made with fewer than three faces; this means that three edges at least meet at the corner or *vertex*. Children can examine the vertices of pyramids, cubes, etc., and notice the different shapes of the corners.

The idea of an angle begins to form when the corner of a face or of any two-dimensional shape is noticed. At this stage a child discriminates between such corners only as right (square), blunt or sharp angles (Figure 10 : 7). A clearer idea of angle develops with experience of rotation. Chapter 12 carries the study of angles further.

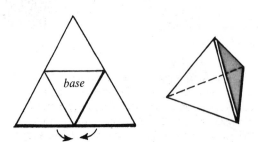

Figure 10 : 5

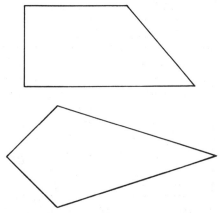

Figure 10 : 7

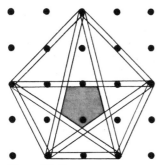

Figure 10 : 8

When a plane figure is made on a nail- or peg-board the vertices define the shape. Suppose that five points are chosen as vertices. An elastic band can be placed round every pair of nails or pegs, as shown in Figure 10 : 8. Five of these bands enclose a region, but another five form a star-shaped figure inside it. How many bands pass round each nail? We see that 4 line segments (lines of limited length) begin at each vertex. Each of the 5 vertices is the end-point of 4 line segments, but of course each line segment has 2 end-points. The number of segments is therefore $(5 \times 4) \div 2$, i.e. 10. Other figures made in this way can be studied and children may discover a rule for the number of lines.

This is a good example of the way in which a spatial structure and the number relationship embodied in it illustrate a more general mathematical pattern. It can be compared with the process of finding how many pairs of children could be formed from a set of five children. Each child could have any one of four partners. This makes 5 sets of 4 pairs, i.e. 20 pairs. But if Ann has Betty for a partner the same pair is formed as when Betty has Ann for a partner. The number of pairs is therefore half of 20, i.e. 10. Figure 10 : 9 shows the possible pairs and the identity of such pairs as (Ann and Betty) and (Betty and Ann).

	A	B	C	D	E
Ann		AB	AC	AD	AE
Betty	BA		BC	BD	BE
Carol	CA	CB		CD	CE
Dora	DA	DB	DC		DE
Enid	EA	EB	EC	ED	

Figure 10 : 9

Symmetry: folding

When children have made a simple balance bar (*see page 66*), they can go on to find *shapes* that look balanced; a glass, a spoon, a chair, an animal, etc. Two halves look alike. Making shapes that balance is a fascinating game that has plenty of variety and yet leads to a practical appreciation of one of the most important concepts of mathematics—the idea of symmetry. Here are some suggestions:

i) A blob of mixed paint or ink can be put next to a fold on a piece of paper. If it is then pressed down firmly along the fold and opened out, the result is surprising and often beautiful (Figure 10 : 10).

Figure 10 : 10

ii) A piece of paper is folded in half and a pattern torn or cut out along the edges. The result is opened out. The children will produce some amusing or pretty designs (Figure 10 : 11).

Figure 10 : 11

iii) Using a folded piece of squared paper, half of a given shape is copied. The squares can be counted to give accuracy. The other half is obtained by pricking through. This method brings out clearly that in a symmetrical shape each point on one side is matched by a point

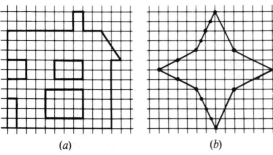

(a)   (b)

Figure 10 : 12

on the other side which is the same distance from the fold (Figure 10 : 12).

Up to the age of about seven children do not distinguish left from right with any certainty. This is understandable because it depends on the point of view of the observer which of two points is seen as left and which as right (Figure 10 : 13).

Figure 10 : 13

Making symmetrical shapes helps children to know left from right. Shoes and gloves and double swing doors have this symmetrical relationship and one of the pair must be distinguished as left. Turning a pair of shoes upside down makes it difficult for a child to identify which is the left one.

Folding a sheet into quarters introduces symmetry about two axes, and children can make interesting patterns by tearing or cutting round the edge and cutting out holes. (See Figure 10 : 14).

It can be seen that Figure 10 : 12 (b) has symmetry about four axes, and this pattern could have been made by folding the paper into eighths. As children's dexterity grows they will invent ways

Figure 10 : 14

of making very attractive paper mats using four-fold symmetry.

In a regular two-dimensional figure, all the sides are equal and all the angles are equal, so that every corner is exactly like every other corner. This involves symmetry about more than one axis. The triangle is a special case because if its sides are equal its angles must also be equal. In other shapes equal sides can be accompanied by unequal angles, as Figure 10 : 15 shows. As can be seen, the equilateral triangle is a regular figure and has three axes of symmetry.

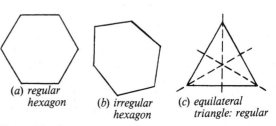

(a) regular   (b) irregular   (c) equilateral
   hexagon   hexagon   triangle: regular

Figure 10 : 15

RIGHT ANGLES AND SYMMETRY

Children can look at squares, rectangles, circles, etc. and see which of them can be folded to make two halves which fit. Any shape can be folded but the two parts are not, of course, usually the same shape. But even the most irregular flat shape, a leaf or a jagged piece of paper, can be folded flat so that the fold is a straight line. Stiff paper folded in this way makes a good edge for ruling a straight line. A further fold, keeping the parts of the first fold together, will make a square corner or right angle. Notice the irregularity of the paper used in Figure 10 : 16; this makes the right angle stand out clearly.

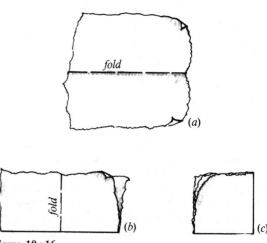

Figure 10 : 16

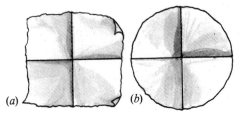

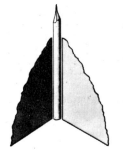

Figure 10 : 17

Figure 10 : 20

A circle folded in this way is a useful alternative to the jagged paper. The intersection of the folds gives the centre; the folds divide the circle into quarters.

If the paper is unfolded the creases show the fitting together of four right angles (Figure 10 : 17). A right angle made in this way will serve as a home-made set square, and children can use it to check right angles which occur in the classroom, and in particular to discover the way in which three right angles fit together at the corner of a room. See Figures 10 : 18 and 10 : 19.

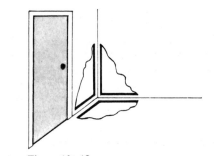

Figure 10 : 18

Figure 10 : 19

They will also find (Figure 10 : 19) that if an open book is standing upright on a table, in one position three right angles fit together, but that the book will also stand with its parts farther open than a right angle, or less far open than a right angle. A pencil is vertical when it stands upright on a horizontal table if the set square fits against it *in any position.*

Two arrangements such as those shown in Figure 10 : 20 can also be produced with a pile of coins.

The set square has many practical uses. Put against a plumb bob it can be used to test a horizontal. It is also needed in drawing squares and rectangles. The first rectangles which children can draw accurately are on squared paper where the right angles are already drawn.

Particular lengths can be drawn accurately by counting squares. A first box can be made in this way; children draw a rectangle on squared paper and draw equal squares in each corner. They cut along one side of each of these squares and fold up along the dotted lines shown in Figure 10 : 21. They then fold the squares round and stick them to the sides of the box.

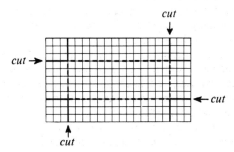

Figure 10 : 21

If a box made in this way can first be shown to the children and then opened out to show how it was made, the children can invent their own way of making a similar box. They can then experiment with making a box with a lid. The same construction will enable them to make a counter or stall for a shop or the body of a truck.

When children have learned to measure and to draw straight lines with a ruler (at 7 or 8 years of age) they can draw a rectangle on plain paper or card. They can now use their set squares to make the corners the right shape.

Movements

Previously, we have considered shapes in themselves without regard to any changes which might take place. We now turn to a dynamic study and examine the effects of movements. Children explore space spontaneously through the natural movements of their bodies, particularly of their limbs. There are three main types of movement:

i) a jabbing or pointing movement

ii) movement to and fro or up and down

iii) moving round and round, with head, hand or the whole body.

These movements can be seen in children's early attempts at drawing and writing (Figure 10 : 22).

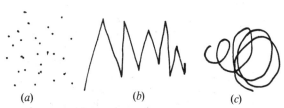

(a)   (b)   (c)

Figure 10 : 22

Children make similar movements in their play with toys and materials. The observation of vehicles, machines, living creatures and other natural objects shows the same types of motion. Through these experiences children become aware of certain spatial relationships.

(1) Pointing, taking aim, interpreting an arrow sign all indicate a straight line in a particular direction and also indicate the point to which the line leads. The abstract idea of a line is thus forming in the mind of a child, since in these instances the line from the observer to the object is not drawn or marked. A point begins to be understood as marking a position (Figure 10 : 23). Further experience of movement will bring clearer understanding of the relationship between points and lines. For example, copying a shape by pricking through a succession of points, or pegging out a path, will bring out the idea that a line or path is a set of points.

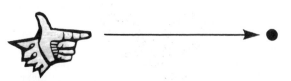

Figure 10 : 23

(2) Moving a body may change its apparent size or shape. It is important to discover which properties change and which remain invariant when the position of the body is altered. The movement to-and-fro or up-and-down takes place in a straight line, as when an engine moves along a straight track or a lift goes up and comes down. The shape and size of the object are easily seen not to change during such movements. Nor does any turning take place. The *site* of the object is simply moved along a straight line. Such a movement is called a *translation*. It will be noticed that the motion could be continued along the line without limit. It can also be seen in Figure 10 : 24 that the edges of the

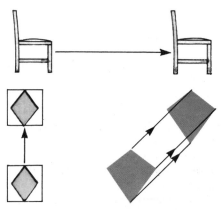

Figure 10 : 24

shape remain parallel to their original positions.

(3) Turning, or moving round and round, is probably the earliest arm movement which infants make. They see human beings and animals turn round and become accustomed to different views of the same object. As we saw in Chapter 2 young children soon recognise that the various views belong to the same object. Nevertheless, a child may not see that the *shape* of the thing is not itself changed by this turning movement or *rotation*. In fact, the inherent shape is invariant but the orientation or lie may be changed by a particular rotation. Turning takes place about a fixed point, as in the movement of the hands of a clock. This turning movement could be reversed and the shape brought back to its original position. The shape can be turned about a fixed point in itself. It may be fixed by a pin and then given a spin. In Figure 10 : 25 various shapes are given a succession of turns and their new positions drawn out separately. The arrows help to indicate the amount of turning.

Rotation is a very important movement, not only in the turning movement of wheels but also in

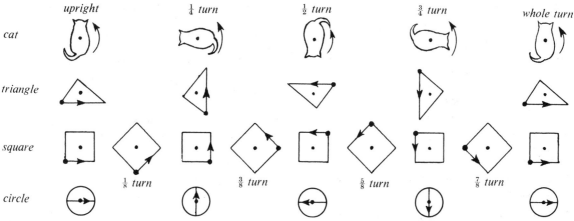

Figure 10 : 25

various forms of measuring dial (for time, pressure, electricity, etc.). As we shall see in Chapter 39 it helps us to understand certain numerical and algebraic structures. Translation along a line illustrates the basic operations of addition and subtraction of numbers (*see Chapter 9*); such a movement may be continued *without limit* in either direction and needs negative as well as positive numbers for its description; the movement of rotation, as on a clock-face, gives rise to a *finite* number system limited to the numbers placed on the dial (Figure 10 : 26). When a second revolution is carried out the numbers are repeated, and so on for succeeding revolutions; the number readings are the same.

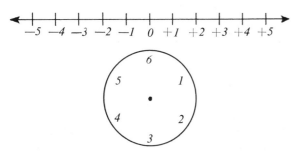

Figure 10 : 26

Children can learn about rotations through experimenting with a pendulum, using a trundle wheel, and marking out circles. They can graduate their own compass card or a clock-face by folding a disc. With some help, they may be able to make a model with a dial to measure the compression of a spring when weights are placed in a scale pan resting upon it.

(4) In addition to the movements which children can make with their own limbs there are other operations on shapes which change them in significant ways. *Reflection* is one which children understand readily because they can actually produce a reflected image of a shape by a simple fold. Alternatively, they can see the reflected image in a mirror. The important property of reflection is that it produces a shape which, though corresponding closely with the original, has a substantial difference: an irregular figure in a plane has a reflected image which cannot be made to fit on to the original by a movement in *the plane*, such as a translation or a rotation or any combination of these two movements. For example, to obtain the reflected shape shown in Figure 10 : 27(*a*), one might rotate the figure about the axis of reflection, but this movement would carry it out of the plane.

In three dimensions a mirror image is familiar in the right-hand/left-hand pairing of gloves, shoes, houses, etc. These forms cannot be fitted into the same site by any translation or rotation. The right-hand glove can be made to look like a left-hand glove only by turning it inside out. This fact of real space is remarkable enough for children to be allowed to discover it for themselves (Figure 10 : 28).

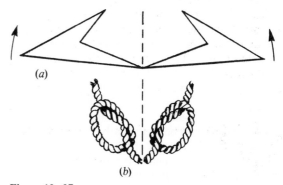

Figure 10 : 27

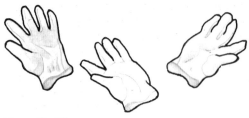

Figure 10 : 28

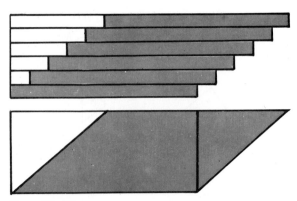

Figure 10 : 30

(5) *Stretch* or *enlargement*. When a picture is projected on to a screen or a blown-up balloon is blown up still further, the shape remains the same but the *size* is *increased*. This movement outwards from a centre is thus different in its effects from the movements already studied. A set of points sited in space could also be moved so that the distances between any pair of points were increased in the same ratio. The shape of the set remains the same. The movement which enlarges distances could be reversed. Any given shape can be made smaller, all lengths being *reduced* in the same ratio. This kind of movement is clearly the basis of scale drawing and map reading (Figure 10 : 29).

(6) *Shear*. Children sometimes notice that books or

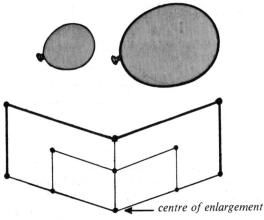

— *centre of enlargement*

Figure 10 : 29

a set of cuboid rods arranged in a pile may be moved, so that each book or rod projects a certain distance beyond the one below it and yet the pile does not collapse. The base of the pile and its height remain the same. If a thick packet of paper is treated in the same way a change in the face of the pile can easily been seen: the rectangle has become a parallelogram. The amount of surface area has not altered because clearly the face still consists of the thicknesses of the sheets of paper. The study of this movement is most suitably undertaken when the area of rectangular shapes has been understood and the question of finding the

area of other shapes has been raised. The position of each sheet has been changed, and this has altered the *shape* of the face, but the *area* has not been changed (Figure 10 : 30).

TRANSFORMATIONS

A mathematician studying the effects of movements on sets of points or shapes describes the procedures by which new points are found as *transformations*. An original point is transformed or mapped into another point by some rule which is applied to the whole set. Each point of the *transform* is called the *image point* of the original point. In the process of transformation some properties of the set of points will be changed; others remain unaltered, i.e. they are invariant. We will now examine the transformations that are related to the movements described in the preceding paragraphs.

TRANSLATION

The transformation of *translation* can be developed in the early years through making patterns. Children have seen already how to make a good pattern by *reflection* or folding; they can now see that repeating a shape along a line produces an interesting pattern too. For example, the rhombus (or diamond), circle, spiral can all be effectively used in simple repeats (Figure 10 : 31). Colour may disguise the repeat but it adds interest.

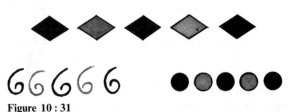

Figure 10 : 31

A combination of two shapes can form a unit and this unit can be *translated horizontally*, or the movement could be vertical instead of horizontal (Figure 10 : 32), or in a sloping direction.

Figure 10 : 32

A further variation is to reflect a shape and then to translate the new shape (Figure 10 : 33).

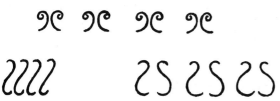

Figure 10 : 33

Making border patterns using these ideas can give rise to some very pleasing designs; for example, the translation of a pattern drawn on a square.

We can describe translation mathematically by noticing that each point of the set is transformed into a point a certain distance away in a given direction. The lines which show this movement are *parallel* (Figure 10 : 34).

We now have two sets of points, the original set and the image set created by the transformation. In Figure 10 : 34 we see, for instance, two crescents, the original and its transform. Shape and size are invariant. The appearance of the shapes is the same; measurement of lengths such as sides, diagonals, perimeters will confirm that these are unchanged. The new shape could be fitted into the site of the original; when this is true the two figures are said to be *congruent*. Corresponding angles are equal. The orientation of the shape is also

unaltered. Any line remains parallel to its original position. These invariants can be seen in the illustrations of Figure 10 : 34.

In Chapter 9 the use of a tape-measure slide-rule was shown to involve movements which give an addition or subtraction transformation of a set of *numbers*. In this situation the numbers are represented on a number line by points. If the numbers are to be transformed by the addition of 3, each of the points representing them will be translated 3 units to the right. The image points represent the transformed numbers (Figure 10 : 35).

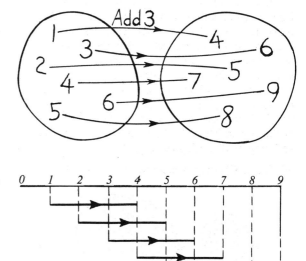

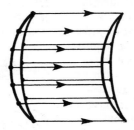

Figure 10 : 35

Later on, when children have learned to name the position of a point by its co-ordinates, they will see how to describe a translation of a point by the change in its co-ordinates. For example, in Figure 10 : 36 the point (1,3) is translated 2 units parallel to the *x*-axis. Its new co-ordinates are (3,3). The point (2,4) is translated 1 unit parallel to the *y*-axis; its new co-ordinates are (2,5). A point may receive

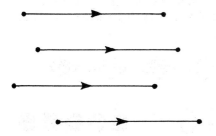

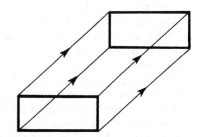

Figure 10 : 34

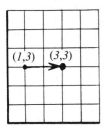

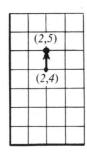

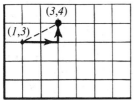

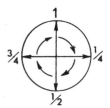

Figure 10 : 37

Figure 10 : 36

two translations, one parallel to the *x*-axis, the other parallel to the *y*-axis. The effect will be to change both co-ordinates and obtain an image point which could have been found by a single translation, as shown in Figure 10 : 36. Point (1,3) is transformed into (3,4) by performing *both* translations.

These translations can be expressed by formulae. If a point (*x, y*) is translated *a* units parallel to the *x*-axis its transform is (*x* + *a, y*); if it is next translated *b* units parallel to the *y*-axis its new transform will be

$$(x + a, \; y + b)$$

Although only the ablest children are likely to be able to discover such a formula while still at the primary school, it is helpful for a teacher to be aware of this possibility. The use of an arrow to show a transformation is the accepted notation. We write

$$(x, \; y) \rightarrow (x + a, \; y + b)$$

ROTATION

The movements of the hands of a clock, the turning of wheels and children's own power of turning round give them a good idea of what *rotation* means. As we have seen in earlier sections children cannot always recognise the results of a rotation. They have to have experience of watching things turn, to notice the results, and to discover that we can measure how much rotation has taken place. When children learn to tell the time they are in fact using a whole revolution of the minute hand to measure 1 hour, half a revolution to measure half an hour, and so on (Figure 10 : 37).

Children should also watch and draw on the ground the shadow cast by a stick on a sunny day hour by hour and notice how the shadow has turned during each hour. This will lead them to find the North–South line and to make a compass card to show the four main points, and later to add NE, SE, SW, NW (Figure 10 : 38).

Figure 10 : 38

A compass with a simple compass card will show children how the needle swings and how the compass must be turned until North lies along the needle when it comes to rest. They can express the turning as a quarter, three eighths, three quarters, etc., of a revolution. This measure of rotation is developed further in Chapters 12 and 27.

Rotation can also be used to make more complex patterns. The familiar square can be rotated through a quarter of a revolution and the 'diamond' appears. Shapes cut out in card can be rotated about a pin through their central point and the new shapes drawn (Figure 10 : 39). At this stage a child can make a wheel turn about a fixed pin.

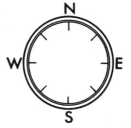

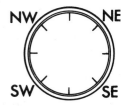

Figure 10 : 39

The shapes can be drawn side by side to form a unit for translation and so produce a new type of border pattern (Figure 10 : 40). They can also be drawn round the rim of a disc and so reveal the

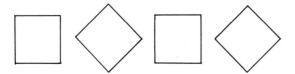

Figure 10 : 40

appearance of the shape in different orientations (*see plate 4*).

We can describe rotation mathematically by saying that a set of points or a shape is transformed by matching each point in the given set with one that could be reached by turning. There must be a fixed point as the centre of rotation and the amount of turning must be the same for each pair of corresponding points. This amount can be expressed as a fraction of a whole turn, a revolution, or an angle measured in degrees.

We can imagine a rod 3 units long being rotated about one end, O, and can think about the other end-point. If the rotation is one eighth of a turn the image of the end-point will stay the same distance from O but it will move into a different position; there is an angle between the lines joining O to the original point and to its image, an angle which is one eighth of a turn. The position of the image of the point relative to the original position of the rod can be stated as (d, θ) where d is the distance of the point from O and θ is the angle of rotation. Figure 10 : 41 shows the image points for several rotations. Their positions could be given as $(3, \frac{1}{8}$ revolution), $(3, \frac{1}{4}$ revolution), $(3, \frac{1}{2}$ revolution) where the angle is stated as a fraction of a turn. It will be noticed that under rotation only the angle changes. Measures of length and angle used to define a position are called *polar co-ordinates*. They are particularly convenient for points related by rotation.

Now suppose that the angle of rotation is one complete turn, or 360°. The image of A under this rotation is *itself*. Succeeding complete rotations will produce the same image points as the first one. This property of rotations raises some interesting questions about the successive transformations of shapes under rotation.

Figure 10 : 42 shows an equilateral triangle ABC with its corners marked so that we can distinguish them. The shaded triangle PQR represents the hole left by the triangle when it was cut out. ABC would fit into PQR in its original position with A upon P. If triangle ABC is rotated when will it again be in a position to fit into PQR? After one third of a turn B would lie on P if the triangle were fitted into the hole. It can be seen that a further rotation of one third of a turn would bring C on to P. If the triangle is rotated another third of a turn it will lie in its original position with A on P.

There are thus three different positions in which the image will fit into the hole, i.e. after one-third or two-thirds of a turn or a whole turn. These are called the rotational symmetry operations of the triangle. Children can experiment with a number of plane shapes to discover their angles of rotational symmetry; suitable shapes are a square, hexagon, circle, rectangle, kite, parallelogram. For a circle any rotation will do; for a kite, only a complete turn (Figure 10 : 43).

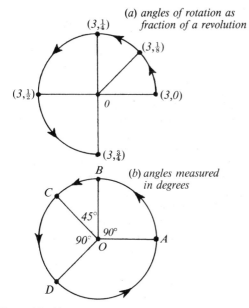

(a) angles of rotation as fraction of a revolution

(b) angles measured in degrees

Figure 10 : 41

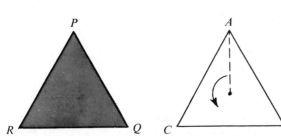
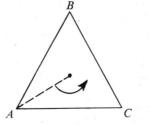
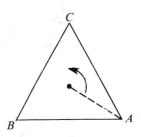

Figure 10 : 42

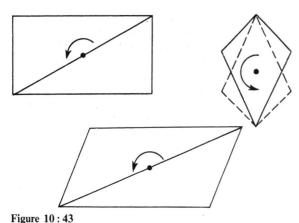

Figure 10 : 43

To summarise, we see that under rotation there is a point of the plane which remains unchanged; the distance of any point from the centre of rotation is also invariant; lengths and angles of a figure are unchanged but the *position* of a point is changed and the *orientation* of a figure changes. A complete turn always fits the image onto the original.

REFLECTION

This is the transformation which shows most clearly a rule for finding the position of a transformed point. When a plane figure is reflected by folding a piece of paper about a line in its plane, the fold represents the axis of the reflection. After the fold has been made a prick can be made through any point of the original and will mark the corresponding point which lies beneath it. On opening out the paper the pairs of corresponding points are seen to lie on a line *perpendicular* to the axis, on *opposite sides* of it and at *equal distances* from the axis. A point *on* the axis will transform into itself. In Figure 10 : 44(a) the points A and E belong to both the original and the transform.

Figure 10 : 44(b) shows a series of reflections of the letter p about equidistant parallel axes. The transforms are all either like the original or are its mirror image.

In Figure 10 : 44(c) the point labelled R_0 and the set of points making up this form of p have been reflected in the y-axis. The image of R_0 is R_1. We next reflect this reflection in the x-axis, so that the image of R_1 is R_2. If this image is compared with the original, it will be seen that it could have been obtained by rotation about O. Thus the two reflections have the same effect as one rotation through half a turn. If R_2 is now reflected in the y-axis, R_3 is obtained. This is related to R_1 by rotation in the same way that R_2 is related to R_0. The reflection of R_3 in the x-axis then finally brings us back to R_0. The position of these four points suggests the use of a special sign to represent a distance to the *left* of the vertical axis, or *below* the horizontal axis. If R_0 is two units from one of these axis, then $^+2$ could represent the distance to the right (or above) and $^-2$ the distance to the left (or below).

The symmetry created by a reflection is a valuable tool for discovering properties of shapes, for instance the properties of rectangles. Recognising symmetry in a mirror image can lead to new insights (Figure 10 : 45).

There is another kind of pattern which children see in the shapes of some flowers, in pictures of snow crystals, or in some decorative designs. The

Figure 10 : 45

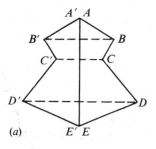

(a)

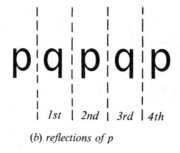

(b) *reflections of p*

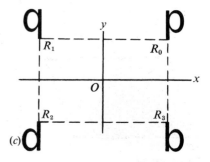

(c)

Figure 10 : 44

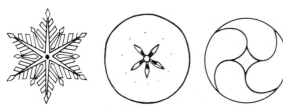

Figure 10 : 46

pattern has parts which are of the same shape and size as one another and are arranged round a centre. Figure 10 : 46 shows some examples of this arrangement.

It can be seen that the whole shape could be rotated about a centre and after a certain fraction of a complete turn the shapes would fit on to its original position. In a five-petalled flower a turn of $\frac{1}{5}, \frac{2}{5}, \frac{3}{5}, \frac{4}{5}$ or a complete revolution would bring the shape to a position where it would fit into its original place. For the three-legged shape $\frac{1}{3}, \frac{2}{3}$, or a complete revolution would be required (Figure 10 : 47). This form of symmetry is called *rotational*

Figure 10 : 47

or *cyclic* symmetry.

A special case of rotational symmetry is seen in those shapes which require half a complete turn to bring them to a position that fits on to the original. The latter S, a parallelogram and such an irregular shape as that shown in Figure 10 : 48(*c*) illustrate this type of symmetry.

Each of these shapes could be given a half-turn about a point marked in the diagram and would then fit into the same position as it originally occupied. Symmetry of this type is known as *half-turn symmetry.*

In three dimensions solids can be reflected in a plane. The perpendicular distances of corresponding points from the plane are equal. Distances, angles, shape and size are all preserved. A change occurs in the reversal of the directions of line segments perpendicular to the plane of symmetry.

ENLARGEMENT

To effect this transformation a centre of enlargement must be chosen. Distances from this centre to all points of the given set of points are increased in a fixed ratio, say, two to one. Experiment will show that the position of the centre will make no difference to the shape and size of the transform but it will affect its position.

Shape is invariant under enlargement but lengths such as sides and diagonals are increased in a constant ratio. See Figure 10 : 49. We may ask what is the effect of this transformation on the area of a two-dimensional shape or on the volume of a three-dimensional shape. These questions are discussed in Chapter 29.

If a shape is to be enlarged in a certain ratio it is possible, of course, to calculate the lengths of the sides of an enlargement and then to construct it in any position we choose. In this chapter, however, we have described the way in which an enlargement can be produced by transforming each point of the original by movement. No calculation is necessary because when the enlarged length corresponding to one original side is known, all other lengths can be

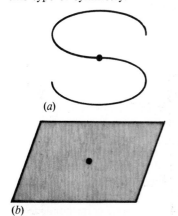

(*a*)

(*b*)

(*c*)

Figure 10 : 48

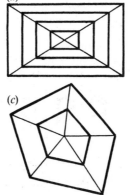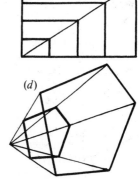

(*a*) (*b*)

(*c*) (*d*)

Figure 10 : 49

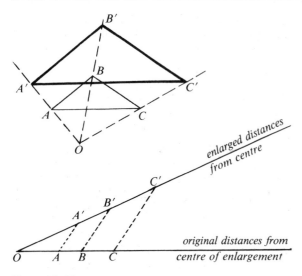

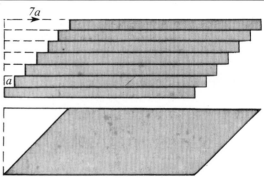

Figure 10 : 51

Figure 10 : 50

found from such a mapping as is shown in Figure 10 : 50. Work on maps which show a known real distance brings home very clearly the underlying principle of ratio in a more general way than do numerical exercises.

SHEAR

This is the most difficult transformation which primary pupils can profitably study and it is best left to the later years. But teachers need to know how it produces changes in shape without affecting areas.

Equal rods, such as the ten-rods of Cuisenaire, can be placed one upon another to show a rectangular face. Each rod is then made to slide so that it projects a given distance, say a units, beyond the one below it. The face of the rods has now changed so that the ends lie on a parallelogram (*see page 122*). In this transformation each point has been translated horizontally through a distance proportional to its height above the base. If a point 1 unit above the base is translated a units to the right, a point 2 units above the base will move $2a$ units to the right. The general rule is that a point b units above the base will move $b \times a$ units horizontally. The length of the base and the height of the face are invariant. If the rods become very thin strips, like the edges of very fine paper, the face is seen to change from a rectangle to a parallelogram when sheared. For any value of a, and so for any parallelogram made in this way from a given rectangle, the area of the parallelogram is the same as that of the rectangle (Figure 10 : 51).

A nail-board can show this transformation. A rubber band is placed so as to enclose a rectangle. Another band is put round the ends of the base line and about two points at equal distances to the right of the other vertices. It will enclose the parallelogram which is the image of the rectangle under shearing (Figure 10 : 52).

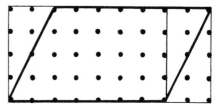

Figure 10 : 52

This property is brought out clearly if shearing is contrasted with the effect of deforming a rectangular framework made of two pairs of equal Meccano strips, bolted at their ends. If the framework is deformed into a parallelogram the lengths of the sides remain unaltered but the area of the enclosed region is changed.

The situation shown in shearing is important because it makes clear that area (and volume in three dimensions) can remain unaltered even when length and angle are changed.

STATIC AND DYNAMIC PROPERTIES

The investigation of space outlined in this chapter includes both the study of shapes when they are static and their properties can be observed and recorded, and also the effects of movement. This dynamic treatment is of practical value today. When it is handled mathematically in a more abstract way as a study of transformations we can recognise that spatial forms can be handled in ways which are similar to those which we use for numbers. Invariance, sets, one–one correspondence and number operations all find a place in a study of space and movement. In Chapters 13 and 31 investigations are suggested to discover spatial connections which can form simple mechanisms that will extend our powers of movement, communications, transport of goods and designs of constructions.

Shapes and their transformations in the National Curriculum

Much of the work in this chapter is to be found in Attainment Target 4 of the National Curriculum. In this target, pupils are expected to 'recognise location and use transformations in the study of space'. In particular, at Level 2, pupils are asked to:

- understand angle as a measurement of turn.
- understand instructions for turning through right angles.
- recognise types of movement: straight (translation); turning (rotation).

(AT4: Shape and space, Level 2)

By Level 3, pupils should recognise symmetry:

- recognise (reflective) symmetry in a variety of shapes in two and three dimensions.

(AT4: Shape and space, Level 3)

While children are carrying out this work, they will become familiar with the names and properties of a variety of shapes.

- recognise squares, rectangles, circles, triangles, hexagons, pentagons, cubes, rectangular boxes (cuboids), cylinders, spheres and describe them.
- recognise right-angled corners in 2-D and 3-D shapes.

(AT4: Shape and space, Level 2)

The early study of shapes and their properties and transformations, which is required in the National Curriculum, lays the foundation for a great deal of later work in two and three dimensions.

11 | USING THE COMPUTER IN THE EARLY YEARS

COMPUTERS IN THE PRIMARY SCHOOL

In 1991, when this chapter is being written, almost every primary school in Britain has at least one computer, and in some schools there are enough computers for each class to have a computer permanently available in the classroom. A considerable proportion of children also have access to a computer at home. Consequently, almost all primary pupils now have some acquaintance with computers. In primary schools, computers are used in many curricular areas, and their use is not confined to mathematics. Almost all primary teachers are now able to load programs for children to use. However, teachers vary considerably in whether, and how much, they integrate computer use into the ongoing work of the classroom. In some classrooms, computer use remains an additional and separate activity; in others, ideas developed on the computer are explored further in activities away from the computer. In these classrooms, the computer has become a piece of classroom equipment like any other, to be used whenever it can contribute to learning or enrich the curriculum.

The question therefore arises as to how much, if at all, the availability of computers will affect the mathematical learning which children undertake at the primary stage. In this chapter we discuss some uses to which computers may be put in the early years of primary school mathematics, and describe a few of the computing concepts which young children can master.

THE PARTS OF A COMPUTER

A computer consists of a great many electronic devices, linked together to do various jobs, and arranged so as to be under the control of the user. The most important parts of a computer, for the person who meets it for the first time, are the devices by means of which a person can communicate with it. The user sends messages into the computer by typing them in at the *keyboard*. After processing these messages the computer responds, usually by showing a display on the *screen*, which can display words and pictures.

The other essential parts of the computer are the *Central Processing Unit*, the *short-term memory* and

Figure 11 : 1

the *long-term memory*. The Central Processing Unit and the short-term memory are concealed inside the computer, but long-term memory needs to be accessible to the user. The short-term memory is used in the computer's internal operations, but its contents are lost when the computer is switched off. Programs and data which the user wishes to preserve for future use must be permanently stored in long-term memory. The most usual form of long-term memory found in the personal computers used in schools is a *floppy disk*. A floppy disk can be put in the computer's *disk drive* when needed, removed for storage, and replaced by another disk. The more powerful personal computers also have an internal *hard disk*, which provides a great deal of storage space for many programs and data. The hard disk is permanently sited within the computer, but its contents are not lost when the computer is switched off. Some older school computers may still use cassette tapes as a form of long-term storage, but most cassette storage has now been replaced by floppy disk storage. The fact that many programs can be stored, either on different floppy disks or on a hard disk, makes the computer a very flexible machine, able to carry out any task for which a program is available.

Most computer users need *printed output*, in addition to the visual output displayed on the screen. A *printer* is therefore an important element of most computer systems. Figure 11 : 2 shows the structure of a simple computer system.

A *program* is a set of instructions to the computer to perform a task. Programs are written in codes known as *languages*. Some computer languages are comparatively simple, and can be learnt quite easily by children; other languages are more powerful and complex, and are largely the province of professional computer programmers. The most important languages for school use are LOGO and BASIC. The early stages of LOGO are so simple that children from the age of about six can produce results in LOGO that satisfy and excite them. The results of BASIC programming are not usually so visually exciting, but the language is simple enough for a teacher to learn enough in a few hours to produce BASIC programs, because BASIC has a strong resemblance to English. The references to programming in this chapter are to LOGO, which has many interactions with mathematics. BASIC is briefly discussed in Chapter 28. However, many of the programs used in schools are written not by children or teachers, but by professional programmers; they need only to be loaded into the computer so that children can use them.

TYPES OF COMPUTER SOFTWARE

The published computer programs, or *software packages*, which are available to schools fall into several categories, each with its own uses and advantages. First, there are programs which allow a child to play a game. Computers can play competitive games such as chess, backgammon, and even noughts and crosses against a human opponent. Computers can also provide boards for playing individual games such as Solitaire and Mah Jong. There are also many games at every level which have been developed specifically for use with the computer.

Children can learn much from these games. First, they learn to interact with the computer. Many games packages require the player to enter moves at the keyboard, so that children become familiar with the arrangement of letters and figures on the keyboard. If a child types inaccurately, or enters an illegal move, a good program points this out and asks the player to enter another move. Children learn not to be afraid of making mistakes when they interact with the computer; the computer program corrects mistakes in an uncritical way. In computer games, children also learn all the thinking skills of the game itself. For example, in noughts and crosses or chess, they learn to take the opponent's probable response into account in planning their own moves. These skills in reasoning and planning are most important for children's mathematical development. Playing the games which need reasoning is an important way of exercising and developing reasoning. Some children play these games at home with parents whose own skilled reasoning enables the children to develop their powers. Other children

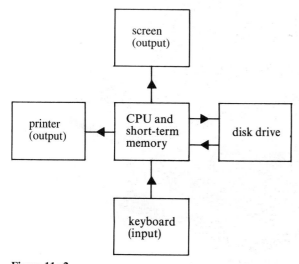

Figure 11 : 2

learn games at school, and the computer provides an additional resource for the player. Many chess programs, for instance, can be set to play at different levels.

Adventure games form a similar type of software. An adventure game simulates a visit to some imaginary, and often fantastic, location. The adventurer regularly makes choices about which way to turn and where to go; in order to progress, the adventurer needs to solve problems along the way. Not only must children work to solve the problems, but it soon becomes advisable to make a record of the route; this encourages children to make rough maps and plans of the location. In a few adventure games, the problems are specifically mathematical in content. If a small group of children play the adventure game together, much discussion is engendered, as the group argues about the best way to go, and how to solve the problems.

Another group of programs enables children to practise specific mathematical skills, often disguising the practice within a 'real life' situation which is intended to motivate the practice. For example, in one program children are given a certain amount of money to visit a fair. After visiting each stall, they have to work out how money they have left, thus practising subtraction skills. Programs such as these may sometimes be useful, but children have little control over the activity. They are required to make correct responses, in the same way that they are required to make correct responses when working through a page of arithmetical practice in a textbook.

In recent years, another type of software – *content-free* software – has become favoured as giving a more appropriate experience of computer use in school. Content-free software allows children to take much more control of their own learning than does the software previously described. Children can decide for themselves what to do with content-free software, and they can do it in their own way, subject to very few restrictions. A *word processor* is an important example of content-free software. Children can decide what they will write with a word processor, which provides no help in composing the writing. However, the word processor makes it very easy to revise and improve the writing, and to produce a neatly printed finished copy.

Some content-free software is mathematical in orientation. *Spreadsheets* can be used to generate and store numerical data, and they make tabulation and calculation very easy; they can often produce graphs from the tables. *Databases* enable data gathered in surveys to be systematically stored, manipulated, and displayed. This encourages children to draw sensible conclusions from their data. Computer *languages* such as LOGO enable children to write programs to make the computer carry out tasks of their own choosing. In all these cases, the software provides a tool which enables children to carry out their own tasks. These tasks could sometimes have been carried out without the computer, but more laboriously; sometimes the task would not have been possible without the computer. The computer has become a tool which expands the possibilities of classroom work, in the same way that the computer has become a tool for use by adults in the workplace and the home.

Another value of content-free software is that the same software can be used for a great variety of tasks, thus cutting down the time taken to learn how to use new pieces of software. A child who learns in the primary years how to use a word processor, a database, a computer language such as LOGO, and perhaps a spreadsheet, is well-equipped for life in the age of the computer. In this chapter, we discuss LOGO and databases, which are the most important pieces of mathematically oriented content-free software for younger primary children. Spreadsheets and BASIC programming are discussed in Chapter 28.

LOGO

LOGO is a full computer programming language, but it seems at first to young children to be a way of making the computer either drive a robot around the floor, or draw pictures on the screen. When introducing LOGO to children, it is usual to attach to the computer a small robot on wheels, known as a *floor turtle*. The computer can be used to steer the turtle round the floor; the turtle can also carry a pen, and be used to draw pictures on large sheets of paper on the floor. Figure 11 : 3 shows a floor turtle.

Alternatively, the computer can draw pictures on the screen. A small arrow moves around the screen,

Figure 11 : 3

leaving a trail as it goes; this arrow is called the *screen turtle*. Most versions of LOGO also allow pictures drawn on the screen to the printed by the computer's printer. Many young children are greatly attracted by the turtle, and wish to find out how to make the computer control it, so that they can draw their own pictures. A few simple LOGO commands steer either the floor turtle or the screen turtle. These commands are FORWARD, BACK, LEFT and RIGHT. Each of these commands must be followed by a number, which tells the turtle how much to move. For example, FORWARD 100 tells the turtle to move 100 'turtle steps' forward. Turtle steps are small, so that children have to use numbers as large as 100 if they are to make the turtle move appreciably. LEFT 100 tells the turtle to turn to the left through an angle of 100 degrees, so as to face in a different direction. Even children who have not previously studied angles soon grasp that larger numbers tell the turtle to turn further, and they learn readily that an amount of turning is called an angle. Two further commands are needed for drawing with the screen turtle. CLEARSCREEN clears previous drawings from the screen, and HOME moves the turtle to a position in the middle of the screen, facing upwards and ready to start drawing.

In order to prevent young children from becoming frustrated by errors in typing long commands, each LOGO command has an abbreviation. For example

FD 100

can be used as an abbreviation for

FORWARD 100.

However, different versions of LOGO use slightly different abbreviations, so the teacher should consult the manual for the version of LOGO being used. Children need to be taught very little about LOGO before they can start to experiment for themselves. They only need to be told the basic drawing commands, the fact that the commands for moves must be followed by a number, and the abbreviations for the commands.

A few further commands make drawing easier and more realistic. The pen can be raised and lowered from the drawing surface by the commands PENUP and PENDOWN; these commands enable children to make drawings with gaps in them. The screen turtle is also provided with a means of erasing mistakes; PENERASE controls this very useful feature.

Young children usually start by trying to draw objects such as houses and cars. Right angles are essential if these drawings are to look realistic, and many young children put a great deal of effort into finding the 'magic number' which makes the turtle turn through a right angle. In fact, 90 seems an unlikely number to be important, especially at a stage when children are usually beginning to learn about place value.

GEOMETRICAL SHAPES IN LOGO

After some free drawing, children can be challenged to draw geometric shapes in LOGO. For example, the set of commands

FORWARD 100   RIGHT 90
FORWARD 100   RIGHT 90
FORWARD 100   RIGHT 90
FORWARD 100

will draw a square, but it involves quite a lot of typing. An additional RIGHT 90 is also needed at the end if the turtle is to face the same way at the end as at the beginning; this is often a convenient feature if the square is to be combined with other drawings. The command REPEAT can be used to avoid repetitive typing. The commands

REPEAT 4 [FORWARD 100   RIGHT 90]

draw the same square, and save typing. Notice that square brackets [and] must be used to enclose the repeated commands. The spaces between words are also an essential feature of LOGO syntax; the computer complains if they are omitted.

Children who can use REPEAT can now draw other regular polygons, challenging themselves to discover the correct angle of turn. For example,

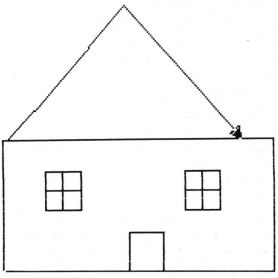

Figure 11 : 4

REPEAT 6 [FORWARD 100   RIGHT 60]

draws a regular hexagon. Children often make errors in the angle of turn; these lead to the discovery of beautiful lacy star-shaped patterns, such as that in Figure 11 : 5.

Figure 11 : 5

Much work on angles, symmetry and properties of shapes can come from LOGO, away from the computer as well as at the computer. Two of the many possible examples are the following: children can find the numbers of axes of symmetry of different regular polygons and other shapes, by drawing them on the computer, making a printout of the drawing, cutting it out and folding (*see page 118*); knowledge of the relations between angles is needed to draw a parallelogram on the screen (Figure 11 : 6), in order to study its symmetry. Starting at A, the commands are as shown, and can be combined into

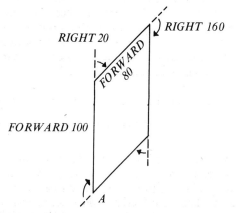

Figure 11 : 6

REPEAT 2 [FORWARD 100   RIGHT 20
FORWARD 80   RIGHT 160]

LOGO PROCEDURES

The drawings in LOGO described earlier in this chapter were carried out in *direct drive*. In direct drive, each command is carried out immediately it is typed in, and the command is then lost. If a child wants to draw the same picture again, it has to be typed in again. The full power of the computer is not being used, and the child is not yet programming the computer to make drawings.

However, it is possible to write programs in LOGO. The computer will retain these programs in its short-term memory until the computer is turned off, and the program can be carried out again and again. LOGO programs are called *procedures*. Procedures can be *saved* on disk and loaded into the computer again, and they can be *edited* with a specialist word processor which is built into LOGO. Thus, children can continue to work at a procedure whenever the computer is available, and they can combine procedures and build up more complex procedures.

When a LOGO procedure is written, it must be given a *name*. For example, a child might give a procedure to draw a square the name SQUARE. A procedure always starts with the world TO, followed by its name, and it ends with the word END. Between the beginning and end of the procedure are written the commands to carry out the procedure. These commands are exactly the same as those used in direct drive. Thus, a procedure to draw a square might be:

```
TO SQUARE
REPEAT 4 [FORWARD 100 RIGHT 90]
END
```

All that is needed to run the procedure is to type its name: SQUARE. The square will be drawn, starting from whatever position the turtle is in when the name of the procedure is typed.

Procedures can be used as parts of other procedures, so that complex drawings can be built up in parts. A valid procedure would be:

```
TO FLAG
CLEARSCREEN
HOME
FORWARD 100
SQUARE
END
```

This procedure clears the screen, moves the turtle to

the centre, and draws a flag consisting of a stick and a square (Figure 11 : 7).

Figure 11 : 7

VARIABLES

Children may sometimes want to draw the same shape in LOGO in several sizes, or they may need to experiment to find out what size a shape should be drawn in a particular picture. *Variables* enable numbers in a procedure to be chosen when the procedure is run, after it has been written. A LOGO variable is a word which will be replaced by a number, called its *value*, when the procedure is run. For example, the following procedure contains a variable for the length of the side of the square:

```
TO SQUARE "SIDE
REPEAT 4 [FORWARD :SIDE RIGHT 90]
END
```

The title line of the procedure must contain not only the name of the procedure, but also the word used for the variable. The word used for the variable is preceded by the symbol " (some versions of LOGO use slightly different notation; consult the manual). The notation :SIDE indicates that when the procedure is run, the *value* of the variable will be used in this command. To run the procedure, and to give the variable the value 200, for example, we type SQUARE 200. LOGO draws a square with sides 200 turtle steps long.

A procedure can contain several variables. For example, the procedure

```
TO POLY "NUMBER "ANGLE
REPEAT :NUMBER [FORWARD 100
RIGHT :ANGLE]
END
```

will, for appropriate choices of the number of repeats and the angle, draw any regular polygon or a lacy, overlapping star.

LOGO has many other features in addition to those described here. As children grow older, they may find those features useful, but the part of LOGO

described here will enable them to enjoy using this program, and to learn a great deal of mathematics as they do so.

LOGO *and the National Curriculum*

LOGO is mentioned in several of the examples which appear alongside the National Curriculum Attainment Targets, from Level 2 to Level 6. These examples are:

Turn to left or right on instruction (in PE, games using turtle graphics or programmable toys).

(AT5: Shape and space, Level 2)

Use doubling and halving, adding and subtracting, FORWARD and BACKWARD (in LOGO) etc, as inverse operations.

(AT3: Algebra, Level 3)

Create shapes by using DRAW and MOVE commands by using turtle geometry in an appropriate computer language.

(AT3: Algebra, Level 4)

. . . Use turtle graphics for distance and direction.

(AT4: Shape and space, Level 4)

It would seem that the National Curriculum expects children to have some acquaintance with LOGO from Level 2, although all the mentions of LOGO are in the examples, rather than in the Attainment Targets, and so are not compulsory.

LOGO can help children to acquire understanding in many areas of mathematics where LOGO is not mentioned in the National Curriculum. For example, beginners in LOGO find that they need to use numbers over 100. Six-year-olds often surprise their teachers by their ability to do this, but at Level 2, children are only expected to use numbers up to 100. The measurement of angles appears in the National Curriculum at Level 5:

• measure and draw angles to the nearest degree.

(AT 4: Shape and space, Level 5)

However, six- and seven-year-olds often find a 360° protractor a very useful tool as they work with LOGO, and they can be seen measuring on the screen with it. The word 'variable' does not appear in the National Curriculum, but much of AT 3 (Algebra) is in fact concerned with variables. For example, at Level 2:

- understand the use of a symbol to stand for an unknown number.

(AT3: Algebra, Level 2)

The box used in early number work is a symbol for a variable, as are many of the algebraic notations used at later levels of this target.

Most important of all, children need to use a great deal of planning and logical thinking if they are to carry out any substantial project in LOGO. This gives many opportunities for the skills described in AT 1 (using and applying mathematics). In LOGO, children constantly 'Ask and respond to questions e.g. "What would happen if . . .?" ' (Level 2); they also 'Work methodically and review progress' (Level 5) and can usually 'Explain work and record findings systematically' (Level 3).

DATABASES

A property which gives computers great power is their capacity to store large amounts of information and to display it in different ways for different purposes.

Children acquire a great deal of information about the subjects they study when they are doing topic work, and some of this information can be processed. For instance, a list of basic information about each bird the children have studied could be kept on a card, as in Figure 11 : 8. The structure of this information is the same for every bird:

Size: large, medium, small
Land or water?
Food: insects, fish, . . .
Migratory?
Nesting places: ground, hedgerow, trees, cliffs
Colour of eggs: white, brown, blue, mottled.

The card for each bird contains information under the same headings: size, habitat, food, migration, nests, eggs. Each card could be given the same layout. The complete set of cards forms a *database*. If a nest containing mottled eggs is found in a hedgerow, the database needs to be sorted so that a list of all the birds whose nests satisfy this description can be made. This sorting process is made easy by means of punched cards, as shown in Figure 11 : 9. A slot is cut whenever the answer to the corresponding question is 'Yes'. The cards can be sorted by placing them in a box without a base, and inserting knitting needles through the pack of cards at the appropriate holes. All the cards with 'Hedgerows' *and* 'Mottled' on them will drop through when the box is lifted up. If we want to find all the birds which nest on the ground *or* in hedgerows, we need to eliminate those which nest in trees and those which nest on cliffs, so knitting needles need to be inserted to prevent those cards from dropping through.

This simple mechanical process gives children a concrete introduction to the essential features of a database. Each *record* must have the same structure, so that it contains the same items of information. In computer databases, these items of information are called *fields*; each record must have the same fields. The database can be *sorted* and *searched* to extract information from it.

Children can keep a database about numbers in the same way that they can keep databases about other types of information. When factors are studied, a set of cards such as those in Figure 11 : 10 can be made. Not only can prime numbers up to 100 be found by using these cards, but children can see that finding the numbers

divisible by 2 *and* divisible by 3

has exactly the same effect as finding those which are

divisible by 6,

and that a number which is

divisible by 9

is also divisible by 3. Statements involving the structure

IF . . . THEN . . .,

The Robin

Small European land bird;
insect-eating.
Does not migrate.
Nests in hedgerows.
Eggs : mottled.

Figure 11 : 8

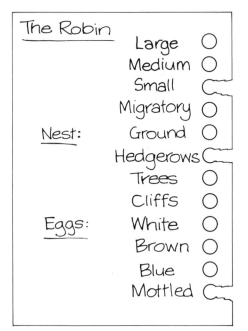

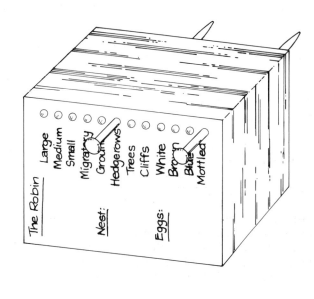

Figure 11 : 9

	Code	
Divisible by 2		○
Divisible by 3		○
Divisible by 4		○
Divisible by 5		○
Divisible by 6		○
Divisible by 7		○
Divisible by 8		○
Divisible by 9		○
Divisible by 10		○
		○

24	Code	
Divisible by 2	u	⊂
Divisible by 3	u	⊂
Divisible by 4	u	⊂
Divisible by 5	N	○
Divisible by 6	u	⊂
Divisible by 7	N	○
Divisible by 8	u	⊂
Divisible by 9	N	○
Divisible by 10	N	○

Figure 11 : 10

can be made. For instance,

IF (it is divisible by 9) THEN (it is divisible by 3).

The converse statement

IF (it is divisible by 3) THEN (it is divisible by 9)

is false, and children can see this by finding numbers which are divisible by 3 and NOT divisible by 9.

Several computer database packages which primary children can use are available. However, it is sensible for children to make databases on sets of cards until they have thoroughly understood the fact that each record in a database must have the same field structure. A computer database package allows children to choose field names for the database, enter records, amend and delete records, sort and search the database, and print out the whole or part of the database. For example, in a computer version of the database of numbers described above, children can print out lists of numbers which are:

divisible by 3
divisible by 9
divisible by 3 AND divisible by 9.

Thus, the computer database can be interrogated to verify or refute a child's hypotheses.

The creation and use of databases is a major way in which computers are used in the adult world, and today's children need to become aware of the many uses of databases, and to use them as a way of organising their learning.

Databases in the National Curriculum

In the National Curriculum, children are expected to use databases as part of their work on Attainment Target 5 (handling data). Unlike LOGO, which is mentioned only in examples, the use of databases is built in to the Attainment Targets themselves. At Level 3, children are expected to use a simple database:

- Access information in a simple database.

(AT5: Handling data, Level 3)

By Levels 4 and 5, the interpretation of data is expected, and children are required to draw conclusions from the data:

- Interrogate and interpret data in a computer database.

(AT5: Handling data, Level 4)

- Use a computer database to draw conclusions.

(AT5: Handling data, Level 5)

The use of databases gives children many opportunities to systematise their mathematical knowledge; for example, children may bring together work on quadrilaterals by constructing a database of the properties of different types of quadrilaterals. This will contribute to part of the Programme of Study on shape and space:

- Classify and define types of quadrilaterals.

(Level 6)

- Know and use angle and symmetry properties of quadrilaterals and other polygons.

(Level 6)

Most of all, the use of databases gives children many opportunities for making and testing predictions, a skill which appears throughout Attainment Target 1 (Using and applying mathematics). For example, children who interrogate databases are always using this statement in the Programme of Study:

- Use examples to test solutions, statements or definitions.

(Level 4)

12 | PLANE SHAPES AND THE IDEA OF AN ANGLE

PATTERNS OF BRICKS AND TILES

Builders make brick walls by fitting together large numbers of equal geometrical solids in the shape of bricks; bathroom walls are often covered with equal square tiles; floors may be covered with parquet, made of equal rectangular wooden blocks. The study of shapes which can be fitted together to build a wall, or to cover a floor, can be a useful source of geometrical experience.

A suitable experience for young children is making a pattern with flat square tiles of different colours. Basically, the only possible regular repeating patterns are those in Figures 12 : 1, 12 : 2, and 12 : 3, if the multitude of different ways of colouring such patterns is ignored. In this chapter we shall look only at the *shapes* which make patterns, and so we shall ignore variations produced by different colouring, but children will want to colour and decorate the patterns they make, and will learn much by doing so.

If rectangular tiles are used instead of square ones, a greater variety of patterns is possible. Those shown in Figures 12 : 4 to 12 : 7 can be made out of equal rectangles of any size and shape, but the pattern shown in Figure 12 : 8 can only be made when the rectangle has been obtained by cutting a square into equal parts.

In all these patterns, the arrows show the movements from a tile to the next one. Each tile is derived from the shaded one by translation or rotation (*see page 122*). A particular example of Figures 12 : 5 and 12 : 6, in which each row of bricks is displaced half the length of a brick, is commonly found in those brick walls which are only the thickness of one layer of bricks, and is shown in Figure 12 : 9. Bricklayers call it *stretching bond*.

Children may find other rectangular patterns in parquet floors, and may also notice in buildings two common brick patterns known as *Flemish bond* (Figure 12 : 10) and *English bond* (Figure 12 : 11) in which bricks are placed both as 'headers' (end on) and 'stretchers' (lengthways). Viewed as patterns

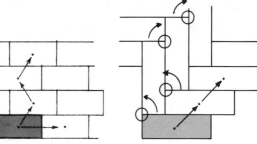

Figure 12 : 4

Figure 12 : 5

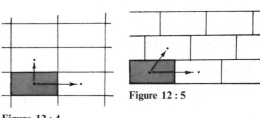

Figure 12 : 6   Figure 12 : 7

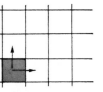

Figure 12 : 1   Figure 12 : 2

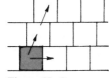

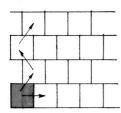

Figure 12 : 3

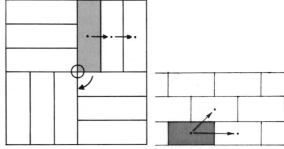

Figure 12 : 8   Figure 12 : 9

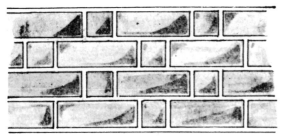

Flemish bond

Figure 12 : 10

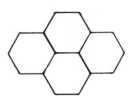

Figure 12 : 12

Figure 12 : 13

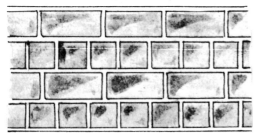

English bond

Figure 12 : 11

these are coverings of the plane using rectangles of two shapes, instead of rectangles of one shape only.

Collecting the different repeating patterns used for covering plane surfaces in walls, floors, patchwork quilts and wallpaper patterns is a valuable activity; it leads to children making drawings and models of the patterns and inventing their own repeating patterns.

All these patterns of bricks and tiles are examples of covering a plane using rectangles of one or more shapes. Tiles in the shapes of polygons other than rectangles or squares can also be used to cover a plane. When the plane is covered completely so that no gaps are left between the tiles, the pattern is called a *tessellation*.[1] The tiles are the *faces* of the tessellation, and the points where two or more corners of the tiles meet are *vertices* of the tessellation.

An interesting problem for children is making tessellations using shapes which are not rectangular. They may be successful, as they will be if they use regular hexagons and produce a honeycomb pattern (Figure 12 : 12), but they will be unsuccessful if they use regular dodecagons (Figure 12 : 13).

Children can only succeed if the angles of the tiles which meet together at the vertex of the

tessellation completely fill the space around that vertex. When we look at the tessellations of squares and rectangles, the tessellation is successful in each case because any vertex has the space around it completely filled either with four right angles (Figure 12 : 14) or with two right angles, which make up a straight angle, together with another straight angle (Figure 12 : 15).

These are two important properties of right angles: two right angles together make a straight angle; four right angles together completely fill the space around a point.

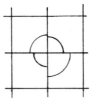

Figure 12 : 14

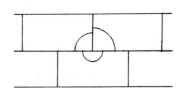

Figure 12 : 15

THE IDEA OF AN ANGLE

Through their work in collecting and making geometrical shapes and patterns, children grasp the concept of an angle, and come to realise the importance of right angles, and the existence of other angles which are wider open or less wide open than right angles.

Two different types of experience of angles need to come together and to combine if children are to have a thorough understanding of the concept of angle.

The first set of experiences is static. An angle is the shape of a corner. It may be sharp or blunt, or right angled. It can be compared with a right angle by seeing whether a set square will fit into it or not (Figure 12 : 16)

Much more fruitful than the static conception of an angle is the dynamic conception of the measure of an angle. If a book is gradually opened, its pages make a growing angle with each other (Figure 12 : 17).

The growth of an angle when one of its arms is

---

[1] In a Roman tessellated pavement the tiles were usually more or less square, but were set in cement with gaps between them.

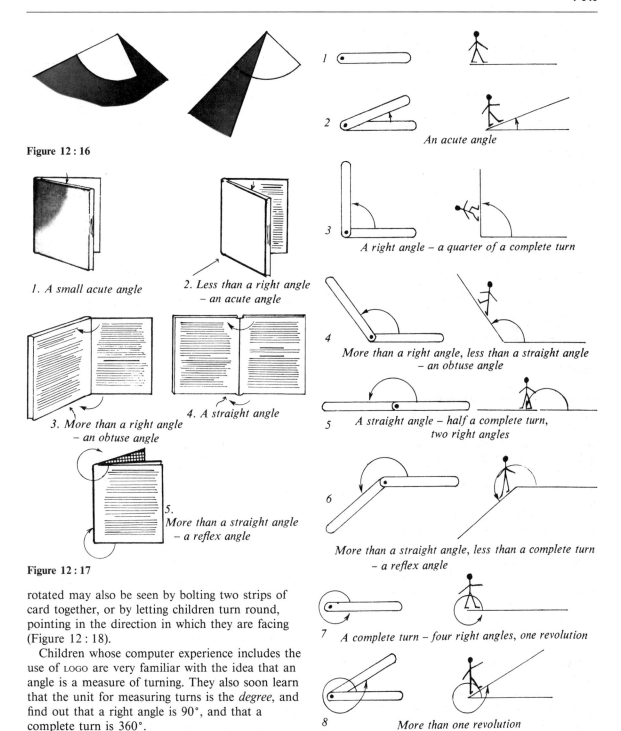

Figure 12 : 16

1. A small acute angle

2. Less than a right angle – an acute angle

3. More than a right angle – an obtuse angle

4. A straight angle

5. More than a straight angle – a reflex angle

Figure 12 : 17

1 *An acute angle*

2 *An acute angle*

3 *A right angle – a quarter of a complete turn*

4 *More than a right angle, less than a straight angle – an obtuse angle*

5 *A straight angle – half a complete turn, two right angles*

6 *More than a straight angle, less than a complete turn – a reflex angle*

7 *A complete turn – four right angles, one revolution*

8 *More than one revolution*

Figure 12 : 18

rotated may also be seen by bolting two strips of card together, or by letting children turn round, pointing in the direction in which they are facing (Figure 12 : 18).

Children whose computer experience includes the use of LOGO are very familiar with the idea that an angle is a measure of turning. They also soon learn that the unit for measuring turns is the *degree*, and find out that a right angle is 90°, and that a complete turn is 360°.

There is no limit to the size of an angle when it is thought of as a measure of turning. The turtle can turn round as many times as the child wishes. Another familiar example is the turning of the hands of a clock. Between mid-day and midnight the minute hand of a clock turns through an angle of 12 revolutions, whereas the hour hand turns

through an angle of 1 revolution. Between 3 o'clock and 6 o'clock the minute hand of the clock turns through 3 revolutions, while the hour hand turns through $\frac{1}{4}$ of a revolution (Figure 12 : 19). Since the clock-face is marked to show minutes, 60 in each

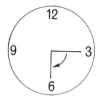 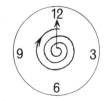

Figure 12 : 19

Figure 12 : 20

revolution, the rotation of the minute hand through 1 minute of time is 6°.

It is important that the static and dynamic conceptions of angle should fuse in children's minds, so that when they look at a shape like the one in Figure 12 : 20 they realise that the measure of the angle at A is a measure of how far open its arms are, or by how much the line AB would have to rotate in order for it to lie along AC. It then becomes clear that the natural measures of angle are the right angle, the straight angle, and the revolution, and that these measures are connected by the relationships:

1 right angle $= \frac{1}{2}$ straight angle
$\qquad = \frac{1}{4}$ revolution $= 90°$
1 straight angle $= 2$ right angles
$\qquad = \frac{1}{2}$ revolution $= 180°$
1 revolution $= 4$ right angles
$\qquad = 2$ straight angles $= 360°$

MORE PLANE TESSELLATIONS

Children who have used an isosceles right-angled triangle as a tile in tessellations may decide to make new tiles by combining several of the original ones. Among the polygons which can be produced from these triangles is a hexagon made from six triangles (Figure 12 : 21). This hexagon has angles of either $1\frac{1}{2}$ right angles (135°) or 1 right angle (90°), and gives an interesting tessellation of non-regular hexagons. The hexagons tessellate because they are such that the sum of the angles at each vertex is 360°:

sum of angles at $A = 135° + 135° + 90°$
$\qquad = 360°$

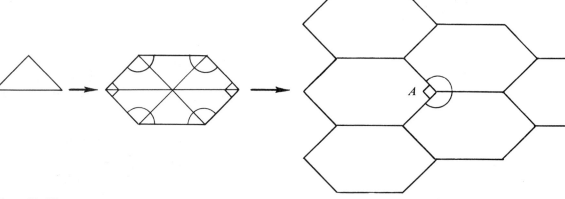

Figure 12 : 21

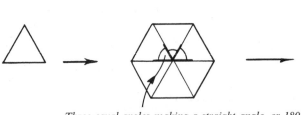

Three equal angles making a straight angle, or 180°

Three equal angles making a revolution, or 360°

Figure 12 : 22

Children will also discover that a *regular* hexagon can be made out of six *equilateral triangles* (Figure 12 : 22). By looking at the way equilateral triangles fit into a regular hexagon, they will find that the angles of an equilateral triangle are each $\frac{1}{3}$ of 180°, or 60°, and the angles of a regular hexagon are twice this size, or 120°. Children who work with LOGO will realise that the turtle makes one complete turn, or turns through 360°, in drawing a polygon. Thus, at each angle of an equilateral triangle, the turtle turns through $\frac{1}{3}$ of 360°, or 120°. It follows that each angle of an equilateral triangle is 60° (Figure 12 : 23). A similar argument applies to regular hexagons.

Tessellations can also be made by using a triangle of any shape as a tile. So that children can recognise its different positions in their patterns, the triangle used should have sides which are of clearly different lengths, and none of its angles should be a right angle. Children will discover such patterns as those in Figure 12 : 24 and 12 : 25.

When children have been introduced to degrees, they will then use a protractor easily to measure angles in the triangles they have made. It is, however, unnecessary for a protractor to be used when a teacher wishes the children to find out that the sum of the angles of any triangle is a straight angle. The hexagon shown in Figure 12 : 25 is made from six equal triangles which can be of any selected shape. In Figure 12 : 26 the angles of the top three triangles which are equal to one another are marked.

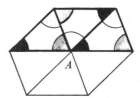

Figure 12 : 26

It will be seen that the three angles which together make up the straight angle at A are the three angles of the basic triangle. The same arrangement of three angles which together make a straight angle can also be found in the tessellation of Figure 12 : 22. Other ways of showing that the sum of the angles of any triangle is a straight angle are shown in Figures 12 : 27 and 12 : 28, where the

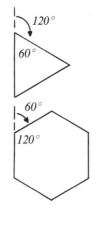

Figure 12 : 23

Figure 12 : 27

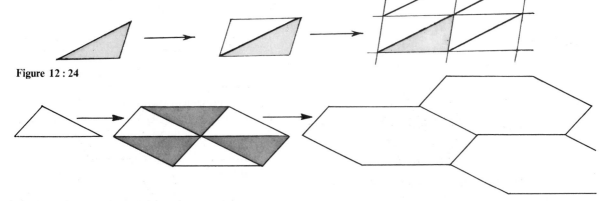

Figure 12 : 24

Figure 12 : 25

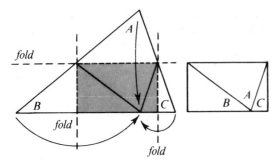

Figure 12 : 28

angles of a paper triangle are torn off or folded together to make the straight angle.[2]

A child should have no difficulty now in finding several ways of showing that the sum of the angles of any quadrilateral is 360°, by making a tessellation (Figure 12 : 29), by tearing off the angles (Figure 12 : 30), or by cutting up the quadrilateral into two triangles (Figure 12 : 31).

[2]Each of the unshaded triangles in Figure 12 : 28 has been reflected in its 'fold line' to give its new position. See page 125.

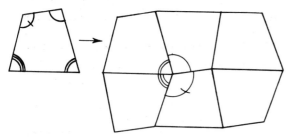

Figure 12 : 29

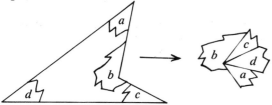

Torn-off corners of quadrilateral are rearranged as shown.

Figure 12 : 30

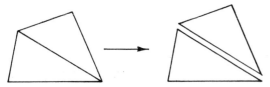

The quadrilateral is cut into two triangles.

Figure 12 : 31

Some children will wish to explore further, and find the sum of the angles of polygons with five, six or more sides. They will discover that only in a few particular cases can tessellations be made with such polygons.

The last method of finding the sum of the angles of a polygon, that of dividing the polygon up into triangles, is the most convenient, and is mathematically the most important method, because it works for a polygon with any number of sides. The results may be tabulated and a graph drawn (Figure 12 : 32).

Number of side	3	4	5	6
Number of triangles	1	2	3	4
Sum of angle	180°	360°	540°	720°

The sum of the angles of a polygon

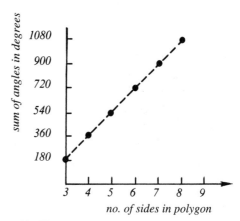

Figure 12 : 32

REGULAR POLYGONS

A *regular polygon* is a polygon in which all the sides are of equal length, and all the angles are equal to one another. Both these conditions are necessary. Children might try making a polygon with, say, six equal sides out of Meccano strips, and examining how the angles can be altered. They might also make a polygon with six equal angles, each of 120°, and see that the sides are not necessarily equal.

From their previous experience, they should know by now at least three regular polygons:

NAME	NUMBER OF SIDES	MEASURE OF EACH ANGLE
Equilateral triangle	3	60°
Square	4	90°
Regular hexagon	6	120°

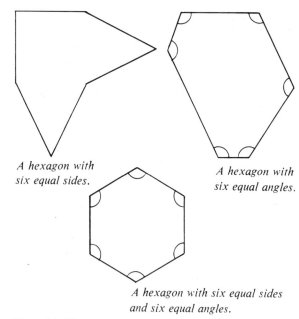

A hexagon with
six equal sides.

A hexagon with
six equal angles.

A hexagon with six equal sides
and six equal angles.

Figure 12 : 33

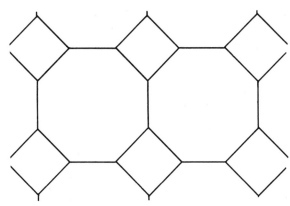

Figure 12 : 34

Other common regular polygons are the regular
octagon (8 sides) which appears in the tessellation
of Figure 12 : 34, but which cannot be used alone to
make a tessellation, and the regular dodecagon (12
sides).

It can be seen from Figure 12 : 34 that each angle
of the regular octagon is or 135°. The table of
regular polygons now takes the form:

NAME	NUMBER OF SIDES	MEASURE OF EACH ANGLE
Equilateral triangle	3	60°
Square	4	90°
Regular *penta*gon[3]	5	
Regular *hexa*gon	6	120°
Regular *hepta*gon	7	
Regular *octa*gon	8	135°
Regular *nona*gon[4]	9	
Regular *deca*gon	10	
Regular *hendeca*gon	11	
Regular *dodeca*gon	12	

The incomplete information provided by this table
gives rise to an interesting graph (which is not a
straight line) (Figure 12 : 35). The missing angles
may be filled in by reference to the table above
Figure 12 : 32. For instance, sum of angles of any
pentagon = 540°.

In a regular pentagon all these angles are equal,

so each angle of a regular pentagon = 540° ÷ 5
= 108°

A simple way to make a regular pentagon is to
make five equally spaced marks on the
circumference of a circle, and join them up (Figure
12 : 36). To do this, we must make each angle at

[3]The names of the polygons could be compared with the
Greek names of the numerals from 1 to 12.

[4]Or *ennea*gon.

The angles of a regular polygon[5]

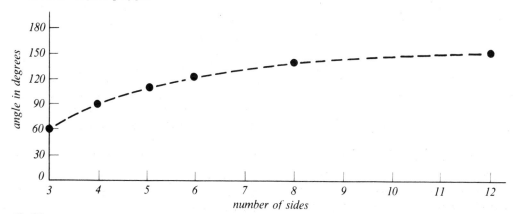

Figure 12 : 35

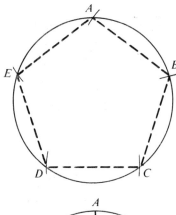

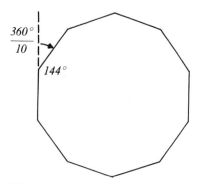

Figure 12 : 37

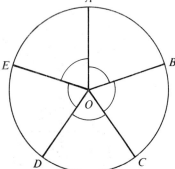

Figure 12 : 36

the centre (AÔB, BÔC, ...) equal to $\frac{1}{5}$ of a complete revolution. This is,

$$\begin{aligned} \text{AÔB} &= 360° \div 5 \\ &= 72° \end{aligned}$$

When children know how to use a protractor, they can construct any regular polygon within a circle in this way. Children who use LOGO have an alternative way of working out the angles of any regular polygon. Suppose the polygon has ten sides. The turtle has to turn through 360° as it draws the whole polygon, so it must turn through (360° ÷ 10) at each corner, or 36° at each corner. Hence each angle of the regular decagon is (180 – 36)°, or 144° (Figure 12 : 37).

FOLDING AND KNOTTING REGULAR POLYGONS

In this section we describe some methods of making regular polygons which do not involve the measurement of angles. Children who do not use LOGO may find these methods convenient, and even some who do use LOGO may find other methods of interest.

Filter paper is very suitable for making regular polygons; it provides a cheap source of paper circles of a convenient size. The centre of a piece of filter paper can be found by folding it in quarters. It is then simple to fold the paper to make a square (Figure 12 : 38) or a regular octagon (Figure 12 : 39). Regular 16-gons, 32-gons, etc., could be made in the same way.

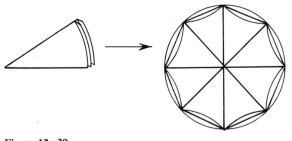

Figure 12 : 39

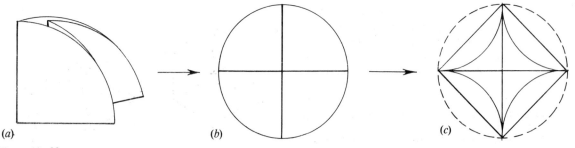

(a)   (b)   (c)

Figure 12 : 38

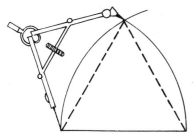

Figure 12 : 40

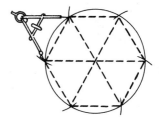

Figure 12 : 42

Other regular polygons can be based on the equilateral triangle. This is very easily constructed with ruler and compasses (Figure 12 : 40), or it can be folded out of a paper circle by folding a point on the edge of the paper to the centre of the circle (Figure 12 : 41).

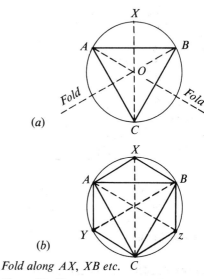

Fold along AX, XB etc.

Figure 12 : 43

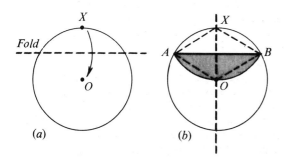

Figure 12 : 41

A regular hexagon is made up of six equilateral triangles within a circle, and so can be constructed by using compasses to step the radius of a circle six times round the circumference (Figure 12 : 42), or by refolding the circle from which an equilateral triangle has been folded (Figure 12 : 43). A regular dodecagon may be made similarly by refolding a regular hexagon.

[5] In diagram (b) AX and XB fold down on to AO and OB, and so are equal in length to the radius of the circle. Therefore, triangles AOX and XOB are equilateral, and $A\hat{O}B = 120°$.

Other regular polygons are more difficult to make by folding, but approximations to them, which may be sufficiently accurate for children to use, can be made by cutting up the regular polygons which have already been folded. If the regular hexagon ABCDEF (Figure 12 : 44) is cut along AO, and stuck together with triangle AOB covering triangle FOA, it will take the shape of a pyramid with an approximately regular pentagon as its base.

The vertices of the regular pentagon ABCDE can then be marked on paper and the pentagon cut out for use as a template. Similarly, a regular nonagon

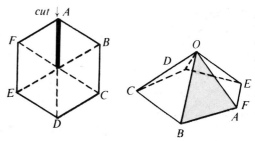

Figure 12 : 44

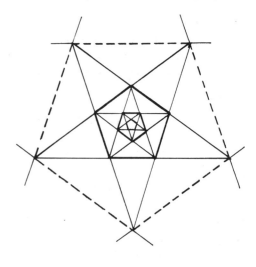

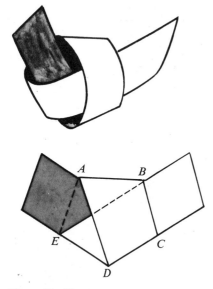

Figure 12 : 45

Figure 12 : 47

could be approximated by removing three of the twelve triangles formed in making a regular dodecagon, and sticking the resulting figure together in the form of a pyramid whose base is an approximately regular nonagon.

A regular pentagon may also be made by making a single knot in a long strip of paper. When the knot is pulled up and flattened, it takes the shape of a regular pentagon (Figure 12 : 45).

If all the diagonals of a regular pentagon are drawn, a five-pointed star, a *pentagram*, appears. This has a smaller regular pentagon in it, which has another pentagram in it (Figure 12 : 46). A child could go on for ever making smaller and smaller pentagrams.

Similarly, larger and larger pentagons could be made without limit by producing the sides of the pentagon until they meet and make another pentagram (Figure 12 : 47).

The pentagram is very like a regular pentagon in many ways; it can be drawn without lifting the pencil from the paper, and has five equal sides and five equal angles. It can be called a 'stellated' regular pentagon.

Children may examine the possibility of obtaining other stellated regular polygons, by producing the sides of regular polygons (Figures 12 : 47 and 12 : 48). Suitable questions for investigation include:

i) Can the stellated polygon be drawn without lifting the pencil from the paper?

ii) If so, how many times has the pencil encircled the centre of the polygon?

iii) Can an equilateral triangle be stellated?

iv) Can a square be stellated?

The question of how many times the pencil ·encircles the centre of the polygon links with the drawing of stars in LOGO.

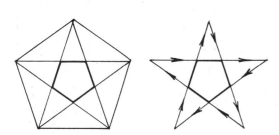

Figure 12 : 46

Figure 12 : 48

A few more tessellations

It is now clear that the only *regular* polygons which can be used *alone* for tessellations are equilateral triangles, squares and regular hexagons. This is so because two conditions are necessary for a tessellation to be possible:

i) the sum of the angles of the polygons which surround any vertex of a tessellation is 360°, because the space around a vertex must be filled.

ii) at least 3 polygons meet at each vertex.

The only possibilities are:
6 equilateral triangles meeting at each vertex,
4 squares meeting at each vertex,
3 regular hexagons meeting at each vertex.

These possibilities are all shown in Figure 12 : 49, together with an attempt to make a tessellation with regular pentagons. This is impossible, since each angle of a regular pentagon is 108°.

No regular polygon with more than six sides can be used *alone* to make a tessellation, for the graph of Figure 12 : 35 shows that the measure of each angle of a regular polygon increases as the number of sides increases. Three regular hexagons meeting at a vertex give an angle sum of 360°, so three regular polygons with more than six sides would give an angle sum of more that 360°. This makes tessellation impossible (Figure 12 : 50).

We conclude this section with an example of a tessellation which uses more than one regular polygon, and two which use irregular polygons (Figure 12 : 51). Further examples will be found in, for instance, Cundy and Rollett's *Mathematical Models.*

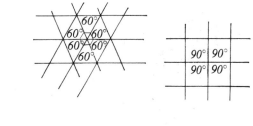

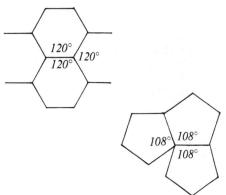

Figure 12 : 49

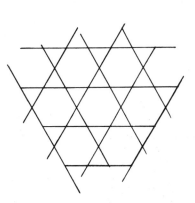

Three regular heptagons meeting at a vertex (with overlapping)

Figure 12 : 50

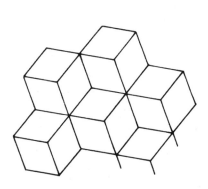

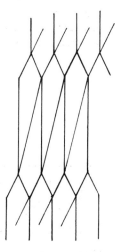

Figure 12 : 51

Polygons and angles in the National Curriculum

The work described in this chapter will give children much experience which contributes towards Attainment Target 4 (shape and space). For example, at Level 4, children are expected to:

- understand and use language associated with angle.
  EXAMPLE: *Know 'acute', 'obtuse', 'reflex', 'parallel', 'perpendicular', 'vertical', 'horizontal', etc.*

  (AT4: Shape and space, Level 4)

At Level 4, children are also expected to be familiar with simple shapes, and be able to construct them.

- construct simple 2-D and 3-D shapes from given information and know associated language.
  EXAMPLE: *Construct rectangles, circles, nets for cubes, pyramids and prisms.*

  (AT4: Level 4)

13 | TOOLS AND SIMPLE MECHANISMS

MAKING USE OF SHAPES

In preceding chapters we have considered children's growing awareness of some of the regular shapes that they have encountered at home, in the streets, on building sites and elsewhere. They have found such shapes as rectangles and circles in natural forms, in vehicles and in machines; they have identified squares and cuboids, triangles and pyramids, cylinders and cones. Of even more importance is their experience of the effects of the basic movements, translation and rotation, on some of these shapes. They have seen how such properties as symmetry and rigidity can be used in making decorative patterns with one or more regular shapes as the basis. Beyond this they may have noticed that people have arranged or combined simple shapes, fitting them together to make useful instruments to help with necessary tasks. We now turn to considering how children can begin to understand the construction and operation of many different objects that we constantly use to help us to satisfy essential human needs in home, farm, office or factory.

TOOLS AND MACHINES

By the time children reach the middle years of primary schooling they will have had considerable experience of the wide variety of inventions which have been designed to enable people to do things for which their own unaided bodies are not adequate. Such an object may give us extra strength; for instance, a hammer concentrates our efforts; or it may help us to reach something that is inaccessible to us with hands and feet only, e.g. a fireman's ladder or a boat; it could increase our speed and range of transport well beyond our capacity in walking or running, as a bicycle does. How do these aids work?

Some aids may be designed for one particular kind of use, for instance, a knife for cutting, a corkscrew for extracting a cork from a bottle. Such simple aids are spoken of as *tools*. The principles on which they work can usually be easily understood at a superficial level — *how* rather then *why* they work. Other aids are more complex; they consist of parts (which may themselves be tools) that are connected in such a way that they can carry out the specific

Figure 13 : 1

task for which they are needed. For example, we can recognise the complexity of the many parts of a car, a vacuum cleaner, or a lawn mower. Such aids are called *mechanisms* or *machines*.

CHILDREN'S RESPONSE TO MACHINES

In our technical age individual children learn about machines chiefly through contemporary toys, including the cycles and toy 'cars' on which they propel themselves. They are accustomed to models which simulate highly complicated inventions, e.g. a helicopter, a fork-lift truck, a tractor. At first children are content to make the toy 'work', and are satisfied if they can push or twist the control that makes the toy move in the way intended. They can select the knob or push button which will stimulate one particular movement, for instance the switch which starts the rotation of a helicopter's rotors and the knob which controls the winding up of a load. In their minds children connect the control with the form of movement it operates (see Figures 13 : 1 and 13 : 2); yet they may have no interest in the actual connecting parts which cause the machines to respond in a precise way to the starting action. Children can identify the visible moving parts but are unaware of how one actuates another. This is evident in the young primary school child's drawing of a bicycle (see Figure 2 : 5). All the essential parts are clearly shown but the pedals are not connected with a wheel; the handlebars and frame are not in the right positions for functioning. Drawing such complex constructions is difficult and we must allow for such limitations. Nevertheless it is clear that the

rider and the wheels are the dominant elements though not actually connected in the drawing.

This question of how to fit together the parts so that they carry out a particular process is essentially mathematical: we are asking how the different parts move and how they must be related to make a specific movement under given conditions. The first experiments and investigations in such tasks will not usually yield numerical results but they should enable children to identify some of the spatial forms and the kind of movement (if any) that the parts can make. They may even discover how to start a mechanism moving with a push, pull, stretch, slide, or turn. But questions of force, speed and acceleration are left to later discussion in Chapter 31. We shall confine ourselves here to such simple rates and ratios as may emerge.

CHILDREN'S USE OF MACHINES

At this stage, constructive play is moving on from representative models built from separate blocks, such as Poleidoblocs, with no adhesion, to integrated types of structures made from specialised sets of building and constructional materials, for instance Meccano with its pierced strips, bolts, nuts and pulleys, or the interlocking Lego bricks. The *connections* between parts are now paramount. It is important to have a variety of such satisfying apparatus available for experiments so that children develop insight into possible uses of the various pieces of the set, sometimes by following a set of instructions but also by taking valuable opportunities for imaginative constructions.

As well as using sophisticated toys and noticing the powerful complex machines that are so impressive a feature of today's roads, fields and factories, children have personal experience of using simple tools at home and several types of apparatus in school, particularly when they are learning to measure length, mass and time (*see Chapter 7*). They will be familiar with the balance bar, the stretched (or compressed) spring, the trundle wheel and the pendulum. The balance bar will have shown them the effects of unequal masses attached to the bar and thus provides an introduction to the lever. The spring with its spiral form suggests the shape of a screw. The trundle wheel illustrates in a direct way the action of wheel and axle.

There are five fundamental machines from which all others are designed; they are

the lever
the wheel and axle
the screw

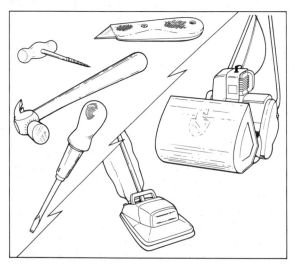

Figure 13 : 2

the pulley

the inclined plane and wedge.

The first three of these children meet in balance bars, trundle wheels and screws and bolts, so their practical uses can be studied at this stage. The other two machines, the pulley and the wedge, will probably be encountered later but if children meet them at this time they can discover their elementary uses in their own constructions and observation.

BALANCE BAR AND LEVER

When children first learn to weigh they probably use a bar supported at its mid-point so that it can turn freely about this point (the *fulcrum*) when masses are placed in pans at its ends. As we have seen in Chapter 7, when the children try to find the number of standard units of mass that will balance the given mass they sometimes put too many units in the pan. At once that pan falls and the other pan is lifted. Or they may put too few units in the pan; immediately, the given mass falls and the other pan rises (see Figure 7 : 19). Always they find that it is the heavier mass that falls and makes the lighter mass rise. Although it is useful to know which of two masses is heavier, the bar balanced about its middle point gives no hint of the possibility that it can help in trying to lift a heavy mass.

Play on a seesaw may give such a hint, when a small child tries to make it work with a heavier child on the opposite end. Children discover that if the lighter child is seated as far away as possible from the fulcrum and the heavier child moves nearer to the fulcrum the lighter mass can make the heavier mass rise (Figure 13 : 3).

Figure 13 : 3

This experience of finding distances from the fulcrum which will enable a light mass to lift a heavier mass is reinforced by experiments on a balance bar whose two arms are marked at unit intervals from the fulcrum. A number of equal masses, for instance standard metal rings, can be placed at a particular point on the bar; then different numbers of rings can be placed in turn at points on the opposite side where they balance the original mass (Figure 13 : 4).

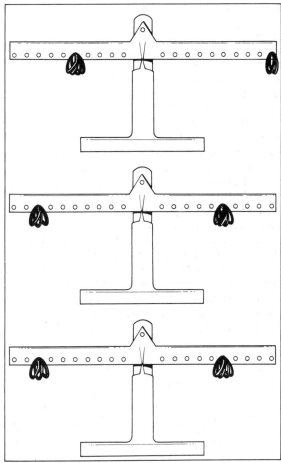

Figure 13 : 4

A slight pressure, or a small movement outwards, of the balancing rings will cause the original rings to rise. Similarly, other light masses can be used to lift a heavier mass (Figure 13 : 5).

It is clear that distance from the fulcrum makes a marked difference to the effect of one mass on another. It is possible to use a bar in such a way that a small effort will have a big effect in a lifting operation. Such an instrument is called a *lever*.

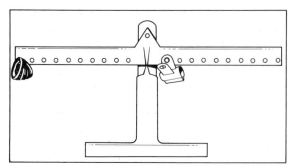

Figure 13 : 5

Figure 13 : 6

taking a lid off a tin with a coin or spoon handle (Figure 13 : 8). Children can make a large collection of such usages, and can record examples, or make models of special uses.

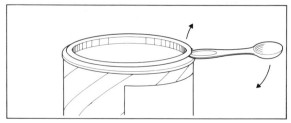

Figure 13 : 8

The numerical connections between masses and distances from the fulcrum will probably not be realised until the results of experiments from the graduated balance bar are recorded, as shown in Chapter 31. But expressions such as 'twice as far' or 'half as many' may well be used and will be evidence that ideas of multiple and ratio are beginning to develop (*see Chapter 17*).

Figure 13 : 6 shows a crowbar used in this way to lift a heavy rock.

The uses of levers are widespread. Even apes use a long stick to reach and push round into their cage food which is otherwise inaccessible.[1] In primitive tribal communities a simple lever is used to lift water out of a river or pond for use in irrigation. A long rod is supported on a post near the water's edge. A short arm carries a bucket which can be lowered into the water. A child can then run to the end of the long arm and pull it down, thus raising the pail of water which can be pulled round and emptied into a container or channel (Figure 13 : 7).

In our own society the lever is so frequently used as to be taken for granted. A common instance is

[1]See Wolfgang Köhler, *The Mentality of Apes.*

A TOOL FOR DRAWING A CIRCLE

So far our study of the action of a lever has been chiefly confined to making use of *weight*, the pull of the earth on masses. In practice it is often a human or a mechanised effort which causes the movement. One instance of this is the tool which young children may use to draw circles. A strip of card can be fastened to a sheet of cardboard so that it can move freely about the drawing pin or other device which holds it. A pencil can be fixed through one of several holes in the strip at its other end. As the child pushes (or pulls) this end at right angles to the strip the pencil will move until it has completed a circle (Figure 13 : 9).

The pressure at the end of the strip is conveyed to the pencil. Hitherto the children have used discs or diagrams in their study of circles. Now they can

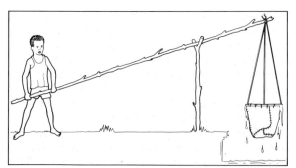

Figure 13 : 7

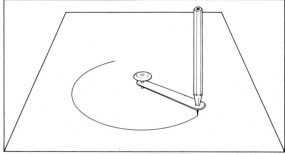

Figure 13 : 9

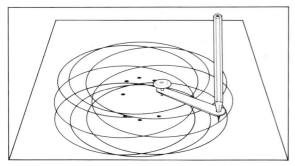

Figure 13 : 10

use their own tool to draw circles of different radii and to make the patterns that they enjoy so much, and in the making to discover many interesting properties of circles.

Modern safety compasses work on this principle. The child holds down the knob at the centre of the circle, puts the pencil through the hole, and rotates (Figures 13 : 11).

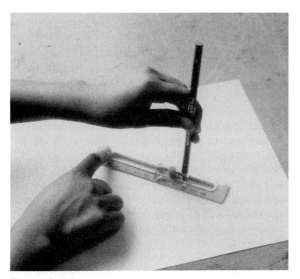

Figure 13 : 11

THE WHEEL

The most familiar of the basic machines in an urban area is undoubtedly the *wheel*. It is even seen in remote agricultural areas on a tractor or harvester or pump, yet there are many simple communities where it was never invented and is now regarded with wonder when it is seen in an imported sewing machine or record player. The most popular toy for young boys in tribal Africa is a kind of hobby-horse, a long stick with a small (imported!) wheel at its end; sometimes it has a

kind of handlebar which helps him to steer when he vigorously pushes his 'machine', delighting in the speed he can attain.

Originally, it is thought, rollers made from suitable tree-trunks were used to convey planks bearing heavy loads. Their usefulness was limited because the plank would go beyond the rear roller which had then to be moved to the front. If children make such a device using equal cylinders as rollers they will quickly find that two rollers are insufficient since the plank tilts when it goes beyond the rear roller. How many rollers are convenient? A similar question will arise later in regard to the number of wheels on large lorries, but in this case the wheels are fixed to the body of the lorry and keep their places as the lorry moves forward. The question arises: *How* are they fixed to the lorry? The idea of an *axle* can be clearly seen in the making of a windvane in which the pointer is fastened to an upright stick so that it is free to turn when the wind blows and is able to turn full circle. It must also be supported in its position on the post (Figure 13 : 12).

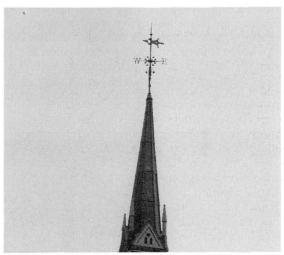

Figure 13 : 12

A more scientific enquiry will arise from the children's use of a trundle wheel (see Figure 7 : 27) for meauring distances. *How* is the wheel fixed to the handle? *Why* is it free to turn? *Why* does it move along as it turns? The making of a model can make the answers clear. The fact that there is only one wheel simplifies the problem but it also means that the trundle wheel cannot stand alone; the wheelbarrow has two legs to help its wheel keep upright. Even two-wheeled structures such as the bicycle or a luggage trolley cannot stand alone. The three-wheel car and the tricycle are able to stand alone but they are not as stable as the four-wheel car or cart. Long lorries with six or more wheels are even more stable and remain upright, even if one or two wheels are damaged. It is instructive for children to make a model of a four-wheel vehicle and to solve the problems of the axle, its attachment to the wheels and to the rectangular body. The making of the open box body is described in Chapter 5. Each of the two pairs of wheels can be attached to a strip of card firmly fixed to the underside of the body. The ends of the strip must be folded downwards so that a pin can connect the centres of the wheels to them. Thus an axle is provided. Clips will be needed to keep the wheels on the axle as the model moves along. The making of a model of this kind shows the essential connections. It can be reinforced by making a more technical version with Meccano (or similar) parts.

SPECIAL KINDS OF WHEEL: PULLEY AND GEAR

The importance of the wheel in facilitating transport is immense, but it is matched by the extensive use that is made of specially designed wheels. Whereas the rim of a car wheel is a tyre with a special surface designed to run well on a road, the *pulley* has a grooved rim which can take a rope or cable and change its direction. A more detailed study of the roles of pulley systems is given in Chapter 31.

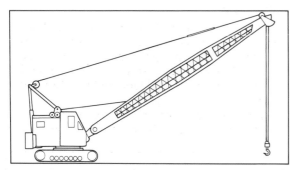

Figure 13 : 13

Another type of wheel has a circumference of teeth which can be fitted into teeth of the same size and shape on the rim of another wheel. When one wheel turns the other turns, but in the opposite direction. For a child with a bicycle or pedal car the use of a chain to connect the two wheels is of special interest.

Children can identify these mechanisms, the pulleys and the gear wheels, in many complex machines and can make working models to demonstrate their usefulness in increasing speed or changing direction.

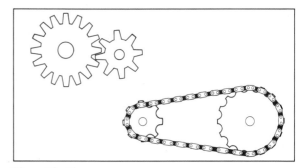

Figure 13 : 14

PISTONS AND PUMPS

Quite young children are familiar with cylinders. They may have played with them as part of a set of building blocks, using them as supporting pillars in a model or to represent wheels. They have seen hollow cylinders as cardboard rolls in which maps are stored, or cylinders round which kitchen foil and paper towels are packed.

The fact that one cylinder can slide within another cylinder, closely fitting all the time, makes this combination a powerful part of many instruments. It is a very important form in a technical age, often seen as the action of a piston. Children can see it in a syringe when they are inoculated or in using a pump to fill a bicycle tyre. They hear about pistons in a petrol-driven car. These all depend on a solid cylinder (perhaps rather thin) moving backwards and forwards within a close-fitting hollow cylinder. Children can experiment with a syringe, taking up coloured water in various quantities and delivering it to a container with varying efforts (Figure 13 : 15). A garden spray will also illustrate the mechanism. If children use a bicycle pump they can *feel* the intake of air and its expulsion, perhaps with some force. They can also use a pump to fill a toy balloon with air and see how its power makes the balloon expand.

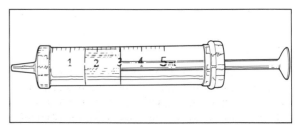

Figure 13 : 15

SPRINGS

One of the devices children use for weighing is the spring. If the spring is hung vertically with a mass attached to the lower end it will stretch and the mass will fall (*see Chapter 7 for the measuring procedures*). When the mass is removed the spring returns to its normal length (Figure 13 : 16). In some weighing scales a spring is *compressed* when a mass is placed in the pan above it.

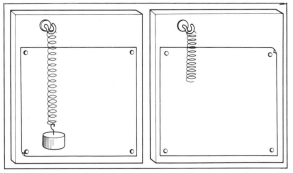

Figure 13 : 16

When the mass is removed the spring again returns to its normal length. This property of a spring is widely used to control latches on doors and the movement of many toys, including the Jack-in-the-box. Children can make a simple version of this toy; they can even make the spring it requires. Plastic-covered garden wire can be wound tightly round a pencil or a wooden cylindrical handle, making about ten turns. When it is taken off the handle, with a sliding movement, the wire forms a spring which can be either stretched or compressed, afterwards resuming its natural length (Figure 13 : 17).

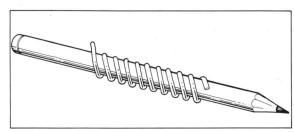

Figure 13 : 17

THE SCREW

It will be noticed that the spring was formed round a cylindrical shape. The uses of cylinders in pipes, rods, saucepans, tanks, etc., are so numerous that children can make an immense collection. But the shape of the spring itself is interesting. It is a kind of spiral called a *helix*. If children look for helices they may notice a corkscrew (Figure 13 : 18). This is made from such hard metal that it does not stretch or compress when it is pulled or pushed but can be used to penetrate a cork. Children can follow the twisting metal with the fingertip from the handle to the point and will realise the continuity of shape; as the finger follows the curve round it also moves down. The helix is also the shape of the edge of a screw or bolt.

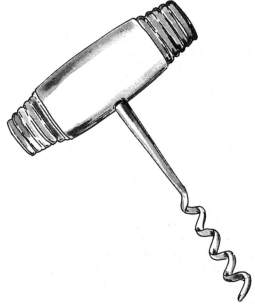

Figure 13 : 18

It is clear that it will be much more difficult to pull out a screw with its spiral shape than to extract a nail which has a smooth cylindrical shaft (Figure 13 : 19). The screwdriver, shaped to *turn* the screw, will necessarily lift it as it turns and so take it out of the wood.

In making simple models from wood children soon discover that nails do not always fasten

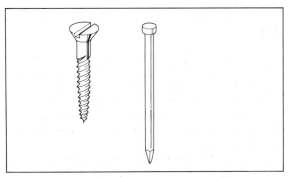

Figure 13 : 19

wooden joints securely, whereas screws will hold them firmly.

THE PENDULUM

In this investigation of children's increasing interest in the use of tools and mechanisms we see that some inventions are founded on the observation of natural phenomena. One instance is the behaviour of fruits dangling on trees and moving in a gentle breeze. Watching them more closely people have discovered how regularly they move, backwards and forwards. Suspending a mass from a point by a piece of string, children can check that the swing is regular and that it gradually fades away unless the mass is given another impetus. In Chapter 7 it is suggested that children might count the swings of three pendulums with strings of different lengths; each has its own rhythm but their rates of swing are different. A tall clock has a pendulum. Could the length of a constructed pendulum be adjusted to swing in seconds? A seconds hand on a watch can supply a count and a metre rod can be used to measure the distance from the point of support to the centre of a mass attached to a piece of string (*see Chapter 31*). It is a memorable realisation that this length is almost exactly 1 metre.

To start a clock pendulum and to keep it going, it must have some energy supplied to it. Children may know that mechanical clocks and watches have to be wound up and this suggests that they have a spring to maintain the impetus.

The pendulum is not as widely used as the wheel and the screw but one dramatic instance of its use can be seen in a television recording of the demolition of an unsafe building. A huge pendulum with a massive ball is mounted on a tall crane and allowed to swing so that the ball hits the wall with sufficient strength to make the building collapse (Figure 13 : 20).

LINKAGES

Modern buildings are often constructed on a frame of great girders enclosed later in concrete. Children can make such frames using the strips and bolts of Meccano. Wooden frames are also used, for example in folding chairs and such toys as a rocking horse. They all need to be safe and stable when at rest and strictly controlled when they move. The structures made from jointed rods or strips are called *linkages* and their capacity for controlled movement ensures that they fulfil many purposes

Figure 13 : 20

both in moving vehicles and in holding frameworks temporarily at rest. Children can search for instances and sometimes make simplified copies of their structure. For this purpose the Meccano strips are invaluable.

Among the earliest shapes that children make with Meccano are rectangles which may represent a floor or a wall or a fenced plot. They soon find that the frame easily goes out of shape. They tighten the bolts but the frame is still not rigid. They may notice that the corners change their shape, or that the opposite corners move closer. They may try putting a strip to hold the opposite corners fixed; the frame is now firm, as two triangles have been made. Children may reflect on the different ways in which Meccano strips can be used. *One* strip can make a balance bar or a tool for drawing a circle, or it can be used as a lever. With *two* strips, a corner or a cross can be made; the strips behave like hinges, opening out or closing up. As soon as the two strips are joined with a third strip, the structure becomes rigid; a triangle has been made. Whenever children need a firm corner in their constructions, they will use a *third* bar to make a rigid triangle (Figure 13 : 21).

Since a linkage of *four* rods is not rigid and can always be deformed unless some restraint is imposed children can investigate the movements that can take place and whether any of them could prove useful. If the four bars are unequal no common form of resultant movement is

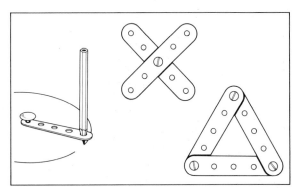

Figure 13 : 21

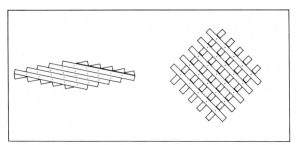

Figure 13 : 22

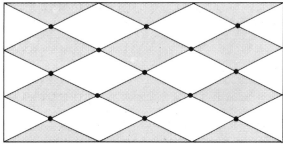

Figure 13 : 23

recognisable. But when the strips are all equal the symmetries of the shapes made (a rhombus or the special case of the square) make a framework which is useful in its flexibility. In particular, this shape is seen in the trellis frequently used in gardens. The rhombus has two pairs of opposite equal bars which remain parallel as the shape is changed. Its diagonals vary in length but are always perpendicular to one another. The trellis therefore changes length and breadth when it is stretched (Figure 13 : 22).

Figure 13 : 23 shows a rhombus unit used to cover a sheet of paper. The lines represent the strips; the verticles show the points where the connecting bolts or nails are used. It will be seen that these points lie on lines which are at right angles, as we would expect because they are end-points of diagonals.

The trellis framework, adjustable as it is in length and breadth, can be made with Meccano rods and recorded in diagrams drawn to show some of the shapes it makes. A fuller treatment of shapes which can make an all-over pattern is given in Chapter 12.

If a quadrilateral linkage is made from a pair of equal long rods and a pair of equal short rods, placed so that the equal rods are opposite one another, when the shape is deformed the opposite rods will remain parallel, and children can learn the name of the shape, *parallelogram*. The diagonal rods which would fix the framework will in general be unequal but when they are equal a rectangle is formed. See Figure 13 : 24.

The property that the opposite sides of a parallelogram are always parallel makes it possible for children to make their own parallel rulers. Two rectangular strips of the same size are connected by two linking bars as shown in Figure 13 : 25. The strips can now move together or open out to make sets of parallel lines. The four pegs which hold the framework together are corners of the various parallelograms formed, including a rectangle. If the

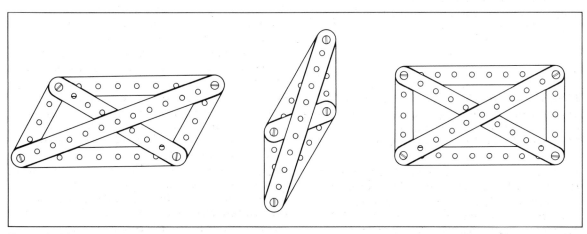

Figure 13 : 24

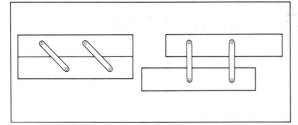

Figure 13 : 25

lower strip is held firmly against a line the other strip can be moved and lines drawn along its upper edge in any required position; these lines will be parallel to the fixed lower edge, as the parallel property of the pegs determines.

If in a quadrilateral linkage only *one* pair of opposite sides are equal the movement is more complicated. In the symmetrical position a trapezium is formed, with the unequal sides parallel. But if *one* of these unequal sides is held firmly the opposite side can be moved out of the parallel position and will tilt within a fairly narrow range. This surprising movement has its uses. In particular children can use it to make a model rocking horse. In Figure 13 : 26 *PQ* and *AB* are the unequal rods. *PQ* could carry a horse with the rider at *M*, the mid-point of the bar. *AB* is fixed. *AP* and *BQ* can rotate about *A* and *B* respectively. As the rider tries to move forward in the direction of *P* the rod *PQ* will move so that *P* must turn about *A* which causes *Q* to turn about *B*. *P'Q'* is the new position of *PQ*. *M'*, the new position of *M*, is *lower* than *M* as well as to its left. If *M* moves in the direction of *Q* the rod *PQ* moves to *P"Q"* as *P* and *Q* turn in the other direction so that *M"* is to the *right* of *M* as well as below it. Thus the rider moves up and down, backwards and forwards, with a sensation similar to that of galloping on a horse. A full-size rocking horse will show the movement.

The action of this linkage is not easy for children to follow but it is simple to make with Meccano

Figure 13 : 27

strips and has the great value that children see an unexpected result from an easy construction and come to be aware of the power that mathematical patterns can have in physical phenomena as well as in logical thought.

FURTHER DEVELOPMENTS

Early studies of tools and mechanisms based on familiar shapes and elementary principles are expected to extend a child's knowledge of shapes, the connections of their parts, their possibilities of movement and the ultimate outcome when movement is investigated. Such investigations give children the opportunity for discovering their usefulness and realising how widespread is their use. They will explore the tools used by the cook and the carpenter, the car mechanic and the electrician. There is no need to plan a separate course of activities; tools and toys can be studied when they appear in the classroom or the construction area. One important observation should have been made after a good series of studies: the great part that is played in mechanics by *rotation*. This and other ideas, involving measuring, number relations, more intricate shapes and new concepts (acceleration, moments, momentum, for instance) are considered in other chapters; particularly Chapters 12, 16, 25, 31, 39.

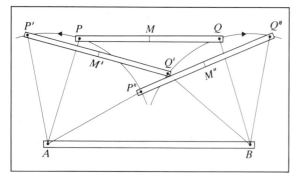

Figure 13 : 26

14 | SOME TYPES OF NUMBERS

THE NATURAL NUMBERS

In previous chapters we have seen how children acquire their first knowledge of numbers, and how they begin to combine these numbers by the operations of addition and subtraction. The numbers which the children are using are only a limited selection from a much wider range of numbers used in mathematics. The fractions and the positive and negative directed numbers have not yet been used systematically. However, children will have begun to use halves and perhaps tenths in their measuring, and they may have discovered negative numbers on their calculators. These types of numbers are like the whole numbers in some ways but unlike them in other ways.

We shall need to distinguish the set of numbers 0, 1, 2, 3, . . . from the other types of number which appear in later work. The set of numbers 0, 1, 2, 3, . . . is called the set of *natural numbers*.[1] We shall use the letter N to stand for the set of natural numbers. The set N has no end, and there is no largest, or last, natural number. None of $\frac{1}{2}$, (-4), 0.333 . . ., is a natural number. The natural numbers are those numbers which arise only from counting, combining and partitioning sets of things. At the stage which we are discussing, children will only have a hazy idea of the existence of numbers such as $\frac{1}{2}$, which are not natural numbers, and their thought may not have developed to a stage when they think of (-4) as a number.

The natural numbers are the building blocks from which a large part of mathematics is constructed. But the construction of mathematics starts, not with numbers in isolation, but with combinations of numbers, the patterns which numbers make when they combine, and the laws which these operations obey. In previous chapters we saw how children begin to combine numbers and to build up the operations of addition and substraction. We now look at some mathematical features of the operations of adding and subtracting the natural numbers.

[1]Some authors use natural numbers as a name for the set 1, 2, 3, . . . excluding 0, but we shall prefer to include 0, so that the set of natural numbers is the set of numbers used in a child's first experiences of counting, adding and subtracting.

CLOSURE

Although we have only discussed children's discovery of two operations on natural numbers, addition and substraction, these operations will lead them to multiplication and division, and it will be useful when discussing the mathematical structure of operations on numbers to take examples from multiplication and division as well as from addition and subtraction.

The first point which we notice about the four operations on numbers – addition, subtraction, multiplication and division – is that the numbers with which we operate have always been (so far) chosen from the set of natural numbers, but the resulting number may or may not be a natural number. Consider the numbers resulting from applying the four operations of arithmetic to 3 and 7:

  i) $3 + 7$ is a natural number;

 ii) $3 - 7$ is not a natural number, although $7 - 3$ is;

iii) 3×7 is a natural number;

 iv) neither $3 \div 7$ nor $7 \div 3$ is a natural number.

Children who know only the natural numbers will express this by saying that they can do $3 + 7$, $7 - 3$ and 3×7, but they cannot do $3 - 7$ nor can they divide 3 by 7, nor 7 by 3 without leaving a remainder.

We have brought out a property which is true for addition and multiplication, but not true for subtraction and division. The result of adding or

$+$	0	1	2	3	4	5	.
0	0	1	2	3	4	5	.
1	1	2	3	4	5	6	.
2	2	3	4	5	6	7	.
3	3	4	5	6	7	8	.
4	4	5	6	7	8	9	.
5	5	6	7	8	9	10	.
.	.	.	.	.	.	.	.

Figure 14 : 1

multiplying any two natural numbers is *always* a natural number. But, if we are given any pair of natural numbers, such as 3 and 7, it is not always possible to subtract them or divide them *in that order* and obtain a natural number. We describe this situation by saying that *the set of natural numbers is closed for addition* and is *closed for multiplication*, but *the set of natural numbers is not closed for subtraction or for division*.

The set of natural numbers is incomplete for subtraction. Any addition of natural numbers can be done, but only some subtractions have natural numbers as answers. We can visualise the construction of a complete addition table for the natural numbers (Figure 14 : 1). This table is symmetrical about its leading diagonal (Figure 14 : 2). The table for any commutative operation

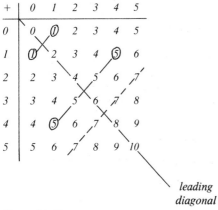

Figure 14 : 2

(*see page 164*) possesses this symmetry. This table is arranged so that the result of the addition 3 + 4 is read from the *row* marked 3 (the first number) and the *column marked* 4 (the second number). The order in which the table is read is shown in Figure 14 : 3. This order becomes important if we construct a natural number subtraction table. There is no entry for 3 – 4, as this is not a natural number, but 4 – 3 = 1 has an entry (Figure 14 : 4). The beginning of the subtraction table is shown in Figure 14 : 5, blank spaces being left when a

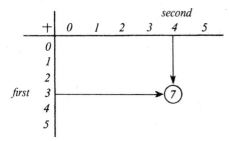

Figure 14 : 3

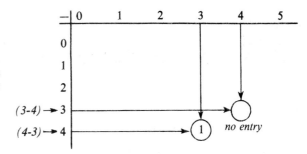

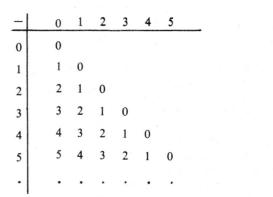

Figure 14 : 4

−	0	1	2	3	4	5
0	0					
1	1	0				
2	2	1	0			
3	3	2	1	0		
4	4	3	2	1	0	
5	5	4	3	2	1	0
.	.	.	.	.	.	.

Figure 14 : 5

subtraction is not possible in the set of natural numbers.

There are some stages in children's development when the property of closure limits the freedom of their work. Children who can only deal with numbers in tens and ones, that is the set of numbers 0, 1, 2, ... 99, cannot yet tackle the sum 98 + 99. The answer is out of range; the set of numbers 0, 1, 2, ... 99 is not closed for addition. This fact gives a motive for the extension of the children's number system; more than 9 tens will turn up at some time in their experience, so they are led to discover a new, extended set of numbers, the set 0, 1, 2, ... 999. Eventually children extend their set of numbers until they can add any pair of numbers belonging to the infinite set of natural numbers *N*, which is closed for addition.

Sets of numbers which are not closed for some arithmetical operation often give a motive for the discovery of new mathematical systems. The set of natural numbers is inadequate; it is a frustrating limitation that not every subtraction is possible. Can a new set of numbers be constructed in which every subtraction has an answer? In the search for answers to such questions as this, mathematics grows and adapts itself to changing situations. As children grow older, they need help in finding the limitations of their mathematics, and in seeing the need for new extensions and discoveries. The problem of finding a set of numbers which is closed for subtraction reappears in this book, and is finally answered in Chapter 33.

DIGRESSION ON LANGUAGE

The definition given on page 162 of the *closure* of a set of numbers for an operation, illustrates a feature of mathematical language which may not be obvious at first sight. The technical words of mathematics are not always new words, invented for the purpose, but words which have a common everyday use. When a word like 'closed' is taken into mathematics, it is given a precise meaning which is not quite the same as its everyday one; the everyday meaning, however, reminds us of the mathematical meaning. 'Closed for addition' is a sensible description of a set of numbers such that we never get outside them by the operation of addition. It is as if the numbers were in a room with a closed door. But the set of natural numbers is not closed for subtraction; the door is open for the construction of new numbers which will make 3 – 7 possible.

This way of inventing technical words helps the memory, but we must remember that mathematical words, whether or not they are used in everyday language, have a precise, clear, exact meaning. As children gain mathematical experience, they must be helped to learn the language of mathematics by building up a vocabulary of mathematical words which they will use to describe their mathematical ideas. Words such as 'minus', 'rectangle' and 'cuboid' are not too difficult for young children if these words precisely express real mathematical experience. 'Television' is a difficult word, but it is meaningfully used by young children because they are involved in watching the television. In the same way, children use mathematical words correctly and meaningfully if these words express what they have handled and understood.

In helping the children to learn the vocabulary of mathematics, the teacher should be aware of the need to notice two types of words:

i) words such as 'minus', which are *only* used in mathematics;

ii) words such as 'difference', which have a specialised mathematical meaning, as in, 'Find the *difference* between 7 and 10' and a more common everyday meaning, as in, 'What *differences* are there between these two Logiblocs?'

Words of the second type will puzzle children greatly if they only know one of the meanings.

THE COMMUTATIVE LAW

A feature of the addition of natural numbers is that the order in which the operation is performed makes no difference to the answer. This feature is more interesting when it is absent than when it is present. In the subtraction of natural numbers, the order of subtraction makes a good deal of difference; 7 – 3 = 4, but 3 – 7 has no answer in the set of natural numbers, and even if we work in the set of the positive and negative integers (*see page 171*), where 3 – 7 = – 4, it is certainly not true that 3 – 7 is equal to 7 – 3.

The order of the numbers in subtraction is vital, but the order of the numbers in addition is immaterial. It is much more convenient to perform an operation when order does not matter, and when the numbers can be arranged in whatever order suits us best; that is when the order of the numbers can be interchanged, or *commuted*, without making any difference to the result. The operation of addition is *commutative*, and for any pair of numbers a and b,

$$a + b = b + a,$$

but the operation of subtraction is not commutative, and in general

$$b - a \neq a - b.$$

Children who put out structural apparatus for 4 + 3 (Figure 14 : 6) do not know whether it was arranged to show 4 + 3 or 3 + 4; thus they intuitively absorb the fact that addition is commutative. However, if a number track is used to order the

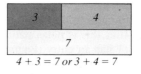

$4 + 3 = 7 \ or \ 3 + 4 = 7$

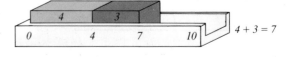

$4 + 3 = 7$

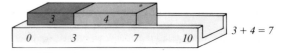

$3 + 4 = 7$

Figure 14 : 6

rods, a child can see that the arrangements of 4 + 3 and 3 + 4 are different, although the total length is the same. Similarly, on the calculator, the order of keystrokes $\boxed{4}\ \boxed{+}\ \boxed{3}\ \boxed{=}$ and $\boxed{3}\ \boxed{+}\ \boxed{4}\ \boxed{=}$ is different, but the results are the same.

In subtraction, the rods 7 and 4 show the *difference* 7 – 4 = 3. On the calculator

$$\boxed{7}\ \boxed{-}\ \boxed{4}\ \boxed{=}$$

gives the expected result of 3, whereas

$$\boxed{4}\ \boxed{-}\ \boxed{7}\ \boxed{=}$$

shows – 3. The teacher may want to start some discussion of negative numbers (*see page 172*), or, for the time being, the negative sign may be explained as an indication that the child attempted to subtract the larger number from the smaller.

Multiplication is commutative, so that for instance 3 × 4 = 4 × 3; but division is not commutative, and 3 ÷ 4 ≠ 4 ÷ 3.

We often automatically use the commutative property of addition. When calculating 3 + 22 mentally it is usual to change the order, and staring with 22, add 3 to it, so replacing 3 + 22 by 22 + 3. When we add up a bill, we often check the result by adding in the opposite direction, in the certainty that addition is commutative. Some mistakes which children make in subtraction are due to a failure to understand that subtraction is not commutative. A child may write, when doing written subtraction,

$$\begin{array}{r} 34 \\ -\ 15 \\ \hline 21 \end{array}$$

The child replaces the apparently impossible subtraction 4 – 5 by the possible subtraction 5 – 4, not realising that subtraction is not commutative. Children make this mistake because they have not had enough experience of subtracting real things which are grouped in tens and ones; to them, subtraction is a process which is performed with symbols on paper. They need to return to concrete materials until they see subtraction as a real operation which is very obviously not commutative. Children will also find that the calculator gives the same answer to a subtraction as they obtain with concrete apparatus; however, it does not give the same answer as the incorrect subtraction method above. This may also help children to realise that their method is incorrect.

We shall discuss more examples of commutative and non-commutative operations as the work proceeds, and we shall notice how much children use the commutative law in calculation, and how much it contributes to their understanding, in particular, of the operation of multiplication (*see page 208*).

ADDITION AND SUBTRACTION

So far in this chapter we have treated addition and subtraction as if they were two unrelated operations. This was possible while we discussed closure and commutativity, which are properties belonging to an operation on a set of numbers. Both addition and subtraction are operations and can be used to illustrate these properties; but we must not lose sight of the close connection between addition and subtraction.

The statement 8 – 5 = 3 is another aspect of 5 + 3 = 8, and '8 – 5' can equally well be thought of as 'subtract 5 from 8' or 'What must be added to 5 to give 8?' Subtraction is inverse addition in the sense that we are asked to find the missing number in an addition sum. We shall use the conventional empty box to represent a missing number. This is a very useful symbol for children to use, because they can write the missing number in the box. We see that 8 – 5 = □ is another way of writing 5 + □ = 8, and children will use their knowledge of the addition fact 5 + 3 = 8 to fill the box in 8 – 5 = □. Until children see this connection between addition and subtraction, they either have to use apparatus to 'take away 5 from 8', or count back 5 from 8. The use of structural apparatus helps children to realise in how many different ways the language of mathematics describes the same situation (Figure 14 : 7) so that they can move freely between the descriptions, and form a unified concept of addition and subtraction.

The calculator cannot accept sentences with missing numbers in them, such as 5 + □ = 8. Children may use a combination of calculator and counting:

$$\boxed{5}\ \boxed{+}\ \boxed{1}\ \boxed{=}\ \boxed{=}\ \boxed{=}$$

The same arrangement of rods answers all these questions

5 + 3 = □	3 + 5 = □
□ = 5 + 3	□ = 3 + 5
5 + □ = 8	□ + 3 = 8
8 – 5 = □	8 – 3 = □

Figure 14 : 7

shows 6, 7, 8, on successive pressings of the $\boxed{=}$ key. Alternatively, they may use a 'trial and improvement' method, perhaps guessing that the missing number is 4, and finding from the calculator that $5 + 4$ is too large. However, the best method is to replace $5 + \square = 8$ by $8 - 5 = \square$.

Similarly, $\square = 5 + 3$ has to be transformed into $\boxed{5}\ \boxed{+}\ \boxed{3}\ \boxed{=}$ for calculator use. The exploration of keystroke sequences such as

$$\boxed{3}\ \boxed{+}\ \boxed{5}\ \boxed{=}\quad \boxed{-}\ \boxed{5}\ \boxed{=}.$$

provide a useful reinforcement of the link between subtraction and addition.

SENTENCES IN THE LANGUAGE OF MATHEMATICS

By this stage, children are using the language of number freely, and are writing sentences in mathematical language to express their discoveries.

$5 + 3 = 8$ is a simple mathematical sentence, consisting of a subject (five plue three), a verb (is equal to) and a complement (eight). It is also a *true* sentence. If children make a mistake and write $5 + 3 = 7$, they have still written a mathematical sentence, but this sentence is *false*. A sentence such as $5 + \square = 8$ is neither true nor false until it is completed by writing a number in the box. It is an *open sentence*, and we ask children to complete it by filling in a number which will make the sentence into a true statement. An *open sentence* is a sentence which has some number or numbers in it missing, so that we cannot decide whether it is true or false. All the statements in Figure 14 : 7 are open sentences. They become true or false statements when the child writes a number in the space.

Some open sentences can be truthfully completed in more than one way. The sentence $\square \times 0 = 0$ is true whatever number is written in the box. For example

$$2 \times 0 = 0, \ 3 \times 0 = 0, \ 5\tfrac{1}{2} \times 0 = 0, \ (-2) \times 0 = 0$$

and so on. Some open sentences can never be completed truthfully. It is not possible to put a number in the box in the open sentence $\square \times 0 = 1$ which will make the sentence into a true statement. The empty box serves as a *place-holder* in an open sentence. It holds open the space, which can be filled by any number. We always try to fill the space so as to convert the open sentence into a true sentence.

As children get older, they will progress to the more abstract symbolism of writing a letter instead of the empty box as a place-holder in an open sentence. The sentence $5 + \square = 8$ becomes the sentence $5 + x = 8$. Instead of writing $5 + \boxed{3} = 8$ to make the open sentence into a true statement, a child will now write

$$5 + x = 8$$
$$\Rightarrow x = 3$$

The sign $\Rightarrow$ shows that the second statement follows from the first. It is usually read 'if (first statement), then (second statement). The above sentence is read: 'If $5 + x = 8$, then $x = 3$'. Thus the child has written down the value of x which makes the open sentence $5 + x = 8$ into a true sentence. The change of symbolism from $\square$ to x is only meaningful when children realise that x stands for a number which is at present unknown to them, but fixed.

Open sentences such as $n \times 0 = 0$, which are true for any value of the place-holder, are called *identities*. Another important identity is the commutative law of addition

$$a + b = b + a$$

This is a true sentence whatever numbers are substituted for the place-holders a and b. Of course, throughout a particular sentence, a symbolises the same number whenever it occurs, as does b. Children become convinced of the truth of identities by seeing that they work in a large number of particular cases, and that they cannot find cases in which the identity is not true.[2] If the teacher wishes children to think about the commutative law explicitly rather than to accept it intuitively, filling in values of the place-holders which make a series of open sentences such as the following into true statements may be helpful.

$$\square + 1 = 1 + 3, \quad \square + 5 = 5 + 8$$
$$2 + 4 = 4 + \square, \quad 6 + \square = \square + 6$$
$$\square + 0 = 0 + \square, \quad \square + 2 = \triangle + \square$$
$$\square + \triangle = \triangle + \square$$

Some of these sentences can be made into true sentences in one way; others are identities, which can be completed in a variety of ways. The convention is used that different shaped boxes are shown when more than one place-holder occurs in a sentence.

---

[2]As a warning, the teacher might consider the open sentence, 'If x is a natural number, $x^2 - x + 41$ is a prime number' (*see page 271*). This is true if $x = 0, 1, 2, 3, \ldots$, 40, but is false when $x = 41$. It looks at first sight like an identity, but it is not always true.

We can now express the statements made on page 165 in a different way. Children do not have an adequate conception of subtraction until they realise that open sentences such as

$$8 - 5 = x \quad \text{and} \quad 5 + x = 8$$

are equivalent; that is, that they are two different ways of saying the same thing, and that they are satisfied by the same value of x. During their primary education, most children's understanding of this relationship will be intuitive and informal rather than precise and formalised, and most children will only formalise it in later years. The teacher should, however, help children to make a firm link between addition and subtraction from the beginning.

THREE-NUMBER ADDITION AND THE ASSOCIATIVE LAW FOR ADDITION

Children's shopping activities, their increasing skill at measuring and their greater facility in the use of numbers will lead them to situations where they wish to add three or more numbers together, for instance, to find the distance all the way round a triangle.

At the stage at which apparatus is used for addition, adding three numbers is not much more complicated than adding two numbers. However, as children progress to the very important skill of being able to add mentally and to hold a number in mind while adding another number to it, we find that addition of three numbers uses the same skills which have been learned in adding two numbers, together with an extra skill. For example, consider $6 + 9 + 7$. Children know that $6 + 9 = 15$, and then have to deal with $15 + 7$. This can be done mentally with ease if the child realises that $5 + 7 = 12$, and that $15 + 7$ is ten more than $5 + 7$. In fact, the 15 is split up into $10 + 5$, and then $(10 + 5) + 7$ is regrouped into $10 + (5 + 7)$, so that the knowledge of $5 + 7$ can be used. Then $5 + 7$ is regrouped into $10 + 2$, and finally the tens are combined:

$$\begin{aligned}
15 + 7 &= (10 + 5) + 7 \\
&= 10 + (5 + 7) \\
&= 10 + (10 + 2) \\
&= (10 + 10) + 2 \\
&= 22
\end{aligned}$$

In practice, the thought-process is much briefer than this, and children just focus attention on $5 + 7$, and then add one ten. Similarly, 35 and 7 can be added by performing $5 + 7$, and then adding 1 ten to the 3 tens to obtain 42.

We see that all three-number addition depends on the regrouping of the numbers to make the addition easier. The fact that such regrouping is possible is known as *the associative law for addition.* This states that for any numbers a, b and c,

$$(a + b) + c = a + (b + c)$$

We see another example of the associative law at work in the thought-process of a child who prefers to add 15 and 7 mentally by regrouping the 7 and using 20 as an intermediate resting place:

$$\begin{aligned}
15 + 7 &= 15 + (5 + 2) \\
&= (15 + 5) + 2 \\
&= 20 + 2 \\
&= 22
\end{aligned}$$

Children who do not understand the regrouping implied by the associative law, and so cannot make use of their previous knowledge of addition, can only add 15 and 7 by counting 7 on from 15. It is fairly common to find children who know that $5 + 7 = 12$, but have not yet seen how to make use of this knowledge when they need to do $15 + 7$ or $35 + 7$, and so they count on laboriously.

The teacher will realise how much use is made of the associative law for addition to regroup the numbers as a column of figures is added. Figure $14 : 8$ shows a likely thought-process in adding down a column of figures, although in practice this is much abbreviated. The numbers in heavy type show where the associative law is used.

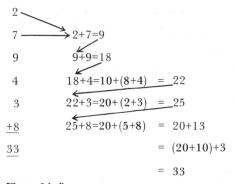

Figure 14 : 8

We shall see later than an associative law is also true for multiplication (*see page 234*).

Changing the order in which a calculation is done is very easy with a calculator. Children can be asked to do

$$\boxed{2}\ \boxed{+}\ \boxed{7}\ \boxed{+}\ \boxed{9}\ \boxed{+}\ \boxed{4}\ \boxed{+}\ \boxed{3}\ \boxed{+}\ \boxed{8}\ \boxed{=}\ ,$$

and then to write down the same calculation in several different orders and do it, until they are convinced that changing the order of addition makes no difference.

VECTORS

In their early experiences of addition children meet two very different situations: sometimes the arrangement of the things which are added is unimportant; sometimes the arrangement is vital. Five things and three things together make eight things however the things are arranged, but if children use structural apparatus for addition they must put the rods end to end; no other arrangement will do (Figure 14:9). If children use the tape-measure slide-rule to find 5 + 3, they must measure *onwards* three units from the 5-unit mark (Figure

14:10). Lengths are only added when they are placed *end to end*. In these situations addition is associated with movement *onward in the same direction*.

We very often associate a measurement with a direction. When children measure a corridor with a rod, they move the rod on and on along the corridor, moving along the corridor in a particular direction. If they are to measure the length accurately, they must keep moving in the same direction.

A child who goes 10 metres North from the school door will arrive at a different spot from a child who goes 10 metres East from the same place. The direction of the movement is as important as the distance. When adding with structural apparatus, and placing a second rod end-on to a

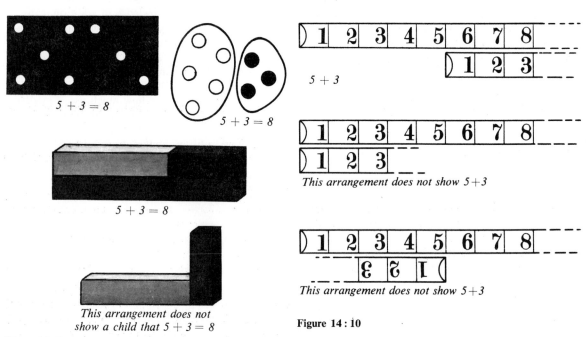

$5 + 3 = 8$

$5 + 3 = 8$

$5 + 3 = 8$

This arrangement does not show a child that $5 + 3 = 8$

Figure 14:9

5 + 3

This arrangement does not show 5+3

This arrangement does not show 5+3

Figure 14:10

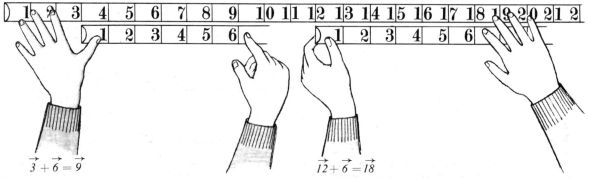

$\vec{3} + \vec{6} = \vec{9}$

$\vec{12} + \vec{6} = \vec{18}$

Figure 14:11

first, the rods must be in the same direction. The direction is as important as the length of the rods.

Mathematics is full of examples of lengths which are measured in particular directions. These quantities are instances of *vectors*.[3] A movement of 6 units to the right along the tape-measure is a vector, and is a different vector from the one which represents a movement of 6 units to the left. A person travels along a different vector when pacing 50 metres to the East from the vector covered when pacing 50 metres to the North. When children add with the tape-measure they are adding vectors. Figure 14 : 11 shows the addition of a vector 6 centimetres to the right to a vector 3 centimetres to the right and to a vector 12 centimetres to the right.

The statement $\vec{3} + \vec{6} = \vec{9}$ conveys the idea: 'A movement of 3 units to the right *followed* by a movement of 6 units to the right *has the same effect as a single movement* of 9 units to the right.' The addition sign stands for the operation of combining two vectors by placing them end-on (Figure 14 : 12).

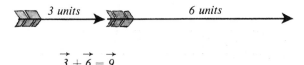

$$\vec{3} + \vec{6} = \vec{9}$$

Figure 14 : 12

Vectors can be combined even if their directions are not the same. Figure 14 : 13 shows a person's walk home. He or she went 30 metres along the road from the bus stop, and then 40 metres along the path home. The person could go home in a straight line across the field. The movement in

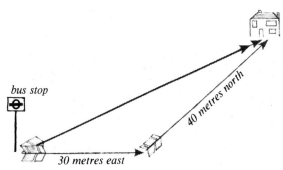

Figure 14 : 13

[3]Later, the word *vector* will also be used to describe other quantities, such as *force* and *velocity*, which have direction as well as magnitude, but which are not distances.

a straight line across the field is the *sum* of the two movements of 30 metres East and 40 metres North. We write

(30 metres East) + (40 metres North)

As was the case for the addition of vectors in the same direction, the plus sign means 'one vector *followed by* the other vector'. If we draw to scale a plan of the journey home (Figure 14 : 14) and

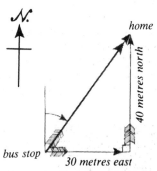

Figure 14 : 14

measure the length and direction of the short cut on it, we find that

(30 metres East) + (40 metres North)
  = (50 metres N37°E)

The sum of two vectors can be found by scale drawing. However, this is not necessary when the two vectors happen to be in the same direction (or opposite directions).

On the tape-measure we can add vectors in opposite directions.

Both diagrams in Figure 14 : 15 show

(a movement of 9 centimetres to the right)
followed by (a movement of 3 centimetres to the left)
= (a single movement of 6 centimetres to the right).
(9 centimetres to the right) + (3 centimetres to the left)
  = (6 centimetres to the right).

Here two vectors in opposite directions along the same line have been added. The subtraction of vectors will not be discussed until Chapter 33.

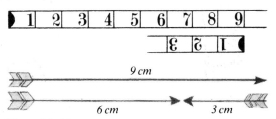

Figure 14 : 15

THE LAWS OF OPERATIONS FOR VECTORS

A vector of length 3 units in a direction moving from West to East is certainly very different from the natural number 3, which has no direction. But we constantly use the addition of vectors as a model for the addition of natural numbers, both on the tape-measure and in structural apparatus, so there must be a very close resemblance between the structure of addition of natural numbers and of vectors. This resemblance enables us to substitute one for the other, and to use the tape-measure as a model when a child wishes to find the total number in the class of 17 boys and 14 girls, although the numbers in this example certainly do not have a direction. In this section we shall pick out a resemblance and a difference in structure between vectors and natural numbers.

The addition of natural numbers is commutative (*see page 164*); the order of addition does not matter. For vectors, the commutative law is also true. A movement of 6 units to the right followed by a movement of 3 units to the right is a different action from a movement of 3 units to the right followed by a movement of 6 units to the right (Figure 14 : 16).

(6 units to the right)+(3 units to the right)

(3 units to the right)+(6 units to the right)

Figure 14 : 16

The result is the same, but the actions are different. If the order of addition in Figures 14 : 13 and 14 : 14 is reversed, the situation is altered. Figure 14 : 17 shows what happens if the person does

(40 metres North) + (30 metres East)

Again, the result is the same, but the situation is different from that of Figure 14 : 14.

The addition of vectors is commutative; for any pair of vectors $\vec{a}$ and $\vec{b}$,

$$\vec{a} + \vec{b} = \vec{b} + \vec{a}$$

Figure 14 : 18 shows the commutative law for addition of vectors in a more general situation, where $\vec{a}$ and $\vec{b}$ are neither in the same direction nor at right angles.

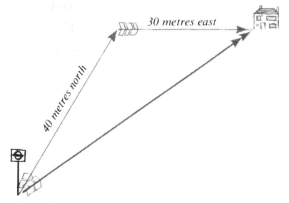

Figure 14 : 17

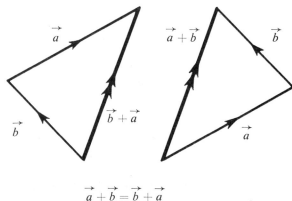

$$\vec{a} + \vec{b} = \vec{b} + \vec{a}$$

Figure 14 : 18

The addition of vectors resembles the addition of natural numbers in that both additions are commutative. We now discuss a most important difference between the two systems. Every vector has an *opposite*. If a person has moved over the vector (3 paces forward) and wants to go back to where they were, they can move over the vector (3 paces back). The *opposite* of (3 paces forward) is (3 paces back). The opposite of any vector $\vec{a}$ is *the vector which undoes the effect* of the movement $\vec{a}$. The opposite of a vector is often called the *negative of the vector*, and is written $(-\vec{a})$ (Figures 14 : 19 and 14 : 20).

If we move over the vector $\vec{a}$, and then over the vector $(-\vec{a})$, we are back where we started. In symbols

$$\vec{a} + (-\vec{a}) = 0$$

This statement says nothing about *negative numbers.* It only says

(movement $\vec{a}$) followed by (the opposite of $\vec{a}$)
= ('movement' of standing still)

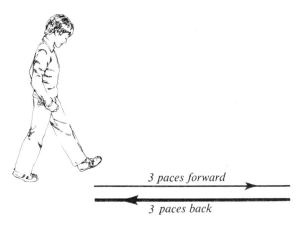

Figure 14 : 19

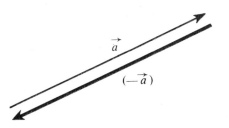

Figure 14 : 20

The ' + ' sign here is the sign for addition of vectors, not the sign for addition of natural numbers; the ' – ' sign in $(-\vec{a})$ is the sign for the opposite of a vector, not the sign for the subtraction of natural numbers. It would no doubt be better in some ways to have two different signs to stand for the 'plus' in

$$3 + 5 = 8$$

which is addition of natural numbers, and in

(3 paces to the right) + (5 paces to the left)
= (2 paces to the left),

which is addition of vectors, but these two operations are alike in so many ways that no confusion usually arises in making the same sign do for both.

We have used the symbol **0** for the vector of (not moving at all). This vector is the *zero vector*, and behaves very like the zero of the natural numbers. We can now state mathematically a major difference between natural numbers and vectors. Every vector has an opposite, but with the single exception of zero no natural number has an opposite. We cannot fill in with a natural number the blank spaces in the sentence

$$3 + \square = 0;$$

there is no natural number which added to 3 gives 0, and so 3 has no opposite natural number. But we can fill in the blank space in the vector equation

(3 paces to the right) + $\square$ = **0**,

so the vector has an opposite. For any natural number a which we start with (apart from the exception $a = 0$) we cannot find a natural number x which makes the sentences $a + x = 0$ true; but for any vector $\vec{a}$ with which we start, we can *always* find a vector $\vec{x}$ which makes the sentence $\vec{a} + \vec{x} = \mathbf{0}$ true.

As we progress in mathematics, we shall find the limitation that the natural numbers do not have opposites more and more inconvenient; vectors and those numbers which have opposites will be used more and more. We shall see that children are often unable to understand directed numbers because their idea of number is limited to the natural numbers and the counting of sets of things, and does not include vectors and the idea of movement.

DIRECTED NUMBERS AS VECTORS: THE ADDITION OF DIRECTED NUMBERS

Ways in which children can be introduced to directed numbers (positive and negative numbers) will be discussed in Chapter 15. In this section, we describe the link between directed numbers and vectors.

Following the movement of a lift up and down a tall building may help children to associate directed numbers with movements. In Figure 14 : 21 the floors above the ground floor are labelled $^+1$, $^+2, ^+3, \ldots$ the ground-floor stopping place is 0, and the basements are $^-1, ^-2, \ldots$. A series of movements of the lift can be charted as shown in the diagram, and statements of the type shown below will be made:

(up 2 floors) followed by (up 3 floors)
= (up 5 floors)
(down 2 floors) followed by (down 3 floors)
= (down 5 floors)
(up 2 floors) followed by (down 3 floors)
= (down 1 floor)
(down 2 floors) followed by (up 3 floors)
= (up 1 floor)

These statements are statements about movements or vectors, and are true *whatever floor the lift starts from*. The notation, however, is cumbersome, and needs to be replaced by a shorter and more conventional notation.

We have defined the addition of vectors to mean:

Chart of a lift's journey

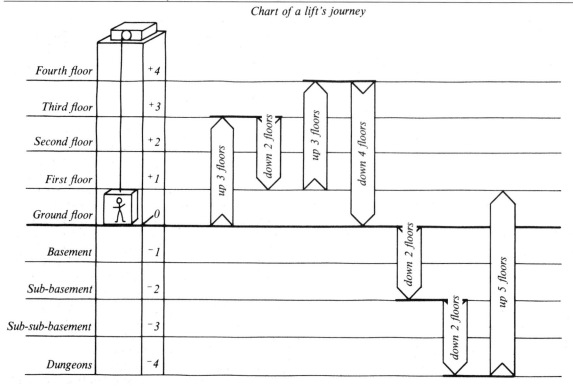

Figure 14 : 21

(one vector) followed by (another vector).

If we use this convention the lift's first two movements become

(up 2) + (up 3) = (up 5)
(down 2) + (down 3) = (down 5)

These statements clearly fit well with the use of the addition sign for natural numbers, but the other two statements are less fortunate:

(up 2) + (down 3) = (down 1)
(down 2) + (up 3) = (up 1)

It is necessary, however, that the same sign must be used in all circumstances for the same operation, and having chosen ' + ' as the sign for the operation 'followed by' for vectors, this use must be maintained.

We now change the notation for (up 3) and (down 3). Since a movement (up 3) from the ground floor takes the lift to floor ($^+$3), the movement (up 3) is written ($^+$3) and the movement (down 3) is written ($^-$3). The statements about the lift now become:

($^+$2) + ($^+$3) = ($^+$5)
($^-$2) + ($^-$3) = ($^-$5)
($^+$2) + ($^-$3) = ($^-$1)
($^-$2) + ($^+$3) = ($^+$1)

The introduction of the addition of directed numbers has been derived from the illustration of the lift, but is clearly a general idea. There are two stages:

i) the notation ($^-$3) is used not only for a point on the number line, but also for the vector, or movement, of 3 units in the negative direction,

ii) the addition of directed numbers is defined as vector addition.

For example, ($^-$5) + ($^+$3) = ($^-$2) means that (5 units in the negative direction) followed by (3 units in the positive direction) gives the same result as (2 units in the negative direction). This is shown in Figure 14 : 22.

Children will find that the calculator does vector addition; ($^+$2) + ($^-$3) is entered by the key strokes

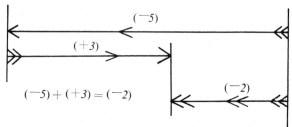

$$(-5) + (+3) = (-2)$$

Figure 14 : 22

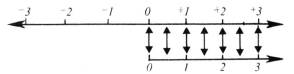

Figure 14 : 24

and Me es the display – 1. Sets of related additic Ex h as the following, can quickly be explored Ar e calculator, and the patterns noticed: Su Int

$$(^+2)+(^+1) = \quad \quad (^-2)+(^+1) = (^-1)$$
$$(^+2)+(0) = (^+2) \quad (^-2)+(0) = (^-2)$$
$$(^+2)+(^-1) = (^+1) \quad (^-2)+(^+1) = (^-1)$$
$$(^+2)+(^-2) = (0) \quad (^-2)+(^+2) = (0)$$
$$(^+2)+(^-3) = (^-1) \quad (^-2)+(^+3) = (^+1)$$

Every vector has its opposite, or *negative* (*see page 170*), which is a vector of the same length in the opposite direction. Clearly the opposite of $(^+3)$ is $(^-3)$ and the opposite of $(^-3)$ is $(^+3)$. We write the opposite of a vector **a** as – **a**. In symbols, we therefore write

$$-(^+3) = (^-3) \text{ and } -(^-3) = (^+3)$$

because

$$(^+3)+(^-3) = 0$$

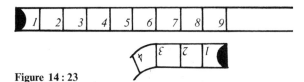

Figure 14 : 23

When children perform subtraction of natural numbers by measuring forwards and backwards with a tape-measure (*see page 109*), they often do it by *addition of* vectors. Figure 14 : 23 (which is the same as Figure 14 : 15) illustrates not only 9 – 3 but also $(^+9)+(^-3)$. The child has replaced the subtraction of natural numbers 9 – 3 by the *addition* of $(^+9)$ and $(^-3)$, which is the opposite of $(^+3)$. The addition of vectors in opposite directions therefore resembles the subtraction of natural numbers. The addition $(^+9)+(^-3)$ is similar to the subtraction 9 – 3. The addition of vectors, however, has a feature not shared by the subtraction of natural numbers; the subtraction of natural numbers 3 – 9 is not possible, whereas the addition of vectors $(^+3)+(^-9)$ is possible, and has the vector $(^-6)$ as its result.

The addition of vectors in the *same* direction, on the other hand, is exactly similar to the addition of natural numbers. Both

$$(^+3)+(^+2) = (^+5)$$

and

$$(^-3)+(^-2) = (^-5)$$

are similar to 3 + 2 = 5. It would therefore be natural, when we are dealing with addition, to

identify one half of the number line of directed numbers with the (signless) number line of natural numbers, as shown in Figure 14 : 24, and to extend this correspondence so that the positive fractions correspond to their signless equivalents. When this identification is made, the positive directed numbers are often written without their signs; $(^+3)$ is written as if it were the natural number 3. Then $(^+3)+(^-2)$ may be written as $3+(^-2)$, and $(^+3)+(^+2)$ as 3 + 2. The '$^-$' sign in a negative directed number must not, of course, be omitted.

When we read 3 + 2, it does not matter whether we think it refers to the natural numbers 3 and 2, so that 3 + 2 = 5, or whether we think it refers to vectors and is an abbreviation for $(^+3)+(^+2) = (^+5)$, since the result in natural numbers and the result in vectors always correspond. But $2+(^-3)$ must be an operation on vectors, as $(^-3)$ does not belong to the set of natural numbers.

SUBTRACTION OF DIRECTED NUMBERS

Children will probably first meet the subtraction of directed numbers on the calculator, setting up subtraction patterns similar to the addition patterns of the last section. For example:

5 – 4 = 1	$(^-5)-4$	$= (^-9)$
5 – 3 = 2	$(^-5)-3$	$= (^-8)$
5 – 2 = 3	$(^-5)-2$	$= (^-7)$
5 – 1 = 4	$(^-5)-1$	$= (^-6)$
5 – 0 = 5	$(^-5)-0$	$= (^-5)$
5 – ($^-$1) = 6	$(^-5)-(^-1)$	$= (^-4)$
5 – ($^-$2) = 7	$(^-5)-(^-2)$	$= (^-3)$
	$(^-5)-(^-5)$	$= 0$

Thus, subtracting a negative number appears to give the same result as adding its opposite. To see why this is so, we need to refer back to the subtraction of natural numbers. When the subtraction of natural numbers was defined, we thought of it as *inverse addition*; 9 – 3 means, 'What must be added to 3 to make 9?' (*see page 108*). Subtraction is addition with one of the components of the sum missing, or a process of finding the missing number in addition. This idea extends to the subtraction of directed numbers. If the lift of page 172 is in the sub-basement floor ($^-2$), and it is needed on floor ($^+3$), it must make a journey of ($^+5$) floors. That is:

$$(^-2) + \square = (^+3)$$

is completed to make

$$(^-2) + \boxed{^+5} = (^+3)$$

In subtraction language this is written

$$(^+3) - (^-2) = (^+5)$$

The subtraction ($^+3$) – ($^-2$) can be read, 'What journey must the lift make from ($^-2$) to reach ($^+3$)?'

Children will find no difficulty in subtracting directed numbers if they regard the subtraction purely as addition with a missing number. The question ($^+5$) – ($^+2$) means, 'If you have gone ($^+2$), and you want to go ($^+5$) altogether, what must you do to finish the journey?' That is, the missing number in ($^+2$) + $\square$ = ($^+5$) is to be found, and so $\square = (^+3)$. This example shows the obvious analogy with subtraction of natural numbers, but the same method applies equally easily to other examples, and only demands visualisation of the directed number line. For instance,

$(^+5) - (^-2) = \square$ comes from ($^-2$) + $\square$ = ($^+5$),
 and so $\square = (^+7)$,
$(^-5) - (^-2) = \square$ comes from ($^-2$) + $\square$ = ($^-5$),
 and so $\square = (^-3)$,
$(^-5) - (^+2) = \square$ comes from ($^+2$) + $\square$ = ($^-5$),
 and so $\square = (^-7)$.

SUBTRACTION AS ADDITION OF THE OPPOSITE DIRECTED NUMBER

We saw on page 172 that children sometimes perform a *subtraction* of natural numbers by an *addition* of vectors. Instead of 9 – 3 they do ($^+9$) + ($^-3$). There is another alternative open to them. They may replace 9 – 3 by ($^+9$) – ($^+3$); that is, they may ask what they must add to ($^+3$) to make ($^+9$) (Figure 14 : 25). The addition ($^+9$) + ($^-3$) and the subtraction ($^+9$) – ($^+3$) give the same result, but the addition is easier to perform, as it only consists of following one movement by another and does not involve going back to the beginning and starting again. We have

$$(^-9) - (^+3) = (^-12)$$
$$\text{and } (^-9) + (^-3) = (^-12)$$

Similarly, the subtraction of ($^-3$) and the addition of its opposite vector ($^+3$) give the same result:

vector methods of performing 9—3

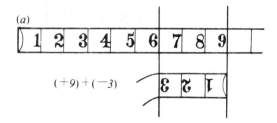

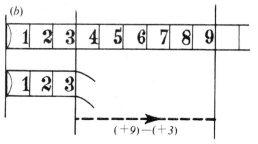

Figure 14 : 25

$(^-9) - (^-3) = (^-6)$ and $(^-9) + (^+3) = (^-6)$;
$(^+9) - (^-3) = (^+12)$ and $(^+9) + (^+3) = (^+12)$;

In each case the subtraction of a directed number has been replaced by the addition of its opposite without affecting the result. We see that this is no coincidence, for if

$$\square = (^-9) - (^-3)$$
$$\text{then } \square + (^-3) = (^-9),$$

replacing the subtraction statement by its original meaning. If we now add the opposite of ($^-3$), which is ($^+3$), to both sides of this equation, we obtain

$$\square + (^-3) + (^+3) = (^-9) + (^+3)$$

But ($^-3$) + ($^+3$) = 0, since ($^-3$) and ($^+3$) are opposites,
and therefore $\square = (^-9) + (^+3)$
But also $\square = (^-9) - (^-3)$
Therefore $(^-9) - (^-3) = (^-9) + (^+3)$

Similarly the subtraction of any directed number can always be performed by *addition of its opposite*. The child who performs subtraction by stepping backwards and forwards on a tape-measure does this, preferring ($^+9$) + ($^-3$) to ($^+9$) – ($^+3$).

Throughout the primary years, exploration of directed numbers and their properties should be informal and intuitive, conducted with the aid of number lines, tape-measures and calculators. The time for formalisation of this knowledge is not reached by most children until well into the secondary years, if then.

15 | *Number and its Notation*

The beginnings of number notation

Large numbers were needed by people as soon as they began to live in communities. When famines came, food had to be stored, listed and shared. Big buildings required planning; lengths had to be decided and the amount of necessary material estimated. Herds of cattle had to be counted to avoid disputes about ownership. For many such purposes records of the numbers involved had to be kept. Some method had to be devised for writing numbers in a concise way. The first way of recording was to make a stroke for each object involved. As soon as large numbers had to be written, dealing with the long row of strokes became intolerably clumsy. For numbers from one to five the pattern of the strokes could easily be recognised and these numbers were given names. The next important step, taken by various peoples at different periods, was to group the strokes and record the groupings. If the number of groupings was small they could count the groupings using the number names they already had.

These strokes would be counted as 3 sets of 4 and 2 strokes.

Figure 15 : 1

Various groupings were used by different peoples; e.g. five, ten, twenty, sixty, but ten has become the established counting set and the number we call twenty three is generally organised into two sets of ten and three single things. A name and a symbol were devised for the counting set; for example the Romans, counting in tens, wrote twenty three as XXIII. The number shown in Figure 15 : 1 could be more economically written in some such way as

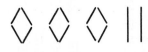

where each grouping of four has been formed into a concise symbol.

To make a second grouping was now an easy step forward. A hundred was a grouping of ten tens. Then a thousand was used for ten hundreds, and so on. Even when the number of times each counting set was used was written as a symbol, e.g. 3 tens, to write a large number as 3 thousands 7 hundreds 2 tens and 3 ones was clumsy. Abbreviations for the names shortened the writing but a new idea was needed before our modern system came into being. This idea, which opened the way to new understanding of numbers, was that the *names* of the groupings should be dropped entirely. A code was adopted by which the *position* of the figures should tell which groupings they referred to. Thus 4723 could be read at sight as four thousand seven hundred and twenty three because it was known that groupings increase in size with each move to the left from the ones. A single new sign only was required, a symbol to put into a place that turned out to be empty when the groupings were made. Hence the invention of 0 for use as a place-holder, as in writing 806, where 8 is seen to occupy the hundreds place because a zero has been written in the tens place.[1]

Children's first introduction to number notation

In earlier chapters we have shown how children come to understand and use the accepted notation for the smaller numbers that occur in their experience. They pass through stages which are similar to those outlined above for our invention of a system that enables any number to be written concisely. Very few additional symbols have had to be invented to express the other kinds of numbers, such as fractions, negative numbers, and irrational numbers, by which the natural numbers have been supplemented to form the whole system of real numbers (*see pages 461–463*). The importance of children's thorough understanding of their first steps in number notation is evident if they are to follow easily the later developments.

[1] A fuller account of the historical development of number notations is given in Chapter 18.

At first children record and compare sets without counting. They use beads, pictures, cubes, squares, and may even use strokes as their ancestors did. Names and symbols for the small and easily recognised numbers are soon learned. The sequence of number names to one hundred and beyond may be familiar before the written forms are known. But as soon as numbers greater than ten need to be written the first introduction to the structure of our notation has to be made. The important operation of grouping must be undertaken and the idea of recording the number of equivalent counting sets made by the grouping has to emerge. The use of a rod to represent a counting set helps children in this recording. For instance, as they group cubes in fives they can replace each set of five by a five-rod. When they group in tens they replace each set of ten by a ten-rod. It is common practice to introduce tens early to children. Frequently children experience no other counting set. For example, the number twenty nine is known to them in only two ways: as the number which occurs after twenty eight when the number names are recited in order, and also as the number which is equivalent to two tens and nine ones. Because we use ten as the counting set successively throughout our number system from tens to millions and beyond, it is important that the structure of numbers in terms of tens and ones should be well understood. Nevertheless, number notations based on other counting sets have some uses and children should have opportunities of organising numbers by means of groupings other than in tens. The experience of using a variety of

bases or counting sets for number notation helps children to generalise the formation or structure which is common to all the resulting systems.

Groupings should be carried out with actual objects. For example, children may take twenty five rods or matchsticks and make as many *triangles* as possible from them. They are then grouping in threes (Figure 15 : 2). They can write

25 = 8 threes and 1 one.

If they make squares instead they will be able to write, as in Figure 15 : 3, 25 = 6 fours and 1 one.

If they pack the sticks in sets of five they will write 25 = 5 fives and 0 ones (Figure 15 : 4).

Putting each pair of fives together children make groupings of ten and write 25 = 2 tens and 5 ones. At this point the way of writing twenty five takes on new meaning: the 2 and the 5 are explained.

Cubes and rods of the Multilink, Cuisenaire, or Dienes type can show similar number structures. Children can match cubes to a set of things which are to be counted, and then either link the cubes together, or exchange them for rods. For example, 17 unit cubes can be converted into 3 five-rods and 2 ones (Figure 15 : 5). The grouping process can conveniently be structured on a piece of card.

Six-rods and eight-rods give two new groupings for 17, as shown in Figure 15 : 6.

With ten-rods children obtain the pattern that matches the notation 17, as shown in Figure 15 : 7.

Such constructions make children familiar with the number patterns they will find in multiplication and division. Here the emphasis is on the practical

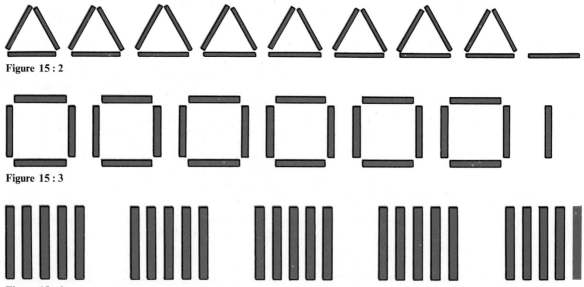

Figure 15 : 2

Figure 15 : 3

Figure 15 : 4

(i)

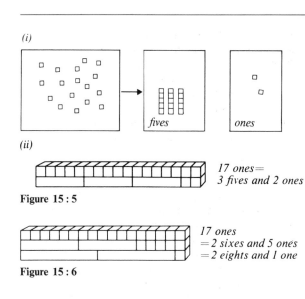

Figure 15 : 5

(ii)

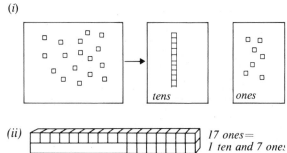

17 ones=
3 fives and 2 ones

17 ones
= 2 sixes and 5 ones
= 2 eights and 1 one

Figure 15 : 6

(i)

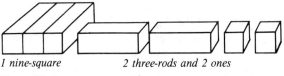

tens   ones

(ii)

17 ones=
1 ten and 7 ones

Figure 15 : 7

experience of grouping. The manipulation of cubes and rods has the further advantage that it shows how such a grouping can be continued. Children quickly discover that 3 three-rods placed side by side form a square. Given 17 unit cubes and some three-rods they can replace the 17 cubes with 1 square layer, 2 three-rods and 2 unit cubes (Figure 15 : 8).

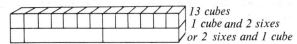

1 nine-square   2 three-rods and 2 ones

Figure 15 : 8

The square trays included in the Stern apparatus provide for varied experiences of this kind, using squares which have 2, 3, 4, ..., 10 units along an edge (Figure 15 : 9).

At this stage no formal work is developed beyond recording the squares, rods and unit cubes that have been used. But it can be seen that basically the children are learning the structure that they will use

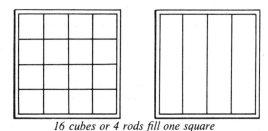

16 cubes or 4 rods fill one square

Figure 15 : 9

when they write hundreds and tens and ones in such a number as 322.

When we write 28 the 2 tells us how many tens and 8 tells how many ones together make twenty eight. A child who has grouped in tens knows at once that 2 ten-rods and 8 unit cubes represent 28. In Chapter 18 we show how number systems using counting sets other than ten, say five, six or eight, as in Figures 15 : 5 and 15 : 6, can be written so that the number of fives, sixes or eights and their squares, cubes, etc., can be read at sight.[2] In the present chapter we are suggesting only the *practical* experience of grouping in such sets so that children fully understand the procedure of grouping and do not think of tens and ones as providing the only means of organising a number.

So far we have made no attempt to develop the idea that the *order* of writing the figures has any importance, although we have consistently written the number of counting sets on the left of the number of ones. Up to the age of seven many children reverse this order sometimes, writing 82 instead of 28 when they mean 2 ten-rods and 8 cubes. From their point of view there is no reason why they should not work from right to left in placing the rods to match the equivalent number of cubes, as in Figure 15 : 10.

13 cubes
1 cube and 2 sixes
or 2 sixes and 1 cube

Figure 15 : 10

The teacher's consistent use of a left to right movement will help the children to develop the same habit, as will the use of cards ruled with labelled boxes in which children can place pieces of different sizes as they make the groupings (Figure 15 : 11). The first and second groupings may also be called *rods* and *squares*; later, the rod will be the *base* of the number system.

[2]Grouping in this way is an essential foundation for multiplying, since the children are counting, say, 3 fives as 15 and vice versa.

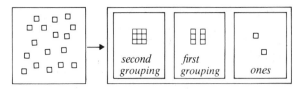

Figure 15 : 11

The next step in the establishment of notation is the introduction of some form of abacus.

THE ABACUS

The abacus has already been suggested in Chapter 2 as a useful way of recording sets so that they may easily be compared. For this purpose the beads placed on any column have the same value; each represents *one* member of a set. Figure 15 : 12 shows five sets.

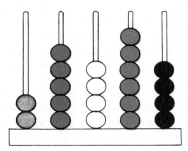

Figure 15 : 12

In Chapter 6 a two-column abacus was used to illustrate the structure of the numbers from ten to twenty. In this case the left-hand column records the number of ten-rods or sets of ten things that can be found when a given number, say seventeen or twenty, is organised in a grouping of ten.

The value of each bead on the left-hand column is ten. The right-hand column still represents ones. Notice the empty column in the representation of twenty in Figure 15 : 13. At first each column should be labelled, and it should be emphasised that the *ones* are always at the right. When counting sets

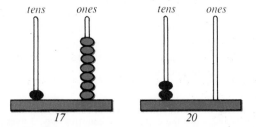

Figure 15 : 13

other than ten are used, groupings beyond the first can be shown on the abacus. The abacus of Figure 15 : 14 goes with the groupings shown in Figure 15 : 11.

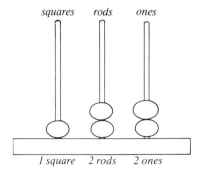

Figure 15 : 14

Beads of a different colour on each rod help children to remember the difference in value of the beads but this distinction should shortly be dropped so that the *position* of the beads is emphasised.

The emphasis can now be placed on grouping in tens, and extensive use made of the two-column abacus to record counts and to translate into written form numbers up to 99. Many different counts which are of interest to children should be made: children present in class, pencils, coins, distances measured in metres, windows or doors in the school, the numbers of various shapes in a room, the number of balls in a box, cars in a car park, berries on a branch, and so on. Children show their count on an abacus and then write the number in symbols. The abacus may be drawn on paper and rings or squares used for the count. Grooves in a sand-tray with pebbles as counters serve equally well and remind us that such an abacus was in use two thousand and more years ago. The purpose of this work is to establish notation using ten as the counting set on a firm basis. This is a necessary preliminary to learning to add and subtract two-digit numbers, either mentally or on paper. Coins also help children in dealing with a counting set of ten. A ten-pence coin can replace ten pennies, and a pound coin is equivalent to ten ten-pence coins.

SPOKEN NUMBERS AND NOTATION

The link between spoken numbers and the ways in which they are recorded needs also to be established, starting from the spoken number. Children who have counted twenty three objects, one by one, may want to record their result as 203, because 20 is the symbol for twenty. As well as grouping in tens, and using the abacus, the calculator can help with this difficulty. Adding 1 successively to 20 shows how numbers in the twenties are written. Keystrokes and displays are shown in Figure 15 : 15.

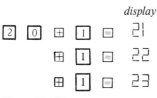

Figure 15 : 15

Similarly, the way in which 'seventy five' is written can be found by adding 70 and 5: $\boxed{7}\boxed{0}\boxed{+}\boxed{5}\boxed{=}$.

MEASURES EXPRESSED IN TWO UNITS

Practical work with two measuring units of different value, e.g. ten-rods and unit cubes, or decimetres and centimetres, provides a variety of experience in grouping. The many activities suggested in Chapter 16 give rise to recording in two-unit form the results of measuring length, capacity, mass, time, etc., as well as the value in ten-pences and pence of sets of coins. In many instances only two distinct units are necessary, and familiarity with two-unit procedures should be well established before a third measuring unit is introduced. For example, metres and decimetres are used together for measuring a path, decimetres and centimetres are sufficient for shorter lengths.

As children work with pairs of units in these different fields, writing their experiences with coins, tape-measures, clock-faces or litre jugs, they can be led to see that the operations they are carrying out are of the same kind as those they perform on tens and ones. When they record a height in centimetres only, or a mass in grams only, they express the number in tens and ones, e.g. 47 cm; to convert the measure to a pair of units they read 47 as 4 tens and 7 ones and 47 cm as 4 dm and 7 cm. A measuring strip can be made to show both forms of stating the length. So long as children confine their working to two measuring units the parallel between this work and the use of tens and ones is clear. It is a great advantage if practical work with measures, and the statements and calculations that record it, can be developed alongside activities with numbers written in tens and ones. This stage is a very important one for understanding the procedures needed to carry through addition, subtraction, multiplication and division of large

numbers when two different values (such as ten and one) must be given to the figures used in writing the numbers. If sufficient time is allowed for the range of practical activities which should be the basis of learning the patterns of these operations involving 2-figure numbers, the extension to 3-figure and 4-figure numbers will be mastered later without difficulty.

MENTAL AND WRITTEN PROCEDURES FOR ADDITION AND SUBTRACTION OF TWO-UNIT NUMBERS AND MEASURES

In the age of cheap pocket electronic calculators, the importance of written calculation procedures is diminishing fast. However, the importance of understanding numbers and their behaviour will certainly not diminish, and the ability to add and subtract two-digit numbers mentally is an important part of the facility with numbers which will continue to be necessary. This type of calculation is not most easily done by trying to visualise a written calculation 'on the blackboard of the mind', but by making use of the grouping in tens and ones in ways which are more natural mentally. Children often discover good procedures for themselves, but may need encouragement to become skilful in them.

Numbers are usually spoken of, and thought about, starting with the left-hand or *most significant* digit, which tells us the most important part of the size of the number. We say 28 as *twenty* eight. But traditional written addition and subtraction conventionally start with the right-hand or least important digit, so that children do not know the size of answer to expect until they have completed a calculation. In mental procedures, many people prefer to work with the most important digit first, and to add or subtract one digit at a time. Thus 36 + 27 may be done as

$$36 \xrightarrow{+20} 56 \xrightarrow{+7} 63$$

Two skills go into this calculation. The first is an ability to add *tens* to any number. Children may be encouraged to count in tens, twenties, thirties, and so on from any starting-point:

36, 46, 56, 66, ...
36, 56, 76, 96, ...
36, 66, 96, ...

and the calculator may also be used to explore patterns such as

36 + 10 =
36 + 20 =

$36 + 30 =$

and so on.

The second skill is the knowledge of facts such as

$36 + 7 = 43$
$46 + 7 = 53$

and so on. These are derived from $6 + 7 = 13$ by 'moving up ten'. A child who is not yet sure of this often 'bridges the ten', saying

$$36 \xrightarrow{+4} 40 \xrightarrow{+3} 43 \xrightarrow{+20} 63$$

A child who cannot carry out the whole process mentally may use some form of intermediate recording, such as

$$36 \xrightarrow{10} 46 \xrightarrow{10} 56 \xrightarrow{4} 60 \xrightarrow{3} 63$$

or

$$36 \xrightarrow{20} 56 \xrightarrow{7} 63$$

When children realise that they can add 36 and 27 by adding the 30, 6, 20, and 7 in any order, they will easily be able to understand the traditional written procedure. It may be helpful at first if the results of adding 20 and 30, and 6 and 7, are recorded in full (Figure 15 : 16). This can be done in either order. Labelling the columns to show the equivalences may be a useful reminder.

tens	ones
3	6
2	7
5	0
1	3
6	3

10's m	dm
3	6
2	7
1	3
5	0
6	3

Litres	tenths
3	6
2	7
5	0
1	3
6	3

Figure 15 : 16

The usual mental procedures for subtraction do not involve methods such as decomposition or equal additions, but proceed directly. One common method of doing $45 - 17$ is

$$45 \xrightarrow{-10} 35 \xrightarrow{-7} 28$$

or

$$45 \xrightarrow{-10} 35 \xrightarrow{-5} 30 \xrightarrow{-2} 28$$

but *complementary addition* is another method which is often used:

$$17 \xrightarrow{+\square} 37 \xrightarrow{+\square} 45$$

The child mentally supplies 20 to bring 17 nearly up to 45, and then 8 to complete the process. This is the process used in giving change when something costing 17p is bought using a 50p piece. The shopkeeper counts out the coins:

$$17 \xrightarrow{+3} 20 \xrightarrow{+10} 30 \xrightarrow{+10} 40 \xrightarrow{+10} 50$$

and finds that she has 33 pence in her hand.

Some children who know at an early stage about negative numbers make use of them in subtraction. The subtraction $45 - 17$ can be done by saying $40 - 10$ is 30, and $5 - 7$ is -2, so the result is 28.

The methods can easily be formalised in such a way as to become useful pencil-and-paper methods. For instance,

$$
\begin{array}{ll}
17 \rightarrow 20 & 3 \\
20 \rightarrow 40 & 20 \\
40 \rightarrow 45 & 5 \\
\hline
& 28
\end{array}
$$

shows a clear recording of building 17 up until 45 is reached.

The third method can be recorded as

$$
\begin{array}{ll}
40 - 10 & 30 \\
5 - 7 & -2 \\
\hline
& 28
\end{array}
$$

If the teacher still requires children to learn a traditional pencil-and-paper method for subtraction, this can be developed by a process which continues to stress the close link between addition and subtraction; this is explained below. However, most children can subtract two- and three-digit numbers by one of the more informal methods illustrated above; they often find these methods more intelligible. For larger subtractions, they will, throughout their lives, use a calculator.

To develop a traditional pencil-and-paper subtraction technique, addition should be learnt first. Then addition and subtraction can be carried out side by side, using structural apparatus to show the regrouping (Figure 15 : 17). Finally, the written procedures can be set out in full as in Figure 15 : 18.

Notice that the addition operation reminds children of what they should already know about the number 15, viz. that $15 = 8 + 7$, a fact that should be linked with $15 - 7 = 8$.

The idea of regrouping can be reinforced by writing it in full, as in Figure 15 : 18, until children can carry it out in their minds.

It will be seen that regrouping is similar to the method of subtraction called *decomposition* but it uses a more fundamental idea. It assumes that such relationships as $15 - 7 = 8$ are remembered without requiring that the ten shall be *decomposed* into ten

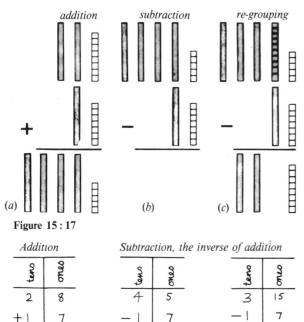

addition   subtraction   re-grouping

(a)   (b)   (c)

Figure 15 : 17

Addition

tens	ones
2	8
+ 1	7
1	5
3	0
4	5

Subtraction, the inverse of addition

tens	ones		tens	ones
4	5		3	15
− 1	·7		− 1	7
			2	8

Figure 15 : 18

ones. The linking of subtraction with addition also makes it possible to formalise *complementary addition* into a written procedure. This is easily seen as a 'missing number' addition, as in Figure 15 : 19. Children should not learn it until they are very familiar with the corresponding addition technique. When the method is thoroughly understood as complementary addition, it can then be recorded in the conventional subtraction layout, but a child will continue to think of it as complementary addition.

The written subtraction procedure known as *equal additions* consists of transforming an inconvenient

(i)

$$17$$
$$+ \boxed{}\boxed{}$$
$$\overline{45}$$

'7 + $\boxed{8}$ = 15; write down 8, carry 1 ten.'

(ii)

$$17$$
$$+ \boxed{}_{,}8$$
$$\overline{45}$$

'2 tens + $\boxed{2}$ tens = 4 tens; write down 2 tens.

Figure 15 : 19

subtraction into an easier one. Children may use it as a mental method. The subtraction 57 – 19 can be replaced by the easier one 58 – 20; if John is 7 years old and Jane is 12 years old, then in three years' time John will be 10 and Jane 15, but the difference in their ages will be the same. The calculator enables this idea to be freely explored as many times as a child wishes (Figure 15 : 20).

	John	Jane	Difference
Now	7	12	5
Next year	8	13	5
5 years' time	12	17	5
43 years' time	50	55	5
50 years' time	57	62	5

Figure 15 : 20

In the written algorithm, 1 ten is added to each of the numbers whose difference is to be found. The writing pattern is illustrated in Figure 15 : 21.

tens	ones
4	5
− 1	7

(a) is rewritten as in (b)

tens	ones
4	15
− 2	7

(a)   *(b)*

Figure 15 : 21

It should be noticed that in adding a ten to each number, 5 in the ones column of the larger number becomes 15, and the 1 in the tens column of the smaller number becomes 2. This method is more difficult than regrouping because tens are introduced from outside; the numbers which are actually

hours	min		hours	min		hours	min
9	15		8	60+15		8	75
− 7	30		− 7	30		− 7	30
						1	45

$$7.30 \longrightarrow 8.00$$
$$8.00 \longrightarrow 9.00$$
$$9.00 \longrightarrow 9.15$$

hours	mins.
	30
1	00
	15
1	45

Figure 15 : 22

subtracted are not those which were given. The procedure is thus somewhat artificial and is based on notational convenience rather than developed from a real situation which leads to subtraction.

In subtraction involving two measuring units connected by a counting set other than ten the same principles can be used: e.g. finding the interval between two times stated in hours and minutes (Figure 15 : 22).

THE SECOND GROUPING: SQUARE LAYERS

Many counting experiences will lead children beyond one hundred; e.g. the number of steps a child takes to cross the playground, the number of acorns in a class collection, the number of visitors who attend a school concert (and the chairs to be placed for them). The written numerals which represent such large numbers must be understood as expressing successive groupings in tens. This can be made clear by the rhythm of the count, each complete ten being stressed ... *ten ... twenty ... thirty ... one hundred*. The acorns in a class collection can be counted in tens, put into boxes or plastic bags and these tens assembled into hundreds; the number is then written so that each digit has its meaning, e.g. 2 sets of 100, 7 bags of 10 and 5 acorns: 275. When a child steps across the playground, markers can be placed at the end of each set of 10 steps and a large marker put at the end of 100 steps, and so on. Children enjoy exercising their skill in these large counts and will extend a numbered strip beyond 100 units until it reaches along a whole wall or even round the room.

All the available ten-rods in apparatus of the Cuisenaire type can be placed end to end and a count made of the equivalent cubes (Figure 15 : 23).

The calculator should also be used to record these counts, so that for the class collection of acorns, we have

	calculator
2 hundreds	$\boxed{2}\boxed{0}\boxed{0}\boxed{+}$
7 tens	$\boxed{7}\boxed{0}\boxed{+}$
5 ones	$\boxed{5}\boxed{=}$

The calculator gives the result of the addition, on pressing $\boxed{=}$, as 275. Work such as this confirms for children the fact that the number which is said as 'two hundred and seventy five' is actually written 275, not 20075, as some children expect.

Similarly, the count in successive tens of all the decimetre rods in the room can be recorded on the calculator by pressing $\boxed{1}\boxed{0}\boxed{+}$ and then pressing $\boxed{=}$ repeatedly. The display should be recorded on each occasion, so that the change from 90 to 100 to 110, and so on, can be discussed.

If the children have already made square layers of 3 three-rods, 4 four-rods, etc., they will know that 10 of the ten-rods will make a square layer which is equivalent to 100 cubes. The square becomes the shape associated with *any* second grouping using the same counting set as the first grouping. The structure of a three-digit number can then be represented by square layers, rods and unit cubes, whatever counting set is used (Figure 15 : 24).

Two successive groupings of sevens

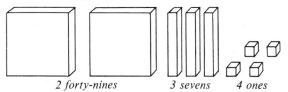

2 forty-nines   3 sevens   4 ones

Two successive groupings of tens

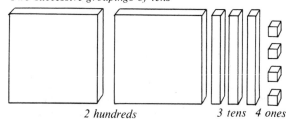

2 hundreds   3 tens   4 ones

Figure 15 : 24

It will be noticed that no new principle is required in carrying out calculations with numbers greater than 99. The step to adding and subtracting numbers between 100 and 1000 should be made easily after the counting and recording activities that we have suggested.

It mental calculation, the same skills as used previously should be extended. Counting in hundreds from any starting-point

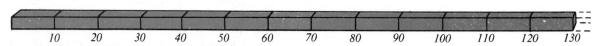

Figure 15 : 23

234, 334, 434, 534, ...

enables a child to progress to mental addition of
234 + 500 = 734. It is then easy to do 234 + 587 in
stages:

234 + 500 = 734
734 + 80 = 814 (or 734 + 70 = 804; 804 + 10 = 814)
814 + 7 = 821

Subtraction can be performed by similar extensions
of previous mental methods. For instance,
821 – 234 may be done as

234 → 300	56
300 → 800	500
800 → 821	21
	577

or more simply in more steps, recording
intermediate totals. By the end of the primary
years, the majority of children should be able to
add and subtract two-digit numbers mentally, to use
a calculator with understanding whether its results
are correct, and to add and subtract numbers over
100 without a calculator, by some method. Whether
the traditional formal written procedures for
addition and subtraction will survive the calculator
revolution is doubtful. Nevertheless, the written
recording of calculations, in some style, will
continue to be important.

COINAGE: HUNDREDS

In the British currency there is one main unit, the
pound. This is equivalent to 100 pence. An
intermediate coin represents 10 pence. Thus it is
possible to symbolise the notation for numbers from
1 to 100s by coins representing pennies, ten-pences,
and pounds. Sums of money which contain other
intermediate coins worth five pence or two pence
can be written in three columns labelled £, 10p, p,
as shown in Figure 15 : 25. Thus money can be
used to illustrate grouping in hundreds, tens and
ones. Children will also use the decimal point as a
marker, when writing, for instance, £2·38.

Among the most important calculator skills are
those concerned with money calculations. Sums of

In columns			In pence	As a decimal
£	10p	p		
2	3	8	238p	£2·38
5	0	7	507p	£5·07
1	9	0	190p	£1·90

Figure 15 : 25

money over £1 can be recorded on the calculator
both in *hundreds of pence* and in *decimals of £1*,
and parallel additions and subtractions observed
with and without decimal notation. It is most
important for children to learn the two ways of
entering a sum such as

£1·35 + 20p

on the calculator, so that the disaster of entering
1·35 + 20 can be avoided. Children also need to
know that when they add £1.35 and £2.25 on the
calculator, by doing 1.35 + 2.25, the calculator
displays the result as 3.6, not 3.60. This may
confuse a child whose grasp of decimal place value
is not yet secure.

Children need to be able to perform money
calculations both mentally and with a calculator.
They should also be able to record them in
conventional form on paper. Figure 15 : 26 shows
some of the many ways of finding the change from
a £5 note when something costing £2·38 is paid for.

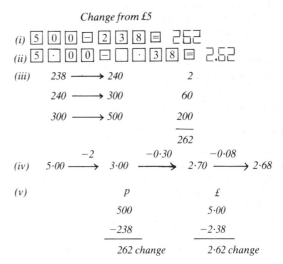

Figure 15 : 26

EXTENSION TO LARGER NUMBERS

When children use structural apparatus and
diagrams to represent the ones, tens and hundreds
that they write in columns, they become aware of
the relation between the values represented by
neighbouring columns. For example, they come to
realise that a 3 in the tens place is worth ten times
a 3 in the ones column, and conversely a 3 in the
ones column is worth one-tenth of a 3 in the tens
column. A ten is 10 times a one, and is also
one-tenth of a hundred (Figure 15 : 27).

As children look at the columns to the left of the
ones column they see that each has a value *ten*

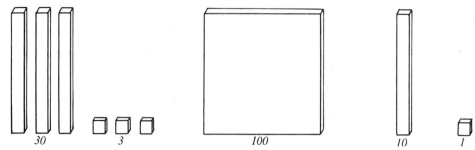

Figure 15 : 27

times that of the column on its *right*. If, however, they begin at the left-hand column, say the hundreds, and move to the right, the value of any column is *one-tenth* of that of the column to its *left*; a ten is one-tenth of a hundred and a one is one-tenth of a ten. This introduction of the link between adjacent columns in both directions is an important step towards understanding of decimal fractions; the facts that a ten is one-tenth of a hundred, and a one is one-tenth of a ten, lead towards the extension of the number system to one-tenth of a one, and one-tenth of a tenth. In just the same way, the facts that a ten is ten times a one, and a hundred is ten times a ten, lead to the extension to larger and larger groupings, of thousands, ten-thousands, and so on.

The first extension may be that to larger and larger groupings. In general children may not master the concept of an unending process of grouping until they are about 9 years of age. It has to be built up by extending the notation through thousands to millions and then evoking awareness that counting in millions can be carried forward indefinitely. The realisation that counting can never reach an end is a startling and memorable experience for most children. Our vast number structure can hardly have much meaning for children unless they encounter some of the very large numbers necessary for recording air journeys, astronomical distances, population figures, etc., and can relate them to their own experiences of crowds and large collections. Nevertheless, children are fascinated by numbers so large that they are difficult to imagine, and they will sometimes undertake prodigious counts. One class of 9 to 10-year-old children used squared paper to make a count beyond 10 000. One small square represented 1 unit. Small squares were grouped in 10 × 10 large squares, so that a row of ten large squares represented 1000. Ten rows represented 10 000. Repeating this large square to make a row of ten made 100 000 and so they continued. Another class of this age spent their spare time for several weeks

in a determined effort to count out, in successive groupings of ten, a million barley corns. At the end of this task they certainly understood our tens notation.

EXPERIENCE LEADING TO DECIMAL FRACTIONS

Experience of writing sums of money using a point to separate the pounds and pence, as in £2·38, prepares children for the extension of number notation to the *right* of the units column. The ten to one relationship of £1 to a tenpence and of a tenpence to a penny leads children to recognise that a penny is a tenth of 1 ten-pence and a tenpence is a tenth of £1. The columns in which money is written can now be described as pounds, tenths and hundredths, because 100 pence make £1 (Figure 15 : 28).

100p	10p	.	p		£	tenths of a £	hundredths of a £
2	3		8		2	· 3	8
		238p				£2·38	

Figure 15 : 28

The point separates the pounds from the tenpences and thus comes between pounds and tenths of a pound. This is the fundamental step in realising the *general* use of the decimal point, which always separates the *ones* from the *tenths*.

When children begin to need to measure lengths with an accuracy greater than to the nearest unit they will use a sub-unit for the piece smaller than 1 unit. Now they should be introduced to *tenths* of a unit in place of a named sub-unit. For instance, instead of recording a length as 2 metres 7 decimetres they can *say* two and seven tenths

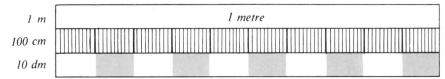

Figure 15 : 29

metres. They will *write* this as 2·7 metres, as the first place after the decimal point shows *tenths*.

It is desirable to use the metric system alongside the decimal system of notation, in order to provide experience of a set of measuring units in which the principal unit (the metre in the measurement of length) is subdivided into tenths and hundredths. The use of a metre ruler for measurement will lead children to know that one metre is equivalent to 10 decimetres or to 100 centimetres. Children should know that they can describe their heights in a variety of ways, of which the following are examples:

> 1 metre 2 decimetres 4 centimetres
> = 12 decimetres 4 centimetres
> = 124 centimetres

The use of decimals gives further expressions, such as:

> 1 m 2dm 4 cm = 12·4 dm
> = 1·24 m

The usual way of giving this height as 1·24 m leads to the introduction of the second decimal place, the hundredths place (Figure 15 : 29).

Children should be aware of a slight irregularity in the way decimals of a pound are written. A length of 1 m 2 dm is usually written in metres as 1·2 m, rather than 1·20 m. However, £1 and 20 pence is always written as £1·20, rather than £1·2. In all cases other than that of money, *non-significant* zeros in later decimal places are usually omitted. In money, the opportunity fraudulently to convert £1·2 to £1·29 makes it necessary to fill in the second decimal place, or the pence place.

The extension of decimal fractions beyond hundredths will occur because of the 1000 to 1

relationship between the standard metric units which gives in reverse the 1 to 1000 relationship. For example:

> 1 km = 1000 m 1 m = 1 thousandth of 1 km
> = 0·001 km
> 1 litre = 1000 ml 1 ml = 1 thousandth of 1 litre
> = 0·001 litre
> 1 kg = 1000 g 1 g = 1 thousandth of 1 kg
> = 0·001 kg

The millimetre and the gram are too small for a single unit to have much practical value but a medicine spoon holds 5 ml, which can be written as 0·005 litres, and a standard litre measure has minor markings in 50 ml. The mass of the contents of a tin of meat is given on the outside, correct to 1 gram or 0·001 kg. Millimetres are not very practical for children's use, but they will be found marked on rulers and tape-measures and as a ruling on cm/mm graph paper. They serve to give a greater accuracy in graphs and scale drawings where decimal fractions are commonly used. From the notational standpoint they have some importance in suggesting that further extensions of the decimal fraction system could be made.

SITUATIONS WHICH LEAD TO DIRECTED NUMBERS

A number of situations within children's experiences lead them to the ideas of directed numbers. If a thermometer is kept in a refrigerator or out of doors in winter, children may obtain a graphical record containing temperatures below freezing point, as in Figure 15 : 30, and they will discuss how many degrees above or below freezing point the temperature is. The vertical axis of the graph may be labelled as in Figure 15 : 31, and a

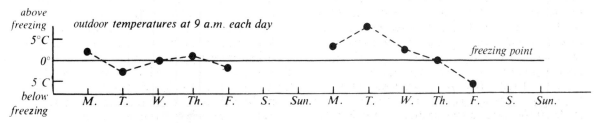

Figure 15 : 30

similar graph of indoor temperatures can be obtained by using a thermometer on which 20°C is marked as 'room heat'. Children may supplement a temperature graph by a diagram showing the rises and falls in temperature (Figure 15 : 32). In this

situation, children need to measure in two opposite directions from a starting-point, and they also use *movements* of temperature in two directions, that is, rises and falls in temperature.

A similar situation, in which measurements can

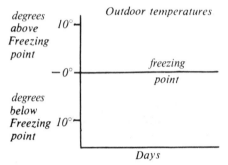

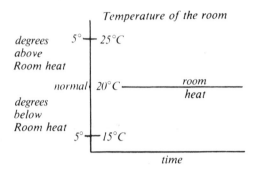

Figure 15 : 31

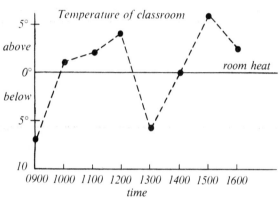

Figure 15 : 32

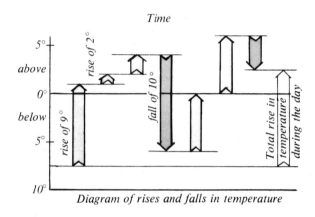

Diagram of rises and falls in temperature

(a)   Block graph of children's heights

(b)   Masses above and below 25 kg

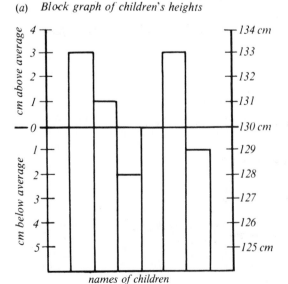

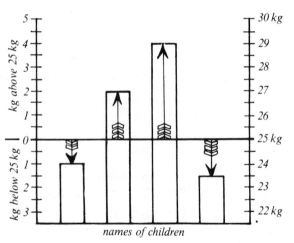

Figure 15 : 33

Ways of measuring time

(a) *A count-down before firing a missile*

(b) *June 1944*

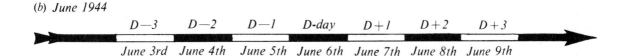

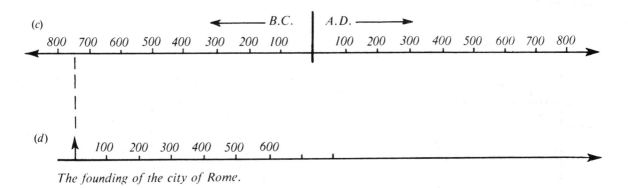

The founding of the city of Rome.

Figure 15 : 34

The number line extends in both directions

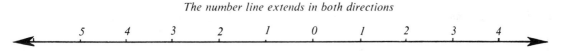

Figure 15 : 35

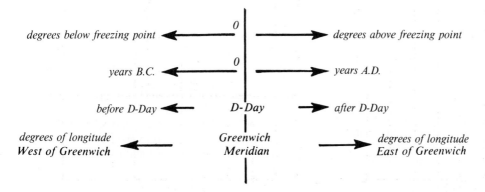

Figure 15 : 36

be taken in two directions, arises when the children's average height is shown on a graph. Each child will know how much above or below the average height of the group they are (Figure 15 : 33(*a*)). The starting-point of measurement need not, of course, be the average for the group. Figure 15 : 33(*b*) shows how far the children's masses are above or below 25 kilograms.

Children will be familiar with the 'countdown' before the firing of a rocket. A time in history from which dates are measured in both directions is the year of Our Lord's birth, but many Roman chronologers reckoned dates from 'the founding of the city' (Figure 15 : 34).

A variety of such examples will make it clear to children that it is often possible and convenient to measure in two opposite directions from a starting-point or *origin*. When measuring time, it is *necessary* to measure in both directions from an arbitrary starting-point such as 'the founding of the city' as we cannot measure forward from the beginning of time. Temperature, too, must be measured in both directions from an arbitrary origin, unless we always measure temperatures from the absolute zero (– 273°C). These examples drive us to use the scale of measurement or number line shown in Figure 15 : 35, which can be indefinitely extended in both directions.

It is clearly necessary to distinguish between the two possible directions of measurement. This is done in a variety of ways, some of which are shown in Figure 15 : 36. Children may invent their own symbolism to show the two directions of measurement. Such a notation as (2 cm *A*) for '2 cm *above* average' and (3 cm *B*) for '3 cm *below* average' might be shortened to 2*A* and 3*B*, the letters *A* and *B* indicating opposite directions of measurement. A Celsius thermometer shows the usual convention of indicating a temperature such as 3°C below freezing point as (– 3)°C. The calculator shows the same convention; a downward count from 5 is produced by the keystrokes

$$\boxed{5} \; \boxed{-} \; \boxed{1} \; \boxed{=} \; \boxed{=} \; \boxed{=} \; ...$$

and gives the successive displays

5, 4, 3, 2, 1, 0, – 1, – 2, – 3, ...

On many calculators, the – sign appears at the extreme left-hand edge of the display; a calculator in which the – sign is placed adjacent to the displayed digits is more helpful at first.

Now the classroom number line can be extended to show steps in both directions from zero, and children can show their skill in successively adding or subtracting the same number from any starting-point:

10, 8, 6, 4, 2, 0, – 2, – 4, – 6, ...
9, 7, 5, 3, 1, – 1, – 3, – 5, – 7, ...
– 17, – 7, 3, 13, 23, ...

In the last example, 10 has been added on each occasion; the correctness of the step from – 7 to 3 may need to be checked, using the number line and the calculator.

NOTATION FOR DIRECTED NUMBERS

The temperature (– 3)°C means 3° below zero, and the minus sign shows a *direction*. In other uses of the minus sign, the sign appears between two numbers, as in 8 – 6, where it means, 'What must be added to 6 to make 8?' or 'from 8, take away 6'. These two uses of the minus sign are very different; the second asks for the performance of an *arithmetical operation*, the first indicates a *direction of measurement*. It is undesirable that the same symbol should be used in such different contexts, but there is a strong pull towards conforming with long-accepted usage in notation. Some calculators help us to distinguish between the two uses of the – sign by providing two keys. The $\boxed{-}$ key is usually situated just above $\boxed{+}$, and it indicates the *arithmetical operation* of subtraction. The keystrokes

$$\boxed{5} \; \boxed{-} \; \boxed{3} \; \boxed{=}$$

produce the display 2. The $\boxed{+/\text{--}}$ key produces a *change of direction*; the keystrokes

$$\boxed{5} \; \boxed{+/\text{--}}$$

produce – 5. We notice that the digits are keyed in first, and then the direction changed by means of $\boxed{+/\text{--}}$, if necessary. Confusion of the two keys will produce either error messages or strange results, and children soon distinguish the different purposes of the two keys.[3]

In written language, the use of the – sign for two different purposes can hinder understanding of directed numbers. A convention which may help to overcome this difficulty, and which is in fairly common use in schools, is now stated.

It is desirable that *both* directions of measurement should be labelled, rather than only the 'below zero' direction, for they are of equal importance. If 3°C below zero is described as (– 3)°C, then 3°C above zero should be labelled (+ 3)°C. Thus the signs (+) and (–) are used to

---

[3]The simplest calculators are not designed for directed numbers, and do not have a $\boxed{+/\text{--}}$ key.

Figure 15 : 37

show the two directions of measurement. Although these signs are the same as the signs for the arithmetical operations of addition and subtraction, children should realise that the signs are used in a different sense. Therefore a temperature of 3°C above zero may be written ($^+$3)°C, and a temperature of 3°C below zero may be written ($^-$3)°C. The changed position of the + and − signs shows their changed use. The sign ($^+$3) may be read as '*positive three*' and ($^-$3) as '*negative three*', the words 'plus' and 'minus' being reserved for the arithmetical operations of addition and subtraction. Using this convention, $^+$3 is entered on the calculator as $\boxed{3}$, while $^-$3 is entered as $\boxed{3}$ $\boxed{+/-}$. With this convention, the double-ended number line, on which measurements can be made in both directions, takes the form shown in Figure 15 : 37. Fractions as well as whole numbers can be placed on the double-ended number line, or the *line of directed numbers*, as fractions of a unit can also be measured in both directions.

In Chapter 14, page 168, lengths which were measured in particular directions were called *vectors*. Directed numbers are examples of vectors. The directed number ($^+$3) describes a measurement, or movement, of 3 units in the positive direction of the number line, and the directed number ($^-$4) describes a measurement or movement of 4 units in the negative direction along the number line. It is important that the idea of movement should be associated with directed numbers, for it is only by thinking of directed numbers as vectors, and so associating them with movement, that children will be able to perform the operations of addition and subtraction on them. Although directed numbers are examples of vectors, they are, however, vectors which are exceedingly limited in direction. Vectors used in two or three dimensions to show movements can be in *any* direction in the space, but for directed numbers, the directions are limited to backwards and forwards on the number line. Directed numbers are one-dimensional vectors.

Numbers and number operations in the National Curriculum

The work discussed in this chapter covers a good deal of that described in the earlier levels of Attainment Target 2 (Number). For example, at Level 3, children are expected to be able to:

• read, write and order numbers to at least 1000, and use the knowledge that the position of a digit indicates its value.

(AT2: Number, Level 3)

At Level 4, numbers of any size may be used:

• read, write and order whole numbers.

• understand and use the relationship between place values in whole numbers.

(AT2, Level 4)

Children are expected to be able to use three methods of calculation: in the head, using a calculator, and without a calculator, according to the size of the numbers used. The level of non-calculator addition and subtraction expected is indicated by the target at Level 4, which is the highest level at which addition and subtraction of whole numbers are mentioned.

• add or subtract mentally two 2-digit numbers; add mentally several single-digit numbers; add and subtract two 3-digit numbers without a calculator ...

(AT3: Number, Level 4)

It should be noted that children are not required to use a particular method for non-calculator addition or subtraction, and that 3-digit numbers are the largest numbers which children are expected to add or subtract without a calculator.

Both decimals and directed numbers make an early appearance in the National Curriculum.

• use decimal notation in recording money.

(AT2, Level 3)

• use, with understanding, decimal notation to two decimal places in the context of measurement.

(AT2, Level 4)

• recognise negative whole numbers in familiar contexts.

(AT2, Level 3)

16 | MEASURING SYSTEMS AND THEIR USES

THE CHOICE OF UNITS

When children begin to measure quantities which interest them – mass, capacity, length, for instance – they use a unit which seems suited to the object they are concerned with. It may be an improvised unit such as a piece of string, a marble, an empty tin, but it is chosen because it seems likely to produce a fairly small number when it is compared with the quantity to be measured. The history of measures shows how through the centuries a people would agree on the units they would use for particular ranges of objects, such as gallons that a milkpan would hold, yards for the distance across a plot of land. There was no thought of inventing a whole *system* of units of length or mass. In order to measure the length of a track, the size of a brick, the amount of ploughing done in a day, the weight of a bag of corn or of a silver coin, a special unit was required in each case. So unconnected units such as the mile, inch, yard, pint, gallon, furlong, stone, ounce continued in use for many years. For ordinary folk in their daily activities these separate measures were adequate but for the merchant or the builder recording and accounting such units demanded numerical skill. Numbers had been organised into a system of tens at an early stage and this system had to be used for each separate unit of measurement without the possibility of converting one unit into another. There was also the problem of ensuring that *each* separate unit was kept at a standard quantity since it was not related to another unit as our measures are today. Few attempts were made to create new systems of measurement until the end of the eighteenth century, when the metric system was devised. Until then systematising consisted of standardising existing units and relating them by the nearest whole number to the ratio which tradition had developed. Consequently we find the prime numbers 2, 3, 5, 7, 11 all occurring as factors in our traditional tables of measure.

LINKING UNITS

The system of the British measures of length illustrates well the complicated history of the different units. Parts of the human body were natural choices for measuring units: the inch as the width of the thumb (or the length of the top joint), the foot from the heel to the toe, the yard as the girth of a man (or the distance from the nose to the tip of the outstretched arm). The now rarely used cubit and fathom were respectively the length from the elbow to the finger tip and the width of the outstretched arms. Such measures varied from one individual to another and any connection between them was an approximate ratio as it chanced to occur in nature. Neither the length of a particular unit nor the ratio of one unit to another was at first fixed by statute but gradually it became necessary to safeguard traders by having a legal standard for a unit and a compulsory system of equivalences. The approximate equivalences of 12 thumb-joints to one foot-length became a fixed artificial relation and both inch and foot were prescribed fractions of the standard yard. Thus the 12 and the 3 which were among the first ratios of units of length sprang from the proportions of two parts of the human body.

Twelve has a long history from before Roman times; it has the advantage of having 2, 3, 4 and 6 as factors and the Romans found its properties so useful that they had a special column for twelfths on their abacus (Figure 16 : 1). The still surviving use of the dozen and the gross demonstrates its usefulness. But with the adoption of metric measures in industry and commerce and the use of decimal currency this special familiarity with twelve is declining.

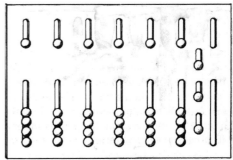

A Roman abacus showing places for twelfths on the right

Figure 16 : 1

Some of our units of length derived from the need to measure the amount of work done. The *furlong* was the length that an animal could draw a plough before resting. This is the unit on which our mile was based. The *rod* (pole or perch) is thought to have been the yoke pole used in Anglo-Saxon times for the four pairs of oxen used in ploughing. The rod was also the basis of land measuring and was originally quite distinct from the yard used for cloth. When yards and rods were linked to fit into a complete length-measuring *system,* the inconvenient $5\frac{1}{2}$ yards appeared as the equivalent of a rod. Children may be interested to know that it is through the use of the rod that eleven appeared as a factor in the number of yards in a chain, a furlong and a mile, i.e. 22, 220 and 1760 yards respectively.

The mile was built on the furlong and we see that the $\frac{1}{4}$-mile, $\frac{1}{2}$-mile and mile were obtained from the furlong by successive doubling, a pattern which is seen frequently in other measures.

The *chain* is a particularly interesting unit. It is derived from the measuring rope which was used in Egypt and other ancient cultures. A chain was equal to 4 rods and to one-tenth of a furlong. It has another link with tens; since the seventeenth century it has been used by surveyors as a measuring chain divided into 100 links. This means

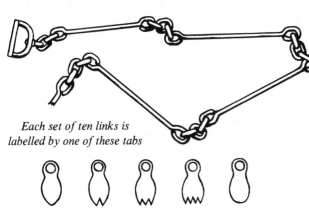

Each set of ten links is labelled by one of these tabs

Figure 16 : 2

that work with these two units, chains and links, follows the pattern of hundreds, tens and units, with 1 chain used as the name for 100 links. A Gunter chain is literally made up of 100 links. See Figure 16 : 2. The measurement of land area also uses the chain. The acre is equal to the area of a rectangle 10 chains long and 1 chain wide. Although the chain does not occur frequently in daily usage, the chain of 22 yards is well known as the length of a cricket pitch.

THE INFLUENCE OF TEN

Calculations are considerably eased when one unit is equivalent to ten smaller units, or a multiple or a power of ten of a smaller unit. The practically minded Romans made their mile equal to 1000 paces[1]. Measurements could be easily be recorded in their decimal notation with its symbols for a thousand (M), a hundred (C) and ten (X).

Ten occurs as a factor of sixty in relating minutes and seconds to hours. This goes back to the Babylonians and their interest in astronomy. The apparent movement of the sun across the sky and the rotation which we observe in the stars in the night sky led to the use of the circle as the image of these movements. The six arose because it is easy to divide a circle into six parts by drawing the inscribed hexagon. The further division by ten gave the rotation 60 parts which matched the counting set of 60 which was the Babylonian number base. It was natural to link 60 with the number of days in the year which was thought to be 360 by the Babylonians. Although we now have discarded 360 as the number of days in a year we keep it as the number of degrees in a complete revolution and we still use 60 seconds to the minute and 60 minutes to the hour.

These are all separate and unsystematic uses of ten in linking units of measure. No measuring system based exclusively on ten came into use until the metric system was adopted in France in 1795 AD.

THE INTRODUCTION OF A METRIC SYSTEM

In that great period of scientific initiatives in Europe, the seventeenth century, it was proposed in England to adopt a set of measuring units which would be convenient to use for practical purposes, would have world-wide validity, and would be likely to produce numerical results of recognisable accuracy. It is not surprising that the unit of *length* was considered to be basic, because not only is it extensively used, but also it can be measured directly (when accessible) by placing the unit repeatedly along the actual length. Various suggestions were made for a new unit of length from which successive powers of ten could be derived to serve as larger units. These ideas came to nothing until, over a hundred years later, at the time of the Revolution, France devised and adopted the metric system which was to become the recognised system for scientific use throughout the

[1]The Roman pace was about one and a half metres long, the same as a Scout pace today.

world. It was built on the basis of the metre, then defined as one-forty-millionth of the length of the meridian through Paris and now recognised as 1 650 763·73 wavelengths of the light emitted by the orange-red spectrum line of the gas krypton–86, measured in a vacuum. Each successive unit was linked to the next larger in the ratio 1 to 10; therefore in any calculations these units can be handled like numbers in the decimal notation.

It is remarkable that a very few highly developed nations have not yet adopted metric units for general public use. When the metric system is established, the simplification of the arithmetic required by the ordinary citizen has welcome repercussions on the curriculum of primary schools. The decrease in the time spent on learning to calculate, and the use of the calculator for calculations in metric units, means that more time can be given to teaching important mathematical ideas.

Halving and doubling

Alongside the tendency to use tens when larger quantities had to be measured, there persisted the primitive method of halving or doubling units to make counting easier. In fact, some systems show complete dependence on these two basic procedures. The traditional measure of capacity used in daily life is one good example, with its gallons, $\frac{1}{2}$-gallons, quarts, pints and $\frac{1}{2}$-pints.

The 'weights' traditionally provided with kitchen scales gave an outstanding example of repeated halving. In addition to 4-lb and 2-lb weights there were single weights of 1-lb, $\frac{1}{2}$-lb, $\frac{1}{4}$-lb, 2-oz, 1-oz, $\frac{1}{2}$-oz and $\frac{1}{4}$-oz. This means that they gave a run of eight successive halvings, and can be compared with the binary sequence: 1, 2, 4, 8, 16, 32, 64, 128, 256, which shows successive doublings. Similarly, the 7 days of the week depend on halving the 28 days of the moon's cycle, to give a fortnight, and halving those 14 days to give a week. In this case the seven seems inevitable.

It is interesting to compare the traditional weights from 1 oz upwards, obtained by repeated doubling, with the traditional units made in Ghana for weighing their main product, gold. These increase by *equal steps* of approximately $\frac{1}{2}$ oz, starting at 1 oz and continuing to $8\frac{1}{2}$ oz at least. A large number of weights is required because combinations are not provided for. This contrasts with the binary system of weighing where numbers of ounces can be expressed as the sum of a few of the binary weights supplied. For example, no special weight is needed for 3 oz because it is the sum of 2 oz and 1 oz. As can be seen in Figure 16 : 3 the form of the Ghanaian weight is significant and their manufacture one of the most pleasing of traditional crafts. There was no desire to economise in their number. Indeed the variety of form is immense, there being several figures to each weight. They are made of brass and are therefore reliable in use, but they also have a cultural meaning: each piece represents either a familiar activity or a commonly used proverb (Figure 16 : 3).

Figure 16 : 3

plate 1a: Cuisenaire rods

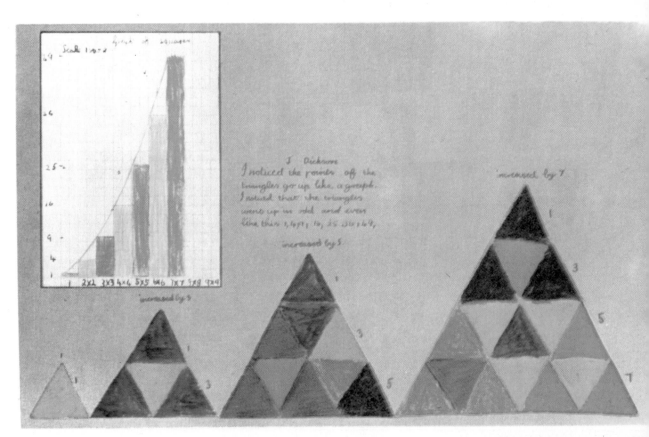

plate 1b: Sequence of triangles

plate 2: Child's model using all the pieces of Poleidoblocs G

this is a garden
with a tree
They are made of
rectangles. It has 4
windows and a
garage.

I   have
use circles

the   nand   is   on   the   tractor

plate 3: Children's patterns

JILL·keenon

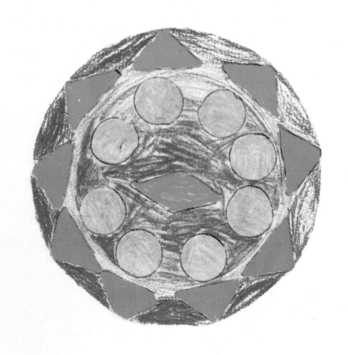

I have made a

plate for my mummy

There are eight yellow 8

circles.

I have nine red triangles 9

There is one orange

1

plate 4: A child's pattern

diamond.

The tendency to use tens and twos in systems of measures is interesting in view of the modern use of the denary and binary scales. Our number system is decimal and we now use a decimal system of measures. At the same time, digital computers work internally on a binary scale.

USING METRIC UNITS

Although children in a modern society begin by using any convenient object for a measuring unit they do not have to pass through humanity's historical phases to reach a unified system of measuring units. As we have seen in Chapter 7 they become familiar with metres, centimetres, kilograms and litres as seen in daily use. But they still have to learn how such units have been developed and related to form a coherent system. They begin by recognising that 100 cm make 1 metre, as they can see on a metre-rod or tape-measure. They use this equivalence to give a measurement in metres with extra centimetres to get as near as possible to the exact length they are measuring. They build up centimetres to 100 to make 1 metre, and also need to think of splitting up 1 metre into 100 small equal parts. This is similar to their recognition of pennies building up to 1 tenpence and 10 tenpence pieces into 1 pound. Children can easily express 237 pence as 2 pounds and 37 pence or £2·37, and also 135 cm as 1m 35 cm. Within this range of understanding they can do many interesting measuring tasks. They can also use halves and quarters in association with the metric units they have chosen for particular measurements.

MEASURING AS AN AID TO UNDERSTANDING

Measuring activities lead young children to informal combining and comparing of quantities such as lengths, capacities and masses. Simple statements can be made to describe the results of these activities. When children are learning about the addition and subtraction of numbers up to 100 or beyond, the practical tasks of measuring give them situations in which adding and subtracting are seen to be operations of wide usefulness, and thus a fuller understanding results. As children's scientific curiosity about the physical world grows, they find an increasing need to investigate through measuring and the recording of measures. Daily or weekly measuring of the length or mass of a growing plant or animal can lead to a discussion about the actual increase during each interval. Subtraction provides the means of measuring the increases; a record can be made and studied. After some weeks the records made week by week can be converted by addition into fortnightly records. If graphs are drawn for the two recordings, weekly and fortnightly, their shapes can be compared. The value of graphical representation can be seen because increases and decreases can be read directly. No formal subtraction is needed but the *differences* are obvious and can be recorded (Figure 16 : 4).

Many of the most interesting instances of what can be learned from a set of measurements will arise in this way from recording a set of observations. A close link with scientific and geographical inquiries is as important as maintaining a connection between concrete procedures with quantities and the abstract operations with numbers.

weekly observations

week	1	2	3	4	5	6	7	8	9	10	11
height	7	8	10	12	15	19	22	24	26	27	28

weekly increases

end of week	1	2	3	4	5	6	7	8	9	10
increase	1	2	2	3	4	3	2	2	1	1

fortnightly increases

end of fortnight	1	2	3	4	5
increase	3	5	7	4	2

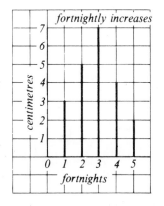

Figure 16 : 4

THE ADDITION OF QUANTITIES

Two quantities, say two masses, can be added in the sense that a single quantity can be found which will match, balance or produce the same effect as the two separate quantities taken together. Children have already added lengths by placing rods end to end. They have used a tape-measure as a slide-rule for adding and subtracting numbers. This has implied the addition and subtraction of lengths. Now they are ready to add *measured lengths,* using the numbers that measuring has provided. The statements that can be made about the quantities are exactly similar to number statements.

> For two collections of shells   24 + 13 = 37
> For two lengths   24 cm + 13 cm = 37 cm

So long as measurements are expressed in a single unit the similarity of the two statements is very clear. The addition of lengths and the addition of numbers can profitably be learnt side by side because the same structure can be seen in both; numbers and lengths combine in the same way, obeying the same rules. For example, a change of order does not affect the result of adding in either case; both additions are commutative.

> 29 + 18 = 18 + 29
> 29 cm + 18 cm = 18 cm + 29 cm

THE ADDITION OF LENGTHS

Every opportunity that classroom or outdoor activities can provide should be taken to let children find total lengths in a particular unit, choosing the one most suited to the length to be measured. The following examples of measuring show three different situations.

i) 'A toy lorry is 16 cm long; a trailer is 13 cm long. Use a tape-measure to find how long they are when placed end to end.'

16 cm + 13 cm = 29 cm

Together they are 29 cm long (Figure 16 : 5).

ii) If two tables were to be placed side by side how long would the length be altogether? If the tables are placed together in fact the total can be found by measuring; but this is an addition situation and if we add we can say how long they will be without moving them (Figure 16 : 6).

The first table measures	96 cm
The second table measures	93 cm
Together they measure	189 cm

The result would be confirmed if the tables were actually moved, of course.

iii) Two bookshelves are fixed one above the other. The top one is 44 cm long and the bottom one is 78 cm long. What length of bookshelf is there altogether? We cannot put these shelves side by side but we can add their lengths (Figure 16 : 7).

    This can be checked practically in several ways. A 150-cm measuring-tape or a 10-cm strip marked in cm can be used to mark first 78 cm and then 44 cm beyond it along a line, or the two lengths can be marked off in succession along a graduated strip.

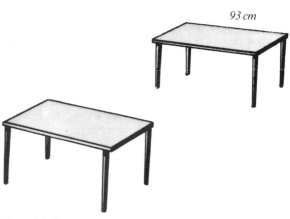

Figure 16 : 6

Figure 16 : 5

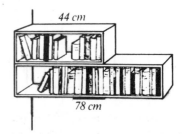

Figure 16 : 7

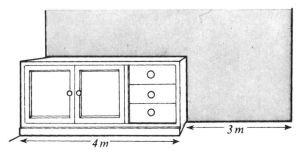

Figure 16 : 8

An example of addition of measures in *metres* occurs when a cupboard prevents the continuous measurement of the length of a wall (Figure 16 : 8).

The width of the cupboard, say 4 m, must be added to the length of the accessible part of the wall:

$$4 \text{ m} + 3 \text{ m} = 7 \text{ m}$$

Addition of lengths in *metres* also arises when children wish to know the length of a path which consists of several parts, one of which is curved. A tape can be used to measure the straight sections and a trundle wheel gives the length of the curve. This involves the addition of several lengths.

In the example illustrated in Figure 16 : 9, the children will probably add 16 and 27 first and then add 14 to 43. The addition of the lengths shown in Figure 16 : 9 cannot easily be checked by measuring on the ground, though a trundle wheel will serve. It is possible to check the numerical work on a number line or track, but this involves using a scale, one unit of the track representing 1 metre. It is also very easy to check it on a calculator.

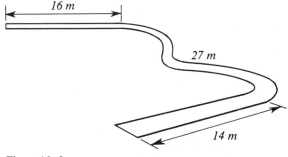

Figure 16 : 9

THE VALUE OF CHECKING

It must be noted that checking an arithmetical operation by measuring or vice versa does not mean

that the one operation can prove that the other is correct. We know that measuring is liable to error and in any case that it is never *exact*. The value of finding a solution to a problem, such as finding a total length, by two different methods is to provide two results which can be compared. If they do not agree the discrepancy must be investigated. Has there been an error in addition, or a mistake in measuring? The error can be discovered and put right. If the two results *do* agree there is a very good chance that they are right but, of course, there is a possibility that there has been a mistake in both operations.

The procedure of checking a calculation by a practical method is important in another way; it recalls the actual situation which gave rise to the number operation, addition for example; it may also show the detailed steps which are taken in a complex calculation, such as adding tens and ones. For instance, in example (iii) in the preceding section, 44 must be marked along a number line starting from the 78 mark. This may be carried out by merely reading off the final number on the line, 122. Children, however, may count 10, 20, 30, 40, 44, along the line, reading on from 78 : 88, 98, 108, 118, 122; or they may count 4, 14, 24, 34, 44 along the line, reading 82, 92, 102, 112, 122 (Figure 16 : 10).

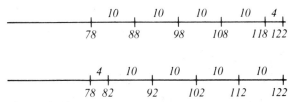

Figure 16 : 10

Each of these procedures gives meaning to the calculation. A child who is flexible enough to use *either* of these counting methods well understands the structure of tens and ones.

When practical measuring is carried out first, the calculation which follows is a way of ensuring that on another occasion children will know that they could find a total length without the need to measure. They could find it mentally or with a calculator.

PERIMETERS

The lengths of boundaries, walls and fences provide many occasions when measuring discloses some of the properties of important shapes, particularly of rectangles, including squares. Finding the perimeter

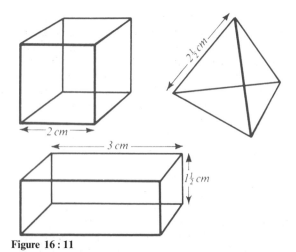

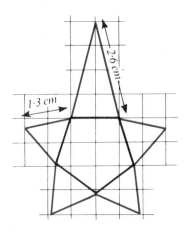

Figure 16 : 11

Figure 16 : 13

of the classroom, of a games pitch or a garden bed will ensure that children see the equality of the opposite sides of a rectangle and use this property to save some of the measuring. It will also show them that when two sides are equal the length of one can be doubled to give the total. Thus an introduction to multiplying quantities occurs. Sketches of the measured shapes can be drawn and the lengths shown on them. If the sketches are drawn on squared paper children will often devise simple scales for themselves.

Measuring the boundaries of interesting two-dimensional shapes, such as triangles, hexagons, and stars of various kinds, extends the knowledge of forms in common use. Children will compare different shapes which have equal perimeters and also shapes which differ only in size.

Three-dimensional shapes made with straws or plastic wire show their form through their edges only. These can be measured and the total length found. Cubes, cuboids and pyramids, etc. can be compared (Figure 16 : 11).

The kites in Figure 16 : 12 have the same shape but the sides of the larger are twice as long as those of the smaller. What can be said about their

perimeters? Shapes of this kind can be cut out in card. If the sides sometimes have an odd $\frac{1}{2}$-cm or $\frac{1}{4}$-cm in their lengths children will discover for themselves how to add or double the half or quarter. Alternatively, they can measure with a strip marked in $\frac{1}{2}$-cm and change to whole cm by counting in twos.

The star in Figure 16 : 13 is based on a pentagon. The long point has sides twice as long as those of the shorter sides. Children may find the perimeter of the star, and how much tinsel would be needed to go round a star which has sides twice as long.

Children can compare the lengths of the boundaries of the different rectangular faces to be found in a set of varied blocks (*see plate 2*). They can find which of the faces are squares.

The cylinder with its curved edges is of special interest, in view of its widespread use in daily life. A cylinder's circumference can be measured by placing a tape-measure tightly round the edge, but it is also valuable to make a cylinder from a rectangle of stiff paper and to realise that the length of the rectangle gives the length of the curved edge, allowing, of course, for any overlap needed for sticking. The diameter of the cylinder can also be found reliably enough by taking the greatest distance across its circular face, as shown by moving a ruler over the surface (Figure 16 : 14).

Such sets of measurements can be found in cylindrical tins and for the three cylinders from the set of Poleidoblocs. See Figure 16 : 14.

A comparison of the three cylinders included in G Poleidoblocs gives interesting results. Their diameters and heights can be compared. Do they increase in the same way? If they are placed in a line or in a tower will the length of the line or the

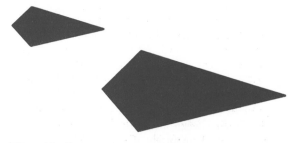

Figure 16 : 12

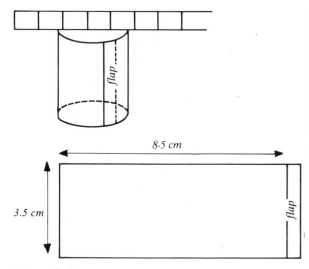

Figure 16 : 14

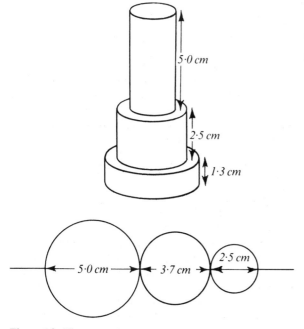

Figure 16 : 15

height of the tower be greater? Tenths of centimetres will occur again here (Figure 16 : 15).

THE DEVELOPMENT OF FRACTIONS

When a small unit is iterated to measure a quantity the resulting number may be large. The small units can then be grouped to form a larger one, e.g. 100 cm to make one metre, 1000 grams to make one

kilogram. But the formation of a second unit may arise in another way. A piece less than a unit may remain to be included in the total measure. This piece may look like half a unit and may be so called: half a litre, half a centimetre etc. With experience, $\frac{1}{4}$ and $\frac{3}{4}$ become recognisable too. It is also possible to split a unit into a number of parts other than two or four (though it may be difficult to carry out), and thirds, eighths, fifths and twelfths can be imagined. Where children have a tape-measure or ruler graduated in small parts they will readily use them, saying how many parts there are, say, in 1 cm and how many are required to make up the quantity they are measuring, e.g. 3 tenths of a cm. They have two ideas in mind: that one unit is equal to a certain number of equal parts, and that the number of these parts required for the measuring must be counted and given a name. Thus the two-number notation for fractions is built up, e.g. three quarters of a litre using the numbers three and four; $\frac{7}{10}$ in using 7 and 10.

THE TWO-NUMBER STRUCTURE OF FRACTIONS

i) *Notation.* The naming of a part as one-third, one-eighth, etc., is straightforward. Fractions with numerator 1 were well-known to the Egyptians, but of all the other possible fractions only $\frac{2}{3}$ was actually used by them. Such a fraction as $\frac{3}{5}$ had to be written as $\frac{1}{2}+\frac{1}{10}$ before they could calculate with it.

For the Greeks a fraction such as $\frac{3}{5}$ was seen as the ratio of 3 to 5, and they had a clear idea that a fraction involved a *pair* of numbers, even when, as in the case of $\frac{1}{8}$, one of the pair is 1. This concept of a fraction as a pair of numbers with a ratio will develop as children have experience of scale in drawings and maps. For the moment they see only a comparison of quantities, principally the comparison of one part to the whole, e.g. $\frac{1}{4}$ litre to 1 litre. But they will also realise the relation of fractional parts of the same kind to one another, for example the relation of $\frac{1}{4}$ to $\frac{3}{4}$ and of $\frac{1}{10}$ to $\frac{3}{10}$.

When children tabulate the equivalences of quantities expressed in different units, e.g. cm and metres, they will see that the *number* of cm is 100 *times* the corresponding *number* of metres, and also that the number of metres is $\frac{1}{100}$ of the number of cm. For instance, 3 metres is equal to 300 centimetres. It is also wise to match the statement 1 cm = 10 mm with 1 mm = $\frac{1}{10}$ of 1 cm, or 1 mm = 0·1 cm.

The equivalence of fractional parts, e.g. $\frac{1}{2}, \frac{2}{4}, \frac{5}{10},$

is seen very clearly in measuring activities. It is the *same quantity* which is expressed as 1 half, or 2 quarters, or 5 tenths, and the relation between the two numbers which express the fraction appears as the result of partitioning each part. For instance, *each half* has been partitioned into 5 equal parts to give $\frac{5}{10}$; hence the 5 corresponds to *1 half* and the 10 to *2 halves*.

To achieve a confident handling of metric measurements children have to build up through experience a familiarity with units and tenths, then with hundredths and tenths, and finally with the range from thousands to thousandths of the basic unit. They will begin by using units and tenths to record measurements actually made, and will discover the value of the standard decimal notation when they need to add and subtract in order to solve problems involving other measurements.

The two-number structure of fractions is still seen in the decimal forms: the place value shows the magnitude of the parts; the digit records how many of such parts have been found in the measurement. For instance, 0·07 shows a number of hundredths; the precise number of hundredths is stated in the 7.

ii) *Tenths and hundredths.* So long as grams or centimetres are used alone the special tens structure of the metric system is not apparent. We have seen in Chapter 7 that children begin measuring with one unit and state the result to the nearest unit, *about* 9 cupfuls, *nearly* 3 handspans, *between* 3 and 4 blocks. In an effort to be more precise they may use a smaller unit and state the result in the two units: 4 ten-rods and 3 cubes; and, later, 4 decimetres and 3 centimetres. Even abbreviated to 4 dm 3 cm this is still a little clumsy. Since children are familiar with the use of a point in stating money in the form £2·58 it is simple to adopt 4·3 dm as a briefer statement and to realise that the 3 after the point is the number of centimetres beyond the 4 dm. Addition of lengths is now exactly as for the natural numbers except for the point needed to identify the unit. It is also important for children to be able to write the length as 43 cm so that they can add the length if necessary to other lengths measured in centimetres.

Children often find that the decimal point symbol is easier than the fractional form, provided that its use is begun in practical situations. Similar work with metre sticks and decimetre rods, and with litres and graduations in tenths will make the common structure (unit and tenths) clear. Although the decimal fractions are confined to tenths at this stage the numbers used will be in the range of 3- and 4-digit numbers. For example, a trundle wheel graduated to show metres and decimetres may well be used for lengths in excess of 10 metres.

The extension to the second decimal place is particularly simple because the children know the notation for pounds and pence so well. The tenpence piece is 1 tenth of £1 and the penny is 1 tenth of a tenpence and so, since this makes 100 pence in the £, a penny is 1 hundredth of £1. The decimal fractions of £1 will be thought of as tenpences and pence for the tenths and hundredths places.

When the metre and the centimetre are used together the same 100 link occurs as in money. The relation between pounds and pence should strengthen the understanding of the hundreds and hundredths used in the number system and metric measures.

Actual measuring, using a tape-measure or metre-rod graduated in centimetres, will make many interesting discoveries possible in the classroom and out of doors. Total lengths, perimeters, comparisons of heights, lengths of jumps, comparisons of shapes and sizes will readily be proposed and carried out; checking by calculation, and checking computations by alternative methods or orders of operation will ensure careful mathematical thinking. During this stage the usual practice of writing a 0 in the units place if the measurement is less than 1 unit should become well established.

MEASURING DISTANCE

In the previous paragraphs all the lengths to be measured (except the diameters of the cylinders) were along lines or edges which permitted a ruler or tape to be placed alongside. Where a distance from one object to another or the distance across a space has to be measured children must visualise the line and iterate the unit along it. See Chapter 7, page 86. If a rope will not stretch across the whole distance they must measure in sections, ensuring that the sections are in a straight line. This introduces a new property of the straight line: we *look* in straight lines; the line of sighting is straight. We can therefore mark a straight line by placing children so that an observer sees one behind another. Or we can place upright sticks so that they are covered when sighted. To measure the diagonal distance across part of the playground it may be necessary to have two or three sections marked in this way, at distances which are short enough for the rope to stretch across the section (Figure 16 : 16).

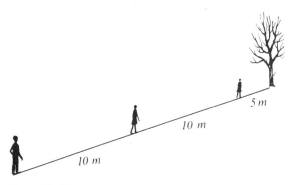

Figure 16 : 16

The line of sight can now be used to find the shortest distance between two points of interest or to mark out a distance, say 25 m, for a race. In the latter case a subtraction situation arises, since the 10-m rope will only measure up to 20 m; to reach 25 m a further 5 m must be measured. We now consider other ways in which the operation of subtracting lengths may occur.

Comparison of the distances that two children can hop in a given time, or the lengths of two walls, will entail the questions, 'How much longer?' and 'How much shorter?' If a measuring-tape is used the subtraction operation is recognised because a tape has already been used for the subtraction of numbers.

One wall is 23.4 m wide; the other is 16.8 m wide.

23·4 m – 16·8 m = 6·6 m

This statement says what the measuring-tape *shows*. We *write*, 'The first wall is 6·6 m longer than the other wall.'

In some kinds of model-making which children undertake, a certain length of material may be required. From a strip 24 cm long a piece 15 cm long is wanted. How much will be left? Will this piece fit a 6-cm edge?

24 cm – 15 cm = 9 cm

The 9-cm length is too long to fit the 6-cm edge exactly.

9 cm – 6 cm = 3 cm

There will be 3 cm left.

It is noteworthy that in these practical activities the necessity to decide *which* is longer and therefore which number can be subtracted from the other becomes obvious.

MEASURING HEIGHTS

Comparison and addition of heights
Children are familiar with the method of finding their own heights by standing against a vertical strip, using a sliding horizontal rod or a book to mark the tops of their heads. They can now compare heights and find how much one is taller than another by the operation of subtraction. Differences of reach can also be found when children stand on tiptoe and touch the highest possible point. They can stand on a chair or table and find by addition their highest reach from that vantage point. A weighted string will show the vertical line along which to measure. The line will be graduated usually in metres and centimetres. The measurements can be written in metres and decimals.

A more difficult problem is to find how high a pile of boxes will be. The height of each box can be measured and added. But how can the answer be checked if the height is beyond the children's reach? After experiment they may hit upon the idea of using a stick to reach the top. They can then measure from the top of the stick to the point where it is held and add this length to the height of the point above the ground, say 1·6 m + 0·9 m.

The same device can be used to find the height of the classroom. A long rod or slat of wood can have a plumb bob attached; the rod is held so that the plumb line hangs parallel to the edge of the slat. Alternatively, a large set square of stiff paper can be used. One edge from the right-angled corner must be placed along a known horizontal such as the top or bottom edge of the blackboard. The other edge will show where the slat must be held. Now the distance from the ceiling to the blackboard edge must be added to the height of this edge above the floor. See Figure 16 : 17.

The height of two cones or two plants can be compared if a technique similar to that of finding a child's height is used. A set square slides down a vertical wall or stake until one edge just touches the top of the cone or plant. The two heights can be marked on the same line and the subtraction checked. In these instances heights have been found when there is no visible line to measure (Figure 16 : 18).

These investigations provide opportunities of handling metres and centimetres together and also

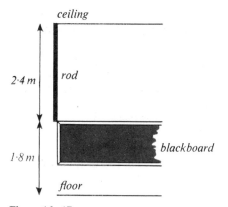

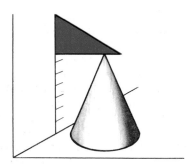

Figure 16 : 17

Figure 16 : 18

of the decimal notation for expressing a length in metres and a decimal fraction.

Position in a room; distances from a wall
When two children wish to know which of them is nearer to a wall they must decide how to measure their distances. They may experiment with a rope to find the distance of each child from the nearest point on the wall. They may place a large set square so that its right-angled corner fits between the taut measuring-rope and the wall. This gives the shortest or perpendicular distance, and shows the proper line to measure. If at the outset children estimate which child is nearer, and by how much, the

estimate can now be checked. In the classroom the distances of two children from the front can be found, and also their distances from a side wall. Pam may be nearer the front but Tim may be nearer the side. A first hint of two co-ordinates for fixing position may thus be given (Figure 16 : 19).

THOUSANDTHS AND MAIN UNITS

Much of the early work on the addition of lengths will be adequately carried out with two places of decimals in the measurements. However, children cannot remain long at this stage in view of the accepted practice of using International (SI) Units (linked by the 1000 to 1 ratio) and decimal fractions of those units, e.g. 3·742 metres for a length correct to 1 mm. The International Units for length – kilometre, metre and millimetre – will all have a useful role in the investigations children undertake to discover the spatial properties that are constantly used in the movements and constructions in their immediate surroundings. Grams and kilograms are in evidence in the masses marked on packages and in the weight measurements quoted in various sports. Milligrams are so small that they are best deferred until they are required in science. But tonnes (1000 kilograms) are widely used in industry and agriculture. Litres and millilitres are the usual units of capacity that children will encounter at this stage. The availability of a calculator is necessary now that children are using numbers larger than 1000.

When the thousandths place is introduced it is well to stress its importance in using the International Units of measuring which are linked by the 1000 to one relationship. For instance

1000 mm = 1 m   1000 m = 1 km
1000 mg = 1 g   1000 g = 1 kg

For heavy loads there is an additional unit of mass

1 tonne = 1000 kg

Also 1000 ml = 1 litre

Most of these units can be used by the children in the classroom or outdoors, but the milligram is too small for handling, though it can be seen on the labels of medicine bottles. The millilitre is likely to be seen only in graduations of 50 ml or 100 ml until its connection with the cubic centimetre is made in the fuller study of volume (see Chapter 29). A kilometre may be set out on the ground and used for timing various rates of walking, running, etc. A tonne will become familiar from observing lorry loads, registered masses, etc. The most vivid

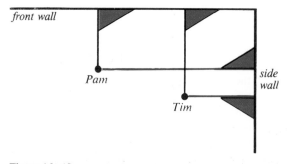

Figure 16 : 19

presentation of a thousandth part of a unit is probably the metre-length tape-measure marked and numbered to show 100 centimetres, with the multiples of ten in bolder figures, and graduated in millimetres throughout. The equivalent of 1 metre, 10 decimetres, 100 centimetres, 1000 millimetres is clearly shown and 1 mm is seen to be 1 thousandth of 1 metre.

The emphasis on international units demands a good mastery of demical notation. Zero will be needed frequently to ensure the correct placing of the digits when the measuring unit is changed. For instance, 7 m = 0·007 km. The 1000 to 1 relationship will be seen to have special meaning later when the volume of solids is studied.

ADDITION AND SUBTRACTION OF MASSES

The need to combine and compare masses occurs much less frequently in a child's experience than operations with length. Making up a parcel or finding the mass of a basket of shopping may arise from the class post office or shop. For example, the tins in the shop may be labelled 480 g, 440 g, 250 g, though if they are empty a child who handles them will not experience the masses. They can have sand put in until their masses match the labels. Addition gives the total mass which can then be checked by weighing. A kilogram can be used for 1000 g and the checking count of the masses then goes thus:

grams	masses in balance pan
	1 kg
480	100 g
440	50 g
250	20 g
1170	1 kg 170 g

The total mass is 1·170 kg.

It will be seen that children use trial and error at first in finding the actual masses to balance the scales rather than working systematically through the combinations of weights. It is much easier to use a spring balance and watch the pointer move to 480, 920, 1170 as the tins are put on the scale-pan one by one.

Parcels of books may be made up and weighed to find the total, or the difference, of their masses, or the number required to make up to a specified mass.

The mass in kilograms of pairs of children can be compared for the purpose of getting reasonably balanced partners for games. Scientific observations will also involve comparison, e.g. of the masses of equal cubes of different materials such as wood, plastic, brass.

Today labels often state mass in grams, especially on many tins of food. The numbers often run to hundreds. It therefore seems that grams should be introduced when hundreds are being learned. The use of thousands will accompany using grams and kilograms together. The investigation of the loads carried by lorries and railway trucks will involve tonnes (1000 kg = 1 tonne) and further calculations with thousands.

TEMPERATURE

Weather reports make children familiar with temperatures and the presence of a thermometer in the classroom may suggest recording the temperature at certain times in the day. The existence of the two scales, Celsius[2] and Fahrenheit, may present some difficulty but children will use only the Celsius scale in school, reading degrees Celsius on the graduated strip. An outdoor thermometer provides much greater variation than one in the classroom and records of its readings can be linked with weather observations. Changes in temperature and differences between outdoor and indoor recordings can be found. If water is studied

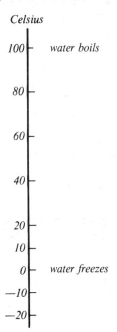

Figure 16 : 20

[2]Degrees Celsius are often called degrees Centigrade in Britain.

as a topic in science, the temperatures at which water boils and freezes should be read on the Celsius scale.

The indirect measurement of temperature through the expansion of a column of liquid is a good example of the use of a graduated strip. It is very impressive that our rather vague sensations of cold and heat can be converted into marks on a number line which give us remarkably exact and important information. An outdoor thermometer will sometimes fall below freezing point during the winter. The readings − 1, − 2, − 3, etc., on the Celsius scale will have the obvious meaning of being *below* freezing point. The use of negative numbers in this simple sense of 'below a level named as zero' may be introduced when children are made aware of it on a thermometer (Figure 16 : 20).

CAPACITY

The numbers involved in using two units of capacity are the familiar 10s, 100s, 1000s used in graduating a litre in millilitres. There are only a few occasions when computations are needed with litres and millilitres but some comparisons of the capacities of different containers is useful. Combinations of fluids may occur in cooking and gardening projects. Medicines to be taken in water are prescribed in millilitres. Concentrations of fruit juice can be diluted to taste and the recipe written in millilitres and litres.

TIME

Children see hours and minutes marked on a clock-face and hear the names frequently at home and at school. As they learn to tell the time they use some of the sets of five shown on the clock: 5, 10, 20, or 25 past the hour; but the rhythm is broken by the quarter past, half past and quarter to the hour. The minutes reappear with 25 to and 20 to the hour, but these do not build up to the 60 minutes of a whole hour. Before children can add or subtract intervals of time they must be able to give the time in hours and minutes, i.e. in digital form. By adding fives they can build the sequence 5, 10, 15, 20, . . . , 50, 55, 60 round the clock and practise converting from ordinary to digital ways of stating the time and vice versa. Addition and subtraction of time are needed only for discovering the end or the beginning or the duration of an interval, as in cooking or travelling, or for

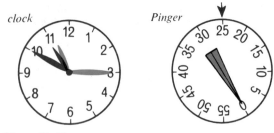

Figure 16 : 21

combining or comparing two intervals. The use of a kitchen pinger to record an interval combines well with a clock to show the result of adding and can check a calculation. For example, a cake needs 25 minutes to cook. The time is now ten to eleven, i.e. 10.50. Set the pinger at 25 minutes. Add 25 minutes to 10 hours 50 minutes. In place of a formal sum a child will almost certainly say, '10 minutes and it will be 11 o'clock; 15 minutes still to go.' The cake will be ready at 11.15, or a quarter past 11. The pinger will in fact check this when it rings at 11.15 on the clock (Figure 16 : 21).

The problem now arises of calculating an interval that stretches from a time before noon to a time after noon. Children can work this out by adding the two intervals which are separated by noon. The difficulty is completely avoided by using a 24-hour clock, so that, say, 2 p.m. is read as 14 hours and 6.25 p.m. as 18.35. Because of the greater distances now frequently travelled and the consequent longer times involved, 24-hour clocks and watches are being more widely used.

The activities of a class will include races, competitions and journeys which call for a great deal of totalling and comparing of times; these may well involve hours and minutes together. A digital watch is particularly useful in working out such comparisons. If the watch has a seconds reading children can measure and calculate timings in minutes and seconds together, since the minutes to seconds relationship is the same as for hours and minutes.

DECIMAL SYSTEMS

All the metric measuring systems are decimal systems of the same pattern as the length system although they measure different properties such as mass and volume. Each has a basic unit (metre, gram, litre) with larger and smaller units derived from it by successively using the factor 10 or 1-tenth. Although these units are named from the basic unit by a prefix which tells the relation of the derived to the basic unit, e.g. kilometre, hectometre, dekametre, metre, decimetre, centimetre, millimetre, very few of these are in common use. Yet they show the tens pattern which is found in the denary notation for numbers.

numbers	1000	100	10	1	$\frac{1}{10}$	$\frac{1}{100}$	$\frac{1}{1000}$
metres	kilo	hecto	deka	metre	deci	centi	milli

We can therefore identify the unit to which any digit in a number of metres relates. For instance, 2137·485 m means the sum of 2 km 1 hm 3 dam 7 m 4 dm 8 cm 5 mm. It is easy too to write this length in km as 2·137485 since the relation of one unit to the next is unchanged. In fact it is usual to write a metric quantity in terms of one unit, using a decimal fraction for any part less than the unit. For this purpose the units of the Système International are commonly used, that is, the kilometre, the metre and the millimetre and the corresponding units of mass and volume, e.g. 7·36 kg, 305 ml. It will be noticed that the recognised units (the basic unit and the kilo- and milli-units) are linked by a factor of 1000 which is a convenient bond but too large for young children to handle in one step.

THE USE OF GRAPH PAPER

Since graph paper is ruled in metric units of length it is useful in many ways when children are able to draw and measure in cm and mm units. In the first uses of squared paper the unit is unimportant and a variety of units will have been encountered. As measurement becomes important children will realise that the paper they use for recording patterns made with Cuisenaire rods is ruled in centimetre squares. But other rulings, 5-cm and 2-cm, are useful and provide occasions for valuable comparisons. A cheap quality of 1-cm squared paper is obtainable and is very generally used for finding perimeters and other lengths in shapes drawn or placed upon it. It can also provide strips for measuring fixed objects and furnishings. Scale models can also be made from squared paper nets and measurements can be compared and recorded. When the graph paper is ruled in tenths as well as units it can offer more varied experiences; graduating strips to measure the stretch of a spring; enlarging a shape in the ratio 10 to 1, etc. The most useful ruling for primary school children is probably 2 cm/2 mm, in which 2 cm is the unit and 2 mm is 0·1 of a unit: an instructive situation for children at this stage.

GRADUATION ON STRIPS AND DISCS

A characteristic of modern measuring is the mechanisation which enables many different properties to be expressed in numbers and read on a scale or a dial. Making and using graduated strips for measuring capacity and mass are recommended in Chapter 7. The construction of such strips will help children to study the use of graduation in thermometers, weighing machines, speedometers, pressure gauges, etc., and so to learn how wide a range of properties are quantified today and to recognise the units in which they are measured.

The graduated strip has the obvious defect that it becomes inconveniently long if a quantity varies from a very small to a very large measure, as in recording time in a 24-hour day when accuracy to a minute is needed. The trundle wheel is an example of a device which economises space. The revolving wheel measures a distance in small units, metres and centimetres, and each whole rotation is marked by a click which can be counted. The measuring scale is limited to the circumference of the wheel but the distance measured can be extended indefinitely. The clock-face shows a similar dual count, one hand recording the minutes and the other showing the number of revolutions made by the minute hand, i.e. the hours. Two revolutions are usually needed to show the full 24-hour clock, since few clocks are graduated to show 24 hours. Now that timetables are based on a 24-hour day it is well to let children see the hours from 13 to 24 on an outer rim of a classroom clock. The economy of space and the ease of reading a dial have led to a variety of other uses which children can discover and record.

Another device is to have a system of wheels which record the digits of the measuring number. As the geared wheels turn, the number seen through a window changes. An example familiar to many children is the odometer on a car or bicycle. On this there is often a place for tenths of a kilometre and this may be a child's first encounter with a mechanism recording tenths by putting them to the right of the ones.

FURTHER DEVELOPMENTS THROUGH MEASURING

It is apparent that the occurrence of equal quantities, as in the sides of a square, the masses of standardised packets or the certified contents of some bottles, opens the door to multiplication. The tabulation of equivalence of units, e.g.

bucketfuls 1 2 3 4 5 . . .
litres   8 16 24 32 40 . . .

is also an iteration which leads to multiplication. Experiences of this kind are useful in developing the concept of the multiplication of numbers. In the concrete situation of adding equal quantities, say 5 metres + 5 metres + 5 metres, and rewriting it as 3×5 metres, we see clearly the distinction between the kinds of answers which must be given when we ask, 'How many pieces of length 5-metres can be cut from a strip 15 metres long?' and, 'What is the length of each strip when a strip 15 metres long is cut into 3 equal pieces?' These questions suggest the kind of activities that children need before multiplication and division can be treated in an abstract way. Certainly they need many such experiences before they are able to select multiplication or division as the operation required to solve an entirely new kind of problem.

As we have seen, fractional parts appear in measuring; the use of $\frac{1}{2}, \frac{1}{4}, \frac{1}{10}$, in connection with lengths, masses, times, etc., builds up a knowledge of the ways in which some of these fractions are related. Even more important is the growth in understanding of the decimal notation for fractions and the consequent grasp of the usefulness of place-value notation in stating quantities to a required degree of accuracy. This is of particular importance now that calculators, which use decimal fractions and not the traditional form, have come into everyday use.

In this chapter we have outlined the remarkable growth of measuring and its dependence on number: the development of the one influences the understanding of the other. For penetration into the physical nature of the universe ever smaller units of length and mass are required. For the exploration of space by spacecraft and telescopes greater units of length are necessary. Moreover measurement has spread into other properties of objects and events; new compound units have been adopted for measuring area, volume, speed, density, etc. These are discussed in Chapters 26, 29 and 36.

Measures in the National Curriculum

In this chapter we have seen how children acquire much of the knowledge of measures required at Levels 3, 4 and 5 of the National Curriculum.

Some statements in the Programme of Study which are covered are:

- Use a wider range of metric units of length, capacity, 'weight' and standard units of time.

- Choose and use appropriate units and instruments; interpret numbers on a range of measuring instruments, with appropriate accuracy.

- Make estimates based on familiar units.

(AT2: Number, Level 3)

- Make sensible estimates of a range of measures in relation to everyday objects.

- Understand the relationships between units of length/'weight'/capacity/time.

(AT2: Level 4)

- Use Imperial units still in daily use and know their rough metric equivalents.

- Convert one metric unit to another.

(AT2: Level 5)

17 | MULTIPLICATION AND DIVISION

ITERATION OF THE COUNTING SET

As children use a small counting set in making counts of things around them, they quickly acquire skill in counting in twos, threes and other numbers. Some things, such as eyes, gloves or feet will naturally be counted in pairs, counting 'two, four, six, eight,. . .'. The wheels of toy cars will be counted 'four, eight, twelve,. . .'. When children have grouped sticks into triangles to make counting sets of three (*see page 176*), they will count again the total number of sticks, using the count 'three, six, nine,. . .'. From such experiences the idea of adding equal numbers, or of multiplication, develops.

A convenient way of recording such facts as they are discovered is to tabulate them (Figure 17 : 1):

Figure 17 : 1

Triangles	1	2	3	4 . . .
Sticks	3	6	9	12 . . .

The facts can also be shown in a picture graph on squared paper. A very simple arrangement is shown in Figure 17 : 2. Above the line, each in one square, are arranged the sticks, and below the line the equivalent number of triangles.

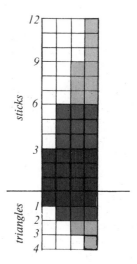

Figure 17 : 3

Children who are used to recording counts on squared paper will find this a natural arrangement, and it is one which develops very easily, as the children grow older, into a conventional straight-line graph. In order to show this development Figures 17 : 3 to 17 : 6 show the same graph constructed at four stages in the development of children's graphical work.

In Figure 17 : 3 the sticks and triangles used in the first graph are replaced by squares of coloured paper, making a block graph. In Figure 17 : 4, the number of triangles is no longer shown by blocks, but is written along the horizontal axis.

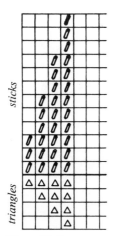

Figure 17 : 2

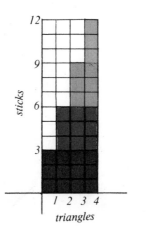

Figure 17 : 4

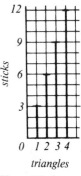

Figure 17 : 5

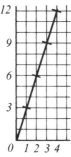

Figure 17 : 6

In Figure 17 : 5 the blocks of the bar graphs are replaced by lines (the lines of the graph paper have been used). At this stage the additional fact that 0 triangles have 0 sides has been shown on the graph.

In Figure 17 : 6 only the highest points of the vertical lines are marked, and these are joined by a line. The line is an aid to visibility and can also be used for interpolation. The graph has also become an abstract graph of threes, instead of a representation of triangles, and from it can be read such information as

$$1\tfrac{1}{2} \text{ threes} = 4\tfrac{1}{2}$$

which has no meaning in terms of triangles and sides.

From the time children begin to count in twos and threes, they will record their counts in writing as well as in graphs or pictures. A count of Wellington boots in the classroom on a wet day might be recorded as in Figure 17 : 7.

A table of twos can be built up from this (Figure 17 : 8). At first, children read $2 + 2 + 2 + 2$ as 'four twos', and learn that another way of writing it is 4×2. The meaning of the multiplication sign is extended later (*see page 208*). Children can also verify on their calculators that the keystrokes

4 × 2 =

give the same result as

2 + 2 + 2 + 2 =

Children can build up other multiplication tables by using equal groupings of things which they can find. An example is shown in Figure 17 : 9.

Five is the number of fingers on a hand, and seven the number of days in a week. Ten is the number of pence in a ten-pence piece, and is the base of our notational system. It is this last property which makes the table of tens both the easiest and the most important of the multiplication tables. Figure 17 : 10 shows the beginning of the

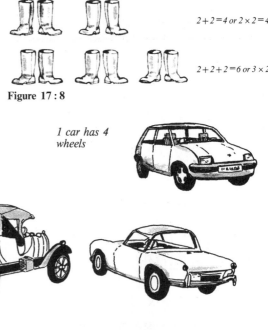

$2 \text{ or } 1 \times 2 = 2$

$2 + 2 = 4 \text{ or } 2 \times 2 = 4$

$2 + 2 + 2 = 6 \text{ or } 3 \times 2 = 6$

Figure 17 : 8

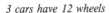

$$2 + 2 + 2 + 2 = 8$$

Figure 17 : 7

1 car has 4 wheels

2 cars have 8 wheels

3 cars have 12 wheels

Figure 17 : 9

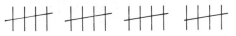

Cuisenaire ten-rods

Figure 17 : 10

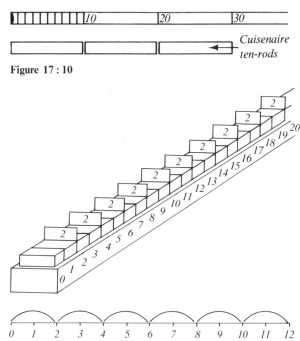

Figure 17 : 11

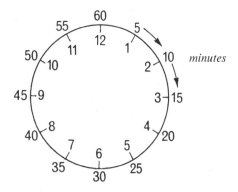

minutes

Figure 17 : 12

table of tens laid out using structural apparatus and a tape-measure.

The number tracks of structural apparatus are also very useful in building up tables, as is drawing jumps in equal steps along a paper number line (Figure 17 : 11).

When children are learning to tell the time, they count minutes round the clock in fives, and so build up the table of fives (Figure 17 : 12). They can also learn the 'gate' method of recording counts, which is useful in such activities as making a traffic census. Every time a car goes by a mark is made, but a long row of marks is confusing to count.

The largest number of things which can easily be recognised without counting is 4, so the fifth mark is made across the first four

and a new 'gate is then started. The number 18 would be represented by

This gives further practice in counting in fives. The calculator can also be used in the building up of tables by repeated addition. Figure 17 : 13 shows

the table of fours built up both by repeated addition and by using the multiplication key. On many calculators, the *constant facility* provides a short-cut in repeated addition so that the sequence of keystrokes $\boxed{4}$ $\boxed{+}$ $\boxed{=}$ $\boxed{=}$ $\boxed{=}$ $\boxed{=}$ produces the displays 4, 8, 12, 16, 20.

When they use calculators, children are not restricted in the size of number whose table of multiples they build up. They may usefully build up, and record, tables of multiples of such numbers as 20, 30, 40, . . . , 100, 200, . . . , 25, 250, and so on, thus building up knowledge of the way multiples of these important numbers behave.

The fact that calculators are increasingly used in arithmetical calculation does not mean that children no longer need to learn the multiplication tables for numbers up to 9. The ability to multiply single-digit numbers mentally remains very important, both for convenience and for checking that the calculator is producing an answer of the expected size in some complicated calculation. Calculators do not always produce correct answers, occasionally because they malfunction, but more often because the human operator presses a wrong key without noticing it. Thus the ability to estimate results has become more important in the calculator age, and the ability to multiply single-digit numbers is the foundation of estimation.

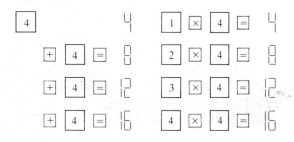

Figure 17 : 13

THE COMMUTATIVE LAW FOR MULTIPLICATION

When children write 3×4, they may arrange the three fours as three rows of four things, or if they use structural apparatus they may make a rectangular block from the rods. A rectangular block of the same size and shape can be made from four threes (Figure 17 : 14).

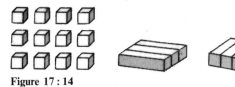

Figure 17 : 14

From this arrangement it can be seen that four threes are equal to three fours.

The fact that the order of a multiplication does not matter, that $3 \times 4 = 4 \times 3$, and in general that $a \times b = b \times a$, becomes so familiar to us by constant use that it is difficult to remember how surprising it can be at first. This law is known as the *commutative law for multiplication*. For any two numbers a and b,

$$a \times b = b \times a.$$

Children need a good deal of experience of the commutative law for multiplication if it is to become part of their mathematical equipment; it is very necessary that they should be able to use it spontaneously. At first, 3×4 means $4 + 4 + 4$, and 4×3 means $3 + 3 + 3 + 3$. The two situations look very different, and when illustrated in a concrete way, the illustrations of them are very

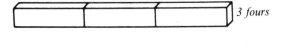

3 fours

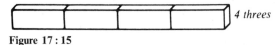

4 threes

Figure 17 : 15

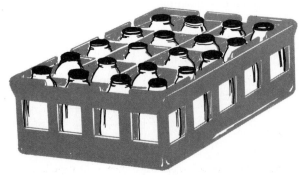

Figure 17 : 16

different (Figure 17 : 15).

The rectangular crate of milk bottles (Figure 17 : 16) provides a useful example where

5 rows of 4 bottles = 4 rows of 5 bottles.

During the first few school years children are abstracting the concept of number from many concrete situations involving numbers of things and they also begin to abstract the concept of multiplication of numbers from varied experiences of counting equal groupings of things. If they are given enough suitable concrete experiences like those suggested above, in which they can arrange equivalent sets in two different ways, they will abstract from these experiences the fact that the order of the numbers which are multiplied together does not matter. When they have reached this stage, children who count the milkbottles in the crate can think of the number of bottles as 5 multiplied by 4, irrespective of whether they have counted 5 rows of 4 or 4 rows of 5. Then the commutative law for multiplication has become meaningful, and they can write 5×4 for either 5 fours or 4 fives.

The calculator provides a further method of verifying the commutative law, and children are not restricted to numbers small enough for them to be able to multiply with apparatus, or mentally. They can verify that, for instance

$$27 \times 45 = 1215$$
$$\text{and} \quad 45 \times 27 = 1215$$

Many such examples can be tried very quickly, and children can choose them for themselves, so that they generalise from an arbitrary choice of examples. However, the calculator only shows *that* the commutative law for multiplication works, and not *why* it works. Hence, some concrete method should be used as well.

'THREE TIMES AS MUCH. . .'

In many of its uses the idea of multiplication has a slightly different emphasis from that stressed in the previous sections. This emphasis is found in the words 'three times as much' or 'multiplied by three'. This is the aspect of multiplication which is used in working out the cost of 3 metres of cloth, in enlarging a plan to 3 times its original (linear) dimensions, or in adapting a recipe for 3 times the number of people. In each of these examples, every quantity is increased so that it becomes three times the original size, and every number becomes three times the original number. A relation diagram shows clearly the 'three times as much' aspect of multiplication by three.

The three times table

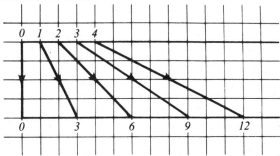

Figure 17 : 17

Each length on the upper number line of Figure 17 : 17 is increased on the lower number line to three times its original length.

The multiplication table which is needed for this operation has a different appearance from the table of threes which the children have built up earlier. Figure 17 : 18 shows the *table of threes* and the *table of 'three times as much'* together, arranged as block graphs.

By the commutative law, the two tables in Figure 17 : 18 are equivalent to one another and can be used interchangeably, but only when children have reached an understanding of the commutative law can they move freely from one to the other. Children who have built up their concept of multiplication through a sufficient variety of

experiences will eventually use 3 × 4 as an expression of all the interchangeable ideas:

  i) three fours,
 ii) four threes,
iii) three times [as much as][1] four,
 iv) four times [as much as] three,
  v) three multiplied by four (that is, three increased to four times its size),
 vi) four multiplied by three.

THE MULTIPLICATION TABLES AND THEIR PATTERNS

The basic multiplication facts are much more valuable when known separately, rather than only as parts of a table. After much use children should know each fact as well as they know the addition bonds, so that the mention of any two of the three numbers 7, 8 and 56 in a multiplication situation will immediately call to mind the remaining one, just as in addition situations the three numbers 7, 8 and 15 are indissolubly linked together.

Using multiplication operations in such contexts as the shop, and in weighing and measuring, will provide some of the practice in multiplication which children need in order to remember the facts. Several other activities such as graphical work and the search for pattern in the tables will be suggested in this section. All these activities help to fix the multiplication facts in the memory, to make them more meaningful, and so cut down the burden of rote learning.

1×1

$2 \times 1 \; 2 \times 2$

$3 \times 1 \; 3 \times 2 \; 3 \times 3$

$4 \times 1 \; 4 \times 2 \; 4 \times 3 \; 4 \times 4$

$5 \times 1 \; 5 \times 2 \; 5 \times 3 \; 5 \times 4 \; 5 \times 5$

$6 \times 1 \; 6 \times 2 \; 6 \times 3 \; 6 \times 4 \; 6 \times 5 \; 6 \times 6$

$7 \times 1 \; 7 \times 2 \; 7 \times 3 \; 7 \times 4 \; 7 \times 5 \; 7 \times 6 \; 7 \times 7$

$8 \times 1 \; 8 \times 2 \; 8 \times 3 \; 8 \times 4 \; 8 \times 5 \; 8 \times 6 \; 8 \times 7 \; 8 \times 8$

$9 \times 1 \; 9 \times 2 \; 9 \times 3 \; 9 \times 4 \; 9 \times 5 \; 9 \times 6 \; 9 \times 7 \; 9 \times 8 \; 9 \times 9$

Figure 17 : 19

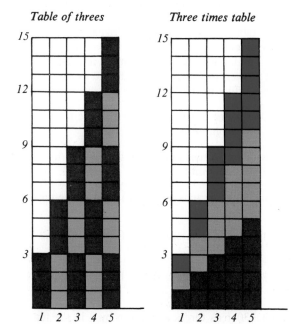

Figure 17 : 18

[1]The words in square brackets are often left unsaid, but are implicit in 'three times four'.

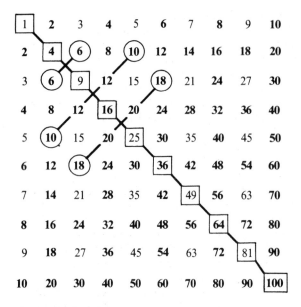

Figure 17:20

Multiples of 4

1	2	3	4	5	6	7	8	9	10
2	4	6	8	10	12	14	16	18	20
3	6	9	12	15	18	21	24	27	30
4	8	12	16	20	24	28	32	36	40
5	10	15	20	25	30	35	40	45	50
6	12	18	24	30	36	42	48	54	60
7	14	21	28	35	42	49	56	63	70
8	16	24	32	40	48	56	64	72	80
9	18	27	36	45	54	63	72	81	90
10	20	30	40	50	60	70	80	90	100

Figure 17:22

By using the commutative law for multiplication, the number of multiplication facts which must be known for future use in the multiplication and division of larger numbers is reduced to 45. These are shown in Figure 17:19, and only the facts in the lower right-hand part of this table are likely to be troublesome to the memory.

When children make the conventional multiplication square (Figure 17:20), they should notice its symmetry about the leading diagonal as an expression of the commutative law, and should notice that the square numbers (*see page 274*) lie on the leading diagonal. Other patterns in the numbers will be suggested later, and it is an interesting activity for children to find, and explain, as many patterns as possible in the square. Underlining every even number or every multiple of 3 in the square will provoke discussion. Figures 17:21 and 17:22 show the patterns made by colouring multiples of 3 and 4.

The table of 10 is intimately linked with the place-value system, and an *understanding* of it is vital. The table of ten appears more impressive when written in symbols than are the words corresponding to the figures.

$1 \times 10 = 10$ one ten is shown by 1 in the tens column

$2 \times 10 = 20$ two tens are shown by 2 in the tens column

$3 \times 10 = 30$ three tens are shown by 3 in the tens column

$10 \times 1 = 10$ ten ones are shown by 1 in the tens column

$10 \times 2 = 20$ ten twos are shown by 2 in the tens column

$10 \times 3 = 30$ tens threes are shown by 3 in the tens column

Multiples of 3

1	2	3	4	5	6	7	8	9	10
2	4	6	8	10	12	14	16	18	20
3	6	9	12	15	18	21	24	27	30
4	8	12	16	20	24	28	32	36	40
5	10	15	20	25	30	35	40	45	50
6	12	18	24	30	36	42	48	54	60
7	14	21	28	35	42	49	56	63	70
8	16	24	32	40	48	56	64	72	80
9	18	27	36	45	54	63	72	81	90
10	20	30	40	50	60	70	80	90	100

Figure 17:21

Children enjoy searching for patterns in all the tables, and once a pattern has been found it helps them to remember the table. A useful piece of apparatus for showing multiplication patterns visually is paper marked in a grid of 100 squares, each square with sides about 1 cm long. The squares can either be blank or numbered from 1 to 100. This can be used in different ways at different stages. Children can colour successive blocks of 2 squares, 3 squares, etc., in different colours. Counting such equivalent sets leads to multiplication, and also produces attractive patterns. Later on every second square, every third square, etc., on the numbered grid can be coloured, familiarising the children with the numbers in each table, and associating the tables with visual patterns, a few of which are shown in Figure 17 : 23.

Older children, by superimposing the patterns of different tables upon one another, can begin to study factors, multiples and prime numbers.

As well as spatial patterns among the digits of the numbers in the tables. An obvious example is that in the table of nines the tens digit *increases* by one and the units digit decreases by one on each line of the table (Figure 17 : 24). Consideration of the reason for this may lead older children to feel a need for algebraic symbolism, and to examine similar patterns in other bases.

Using a calculator, such a pattern can be explored much further. Figure 17 : 25 shows the multiples of 9 up to 50 × 9. Many further facts are now noticeable, and children should be encouraged to find all the patterns they can. For instance, at the bottom each column,

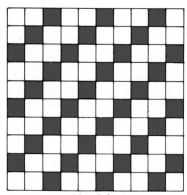

Table of threes

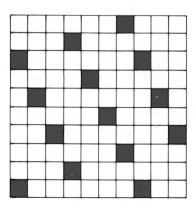

Table of sevens

1	2	3	4	5	6	7	8	9	10
11	12	13	14	15	16	17	18	19	20
21	22	23	24	25	26	27	28	29	30
31	32	33	34	35	36	37	38	39	40
41	42	43	44	45	46	47	48	49	50
51	52	53	54	55	56	57	58	59	60
61	62	63	64	65	66	67	68	69	70
71	72	73	74	75	76	77	78	79	80
81	82	83	84	85	86	87	88	89	90
91	92	93	94	95	96	97	98	99	100

Table of eights

Figure 17 : 23

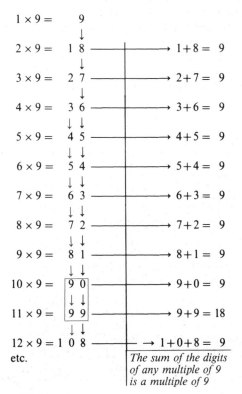

$$1 \times 9 = \quad 9$$
$$2 \times 9 = \quad 1\ 8 \longrightarrow 1+8 = 9$$
$$3 \times 9 = \quad 2\ 7 \longrightarrow 2+7 = 9$$
$$4 \times 9 = \quad 3\ 6 \longrightarrow 3+6 = 9$$
$$5 \times 9 = \quad 4\ 5 \longrightarrow 4+5 = 9$$
$$6 \times 9 = \quad 5\ 4 \longrightarrow 5+4 = 9$$
$$7 \times 9 = \quad 6\ 3 \longrightarrow 6+3 = 9$$
$$8 \times 9 = \quad 7\ 2 \longrightarrow 7+2 = 9$$
$$9 \times 9 = \quad 8\ 1 \longrightarrow 8+1 = 9$$
$$10 \times 9 = \quad 9\ 0 \longrightarrow 9+0 = 9$$
$$11 \times 9 = \quad 9\ 9 \longrightarrow 9+9 = 18$$
$$12 \times 9 = 1\ 0\ 8 \longrightarrow 1+0+8 = 9$$
etc.

The sum of the digits of any multiple of 9 is a multiple of 9

Figure 17 : 24

9	99	189	279	369
18	108	198	288	378
27	117	207	297	387
36	126	216	306	396
45	135	225	315	405
54	144	234	324	414
63	153	243	333	423
72	162	252	342	432
81	171	261	351	441
90	180	270	360	450

Figure 17 : 25

it can be seen that

$$10 \times 9 = 90$$
$$20 \times 9 = 180$$
$$30 \times 9 = 270$$
$$40 \times 9 = 360$$
$$50 \times 9 = 450,$$

and so ideas needed for the multiplication of large numbers are building up. Reading across the first row, we have

$$9 \xrightarrow{+90} 99 \xrightarrow{+90} 189 \xrightarrow{+90} 279 \xrightarrow{+90} 369,$$

so that $1 \times 9 \xrightarrow{+(10 \times 9)} 11 \times 9 \xrightarrow{+(10 \times 9)}$

$$21 \times 9 \xrightarrow{+(10 \times 9)} 31 \times 9 \xrightarrow{+(10 \times 9)} 41 \times 9$$

and similarly in the other rows. It is now a very small step to saying that

21 nines = 20 nines + 1 nine

When facts such as this are found, other tables can be searched for similar patterns.

Children may also plot all the multiplication tables which they are using on the same graph for comparison (Figure 17 : 26).[2]

As they draw this graph, children are gaining experience which will lead to the development of concepts such as that a straight-line graph shows steady growth, and that more rapid growth is shown by a steeper graph.[3]

Discussion of graphs which would occupy the area of Figure 17 : 26 below the 'one times table', and of interpolation (*see page 261*) on the graph, will lead to the multiplication of decimal fractions. The graph can also be used to answer such questions as, 'How many 8s in 96?'.

---

[2]It may be advisable to reduce the scale on the vertical axis, for if this is not done a piece of graph paper whose height is at least 10 times its width will be needed. As a wallchart, this gives a real impression of the rates of growth.

[3]This will lead on to the gradient of a line, the tangent of an angle, and the ideas of differential calculus at the Secondary stage.

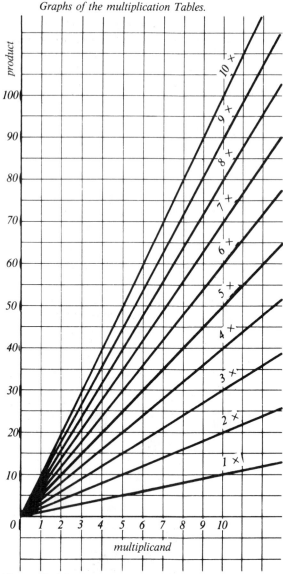

Graphs of the multiplication Tables.

Figure 17 : 26

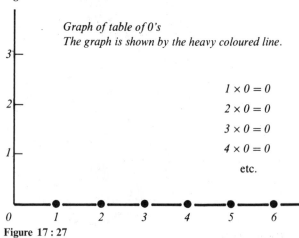

Graph of table of 0's
The graph is shown by the heavy coloured line.

$$1 \times 0 = 0$$
$$2 \times 0 = 0$$
$$3 \times 0 = 0$$
$$4 \times 0 = 0$$

etc.

Figure 17 : 27

Multiplication facts involving zero are shown in Figure 17:26, as each of the graphs passes through the origin. These facts call for special mention, as children often make mistakes such as $5 \times 0 = 5$ which are due to failure to visualise the situation. A child who knows that 5×0 means $0 + 0 + 0 + 0 + 0$ will not make this mistake, and a graph of the 'table of 0's' is sufficiently startling to fix it in the memory (Figure 17:27).

The sequence of keystrokes

$$\boxed{0} \ \boxed{+} \ \boxed{0} \ \boxed{=} \ \boxed{=} \ \boxed{=} \ \ldots$$

on a calculator with a constant facility gives an unchanging 0 on the display.

OTHER PICTORIAL REPRESENTATIONS OF MULTIPLICATION

Children who have seen the effect of such a transformation as 'add 7' on a set of numbers (*see page 106*) will also think of multiplication by a fixed number as a transformation which can act on any set of numbers. The transformation 'multiply by 4' transforms the numbers 1, 2, 3, . . ., 10 into 4, 8, 12, . . ., 40. Each multiplication table states the result of applying a multiplication transformation to the set 1, 2, 3, . . ., 10. Figure 17:28 illustrates two of these transformations, using both function machines and relation diagrams.

Such transformations can be illustrated more clearly by number lines. Figure 17:29 shows a

The transformation '×4'

Figure 17:29

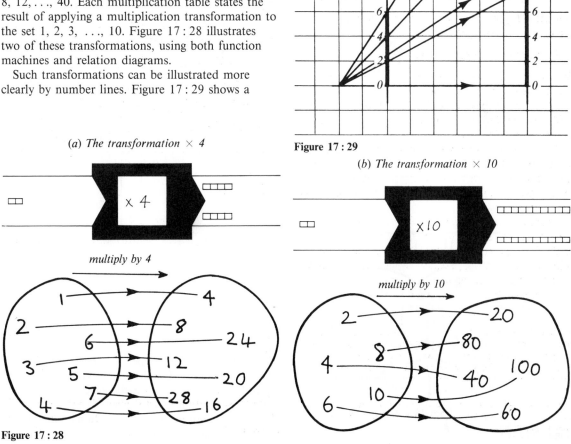

(a) The transformation × 4

multiply by 4

(b) The transformation × 10

multiply by 10

Figure 17:28

relation diagram of the transformation 'multiply by 4'. For an addition transformation, the lines joining each point of the number line to its image are parallel (*see page 106*); for a multiplication transformation, these lines are not parallel, but radiate from a point. The diagram shows very clearly the result of multiplying *any length* on the number line by 4. For example, we see that a line of length 6 units, enlarged to 4 times its length, becomes 24 units long. Also, although 10 does not belong to the set of whole number multiples of 4,

$$10 = 2\tfrac{1}{2} \times 4$$

Children may also use a set of cards, each one bearing a number, for instance up to 30, to sort out the sets of multiples of 2, 3, etc., and will illustrate their results in Venn diagrams as in Figures 17 : 30 and 17 : 31. They will find that numbers which are multiples of both 2 and 3 are in fact multiples of 6, and this will lead on to later work on factors. As children become older and more able to handle complicated classifications, they may extend their diagrams to illustrate classifications such as those shown in Figures 17 : 32 and 17 : 33.

multiples of 3

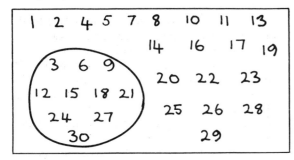

Figure 17 : 30

multiples of 2 and of 3

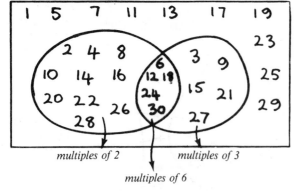

Figure 17 : 31

(*a*) *multiples of 2, 3, 4 and 9*

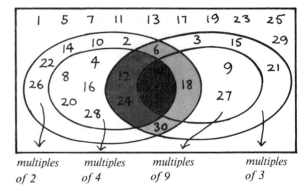

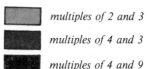 *multiples of 2 and 3*

multiples of 4 and 3

multiples of 4 and 9

Figure 17 : 32

	multiples of 2	not multiples of 2
multiples of 3	6 12 18 24 30	3 9 15 21 27
not multiples of 3	2 4 8 10 14 16 20 22 26 28	1 5 7 11 13 17 19 23 25 29

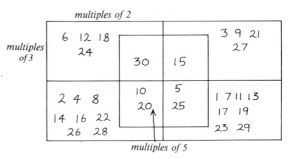

Figure 17 : 33

THE BEGINNING OF DIVISION

Division is the inverse operation of multiplication, and is related to it in the same way that subtraction, the inverse operation of addition, is related to addition. Children, however, first use the idea of division at a very early stage, long before the concept of multiplication has become at all precise. Children use two fundamentally different types of division, the first of which occurs when they share out sweets with friends, and the second when they try to find out how many two-penny bars of chocolate they can buy with a ten-pence piece.

The first type of division, *sharing*, is mathematically less simple, but children usually use it earlier, as no counting is needed at first. Sweets can be shared, or cards dealt out, without the child knowing either how many sweets there are, or how many children they are to be shared between. All the child has to do is to go round and round the set of children, giving one sweet to each child until there are no more sweets, or until there are not enough for another round. This is a mathematical experience of sharing, but it does not become numerical until the child knows that there are 12 sweets and 4 children, so that any mishaps in the sharing can be checked by all the children seeing that they have 3 sweets.

In sharing, the *number in the total set* (12 sweets) to be shared is known, and the *number of subsets* into which it is to be shared is known (there are 4 children). The unknown quantity is the *number in each share*. Sharing is mathematically a rather advanced operation, as children cannot predict the size of a share until they can answer the question, 'Four times what equals twelve?', and this demands considerable familiarity with the numbers. Of course they can *do* the sharing much earlier, and should have the experience of sharing things out and recording the results.

To look further at the mathematical difficulty of sharing, we shall use structural apparatus to solve the sharing problem, 'Divide 20 centimetres of string into 4 equal parts.' Structural apparatus is certainly not ideal for this problem; it is much easier with a piece of string, which can be folded into four equal parts. But children equipped with structural apparatus will put out 20, and then have to find four equal rods which together make the 20. Unless they know that four fives equal 20, they can only use an estimate of length, and trial and error, to guide them in the choice of five-rods (Figure 17 : 34).

The other aspect of division, *grouping*, is mathematically rather simpler, but seems at first to children to be completely unrelated to the operation of sharing. *Grouping* is splitting up a set into counting sets of known number. How many two-penny bars of chocolate can be bought with a ten-pence coin? How many triangles can be made with 12 sticks? How many 2-centimetre-wide strips of paper can be cut from a 12-centimetre-wide piece? Children group a set of 10 pennies into subsets each containing 2 pennies, or make triangles with the sticks and see that they have 4 of them. They measure 2 centimetres on the piece of paper and cut off a strip, and then another and another until there is nothing left. In grouping, the *size of the total set* is known, and the *size of each part* or subset is known. The unknown quantity is the *number of subsets*.

Grouping problems are more easily solved by the use of structural apparatus than are sharing problems. The problem of finding how many two-penny bars of chocolate can be bought with 10 pence, or of finding how many 2s there are in 10, is solved by putting two-rods end of end to make up 10, and counting how many rods were used. Children know which rod to choose, and have to find how many are needed to make 10.

To sum up, a *sharing* problem is of the type

divide 12 into 4 equal parts,

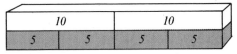

Figure 17 : 34

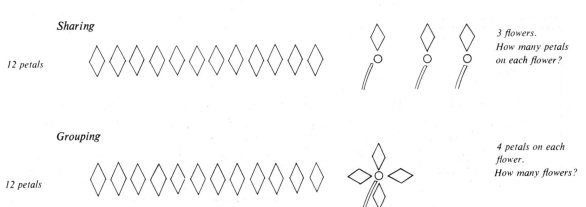

Figure 17 : 35

whereas a *grouping* problem is of the type

how many 4s are there in 12?

(See Figure 17 : 35.)

THE RELATION BETWEEN SHARING AND GROUPING

It is usual to give the name of *division* to both sharing and grouping problems, and to represent both situations by the same symbols $\frac{12}{4}$ or $12 \div 4$, but when children first use division ideas these should always be set in a practical situation so that an appropriate method can be used: a sharing method for a sharing problem, or a grouping method for a grouping problem. Children's power over division increases when they begin to understand the connection between sharing and grouping, and to connect both operations with other operations on numbers.

Grouping they may think of as repeated subtraction. They want to find how many fours there are in 12, so they take four away from 12, and then take away another four and another four until they cannot go any further.

$$12 - 4 - 4 - 4 = 0$$

They see that they have taken away 3 fours, so there are 3 fours in 12. A calculator with a constant facility enables division by repeated subtraction to be done very simply. The sequence of keystrokes is shown in Figure 17 : 36. Children count the number of times 4 has been subtracted. They are not restricted to numbers within the range of the tables so that the sequence

$$\boxed{1}\ \boxed{7}\ \boxed{2}\ \boxed{-}\ \boxed{2}\ \boxed{3}\ \boxed{=}\ \boxed{=}\ \boxed{=}\ \dots$$

produces the successive displays

172, 149, 126, 103, 80, 57, 34, 11.

Hence 23 can be subtracted from 172 seven times, leaving a remainder of 11.

display

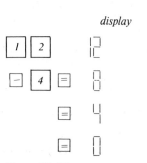

Figure 17 : 36

Alternatively, children may think of grouping as the inverse of repeated addition. They want to find out how many fours there are in 12, so they build up in fours until they reach 12. Figure 17 : 37 shows this done with structural apparatus. The calculator can also be used to build up in this way, and to perform division by counting how many times the divisor must be added on to make the dividend.

Division is also *inverse multiplication*. In the example of Figure 17 : 37 we supply the missing number in the multiplication, 'What number of fours is equal to twelve?' or

$$\boxed{n} \times 4 = 12$$

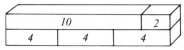

Figure 17 : 37

Sharing, however, presents a different arrangement. 'Divide a set of 12 things into 4 equal parts' requires the choice of 4 subsets with the same number of members which together give 12, or finding the missing number in the multiplication, 'Four times what number is equal to twelve?' or

$$4 \times \boxed{n} = 12$$

Both types of division are inverse of multiplication; that is, multiplications in which the produce is known and one of its factors is missing. Similarly, subtraction is inverse addition, in which the sum is known and one of the parts is missing. The subtraction of 4 from 12 requires the finding of the missing number in

$$4 + \boxed{n} = 12$$

The division of 12 by 4 requires the finding of the missing number in either

$$4 \times \boxed{n} = 12 \text{ (sharing)}$$

or

$$\boxed{n} \times 4 = 12 \text{ (grouping)}.$$

There are two different division arrangements because the missing number may be either the number of sets or the number in each set. In concrete situations these two numbers have clearly differentiated functions and are not interchangeable. So at the concrete stage grouping and sharing are very different to children, and must be distinguished.

This complication does not arise in subtraction, as the order of the two numbers n and 4 in

$n + 4 = 12$ is unimportant. Children know that addition is commutative long before they know that multiplication is commutative, for concrete situations involving multiplication are not symmetrical.

When the commutativity of multiplication is understood, it becomes clear that there must be a close connection between sharing and grouping, since $4 \times n = n \times 4$, so that a solution of $4 \times n = 12$ is also a solution of $n \times 4 = 12$. Grouping is also the method usually chosen for the division of large numbers. The division $324 \div 9$ is usually worked by finding how many nines there are in 324 (grouping), rather than by dividing 324 into 9 equal parts (sharing). Even if 324 is the number of children to be shared between, and taught by, 9 teachers in a school, the method of calculation used by many adults seems to be based on the grouping method of finding how many 9s there are in 324.

We shall now examine the connection between concrete situations involving sharing and those involving grouping. Suppose that 12 cards are to be dealt out to 4 children. This is the sharing process of dividing into 4 equal parts, but if the dealing is done one round at a time it becomes a grouping process. For the first round of dealing a set of 4 cards is used, and one of them is given to each child (Figure 17 : 38).

A   B   C   D

Figure 17 : 38

In the next round another set of 4 cards is used, and so on until the cards are exhausted. Each child receives one card from each set of four cards. The problem of dividing 12 cards into 4 equivalent sets has been replaced by the problem of dividing 12 cards into sets containing 4 cards (Figure 17 : 39). The sharing has been replaced by a two-stage process:

  i) grouping in sets of 4, and then

  ii) sharing each set of 4, one card to each child.

This method can be used for any sharing problem, and children often use it spontaneously. If you watch a child sharing bricks between himself and a friend, you will find that the child will often take a brick in each hand, forming a set of 2 bricks, and then put one of these bricks in each pile. Most children, however, need to have this natural process

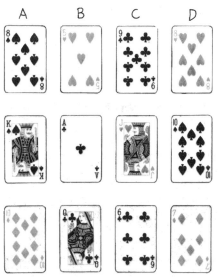

Figure 17 : 39

made explicit to them, so that they realise that sharing and grouping are interchangeable as far as the *numbers* are concerned.

INVERSE MULTIPLICATION

If division is to become a meaningful rather than a mechanical process, children must pass through the three stages of:

  i) using grouping and sharing as two different operations and solving problems by the use of concrete apparatus,

  ii) relating sharing to grouping,

  iii) using their knowledge of multiplication to deal with both types of division by the same numerical procedure.

At the last stage the long descriptions which were necessary in order to express sharing and grouping situations can be replaced by the abstract 'divide 12 by 4'. *Divide* is a general, neutral word which is not tied to either sharing or grouping; it is appropriately used at the stage at which it no longer matters to children whether they are sharing or grouping. They are now performing the operation inverse to multiplication, and are performing that operation with abstract numbers. 'Divide 12 by 4' corresponds to either

  i) 'how many 4s equal 12?' or

  ii) '4 times what number equals 12?', and the answer is '3, because 3 multiplied by 4 = 12'.

SOME DIVISION ACTIVITIES

As children move into the final stage of seeing division as inverse multiplication it may be helpful to describe some of the multiplication activities suggested on page 212 in the language of division. Figure 17 : 40 shows the use of the graph of multiplication tables to find $96 \div 8$.

Older children may like to take a number such as 24, which has many factors, and draw a graph of the results of dividing it by 1, 2, 3,... (Figure 17 : 41).

The spaces left blank in this table may be read off from the graph, and also supplied by the calculator, so that results such as

$$24 \div 5 = 4 \cdot 8$$
$$\text{and } 24 \div 7 = 3 \cdot 428 \ldots$$

are available for discussion. Similarly,

$$24 \div 0 \cdot 5 = 48$$
$$\text{and } 24 \div 0 \cdot 8 = 30$$

are shown on the calculator, and fit the pattern of the graph. Children then need to understand why these results work as they do (*see page 223*).

This graph is also a useful example of a curved graph. Some points on the same graph (which is a rectangular hyperbola) (*see page 396*) can also be obtained by marking all the positions of the number 24 in the multiplication table of Figure 17 : 20 (see Figure 17 : 42). The equivalence of Figures 17 : 41 and 17 : 42 can be discussed.

Older children should also investigate divisions involving 0, and may realise not only that

$0 \div 2 = 0$, since the solution of $\boxed{n} \times 2 = 0$ is $n = 0$,
$0 \div 5 = 0$, since the solution of $\boxed{n} \times 5 = 0$ is $n = 0$,

and so on, but that

$2 \div 0$ has no answer, since $\boxed{n} \times 0 = 2$ has no solutions

and that

$0 \div 0$ may be any number,

since the equation $\boxed{n} \times 0 = 0$ has every number as a solution.

The calculator very helpfully supplies an error message when either

$$\boxed{2} \ \boxed{\div} \ \boxed{0} \ \boxed{=}$$
$$\text{or } \boxed{0} \ \boxed{\div} \ \boxed{0} \ \boxed{=}$$

is attempted.

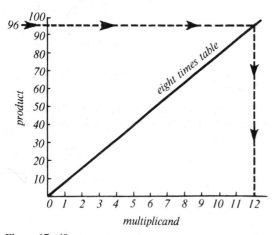

Figure 17 : 40

$24 \div$	1	2	3	4	5	6	7	8	9
quotient	24	12	8	6		4		3	

The division of 24

Figure 17 : 41

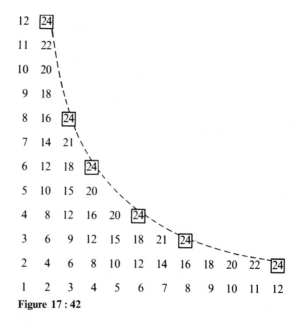

Figure 17 : 42

THE LANGUAGE OF DIVISION

Some very odd forms of wording are occasionally used in the hope of making multiplication and division clear to children. The words which can be heard on some children's lips: 'You times it by 3' are objectionable, but the reading of $12 \div 3$ as 'share 12 by 3' is not much better. 'Share 12 between 3 people' and 'divide 12 by 3' are both correct, but the hybrid will have to be unlearnt later, and is restrictive in idea, although the word 'share' must be used in sharing situations.

The very common reading of $8\overline{)72}$ as 'eights into 72' is not clear, and could be replaced by, 'How many eights are there in 72?', or 'one-eighth of 72', either of which is a correct reading of the symbols $72 \div 8$. Division is not commutative, so that the order is important;

$$72 \div 8 = 9,$$
$$\text{but } 8 \div 72 = 0 \cdot 111 \ldots$$

The symbols 8 and 72 in $8\overline{)72}$ occur in the reverse order from those in $72 \div 8$, and this is a frequent cause of confusion at the later stage at which both divisions are meaningful and children have to decide which is appropriate to the problem.

The calculator brings home the importance of order in division very clearly:

[7] [2] [÷] [8] [=]

produces the expected answer of 9, which can be verified by the keystrokes

[7] [2] [÷] [8] [=] [×] [8] [=]

On the other hand,

[8] [÷] [7] [2] [=]

produces what a child will probably at this stage think of as rubbish.

Until decimals are understood, division with a remainder can produce problems for children who are using a calculator. For instance,

[7] [3] [÷] [8] [=]

gives $9 \cdot 125$. Children can learn that the part of the display after the point indicates that there is a remainder. The answer is the part before the point, or 9, and the remainder can be found by working out 9×8 and subtracting it from 73.

Children who regularly use calculators often discover that $\cdot 125$ is 'the way the calculator writes $\frac{1}{8}$'.

Multiplication and division ideas in the National Curriculum

Understanding of the ideas of multiplication and division receives only brief mention in the National Curriculum, but this understanding underlies the mentions of multiplication and division problems and facts. At Level 3, children are expected to know the ideas of multiplication and division:

- solve problems involving multiplication or division of whole numbers or money, using a calculator where necessary.

(AT2: Number, Level 3)

By Level 4, the multiplication facts need to be known:

- learn multiplication facts up to 10×10 and use them in multiplication and division problems.

(AT2, Level 4)

By Level 4, also, children are expected to be able to make use of place value in multiplication.

- understand the effect of multiplying whole numbers by 10 or 100.

(AT2: Number, Level 4)

18 | *The Development of Number Systems*

Early ways of writing numbers

Many children in English-speaking countries have met numbers written in Roman figures. They see them on some clock-faces, on old tombstones, and at the head of chapters in some books. In television credits, dates are given in Roman numerals. The difference between these numerals and those that have come down to us from the Hindus via the Arabs strikes children at once. They notice that familiar letters are used in place of figures and these letters may be repeated. They see that strokes or ones appear at the right of the letters, e.g. LXXIII. These Roman numerals tell us a great deal about how our modern system of notation developed.

The use of a simple sign such as a stroke, or the shape made by pressing the end of a pointed stick into a clay tablet, was very common in early civilisations for recording a count. The Egyptians used strokes for the numbers from one to nine, grouping them to make them more easily recognisable, as in Figure 18 : 1.

The Babylonians used a similar method in wedge-shaped or cuneiform markings (Figure 18 : 2).

Children may record a set similarly, or they may use beads, cubes or sticks as 'counters'. A one–one correspondence is thus made between things (the members of a set) and the strokes or other symbols used. Since there are as many separate symbols as there are things no economy has been made and no true counting may yet have taken place.

Grouping objects and animals was a common experience of primitive people and they soon gave names to the smaller groupings. A great step forward came when they recorded groupings as well as separate objects which are too few to make a grouping. Different cultures have used different groupings but most of them devised a special symbol for a grouping and recorded the number of the groupings of a particular size by repeating the symbol, just as they repeated strokes to write the smaller numbers (Figure 18 : 3).

Roman Symbols	III	XX	XXXII
Arabic Symbols	3	20	32

Figure 18 : 3

Because finger-counting is so convenient, grouping in tens developed in many countries and has replaced the groupings in fives, twelves, twenties and sixties which appeared in some ancient civilisations. We know a great deal about the early use of numbers grouped in tens from the Ahmes papyrus, a remarkable survival from Egypt of about 1700 BC. Much of the papyrus is in the British Museum where a facsimile is exhibited (Figure 18 : 4).

Many of the calculations recorded in the papyrus concern rationing during famines. This reminds us of the famines in the story of Joseph in the Bible. Joseph lived in Egypt during the era of the Ahmes papyrus and when he organised the storage of part

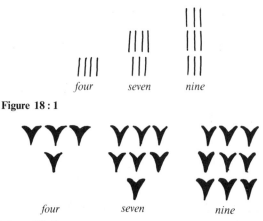

four　　*seven*　　*nine*

Figure 18 : 1

four　　*seven*　　*nine*

Figure 18 : 2

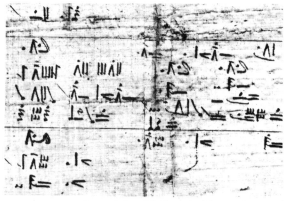

By permission of the Trustees of the British Museum.

Figure 18 : 4

of the harvests during the good years the Egyptian priests were able to work out fair shares for people and cattle in the lean years. The papyrus shows the calculations that were carried out, the ways in which addition and subtraction were performed and the ingenious device for multiplying that was invented to overcome the limitations of the Egyptian number notation. We consider this notation now in some detail as an example of the way that a number system can help or hinder the development of understanding and skill in using numbers.

EGYPTIAN NUMERALS

For a grouping of ten the Egyptians used the symbol ∩. Thus fifty three would appear as

$$∩∩∩ \atop ∩∩ \quad |\,|\,|$$

The next grouping, ten tens or a hundred, was written ⌐. Six hundred and fifty three would be written

$$⌐⌐⌐ \;\; ∩∩∩ \;\; |\,|\,| \atop ⌐⌐⌐ \;\; ∩∩$$

Symbols for one thousand, ten thousand, etc., were also invented and were used in the same repetitive way. No particular order was laid down for writing the symbols; tens could be placed either to the right or left of the units. But addition and subtraction are so much easier when like groupings are placed in the same column that the habit of writing the symbols in order of the size of the grouping became established. The use of a counting tray or abacus stabilised this order. The parallel between the Egyptian notation and the experience with structural apparatus and the abacus which modern children use can be seen in Figure 18 : 5

Figure 18 : 6

Figure 18 : 7

which represents the number three hundred and thirty two.

It seems to us a very short step from this stage to the form of numeral we use today, 332, but in fact it was many centuries before our system became general in Europe.

Addition in Egyptian numerals was cumbersome in appearance but the thought involved in the process was similar to our own, as can be seen in Figure 18 : 6.

Multiplication in such a system involves so many symbols that it would be difficult to memorise the products. For an example, see Figure 18 : 7.

Multiplication by a number greater than two could be performed by continuing to add the multiplicand. To multiply by eleven or more in this way is a tedious proceeding. Instead the Egyptians used a system of successive doubling which is similar to the modern use of the binary scale in computers. In Figure 18 : 8 we show the way in which seventeen × thirteen was carried out in the Egyptian system. Successive doubling of 17 produces 2×17, 4×17, 8×17, and so on; 13×17 can be built up from these. Since $13 = 8 + 4 + 1$, we have

$$13 \times 17 = (8 \times 17) + (4 \times 17) + (1 \times 17).$$

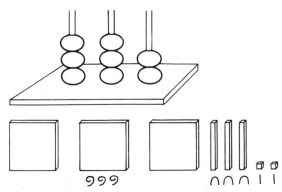

Figure 18 : 5

Figure 18 : 8

In Figure 18 : 8 modern notation is used alongside the hieroglyphics.

With so cumbersome a notation it is not surprising that the Egyptians could only handle unit fractions such as $\frac{1}{2}, \frac{1}{3}, \frac{1}{8}, \frac{1}{15}$. Decimal fractions could not develop without a new advance towards the idea of place value.

ROMAN NUMERALS

Basically, the Romans, like the Egyptians, counted in powers of ten.

X = 10
C = 10 × 10
M = 10 × 10 × 10

They also recorded groupings by repeating symbols:

231 (Arabic) = CCXXXI (Roman)

But a special feature of the Roman notation is a symbol for the five of each grouping, a half-way point to the next main grouping.

V = 5
L = 50
D = 500

This is reminiscent of counting on the fingers of one hand. It has the important advantage of making numerals easier to recognise. LXVI is a neat way to write 66 compared with the Egyptian

∩∩∩ |||
∩∩∩ |||

But the Roman system had the great disadvantage that it was based on alternating groupings, by five and by two. Out of such a notation it would be difficult to evolve a system like the Arabic in which the *position* of a figure is sufficient to tell us its value. However, the Romans made one notable advance; they used position to show whether a number was to be added to or taken from the next higher grouping when writing or reading a number. For example,

VI means V + I, i.e. 6   IV means V – I, i.e. 4
LX means L + X, i.e. 60   XL means L – X, i.e. 40

This is a first step towards making a code based on the relative position of the digits.

THE ARABIC SYSTEM

The numerals 1 to 9 which we use today are thought to have originated in India about 2000 years ago, though their form has changed a good

deal with the passing of the centuries. The Hindus used one of these signs to write the *number* of any grouping in place of repeating its symbol; thus 2674 would be written 2 thousands 6 hundreds 7 tens and 4, of course using the Hindu names. Even if the names were abbreviated this was still a lengthy numeral to write, but names were necessary until an unknown scholar in India thought of using a symbol to show that none of any particular grouping occurred. This idea of emptiness or nothingness still fascinates children and we now encourage them to use a symbol for it at 5 or 6 years of age to represent the emptiness of a plate or bowl.

The round zero is a very suitable symbol for the number of the empty set. Its importance for notation is obvious: with it the count of every set can be given a symbol using only the numerals 0 to 9. The pattern of beads on an abacus, where every rod or groove corresponds to a grouping, can always be expressed as a numeral where the digits match the beads on each column, even on an empty column. The groupings need no written names because there is a digit, beginning with the ones digit on the right, for each grouping (Figure 18 : 9).

In Figure 18 : 9, 6 is the number of tens; the zero shows that there are *no* hundreds; therefore the 3 must count thousands.

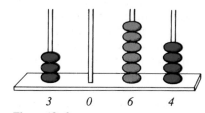

3   0   6   4

Figure 18 : 9

Since the columns can be extended as far as we please to the left we can write a number as large as we wish using only the ten symbols 0, 1, 2, . . ., 9. Because the *position* of any grouping is known, the written forms of computations can be neatly arranged in columns without labels. The simplifications which resulted from the general adoption of this system in Europe in the sixteenth century were of tremendous benefit to the expanding trade of the Renaissance period. In the late twentieth century the importance, for children's mathematical development, of a full understanding of the place-value system of naming and writing numbers cannot be over-estimated.

SYMBOLS FOR FRACTIONS

We have seen that the Egyptians found fractions difficult to handle. The idea of a part was familiar.

It was frequently thought of in relation to measures as being a smaller unit. For example, one-sixtieth part of an hour was called a *minute* or small part. A sixtieth part of a minute was called a *second* part of an hour. Given a name such as minute or second these parts could be expressed in whole numbers and calculations could be carried out in well-known ways. Difficulty arose when multiplication involving fractions was required, as in finding the area of a rectangle with dimensions involving fractions. This problem led to new notations. Symbols were needed which would make the computations easier both to carry out and to understand. The standard way of writing fractions is by means of a pair of numbers separated by a horizontal line. This notation makes it easy to distinguish the name of each part, the *denominator*, from the number of the parts, the *numerator*. This is useful because fractions must frequently be transformed so that their denominators are identical, and the fractions all expressed in parts of the same size. This notation can then allow operations to be carried out in terms of whole numbers.

The decimal notation for fractions

Even this simple notation is too unwieldy to commend itself to those who must deal with fractional parts of small size or those who need to know precisely the degree of accuracy of the numbers they have computed. It is astonishing that it took humankind so long to extend the Arabic notation downwards so that successive columns, moving to the right, would show not only tens and ones but also tenths, hundredths, etc., each having a place value one-tenth of that to the left. Only one symbol was required to make this system intelligible: a sign to show which is the units figure. There is still diversity about this symbol; usage in France differs from that in Britain and the USA. The French use a comma, while in Britain and the USA a point is used, either on or above the line.

Any fraction can be expressed as the sum of decimal fractions, tenths, hundredths, etc., by dividing numerator by denominator, for example

$$\frac{5}{8} = 0 \cdot 625 \quad \text{by division.}$$

Notice the zero in the units place, serving to draw attention to the decimal point. Decimal fractions share the advantage of decimal integers in that they can be arranged in columns. Moreover, we can write them to the degree of accuracy that we need, stopping at the second, third, or nth decimal place. Clearly we can extend decimal fractions as

far as we please since there is no end to the places we can move to the right. This brings out the value of the place-value system: we can write fairly concisely as large or as small a number as we choose to think about. Félix, in *The Modern Aspect of Mathematics*, quotes Lebesgue, 'Our teaching does not yet fully use this historic achievement, perhaps the most important in the history of the sciences, the invention of decimal notation.' A smaller unit is always ready when it is needed, a tenth of the last unit. The system of subdivision into smaller units is based on the *ten* in exactly the same way as the notational system for whole numbers.

The general adoption of the metric system of weights and measures, and of decimal systems of currency, makes it even more important now that children should understand the decimal place-value system. Moreover, children very quickly find decimals on a calculator; even if they do not ask about the ⊡ decimal point key, they will perform division such as $8 \div 5 = 1 \cdot 6$. Thus, the decimal notional now, more than ever, needs to be seen as a natural extension of the notational system, designed to deal with the problem of dividing units into parts. The decimal system has the further advantage that the calculator (electronic or human) carries out exactly the same computations (except for the position of the decimal point) in performing the additions

$$123 + 276 \quad \text{and} \quad 1 \cdot 23 + 2 \cdot 76$$

or in obtaining

$$473 \times 42 \quad \text{and} \quad 47\,300 \times 0 \cdot 42$$

Scientific notation

Further developments of the notation of the decimal system have been brought about by the need to express concisely the very large numbers required in astronomy or social statistics and the very small numbers in modern physics. They have given rise to yet more concise means of symbolising numbers and operations. The velocity of light, 299 800 000 metres per second, can be concisely written in *scientific notation* as $2 \cdot 998 \times 10^8$ metres per second, and the radius of an hydrogen atom,

$$0 \cdot 000\,000\,005\,29 \text{ cm,}$$

is abbreviated to $5 \cdot 29 \times 10^{-9}$ cm. The notation used by computers avoids 10^8, which cannot conveniently be printed, and uses the letter E (for exponent) to symbolise that a number is to be multiplied by the power of 10 following the E. Thus

$$2.998E + 08 = 2.988 \times 10^8$$
and $$5.29E - 09 = 5.29 \times 10^{-9}$$

Many older primary children have access to scientific calculators, which can perform other operations in addition to the four arithmetic operations. These calculators will accept scientific notation, but are unable to display E, so they merely leave a space. In this notation,

$$2.998 \times 10^8 \text{ is displayed as } 2.998 \ 08$$
and $$5.29 \times 10^{-9} \text{ is displayed as } 5.29 - 09$$

Scientific notation is discussed further in Chapter 33, and forms the most recent development of the decimal system.

NOTATION IN VARIOUS BASES

The purpose of notation is to give a neat way of representing numbers so that we can carry them in the mind as well as write them on paper. We can see how a number is organised, what structures it contains, how it is related to other numbers, and what will be the effect upon it of operations we can carry out mentally. The decimal notation enables us to do these things very well. But it is possible to increase understanding and skill if we enrich the *symbolic* representation by spatial images resulting from handling suitable shapes. We can use discs, round beads, cylinders, etc. to illustrate groupings but the shape that gives the closest parallel to a place-value notation is the *cube*. Because its faces are all squares of the same size we can fit a cube to other cubes in three directions. We need not confine our groupings to tens. In Figure 18 : 10 we group cubes in sevens. The shapes are the same if we group in fours, twelves or tens.

These shapes are always rods, square layers, and cubes. We see that when we group in sevens: (seven × seven) small cubes make a square layer, and (seven × seven × seven) small cubes make a large cube. We can now group these large cubes and

obtain long rods to represent seven × seven × seven × seven, and so on. The groupings are now producing the same shapes as before and children can build up to a huge cube that represents seven × seven × seven × seven × seven × seven. If they group in tens they can produce the million cube. Now they could go on grouping for ever in the imagination.

A large number of small cubes can be organised into groupings of threes, fours, etc. For example, a handful of seventy cubes can be organised into three-rods, then into (three × three) layers, and then into (three × three × three) cubes. This gives

2 large cubes (3 × 3 × 3) fifty-four
1 square layer   (3 × 3) nine
2 rods   3 six
1 cube   1 one

We can write this in columns

(3 × 3 × 3)	(3 × 3)	3	1
2	1	2	1

More shortly it can be written without labels using place value only but naming the counting set or *base*, as

2121 (base three)

Children can also set out with appropriate materials a representation of a given number in any base. These activities will lead to discussion of the number of symbols needed to write numbers in different bases and children will find that for base three they need only 0, 1 and 2. They enjoy inventing their own symbols, e.g. 0, /, ∠.

The Dienes Multibase Arithmetic Blocks consist of unit cubes and robs, square layers and large cubes produced in blocks marked to show the equivalent small cubes. These are convenient for children to handle. A counting set of four unit cubes can be exchanged for a four-rod, and four of these rods for a four × four layer, and so on. The material includes bases two, three, four five, six and ten. Large as the blocks seem when working in base six or base ten, children can experience the

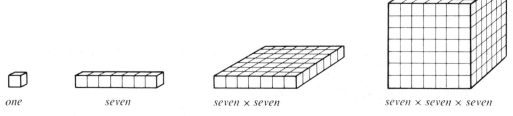

one   *seven*   *seven × seven*   *seven × seven × seven*

Figure 18 : 10

organising of a number into each of these bases. They will then realise that a number of unit cubes can be put together in ways which illustrate a notation based on *any* counting set. The cubes provide a concrete model for the place-value notation because the organisation of the cubes is parallel to the number grouping.

THE INDEX NOTATION

We have seen that in base seven a number can be illustrated with unit cubes as follows:

$$1 \text{ rod} = 7 \text{ ones}$$
$$1 \text{ square layer} = 7 \text{ rods} = 7 \times 7 \text{ ones}$$
$$1 \text{ cube} = 7 \text{ square layers} = 7 \times 7 \text{ rods}$$
$$= 7 \times 7 \times 7 \text{ ones}$$

A similar pattern occurs in any base. For instance, if base five is used:

$$1 \text{ rod} = 5 \text{ ones}$$
$$1 \text{ square layer} = 5 \text{ rods} = 5 \times 5 \text{ ones}$$
$$1 \text{ cube} = 5 \text{ square layers} = 5 \times 5 \text{ rods}$$
$$= 5 \times 5 \times 5 \text{ ones}$$

It is convenient to abbreviate 5×5 as 5^2 (five squared) and $5 \times 5 \times 5$ as 5^3 (five cubed), so that in base five:

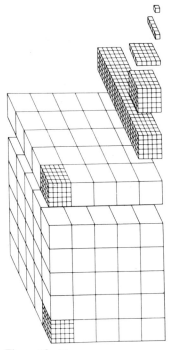

Figure 18 : 11

$$1 \text{ rod} = 5 \text{ ones} \quad 1 \text{ square layer} = 5^2 \text{ ones}$$
$$1 \text{ cube} = 5^3 \text{ ones}$$

The words 'rod', 'square layer' and 'cube' which we have used for the larger groupings of units will be replaced by:

$$\text{base} \equiv \text{rod}$$
$$\text{square (of base)} \equiv \text{square layer}$$
$$\text{cube (of base)} \equiv \text{cube}$$

which reflect their mathematical structure more fully.

This *index* notation is easily extended to accommodate numbers of units greater that the cube of the base. In base five, whenever five pieces of the same size occur, they are grouped together to form a piece of the next size. This process is illustrated in Figure 18 : 11. When five pieces whose size is the cube of the base (5^3) occur, they are grouped together to form a piece which bears the same relation to the 'cube' as does the 'rod' to the unit. This piece is called the *fourth power* of the base, and is written 5^4. Next, five to these pieces are grouped together to form a large square layer, the *fifth power* of the base (5^5), and five of these make a large cube, the *sixth power* of the cube (5^6). The process can clearly be continued indefinitely, so that any number, however large, can be written in base five, or similarly in any other base. It is natural to extend the notation used earlier to

1 one

5 ones = base = 'rod'

5 × 5 ones = 5^2 ones = square of base = 'layer'

5 × 5^2 ones = 5^3 ones = cube of base = 'cube'

5 × 5^3 ones = 5^4 ones = fourth power of base = 'big rod'

5 × 5^4 ones = 5^5 ones = fifth power of base = 'big layer'

5 × 5^5 = 5^6 ones = sixth power of base = 'big cube'

describe the larger pieces. In base five, Figure 18 : 11 shows that:

Base:
 1 base = 5 ones

Square of base:
 1 square = 5 bases = 5×5 ones = 5^2 ones

Cube of base:
 1 cube = 5 squares = 5×5 bases = $5 \times 5 \times 5$ ones
  = 5^3 ones

Fourth power of base:
 1 fourth power = 5 cubes = 5×5 squares
   = $5 \times 5 \times 5$ bases
   = $5 \times 5 \times 5 \times 5$ ones = 5^4 ones

Fifth power of base:
 1 fifth power = 5 fourth powers = 5×5 cubes
   = $5 \times 5 \times 5$ squares
   = $5 \times 5 \times 5 \times 5$ bases
   = $5 \times 5 \times 5 \times 5 \times 5$ ones = 5^5 ones

and so on.

A symbol such as 5^6, 5 *raised to the sixth power*, indicates that six factors, each equal to 5, are multiplied together; that is

$5^6 = 5 \times 5 \times 5 \times 5 \times 5 \times 5$
  6 factors

Similarly, 5 (or any other number) can be raised to any power, the *index* showing the power to which the base has been raised.

The columns in which children write numbers when they use the multibase blocks can appropriately be labelled:

Fourth powers	Cubes	Squares	Bases	Ones

or in base five:

5^4	5^3	5^2	5	1

The number 43 232 (base five) is made up of

$$(4 \times 5^4) + (3 \times 5^3) + (2 \times 5^2) + (3 \times 5) + (2 \times 1)$$

The principles of place-value notation which we have discussed in base five apply equally well to all bases. It is most important that children should fully understand the structure of base ten, so that they see how to build up, with the aid of concrete apparatus, from tens to hundred, and to thousands. The size of the pieces in base ten is too large to permit further building up in successive steps, but Figure 18 : 12 shows the number 1 million, 1 hundred-thousand, 1 ten-thousand, 1 thousand, 1 hundred, 1 ten, 1 one. However, if a *one* is represented by a cubic centimetre (as in Cuisenaire rods), then 1 cubic metre represents 1 million. Children can visualise a million most easily by comparing a cubic centimetre with a cubic metre.

Some of the relationships in the system of notation, which children need to recognise and be able to use, are

1 thousand = 10 hundreds = 100 tens = 1000 ones
 10^3 = $10 \times (10^2)$ = 100×10 = 1000×1
     = $(10^2) \times 10 = (10^3) \times 1$

and

1 million = 10 hundred-thousands
    = 100 ten-thousands = 1000 thousands

The number 1 111 111 (base ten)

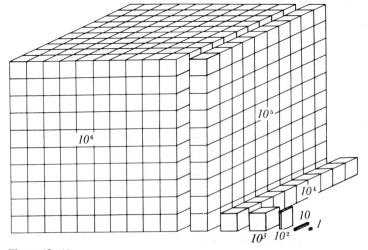

1 one
10 units = 1 ten
100 units = 10^2 units = 1 hundred
1 000 units = 10^3 units = 1 thousand
10 000 units = 10^4 units = 1 ten-thousand
100 000 units = 10^5 units = 1 hundred-thousan
1 000 000 units = 10^6 units $\times$ 1 million
The number 1 111 111 (base ten)

Figure 18 : 12

or $10^6 = 10 \times (10^5)$

$\qquad = 100 \times (10^4) \qquad = 1000 \times (10^3)$

$\qquad = 10^2 \times 10^4 \qquad\quad = 10^3 \times 10^3$, etc.

They will come to know the index form for any power of ten:

$10^2 =$ 100

$10^3 =$ 1 000

$10^4 =$ 10 000

$10^5 =$ 100 000

$10^6 =$ 1 000 000

$10^{12} =$ 1 000 000 000 000

This table may be extended to include smaller as well as larger numbers. Cleary $10^1 = 10$ is sensible, and the pattern is completed by $10^0 = 1$. We notice that an increase of 1 in the index has the effect of multiplying the number by ten, and a decrease of 1 in the index has the effect of dividing the number by ten. The pattern now is:

$10^0 =$ 1

$10^1 =$ 10

$10^2 =$ 100

$10^3 =$ 1 000

$10^4 =$ 10 000 and so on,

and the headings of the columns in the decimal system of notation:

Ten-thousands   *Thousands*   *Hundreds*   *Tens*   *Units*

may be written:

10^4   *10^3*   *10^2*   *10^1*   *10^0*

PLACE-VALUE NOTATION FOR FRACTIONS

The process of building up from unit cubes to larger and larger units can be paralleled by a process of breaking down into smaller units. If we take a large cube as a unit (Figure 18 : 13), it can be broken down into, say, ten square layers, each one of which is made up of ten rods, each one of which is made up of ten cubes, each one of which is made up of ten small square layers, each one of which . . . .

Thus the positional system of notation in base ten can easily be extended downwards to accommodate fractions of a unit as well as whole numbers of units.

Children need to realise that a piece of any size in the multibase blocks can be used to represent one unit, and the other pieces take their value from the piece which is chosen to represent one unit. The pieces shown in Figure 18 : 14 might represent either:

i) 1 one, 3 tenths, 2 hundredths, 4 thousands; that is 1·324, if the large cube represents one; or

ii) 1 ten, 3 ones, 2 tenths, 4 hundredths; that is 13·24, if the square layer represents one; or

iii) 1 thousand, 3 hundreds, 2 tens, 4 ones; that is 1324, if the small cube represents one.

Other values are also possible.

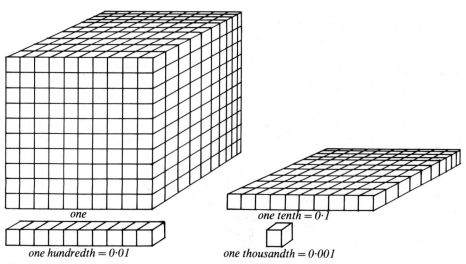

one

one hundredth = 0·01

one tenth = 0·1

one thousandth = 0·001

Figure 18 : 13

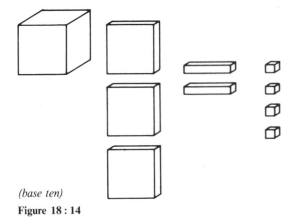

(base ten)

Figure 18 : 14

This free choice of a piece to represent one unit is exactly parallel to the situation in dealing with money; a sum of money can be thought of either as

123 pence,

if a penny is chosen as unit, or as

£1·23,

if a pound is chosen as unit. Similarly, a child's height may be given as either 109 cm or 1·09 m according to the choice of unit.

For a time, until the values are securely established, the columns can be headed when decimals are handled, as shown in Figure 18 : 15.

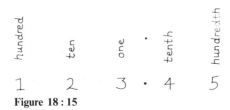

Figure 18 : 15

Children should be encouraged to read 0·45 as

'4 tenths and 5 hundredths',

rather than 'point four five', so that the values become established in speech. There is no need for the fractional notation $\frac{4}{10}$ and $\frac{5}{100}$ to be known before decimal notation is introduced; decimal notation is an extension of the place-value system to parts of one unit, rather than a translation of $\frac{4}{10}$ and $\frac{5}{100}$ into a new and obscure notation. In exactly the same way that 50 stands for 5 *tens*, so does 0·05 stand for 5 *hundredths*.

NOTATION ON THE ABACUS

The calculator is inflexible in notation because it is entirely confined to working in base ten. When children are working in other bases they often find an abacus a useful bridge between multibase blocks and written recording. The columns should be labelled in the base notation, as in Figure 18 : 16. Children can choose a number to show on the abacus with a selected base, and they can also use the abacus to record the results of their organising of cubes, as shown on page 178. This will encourage further discussion of the symbols needed to write what is seen on the abacus. It is very important *not* to use the base-ten words at this stage but to speak a number such as 312 (base four) either as 3 squares, 1 base, 2 ones, or in the way we give a telephone number: three-one-two (base four). It would be quite wrong, of course, to say three hundred and twelve, even if the words 'base four' were added.

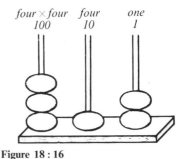

Figure 18 : 16

BASES USED IN COMPUTING

Base two is the smallest base which it is possible for a number system to have. It is very inconvenient to work with, because so many digits are needed to represent quite small numbers. Figure 18 : 17 shows a set of multibase blocks in base two; the number represented by the collection shown is (in base ten) 64 + 32 + 16 + 8 + 4 + 2 + 1, or 127. In base two, this number is written 1 111 111. Although human beings find base two tiresome, it is exactly what is needed to represent a number internally in a computer; only the two symbols 0 and 1 are needed in combination to represent any number. Thus, any device which can be in exactly one to two states can represent 0 and 1; for instance, a semi-conductor can be in either a conducting state (= 1) or a non-conducting state (= 0), and the number 127 (base ten) can be stored in a set of 8 memory cells, or bits, as the base two, or *binary*, number 0111 1111.

Although most people who come into contact with computers do not need to know about their internal workings, children are often interested in

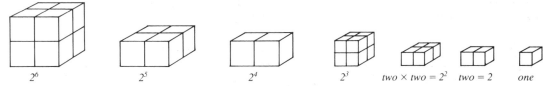

Figure 18 : 17

binary numbers and computer arithmetic. Counting in binary, either using an abacus, or combining Multilink cubes into base two blocks, as shown in Figure 18 : 18, is a useful way of becoming familiar with this strange base.

Another base which is used in computing is hexadecimal (hex) or base sixteen. This base has another feature which will be new to children. Because the grouping is in sets of sixteen, different symbols are needed for the numbers zero to fifteen, and our usual digits from 0 to 9 are not enough. They are conventionally supplemented by the letters A, B, C, D, E, F. Figure 18 : 19 shows the beginning of a count in base ten or *denary*, base two or *binary* and base sixteen or *hex*. It will be seen that one column of hex represents four columns of binary, so that 1111 (binary) is replaced by F (hex). A continuation of this count will show that

$$127 \text{ (denary)} = 111\ 1111 \text{ (binary)}$$
$$= 7F \text{ (hex)}$$

Thus hex is often used as a shorthand replacement for binary. These two bases will become of increasing interest to children.

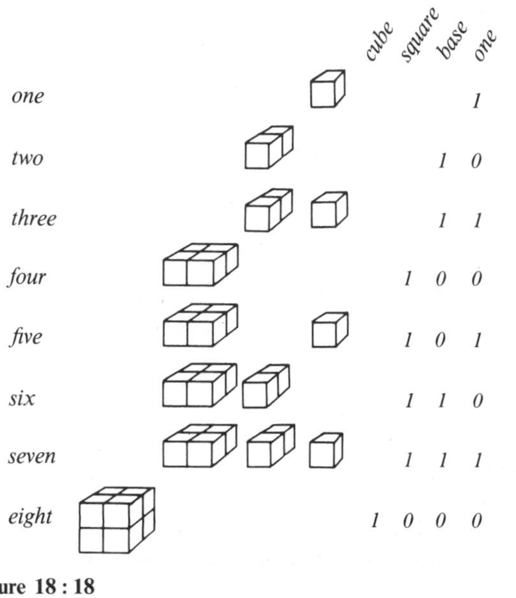

Denary	Binary	Hex
1	1	1
2	10	2
3	11	3
4	100	4
5	101	5
6	110	6
7	111	7
8	1000	8
9	1001	9
10	1010	A
11	1011	B
12	1100	C
13	1101	D
14	1110	E
15	1111	F
16	10000	10
17	10001	11

Figure 18 : 19

THE EMERGENCE OF THE PLACE-VALUE CONCEPT

From the variety of forms in which children experience our number system – the cubes and rods, recordings of sums of money and measuring, graphs, the abacus and symbols for numerals – there develops a capacity to read and write numbers with a confident recognition of their meaning. Behind the symbols children recognise the number itself and can look critically at a number sentence and say whether it is sensible or true. They will be ready to adopt new notations and to understand their scope and usefulness.

Our number notation and the measures in daily use are so closely bound up with our history that new meaning is given to them if their origins are known. There is considerable value in letting children read for themselves about the inventions that have gone to the making of our number system, and the ways in which the number system is continuing to develop to cope with the demands of the computer age. Several interesting books on the history and development of numbers are now available for children, and can provide useful sources of topic work.

	cube	square	base	one
one				1
two			1	0
three			1	1
four		1	0	0
five		1	0	1
six		1	1	0
seven		1	1	1
eight	1	0	0	0

Figure 18 : 18

Decimals and index notation in the National Curriculum

The National Curriculum only demands that children should work in base ten. The teacher will decide whether it is helpful and interesting for them to use other bases in addition to base ten. The more able older primary children are certainly expected to understand decimals:

- order decimals and appreciate place values.
                              (AT2: Number, Level 6)

Index notation appears at Level 5:

- use index notation to express powers of whole numbers.
                              (AT2, Level 5)

However, it is surprising in the calculator age that children are not expected to understand scientific notation until Level 8:

- express and use numbers in standard index form, with positive and negative integer powers of 10.
                              (AT2, Level 8)

Children who have access to scientific calculators will wish to explore this notation at an earlier stage.

19 | LARGER NUMBERS AND THE LAWS OF ARITHMETIC

MULTIPLICATION OF LARGER NUMBERS

As children become familiar with the idea of multiplication, the size of the numbers which they can use increases and gradually they learn the multiplication tables so that eventually they know the result of any multiplication up to 9×9. The method of building up multiplication by continued addition whenever the result is not known is, however, inadequate for mental or written calculations with larger numbers, and can be supplemented by methods which make use of the positional notation for writing numbers. The use of any type of structural apparatus will encourage children to discover such methods for themselves.

Children who use Cuisenaire rods to obtain the answer to 3×14 (three fourteens) may put out a fourteen made up to $10 + 4$, followed by another fourteen and another fourteen, or they may prefer to put out 3 tens and 3 fours (Figure 19: 1).

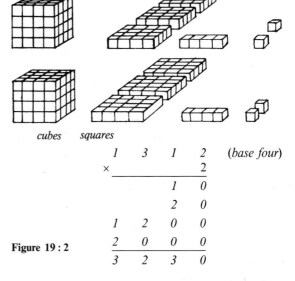

Figure 19 : 1

The result is the same by either method, but the second method forms the basis of non-calculator methods for the multiplication of numbers with more than one digit. As children become less dependent on apparatus, they think this out as

'3 *tens* are 30, 3 *fours* are 12, 30 plus 12 is 42,'

and record it as

$$
\begin{array}{r}
14 \\
\times\ 3 \\
\hline
30 \\
12 \\
\hline
42
\end{array}
\qquad \text{or} \qquad
\begin{array}{rcl}
3 \times 10 & \to & 30 \\
3 \times\ 4 & \to & +12 \\
\hline
3 \times 14 & & 42
\end{array}
$$

The traditional written procedure is obtained by starting the multiplication with the ones instead of the tens, saying

'3 times 4 equals 12, 1 ten and 2 *ones* 3 times 1 ten equals 3 tens, 3 tens plus 1 ten equals 4 *tens*'

and recording this as

$$
\begin{array}{r}
14 \\
\times\ 3 \\
\hline
12 \\
30 \\
\hline
42
\end{array}
$$

In any case, the thinking and the recording correspond exactly to the arrangement which the child constructed in Figure 19 : 1.

Similarly, children who use multibase blocks to multiply

1 cube 3 squares 1 base 2 ones   (base four)

by 2 will put out the apparatus shown in Figure 19 : 2, and if they start with the ones, they will gather together first all the ones, then the bases, then all the squares, then all the cubes; and will record the work, thinking first of the multiplication of the ones by 2, then of the multiplication of the bases by 2, and so on. This thought-process and the method of working based on it persist unchanged as the use of the apparatus is discarded, and form the foundation for all non-calculator procedures for the multiplication of larger numbers.

2 × 1312 (base four)

cubes   squares

	1	3	1	2	(base four)
×				2	
			1	0	
		2	0		
1	2	0	0		
2	0	0	0		
3	2	3	0		

Figure 19 : 2

THE DISTRIBUTIVE LAW

The mathematical law which expresses the idea used above is the *distributive law*.[1] The multiplication 3×14, or $3 \times (10 + 4)$, can be replaced by $(3 \times 10) + (3 \times 4)$. In fact,

$$3 \times (10 + 4) = (3 \times 10) + (3 \times 4)$$

Similarly,

$$3 \times (1 \text{ metre } 4 \text{ centimetres})$$
$$= 3 \times (1 \text{ metre}) + 3 \times (4 \text{ centimetres})$$

In general, the distributive law states that, for any numbers a, b and c,

$$a \times (b + c) = (a \times b) + (a \times c)$$

This law can also be illustrated by building a rectangular layer like the one shown in Figure 19 : 3. This rectangle consists of either

i) a rows of $(b + c)$ bricks, that is $a \times (b + c)$ bricks,

or

ii) a rows of b bricks together with a rows of c bricks, giving $(a \times b) + (a \times c)$ bricks in all, so that

$$a \times (b + c) = (a \times b) + (a \times c)$$

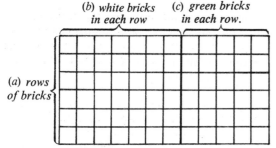

Figure 19 : 3

The calculator can also be used to support this work, so that for instance

$$8 \times (10 + 7) = 8 \times 17$$

can be evaluated directly on the calculator, giving 136; children should be able to work out the other form

$$(8 \times 10) + (8 \times 7) = 80 + 56$$

directly, and add the two elements to obtain 136. They will realise that if they are not using a

[1] The name 'distributive law' expresses the fact that multiplication is 'distributed out' over addition.

calculator, it is necessary to split 17 into $10 + 7$, and multiply each part by 8. There are two methods for recording this:

	17		$8 \times 10 =$	80
	$\times$ 8		$8 \times\ 7 =$	56
8×10	80		8×17	136
$8 \times\ 7$	56			
	136			

Each is a record of the splitting up of the calculation by the distributive law.

MULTIPLICATION BY THE BASE

The next step in understanding multiplication when numbers are written in a particular base is the realisation of what happens when a number is multiplied by the base number. Children need to understand that for instance.

$$10 \times 24 = 240 \text{ (base ten)}$$
and $\qquad 10 \times 2 \text{ pence} = 2 \text{ tenpences.}$
Similarly, $100 \times 2 \text{ pence} = £2$
and $\qquad 100 \times 2 \text{ centimetres} = 2 \text{ metres.}$

This behaviour is surprising, and children may regard it as a curious coincidence, without understanding, but it forms the basis of multiplication of larger numbers. so that it is important that the point should be understood. The following practical experiences may be helpful.

i) Multiplication of ones by 10 (base ten) (Figure 19 : 4).

ii) A slight change of emphasis in an earlier multiplication graph may be helpful (Figure 19 : 5).

iii) The calculator can be used to demonstrate what happens when a number is multiplied by 10. Children should be encouraged as soon as possible to predict the answers, and to use the

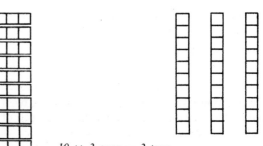

$10 \times 3 \text{ ones} = 3 \text{ tens}$

Figure 19 : 4

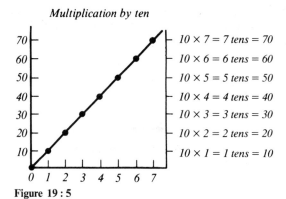

Multiplication by ten

$10 \times 7 = 7$ tens $= 70$
$10 \times 6 = 6$ tens $= 60$
$10 \times 5 = 5$ tens $= 50$
$10 \times 4 = 4$ tens $= 40$
$10 \times 3 = 3$ tens $= 30$
$10 \times 2 = 2$ tens $= 20$
$10 \times 1 = 1$ tens $= 10$

Figure 19 : 5

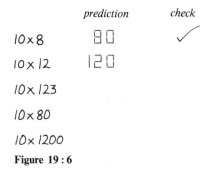

	prediction	check
10×8	80	✓
10×12	120	
10×123		
10×80		
10×1200		

Figure 19 : 6

calculator as a check on their predictions (Figure 19 : 6).

iv) Multiplication of larger numbers by the base shows that

10×3 tens = 30 tens
$\qquad\qquad$ = 3 hundreds,

or

$10 \times 30 = 300$

v) Similarly,

10×30 centimetres $= 10 \times 3$ ten-centimetre rods
$\qquad\qquad\qquad\qquad$ = 30 ten-centimetre rods
$\qquad\qquad\qquad\qquad$ = 3 metres,
and $\quad 10 \times 3$ ten-pence pieces = £3

These last two examples can also be written in decimal notation as

$10 \times 0 \cdot 3$ metres = 3 metres
and $10 \times £0 \cdot 30 = £3 \cdot 00$

The principle which children must grasp here is that multiplication (within a notational system) by the base has the effect of moving each digit of the number multiplied one place to the left. If the working is written down in columns, this becomes very clear.

£ 10p p $\qquad$ £
$\quad$ 2 $\quad$ 0 $\times 10$ or $0 \cdot 20 \times 10$
2 $\quad$ 0 $\quad$ 0 $\qquad$ 2·00

m dm cm $\qquad$ m
$\quad$ 2 $\quad$ 3 $\times 10$ or $0 \cdot 23 \times 10$
2 $\quad$ 3 $\quad$ 0 $\qquad$ 2·3

Similarly, multiplication by the square of the base moves the digits two places to the left. The calculator shows

$100 \times 2 = 200$
$100 \times 20 = 2000$
$100 \times 23 = 2300$
$100 \times 2 \cdot 3 = 230$
$100 \times 0 \cdot 23 = 23$

and the vertical arrangement is again helpful.

£ 10p p $\qquad$ £
$\qquad$ 2 $\times 100$ or $0 \cdot 02 \times 100$
2 $\quad$ 0 $\quad$ 0 $\qquad$ 2·00

m dm cm $\qquad$ m
$\quad$ 2 $\quad$ 3 $\times 100$ or $0 \cdot 23 \times 100$
23 $\quad$ 0 $\quad$ 0 $\qquad$ 23

Children will notice from their experience of money and measurement that the principle of multiplying by the base (in this case ten) by moving the digits one place extends to numbers which are written with a decimal point.

The next step is to see what happens when a number is multiplied by 20, or 30, or 40, ... and by 200, 300, 400, ... Patterns such as those in Figure 19 : 7 can easily be worked out with a calculator. Children should be encouraged to look for and predict patterns, using the calculator as a check, and to make generalisations such as:

to multiply by 20:
$\quad$ multiply by 10,
$\quad$ multiply the answer by 2.

$1 \times 23 = 23$	$10 \times 23 = 230$	$100 \times 23 = 2300$
$2 \times 23 = 46$	$20 \times 23 = 460$	$200 \times 23 = 4600$
$3 \times 23 = 69$	$30 \times 23 = 690$	$300 \times 23 = 6900$
$4 \times 23 = 92$	$40 \times 23 = 920$	$400 \times 23 = 9200$
$5 \times 23 = 115$	$50 \times 23 = 1150$	$500 \times 23 = 11500$
$6 \times 23 = 138$	$60 \times 23 = 1380$	$600 \times 23 = 13800$
$7 \times 23 = 161$	$70 \times 23 = 1610$	$700 \times 23 = 16100$
$8 \times 23 = 184$	$80 \times 23 = 1840$	$800 \times 23 = 18400$
$9 \times 23 = 207$	$90 \times 23 = 2070$	$900 \times 23 = 20700$
$10 \times 23 = 230$	$100 \times 23 = 2300$	$1000 \times 23 = 23000$

Figure 19 : 7

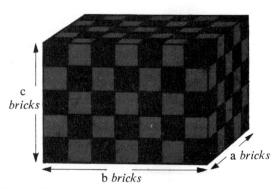

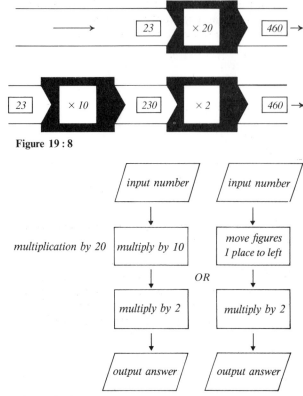

Figure 19 : 8

Figure 19 : 9

Figure 19 : 10

which plays an important part in simplifying the addition of large numbers.

A further illustration of the truth of the associative law for multiplication may be obtained from the building of a cuboid out of cubical bricks (Figure 19 : 10). The floor contains a rows of b bricks, or $(a \times b)$ bricks, and so the cuboid, which has c layers of bricks, contains $(a \times b) \times c$ bricks. Alternatively, the front wall has $(b \times c)$ bricks in it and the cuboid is a layers thick, so that

$$a \times (b \times c) = (a \times b) \times c$$

Children do not easily connect this experience of the associative law for multiplication with its use in the multiplication of a number by a multiple of the base unless the link between the experiences is made clear. The evaluation of triple multiplications such as

$$(8 \times 9) \times 7 = 72 \times 7 \qquad 8 \times (9 \times 7) = 8 \times 63$$
$$= 504 \qquad\qquad = 504$$

and

$$(2 \times 10) \times 23 = 20 \times 23 \qquad 2 \times (10 \times 23) = 2 \times 230$$
$$= 460 \qquad\qquad = 460$$

may help to make the link clearer.

Although an associative law is true for both addition and multiplication, it is not true for subtraction or division. For instance,

$$60 \div (6 \div 2) = 60 \div 3 = 20,$$
$$\text{but} \quad (60 \div 6) \div 2 = 10 \div 2 = 5,$$
$$\text{so that } 60 \div (6 \div 2) \neq (60 \div 6) \div 2$$

Function machines can also be used to examine the possibility of doing multiplication in two stages (Figure 19 : 8), and the generalisations can be expressed in flow charts (Figure 19 : 9).

The mathematical law upon which the process of multiplying by a multiple of the base rests is seen when in 30×1486 the 30 is written as 3×10. Then

$$30 \times 1486$$
$$= (3 \times 10) \times 1486$$
$$= 3 \times (10 \times 1486),$$

where the brackets show that multiplication by 10 is performed first, and the result is then multiplied by 3. In general, if a, b and c are any numbers,

$$(a \times b) \times c = a \times (b \times c)$$

This law, the *associative law for multiplication*, in effect states that if three numbers are to be multiplied together, the order in which the multiplication is performed may be varied according to convenience. The associative law for multiplication will be seen to correspond extremely closely to the associative law for addition (*see page 167*)

$$(a + b) + c = a + (b + c)$$

A SECOND FORM OF THE DISTRIBUTIVE LAW

The final stage in multiplication is reached when children realise that if they wish to multiply for instance 476 by 23 (base ten) without a calculator, they can do so in three steps, by multiplying 476 by 20 and multiplying 476 by 3 and adding the results together. This construction is implicit in the very first stages of multiplication. When young children put out apparatus to find 3×8 they will often put the eights out one at a time, and when they put out two eights they know they need another one; that is, they know that

$$3 \times 8 = (2 \times 8) + (1 \times 8)$$

Exactly the same law is used in the multiplication of larger numbers;

$$23 \times 476 = (20 \times 476) + (3 \times 476);$$

and children who have understood the previous stages find little difficulty in grasping this, either with structural apparatus or an abacus or in calculation on paper. When calculating on paper it is of course immaterial whether the multiplication by 20 or by 3 is done first.

The law upon which long multiplication is based is a second form of the *distributive law*. The statement:

$$23 \times 476 = (20 \times 476) + (3 \times 476)$$

is a special case of:

$$(a + b) \times c = (a \times c) + (b \times c)$$

This distributive law is noticeably similar to that given on page 232

$$a \times (b + c) = (a \times b) + (a \times c)$$

In one case the multiplier is split up, and in the other case the multiplicand. It is possible that the two distributive laws may appear to children to be different, as the multiplier (in the example the number of times 476 is to be repeated) plays a very different part at the concrete stage from the multiplicand 476, which is set out in concrete form. However, as the commutative law for multiplication (*see page 208*) is assimilated, and as children's ideas of number become more abstract, the two laws become completely interchangeable.

The teacher should notice how often the laws are used in such a multiplication as:

$$\begin{array}{r} 20 \times 76 = 1520 \\ 9 \times 76 = 684 \\ \hline 29 \times 76 = 2204 \end{array}$$

the steps of which can be analysed as:

$$29 \times 76 = (20 \times 76) + (9 \times 76) \text{ (distributive law)}$$
$$= 2 \times (10 \times 76) + (9 \times 76) \text{ (associative law)}$$
$$= (2 \times 760) + (9 \times 76)$$
$$= (2 \times 700) + (2 \times 60) + (9 \times 70) + (9 \times 6)$$
$$\text{(distributive law)}$$

The distributive law also holds for the distribution of multiplication over subtraction. Because $29 = 30 - 1$, we can calculate 29×76 by doing

$$(30 \times 76) - (1 \times 76), \ or \quad \begin{array}{r} 30 \times 76 = 2280 \\ - 1 \times 76 = - 76 \\ \hline 29 \times 76 = 2204 \end{array}$$

In general, this law is

$$(a - b) \times c = (a \times c) - (b \times c)$$

Similarly we have

$$c \times (a - b) = (c \times a) - (c \times b)$$

DIVISION AS INVERSE MULTIPLICATION AND REPEATED SUBTRACTION

The $\boxed{\div}$ key of the calculator undoes multiplication, or performs inverse multiplication, and children should be encouraged to use it in this way, so that the link between division and multiplication is firmly established (Figure 19 : 11).

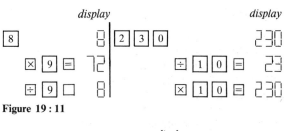

Figure 19 : 11

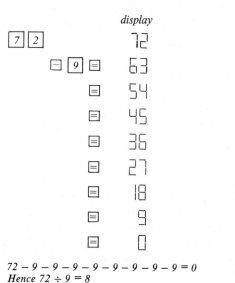

$72 - 9 - 9 - 9 - 9 - 9 - 9 - 9 - 9 = 0$
Hence $72 \div 9 = 8$

Figure 19 : 12

The division $72 \div 9$ can also be regarded as finding how many times 9 can be subtracted from 72. This can be done on a calculator with a constant facility by the simple set of keystrokes shown in Figure 19 : 12.

Human calculators, because they are equipped with a knowledge of the multiplication tables, prefer inverse multiplication for division calculations within the range of these tables. They can say '$73 \div 9 = 8$ remainder 1, because $8 \times 9 = 72$'. However, written algorithms for division, used when the numbers are outside the range of the tables, usually use a combination of repeated subtraction and inverse multiplication.

WRITTEN DIVISION OUTSIDE THE RANGE OF THE MULTIPLICATION TABLES

Division methods used for

$$84 \div 4 = 21$$

are based upon a distributive law

$$(80 + 4) \div 4 = (80 \div 4) + (4 \div 4) = 20 + 1,$$

and the division

$$96 \div 4 = 24$$

is based upon

$$(80 + 16) \div 4 = (80 \div 4) + (16 \div 4) = 20 + 4$$

These are special cases of a *distributive law for division*[2]

$$(a + b) \div c = (a \div c) + (b \div c)$$

For the understanding of two-step division it is therefore necessary for children to know some multiplication facts, and hence some division facts, which lie outside the range of the multiplication tables, such as $20 \times 4 = 80$ and so $80 \div 4 = 20$. These additional multiplication facts are easily found by

[2]It should be noticed that while for the distribution of multiplication over addition there are two distributive laws:

$$(a + b) \times c = (a \times c) + (b \times c)$$
$$\text{and } a \times (b + c) = (a \times b) + (a \times c),$$

only one distributive law

$$(a + b) \div c = (a \div c) + (b \div c),$$

is true for division, and that

$$a \div (b + c) \neq (a \div b) + (a \div c)$$

since division is not commutative.

children who understand multiplication by a multiple of the base (*see page 232*), so that they can use their knowledge of the table of fours to give them such additional facts as

$10 \times 4 = 40$	$100 \times 4 = 400$	$1000 \times 4 = 4000$
$20 \times 4 = 80$	$200 \times 4 = 800$	$2000 \times 4 = 8000$
$30 \times 4 = 120$	$300 \times 4 = 1200$	$3000 \times 4 = 12000$
etc.	etc.	etc.

Equipped with this knowledge, the traditional 'long division' arrangement of

```
   1326
4)5304
   4
   ──
   13
   12
   ──
   10
    8
   ──
   24
   24
   ──
    0
```

is seen to be an abbreviation of an arrangement of

```
   1326
4)5304
   4000      1000 × 4 = 4000
   ────
   1304
   1200       300 × 4 = 1200
   ────
   104
    80        20 × 4 =   80
   ───
    24
    24         6 × 4 =   24
   ───
     0
```

Children may prefer to record their working as:

```
                 5304
    4 × 1000 = 4000
                 ────
                 1304
    4 ×  300 = 1200
                 ────
                  104
    4 ×   20 =    80
                 ───
                   24
    4 ×    6 =    24
          ────   ───
          1326     0
```

This method of recording has the advantage that if too small a multiple is subtracted, it is easy to subtract more without upsetting the pattern of the calculation.

These methods of long division can of course be used whether the corresponding multiplication table is known or not.

Although most divisions involving large numbers are now done on the calculator, long division may not disappear completely, and children should still be able to divide a three-digit number by a one-digit number without a calculator. There no longer seems any value, however, in teaching abbreviated methods.

PECULIAR NUMBERS: **0** AND **1**

In Chapter 17 we discussed the odd behaviour of 0 in multiplication and division (*see pages 213 and 218*). To summarise this behaviour, for every number n

i) $n \times 0 = 0$

Rewriting this statement as a division statement,

ii) $0 \div n = 0$, but

iii) $n \div 0$ has no value if $n \neq 0$, since there is no number which multiplied by 0 gives a non-zero answer;

iv) $0 \div 0$ may have any value, since any number multiplied by 0 gives 0.

The number 1 also has interesting multiplication properties. It is the only number which does not alter the value of any number by which it is multiplied. That is, for any number n,

$n \times 1 = 1 \times n = n$

In this respect, the behaviour of 1 in multiplication exactly parallels the behaviour of 0 in addition. Zero is the only number which does not change the value of any number to which it is added. That is, for any number n,

$n + 0 = 0 + n = n$

A number which behaves in this way is called an *identity*. The *identity for addition* is 0, since

$n + 0 = 0 + n = n$ for all n.

The *identity for multiplication* is 1, since

$n \times 1 = 1 \times n = n$ for all n.

SOME LAWS OF ARITHMETIC FOR THE NATURAL NUMBERS

We have now seen that the operations of addition, subtraction, multiplication and division in the arithmetic of natural numbers are based upon the repeated application of certain laws of behaviour which are true of all the natural numbers. As these

laws are fundamental, not only for elementary arithmetic, but for all further study of numbers, we conclude this chapter by summarising the laws which addition and multiplication of natural numbers obey.

ADDITION

1 *Closure*
The set of natural numbers is closed for addition (*see page 162*).

2 *The commutative law*

$a + b = b + a$

(*see page 164*).

3 *The associative law*

$(a + b) + c = a + (b + c)$

(*see page 167*).

4 *The distributive laws*

$a \times (b + c) = (a \times b) + (a \times c)$ (*see page 232*)
$(a + b) \times c = (a \times c) + (b \times c)$ (*see page 235*)

5 *The identity*
0 is the identity for addition

$n + 0 = 0 + n = n$

(*see page 237*)

6 *Subtraction*
Subtraction is the inverse operation of addition

$\boxed{x} = a - b$

means

$\boxed{x} + b = a$

(*see page 162*)

MULTIPLICATION

1 *Closure*
The set of natural numbers is closed for multiplication (*see page 162*).

2 *The commutative law*

$a \times b = b \times a$

(*see page 208*).

3 *The associative law*

$(a \times b) \times c = a \times (b \times c)$

(*see page 234*).

5 *The identity*
1 is the identity for multiplication

$n \times 1 = 1 \times n = n$

(*see page 237*)

6 *Division*
Division is the inverse operation of multiplication

$\boxed{x} = a \div b$

means

$\boxed{x} \times b = a$

(*see page 217*)

In later chapters, as the set of numbers used in mathematics is extended from the natural numbers to include numbers of other types, we shall see that the above laws are retained and used, but that more extensive number systems also obey laws which are not true for the natural numbers.

Multiplication and divsion in the National Curriculum

The National Curriculum states explicity the largest sizes of numbers that children should be expected to multiply and divide without a calculator.

- understand and use non-calculator methods by which a 3-digit number is multiplied by a 2-digit number and a 3-digit number is divided by a 2-digit number.

(AT2: Number, Level 5)

However, the methods to be used are never specified, and understanding is emphasised. It seems better, therefore, to encourage children to use methods of recording that they understand and feel confidence in, rather than traditional 'long multiplication' and 'long division' methods which are often not understood. For everyday use, it is no longer important for children to know written methods for large multiplication and division calculations – they can always use a calculator.

20 DEVELOPING IDEAS OF PROBABILITY

INTRODUCTION

We live in a world in which some happenings are totally predictable, and others are more random in nature. If a stone is dropped, it will *certainly* fall to the ground, but if a coin is tossed in the air, although it will fall to the ground, it is *uncertain* whether it will come down with the head or tail uppermost. The first event is *deterministic*, and is explained by the law of gravity; the second event is *probabilistic*, and although we cannot predict on any given occasion whether a head or tail will occur, the laws of probability lead us to expect that if a coin is tossed a large number of times, it will come down heads on about half the tosses.

Many of the most important events in life are probabilistic in nature; the next baby in the family will certainly be either a boy or a girl, but which is uncertain. The sun will rise tomorrow, but it is uncertain whether the sky will be cloudy. Combinations of uncertainties govern the national economy, and while 1 person in 150 is involved in a road accident in Britain each year, it is uncertain whether anyone of our own acquaintance will be represented in that statistic.

Probability and statistics give rise to some of the most important uses of mathematics in the modern world, and it is therefore important that children should be introduced to concepts of probability as early as possible in the primary school years, so that they can distinguish between events whose outcome is certain and those which are probabilistic. They also need time to experiment and discover for themselves how chance works.

In recent years, the development of children's ideas of probability has been studied by Piaget and other workers, and work on probability has increasingly been introduced into primary schools. Piaget and Inhelder's work on probability, published in French in 1951, was not translated into English until 1975.[1] In the same year another important study of children's ideas of probability, by

Fischbein, appeared.[2] Fischbein's work shows that children's primary intuitions of probability are not strong. However, he believes that intuition in the field of probability can be developed by teaching, and that this teaching should start during the period of concrete operations. The raw material of children's learning about probability is described as natural 'experiments' which involve prediction and observation of random events.

Children have a good deal of experience of random experiments, because they play so many games with dice, spinners and packs of cards. However, their concentration is usually on what happens after the dice are thrown or the spinner spun, so that the way the dice themselves behave is not really noticed. Hence, early beliefs about chance may persist for a long time.

Figure 20 : 1

CHILDREN'S IDEAS OF CHANCE

Very young children do not yet have the experience to distinguish between events which are controlled by fixed laws and those which have an element of randomness. To examine young children's ideas of randomness, Piaget and Inhelder used an ingenious

[1]Piaget, J. and Inhelder, B. *The Origin of the Idea of Chance in Children*, W. W. Norton, 1975.

[2]Fischbein, E. *The Intuitive Sources of Probabilistic Thinking in Children*, D. Reidel, 1975.

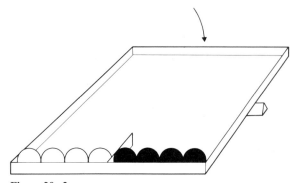

Figure 20 : 2

tray which held red and white balls, and which could be tilted on a seesaw (Figure 20 : 2).

Red balls were originally placed on one side of the partition and white balls on the other side. Children were asked to predict what could happen after the seesaw had been tilted so that the balls rolled to the other end of the tray and back. Before about 7 years of age, many children believe either that the balls will all stay on the same side, or that they will all change places.

If, after the tray has been tilted once, one ball has changed sides, some children believe that this will continue to happen, so the next time another ball will change places, and next time a third ball will change. Some fixed, if invisible, force controls the sideways movement of the balls, in just the same way that a fixed and invisible force makes the ball roll downhill to the other end of the tray. Eventually, after being tilted several times, *'It will come back to the way it was.'*

In other situations also, young children believe in some guiding force which controls what an adult believes to be a random movement. In one experiment, the experimenter first tossed a number of counters which had a circle on one side and a cross on the other, so that some came down 'circles' and some 'crosses'. He then cheated by replacing the counters surreptitiously by 'double-cross' counters. In the age group of 4- to 6-year-olds, one child explained the trick as, *'A trick that you can do with your hands'*, and another said, *'You threw them like that'*. We find children who, when they are playing dice games, shake extra hard and wish for a six; perhaps concentration can get the forces moving!

In another experiment, a set of different-coloured marbles were shaken up in a bag. Children were asked to predict which colour marble they would get by putting a hand into the bag without looking. As a guide, an exactly similar set of marbles was put on the table for them to look at. Here again, 5- and 6-year-olds make predictions which are based on influences other than chance: *'White, because white is the first'* (in the set of marbles on the table); *'White, because there is only one white one'*; or on predicting the colours when two marbles are to be drawn: *'Red and rose, because that's pretty'*.

Fischbein asked children to predict the results of rolling a marble down sloping boards with mazes, such as those in Figure 20 : 3, constructed on them. Almost all the children from the age of 6 upwards were able to predict successfully in the case of maze (*a*); however, for mazes (*b*) and (*c*), performance actually deteriorated with age. On maze (*c*), 78% of the 6-year-olds, but only 64% of the 14-year-olds predicted correctly. Older children believed that the shape of the channel lower down affects the marble's motion at the first junction: *'The marble will come more often down the channel with the longer bend.'* Fischbein believes that our culture and educational system orient children towards deterministic explanations, so that random events become irrational and unscientific.

Another well-documented mistaken belief about

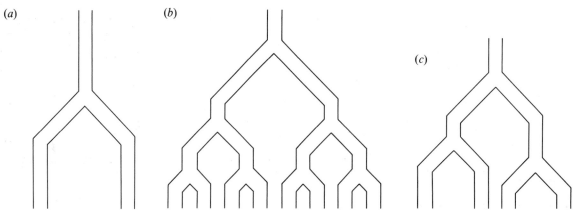

(a)   *(b)*   *(c)*

Figure 20 : 3

THTHHTTHHTTHTHTHTHHTHHTHHTHTTTHHHTTTHHTHHT

HTHTHHTTHTTTHHTTHTHTTHHTTTHHTHTHTHHTTHT

HHTTHTHHTTHTTHTHHHTHHTTHHTHHHHTHTTHTH

HTTHTHTHTHHTTTHTTHHTHTHTHHTTHHHHTHHHHTHTHHT

TTHTTHHTTTTHTTTTHTTHHHHTHTTHTHTHHTTTHHTHHH

HTTHHHHTHHHHHTHTTHHHHTTHTHTTHHHHTTHTTTHHHHTH

HHHHHTHTHTHTHTTTTTTTTHHHHHHTTTTHHTHTHTHTT

HTTHTTHHHHHHHHTHTTHHTTTHHTTTHTTTHHHHHTT

THHHHHTHTHTTTHTHTHTTHHHTHHHHHTTHHHHTHHHHTT

Figure 20 : 4

chance, which often persists into adulthood, is '*the gambler's fallacy*'. This is the belief that because a tossed coin came down heads on the last three occasions, for instance, it is more likely to come down tails next time. This belief imputes some sort of controlling force, which has a memory, to the coin.

Of the two sequences of coin tosses in Figure 20 : 4, one is a genuine random sequence, and the other is a fake produced by a pupil in imitation of a random sequence. It has been found that secondary school pupils usually think, wrongly, the first is the random sequence, being unable to believe that the long runs of heads and tails in the second sequence could have occurred by chance.

Another example of belief in the 'non-randomness' of random behaviour is one found by D. R. Green.[3] Children were told that the roof of a small garden shed had 16 square tiles. At the beginning of a snowstorm 16 snowflakes had fluttered on to the roof. They were asked to choose the most likely arrangement of the snowflakes from those shown in Figure 20 : 5. Among 11-years-olds, 46% chose (*a*), 40% chose (*b*) and 11% chose (*c*). However, among 15-year-olds, only 33% chose (*a*), while 55% chose (*b*). Again, the proportion of those who attribute regularity to chance happenings has risen during the secondary school years.

If children are to gain a real understanding of chance, they need a good deal of experience of random events during the primary years. Moreover, this experience needs to be focused, so that the children do not only play games using dice and spinners, but they discuss what they are doing, record their results, and reflect on what is happening. Work on probability gives a great deal of opportunity for children to use all forms of pictorial representation, and it also gives informal experience of proportion, which can be made use of in the study of fractions. In the remainder of this chapter, some suggestions will be made of experiences of chance which can be used with

(*a*)

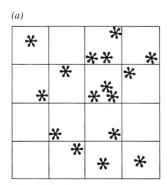

(*b*)

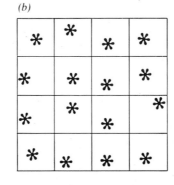

(*c*)

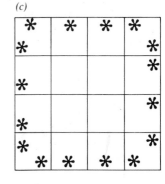

Figure 20 : 5

[3]Green, D. R. The Chance and Probability Concepts Project, *Teaching Statistics*, 1 (**3**), 1979, pp. 66–71.

primary age children. Some of the ideas they may gain from these experiences are also discussed.

RANDOM DRAWING

A bag containing coloured beads or cubes can give young children experience of randomness. Red cubes and blue cubes can be matched one-to-one, so that the same number of each goes into the bag. A block graph can be built up as cubes are drawn from the bag (Figure 20 : 6). If this is done more than once, the graphs can be compared, and the variations discussed. If each cube is put back into the bag when it has been drawn, the numbers of red and blue cubes in the bag stay the same throughout. This is drawing *with replacement*, and is a simpler situation than drawing *without replacement*. The variation in the results shown on different occasions can be discussed, and each child's graph displayed.

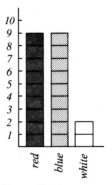

Figure 20 : 7

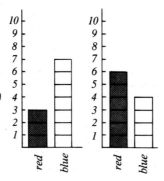

We put 10 red cubes and 10 blue cubes in the bag. We drew out 10, putting them back each time. Then we did it again.

Figure 20 : 6

Changing the number of colours, and the number of cubes of each colour, gives rise to useful discussion. The graph in Figure 20 : 7 was obtained by 20 drawings with replacement from a bag containing 6 red cubes, 3 blue cubes and a white cube. Although the result may surprise the reader, the graph was genuinely randomly obtained.

Similar experiments can be conducted with some

of the many dice and spinners available (Figure 20 : 8). Children should eventually realise that the same chances can happen in very different situations. For example, the chances of getting a red cube out of a bag containing 10 red cubes and 10 blue cubes are just the same as the chances of getting a head or a tail when tossing a coin, or of getting an odd number when rolling the standard cubical die (Figure 20 : 9). In the same way, instead of a bag with 6 red cubes, 3 blue cubes and 1 white cube, an icosahedral die could be used (Figure 20 : 9). These usually have faces numbered from 1 to 10, each number occurring twice. If the numbers of occurrences of scores are recorded in the groupings

6 or under,
7, 8 or 9,
10,

then the situation is exactly the same as 6 red cubes, 3 blue cubes and 1 white cube.

Another useful device for obtaining the same results is a sampling bottle (Figure 20 : 10). This is a bottle with a short glass tube protruding from its stopper. The tube is closed at the top. When the bottle is filled with coloured beads and turned upside down, just one bead appears in the glass tube. The effect is just the same as that of drawing cubes from a bag with replacement.

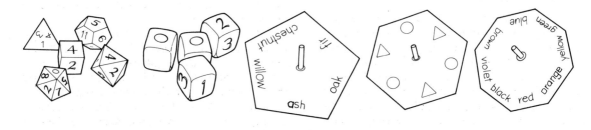

Figure 20 : 8

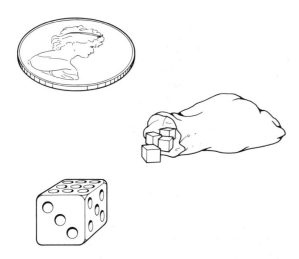

Figure 20 : 9

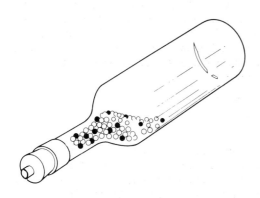

Figure 20 : 10

GROWTH OF THE IDEAS OF RANDOMNESS AND PROBABILITY

As well as sorting objects into sets according to their properties, children may sort future events according to their degree of likelihood: it is *certain* that tomorrow is Friday, and it is possible that it will rain tomorrow. The category of possible events may be split into *likely* and *unlikely* events, and the weather forecast will make a difference to how the event 'It will rain tomorrow' is classified, in class discussion. On the other hand, in January, the event 'tomorrow is Christmas Day' is *impossible*. Drawing

a white cube out of the bag with 6 red, 3 blue and 1 white cube is unlikely, but it sometimes happens. The idea emerges that some events cannot be predicted with certainty; they happen randomly. Other events are either certain or impossible. December 25th is always the day after December 24th. However, many random events have some degree of regularity about them. It is less likely that a six will be thrown with a die than it is that an even number will be thrown. It is more likely to rain when the weather forecast says it will than when the weather forecast says it will be a beautiful sunny day (Figure 20 : 11). *Probability* is beginning to become measurable.

Last week's weather

	Forecast weather	*Actual weather*
Monday	*Rain*	*Rain*
Tuesday	*Rain*	*Cloudy*
Wednesday	*Sunny*	*Sunny*
Thursday	*Cloudy*	*Cloudy*
Friday	*Rain*	*Cloudy*

Figure 20 : 11

At this stage, children also relate *chance* with *perhaps* or *may*: '*It may rain tomorrow*', '*Perhaps I shall get a bicycle for my birthday*', '*I have a chance of landing on the ladder* (in a game of Snakes and Ladders)'.

At first, children have a good deal of difficulty in comparing probabilities. A number of experimenters, including Piaget and Inhelder and Fischbein, have asked children to decide between two bags of coloured beads, out of which one they would have the greater chance of drawing a particular coloured bead. The comparisons which have to be made are of various types. First, the number of one colour may be the same in each bag while the numbers of the other colour are different (Figure 20 : 12(*a*) and (*b*)). Secondly, the numbers in the two bags may be proportional (Figure 20 : 12(*c*)), and finally the numbers of both colours in the two bags are different (Figure 20 : 12(*d*)). In general, (*a*) is the easiest, although a very young child may choose the bag with only one white bead, when they want to draw one white. Piaget and Inhelder found that (*a*) and (*b*) became correct at the stage of concrete operations, some time between 7 and 10 years, but only 74% of Green's 11-year-olds had (*b*) correct. Awareness of the

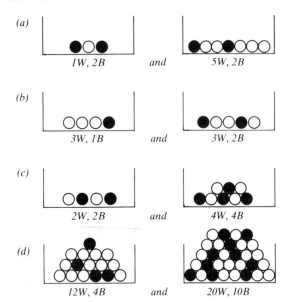

(a)   1W, 2B   and   5W, 2B

(b)   3W, 1B   and   3W, 2B

(c)   2W, 2B   and   4W, 4B

(d)   12W, 4B   and   20W, 10B

Figure 20 : 12

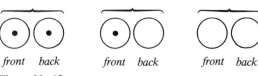

front back   front back   front back

Figure 20 : 13

equality in (c) seems to develop considerably later. Many children prefer 2W, 2B rather than 4W, 4B 'because there are less whites and blacks than in the other bag'. Type (d) is also difficult, as children in both cases (c) and (d) may compare only the actual number of white balls, irrespective of the number of black balls.

Children's views of which is the better choice can be verified in one of two ways. Fischbein found that improvement was produced by teaching a grouping technique; 4W, 4B is the same as two bags each with 2W, 2B, and no difference should be produced by mixing two bags which are the same. Similarly, 12W, 4B is the same as four bags of 3W, 1B; 20W, 10B is the same as ten bags of 2W, 1B. The drawer is more likely to get a white ball out of 3W, 1B than out of 2W, 1B. However, this strategy will not induce belief until a child is sure that mixing two bags does not affect the chances.

The other way of verifying the choice of bag is to try it. However, because of the randomness of drawing a ball from a bag, a single trial, or even a few trials, may be very misleading. Hence, children need to arrive at an intuitive understanding of the fact that over a long period, the random fluctuations tend to even out, so that about the right proportion of each colour tends to be drawn over a long period. This fact is known as the Law of Large Numbers, and it is fundamental to an understanding of probability. Piaget believes that this law is only understood at the stage of formal operations; Fischbein, however, thinks that experience and teaching can accelerate the understanding of probability. An experience quoted

by Sherwood[4] suggests that children of junior school age can come to appreciate the Law of Large Numbers. Three discs were shown to a class of children, marked as in Figure 20 : 13, and the children were then shown one side of a disc and asked to guess what was on the other side. The experimenter suggested to a child what is actually the best strategy: guess whatever is on the side you can see. This child was the most successful over a sequence of 50 tries, and the rest of the class appreciated and discussed the reason for this long-term success. They realised that a long run of tries was needed in order to validate a strategy.

This appreciation of the Law of Large Numbers is necessary in order that children may verify their choice between a 12W, 4B and a 20W, 10B bag in deciding the best bag for drawing a white bead. The first few draws can be very deceptive; for the first twelve draws from two bags the writer obtained the following results:

From the 9W, 3B bag: W B B B W W B B W W B W
From the 10W, 5B bag: W B B W W W B B W B W B

Thus, from each bag six balls of each colour were drawn. However, the writer was able to use a computer to simulate continuing both draws, and divergences eventually became apparent, as shown in Figure 20 : 14. Without a computer, it is not feasible to make such large numbers of draws, but a hundred or more can be made by a group of children.

When children are deciding which bag gives a better chance of success, they tend to compare the numbers of white and black beads. However, in

From the 9W, 3B bag		From the 20W, 10B bag	
No. of draws	No. of white balls	No. of draws	No. of white balls
12	6	12	6
120	88	120	90
1200	814	1200	889

Figure 20 : 14

[4]Sherwood, P. Probability in a Primary School, *Teaching Statistics*, 1(**1**), 1979, pp. 2–7.

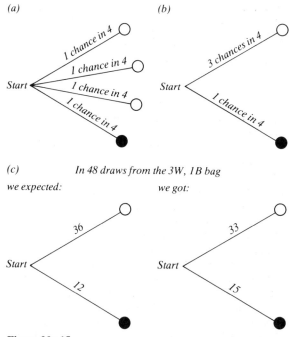

(a)

(b)

(c)

In 48 draws from the 3W, 1B bag

we expected:

we got:

Figure 20 : 15

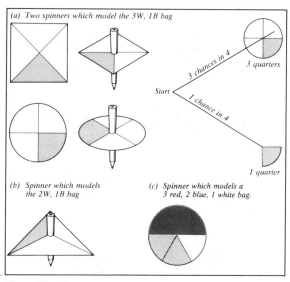

(a) Two spinners which model the 3W, 1B bag

(b) Spinner which models the 2W, 1B bag

(c) Spinner which models a 3 red, 2 blue, 1 white bag.

Figure 20 : 16

order to reach the next stage, they need to compare the number of white beads with the *total* number of beads. If we replace the 9W, 3B bag by the simpler equivalent of a 3W, 1B bag, there are four beads altogether, and only one of them is black. The black bead has only 1 chance in 4 of being drawn; so

does each white bead, but there are 3 white beads. Tree diagrams can be used to record this line of thought, as in Figure 20 : 15. The second diagram puts all the white beads together, as children cannot distinguish between the 3 white beads when they draw. From this diagram, predictions can be made of how many black and white beads to expect in 12 draws, 24 draws, and so on.

A spinner can be used to help children to connect 1 chance in 4 with the fraction one quarter. Either

Spinning the 3W, 1B spinner

Number of spins	Number of 'white'	Proportion of 'white' altogether
10 卌 卌	卌	5 out of 10
20 卌 卌	卌	10 out of 20
30 卌 卌	卌 III	18 out of 30
40 卌 卌	卌 IIII	27 out of 40

	0	1	2	3	4	5	6	7	8	9	10
first 10 spins					white						

	0	2	4	6	8	10	12	14	16	18	20
first 20 spins					white						

	0	3	6	9	12	15	18	21	24	27	30
first 30 spins					white						

	0	4	8	12	16	20	24	28	32	36	40
first 40 spins					white						

Figure 20 : 17

Spinning the 3W, 1B spinner

Number of spins	Number of 'white'	Fraction 'white'
10	5	$\frac{5}{10} = 0.5$
20	10	$\frac{10}{20} = 0.5$
30	18	$\frac{18}{30} = 18 \div 30 = 0.6$
40	27	$\frac{27}{40} = 27 \div 40 \approx 0.68$
50	35	$\frac{35}{50} = 35 \div 50 = 0.70$
60	43	$\frac{43}{60} = 43 \div 60 \approx 0.72$
70	52	$\frac{52}{70} = 52 \div 70 \approx 0.74$
80	60	$\frac{70}{80} = 60 \div 80 = 0.75$
90	69	$\frac{69}{90} = 69 \div 90 \approx 0.77$
100	76	$\frac{76}{100} = 0.76$

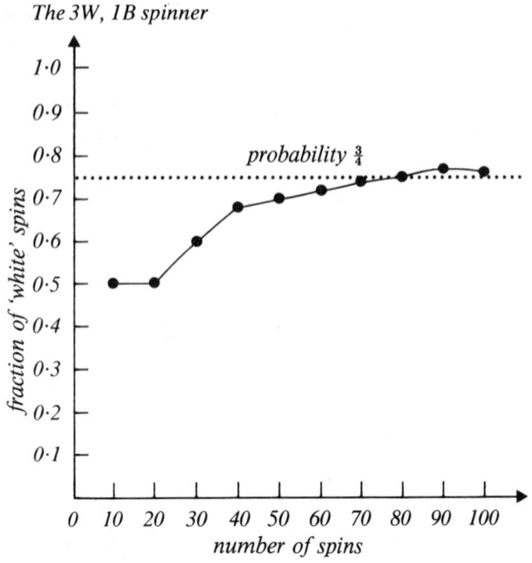

The 3W, 1B spinner

Figure 20 : 18

a square or a circular spinner can be used; and other spinners can be used as models of other bags of beads (Figure 20 : 16).

Children will by now be using the notation $\frac{3}{4}$ and $\frac{1}{4}$ instead of 3 quarters and 1 quarter. In order to make predictions they need to make calculations such as

$$\frac{1}{4} \text{ of } 48 = 48 \div 4$$
$$= 12$$
$$\text{and } \frac{3}{4} \text{ of } 48 = 3 \times 12 = 36$$

Actual experiments can first be recorded by tallying; and bars can be drawn to help children to see the proportions, as in Figure 20 : 17, which shows the spins of the 3W, 1B spinner.

Thus children begin to think of probability as the *long-term proportion*. A few spins of the spinner only approximate to this probability, which, in this case, is $\frac{3}{4}$. Children can use a calculator to help them work out the proportion of 'white' spins at each stage, as shown in Figure 20 : 18, and can draw graphs showing how their proportions approach the expected proportion.

Similar experiments can be made by tossing a coin, where the probability of getting a 'head' on each occasion is $\frac{1}{2}$. Dice can be used, as can packs of cards, where the probability of getting a spade each time a well-shuffled pack is cut is $\frac{1}{4}$.

DISPLAYING ALL THE POSSIBILITIES

Many dice games are played with two dice, and the total score is used. In some games, a double six has

to be thrown to start. The probabilities in these games can greatly surprise children. A game which seems inherently unfair is one in which two players move along a number line according to the throw of two dice. They move *one* step on each move, according to the scores on the two dice. Each player owns various totals, and moves one step when one of their totals shows the following:

Player A: 1, 2, 3, 4, 9, 10, 11, 12
Player B: 5, 6, 7, 8.

Player A, including the fake total of 1, owns twice as many totals as Player B but, in the great majority of games, Player B wins. A typical game is shown in Figure 20 : 19. Children will soon want to devise more equally-balanced games, and to find out why this one is so unfair.

Total on dice	A's score	B's score
6	0	1
8	0	2
4	1	2
6	1	3
5	1	4
8	1	5
9	1	6
7	1	7
12	2	7
5	2	8
7	2	9
5	2	10

Figure 20 : 19

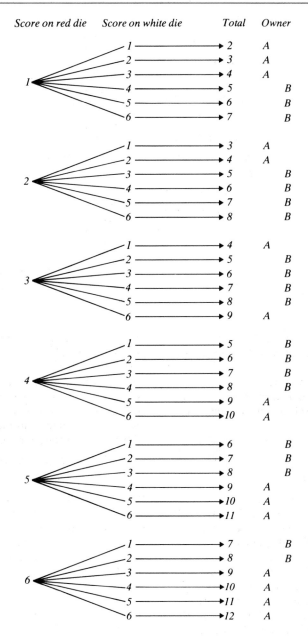

Score on red die	Score on white die	Total	Owner
1	1	2	A
	2	3	A
	3	4	A
	4	5	B
	5	6	B
	6	7	B
2	1	3	A
	2	4	A
	3	5	B
	4	6	B
	5	7	B
	6	8	B
3	1	4	A
	2	5	B
	3	6	B
	4	7	B
	5	8	B
	6	9	A
4	1	5	B
	2	6	B
	3	7	B
	4	8	B
	5	9	A
	6	10	A
5	1	6	B
	2	7	B
	3	8	B
	4	9	A
	5	10	A
	6	11	A
6	1	7	B
	2	8	B
	3	9	A
	4	10	A
	5	11	A
	6	12	A

Figure 20 : 20

A tree diagram can be drawn of all the possibilities; it is helpful if two different-coloured dice are used, so that they can easily be distinguished. This tree diagram needs careful planning, as it has 36 branches! It is shown in Figure 20 : 20. It can be seen that 12 can only occur as 6 + 6, while 7 occurs as 1 + 6, 2 + 5, 3 + 4, 4 + 3, 5 + 2, and 6 + 1. Of the 36 branches of the tree, Player B owns 20, while Player A only has 16. All these branches are equally likely to occur. No wonder the game favours B! Other tabulations can be made, and graphs drawn, of the numbers of ways each score can occur. Children can also graph the results of their own experiments. Some of the possibilities are shown in Figure 20 : 21.

The number of possibilities using dice is rather large; smaller tree diagrams can be obtained by using spinners with fewer sections, or coins. An analysis of the different orders in which boys and girls may occur in a family provides an interesting application of tree diagrams (Figure 20 : 22). Many classes will contain all four possible two-child families: two boys, boy followed by girl, girl followed by boy, two girls. The probabilities may be written on each branch of the tree, on the assumption that a boy and a girl are equally likely.

(a)

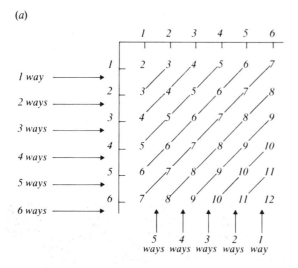

(b)

Score	Ways of getting the score
2	(1,1)
3	(1,2)(2,1)
4	(1,3)(2,2)(3,1)
5	(1,4)(2,3)(3,2)(4,1)
6	(1,5)(2,4)(3,3)(4,2)(5,1)
7	(1,6)(2,5)(3,4)(4,3)(5,2)(6,1)
8	(2,6)(3,5)(4,4)(5,3)(6,2)
9	(3,6)(4,5)(5,4)(6,3)
10	(4,6)(5,5)(6,4)
11	(5,6)(6,5)
12	(6,6)

(c)

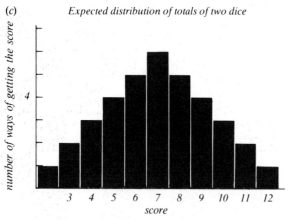

(d)

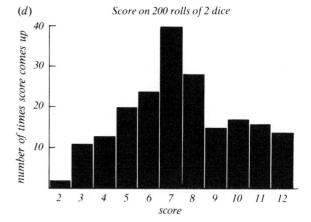

Figure 20 : 21

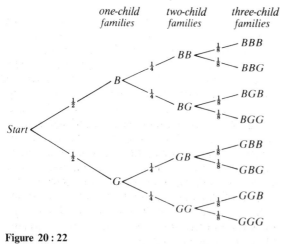

Figure 20 : 22

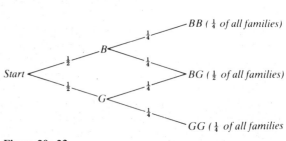

Figure 20 : 23

All possible one-child, two-child, three-child, and so on, families can now be investigated to see how far the actual distribution corresponds to that expected.

For some purposes, the boy-girl or girl-boy order in a two-child family does not matter, so that the families containing a boy and a girl can be grouped

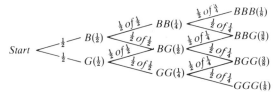

Figure 20 : 24

together, as shown in Figure 20 : 23. Then the diagram for three-child families, without taking account of the order of the children, can be constructed as in Figure 20 : 24. In each branch the method of calculating its probability is shown, and beside each type of family is shown its total probability.

The grouping of probabilities obtained from tree diagrams appears in several other situations which children may investigate. The *binostat*, or Galton's Quincunx, is a machine based on the mazes which Piaget and Inhelder and Fischbein investigated (Figure 20 : 25). Balls are dropped in at the top of the track. At every level, they bounce either to the left or right of fixed pegs, and run in a zigzag way down the maze to be caught in channels in a tray at the bottom.

On some binostats, the tray can be fixed at any level, so that children can look at the number of different paths a ball can take to arrive at any particular channel in the tray. The numbers of different pathways to the points at the top of each peg are shown in Figure 20 : 26. Balls hit peg A and branch either left or right. There is therefore just one route to B and one route to C. However, a ball can hit E having come from either left or right of A, so that there are two routes to E; but a ball that hits D must have come to the left of B, and so to

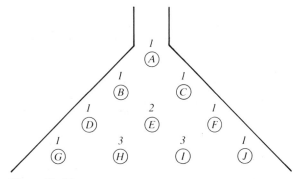

Figure 20 : 26

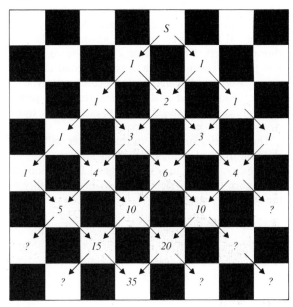

Figure 20 : 27

the left of A. Thus, there is only one way of getting to D.

A similar exploration can be made using a draughts piece, which moves one square diagonally, on a draughts board. The numbers in the squares of Figure 20 : 27 show the numbers of ways of getting to each white square, starting from square *S* at the top of the board, and always moving diagonally forward. It will be seen that the number of ways of getting to each square is the sum of the numbers of ways of getting to the two squares diagonally above it, which the draughts piece must pass through on the way. Some squares are marked with a ?, because the number of ways of reaching them is limited by the edges of the board. On a larger board there are many more ways.

The number pattern of Figure 20 : 27 is called *Pascal's Triangle*. It turns up in many places in probability and other parts of mathematics (Figure 20 : 28). Children will find many instances of the

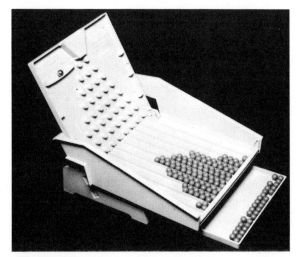

Figure 20 : 25

occurrence of numbers in the first few rows of Pascal's Triangle: 1, 2, 1 and 1, 3, 3, 1, in their listing of all the probabilities in exploration of random situations.

Very simple games of chance and skill can be devised, played and analysed using tree diagrams. An example is 'toss for four', which is played by one player against a coin. Head counts 2 and tails 1, and the current toss is added to the score. The player wins if the score reaches 4; the coin wins if the score reaches 5. The tree diagram shows all progressions in the score. The winning scores are boxed if the player wins, circled if the coin wins. The player should win rather more than $\frac{2}{3}$ of the games, and can work out the exact probability of winning. If two players play one against another, choosing whether to add 1 or 2 to the score, the first player cannot lose if a sensible second choice is made. More complicated games of the same type can be invented and analysed. Unfortunately, games as complicated as noughts and crosses present too many possibilities at each move.

The activities suggested in this chapter will enable children to develop their intuitions about probability, so that they have a good foundation of experience for the systematic study of probability at the secondary stage.

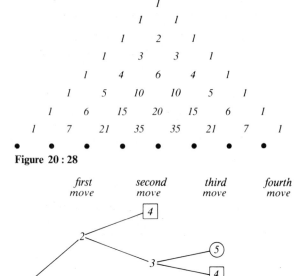

Figure 20 : 28

Figure 20 : 29

Probability in the National Curriculum

Attainment Target 5 of the National Curriculum includes the study of probability. Many primary teachers were surprised that probability makes an appearance as early as Level 1, but we have seen that it takes time for children to build up an appreciation of randomness. At the early levels, the idea of probability makes a gradual, non-numerical appearance. Some statements are:

- recognise possible outcomes of random events.

(AT5: Handling data, Level 1)

- recognise that there is a degree of uncertainty about the outcome of some events and that other events are certain or impossible.

(Level 2)

- place events in order of 'likelihood' and use appropriate words to identify the chance.

- understand and use the idea of 'evens' and say whether events are more or less likely than this.

(Level 3)

At Level 4, the numerical measurement of probability appears, and children are expected to identify all the possible outcomes of an event.

- understand and use the probability scale from 0 to 1.

- list all the possible outcomes of an event.

(Level 4)

At Level 5, children are expected to distinguish between a theoretical probability, which is based on the symmetry of a die or spinner, and an experimental probability, which is based on many repetitions of an experiment.

- recognise situations where estimates of probability can be based on equally likely outcomes, and others where estimates must be based on statistical evidence.

(Level 5)

The probability of combinations of events begins to occur at Level 6, but not until Level 8 are children expected to make calculations of combined probabilities which involve the multiplication of fractions or decimals. These calculations hence lie beyond the primary years.

- identify all the outcomes when dealing with two combined events which are independent, using diagrammatic, tabular or other forms.
  EXAMPLES: *List all the outcomes when tossing two coins: HH, TT, TH, HT.*
  List all the outcomes when tossing two dice and show the total sums arising.

(AT5: Level 6)

Thus, the National Curriculum's approach to probability represents a gradual treatment which develops throughout the primary years, but leaves a more detailed systematic study to the secondary years.

21 | PICTORIAL REPRESENTATION

TYPES OF INFORMATION

When we speak of information which is to be presented mathematically we are often thinking of facts which are quantitative in one or more aspects. They are records of counting or some kind of measuring. They may come to us in no special order and may appear quite haphazard. If we wish to see the significance of the numbers, we *arrange* them and *represent* them in ways which may show some pattern, a regular sequence, perhaps, or repetition, or a trend. On other occasions, the information is not quantitative, but is concerned with properties and their relations: '*all* the red shapes', or '*if* it is a square, *then* all the sides are equal'. Both quantitative and non-quantitative information can be represented pictorially, and the understanding and ability to use suitable forms of pictorial representation is a major mathematical skill which develops during the primary years. In

this chapter we shall summarise the forms of representation which have been used from the beginning of schooling and show how they can develop to form a basis for two important branches of mathematics, the study of relations and functions and the study of statistics.

PRESENTING SETS

From the first experiences of sorting, matching, counting and measuring, children collect information which they want to record and represent, either to help them to see more clearly what they have found out or to display it for other people to see. When they have classified objects and made sets of those with some common property they may put pictures of them or symbols inside a closed boundary. When two such sets have some connection and can usefully be compared their correspondences can be presented by arrows linking elements of the respective sets. Figures 21 : 1(a) and (b) show how relation diagrams (mapping diagrams) can be used to present the first comparison of whether there are more, fewer, or just as many elements in the first set as in the other. Finally, several sets can be compared and put in order. A number sequence is made, as in Figure 21 : 1(c).

The comparisons are made more obvious if the sets are represented on squared paper, one element to each square, in rows or columns with elements

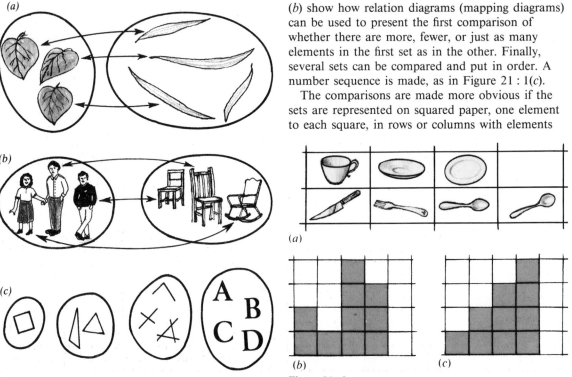

(a)

(b)

(c)

Figure 21 : 1

(a)

(b)   (c)

Figure 21 : 2

side by side so that matching can be seen at a glance, as in Figure 21 : 2. The arrangement may be haphazard or in order of number, each set having fewer members than the one on the right (Figure 21 : 2(c)).

ESTABLISHING AN ORDER

When children really know the counting order of natural numbers they have a sequence which enables them to put all kinds of things in order by matching them to this order of numbers. It is not the only pattern of order. The days of the week, the months of the year, the letters of the alphabet are fixed finite sequences which children will often use. They may record class attendances each school day, the number of birthdays occurring in the class each month, or the number of times a letter occurs on a page of a reading book. The things recorded may not be numbers. A class may list the forenames beginning with A, B, C, ... of the children in the class without counting them.

Anthony
Andy   Carol
Ann   Clare
Afsal   Bob   Colin
Adam   Betty Chris

A group of children may record the colours of cars they see on the way to school. This requires a double order if each child's record is to be kept. In the previous example we were sorting out the set of children into various subsets; we were interested only in their distribution over the range of the alphabet. One child's name could only appear once, in the subset of the initial letter. In the new inquiry there is a set of children and a set of car colours. Neither of these has a particular order. Our record will show each child related to *each* of the colours that is seen. We therefore use a rectangular table, often called a *two-way table, array or matrix*, as in Figure 21 : 3.

	Pam	Ken	Sue	Alan	Mary
black		✓	✓	✓	✓
blue	✓		✓	✓	✓
green	✓	✓	✓	✓	✓
red		✓	✓	✓	✓
white	✓	✓		✓	
yellow	✓			✓	✓

Figure 21 : 3

From this array a number of questions can be answered. For example: which car colour was seen by most children? Which child saw most colours? New orders of arrangement could then be made based on the *number of colours* seen, etc. One of the chief values of these arrays in that they enable us to find a fact quickly.

RECORDING SUBSETS

If a set is sorted using two or more properties, then *sorting trees, decision trees, Venn diagrams* and *Carroll diagrams* can be used to represent the sorting. A sorting tree shows all the possible choices

(*a*) *A sorting tree for birds*

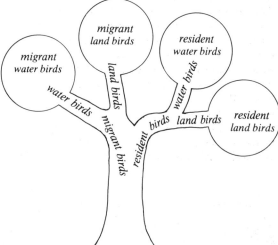

(*b*) *A decision tree for birds*

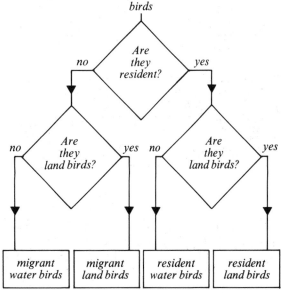

Figure 21 : 4

at each junction. Sorting trees develop into the tree diagrams which are used to analyse all the possibilities in the study of probability. Children who use a sorting tree should be encouraged to label each branch at a junction before using it for sorting (Figure 21 : 4). Thus, a sorting tree clearly separates all the possible subsets.

A Venn diagram (Figure 21 : 5(*a*)) or a Carroll diagram (Figure 21 : 5(*b*)), on the other hand, shows very clearly the *intersection* of the two sets, i.e. the set of elements that have *both* qualities; the *union* of the sets, i.e. the set of elements that have *at least one* of the properties, is also shown.

It will be noticed that drawings or lists of the elements are not necessary if we are presenting classification only and do not wish to show the numbers in the sets. The four *regions* of Figure 21 : 5 tell us that in the bunch of flowers there may be white scented, white unscented, coloured scented, and coloured unscented flowers.

For numerical properties other forms of

presentation may be preferable. A line, strip, or rod can illustrate the case in which there are 10 white flowers of which 3 are scented, and 10 of the flowers altogether are scented. If there are 24 flowers in the bunch the number in each of the four categories can be seen (Figure 21 : 6).

PICTOGRAMS

The use of pictures to record the objects in a set has been mentioned already. Symbolic figures (pinmen, cars, ships, pigs) make an effective means of showing comparable numbers of such things. But they have some disadvantages. If a picture is used for each element of a large set, for instance a traffic count of lorries, vans and cars, the numbers soon become too big to be readily recognised. If a scale is used, 1 pinman representing 10 people working at a certain job, then fractions of a pinman may be required. This form of symbol is best used for numbers which can suitably be rounded off so that 64 people will be shown as 6 pinmen, say, and 89 people as 9 pinmen. It is also a good idea to ensure that each picture symbol occupies the same length, so that comparisions may easily be made by eye. Figure 21 : 7 shows that this may be difficult.

(a)

neither white nor scented

A
white flowers

B

scented flowers

white scented

(b)

	white	not white
scented	white scented	
not scented		

Figure 21 : 5

Pets of children in class

dogs	
cats	
tortoises	

traffic count

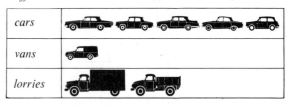

cars	
vans	
lorries	

1 picture stands for 10 vehicles

Figure 21 : 7

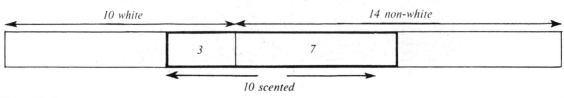

10 white   14 non-white

3   7

10 scented

Figure 21 : 6

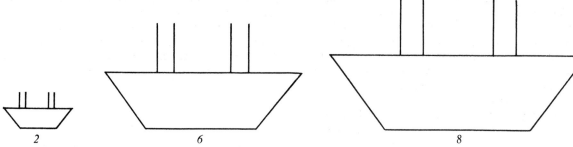

Figure 21 : 8

There is a risk that children who have been using a scale for drawing plans of classroom or playground may use scale wrongly in pictograms. For example, in recording the number of toy boats that three boys severally possess, say 2, 6 and 8, picture boats may be drawn 2, 6 and 8 units long. In *judging* the numbers represented an observer will probably compare the *areas* of paper which the pictures cover. This assumes an increase in height as well as length, so that the numbers represented on this basis are 2, 18 and 32. Even more mistaken is a judgement based on the three-dimensional boat which the flat drawing suggests. Width as well as length and height may now be assumed to have increased and the numbers conveyed to the observer are 2, 54 and 128: a formidable misinterpretation (Figure 21 : 8).

TABULATING MEASUREMENTS: AVERAGE AND SPREAD

When a large number of measurements have been taken, e.g. the height of each child in a class, a tabulation of all the heights will involve first putting them in order, say, from shortest to tallest. Even if only part of the class is taken, perhaps 20, the list is not easy to study. Statements can be made about the shortest, tallest and those about half-way in the list; that many of the children are near to the half-way mark can be noted. But a list of the heights can tell little more. It can be suggested that a set of class measurements is separated into subsets covering intervals of 3 cm. A set of 21 children in a ten- and eleven-year-old class produced the tabulation and block graph in Figure 21 : 9.

Discussing these numbers the pupils noticed the larger numbers of children in the middle; they then found that 147 cm was half-way between 132 cm and 162 cm. They also found the height of the pupil half-way between the shortest and the tallest child, who was the eleventh in order of height; this child's height fell in the 147 cm range.

The next step was to find the *average* height of the class. This was done by asking what would be the height of a class of children *who were all the same height*, and whose total height was the same. Thus some of the pupils found the average height, or *mean* height, by adding the heights of all the individuals and dividing by 21. This average proved

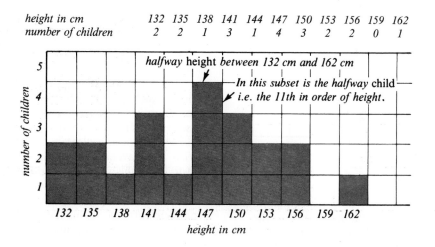

Figure 21 : 9

Average height of children of different ages

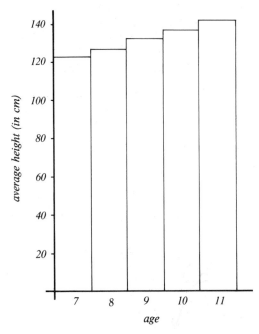

Figure 21 : 10

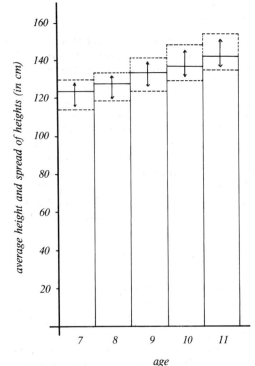

Figure 21 : 11

to be less than the half-way or *median* height and the effect of the one tall child in contrast to the four children in the two shortest groupings was noticed. Both the mean height and the median height of the class contain a lot of information in a single number. Thus, both the mean and the median can be regarded as *good representatives* of the set of numbers from which they are calculated.

The method of finding the mean by totalling and dividing used to be too tedious for practical use, but calculators and computer spreadsheets have changed this. It is now easy to find the average height of a whole class, and to see how the average changes during the school year. In the same way, growth can be studied by finding the average height of all the 7-year-old, 8-year-old, 9-year-old, 10-year-old and 11-year-old children in the school (Figure 21 : 10).

As well as the average, the *spread* of heights is very important. The average height may be 148 cm, but the class contains children of heights between 132 cm and 162 cm. In Figure 21 : 11, an indication of the spread of heights has been added to the graph of average heights.

EARLY IDEAS OF AVERAGE

Ideas of average start to develop earlier than the sophisticated calculations of the last section. When a set of measurements (like the handspans of a group of children) has been recorded in a diagram, it can often be seen that there are several measurements very close to the half-way length and that the other lengths are nearly balanced on either side. The children can decide whether their own hand-spans are more or less than the half-way length. This is an approach to the idea of average.

A child's first idea of an average may well be that of a fair share when unequal shares are pooled and redistributed to give each person the same amount. This leads directly to the method of adding up all the separate unequal shares and dividing the total by the number of people who are to share it. A team of five children have 6, 9, 4, 3, and 8 conkers in their respective collections. They decide to start a game with the same number each. They pool their contributions and have a total of 30. Sharing them among the participants they start with 6 conkers each. This set of numbers might also appear in quite a different situation, for instance as the scores obtained by 5 teams in a contest. The scores are shown in a diagram on squared paper.

What is the average score? The children may want to know this in order to compare their score with that of a set of teams of different size.

Discussion can lead to a guess. It must be somewhere between the highest and the lowest, and so between 9 and 3. They may guess 6. If the guess is right, the scores that are more than 6 must have

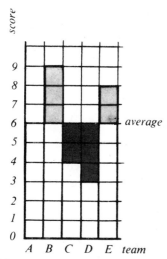

Figure 21 : 12

made up for those that were less than 6. How many scores above 6 are there?

Above 6:   9 – 6 = 3
          8 – 6 = 2
                5 above 6, giving an excess of 5

Below 6:   6 – 4 = 2
          6 – 3 = 3
                5 below 6, giving a defect of 5

The excess and the defect balance, as can be seen in Figure 21 : 12. Thus 6 must be the average score.

In their later calculations, children need to realise that the average, or mean, balances excess and defect. For example, the heights of 6 children, measured at random, may be 142 cm, 148 cm, 151 cm, 144 cm, 149 cm, 148 cm. If these are put in order of size a child may take the half-way measurement for an estimated average (Figure 21 : 13). The lengths greater than 148 cm give:

Above 148 cm   1 cm
                          3 cm
                          4 cm total

Below 148 cm   6 cm
                          4 cm
                         10 cm total

The defect is (10 – 4) cm greater than the excess. The estimated average is not quite right. With the average line where it was drawn on the graph the defect is too great. The line must be lowered to make the defect less. Lowering the estimate will change every difference from the guessed average, so we must spread the total defect of 6 cm over all 6 columns of the graph. Dividing 6 by 6 gives 1 cm

as the distance the line must be lowered. It will then be at 147 cm; this is the true average or *mean*. This should be checked by adding the differences above 147 cm and those below it to see whether, in fact, they give equal totals.

    Above: 1 + 1 + 2 + 4 = 8   *Below*: 5 + 3 = 8

As the amounts above and below balance, 147 cm must be the mean height; the line drawn on the diagram in Figure 21 : 13 shows this.

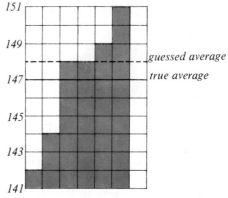

Figure 21 : 13

FUNCTIONS

The sets of measurements discussed in the last two sections were *statistical*: on another occasion a similar pattern is likely to occur, but the pattern will not be exactly the same.

Other sets of measurements which can be tabulated show a greater regularity; these are *determinate* and can be described by functions. The diameters of a set of regular hexagons of different sizes can be measured. Below is a tabulation of some that were measured. The value of such tabulations is that corresponding members of the two sets are placed together and the sequence of corresponding pairs is made evident (Figure 21 : 14).

Side of hexagon (cm)	1	1·5	2	3	3·5	4
Diameter of hexagon (cm)	2	3	4	6	7	8

That the diameter is twice the length of a side is immediately obvious without drawing a diagram. This can be shown by a *function* which multiplies the side by 2; it can be written as $d = 2 \times s$. The diameter of the hexagon with sides 2·5 cm can be found by the rule. The side of the hexagon with diameter 9 cm can also be worked out.

The counting and measuring involved in the surveys and records which are commonly part of the programme of primary schools provide many determinate sets of numbers. If the significance of

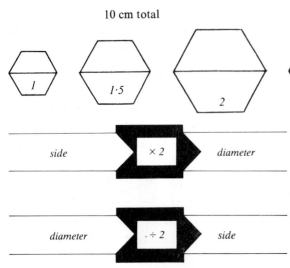

10 cm total

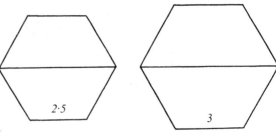

1

1·5

2

2·5

3

side → ×2 → diameter

diameter → ÷2 → side

Figure 21 : 14

the numbers is to be evident they must be organised in some way and the most suitable arrangement for any particular set of results must be devised. We can tabulate the numbers according to some rule or match them to another set of numbers. An example is given below. The numbers on the houses along one side of the street can be listed and placed against the actual count of the houses in the row (Figure 21 : 15).

The house numbers give the odd numbers in order and we can say what the house number is for the fourth house, and so on. From the tabulation we can find a rule for obtaining the house number of any house in the row.

The third number is 5, 1 less than 2×3
The fourth number is 7, 1 less than 2×4
The fifth number is 9, 1 less than 2×5

1   3   5   7

Order of houses in row 1 2 3 4 5 6...
House number   1 3 5 7 9 11...

n   H

6 → □ ×2 → → → □ − 1 →

Figure 21 : 15

This rule might be given by a child as 'double the number and subtract 1'. A symbol can then be

used: the nth house is numbered $(2 \times n) - 1$. We can write

$$H = (2 \times n) - 1$$

The function machine (Figure 21 : 15) illustrates this; a number n is placed in the input of the machine on the left, and is moved to the right, being changed as it moves through the machine. For example, 6 changes first to 12, and then the 12 changes to 11. Which house is numbered 17? The number 17 can be put in the output of a function machine, and moved backwards; the input must have been 8.

TABULATION OF PAIRS

We are often called upon to select partners from two different sets of people or things; partners for a school activity, dishes from two sections of a menu, and so on. When asked in how many ways they can do this children will work through all the possibilities but do not always discover a way of tabulating their results and organising their method so that they are sure of finding *all* possible pairs. A *two-way table* provides a surer way of doing this.

If a choice of four meat dishes and three vegetable dishes is offered on a menu, how many different combinations of one meat dish and one vegetable can be made? If children choose in a haphazard way, e.g. beef and peas, lamb and cabbage, etc., they may reach the correct answer, 12

	peas	cabbage	carrots
pork	pork, peas	pork, cabbage	pork, carrots
beef	beef, peas	beef, cabbage	beef, carrots
lamb	lamb, peas	lamb, cabbage·	lamb, carrots
ham	ham, peas	ham, cabbage	ham, carrots

Figure 21 : 16

(a)

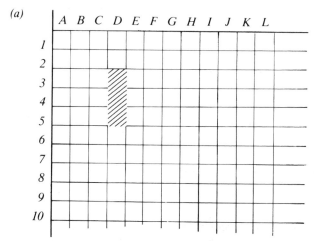

(b)

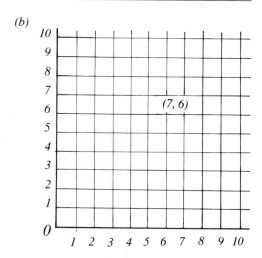

Figure 21 : 17

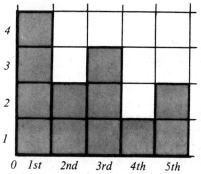

Figure 21 : 18

combinations, but they may not. Tabulation helps them to see all the possibilities. See Figure 21 : 16.

A table of this kind shows the number of choices as the *product* of the *numbers of elements* in each set. This array of ordered pairs is known as the Cartesian product of the sets. Each pair can be named by the row and the column in which it can be found. This reminds us of the co-ordinates (distances from the two axes) which Descartes first used to state the position of a point in a plane.

The game of Battleships provides another opportunity for children to use the Cartesian product of two sets. The player in Figure 21 : 17(*a*) has scored 'hits' in squares D3, D4 and D5. On this particular rectangular board, there are 12×10 squares which might be searched. Older children may use numbers for both rows and columns, and ensure that the conventional ordering of the co-ordinates is used (Figure 21 : 17(*b*)).

PRESENTATION ON SQUARED PAPER

Square ruling provides the easiest method of representing sets of *numbers* because any line on the page is marked in equal segments and can serve as a number line. Each segment carries a square; thus we can use a row or column of squares as the image of a natural number (Figure 21 : 18).

When several sets are to be recorded for comparison we can arrange a succession of columns: first, second, third, and so on. The cardinal number of each set is equal to the number of squares in the corresponding column. Alternatively names or measurements could be used to label the sets and show what kind of elements they contain. For instance, a record could be made of the number of

children who take a certain time to walk to school. The times would be given in intervals (for example, 10 to 14 minutes) and the children would arrange themselves in sets according to which time interval included their time. We can now show on squared paper a set of intervals of time and the number of children corresponding to each interval. These numbers are necessarily natural numbers and can properly be shown by a count of squares as in Figure 21 : 19. This type of diagram is called a *frequency diagram*; it shows the number of people in each *class interval*.

Two sets of records can be shown in this way on the same diagram. It helps comparison if bars are used rather than columns. The two sets can be drawn on opposite sides of an axis; symmetry, or lack of it, can then be readily judged. As an example we can show separately how long boys and girls take to walk to school.

A similar type of diagram will show daily attendances and absences in a class. In a week of infection the graph of Figure 21 : 20 might appear. The children will notice that the two bars for each

minutes to walk to school	5	5 — 9	10 —14	15 — 19	20 —24
number of children	7	14	12	5	1

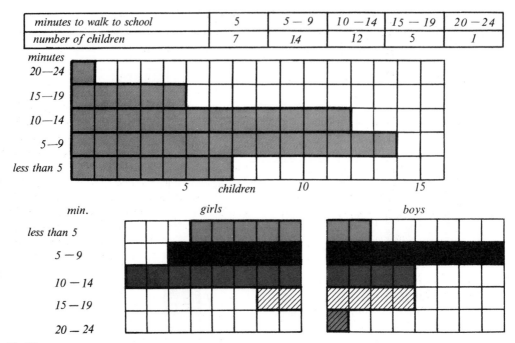

Figure 21 : 19

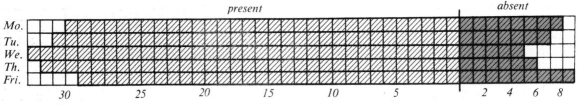

Figure 21 : 20

day put together always show the number of children in the class. A mistake can easily be seen.

Numbers that result from investigations are often too large for the number of squares available on the sheet of paper. Rulings in smaller squares can sometimes be used: 5 mm, or later 2 mm. If only one ruling is available a scale will be suggested by the children. It seems easy for children to think, 'I can say two to a square', or 'five to a square', and so on. They can then read the scale in twos, fives, etc.

BAR GRAPHS: THEIR USES AND LIMITATIONS

If a square sheet of paper is folded once, two pieces can be cut from it. If the pieces are folded again four pieces can be made. If the process is repeated the number of pieces made by successive folds can be tabulated and graphed. Since we are dealing with natural numbers, the *number* of folds and the

number of pieces, a bar graph with squares representing these numbers is quite suitable (Figure 21 : 21).

It is possible to continue this graph, making the next column twice as high as the fifth column, and so to check that the sixth fold would give 64 pieces. But there would be no meaning in asking about a *fraction* of a fold. We turn to another example to look for further developments.

The set of multiples of three can be shown on squared paper in the order 3, 6, 9, . . . using rectangular bars. Here again one can graph the first few multiples, notice that the corresponding corners of the blocks lie on a line, and then read higher multiples by continuing the line (Figure 21 : 22). Because we are dealing with natural numbers the bar graph is adequate; but if we think of multiplying by 3 instead of finding multiples of 3 we realise that we could multiply a *fraction* by 3; it is necessary to find a form of graph which will show relations between fractions. This cannot easily be

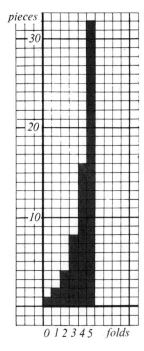

number of folds   0 1 2 3 4 5

number of pieces   1 2 4 8 16 32

Figure 21 : 21

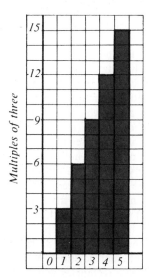

Figure 21 : 22

done with columns of squares. We therefore recall the way in which children have recorded their heights and similar measurements by representative lengths instead of squares.

LINE GRAPHS

The sequence of *multiples of three* gives the following tabulation:

1	2	3	4	5	6	7...
3	6	9	12	15	18	21...

The same sets of numbers would show the transformation of 1, 2, 3, 4, ... into 3, 6, 9, 12, ... by the operation of *multiplying by 3*. The axes of reference can be graduated to show numbers. It is then simple to represent 3, 6, 9, etc., by lines of the appropriate length drawn in succession at the *points* 1, 2, 3, etc. (Figure 21 : 23(*a*)). A similar graph could be drawn to show the number of apples which fall from a tree on each day of a week. Figure 21 : 23(*b*) shows such a representation. The first *bar-line graph* is regular and the tops of the

(a) multiples of three

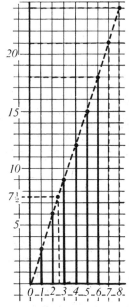

(b) daily fall of apples

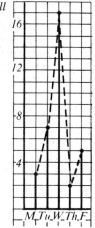

Figure 21 : 23

lines lie on a straight line; the second graph shows no pattern though it tells us something about the variable wind during the week. In the first graph there is a connection between the multiple, say 12, and the number which was *multiplied* by 3, in this case 4. In the second graph there is no connection between the number of apples which fell and the particular day of the week. In such a case where there is no apparent regularity the bar-line graph has only one advantage over the bar graph; joining the tops of the bar-lines by a broken line draws attention to the differences between successive numbers recorded.

In Figure 21 : 23(a) we find that a line drawn upwards from $2\frac{1}{2}$ on the horizontal axis meets the line of the 'tops' to give a length of $7\frac{1}{2}$, 3 times $2\frac{1}{2}$, as we should expect from the regularity of the multiples. If any fraction is marked on the horizontal axis the corresponding number which is 3 times the fraction can be read from the graph.

Sometimes children build up a graph of equivalences between centimetres and inches by comparing a measuring-tape marked in inches with a tape marked in centimetres. They find that 1 inch measures approximately $2 \cdot 5$ cm, 2 inches measure 5 cm, and so on. The graph is shown in Figure 21 : 24. The tape is continuous and *any* distance along it can be measured in inches or in centimetres. If the horizontal axis represents centimetres the upright line from *any point* on it drawn to meet the line of the graph will show the number of inches corresponding to the number of centimetres marked by the point on the axis. This means that any point on the line of the graph, since it comes from a point on the axis, shows $0 \cdot 4$ times the number represented on the axis. The line joining the tops of the plotted multiples can now be a solid line, without any breaks, because every point on it shows the same relation, $0 \cdot 4$ times, connecting the multiple with a number (Figure 21 : 24).

along the horizontal axis and the upright distance from it. These are the co-ordinates of the point and are shown as a number pair, say (2, 5). The tabulation of multiples given at the beginning of this section can, for instance, be replaced by a set of ordered pairs of numbers: (1, 3), (2, 6), (3, 9), (4, 12), (5, 15) (6, 18), (7, 21), ... The second number of each pair is the same *function* of the first member; a function machine may be used to illustrate it. Figure 21 : 25(a) shows the function machine for multiples of 3, and Figure 21 : 25(b) shows two equivalent machines which convert centimetres to inches.

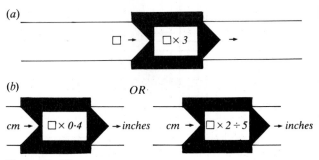

(a)

(b)   OR

Figure 21 : 25

RECTANGLES OF EQUAL AREA: ANOTHER APPROACH TO CO-ORDINATES

A set of rectangles all of the same area provides an interesting study of the relations between the lengths of their sides. The product of the length and breadth of each rectangle is the same number of units. If the rectangles are drawn so that one right angle is common to them all, the arms of the angle form two axes along which the sides of each rectangle can be marked (Figure 21 : 26). Even if only integral values of the sides are considered the corners of the rectangles not on the axes show a pattern. These vertices are fixed by the lengths of the sides of the respective rectangles and can be named by the number pair made by these lengths: (24, 1), (12, 2) (8, 3), (6, 4), (4, 6), (3, 8), (2, 12), (1, 24). It will be noticed that pairs of these rectangles, such as (3, 8) and (8, 3), are the same shape but in different positions. When children try to find all possible rectangles with area 24 units they will include some with fractional sides, e.g. $(0 \cdot 5, 48)$, $(0 \cdot 5, 16)$, $(2 \cdot 5, 9 \cdot 6)$, which are produced by dividing the area of 24 square units by convenient lengths such as $2 \cdot 5$ units to obtain the breadth. The graph and function machine are shown in Figure 21 : 26.

What has emerged is a curve or set of points

centimetres and inches

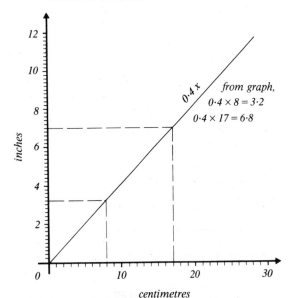

Figure 21 : 24

In a continuous graph such as the last, each point on the graph is fixed by two lengths, the distance

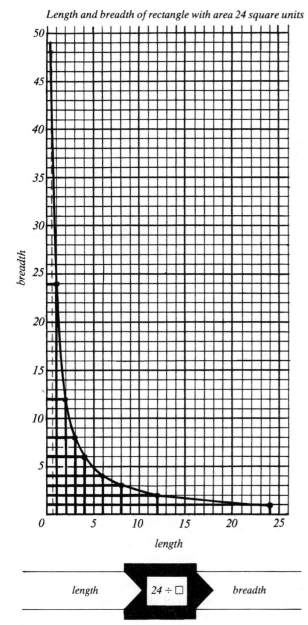

Length and breadth of rectangle with area 24 square units

length → **24 ÷ □** → breadth

Figure 21 : 26

which shows the relation between the lengths and
breadths of rectangles with constant area. The
lengths can be tabulated:

length	24	12	8	6	4	3	2	1	0·5	1·5	2·5
breadth	1	2	3	4	6	8	12	24	48	16	9·6

This tabulation shows a function from the set of
lengths, l, to the set of breadths, b. The relation
shown by the tabulation and graph is that the
corresponding elements of the two sets have the
same product. This can be written in symbols by
the pupils, perhaps as

$$b = 24 \div l$$
$$\text{or } l \times b = 24$$

THE STRAIGHT-LINE GRAPH: EQUAL INCREASES

If a class is carrying out a measuring project using a
7-dm stride as unit they can draw a graph as a
ready-reckoner to convert strides to dm. This graph
will obviously be the straight line produced by
plotting the multiples of 7. But certain properties of
the graph can be made apparent by studying it in
this context; as children stride they realise that at
each stride they move forward 7 dm. The distance
from the starting-point grows steadily 7 dm at a
time. It can be seen that for a straight-line graph it
will always be true that equal increases along the
x-axis produce equal increases in the lengths of the
uprights drawn at these intervals. For *every two*
strides forward a child will be *fourteen dm* further
from the start. This will be so wherever along the
line the two strides are taken. We can say that the
distance increases at a constant *rate* (Figure 21 : 27).

When children have developed, through practical
examples such as these, a good understanding of

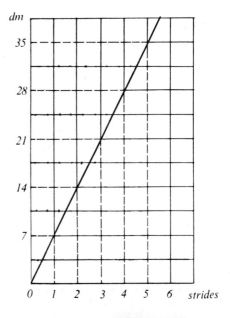

strides → **□ × 7** → dm

Figure 21 : 27

simple functions, with their function machines and graphs, they may begin to use conventional algebraic notation, in which the input to a function is often symbolised by a letter such as x, and output from the function by y. The two axes of the graph of a function are called the x-axis and the y-axis. Conventionally, the x-axis or *input axis* is always drawn across the page, and the y-axis or *output axis*, up the page. The function which shows multiples of 7 is then written

$$y = 7 \times x$$

or, omitting the $\times$ sign,

$$y = 7x$$

Another notation, which symbolises the function machine, is

$$x \rightarrow 7x$$

We can read this as 'x maps to $7x$'. These notations are shown in Figure 21 : 28. In (*c*), a rectangular function machine has the notation for its function written on it; it is tranforming an input of 5 into an output of 35.

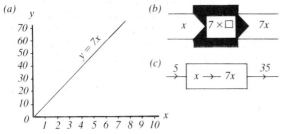

Figure 21 : 28

A graph showing the cost of a number of articles, charged at a constant rate, is a straight line. If a graph is drawn for the cost in pence of milk at 20p a bottle all the points lie on the line $y = 20x$. But if the milkman charges 20 pence per week for delivery of milk at 20p a bottle a graph of the weekly charges for various quantities of milk is of slightly different form: 20 pence must be added to the cost of milk and the rule for finding the charge y in pence for x bottles of milk would be $y = 20x + 20$. The two graphs $y = 20x$ and $y = 20x + 20$ are shown together in Figure 21 : 29. It will be seen that the addition of the extra 20 pence has meant that the graph has been translated upwards in the direction of the y-axis. In fact any point *above* the line $y = 20x$ has a y-number or ordinate *greater* than $20x$.

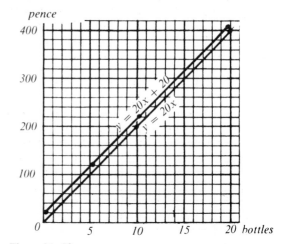

Figure 21 : 29

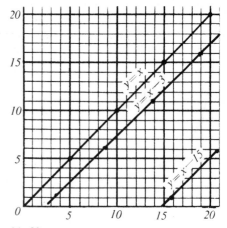

Figure 21 : 30

If, instead of charging for delivery, the milkman had allowed a *discount* of 20 pence for paying the bill each week the charges would be shown on a line below $y = 20x$. The rule for finding the charge in pence would be $20x - 20$.

In Figure 21 : 30 we see the line $y = x$ together with two other straight lines, $y = x - 3$ and $y = x - 15$. All points below $y = x$ have a y co-ordinate less than x. Thus we see that the line $y = x$ divides the plane of the paper into two parts: for all the points above it y is greater than x and for all the points below it y is less than x. Only on the line itself is y exactly equal to x.

Thus, the effect of adding or subtracting a number from the multiple of x is to translate the straight line of the graph parallel to the y-axis.

SQUARE NUMBERS

The sequence of square numbers, 1, 4, 9, 16, ... is both the measure of the areas of squares with sides 1, 2, 3, 4, ... units and the product of two equal factors, 1×1, 2×2, 3×3, 4×4, ... This set of numbers appears frequently in the mathematics which comes from phenomena of everyday life, for instance, the distances which a ball falls under gravity in successive equal times, and the area of the picture obtained when a slide is projected on to a screen from various distances. It is thus important that children should grow familiar with the shape of the graph produced when the natural numbers are mapped on to their squares. Only if the shape is well known can any estimate be given of a square number which lies *beyond* the points plotted. The continuity of the graph must also be realised so that the square of any number which lies *between* the natural numbers on the x-axis can be found.

If the points (0, 0), (1, 1), (2, 4), (3, 9), (4, 16), ... are plotted they are found to lie not on a straight line, but on a curve which, turned upside down, is like the one made by water pouring from a spout. The number of points plotted is insufficient to show the shape of the curve very certainly (Figure 21 : 31).

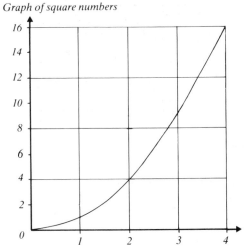

Graph of square numbers

Figure 21 : 31

Now children can use a calculator to put on the graph points corresponding to $1 \cdot 5^2$, $2 \cdot 5^2$, and so on. These additional points, $(1 \cdot 5, 2 \cdot 25)$, $(2 \cdot 5, 6 \cdot 25)$, $(3 \cdot 5, 12 \cdot 25)$, and so on, enable a good curve to be drawn. It can be used to read the square of any number within the interval on the x-axis over which the graph extends. The result will not be very accurate but it gives a pupil the means of stating an approximate result without calculation.

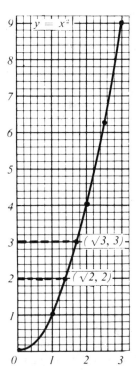

Figure 21 : 32

The inverse reading of the graph, that is, finding a number whose square is known, gives the pupils a way of doing this without using a calculator with a square root $\boxed{\sqrt{}}$ key. They can find an approximate value for the square roots of 2 and 3, lengths which appear in the diagonal of a square and the height of an equilateral triangle respectively (Figure 21 : 32). These are dealt with more fully in Chapter 36.

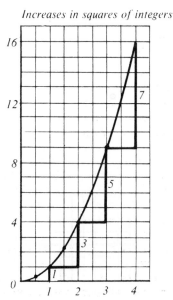

Increases in squares of integers

Figure 21 : 33

The graph of a set of numbers which increase by equal steps is a straight line. Can the pupils find out how the *squares* increase by using their graph? They can draw the vertical ordinates at equal intervals, and find how much longer each of them is than the preceding one. Each square number exceeds its predecessor by an odd number which has a special structure: it is one more than twice the preceding number. The step from 1 to 4 is 3, which is $2 \times 1 + 1$; the step from 4 to 9 is 5, which is $2 \times 2 + 1$ the step from 9 to 16 is 7, which is $2 \times 3 + 1$, and so it will continue if more points are plotted (Figure 21 : 33). In Chapter 22 we discuss another way of handling this pattern. This regularly changing rate of growth is remarkable, quite important, and of considerable interest to children.

EXTENSION TO DIRECTED NUMBERS

The graphs that we have considered so far in this chapter have represented signless numbers using axes which are drawn from the origin (zero) in one direction only. Fractional values are shown on these graphs but we also need to extend to graphs which use positive and negative numbers. This can be done by using the directed number line for each axis, drawing the axis in both directions from the origin. We can thus represent number pairs such as ($^-4$, $^+1$), and ($^-2$, $^-3$) (Figure 21 : 34).

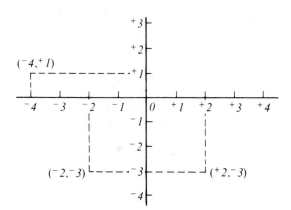

Figure 21 : 34

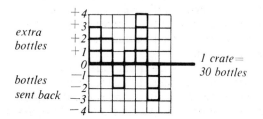

Figure 21 : 35

At early stages, directed numbers may only be needed on one of the axes. If children record how many more bottles of milk than one crate are needed each day, they will probably find one day that not all the bottles in the crate are needed, and a few must be sent back. A block graph will look like Figure 21 : 35.

When children are confident in their use of directed numbers the graph of any of the functions we have discussed in this chapter, such as $y = 2x + 1$, $y = x^2$, can now be extended to cover any suitable intervals of values of x. The values of y may then range between any negative and positive numbers (Figure 21 : 36).

$$y = 2x + 1$$

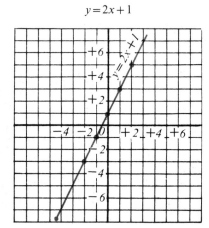

Figure 21 : 36

In the upper classes of the primary school experiments with speed, cooling, scoring with points and penalties, variations from a standard measurement, etc., will provide many occasions for the use of graphs of sets of directed numbers. The reason for the use of the negative numbers needs careful investigation in each situation, for example, in regard to past and future time or movement in opposite directions.

MAPPING DIAGRAMS

As an alternative to the Cartesian graph, a *mapping diagram* or *relation diagram* to illustrate the relation between two sets of numbers may be preferred on some occasions. Here, two number lines are drawn parallel to one another, and arrows join the points of one number line to corresponding points of the other. These diagrams, which have already been used in Chapters 9 and 18, give a different pictorial representation, and show another way of looking at relations between sets of numbers. Used in conjunction with graphs, relation diagrams will broaden children's ideas and pictures of these relations. A collection of examples, which show the different forms diagrams may take, are given in Figures 21 : 37 to 21 : 41. The inverse nature of the relations 'add 3' and 'subtract 3' can be seen in Figures 21 : 37 and 21 : 38.

The form of the relation diagram for 'divide by 3', or $y = \dfrac{x}{3}$, is easily obtained from Figure 21 : 39.

We next show the relation diagram corresponding to the curves of squares (Figure 21 : 40). It will be noticed that the lines joining corresponding points in the mapping do not radiate from a single point, as the relation is not a simple enlargement.

The relation 'add 3' or $y = x + 3$

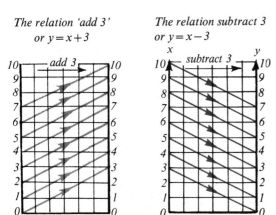

Figure 21 : 37

The relation subtract 3 or $y = x - 3$

Figure 21 : 38

Relation diagram for $x \rightarrow y = x^2$

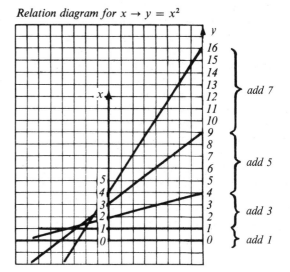

Figure 21 : 40

PIE-GRAPHS

One valuable form of diagram for showing the parts into which a set or a unit of time or money can be partitioned is a circle with subdivisions to represent the parts. The symmetry of the circle enables us to produce sectors in which the area is proportional to the angle at the centre and also to the length of the arc. One third of a day of 24 hours can be represented by a sector with an angle of 120° at the centre and with an arc which is one third of the circumference of the whole circle (Figure 21 : 41).

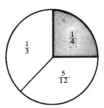

Figure 21 : 41

Therefore, whether we compare the areas of the sectors, the angles which they make at the centres, or the arcs which bound them, the ratios are identical with those of the quantities represented. The risk of misinterpretation is eliminated in this circular diagram.

Children usually learn how to mark out a clock-face and are therefore able to divide a circle into halves, thirds, quarters, sixths and twelfths, so that they can draw simple pie-charts to show how a day was spent.

The relation multiply by 3 or $y = 3x$

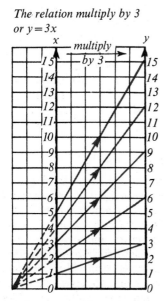

Figure 21 : 39

Some computer software is able to draw pie-graphs of data supplied to it, so that children are able to interpret pie-graphs before they can draw their own pie-graphs very accurately.

When they have mastered the skill of measuring with a protractor, they can draw any angle which is needed in a pie-graph, using the calculator to work out the required angles (Figure 21 : 42). For example, in a pie-graph to show the spending of £1 pocket money, the savings of 35 pence will be shown by a sector calculated as follows:

100 pence is represented by 360°,
so 1 penny is represented by $\frac{100}{360} = 3 \cdot 6°$
and 35 pence is represented by $3 \cdot 6 \times 35 = 126°$

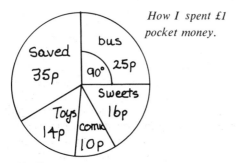

How I spent £1 pocket money.

Figure 21 : 42

There are many occasions when a class will find that a pie-graph is the most suitable way of exhibiting information. It shows well the occupations of a person over an interval of time, or the apportionment of money, or the subsets into which a class of children can be split according to a particular property such as weight, athletic skills, etc. Since the whole circle must be regarded as the whole interval, sum of money, or number of pupils, fractions are required to show the ratio of any part of the whole. This type of fractional work greatly helps the understanding of fractions and their connection with ratio.

The limitation of the pie-graph is that it does not lend itself to the comparison of two situations, for instance the way Alan spends his evening with Derek's occupations during the same time, or the uses of pocket money in a week of term and a week of holiday.

SCATTER GRAPHS

Children often take two measurements for each child in a group, and want to see whether these measurements are connected in any way. For

example, they may measure how far each child can jump, and that child's height. Is it true that taller children can jump further? A *scatter graph* is a very useful visual display here (Figure 21 : 43). It seems that there is some *correlation* between height and length of jump, although the correlation is not very close.

A graph which shows on one axis the ages of a group of children, some very young and some approaching adulthood, and on the other axis the length of time they sleep during a day, would be likely to show a *negative correlation* (Figure 21 : 44).

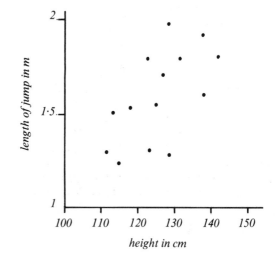

Figure 21 : 43

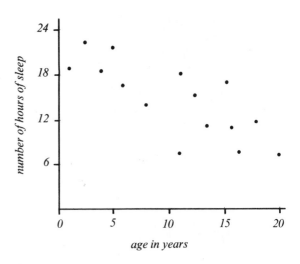

Figure 21 : 44

THE VALUE OF VARIETY

This chapter has set out several forms of
presentation in which the visual pattern is
all-important, whether in tabulation or diagram.
Each form has its own special advantages; pupils
should be able to make their own choices. By this
means they are encouraged to consider carefully the
numbers they are trying to present and thus to
become aware of some of their properties. Instead
of learning a new procedure in terms of symbols
they translate a real situation into an ordered
arrangement or diagram and then can more easily
discover new properties or solve a problem.

Pictorial representation in the National Curriculum

Pictorial representation occurs in two attainment
targets in the National Curriculum. Some
Statements of attainment in Attainment Target 5
are concerned with the representation of
statistical and other real data, while the
representation of algebraic data is found in
Attainment Target 3.

In handling statistical data, children are
expected to become familiar with the wide
variety of forms of representation which have
been described in this chapter. The following are
mentioned between Levels 1 and 6:

mapping diagrams
block graphs
frequency tables
Carroll diagrams
Venn diagrams
bar charts
pictograms
decision tree diagrams
bar-line graphs
line graphs
frequency diagrams
pie charts
scatter graphs
network diagrams

The build-up to the use of algebraic graphs in
Attainment Target 3 starts at Level 4, with the
introduction of co-ordinates. At Level 4 only
positive co-ordinates are used. These are known
as co-ordinates *in the first quadrant*. At Level 5
children are expected to use positive and negative
co-ordinates (*in all four quadrants*). At Level 6
children are required to draw graphs of simple
algebraic functions. The statements in the
Programme of Study are:

- learn the conventions of the co-ordinate
representation of points; work with co-ordinates
in the first quadrant.

(AT3: Level 4)

- understand and use co-ordinates in all four
quadrants.

(AT3: Level 5)

- draw and interpret simple mappings in context,
recognising their general features.
EXAMPLE: $x \rightarrow x+1$ (or $y = x+1$)
$x \rightarrow 2-x$ (or $y = 2-x$)
$x \rightarrow x^2$ (or $y = x^2$)

(AT3: Level 6)

22 | PATTERNS AMONG THE NATURAL NUMBERS

Factorisation of 24

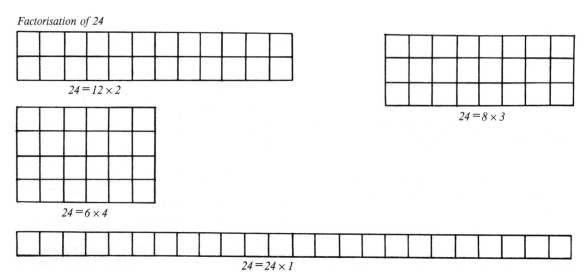

$24 = 12 \times 2$

$24 = 8 \times 3$

$24 = 6 \times 4$

$24 = 24 \times 1$

Figure 22 : 1

INTRODUCTION

For many centuries people have been fascinated by the various patterns which have been found among the natural numbers. Some of these patterns may arise naturally out of children's practical experiments with numbers, and will lead them to make their own simple investigations, and to begin to generalise about the properties of numbers. The fascination which simple number patterns hold for children can be used to give practice in computation and to show the need for accuracy (since patterns will not be found among numbers if calculations are inaccurately made), and to give help in practical learning of multiplication tables. These uses are, however, subservient to the search for order and pattern which is one of the driving forces of all mathematical work with children.

This chapter contains a variety of number patterns with which older primary children will enjoy experimenting, together with a mechanical method of multiplication which is of historical interest.

[1]If the child does not yet understand the commutative law for multiplication, each of these rectangles may appear twice, as for instance 6 × 4 and 4 × 6.

FACTORS AND MULTIPLES

In their work on multiplication and division, children come to know not only that 6 fours are equal to 24, but in reverse, that 24 is made up of 6 fours; that is, they know that 6 and 4 are *factors* of 24. Similarly, 12 is a factor of 24, because $24 = 2 \times 12$; 11 is not a factor of 24, because 24 is not a multiple of 11, and so 24 cannot be divided by 11 a whole number of times without remainder. Children may study the factors of such a number as 24 by taking 24 cubes or bricks and trying to arrange them in rectangular layers in as many different ways as possible. They will obtain the arrangements shown in Figure 22 : 1. No other rectangles are possible; an attempt to make one with a side of 7 units can only produce the

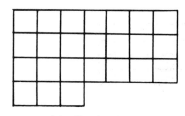

$24 = (3 \times 7) + 3$

Figure 22 : 2

Factors of 24

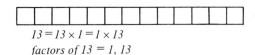

factors of 24 = 1, 2, 3, 4, 6, 8, 12, 24

$$1 \times 24 = 24 \times 1 = 24$$
$$2 \times 12 = 12 \times 2 = 24$$
$$3 \times 8 \;=\; 8 \times 3 = 24$$
$$4 \times 6 \;=\; 6 \times 4 = 24$$

Figure 22 : 3

arrangement shown in Figure 22 : 2. The only factors of 24, that is the only natural numbers by which 24 can be divided exactly without remainder, are 1, 2, 3, 4, 6, 8, 12 and 24. If appropriate pairs of members of this set of factors

1, 2, 3, 4, 6, 8, 12, 24

are multiplied together, the original number 24 will be recovered. The correct linking is shown in Figure 22 : 3.

If children experiment similarly with the factorisation of 36, they will obtain the situation shown in Figure 22 : 4. It will be noticed that 36 is a *perfect square*; that is, the product of two *equal* factors. One of the rectangular arrangements is the square 6 × 6.

PRIME NUMBERS

Every number is divisible by 1 and by itself; some

Factorisation of 13

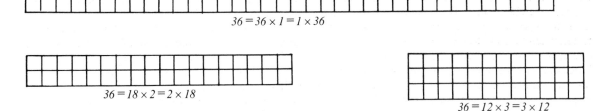

$13 = 13 \times 1 = 1 \times 13$
factors of 13 = 1, 13

Figure 22 : 5

natural numbers have no other factors. The factor pattern for 13 is shown in Figure 22 : 5. A natural number greater than 1 whose only factors are 1 and itself is called a *prime number*.[2] The first few prime numbers, which children will quickly find because they are so familiar with the smaller natural numbers, are 2, 3, 5, 7, 11, 13, 17, ... If children find difficulty in picking out prime numbers, the tabulation of the factors of each number shown in Figure 22 : 6 may be helpful. Here the pairs of factors of each number are listed according to the multiplication table in which they appear. Use may be made of the commutative law to avoid putting each pair of factors into the list twice. If this is done, only the factors in bold type in Figure 22 : 6 will appear. The tabulation can be continued for as long as is desired, and it is extremely easy to pick out prime numbers from it.

If many prime numbers are to be found, a

[2] It is usual not to include 1 among the prime numbers, since 1 is a factor of every number.

Factorisation of 36

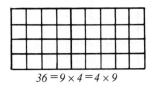

$36 = 36 \times 1 = 1 \times 36$

$36 = 18 \times 2 = 2 \times 18$

$36 = 12 \times 3 = 3 \times 12$

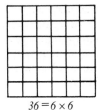

$36 = 9 \times 4 = 4 \times 9$

$36 = 6 \times 6$

Set of factors of 36 = 1, 2, 3, 4, 6, 9, 12, 18, 36

Figure 22 : 4

Prime	number	Table of ones	Table of twos	Table of threes	Table of fours	Table of fives	Table of sixes	Table of sevens	Table of eights	Table of nines
	1	1 × 1								
P	2	2 × 1	1 × 2							
P	3	3 × 1		1 × 3						
	4	4 × 1	2 × 2		1 × 4					
P	5	5 × 1				1 × 5				
	6	6 × 1	3 × 2	2 × 3			1 × 6			
P	7	7 × 1						1 × 7		
	8	8 × 1	4 × 2		2 × 4				1 × 8	
	9	9 × 1		3 × 3						1 × 9
	10	10 × 1	5 × 2			2 × 5				
P	11	11 × 1								
	12	12 × 1	6 × 2	4 × 3	3 × 4		2 × 6			
P	13	13 × 1								
	14	14 × 1	7 × 2					2 × 7		
	15	15 × 1		5 × 3		3 × 5				
	16	16 × 1	8 × 2		4 × 4				2 × 8	
P	17	17 × 1								
	18	18 × 1	9 × 2	6 × 3			3 × 6			2 × 9
P	19	19 × 1								
	20	20 × 1	10 × 2		5 × 4	4 × 5				
	21	21 × 1		7 × 3				3 × 7		
	22	22 × 1	11 × 2							
P	23	23 × 1								
	24	24 × 1	12 × 2	8 × 3	6 × 4		4 × 6		3 × 8	
	25	25 × 1				5 × 5				

Figure 22 : 6

simplified version of this arrangement, known as the Sieve of Eratosthenes[3], is convenient. To operate this Sieve, a list of natural numbers is made.

The number square shown in Chapter 17 will yield all the primes up to 100, and the method is a direct extension of the colouring of multiples suggested in that chapter.

[3]Eratosthenes was a Greek mathematician who was librarian of the University at Alexandria at about 240 BC. He also measured the circumference of the earth by a very ingenious method. See Hogben, L. *Man Must Measure* (Rathbone, 1955), page 36.

Among the multiples of 2, the only prime is 1×2 or 2 itself. We therefore put a ring round 2 on the list, and go through the list crossing out the set of multiples of 2 because they are not prime, i.e. 4, 6, 8, 10, ... The first number remaining on the list is 3, which is 1×3 and is prime. We ring it, and cross out its set of multiples 6, 9, 12, ... Next, $4 = 2 \times 2$ has already been crossed out, and the next remaining number is 5, which is prime. This is ringed and its set of multiples 10, 15, 20, ... crossed out. We proceed by crossing out multiples of primes. Figure 22 : 7 shows the operation of the Sieve to give primes up to 150.

The Sieve of Eratosthenes

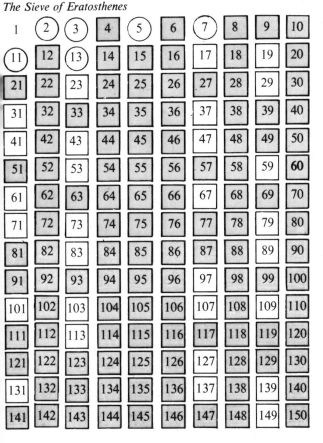

Figure 22 : 7

COMPOSITE NUMBERS AND THEIR PRIME FACTORS

A natural number greater than 1 which is not a prime number is called a *composite number*. The prime numbers are building bricks from which all the composite numbers can be built by multiplication. Children may like to build composite numbers out of the members of a given set of prime numbers, and see how many different composite numbers they can find. Figures 22 : 8, 22 : 9 and 22 : 10 show the building up of numbers from sets of primes, the members of which may or may not be repeated in building the composite numbers. It should be noticed that the set of composite numbers which can be built is the set of factors (other than 1) of the largest of them.

Numbers built from 2, 3, 7

Using 1 prime factor	2	3	7
Using 2 prime factors	$2\times3=6$, $3\times7=21$, $2\times7=14$		
Using 3 prime factors	$2\times3\times7=42$		

Set of factors of $42=1$, 2, 3, 6, 7, 14, 21, 42

Figure 22 : 8

Numbers built from 2, 2, 2, 3

Using 1 prime factor	2	3
Using 2 prime factors	$2\times2=4$	$2\times3=6$
Using 3 prime factors	$2\times2\times2=8$	$2\times2\times3=12$
Using 4 prime factors	$2\times2\times2\times3=24$	

Set of factors of $24=1$, 2, 3, 4, 6, 8, 12, 24

Figure 22 : 9

The use of the Sieve is not nearly as laborious as it looks. A number less than 150 which is not a prime must have a factor less than 13, because $13 \times 13 = 169$. Hence sieving out multiples of all the primes up to 13 will leave all the primes up to 150. In Figure 22 : 7 a circle has been put round all the numbers whose multiples were crossed out; the other numbers left after sieving, which are also primes, are enclosed in squares; shaded squares show the numbers crossed out.

Prime numbers have always interested mathematicians, and there are still many unsolved problems about them. There is an infinite number of primes, but in general they get rarer as their size increases. There are, however, many *twin primes*, such as 11 and 13, 41 and 43, 137 and 139, 149 and 151, which are only 2 apart. It is likely that there is an infinite number of twin primes, but this has not yet been proved.

As a reversal of this process, a tree diagram can be used to break down a composite number into its prime factors. The method is shown in Figure 22 : 11. We see that factorisation of a composite number can often yield several different trees, but that there is only one prime factorisation of any number; this will appear at the end of any tree for that number. It may be interesting in a simple case

Numbers built from 2, 3, 5, 11

Using 1 prime factor	2	3	5	11
Using 2 prime factors	$2 \times 3 = 6$ $3 \times 5 = 15$	$2 \times 5 = 10$ $3 \times 11 = 33$		$2 \times 11 = 22$ $5 \times 11 = 55$
Using 3 prime factors	$2 \times 3 \times 5 = 30$ $2 \times 5 \times 11 = 110$			$2 \times 3 \times 11 = 66$ $3 \times 5 \times 11 = 165$
Using 4 prime factors		$2 \times 3 \times 5 \times 11 = 330$		

Set of factors of 330 = 1, 2, 3, 5, 6, 10, 11, 15, 22, 30, 33, 55, 66, 110, 165, 330

Figure 22 : 10

to construct this family tree practically, using interlocking cubes or rods, as shown in Figure 22 : 12. Children should also notice what happens when they divide a number by one of its factors. For instance

$$24 \div 3 = (2 \times 2 \times 2 \times 3) \div 3$$
$$= 2 \times 2 \times 2$$
$$= 8$$

and

$$24 \div 6 = (2 \times 2 \times 2 \times 3) \div (2 \times 3)$$
$$= 2 \times 2$$
$$= 4$$

Factorisation of 24 into prime factors

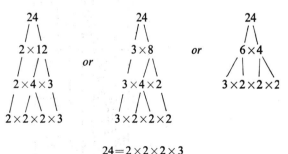

$$24 = 2 \times 2 \times 2 \times 3$$

Figure 22 : 11

$$24 \div 6 = (2 \times 2 \times 2 \times 3) \div (2 \times 3)$$
$$= 2 \times 2$$
$$= 4$$

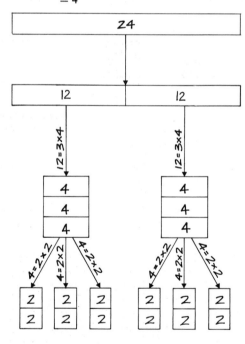

$$24 = 2 \times 3 \times 2 \times 2$$

Figure 22 : 12

SQUARE NUMBERS

Among the most interesting of the natural numbers are those, such as 36, which can be factorised into a product of two *equal* factors. Children will find these numbers at an early stage, when they build up small cubes to make square layers of increasing size. The first few of these *square numbers,* or *perfect*

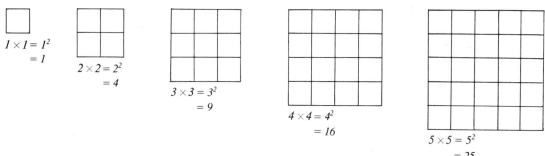

$1 \times 1 = 1^2$
$= 1$

$2 \times 2 = 2^2$
$= 4$

$3 \times 3 = 3^2$
$= 9$

$4 \times 4 = 4^2$
$= 16$

$5 \times 5 = 5^2$
$= 25$

Figure 22 : 13

squares, are shown in Figure 22 : 13. We have already seen that the perfect squares appear in the leading diagonal of the multiplication table square.

The perfect squares increase in size more and more rapidly as the side of the squares increases. The number of unit squares needed to make each perfect square is shown in the block graph of Figure 22 : 14(*b*). This diagram also emphasises the number of unit squares which must be added to each perfect square to construct the next perfect square.

Since the number of units in each perfect square grows so rapidly, it is inconvenient to use the same scale on both axes of the graph.

In Figure 22 : 14(*c*) the scale on the vertical axis is greatly reduced, and the block graph of Figure 22 : 14(*b*) is replaced by a line graph. Children will also see that they can make each square from the one before it by adding a border round two sides of the square, and that the number of squares in the border is always an odd number. They may write as

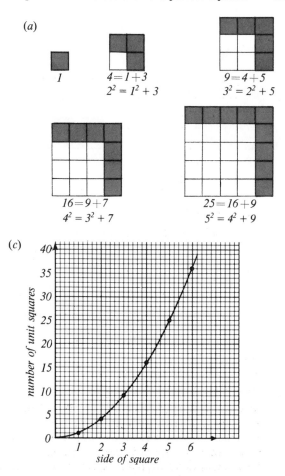

(*a*)

1

$4 = 1 + 3$
$2^2 = 1^2 + 3$

$9 = 4 + 5$
$3^2 = 2^2 + 5$

$16 = 9 + 7$
$4^2 = 3^2 + 7$

$25 = 16 + 9$
$5^2 = 4^2 + 9$

(*c*)

number of unit squares

side of square

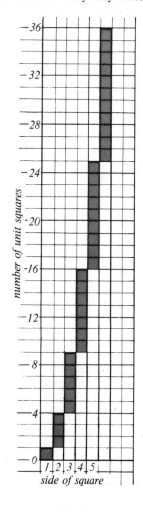

(*b*)

number of unit squares

side of square

Figure 22 : 14

a description of the building up of squares:

$$
\begin{aligned}
1 &= 1 = 1 \times 1 = 1^2 \\
1 + 3 &= 4 = 2 \times 2 = 2^2 \\
1 + 3 + 5 &= 9 = 3 \times 3 = 3^2 \\
1 + 3 + 5 + 7 &= 16 = 4 \times 4 = 4^2 \\
1 + 3 + 5 + 7 + 9 &= 25 = 5 \times 5 = 5^2
\end{aligned}
$$

Situations such as this, where a number pattern is repeated, will often lead children to begin to generalise, at first in words such as, 'if you add together the first 5 odd numbers, the sum is 5^2'; later, the generalisation will be algebraic: 'the sum of the first n odd numbers is n^2'. At this stage a child will confidently predict that the sum of the first 32 odd numbers will be 32^2; predictions such as this are easily verified using a calculator. When long calculations are undertaken, some tabular method of recording intermediate results needs to be devised, so that mistakes are not made (Figure 22 : 15).

	Add	Result	
1st odd number	*1*	*1*	$= 1^2$
2nd odd number	*3*	*4*	$= 2^2$
3rd odd number	*5*	*9*	$= 3^2$
4th odd number	*7*	*16*	$= 4^2$
5th odd number	*9*	*25*	$= 5^2$
. . . .			
31st odd number	*61*	*961*	$= 31^2$
32nd odd number	*63*	*1024*	$= 32^2$

Figure 22 : 15

The growth of other shapes than squares follows the same law. If larger equilateral triangles are built out of small equilateral triangles (Figure 22 : 16), or if larger rectangles are built out of small rectangles such as those represented by Cuisenaire rods (Figure 22 : 17), provided that all the shapes formed are *similar* (*see page 453*), then the law of growth will be that of the perfect square.[4]

The growth of equilateral triangles

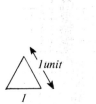
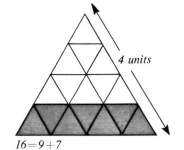

1 unit

1

2 units

$4 = 1 + 3$

3 units

$9 = 4 + 5$

4 units

$16 = 9 + 7$

Figure 22 : 16

The growth of similar rectangles

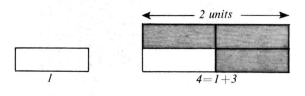
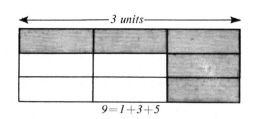

1

— *2 units* —

$4 = 1 + 3$

— *3 units* —

$9 = 1 + 3 + 5$

— *4 units* —

$16 = 1 + 3 + 5 + 7$

Figure 22 : 17

[4]This illustrates the fact that the areas of *similar figures* are proportional to the squares of corresponding sides (*see page 455*).

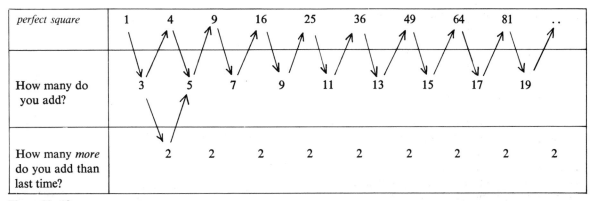

Figure 22 : 18

Children may find the tabulation of the growth of perfect squares interesting (Figure 22 : 18). It can be used to investigate the construction of many other sequences. The second line of the table shows the *differences* between successive members of the sequence, and the third line shows the differences of differences, or *second differences*. The third line of the table is probably unnecessary in this case, but it is useful when dealing with more complicated sequences.

When they have seen how the pattern of 1, 1 + 3, 1 + 3 + 5, 1 + 3 + 5 + 7, ... behaves, children may wish to investigate other regular growth patterns, such as

1, 1 + 2, 1 + 2 + 3, 1 + 2 + 3 + 4, ... (sums of natural numbers)
2, 2 + 4, 2 + 4 + 6, 2 + 4 + 6 + 8, ... (sums of even natural numbers)

or to examine the growth of cubes and other shapes. Some of these growth patterns are investigated in the next two sections.

TRIANGULAR NUMBERS AND RECTANGULAR NUMBERS

If circular counters are used instead of equilateral triangles to build up a growth pattern rather like that of Figure 22 : 16, it will be found that the

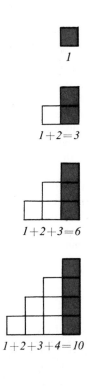

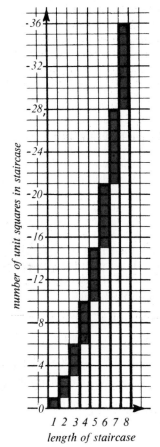

Figure 22 : 20

   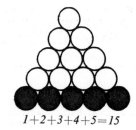

Figure 22 : 19

The triangular numbers make rectangles

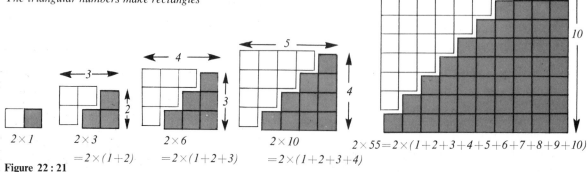

2×1 2×3 2×6 2×10 $2 \times 55 = 2 \times (1+2+3+4+5+6+7+8+9+10)$

        $= 2 \times (1+2)$ $= 2 \times (1+2+3)$ $= 2 \times (1+2+3+4)$

Figure 22 : 21

counters can conveniently be packed as shown in Figure 22 : 19.

The *triangular numbers* 1, 3, 6, 10, 15, 21, ... are also found in the building of 'staircases' with structural apparatus (Figure 22 : 20). The triangular numbers do not follow such an easily recognisable growth pattern as do the square numbers, but two equal staircases can always be fitted together to make a rectangle (Figure 22 : 21) by turning one of them upside down.

All these rectangles have a length greater by one unit than their width; that is, if the width is n units, the length is $(n + 1)$ units.[5] This fact can be used to calculate the value of any triangular number. For instance, the last rectangle in Figure 22 : 21 shows that:

$$2 \times (1 + 2 + 3 + 4 + \ldots + 9 + 10) = 10 \times 11,$$

so that

$$1 + 2 + 3 + \ldots + 9 + 10 = (10 \times 11) \div 2 = 55$$

For successive triangular numbers the pattern is:

first triangular number
   $= 1 = (1 \times 2) \div 2$
second triangular number
   $= 1 + 2 = (2 \times 3) \div 2$
third triangular number
   $= 1 + 2 + 3 = (3 \times 4) \div 2$
fourth triangular number
   $= 1 + 2 + 3 + 4 = (4 \times 5) \div 2$

and in general:

[5]The numbers of unit squares in these rectangles, 1×2, 2×3, 3×4, 4×5, ... were called by the Greeks *rectangular numbers*. This name is confusing, as any *composite* number of unit squares can be arranged in a rectangle.

nth triangular number
   $= 1 + 2 + 3 + \ldots + n = (n(n + 1)) \div 2$

Numerically,

$$1 + 2 + 3 + \ldots \ldots + 49 + 50$$

can be dealt with by adding it twice, as

      $1 + 2 + 3 + \ldots \ldots + 49 + 50$
and $50 + 49 + 48 + \ldots \ldots + 2 + 1$

Each vertical sum is 51, and there are 50 of these sums. Hence

$$(1 + 2 + 3 + \ldots \ldots + 49 + 50)$$
$$+ (50 + 49 + 48 + \ldots \ldots + 2 + 1) = 50 \times 51,$$

so that

$$1 + 2 + 3 + \ldots \ldots + 49 + 50 = (50 \times 51) \div 2$$

This generalisation is sufficiently straightforward for some children to make it spontaneously. Children may also notice that the sum of two successive triangular numbers is a square number (Figure 22 : 22). The series of triangular numbers can therefore be constructed from the series of square numbers by subtracting a triangular number from the appropriate square number to give the next triangular number:

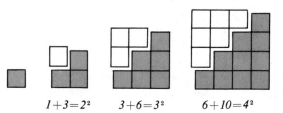

$1 + 3 = 2^2$ $3 + 6 = 3^2$ $6 + 10 = 4^2$

Figure 22 : 22

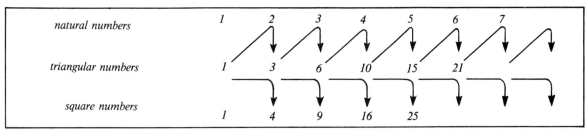

Figure 22 : 23

$$2^2 - 1 = 3$$
$$3^2 - 3 = 6$$
$$4^2 - 6 = 10$$
$$5^2 - 10 = 15 \text{ etc.}$$

Figure 22 : 23 shows the natural numbers, triangular numbers and square numbers arranged in one table. The arrows indicate how the triangular and square numbers can be built up from the natural numbers by addition.

CUBES, TETRAHEDRA AND PYRAMIDS

Children may investigate the growth of cubes, in the same way that the growth of squares was examined, by building up small cubes to make larger cubes. The pattern of growth is shown in Figure 22 : 24, together with a graph of the cubes of natural numbers. Because of the increasingly rapid growth of cubes, it is impracticable to use the same scale on both axes of the graph. The making of this graph will help children to visualise a rate of growth which increases very rapidly, and to foresee without using actual materials what will happen in later

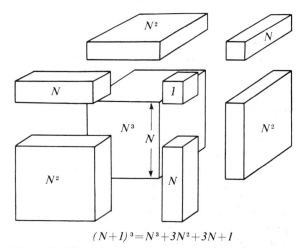

$$(N+1)^3 = N^3 + 3N^2 + 3N + 1$$

Figure 22 : 25

cases, for it rapidly becomes impracticable physically to build larger cubes.[6]

[6]We have seen (very advanced) 6-year-olds building this sequence, using a box of 1000 small cubes. As they built the larger cubes they were able to calculate mentally (without counting) the number of units which each one contained

The growth of cubes

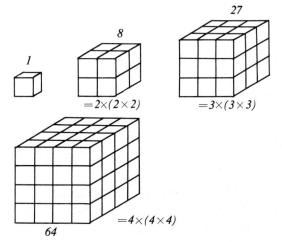

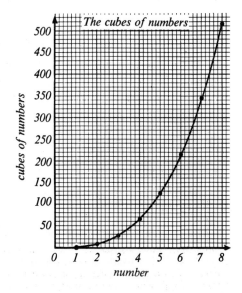

Figure 22 : 24

Side of cube	1	2	3	4	5	6	7	8	9	10
Number of unit cubes used	1	8	27	64	125	216	343	512	.	.
How many do you add?		7	19	37	61	91	127	169	217	
How many more do you add than last time			12	18	24	30	36	42	48	54

Figure 22 : 26

Exploration of the number of units which must be added in order to turn each cube into the next one also gives interesting results. Here multibase blocks are useful, and children will find that in order to turn each cube into the next cube they must add 3 square layers, 3 rods and a unit cube (Figure 22 : 25).

The growth of cubes can now be tabulated as in Figure 22 : 26, and this table can be used to build up the cubes of larger numbers, for the last line of the table is very easily extended.

In the table, the numbers in heavy type have been obtained from Figure 22 : 24; the rest of the table is built up from the last line, as indicated by the arrows.

The way in which cubes grow, according to the law

$$(N+1)^3 = N^3 + 3N^2 + 3N + 1,$$

can be compared with the way in which squares grow, according to the law

$$(N+1)^2 = N^2 + 2N + 1$$

(Figure 22 : 27). It will be noticed that the co-efficients in $(N+1)^2$ and $(N+1)^3$ are

    1 2 1
and 1 3 3 1

These patterns are part of Pascal's Triangle (*see page 249*). At the secondary stage, children will make links between the occurrence of the Pascal's Triangle numbers in probability and in the expansion of $(N+1)^n$.

Other suitable topics for investigation are the growth of piles of spheres in the shape of tetrahedra (Figure 22 : 28) or square pyramids (Figure 22 : 29). Practical experiment with these topics is very easy if spherical beads are used.

The number of beads in each layer of the triangular pyramid is a triangular number.

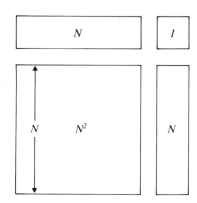

Figure 22 : 27 $(N + 1)^2 = N^2 + 2N + 1$

1 $1+3$ $1+3+6$ $1+3+6+10$

length of base	1	2	3	4	5	6
Number of beads used	1	4	10	20	35	
How many do you add?		3	6	10	15	
How many more do you add than last time?			3	4	5	6

Figure 22 : 28

1 $1+4$ $1+4+9$ $1+4+9+16$

length of base	1	2	3	4	5	6
Number of beads used	1	5	14	30	55	91
How many do you add?	4	9	16	25	36	49
How many more do you add than last time?		5	7	9	11	13

Figure 22 : 29

The number of beads in each layer of the square pyramid is a perfect square.

A doormat forms a suitable base for the pile, and a nail passed through the hole in each bead in the bottom layer will hold it sufficiently firmly in position for a stable pyramid to be built. Alternatively, balls of clay may be used.

MAGIC SQUARES

If numbers are arranged at random in a square array such as

```
11  13  15
 2   4   8
 5   9   7
```

children can use the square when practising addition:

			sum of row
11	13	15	39
2	4	8	14
5	9	7	21
sum of column			
18	26	30	

There are some ingeniously arranged square arrays of numbers such that the sums of every row, every column, and both diagonals are equal. Such squares are called *magic squares*, and have attracted mathematicians as well as children of all ages for thousands of years. The earliest known magic square is the Chinese 'lo-shu', which has the same number of dots in every row, every column and both diagonals. It is shown in its original form in Figure 22 : 30, together with a translation into Arabic numerals; it was known at least as early as 1000 BC, and is engraved on charms worn in the East today.[7] In this the consecutive natural numbers 1, 2, 3, 4, 5, 6, 7, 8, 9 have been used.

We shall call a magic square which uses consecutive natural numbers starting at 1 a *standard* magic square. There are, however, many magic squares which are not standard. Figure 22 : 31 shows a standard magic square of the *fourth order*.[8] The sum of each row, column and diagonal of a

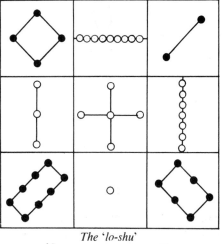

The 'lo-shu'

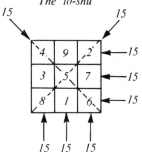

Figure 22 : 30

A standard fourth-order magic square

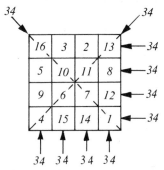

Figure 22 : 31

standard magic square is easily predicted. A fourth-order square contains the numbers 1, 2, 3, ..., 15, 16, so that the sum of all the numbers in the square[9] is

[9]This is a triangular number (*see page 278*).

[10]This magic square appears in an engraving by Albrecht Dürer, entitled *Melancolia*, made in 1514 AD. The two central numbers in the bottom row give the date of the picture. See Gardner, M. *More Mathematical Puzzles and Diversions* (Bell, 1963), page 93.

[7]See Smith, D. E. *History of Mathematics* (Ginn, 1923), I, page 28.

[8]The *order* of a magic square is the number of unit squares in each side.

(a)
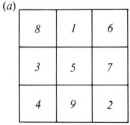

8	1	6
3	5	7
4	9	2

Standard magic square of third order

(b)

16	9	14
11	13	15
12	17	10

Add 8 to every number in the square.
Magic constant = 39
$$= 15 + 3 \times 8$$

(c)
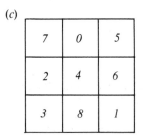

7	0	5
2	4	6
3	8	1

Subtract 1 from every number in the square.
Magic constant = 12
$$= 15 - 3 \times 1$$

(d)
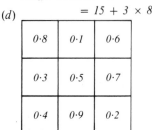

0·8	0·1	0·6
0·3	0·5	0·7
0·4	0·9	0·2

Divide every number in the square by 10.
Magic constant = 15 ÷ 10 = 1·5

(e)

- - -
4	9	2
3	5	7
8	1	6
- - - -

Reflect square in horizontal axis.

(f)

4	3	8
9	5	1
2	7	6

Give square a quarter-turn clockwise

Figure 22 : 32

$$1 + 2 + 3 + \ldots + 15 + 16 = (16 \times 17) \div 2$$
$$= 272 \div 2$$
$$= 136$$

The sum of each row must be $\frac{1}{4}$ of the total for the square, or 34. Similarly, the constant sum of each row, column or diagonal of a standard fifth-order magic square[11] is:

$$\tfrac{1}{5} \text{ of } (1 + 2 + 3 + \ldots + 24 + 25) = \tfrac{1}{5} \text{ of } (25 \times 26) \div 2$$
$$= \tfrac{1}{5} \text{ of } 325$$
$$= 65$$

Once a magic square has been constructed, more magic squares can be made from it, by adding,

---

[11]This constant sum is the *magic constant* of the square.

---

subtracting, multiplying or dividing every number in the square by the same number, or by rotating the square, or reflecting it in one of its axes of symmetry (*see page 64*). Figure 22 : 32 shows some variations on a standard magic square of the third order.

When a teacher or a child has devised a magic square, they will be able to make variations on it. At first, children will be content to find out whether a given square is magic or not; later, they will be able to fill in the missing numbers in squares such as those shown in Figure 22 : 33, and finally some children may wish to make their own magic squares, either by trial and error or by following some of the methods suggested in the books listed below.[12]

		2
3	5	7

16		
	13	15

Magic constant = 39

Figure 22 : 33

MULTIPLICATION DEVICES

Many efforts have been made over the centuries to remove the drudgery from long multiplication and division. The calculator and computer have finally solved this problem. Two earlier devices for multiplying will interest older primary school children. The first of these, finger multiplication, was used in the Middle Ages. The second, Napier's Rods, was invented in 1617, but was an adaptation of a method used much earlier in many parts of the world.[13]

Finger multiplication enables a person who only knows multiplication tables up to 5×5 to obtain products up to 9×9. Each number to be multiplied is represented on the fingers of one hand; the number of fingers raised is the difference between the number and 5 (Figure 22 : 34).

---

[12]Andrews, W. S. *Magic Squares and Cubes* (Dover, 1960). Ball, W. W. Rouse. *Mathematical Recreations and Essays* (Macmillan, 11th ed., 1939). Dudeney, H. E. *Amusements in Mathematics* (Nelson, 1917).

[13]See Smith, D. E. *History of Mathematics* (Dover, 1958), II.

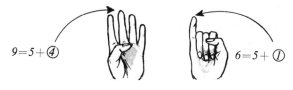

$9 = 5 + ④$ $6 = 5 + ①$

Representing 9 and 6 on the fingers

Figure 22 : 34

Then the tens digit of 9×6 is the *sum* of the numbers of fingers raised; the units digit of 9×6 is the *product* of the numbers of fingers not raised (Figure 22 : 35).

Finger multiplication of 9×6

tens digit $= 4 + 1 = 5$

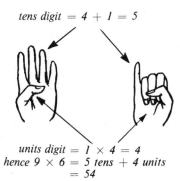

units digit $= 1 \times 4 = 4$
hence $9 \times 6 = 5$ *tens* $+ 4$ *units*
$= 54$

Figure 22 : 35

Finger multiplication of 7×6
tens digit $= 1 + 2 = 3$

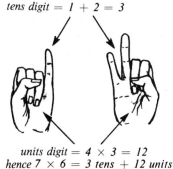

units digit $= 4 \times 3 = 12$
hence $7 \times 6 = 3$ *tens* $+ 12$ *units*
$= 42$

Figure 22 : 36

The explanation of finger multiplication is shown in the general case in Figure 22 : 37.

Finger multiplication gives

$$(a + b) \text{ tens} + (5 - a) \times (5 - b) \text{ units}$$
$$= 10(a + b) + (5 - a)(5 - b)$$
$$= 10a + 10b + 25 - 5a - 5b + ab$$
$$= 25 + 5a + 5b + ab$$
$$= (5 + a)(5 + b)$$

Finger multiplication of $(5+a) \times (5+b)$

tens digit $= (a + b)$

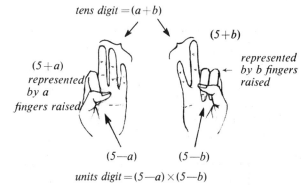

$(5 + a)$
represented by a fingers raised

$(5 + b)$
represented by b fingers raised

$(5 - a)$ $(5 - b)$

units digit $= (5 - a) \times (5 - b)$

Figure 22 : 37

Napier's Rods are an ingenious mechanical device for performing long multiplication. John Napier (1550–1617 AD), laird of Merchiston, Edinburgh, devoted much of his life to the improvement of methods of calculation. The invention of logarithms was undoubtedly his greatest work, but he also published in 1617 AD an account of 'numeration by little rods'. Each multiplication table up to 9 was written on a small rod, as shown in Figure 22 : 38, with the units digit and tens digit of a number each occupying half of a square cell.

In order to form multiples of such a number as 768 the 7 rod, the 6 rod, and the 8 rod are placed side by side. The multiples of 768 can then be read off as shown in Figure 22 : 39. Carrying from one column into the next is performed by diagonal addition, since tens of units and units of tens must occur in the same column, and tens of tens and

Napier's Rods

0	1	2	3	4	5	6	7	8	9
0	1	2	3	4	5	6	7	8	9
0	2	4	6	8	1/0	1/2	1/4	1/6	1/8
0	3	6	9	1/2	1/5	1/8	2/1	2/4	2/7
0	4	8	1/2	1/6	2/0	2/4	2/8	3/2	3/6
0	5	1/0	1/5	2/0	2/5	3/0	3/5	4/0	4/5
0	6	1/2	1/8	2/4	3/0	3/6	4/2	4/8	5/4
0	7	1/4	2/1	2/8	3/5	4/2	4/9	5/6	6/3
0	8	1/6	2/4	3/2	4/0	4/8	5/6	6/4	7/2
0	9	1/8	2/7	3/6	4/5	5/4	6/3	7/2	8/1

Figure 22 : 38

Multiples of 768

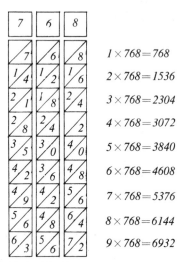

7	6	8

$1 \times 768 = 768$

$2 \times 768 = 1536$

$3 \times 768 = 2304$

$4 \times 768 = 3072$

$5 \times 768 = 3840$

$6 \times 768 = 4608$

$7 \times 768 = 5376$

$8 \times 768 = 6144$

$9 \times 768 = 6932$

Figure 22 : 39

units of hundreds must occur in the same column (Figure 22 : 40).

Dealing with carrying figures:

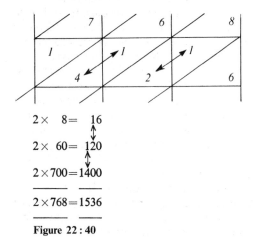

$2 \times 8 = 16$

$2 \times 60 = 120$

$2 \times 700 = 1400$

$2 \times 768 = 1536$

Figure 22 : 40

Napier's invention of his rods is related to an Arabic method of multiplication known as *Gelosia*. In order to multiply 426 by 73, each partial product is written down separately as on Napier's Rods, and the addition is done diagonally as when using Napier's Rods (Figure 22 : 41). Children who have used Napier's Rods will find this method easy to understand.

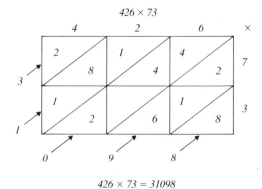

426×73

$426 \times 73 = 31098$

Figure 22 : 41

Number patterns in the National Curriculum

The early level of AT 3 (algebra) are devoted to the exploration of number patterns, and some of the work at later levels is concerned with generalisations made from number patterns. The earlier levels have been covered earlier in this book. Work of the type described in this chapter appears chiefly at Level 5. The statements in the Programme of Study are:

- understand and use terms such as 'prime', 'cube', 'square root' and 'cube root'.

- understand patterns in numbers through spatial arrangements.

(AT3: Level 5)

23 | THE REPRESENTATION OF SPACE

BUILDING UP SPATIAL IDEAS

Children show a keen interest in the spatial properties of their world. From the earliest years they notice and respond to shapes and patterns. Given opportunities of seeing pictures they quickly recognise what they are intended to represent. As we saw in Chapter 1, children's mental life includes representing their experiences in a variety of forms. These representations may be expressed in words or symbols but they often take shape as models or drawings of things that have interested them.

In the early primary school years, children begin to take special notice of distances along roads, the slopes of hills, the shapes of aircraft or pylons, machines such as excavators or bicycles, and the many constructions that are so effective a part of modern life. They become familiar with new words, such as orbit and gradient, and with symbols like those in Figure 23 : 1.

Underlying the phenomena and objects they observe children come to recognise structures which they try to represent in their minds. Gradually they build up an 'ideal space', a body of images and ideas which are somewhat loosely connected but yet serve as the mental space in which they think of themselves as living, and within which objects are situated and movements take place. In this age of satellites and spacecraft most adults have had the experience of enlarging their own idea of space. In children's urge to express their experiences and the relationships that they have perceived they try to show on paper some of the shapes and movements that have struck them as significant. Their drawings show at the outset (and still in imaginative drawing later on) that they are not attempting an exact copy of what they have seen but are trying to represent those features that they have particularly noticed. At about the age of 8 children have acquired a wider range of perception and greater skill of hand. They can now measure and can use instruments with more control and thus can produce fairly accurate and informative representations on paper (*see plate 6*). In turn these drawings become registered in the mind and provide the means for further thought and inquiry.

REPRESENTATION IN MODELS AND DRAWINGS

Three types of drawing or modelling can be distinguished in children's work.

i) Children draw quite spontaneously in response to an inner urge. The spatial relations which they show at first are not at all precise: things are shown in the right relative positions, between or beyond, inside or outside; and their sizes are correctly related, i.e. they are bigger or smaller, but proportions are not maintained nor are objects usually shown in perspective. Gradually children acquire the capacity to draw things of such a size that distance can be inferred, and of such a shape that their true shape is conveyed. But the growth is slow and the ability to show perspective is not usually seen until about 9 years of age when a system of co-ordinated relations is beginning to form. Children vary considerably in their rate of development in this matter. A class of untutored African children about 7 years of age, when given crayons for the first time and told to draw what they liked, produced several pictures of a round hut with the base shown as an ellipse. Others drew a flat triangle for a hut.

ii) Long before perspective is mastered, children make drawings or models which are meant to be a record rather than a picture. A purpose directs such a representation. Children may be drawing types of aircraft or of costume, a house or a bicycle. These will have certain spatial features deliberately embodied but they will be diagrammatic and not in perspective. They draw not what they see from their particular point of view but what they know from experience about the characteristics of the house

Figure 23 : 1

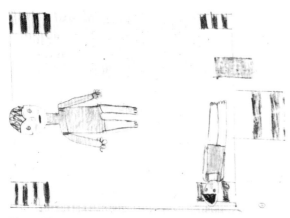

Figure 23 : 2

or tractor or garden they are trying to represent. Figure 23 : 2 shows a 6-year-old child's drawing of a swimming bath.

iii) In the third stage fairly exact copies are modelled or drawn and may actually be reproduced to scale. Experiences of scale models of cars and aircraft as toys or in shop-window displays stimulate thinking about scale. The widespread use of road maps and street plans may enable children to learn to read maps at an early age, long before they understand how they are constructed. They can put themselves 'on the map' and visualise walking or driving along a road. From this point they can begin to draw a map for themselves.

THE DESIRE FOR ACCURACY

Making miniature figures and objects is a very ancient art in human history and children given plastic material will make realistic dolls, animals, lorries, etc. Yet these are not constructed with any reference to their measurements. Similarly, in early civilisations, a design or emblem was varied in size to fit the space it was to occupy. Children will also fit features of the right size to the drawing of a given object, e.g. a door to a house; but they do this without measuring. The question we have to ask is, 'For what reasons does a child begin to seek for *accuracy* in representations?'

As Piaget says, 'Children reconstruct their own movements or changes of position by drawing their own conceptions of the spatial field ... as they grow in maturity the latter become increasingly co-ordinated.' When a scene or object is seen with this unity of relationships children are ready to think about an *exact* reproduction. But why should

they wish to do so? They experience a growing dissatisfaction with drawings or models which *do not look right*. They want to make things which are *exact enough to work*; therefore they must be structurally right and their parts must fit. To quote Piaget again, the child will seek for accuracy when he wishes or 'is asked to make a construction which he recognises sooner or later as one which demands a degree of precision that only measuring can guarantee.' Children know that for a good model the measurements must 'match' those of the original.

There are other pressures: children wish to communicate what they have discovered, to share it and perhaps to obtain co-operation; they also want to convince themselves that they have really mastered a problem or skill; hence the need to make a map, diagram or model. These are the motives which a teacher will use to encourage children to develop their capacity for useful representations.

FIRST IDEAS OF SCALE

Making an accurate model or drawing requires the co-ordination of the measurements of the original with those of the model to be constructed. Children must therefore have reached the stage when they can hold in mind these various lengths and the shapes they make. They must see the way in which the parts of the original are related to one another so that they can co-ordinate the matching parts in the model. Such a complex system of co-ordination is not easily achieved and cannot be expected before about 8 years of age. The capacity to see the relationships in increasingly complex situations develops over a period of years, making it necessary to plan courses in the representation of space for university students of engineering, architecture, etc., as well as for pupils in primary and secondary schools.

The way in which an attempt at representation assists children to take account of several properties of a shape at the same time was well illustrated by a small group of children, 8 to 9-years-old, who were trying to shape the roof of a Butter Cross for a class model of a medieval village. The picture from which they were working showed the roof as a square pyramid. The children inferred that four triangles would be needed. They knew that the bases of the triangles would be horizontal when placed in position and that an edge was shared by two triangles. They therefore placed two triangles side by side, the two bases being equal and in the

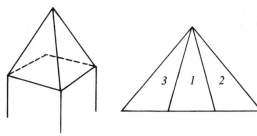

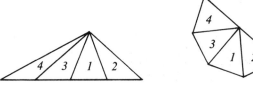

Figure 23 : 3

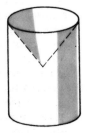

Figure 23 : 4

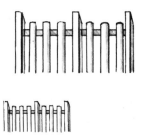

Figure 23 : 5

same straight line. A third triangle was drawn to match the second, as in Figure 23 : 3. At this stage the shape looked to the children as though it would produce the correct roof.

But where should they put the fourth triangle? As soon as it was drawn next to triangle 3 the discrepancy was obvious. The edges clearly would not fit. Lively discussion and renewed observation produced the realisation that the triangles must all be of the same shape as well as having equal bases. Folding would then give a square base and would enable matching edges of triangles 2 and 4 to be fitted together (Figure 23 : 4).

If an accurate model or drawing is to be made smaller than the original children must realise that a short length can represent a longer one. It need not be a measured length but it must always be used for the same length of the original. Any rod or straight stick could provide the unit length. If the original has two pieces of fencing, the model must have two pieces but made from the chosen unit, as shown in Figure 23 : 5. This quickly leads to problems in the number relations involved.

If the sticks which make the fence are smaller in the model than in the real one, how do children

know *how close* to place the sticks to make the fence look right? Children who have done much practical measuring will soon suggest some numerical relations, e.g. a 10-cm stick to represent a 5-m pole, and thus develop the idea of scale. It is essential for children to recognise now that there is a constant relation between the lengths of corresponding sides, edges, diagonals, boundaries, etc., in the real object and in its representation. They may express the relation in various ways, as we shall see on page 435, but to understand it they must have plenty of experience of handling sets of similar shapes of different size in situations where lengths need to be compared, e.g. in fitting pyramids on to prisms, or a cone into a cylinder to make a raingauge, or in projecting a drawing on to a screen (Figure 23 : 6).

In this way the early recognition of a real object seen in a picture (of which children under 2 are capable) is converted into the ability to see the precise connection between two similar shapes, including an object and its model, and a site and its plan.

THE FIRST MAPS

A map is generally understood to mean the representation on a flat piece of paper of some part of the earth's surface. Since the earth is roughly a sphere, making a map is a very skilled mathematical feat. For young children, not yet aware of the earth's shape, the beginning of

   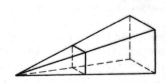

Figure 23 : 6

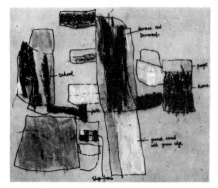

Figure 23 : 7

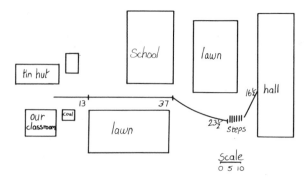

Figure 23 : 8

map-making can most easily be undertaken through an attempt to record the path of a walk they have actually taken. On such a journey children receive a large number of visual impressions, a few clear and memorable, most of them vague pictures not easily recalled but recognised when the path is traversed again. The clear impressions will be of buildings or other sights which have a particular interest for children, a toyshop, a railway bridge, a garage, a bus-stop. Some other places will be linked with these special places which serve as landmarks or points of reference for the children. The whole path may not be sufficiently connected to be open to recall; only separate sections related to the landmarks will show co-ordination.

At this stage a group of children about 6-years-old will draw a sketch-map of their route through their village, or along a road, showing certain bends and turnings and pictures of landmarks, all in the right order but not accurately placed. Figure 23 : 7 shows an example.

Many buildings will be omitted because they have not been truly *seen*; children have not registered mentally what was received by sight. Between the neighbourhoods of the landmarks there will be such vagueness that even the distances cannot be estimated.

Measuring, of course, has not at this point developed sufficiently to be of use. Later on, children will be able to picture themselves walking along the entire path, if it is not too long or complicated, and may even be able to give reliable instructions for a journey to school or to a bus station. The various neighbourhoods about the landmarks have become co-ordinated. With a measuring-tape or marked rope a group of children can measure distances along the road, and between turnings, and fix the position of landmarks by finding the distance from one to another. Some of the larger buildings can have their frontages measured. Notebooks should be available for the children to describe or sketch the measurements made. After the walk a 'map' of the road can be made from these measurements, the map lengths being related in an approximate way to the actual lengths by comparisons of more or less. If a length is chosen to represent the total distance, the lengths of the various sections will be gauged as parts of the whole. But at this stage it is possible that some children will suggest a simple scale such as 1 cm to 10 metres and will draw to the nearest cm or $\frac{1}{2}$-cm. If so, full use should be made of such a good opportunity. See Figure 23 : 8.

This kind of map, involving only drawing a line and marking the features seen along its length, is the easiest for children because they can visualise themselves walking along the line. Various parts of the walk in which they have been interested become linked together and the whole walk is a co-ordinated structure which the map can illustrate to the children. This helps them to see the structure from an outside point of view, independent of their own actions.

THE MAP OF A REGION

A second type of map which children will want to draw is more difficult because it must be based on a number of different perceptions. It is the map of a region, say a wall or floor, or an outdoor site. To make a map of this kind children must be able to see it from outside; it cannot be simply a picture of their own movements, much as they will be helped by personal exploration. They must be aware of its shape, the nature of its boundaries, and the lengths of its bounding sides. It will help them if they have sketched the shape as they visualise it and checked this by a comparison with the original.

The simplest example to start with is a map of a wall which children can see and whose shape they can recognise. On such a map they can place

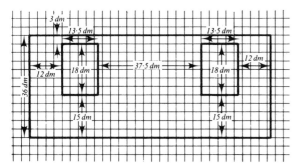

Figure 23 : 9

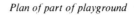

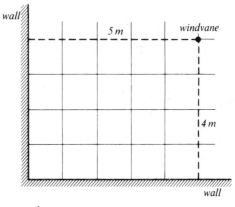

scale:
side of square to 1 m

Figure 23 : 10

windows or door or blackboard in correct position. It is easy to draw this map on squared paper where the right angles are given and the side of a square can represent a particular actual length, e.g. 30 cm, or 3 dm (3 ten-rods).

This drawing follows naturally from the measuring activities suggested in Chapter 16. It will be noticed that fixing the position of a window requires two measurements (in addition to the dimensions of the window), the distance of an edge from the end of the wall and the height of the lower edge above the floor. This is the beginning of the use of co-ordinates, where two measurements are used to fix the position of a point (Figure 23 : 9).

More difficult for children to visualise is a horizontal region such as the floor of the classroom or part of the playground. They must picture this as seen from above, a skill which comes more easily to children who have looked down on a site from a hill or a window, or have seen the ground from an aircraft or looked at aerial photographs. Without such experiences they can imagine the view from above if they have explored the region and attempted to sketch it, inserting the measurements they have made. If objects are to be shown on this map in their true positions children must be able to co-ordinate relations not only in a line, as in the map of a walk, but in two directions: before or behind, and left or right. The effort to show their own seats in the classroom or the spot in the playground where the class has placed a windvane will thus lead again to the use of co-ordinates, that is of two measured distances (Figure 23 : 10). The

possible use of an angle as one of the measures is discussed in Chapter 12.

DEVELOPMENT OF SCALE

The informal uses of scale so far discussed have been based on the idea that one length can represent another and larger length. The selected representative length may be chosen arbitrarily and without considering its measurement. One of the Cuisenaire rods could be used, or the side of a square on squared paper, without reference to its measured length, 4 cm, 2 cm or $1\frac{1}{2}$ cm. A small conventional unit could be chosen, such as 1 cm, to represent a larger unit, say, 1 metre. But scale is not fully understood until it is seen as the ratio of a representative length to the corresponding actual length. This is brought out fully when sets of similar shapes are studied in Chapter 35. At the present stage, when maps are being drawn, the correspondence between scale length and actual length can be emphasised by tabulating the two sets of corresponding measurements. For example, a scale of 1 cm to 4 m may be shown as in Figure 23 : 11.

Scale 1 cm to 4 m

Scale length in cm	1	2	3	4	$\frac{1}{2}$	$\frac{1}{4}$	$1\frac{1}{2}$	$1\frac{1}{4}$
Actual length in m	4	8	12	16	2	1	6	5

Figure 23 : 11

Graph to show scale 1 cm to 4 m

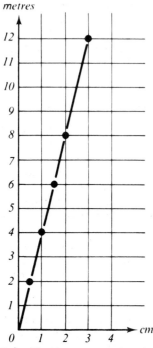

Figure 23 : 12

The other approach to the idea of the ratio of representative length to true length is through drawings of patterns and shapes reduced in size. Occasion for such drawings will be found among the stars, polygons and lattices described in Chapter 12. Copies will be made $\frac{1}{2}$-size, $\frac{1}{4}$size, and so on to fit the available space. Dimensions must be compared; the use of squared paper brings out the relationship (see Figure 23 : 21). Rulings in 5-cm, 2-cm, 1-cm and $\frac{1}{2}$-cm squares are obtainable; a shape drawn on one ruling can be readily reproduced, enlarged or reduced, on another ruling. Comparisons of length can easily be made. In these cases a *scale factor* or a *ratio* can be used to state the scale. For instance, a pattern reduced from 5-cm squared paper to 1-cm squared paper would be reproduced on a scale whose scale factor is $\frac{1}{5}$, or in a ratio of 1 : 5.

A graph could be drawn to enable scale length to be read when the actual length is known and vice versa (see Figure 23 : 12). This scale relationship can be more fully understood if the map is used to find an inaccessible length. A strip of the squared paper used for the map can measure the map length which can then be converted into the actual length of the inaccessible line.

Questions about the actual reduction in size can be considered. This gives the ratio of *actual length* to *scale length* (or vice versa); for instance, in the example shown the ratio of scale length to actual length is 1 to 400. The study of a map with scale 1 cm to 1 km leads to numbers which children find surprisingly large.[1] With the coming of micro-technology it is important for children to realise the accuracy with which immense reductions in size can be calculated and used to produce such complex mechanisms as the digital watch, the calculator and the computer.

GROWTH OF THE USE OF FRACTIONS

Fractions often make their first appearance in connection with partitioning a spatial form or a set. It may be a line or a rectangle or a collection of coins. This is discussed in Chapter 27. It is a valuable method because the equality of the parts which make the whole and the equivalence of different forms of the same fraction are so easily seen. The partitioning of a set into subsets is also splitting up a whole into parts which may be equivalent. A set of 12 cups can be arranged as 4-subsets of 3 cups; $\frac{1}{4}$ of 12 is 3. Similarly, $\frac{1}{4}$ of £2 is $\frac{1}{4}$ of 200p, i.e. 50p; $\frac{1}{4}$ of 1 metre is $\frac{1}{4}$ of 100 cm, i.e. 25 cm. A much wider range of experience with fractions is provided by the practical situations in which measuring and representation are required. If a model or diagram is to have measurements which are $\frac{1}{2}$ or $\frac{3}{4}$ or $\frac{1}{8}$ of the original, operations with fractions will have to be undertaken. Any necessary adding or subtracting can be carried out by using a tape or strip to show the sum or difference required. Thus the result of adding the numbers $2\frac{3}{4}$ and $3\frac{5}{8}$ may be shown on a strip graduated in eighths of a unit to be $6\frac{3}{8}$. See Figure 23 : 13.

When scale factors are used in scale drawings, multiplication and division will concern metric

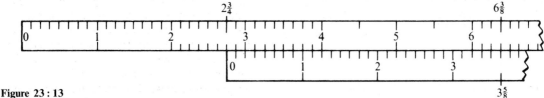

Figure 23 : 13

quantities, involving decimal fractions. Basic practical work is the opportunity for children to use the written forms with understanding. We are concerned here with the *language* of fractions. Children are familiar with such forms as $\frac{1}{2}$, $\frac{1}{4}$, $\frac{1}{3}$, $\frac{2}{5}$, 0·3, etc. Formal procedures for finding scale lengths by using a scale factor of lengths expressed in decimal form will come later.

In the use of scale factors for scale drawing the meaning of a fraction as a ratio is dominant. If the scale factor is $\frac{1}{5}$, every length in the scale drawing must be related to the corresponding length in the original by the ratio 1 : 5. To find $\frac{1}{5}$ of the length we divide by 5. If the original length is 8·5 cm, the scale length is

$\frac{1}{5}$ of 8·5 cm = 8·5 ÷ 5 cm = 1·7 cm

8·5 is represented by 1·7 cm

This can be checked on a ruler. Pairs of numbers obtained in this way can be tabulated and a graph drawn, from which scale lengths can be read, thus avoiding more difficult calculations.

The use of money and measures of length should have familiarised children with such equivalences as £$\frac{1}{2}$ = 50p, $\frac{1}{4}$ metre = 25 cm and such decimal forms as £0·50 and 0·25 m. Then $\frac{1}{2}$ of 0·5 m is $\frac{1}{2}$ of 50 cm = 25 cm = 0·25 cm.

Actual length in *cm*	6	3	2	1	4	5	10
Scale length in *cm*	4·5	2·3	1·5	0·8	3·0	3·8	7·5

Graph to show reduction in lengths in ratio 3 : 4

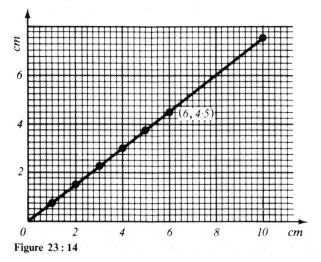

Figure 23 : 14

If a drawing is reduced to $\frac{3}{4}$ of the original dimensions, a tabulation of matching lengths will involve finding $\frac{3}{4}$ of each original measurement in decimal form. It will be noticed that the decimal forms must be stated to the degree of accuracy required for drawing the graph. In the tabulation for the graph in Figure 23 : 14 the lengths are given in centimetres correct to 1 decimal place.

THE USE OF DRAWING INSTRUMENTS

Children appreciate the tools they learn to use from 7 to about 9 years of age for the increased skill and exactness they allow. But these tools are also important for the understanding to which their use can lead. The instruments may serve two purposes: they may be measuring tools, and/or instruments for use in some constructive task. For example, a ruler enables one to draw straight lines, taking the place of the less reliable fold in a sheet of paper; but if it is graduated it can be used for measuring a straight length. We will consider each instrument in turn.

i) *The ruler.* Probably most children think of a ruler first as an instrument for measuring. They take its straightness for granted; they can use printed lines on a page when they wish to draw straight lines. They will be measuring in centimetres before they learn to hold a ruler firmly enough to draw a straight line on plain paper.

A ruler marked in centimetres is a model of part of the number line. Children will have used it to show addition and subtraction of whole numbers by translations along it. If it is also graduated in fractions their idea of numbers will be enlarged to include fractional numbers which can be added and subtracted in the same way as integers along the ruler. The study of the number line in a more systematic manner will follow later. Meanwhile such a ruler will be needed for scale drawings and will demand two skills. It can be used to measure a given length; it can also be used to mark a required scale length along a line. For example, the ruler can be used to measure the width of the blackboard; on the corresponding scale drawing it will show where, on the line representing the edge of the board, the end of the board must be marked. The first skill is fairly well mastered by 7 years of age, but the second demands more precision and standards must be adjusted to the age of the child. As always, children will be encouraged to make their measures as accurate as possible; they can never be absolute (Figure 23 : 15).

Measuring the blackboard

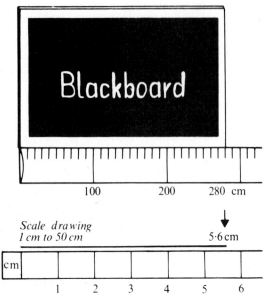

*Scale drawing
1 cm to 50 cm*

5·6 cm

Figure 23 : 15

ii) *Compasses.* The set of points which constitute a circle is often drawn on the ground by children using a piece of string and chalk or a stick. Cotton or a strip of cardboard may be used for a smaller circle on paper, or a disc may be used as a template (*see Chapter 13*). But none of these methods gives as much accuracy or variety in drawing interesting patterns based on the circle as do compasses. To children of 8 or 9 the invention and colouring of such patterns gives great pleasure; it also shows them many surprising relations between the centres and radii of circles of different sizes used in combination. As well as helping children to invent patterns, compasses have a practical function in some scale drawings. With traditional compasses children can mark a length of 5·4 cm along a line with considerable accuracy, fixing the length of the radius carefully on the ruler. Safety compasses have a built in ruler (Figure 23 : 16). Drawing an equilateral triangle is a good example of what children can now do. Compasses may be the most complicated tool they have yet used. They should be encouraged to examine this tool carefully. (*See Chapter 13.*)

iii) *The protractor.* The clock-face with a hand marking out the rotations is usually a child's first informal protractor. At a later stage, folding a disc into 24 parts will give angles at intervals of 15°, as shown on a protractor.[2] This is sufficiently exact for many of the representative drawings children wish to make at this level. Moreover they can copy *any* angle by making a fold to match it in a disc, or half-disc. See Figure 23 : 17.

Nevertheless, using a properly made tool such as a plastic protractor will help children to produce an accurate representation when the time comes for them to fix the position of a tree or other object by its directions from two points of observation (Figure 23 : 18). Children who use LOGO will find a 360° protractor a useful aid from quite an early stage.

iv) *The set square.* Children first used a set square in the form of a folded paper 'corner' or right angle, such as a piece of paper folded

[2] See Chapter 12 and Figure 12 : 43 for a method of folding $\frac{1}{3}$ of a circle to give an angle of 120°.

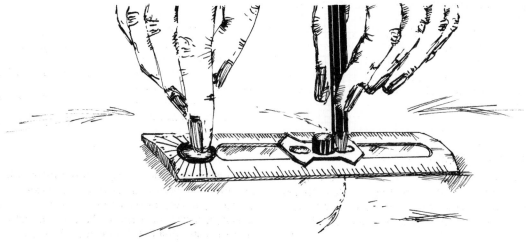

Figure 23 : 16

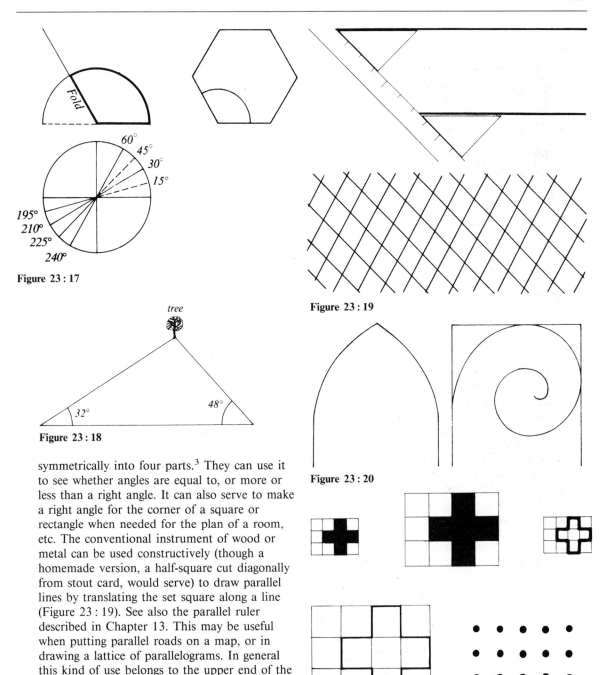

Figure 23 : 17

Figure 23 : 18

tree

32°   48°

Figure 23 : 19

Figure 23 : 20

Figure 23 : 21

symmetrically into four parts.[3] They can use it to see whether angles are equal to, or more or less than a right angle. It can also serve to make a right angle for the corner of a square or rectangle when needed for the plan of a room, etc. The conventional instrument of wood or metal can be used constructively (though a homemade version, a half-square cut diagonally from stout card, would serve) to draw parallel lines by translating the set square along a line (Figure 23 : 19). See also the parallel ruler described in Chapter 13. This may be useful when putting parallel roads on a map, or in drawing a lattice of parallelograms. In general this kind of use belongs to the upper end of the primary school.

DRAWING SHAPES AND PATTERNS

During the exploratory activities which lead to map and plan making children will notice many shapes in buildings, such as towers, windows, doorways and roofs, as well as in bridges, vehicles and

[3]See Chapter 5, page 117.

machinery. Some of the shapes are regular in form and frequently used, e.g. cylinders, triangles, cuboids, parallelograms. These can be recorded in drawings; their properties can be studied, and if the shape is appropriate it can be embodied in a pattern. Less common shapes will be found, as in many church windows; they can be experimentally reproduced and similar shapes devised (Figure 23 : 20).

The important aspect of these experiences for children at this stage is that they develop growing awareness of the dependence of form on properties of lengths and angles. Hence comes the possibility of representing shapes accurately in models or plans through the correspondences of shapes, lines and points between the original and its representation. Drawing on squared paper brings out such relations well because an all-over square pattern can be seen in terms of squares, lines or points, as Figure 23 : 21 shows. The different relations are emphasised by the kind of representation selected.

Representing space in the National Curriculum

The work described in this chapter links ideas of shape with ideas of number, and so contributes to two targets of the National Curriculum. Work on scale factors and ratios occurs in Attainment Target 4 (shape and space) and Attainment Target 2 (number).

- enlarge a shape by a whole number scale factor.

  (AT4: Level 6)

- enlarge a shape by a fractional scale factor.

  (AT4: Level 7)

In fact, 'enlarging' a shape by a fractional scale factor such as $\frac{1}{4}$ reduces it.

In Attainment Target 2, the same ideas are stated in numerical terms by using ratios.

- use unitary ratios.
  EXAMPLE: *Use a ratio of 1 : 50 for drawing a plan of the classroom.*

  (AT2: Level 5)

- calculate using ratios in a variety of situations.
  EXAMPLE: *Adapt a recipe for six people to one for eight people.*

  (AT2: Level 6)

Work of this type also increases children's familiarity with fractions, and their awareness of angle properties of shapes.

- recognise and understand simple fractions in everyday use.

  (AT2: Level 4)

- explain and use properties associated with intersecting and parallel lines and triangles, and know associated language.

  (AT4: Level 5)

24 | THE NUMBER LINE, DECIMALS AND FRACTIONS

THE NUMBER LINE

Many of the physical representations of number which children make use lengths as models for numbers. Among the more important representations of numbers are

i) the ruler or the tape-measure,

ii) types of structural apparatus such as Cuisenaire or Multilink, and

iii) the labelling of an axis of a graph with numbers.

As children grow older, their ideas of how numbers are represented on a ruler change, and the type of ruler which they can handle changes to match their evolving ideas. Length is becoming a *continuous quantity*, rather than a number of separate units.

The distinction between the measurement of continuous quantities and the counting of discontinuous individual units is a very important one. Whole numbers of units can never be good enough for the measurement of continuous quantities such as length, mass, time or volume. Children may balance a book by putting it in one pan of a balance and putting a number of individual 10-gram masses in the other pan. Unless they have been most extraordinarily lucky in the book, or unless the balance is very insensitive, they will find that, for instance, 150 grams do not tip the balance, but 160 grams send it down heavily. The difference of 10 grams between successive masses is too great. The same is true of length, time, capacity, area, volume, temperature, air pressure, and all the other continuous quantities which we attempt to measure. The difference between successive units,

however small they may be, is always too large for total accuracy, so that completely accurate measurement must always be impossible.

Eventually, through much experience of measuring and of graduating their own measures, children visualise a continuously increasing scale of length, mass or capacity, containing some isolated landmarks which represent the units. The ruler, the kitchen scales, and the graduated measuring jug all show units as isolated landmarks on a continuous scale of measurement (Figure 24 : 1).

As a result of these experiences a number comes to correspond in children's minds not only to a set of things, but also to a measurement, and so to a *point on a number line*. The one-unit marks on a ruler have come to represent numbers.

Graph to show number of balls which each class has.

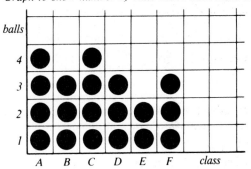

Figure 24 : 2

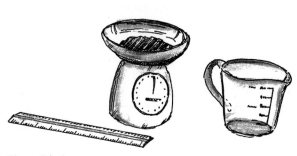

Figure 24 : 1

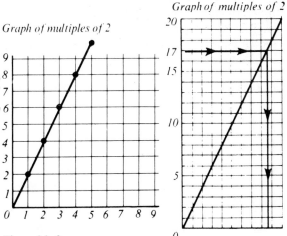

Figure 24 : 3

Figure 24 : 4

The same development in the representation of numbers is shown in a change in children's graphical work. The earliest graphs are always picture or block graphs, in which a number is represented by a number of unit blocks which can be counted (Figure 24 : 2); but block graphs are later supplemented by line graphs such as Figure 24 : 3, in which numbers are represented by equally spaced points on the axes.

In such line graphs as Figure 24 : 3, *interpolation* becomes possible. Children who have used the graph to find how many twos there are in 16 may then try to use it to find out how many twos there are in 17, arriving at a point on the horizontal axis half-way between that which represents 8 and that which represents 9. Interpolation is not possible on a block graph; there is nothing between the block which represents 8 and that which represents 9.

In such ways the representation of the natural numbers by equally spaced points on a number line takes shape, and with it comes the realisation that there are other numbers as well as the natural numbers, and that these other numbers also correspond to points on the number line.

The number line shown in Figure 24 : 4 begins to be seen as *representing* a continuously increasing range of numbers, among which is a sequence of equally spaced landmarks, corresponding to the natural numbers. Other points *between* these natural number points also represent numbers, which lie *between* the whole numbers.

ISOMORPHISM

In what sense can the equally spaced points on the number line be said to *represent* numbers? Equally spaced points on a line are not themselves numbers, but the structure of points on a line mirrors the behaviour of the natural numbers in some of their most important properties, provided that we think

of the line as extending without limit in one direction.

The first such property is that both the natural numbers and the spaced points on a line have an *order*. Each natural number except 0 has unique *neighbours*; 4 has 3 on one side of it and 5 on the other side.[2] Corresponding to this property of natural numbers, each spaced point on the line except for the starting-point of the half-line also has a neighbouring spaced point on each side of it. After any natural number, however large it may be, there is always a *next* natural number; to the right of any point of the line, however far from the starting-point of the half-line it may be, there is always a *next* spaced point. These two properties enable the *one-to-one correspondence* shown in Figure 24 : 5 to be set up between the set of natural numbers and the set of spaced points, so that neighbouring natural numbers always correspond to neighbouring points, and the larger of two numbers always corresponds to the right-hand member of a pair of points.

Children need to be able to visualise the relative positions of different numbers on the number line, so that they are always sure which of two numbers is the larger. They can write

$$5 < 8 \quad \text{or} \quad 8 > 5$$

The larger number always comes at the wide end of the inequality sign. This skill in recognising order, so easy for natural numbers, becomes much more important, and much more difficult, for decimals and fractions.

The one-to-one correspondence which has been set up between the natural numbers and the spaced points on the number line also mirrors the structure of the addition and subtraction of natural numbers by a structure of addition and subtraction on the number line. The structure of addition and subtraction of vector lengths in the same direction

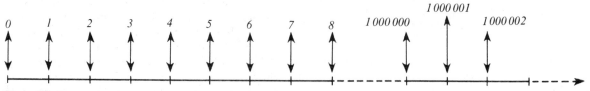

Figure 24 : 5

[1]This 'line' is in fact a *half-line*, starting from the point 0 and extending without limit in one direction.

[2]0 has only one neighbour, the number 1.

along a line is identical with the structure of addition and subtraction for natural numbers derived from sets of things.

(5 cm to the right) + (3 cm to the right)
= (8 cm to the right)
For numbers 5 + 3 = 8

When subtraction is seen as inverse addition, the correspondence would be:

(5 cm to the right) + □ = (8 cm to the right)
For numbers 5 + □ = 8

The correspondence is exact: in the first equation, the vector *3 centimetres to the right* fills the empty space, and in the second equation the corresponding natural number 3 fills the empty space. The structure of the addition and subtraction of vectors measured along the number line is identical with the structure of addition and subtraction of natural numbers.

There are some addition and subtraction structures which do not behave in the same way as these. On the clock, for instance, 5 hours after 8 o'clock the time is 1 o'clock. Symbolically

8 + 5 = 1

But in the arithmetic of natural numbers,

8 + 5 = 13

so that it is not possible to set up a one-to-one correspondence between clock numbers and natural numbers which preserves the structure of addition (*see page 498*).

Because the structures of the natural numbers and of lengths on a line are identical, either can be used as an image or model of the other, and children often make this transference. Children replace one structure by the other when they use a tape-measure or structural apparatus[3] to find the answer to

15 marbles + 17 marbles,

or when they count on their fingers to find the answer to

7 centimetres + 6 centimetres.

Two structures which behave in exactly the same way, so that the results of operations such as additions and subtractions correspond, are said to be

[3]Since structural apparatus uses length as a model of number, its structure is the same as that of the tape-measure.

[4]*Noun:* isomorphism. From Greek ισος (isos) equal, and μορφε (morphe) form, structure, as in *isosceles* (equal sides) and *morphology* (the science of form).

isomorphic.[4] Isomorphic structures are used in mathematics whenever a real situation is replaced by a model like structural apparatus, or by a mental model like the natural numbers. The addition and subtraction of natural numbers is isomorphic with the addition and subtraction of lengths, or masses, or the rods of structural apparatus; but there are other structures, such as the addition of hours on the clock, with which the addition of natural numbers is not isomorphic. It would be foolish to pretend that a two-rod of structural apparatus *is* the number 2, or that placing a two-rod end to end with a three-rod *is* the addition of the abstract natural numbers 2 and 3, but the two structures are isomorphic, so that the concrete structure can be used as a very satisfactory model of the abstract one, or indeed of other concrete structures, such as

2 kilograms + 3 kilograms

Thus children develop the idea that the number line, or its concrete embodiments the tape-measure and the axis of a graph, are models whose structure is isomorphic with the structure of the natural numbers. Of course children do not consciously formulate the isomorphism but it is certainly present.

ZERO ON THE NUMBER LINE

As the idea of the number line develops in children's minds, zero takes a more satisfactory place among the numbers than it has hitherto held. Measurement forwards and backwards with a tape-measure gives such results as

(7 cm) – (7 cm) = (0 cm)

and so 0 becomes the label for the starting-point of the number line, and is a number like other numbers (which are also labels for points on the number line) rather than a symbol for the absence of number, which it may previously have been. The same change in the status of zero is seen in graphical work. In the graph of the number of children wearing jerseys, shown in Figure 24 : 6(*a*), zero is a symbol which to children may stand for the absence of any children wearing jerseys, but it is also the label of the starting-point of the number line. When children have reached the stage shown in Figure 24 : 6(*b*), 2 × 0 = 0 has taken its place alongside 2 × 1 = 2 and 2 × 2 = 4, and zero has become a number which is symbolised on the number line in the same way that other numbers are symbolised. Similarly, on the calculator, 0 behaves in the same ways as other numbers;

children see that the sequence of keystrokes

 gives a display of 0,

and ⟨2⟩⟨×⟩⟨0⟩⟨=⟩ gives a display of 0.

On the calculator, 0 has another useful property: it is the starting-point, the number which appears when the calculator is turned on. The successive displays 1, 2, 3, ... can be produced by turning the calculator on to display 0, and then keying

⟨+⟩ ⟨1⟩ ⟨=⟩ ⟨=⟩ ...

(a)   *Number of children wearing jerseys*

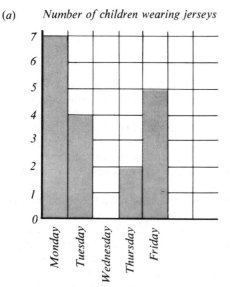

(b)   *Graph of two times table*

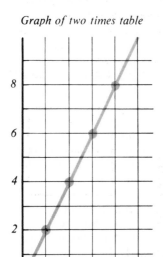

$$2 \times 0 = 0$$
$$2 \times 1 = 2$$
$$2 \times 2 = 4$$
$$2 \times 3 = 6$$
etc.

Figure 24 : 6

THE APPEARANCE OF DIRECTED NUMBERS AND FRACTIONS

The two structures of equally spaced points on the number line and of the natural numbers are isomorphic, but the number line has some additional features which do not mirror the structure of the natural numbers. Two of these features point the way towards extensions of the number system from natural numbers to new types of number.

One feature is that the set of natural numbers extends without limit to give larger and larger numbers, which are represented by points at an increasing distance from the starting-point of the number line. But a line can be extended in both directions. The usual idea of a line is not of the half-line with a starting-point:

$$\longrightarrow$$

but of a line which can be extended in both directions:

$$\longleftrightarrow$$

This property of a line mirrors the extension of the number system to the positive and negative directed numbers. These now come into children's experience much earlier than they used to; the use of Celsius (Centigrade) temperature means that $-2°C$ is a familiar temperature. Moreover, children who perform repeated subtraction on a calculator very soon find that the key sequence

⟨1⟩⟨3⟩⟨−⟩⟨2⟩⟨=⟩⟨=⟩⟨=⟩ .....

gives the sequence of displays

13, 11, 9, 7, 5, 3, 1, -1, -3, ...

Similarly, a mistaken keying of

⟨2⟩⟨9⟩⟨−⟩⟨3⟩⟨7⟩⟨=⟩

instead of

⟨3⟩⟨7⟩⟨−⟩⟨2⟩⟨9⟩⟨=⟩

produces the display of -8.

The second feature of the number line is that although there is no natural number between, for instance, 3 and 4, there are many points on the number line between the point which represents 3 and that which represents 4. Filling in some of these spaces on the number line corresponds to the introduction of fractions into the number system.

Ways in which children gain their early experience of fractions have been discussed in Chapter 23. Here we shall be concerned with some aspects of the concept of a fraction, with the interlocking of these aspects, and with setting fractions, especially decimal fractions, in their places on the number line.

PARTS OF A DIVISIBLE UNIT

Some units can be divided into parts, some cannot. We never halve a child, a dog, a balloon or a glass marble, but a cake, a metre, a litre or an hour can be divided into parts of any size. The units of continuous qantities such as length or mass or time can always be divided into parts, but discontinuous separate units such as people or things usually cannot. In their work in folding and cutting shapes into parts and in weighing, measuring liquids, measuring lengths and telling the time, children gain experience of units which can be divided into parts, and learn the names and the symbols for the simpler fractions of a unit, such as the half, quarter and third. They also learn that the unit must be divided, not merely into a number of parts, but into a number of *equal* parts (Figure 24 : 7). At first, the equality of the parts will be checked by folding or cutting and fitting them over one another, or, in the case of masses, by balancing them against one

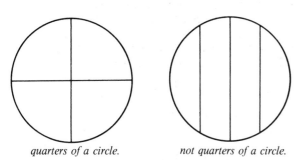

quarters of a circle.   not quarters of a circle.

Figure 24 : 7

another, or for volumes, by seeing that they reach the same level in equal measuring jars.

When the unit is divided into 10 equal parts, decimal notation can be used for the parts; thus, the decimal fraction 0·7 shows that the unit is divided into 10 equal parts or tenths, and that 7 of them are considered. Similarly, using the second decimal place, 0·75 shows that the unit has been divided into 100 equal parts, and 75 of them are considered. This fraction is, of course, the same as the fraction made up of 7 tenths and 5 hundredths.

When the unit is divided into a number of equal parts other than 10, 100, 1000, . . ., decimal notation cannot be used, and *two* numbers are needed to show a fraction, so that when a fraction

Some concrete embodiments of $\frac{3}{4}$ and 0·7

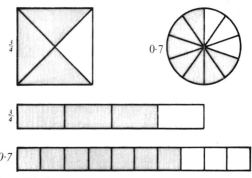

Figure 24 : 8

such as $\frac{3}{4}$ is named, the bottom number or *denominator* of the fraction shows or denominates the number of equal parts into which the unit has been divided, and the top number or *numerator* shows the number of these parts which are being considered (Figure 24 : 8).

It is also important that children should realise that $\frac{3}{4}$ is always three quarters of *some unit* or *whole*, and that $\frac{3}{4}$ will appear in many different forms according to the unit to which it is referred. A fraction only exists in relation to its unit. The shaded area in Figure 24 : 9, taken by itself, consists of 3 squares. If the shaded area is related to the square (*b*) as unit, it is $\frac{3}{4}$ of square (*b*), but if it is related to the rectangle (*c*) as unit, the shaded area is $\frac{1}{2}$ of rectangle (*c*). Similarly, a decimal fraction has many concrete embodiments in relation to different units. Thus, 0·7 may be represented by 7 decimetres in relation to a metre, or by 7 centimetres in relation to a decimetre, or by 7 ten-pence coins in relation to a £1 coin.

The unit is a fracton of itself: it may be visualised as 4 quarters of itself, or 10 tenths of

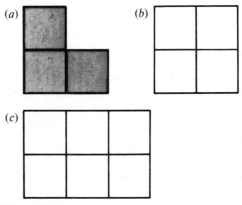

Figure 24 : 9

(b) A sequence of decimal fractions made with Cuisenaire rods

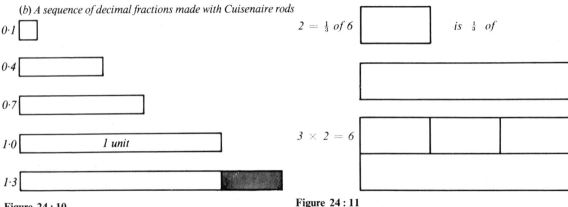

0·1

0·4

0·7

1·0   *1 unit*

1·3

Figure 24 : 10

$2 = \frac{1}{3}$ *of* 6   *is* $\frac{1}{3}$ *of*

$3 \times 2 = 6$

Figure 24 : 11

itself. A quantity which is larger than the unit may also be described as a fraction of the unit. In Figure 24 : 10 each rod is a fraction of the unit rod, although one of the rods is longer than the unit rod.

Two natural numbers are used in naming a fraction; the fraction $\frac{3}{4}$ is described by the *ordered pair* of whole numbers 3 and 4, using the first number as numerator and the second as denominator. The pair of whole numbers used to build a fraction is *ordered*, as the fraction $\frac{4}{3}$, built from 4 and 3, is different from the fraction $\frac{3}{4}$, built from 3 and 4. In later mathematics, this aspect of a fraction as an *ordered pair* of integers or whole numbers becomes increasingly important. New types of numbers are often built up from ordered pairs of numbers of a type already known.

When we use decimal notation, the second number of the pair, or the denominator of the fraction, has to be supplied from our knowledge of the number system. For example, 0·7 is 7 tenths, and so is built up from the ordered pair of integers 7 and 10. Similarly, 1·7 is 17 tenths, and is built up from the ordered pair (17, 10). The decimal fraction 0·23 is 23 hundredths, and so is built up from (23, 100).

FRACTIONS, MULTIPLICATION AND DIVISION

Representations of $\frac{1}{3}$ as part of some unit, using structural apparatus, are closely related to the arrangements of rods which children make when they use structural apparatus to multiply natural numbers. If children need to discover $\frac{1}{3}$ of 6, they will have to find which rod repeated 3 times makes up 6 (Figure 24 : 11), so building a multiplication situation.

The operation of *finding a third of* a number is the inverse of the operation of *finding three times as*

much as a number; that is, it is the inverse of multiplying by 3. The statement

$\frac{1}{3}$ of 6 = 2

is equivalent to

$3 \times 2 = 6$

But the operation of dividing a quantity into 3 equal parts and the operation of finding $\frac{1}{3}$ of that quantity are clearly only different descriptions of the same process. Hence there are three different ways of representing the same situation:

$\frac{1}{3}$ of 6 = 2

$6 \div 3 = 2$

$3 \times 2 = 6$

The graph of 'three times as much' shown in Figure 24 : 12 could equally well be described by saying that the grey columns are $\frac{1}{3}$ of the outline columns,[5] or that the outline columns have been *divided by* 3 to produce the grey columns. Children should use the language of fractions and decimals alongside the language of division from the beginning to describe the relationship between a part and its whole or unit. Any of the relationships shown in Figure 24 : 12 can be described, and children should be accustomed to describing it, in three ways. For instance:

$3 \times 5 \quad = 15$
$\frac{1}{3}$ of 15 = 5
$15 \div 3 \quad = 5$

Decimal representations should be used when they are appropriate, as in Figure 24 : 13 where the

[5]Cf. page 209.

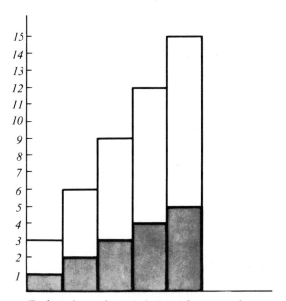

Each outline column is 3 times the grey column.
Each grey column is ⅓ of the outline column.
Each outline column is divided by 3 to produce
the grey column.

Figure 24 : 12

2	2	2	2	2	2	2	2	2	2
20									

Figure 24 : 13

situation can be described by

$$20 \div 10 = 2 \quad or \quad 1 \text{ tenth of } 20 = 2$$

The second description will be written

$$0 \cdot 1 \text{ of } 20 = 2,$$

but there is no ⬚of⬚ key on a calculator. Children will find, however, that ⬚×⬚ produces the result they need, so that

$$0 \cdot 1 \times 20 = 2$$

The calculator can helpfully be used to explore division by 10 and multiplication by 1 tenth or $0 \cdot 1$.

$300 \div 10 =$	$300 \times 0 \cdot 1 =$
$350 \div 10 =$	$350 \times 0 \cdot 1 =$
$354 \div 10 =$	$354 \times 0 \cdot 1 =$

Similarly, division by 100 and multiplication by 1 hundredth, or $0 \cdot 01$, can be linked.

1 unit

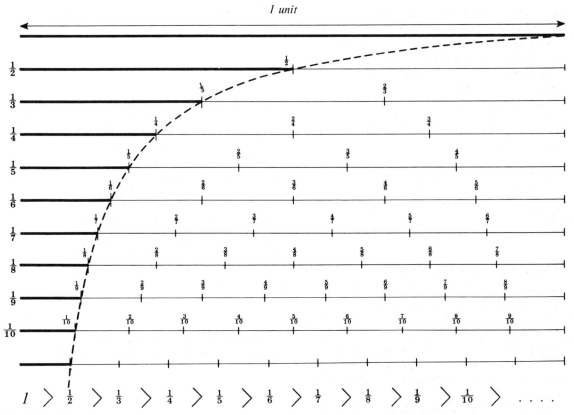

Figure 24 : 14

FRACTIONS ON THE NUMBER LINE

As children make and examine fractions, they will begin to compare the relative sizes of fractions *of the same unit.* Clearly

$$\tfrac{1}{2} > \tfrac{1}{3} > \tfrac{1}{4} > \tfrac{1}{5} \ldots$$

since in each case the same unit has been cut into 2 equal parts, 3 equal parts, 4 equal parts, 5 equal parts, ... so that at each step the size of the parts decreases. Figure 24 : 14 shows this property, the unit being the length of a line.

Children need to become consciously aware of the fact that, for instance, $\tfrac{1}{3} > \tfrac{1}{4}$, since they already know very thoroughly that $4 > 3$, and hence often seem to expect, when they have written down the two fractions, that $\tfrac{1}{4}$ will be greater than $\tfrac{1}{3}$. Frequent reference to a real situation prevents misunderstandings of this sort. Knowledge of the meaning of fractional parts, with their strange notation, and of the relative sizes of different fractions, is much more important at this stage than any formal calculation with fractions. Children may well notice that $\tfrac{2}{4} = \tfrac{1}{2}$, $\tfrac{5}{10} = \tfrac{1}{2}$, and so on, and these relations can be listed when they are found.

It is extremely important that children should realise the relative sizes of decimal fractions. Figure 24 : 15 illustrates the subdivision of the first unit of the number line using decimal fractions.

The unit is first divided into ten equal parts, so that the points of division represent $0\cdot1$, $0\cdot2$, ..., $0\cdot9$. Each of these parts is divided again into ten equal parts, and the points of division correspond, for instance, to $0\cdot21$, $0\cdot22$, ..., $0\cdot29$. This process can, of course, be repeated indefinitely.

Children are often deceived about the relative sizes of decimal numbers by the fact that, for instance, $0\cdot9$ is written with one decimal digit, while $0\cdot21$ has two decimal digits. Knowing that $21 > 9$, a child who does not yet understand place value may think that $0\cdot21 > 0\cdot9$. Marking decimal numbers on the number line, and saying them in unabbreviated form, will help to fix the relative sizes of decimal numbers. It is much clearer to say '9 tenths' at first, rather than 'point nine', and '2 tenths and 1 hundredth', rather than 'point two one'. Then it is immediately clear that 9 tenths > (2 tenths and 1 hundredth) or $0\cdot9 > 0\cdot21$.

When they use money, children can write 21 pence as £0·21; they need to be absolutely certain that 9 pence is 9 hundredths of a pound, and so must be written £0·09, not £0·9. These two ways of writing money need to be related together, and related to the positions of the decimal numbers on the number line.

It is clear that on the number line the smaller of two numbers lies to the left of the larger. When the number line is extended to include negative numbers, the same principle continues to apply. Certainly, $-1 < 4$ causes no surprise, but $-4 < -1$ may surprise children at first, although a temperature of $-4°C$ is colder than a temperature of $-1°C$. Moreover, $-0\cdot9 < -0\cdot21$ (Figure 24 : 16); children need to place points on the number line if they are to feel certain about the order of directed numbers.

The number line has become very much more tightly packed with numbers since, in our earliest description of it, only points corresponding to the natural numbers had any meaning. Now there are points on the number line corresponding to all the decimal fractions with one decimal place, with two

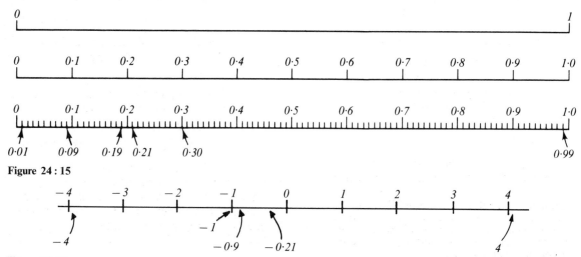

Figure 24 : 15

Figure 24 : 16

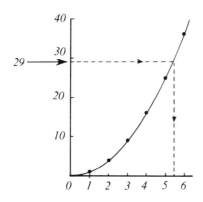

Figure 24 : 17

decimal places, and so on. All the numbers such as

2·1, 3·52, 0·7604

have taken their places on the number line, so have some fractions which are more conveniently thought of in parts of the unit other than tenths, hundredths, thousandths, and so on; these are fractions such as $\frac{1}{2}, \frac{1}{3}, \frac{3}{4}, \frac{5}{8}$, and so on.

That the number line is packed with fractions is implicit in children's minds when they try to interpolate in such a graph as Figure 24 : 17 in order to find a number whose square is 29 (*see page 448*). If they have drawn the graph on a fairly small scale they will probably give the result as approximately 5·4; if the scale of the graph is larger they may be able to estimate 5·38. At this stage children are prepared to think of the same unit as divided up into 10, or 8, or any other convenient number of equal parts. They have implicitly reached a correspondence between the set of all possible fractions and a set of points on the number line, although this correspondence may not be explicitly expressed until the secondary stage.[6]

ROUNDING ON THE NUMBER LINE

In order to check that the results of calculations carried out on a calculator are of a sensible size, and wrong keys have not been pressed, it is necessary to be able mentally to replace a calculation such as

6·27 × 478·3

by 6 × 500, which can be done mentally. The foundation of this skill is using the number line to

[6]It will be noticed that the correspondence has been described as being between *all possible* fractions and *a set of* points on the number line, not *all possible points* on the number line. This leads to a further generalisation of the idea of number. See Chapter 39.

place 'difficult' numbers between landmarks which are 'easy' numbers. For instance, 6·27 is between the landmarks of 6 and 7, and 478·3 is between 400 and 500. The latter number, 500, is a more sensible approximation to use, as 478·3 is nearer to it than it is to 400.

Children should be encouraged to use the number line to decide what 'round numbers' a particular number lies between, and which of these it is nearer to. Usually only *one digit accuracy* is needed, so that 478·3 is rounded to 500 rather than 480. However, sometimes greater accuracy is needed, as in checking the fact that the answer to

478·3 + 17·9

will be approximately 500.

Similarly, numbers less than 1 can be placed between landmarks; 0·67 is between 0·6 and 0·7, and 0·03 is between 0 and 0·1. Children often have difficulty in placing decimals in the right relative order of size when they have different numbers of decimal places; they think that 0·3 < 0·12 because 3 < 12. Placing decimals between landmarks on number lines will help them to understand relative sizes of decimal numbers.

The number line in the National Curriculum

The number line is not explicitly mentioned in the National Curriculum. However, its use is implicit in statements which require children to put numbers in order.

- read, write and order whole numbers.

(AT2: Level 4)

- order decimals appreciate place values.

(AT2: Level 6)

We have seen that the number line is also of considerable use in estimation and approximation.

- estimate and approximate to check the validity of addition and subtraction calculations.

(AT2: Level 4)

However, the major use of the number line is not to build up skills required by the attainment targets, but to give children a vivid mental picture of numbers, which they will be able to use in very many situations.

25 | *THREE-DIMENSIONAL SHAPES*

INTRODUCTION: POLYHEDRA

In Chapter 5 we have seen how children discover
that their world is made up of solids of different
shapes and sizes, and how they begin to classify
solids into sets which have similarities of shape and
to give these solids names.

Among the important subsets of the set of solids
is the set of those solids which are bounded by
plane surfaces only. These solids are called
polyhedra. Children will find and make a varied
collection of polyhedra, which occur in cartons,
packets and in the shapes of buildings. Some are
shown in Figure 25 : 1.

An attempt to sort polyhedra into sets will
probably lead first to the classification and naming
of *cubes* and *cuboids* (Figure 25 : 2). As children talk
about polyhedra, they will need words to describe
the different parts of the shape. Each plane surface
on the boundary of a polyhedron is a *face*; two

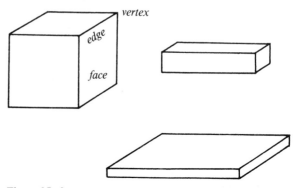

Figure 25 : 2

faces meet in a straight line, an *edge*; and a number
of edges meet at each corner, or *vertex*, of the solid.
A cube has six faces, each of which is a square,
twelve edges and eight vertices. The six faces of a
cuboid may be either oblong rectangles or squares.

Another set of polyhedra of which children will
find many examples are those with a top and a
bottom face which are parallel equal polygons, and
all the other faces are rectangles. These polyhedra
are *prisms*. A hexagonal pencil is a prism. So are
two of the solids in Figure 25 : 1; more prisms are
shown in Figure 25 : 3.

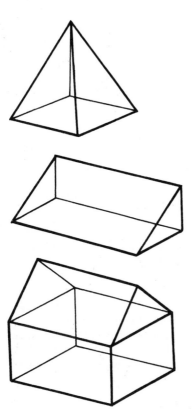

Figure 25 : 1

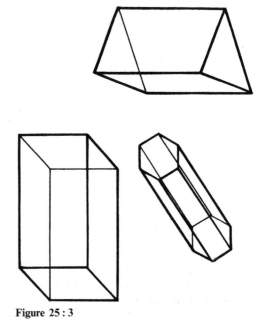

Figure 25 : 3

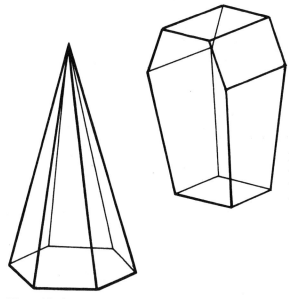

Figure 25 : 4

their *nets* is another useful activity. If children cannot see at once how to arrange the net of a solid, it is often helpful to allow them to cut along the edges of a cardboard model until they can open it out flat. This can usually be done in several ways. A useful form of apparatus consists of cardboard polygons with flaps on the edges. These can easily be held together with rubber bands, and the resulting solid models dismantled into their nets in a variety of ways (Figure 25 : 5). Another useful form of apparatus consists of plastic polygons which

(i) Card shapes for construction of solids

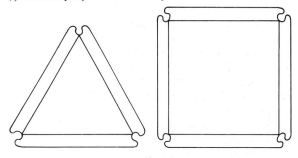

(ii) Clixi shapes

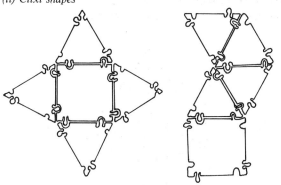

(iii) Two different nets of a square pyramid

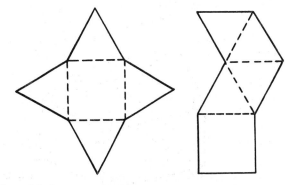

Figure 25 : 5

Many sweet packets are prisms of various shapes, so are garden sheds and swimming baths. Prisms are named according to the shape of their bases, as, for instance, the triangular prism and hexagonal prism shown in Figure 25 : 3. Pyramids are also named according to the shape of their bases. Figure 25 : 1 shows a square pyramid, and the shape obtained by carefully sharpening a hexagonal pencil with a penknife is a hexagonal pyramid (Figure 25 : 4). There are also many polyhedra like the sweet packet in Figure 25 : 4, which cannot be classified as cuboids, prisms or pyramids. All polyhedra can, however, be named according to the total number of their faces. The ending *-hedron* is combined with the Greek word for the number of faces. The solids in Figure 25 : 4 are a heptahedron and an octahedron.

As children find examples of polyhedra, it is useful for them to keep a list of the names of each one, together with the numbers of faces, edges and vertices.

Name	Number of faces	Number of edges	Number of vertices
cube	6	12	8
square pyramid	5	8	5

Even at an early stage, children should be encouraged to look for patterns in this list. The pattern will be discussed later, when more examples have been found. Making models of polyhedra from can be linked together along their edges. Both the nets shown in Figure 25 : 5(*ii*) can be made into the same square pyramid.

In making polyhedra from their nets, children will notice that the edges of two faces which are to be joined together must be the same length, and they will also begin to notice the angles of the polygons which meet at a vertex of the polyhedron.

In Figure 25 : 6, a polyhedron has been cut away until just one vertex, and the faces which surround that vertex, remain. A cut along one edge will now allow the figure to be opened out flat. The sum of the angles which surround the vertex must therefore be less than 360°.[1] The smaller the sum of the plane angles which meet at the vertex, the more 'pointed' the vertex will be. We can also see that at least three faces must meet at a vertex of the solid.

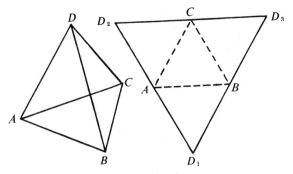

Figure 25 : 7

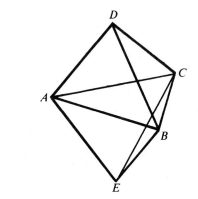

Figure 25 : 8

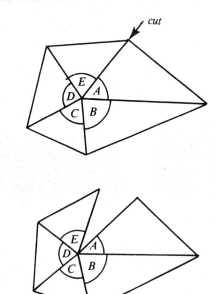

$$\hat{A}+\hat{B}+\hat{C}+\hat{D}+\hat{E} \quad <360°$$

Figure 25 : 6

THE REGULAR SOLIDS

There are some polyhedra whose faces are all equal regular polygons. For instance, all the faces of a cube are equal squares. It would seem natural to call such polyhedra *regular solids*, but only some of them are regular. In two dimensions, a regular polygon must have equal angles as well as equal sides. In three dimensions, for a polygon to be regular, not only must all the faces be equal regular polygons, but *the solid angles at each vertex must*

also be exactly the same shape.

For example, Figure 25 : 7 shows a triangular pyramid, each of whose faces is an equilateral triangle. Whichever face it stands on, it looks exactly the same. The solid angles at all the vertices are the same shape. It is a *regular tetrahedron*.

If two regular tetrahedra are stuck together, we get the solid, shown in Figure 25 : 8, which has six faces, each one an equilateral triangle, but it is not a regular polyhedron. Three equilateral triangles meet at vertices *D* and *E*, but at vertices *A*, *B* and *C*, four equilateral triangles meet. The solid angles at *A*, *B* and *C* are not the same shape as those at *D* and *E*.

So we see that a regular polyhedron is a solid with:

i) each face a regular polygon,

ii) all the faces congruent,

iii) the same number of faces meeting at each vertex.

The cube is another example of a regular solid. We now consider whether there are any more regular solids. The algebraic demonstration which follows is intended for the teacher rather than for children, but it prepares the way for the geometrical

---

[1] This may not be true if the solid angle at the vertex is not convex.

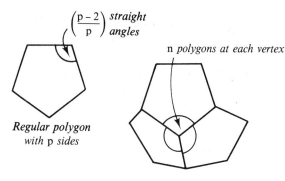

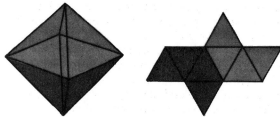

Figure 25 : 10

$\left(\dfrac{p-2}{p}\right)$ *straight angles*

n *polygons at each vertex*

Regular polygon with p *sides*

Figure 25 : 9

work which follows and will lead children to discover more regular solids.

Let us try to build a regular solid, each of whose faces is a regular polygon with p sides (Figure 25 : 9). The sum of the angles of this polygon is $(p-2)$ straight angles, so that each angle of the polygon is $\left(\dfrac{p-2}{p}\right)$ straight angles. Suppose that n polygons meet at each vertex. Then the sum of the angles at a vertex is

$$\dfrac{p-2}{p} \times n \text{ straight angles.}$$

But this must be less than a complete revolution or two straight angles.

Hence $\left(\dfrac{p-2}{p}\right) \times n < 2,$

so that $(p-2) \times n < 2p.$

Now every polygon has three or more sides, so $p \geqslant 3$; and three or more polygons meet at each vertex of the solid, so $n \geqslant 3$. We try various possible values in the inequality.

If $p = 3$, $n < 6$; so n may be 3, 4 or 5.
If $p = 4$, $2n < 8$; so n can only be 3.
If $p = 5$, $3n < 10$; so n can only be 3.
If $p = 6$, $4n < 12$; there are no possible values of n.

It is useless to try values of p greater than 6, for we know that even a plane tessellation cannot be made out of regular polygons with more than six sides. So there is no possibility of using these polygons for the net of a regular solid. There are therefore only five possibilities which we can try.

i) $p = 3$, $n = 3$. Each face is an equilateral triangle, and three faces meet at each vertex. We have already met this solid, the *regular tetrahedron* (Figure 25 : 7). It should be noticed that its net can be cut out from a tessellation of equilateral triangles.

ii) $p = 3$, $n = 4$. Each face is an equilateral triangle, and four faces meet at each vertex. The solid, which has eight faces, and its net are shown in Figure 25 : 10. It is the *regular octahedron*, and can be thought of as two square pyramids stuck together by their bases. Children should turn it round to see that it looks exactly the same from any angle. Again, the net is part of the tessellation of equilateral triangles; several other arrangements of the net are possible.

iii) $p = 3$, $n = 5$. Five equilateral triangles meet at each vertex. The solid, the *regular icosahedron*,[2] has twenty faces, and is shown in Figure 25 : 11.

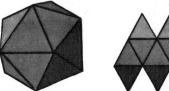

Figure 25 : 11

iv) $p = 4$, $n = 3$. Each face of the solid is a square; three faces meet at each vertex. The solid is the *cube*. The net is part of the tessellation of squares.

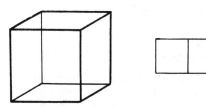

Figure 25 : 12

v) $p = 5$, $n = 3$. Each face is a regular pentagon; three faces meet at each vertex. The solid, the *regular dodecahedron*, has twelve faces. It is most easily made as two bowl-shaped parts, which are easily fitted together.

[2]Greek εικοσι (eikosi) twenty.

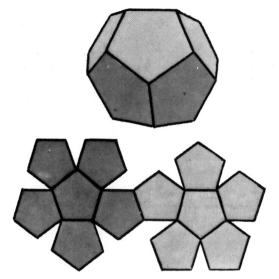

Figure 25 : 13

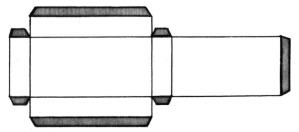

Figure 25 : 15

Alternatively, the nets of the two halves of a dodecahedron can be made separately of strong card, arranged one above the other as in Figure 25 : 14, and laced together with a strong elastic band. If the folds have been scored through, the elastic will pull the model into the shape of a regular dodecahedron, held together by the band round its equator.

If the model-maker wishes to assemble models by sticking together flaps which can be hidden inside the model, rather than by using sticky tape on the outside, it is enough to put flaps on alternate edges of the net, as shown on the net of a cuboid in Figure 25 : 15.

The five regular solids are known as the Platonic solids. They were all known to the Greeks, and Plato associated the tetrahedron, octahedron, cube and icosahedron with the four elements of fire, air, earth and water, and saw the dodecahedron as a symbol of the universe as a whole. While we no longer associate ourselves with such mystical symbolism in mathematics, we can still feel a shock of surprise at the fact that, although in two dimensions it is possible to construct regular polygons with any number of sides, in three dimensions there are only five different regular solids.

It is possible to make four other regular solids, the Kepler-Poinsot polyhedra, if the solid angle at each vertex is not required to be convex, or if the faces of the solid are allowed to be pentagrams (Figure 25 : 16). Details of the construction of these most beautiful star polyhedra will be found in Cundy and Rollett's *Mathematical Models*. The easiest to make is the great stellated dodecahedron. The others are likely to be beyond the technical skill of most primary school children.

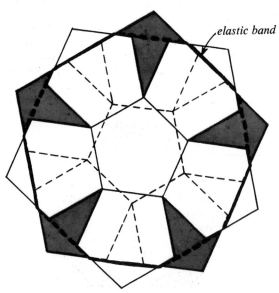

elastic band

Figure 25 : 14

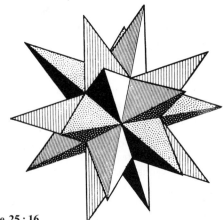

Figure 25 : 16

CHILDREN'S EXPERIMENTAL DISCOVERY OF THE FIVE REGULAR SOLIDS

Children can be led to discover the five Platonic regular solids by cutting up the three regular tessellations. If the faces of a solid are to be regular

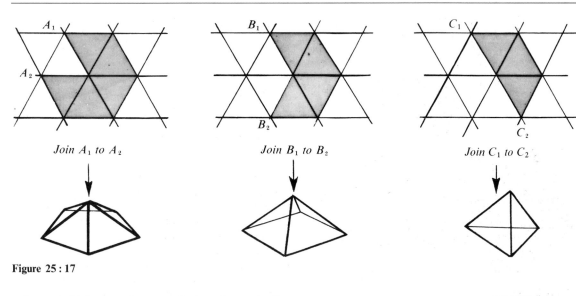

Join A_1 to A_2   *Join B_1 to B_2*   *Join C_1 to C_2*

Figure 25 : 17

polygons which occur in a tessellation, the part of the net surrounding a vertex can be made by cutting out a part of the tessellation.

From the tessellation of equilateral triangles, a solid angle can be made by cutting away one of the six triangles which surround a vertex, and joining the remaining five triangles into a pyramid (Figure 25 : 17). Similarly, four or three triangles at a vertex of the tessellation can be used to make a solid angle.

A solid angle can then be stuck to other equal solid angles until a regular solid is built up. Children will then see that only three regular solids, the regular tetrahedron, octahedron and icosahedron can be made from equilateral triangles.

In the same way, cutting up the tessellation of squares gives a cube (Figure 25 : 18).

Children will see that a solid angle cannot be made from the tessellation of regular hexagons, as three hexagons completely fill the angle of 360° at a vertex, leaving no space for cutting out.

Children who have tried to make a tessellation of regular pentagons will see that they can make a solid angle which has regular pentagons as faces. This leads to the regular dodecahedron (Figure 25 : 19).

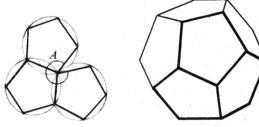

Figure 25 : 19

It is easy to see that a regular solid cannot have faces with more than six sides, because a tessellation cannot be made with regular polygons with more than six sides, and the net of a polyhedron must leave space for cutting out at any vertex.

The construction of the regular solids is made very much easier if cardboard polygons which can be looped together with rubber bands, or plastic polygons which link together, are used. A number of solid angles are made, as in Figure 25 : 20, and linked together.

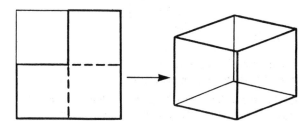

Figure 25 : 18

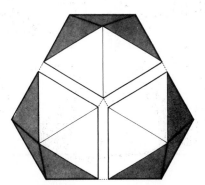

Figure 25 : 20

310 .

EULER'S FORMULA

Children who have kept the list of polyhedra suggested on page 305, with the numbers of their faces, edges and vertices, may search for a pattern in the table. The arrangement of the table shown below may help them.

Name	Number of faces (F)	Number of vertices (V)	Number of edges (E)
Square pyramid	5	5	8
Hexagonal prism	8	12	18
Regular solids			
Regular tetrahedron	4	4	6
Cube	6	8	12
Regular octahedron	8	6	12
Regular dodecahedron	12	20	30
Regular icosahedron	20	12	30

Children will notice that the number of edges is always greater than the number of faces or vertices, and pairing the regular solids may suggest that $F + V$ is important. A graph of E against $(F + V)$ (Figure 25 : 21) will confirm this for all the solids on their list, not only the regular solids.

A curious feature of this graph is that each point of it will usually correspond to several different solids. For each solid, the sum of the number of faces and vertices is two more than the number of edges. Symbolically,

$$F + V = E + 2$$

This formula was proved by Leonard Euler in 1735 AD. Primary school children will be content to

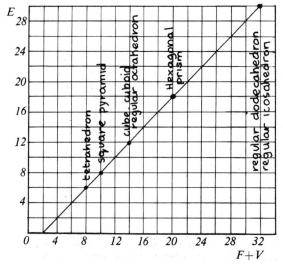

Figure 25 : 21

notice that the formula is satisfied by every polyhedron they know, but the teacher may be interested in a proof of the formula, which is similar to that given by Euler.

Imagine that we build up a polyhedron by adding one face to it at a time, and notice how the number

$$N = F + V - E$$

changes as each successive face is added to the polyhedron. Suppose that the first face is a polygon with n sides (and n vertices). At this stage $F = 1$, $V = n$, $E = n$, and $N = F + V - E = 1$.

Now add another face, a polygon with m sides. It will be built on to one edge of the first face, so it has one edge and two vertices in common with the first face. So one face, $(m - 1)$ edges, and $(m - 2)$ vertices have been added. For the two faces together,

$$F = 2, \quad V = n + m - 2, \quad E = n + m - 1,$$

and

$$\begin{aligned} N &= F + V - E \\ &= 2 + (n + m - 2) - (n + m - 1) \\ &= 1 \end{aligned}$$

It looks likely that N remains equal to one as we add more and more faces. This is so, as we can show that adding another face at any stage does not change the value of N, provided it does not complete the polyhedron. As time goes on, it will be necessary to add polygons which have more than one edge in common with what has already been built (Figure 25 : 22). Suppose that at some stage, when the part already built has f faces, v vertices, and e edges, we add a polygon with p sides, which has k consecutive edges in common with the part already built. It will have $(k + 1)$ vertices in common with part already built, so, at this stage,

$$F = f + 1, \quad V = v + p - (k + 1), \quad E = e + p - k,$$

and

$$\begin{aligned} N &= F + V - E \\ &= (f + 1) + (v + p - k - 1) - (e + p - k) \\ &= f + v - e \end{aligned}$$

So adding another face does not change N. At the beginning $N = 1$, so each time a face is added without closing the polyhedron, N stays equal to one.

When the last face is added to close the polyhedron, the number of faces is increased by one without adding any more vertices or edges. This increases $N = F + V - E$ by one, so for the completed polyhedron

$$N = F + V - E = 2,$$

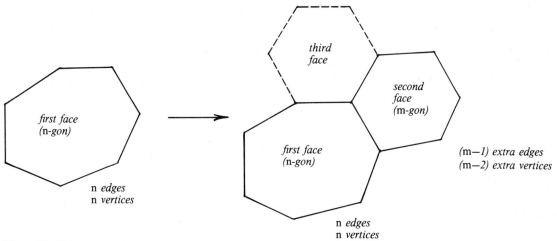

Figure 25 : 22

or

$$F + V = E + 2$$

This formula is true whether the polyhedron is regular or not. The only restriction is that it must be possible to build it up by adding faces which only have *consecutive* edges in common with what has already been built. All polyhedra which children are likely to meet at this stage satisfy this requirement.

RIGIDITY OF POLYGONS AND POLYHEDRA

Children can make polygons and tessellations by using Meccano strips to make the edges of the polygons. The fact that they will find it difficult to tighten up nuts and bolts sufficiently to prevent the strips from moving will lead them to study *rigidity*. They will quickly find that any triangle is rigid, but that any other polygon can be deformed and made to alter its shape in various ways. Squares will turn into rhombuses, and rectangles into parallelograms (Figure 25 : 23). But if a quadrilateral is made with both pairs of opposite sides equal, however it is pushed about, the opposite sides will always stay *parallel*, so that although the shape of the polygon changes, it always remains a parallelogram.

Children can discover a good deal about the diagonals of polygons if they use elastic thread to

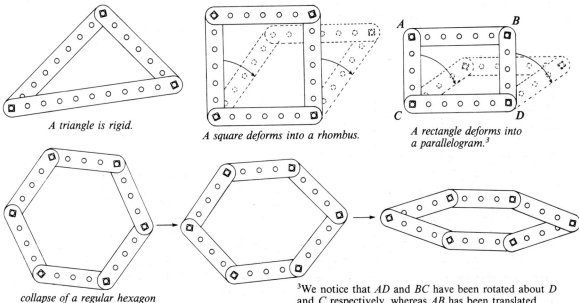

A triangle is rigid.

A square deforms into a rhombus.

A rectangle deforms into a parallelogram.[3]

collapse of a regular hexagon

Figure 25 : 23

[3]We notice that *AD* and *BC* have been rotated about *D* and *C* respectively, whereas *AB* has been translated parallel to itself.

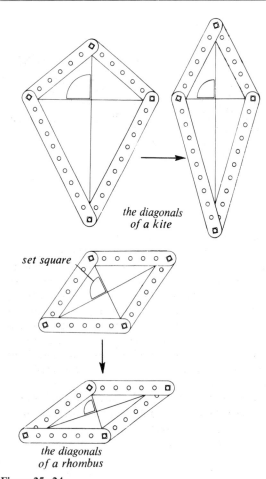

the diagonals
of a kite

set square

the diagonals
of a rhombus

Figure 25 : 24

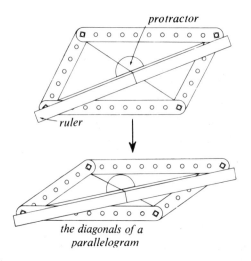

protractor

ruler

the diagonals of a
parallelogram

make the diagonals of the Meccano models, and
watch what happens as they change the shape of a
model (Figure 25 : 24).

Children may also discover how many rigid
diagonals made of Meccano they need to put in
before a polygon is rigid. This experiment lends
itself to graphical treatment, and should be
compared with Figure 25 : 25. The total number of
diagonals which can be put into each polygon also
makes an interesting graph.

Children will soon see that the triangle is the only
rigid polygon, and that other polygons can be made
rigid by struts which make them into triangles.
They will be able to collect many examples of
this fact in use in five-barred gates, electricity pylons,

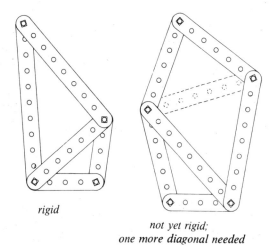

rigid

not yet rigid;
one more diagonal needed

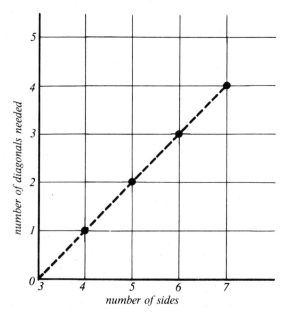

Number of sides in polygon	3	4	5	6
Number of diagonals needed for rigidity	0	1	2	3

Figure 25 : 25

Figure 25 : 26

bridges and roofing girders (Figure 25 : 26).

Tessellations made from Meccano strips are certainly not rigid unless they are made of triangles. An interesting application of this fact is found in lattice-work fencing panels, which stretch to make variable lengths of fence (Figure 25 : 27). A parallelogram lattice, made on this principle from Meccano strips, can be used to enable children to discover all the well-known angle properties of parallel lines (Figure 25 : 28). As the shape of the lattice changes, angles *A*, *B* and *C* change in shape, but remain equal to one another.

In order for children to be able to examine the problem of building rigid shapes in three dimensions, they must be able to use joints which can move in any direction. Meccano will not make such joints, but straws can be used for the edges of solids which are made by threading cotton through the straws and tying them. More permanent models can be made with plastic straws and elastic thread. The commercially produced kits are not suitable for this investigation, as they usually have at least semi-rigid joints.

Children will find that triangles and tetrahedra are rigid figures in three dimensions, but that the

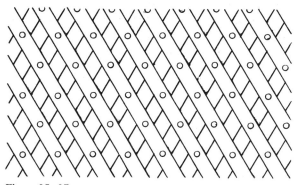

Figure 25 : 27

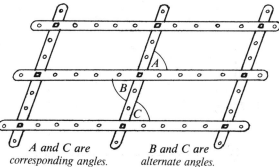

A and C are corresponding angles.

B and C are alternate angles.

A and B are vertically opposite angles.

Figure 25 : 28

A tetrahedron is rigid.

A quadrilateral with one diagonal joined is not rigid.

A square pyramid is not rigid; it folds flat.

Figure 25 : 29

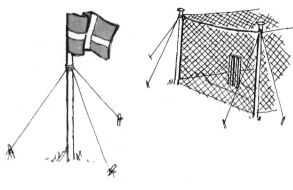

Figure 25 : 30

This is one shape made from a collapsed cube.

Figure 25 : 31

number of struts needed to make a plane polygon rigid in two dimensions is insufficient in three dimensions (Figure 25 : 29).

Many examples of the use of a tetrahedron to make a rigid framework will be found in pylons. Children may also like to examine the number of ropes needed to steady a flagpole, or the corner of a cricket net, and to consider in what ways these situations differ (Figure 25 : 30).

A cube made from straws is quite astonishingly deformable (Figure 25 : 31) and children may enjoy experimenting to see how few struts will make it rigid.

If rigid three-dimensional models of this type are to be built, a firmer joint can be made with a short piece of pipe-cleaner, or one of the commercially available kits can be used (Figure 25 : 32).

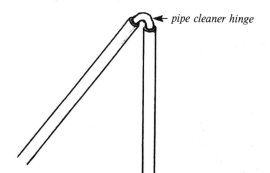

← *pipe cleaner hinge*

Figure 25 : 32

SPHERES, CYLINDERS AND CONES

Some of the three-dimensional shapes with which children are most familiar do not have plane faces. The *sphere* is familiar to all children from their earliest years as the shape of a ball. All spheres are the same shape; they are merely larger or smaller versions of one another. This is a property which they share with cubes and with other regular solids (Figure 25 : 33), but not with cuboids or cones. Shapes which are merely enlargements or reductions of one another are said to be *similar*. This use of the word 'similar' means much more than merely 'having the same name'. All rectangles have the same name, but they are certainly not similar. Children can be asked to collect sets of similar shapes, such as different-sized models of the same car, or different-sized equilateral triangles. They can also collect sets of shapes which have the same name but are not similar, such as cuboids or triangles.

Another property of a sphere which reveals its extreme regularity is that every plane cut through it

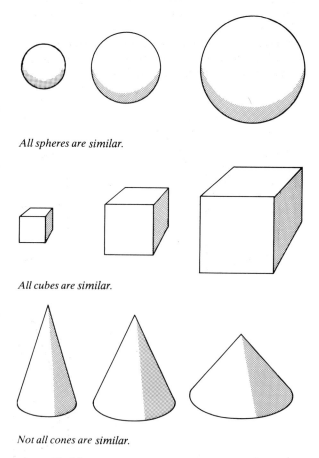

All spheres are similar.

All cubes are similar.

Not all cones are similar.

Figure 25 : 33

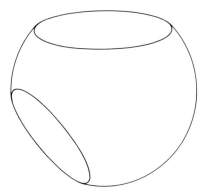

Figure 25 : 34

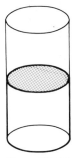 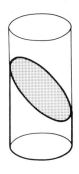 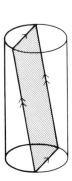

Figure 25 : 35

shows a circle (Figure 25 : 34). Most children know this well from the experience of cutting up apples and other fruit, but they are not aware that they know it, nor that the sphere is the only shape which has this property. Children may experiment by making plane cuts across cylinders, cubes, cones and cuboids made of clay, Plasticine or polystyrene. They will find that, for instance, a cylinder can be cut to make a circle, an oval shape which is called an ellipse, or a rectangle, and other shapes (Figure 25 : 35). A cube can be cut to make a variety of sections, ranging from triangles to hexagons (Figure 25 : 36). But a sphere can only be cut to give plane sections which are circles of different sizes.

A sphere is also the only shape which will roll in any direction, steadily and without wobbling. This is why the balls used in almost all games are spherical. A punctured tennis ball or a rugby football may be compared with a spherical ball for ease of rolling. A sphere may also be used to test whether a surface such as a shelf is horizontal; it rolls downhill if there is a hill.

Cylinders are known to children as pencils and tubes of sweets, and through rolling out dough, and rolling up paper into tubes. A cylinder is a solid of the same type as a prism, but its top and bottom faces are circles instead of polygons. A cylinder will roll if it is placed with its curved face on a

Some sections of a cube

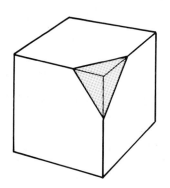 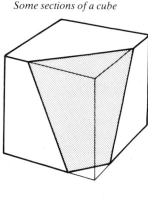 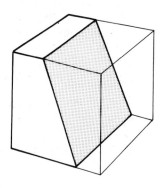

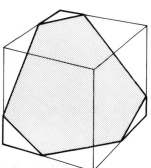

Figure 25 : 36

Some sections of a cone

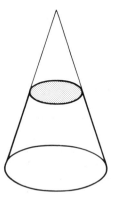 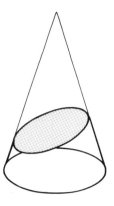 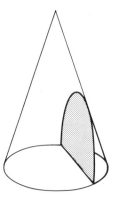 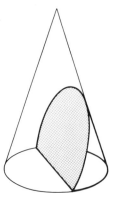

Figure 25 : 37

horizontal surface, but it is stable if it rests on its base; wheels are cylinders, and a vehicle supported by cylindrical wheels travels straight forward.

Cones can be seen as ice-cream cones, and can be twisted from pieces of paper. The pointed ends of sharpened pencils are conical. A cone is a solid of the same type as a pyramid, but its base is a circle instead of a polygon. Sections of a cone may be circles or ellipses (Figure 25 : 37). If the section cuts the base, we get part of a parabola or a hyperbola (*see Chapter 38*). A cone does not roll in a straight line, but rolls round in a circle about its point. Thus we see that the sphere, cylinder and cone all roll in different ways, and different shapes appear as their sections. The sphere is the most regular shape of all; it will roll in any direction, and all its sections are circles.

The sphere is also the shape of the earth. Children will identify different places on a globe of the earth, and they can mark the route which an aircraft flies between them by stretching a piece of string between the places on the globe, and pulling it taut. They may well be surprised that the shortest distance between, for instance, London and New York, goes so far north. This idea is discussed further in Chapter 38.

The sun and the moon are also spheres. Discussion may well need to ensure that children realise that the full moon, which they see as a circle, is in fact a sphere. The effect of an eclipse in blocking out part of the moon from visibility may be deferred until late in the primary years. Knowledge of the exploration of space has now pervaded our culture so deeply that children should develop their spatial ideas to know the inter-relations of the sun, earth and moon during the primary stage of education. If children picture the earth revolving in a circle around the sun, and

the moon revolving in a circle around the earth, their ideas of the shapes of the orbits will only have to be slightly modified as they get older.

> ### Three-dimensional shapes in the National Curriculum
>
> The work described in this chapter relates to Attainment Target 4 (shape and space). Children are expected to be familiar with three-dimensional shapes, to be able to construct them, and to be aware of their symmetries.
>
> - construct simple 2-D and 3-D shapes from given information and know associated language.
>   EXAMPLE: *Construct rectangles, circles, nets for cubes, pyramids, prisms.*
>
> *(AT3: Level 4)*
>
> - identify the symmetries of various shapes.
>   EXAMPLE: *Find the centres, axes and planes of symmetry in a variety of plane and solid shapes.*
>
> *(AT3: Level 5)*
>
> At Level 5, children are also expected to be aware of the angle properties of sets of parallel lines.
>
> - explain and use properties associated with intersecting and parallel lines and triangles, and know associated language.
>
> *(AT3: Level 5)*

26 | *MEASURING AREA*

EARLY EXPERIENCES OF SURFACES

By 8 or 9 years of age children have become familiar with flat or plane surfaces as opposed to those that bulge or are indented. Mounds and dips are seen in the countryside or in road excavations; a saucer right way up looks different from one placed upside down. A smooth plane surface is horizontal when things on it do not roll or slide of their own accord; if a ball placed on a surface does not roll, the surface is horizontal. A vertical surface may suggest balance or stability. If it is sloping it may offer a good slide or look like an unstable tower, the face of a roof or the partly open lid of a box. But none of these examples of surface, flat or curved, appear to raise the question of *how much* surface there is.

Experiences of cutting up paper shapes and reassembling the parts to make a new shape lead children to realise that the *size* of the shape, i.e. the amount of surface, does not vary with a rearrangement of its parts. For example, a unit square centimetre may take up a variety of forms (Figure 26 : 1).

The ancient Chinese puzzle, the tangram (Figure 26.2) consists of a square cut into seven pieces. From these pieces very many shapes can be made, all of which have the same area as the original square. Simpler tangram sets, with fewer than seven pieces, are available, and can be used to give young children experience of the fact that something remains constant when the pieces of a surface are rearranged; that constant is the *area* of the surface.

A set of similar shapes, such as rectangles, circles, triangles, can be compared for size using an intuitive judgement, or by placing one upon another, to test whether they fit or one is larger than the other. Several such shapes can be put in order of size. Folding and cutting show that two equal parts of a shape can be made to fit one on another; thus each is a half of the whole surface. But suppose they cannot be made to fit and each projects in some places over the other; can we tell whether they have the same amount of surface? Can we detect whether a round biscuit is the same size

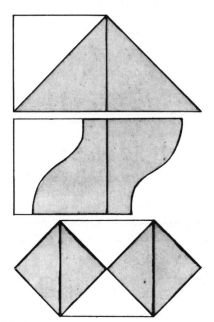

Figure 26 : 1

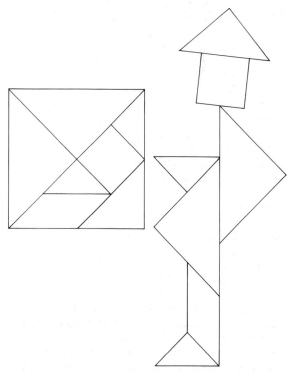

Figure 26 : 2

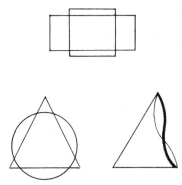

Figure 26 : 3

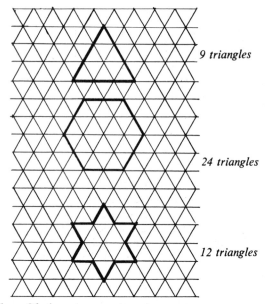

9 triangles

24 triangles

12 triangles

Figure 26 : 4

as a rectangular one (ignoring their thickness)? See Figure 26 : 3.

The surfaces of three-dimensional objects have been interesting hitherto chiefly for their shapes or the properties of their faces. For example, cubes, pyramids and cones have exhibited squares, triangles or parts of circles in their surfaces. Such objects have been made by folding and joining plane shapes. Clearly some forms, the sphere for instance, cannot be produced from a plane surface; yet such objects have a surface and obviously a large ball has more surface than a smaller one. The human body shows similar differences: a tall, broad-shouldered person has much more skin surface than a short, slight person. Children can be given opportunities of inventing ways of comparing such surfaces and can experiment with simple rectangular shapes in the playground. At 8 or 9 years of age children often compare length and breadth or perimeter and show no awareness of the quantity of *surface*.

COVERING A SURFACE

One of the most formative experiences that direct children towards thinking about the measure of a surface is making all-over patterns. Covering a plane surface with repetitions of a particular shape may readily lead to the question, '*How many* such shapes were needed?' Using triangles,

parallelograms, rectangles or hexagons to cover two or more surfaces may lead to the idea that the *number* of one particular shape required to cover a surface enables us to compare it with another surface. There will be a correspondence between the numbers of the unit shapes and the respective sizes of the two surfaces. In fact a way of measuring surfaces will have been discovered. Any paper ruled in a grid, such as the isometric paper in Figure 26 : 4, enables comparisons of shapes drawn on the paper to be made very easily.

A lattice of parallelograms allows a comparison to be made between the regions enclosed by pairs of parallel lines by counting the number of unit parallelograms enclosed. In Figure 26 : 5, parallelogram *A* contains 6 unit parallelograms and figure *B* contains 8 units.

Some valuable experience of quantities of surface can be found from the shapes made by elastic bands stretched round nails on a nail-board or a commercially produced geoboard. These geoboards often have pegs at intervals of 2 cm, but there is an underlying grid of 1-cm squares (Figure 26 : 6).

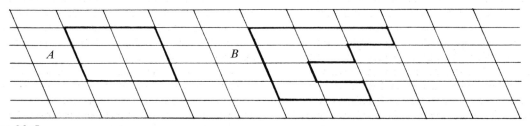

Figure 26 : 5

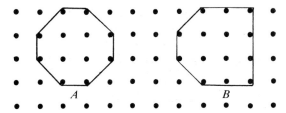

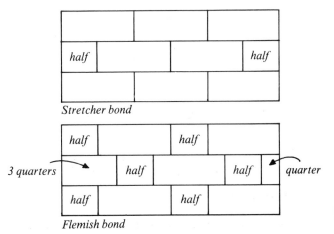

Figure 26 : 6

Children therefore need to come to a decision about the size of square which they will take as a unit of area. The unit will differ according to the circumstances, and children will continually notice that one of the 2-cm side squares contains four 1-cm squares. Many of the shapes which children make on the geoboard contain half-squares. Half a square will be recognised readily from symmetry and this half-unit will often occur.

The amount of surface or *area* in shape *A* is 5 squares and 4 half-squares, the area of shape *B* is 7 squares and 2 half-squares. Thus shape *A* contains 7 square units and shape *B* contains 8 square units.

In Figure 26 : 7 a more complicated problem

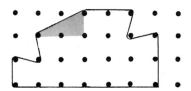

Figure 26 : 7

involves the recognition that the triangular part is half of *two* of the squares. The advantage of using a square as a unit is seen to lie in its symmetry and in the ease of counting in rows.

Children can find other patterns of tiles and floor coverings that enable them to make counts in order to compare the size of the two surfaces. For example, parquet flooring consists of a tessellation of rectangles and a count can be made of the rectangles which have been used for a particular surface.

The surface of a wall can be stated in terms of brickfaces, including the mortar with the brick. Since a brick is half as wide as it is long the various types of bond (*see Chapter 12*) give counts of 'bricks' and 'half-bricks'. Figure 26 : 8 shows rectangular pieces of wall in stretcher bond and Flemish bond. The patterns of whole bricks and half bricks are different and so the counts made in finding the areas of the pieces of wall will be different, although of course the total area of each piece of wall is the same.

Figure 26 : 8

In similar ways the areas of floors, ceilings and windows can be found in terms of tiles, block-faces, panes, etc., and their halves or quarters.

STANDARD UNITS OF AREA

When the principle of measuring surface by counting unit shapes has been established the standard units can be taught, though it frequently happens that children who have used graph paper of various rulings extensively will themselves suggest a *square centimetre* as a unit. The quarters of a square centimetre which can be seen on paper ruled in $\frac{1}{2}$–centimetre squares will be used spontaneously.

The *square decimetre* is a 10-centimetre square, and so contains 100 square centimetres. Some forms of structural apparatus, which use a 1-centimetre unit, contain pieces, representing hundreds, which are square decimetres. The *square metre* can be built up from square decimetres, and pieces of paper which are square metres should be cut out by the children, given a stiff backing, and used by groups of children to form a variety of shapes of specified area. For example, several shapes made by 12 square units could be marked on the floor or playground, using the square unit as a template. The variability of shape for a stated area is thus established and the tendency to think of area as related only to the surface of a rectangle is avoided. If twelve 1-cm cubes are used to make a variety of single layer shapes the surfaces of the tops will have the same area.

It will be noted that a square can be named by the length of a side, for instance, a 2-cm square or a 1-m square. Its area is stated as 4 square centimetres or 1 square metre, and is written as 4 cm^2 or 1 m^2. Children should be encouraged to

Metric units of area (to scale)

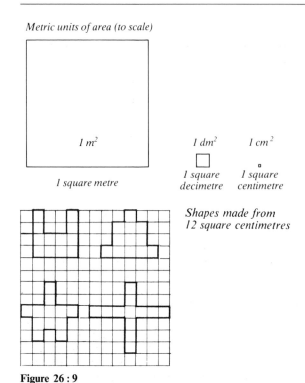

1 m²

1 square metre

1 dm²   *1 cm²*

1 square   *1 square*
decimetre   *centimetre*

Shapes made from
12 square centimetres

Figure 26 : 9

use the symbols cm², dm², and m² for the units of area, as these symbols link with the symbols for the squares of numbers. At first, each size of area unit will be used alone, having been chosen as suitable for the task in hand. At a later stage, children should return to look at several units together, and to see that 1 square decimetre is made up of 100 square centimetres, and 1 square metre is made up of 100 square decimetres. They can write

$$1 \text{ dm}^2 = 100 \text{ cm}^2$$
$$\text{or } 1 \text{ dm}^2 = 10^2 \text{ cm}^2$$
$$\text{and } 1 \text{ m}^2 = 100 \text{ dm}^2$$
$$\text{or } 1 \text{ m}^2 = 10^2 \text{ dm}^2$$

THE AREA OF IRREGULAR SHAPES

Irregular shapes with right-angled corners have probably been encountered in the course of covering floors or parts of walls. Other shapes, with curved boundaries or unequal angles, will occur, for example, in leaves, stars, or a lake on a map. To find the area of such a shape we must endeavour to use one of the standard units and make an approximate count. The outline of the shape can be drawn on squared paper or a sheet of transparent squared paper can be placed over the shape. Children can then carry out the count using one of two rules: in each case first count all the whole

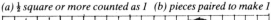
(a) ½ square or more counted as 1 (b) pieces paired to make 1

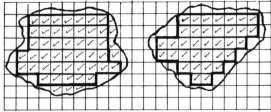

Figure 26 : 10

squares and then *either* (a) count as whole units the pieces that appear to be equal to or more than half of a whole square and ignore the pieces that are less, *or* (b) collect pairs or sets of pieces which together are about equal to a whole square. The total of unit squares obtained by either method usually gives a reasonably good approximation to the area (Figure 26 : 10).

It is as well to stress counting the whole squares in rows, marking them and the pieces which are being counted, e.g. $9 + 8 + 9 + 9 + 10 + 7 + 3$ (Figure 26 : 10).

The study of leaf surfaces, comparing two leaves of different shape or the total leaf surfaces on two twigs of the same length, is interesting (Figure 26 : 11). It is possible, too, to find a rough value for the area of the surface of a child by drawing the silhouettes of the four aspects, front, back and the two sides.

As children get older, they can use a sandwiching technique to approximate to the area. The area of the shape in Figure 26 : 12 is certainly more than 43 cm², and certainly less than 74 cm². The statement

Figure 26 : 11

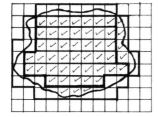

Figure 26 : 12

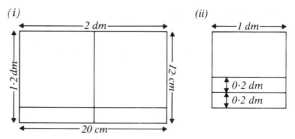

Figure 26 : 13

43 cm² < area < 74 cm²

can be written with certainty. The best *estimate* of the area will be the *average* of these two values, or $58\frac{1}{2}$ cm². However, averaging to this degree of accuracy is not justified in this case, and 60 cm² would be a more sensible estimate. Children should discuss the different estimates of area obtained by different methods.

This idea links with the similar use of estimation in measuring length (page 20), when children can say with certainty that the length of a rod is more than 5 cm, and less than 6 cm, but then have to make the best estimate they can between these quantities.

THE AREA OF A RECTANGLE

Children will usually have discovered by this time how easy it is to find the area of a rectangle when it contains a whole number of rows each consisting of a whole number of squares. No longer do squares need to be individually counted; 5 rows of 6 squares make 30 squares in all. The product of the number of units in the length and the number in the breadth recalls early work on making patterns with rods and strips to show what multiplication means. Now children realise that this product states the area in terms of a square unit.

In general, however, rectangles do not have sides which are an exact number of measuring units in length. Yet they have a quantity of surface and it must be possible to find a way of measuring it. A rectangle whose sides are conveniently measured either in dm or cm provides a good starting-point. For instance, if the rectangle is 12 cm by 20 cm, the area is known to be 240 cm². Since there are 100 cm² in 1 dm², this area is also 2·40 dm². If the rectangle is measured in dm, its sides are 1·2 dm and 2 dm. Children will expect that

$$1·2 \times 2 = 2·4,$$

and the calculator confirms the correctness of this expectation; on entering

it displays 2·4. Children can write

area = 1·2 × 2 dm²
= 2·4 dm²

Children should be encouraged to draw rectangles and estimate their areas before making a full calculation either with a calculator or on paper. In Figure 26 : 13(*i*) the area is expected to be rather more than 1 × 2 dm², since 1·2 > 1. The 2 dm² are clearly seen in the diagram; the only question is the area of the strip along the bottom. This is 0·2 dm by 2 dm. The strip can be cut out and rearranged within a 1-dm square, and is then easily seen to be 4 tenths of the 1-dm square, or 0·4 dm² (Figure 26 : 13(*ii*)).

When one side of the rectangle measures a whole number of decimetres, the problem is comparatively straightforward; if both sides contain decimals of decimetres, a further complication is introduced. If the measurements of the rectangle are 2·3 dm by 1·2 dm (Figure 26 : 14), the area is again estimated to be rather more than 2 dm², because 2·3 > 2 and 1·2 > 1. The three strips around the edges have areas 0·2 dm², 0·2 dm² 0·3 dm². Only the shaded area, which measures 0·3 dm by 0·2 dm, presents a new problem. A number of approaches are possible, as shown below, and they should be used at some time.

The key to an understanding of area in decimal units is an appreciation of the fact that the area of a square 1 tenth of a unit by 1 tenth of a unit is 1 hundredth of a square unit. This is shown in Figure 26 : 15(*a*) where it can be seen that 100

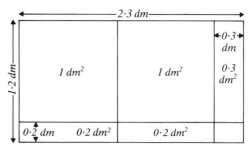

Figure 26 : 14

(a)

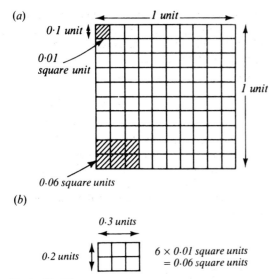

(b)

Figure 26 : 15

small squares, each measuring 0.1 unit by 0.1 unit, fit into the unit square. Thus, the area of a square with sides 1 tenth of decimetre, or a 0.1 dm square, is 1 hundredth of a square decimetre, or 0.01 dm². Similarly, a rectangle 0.2 dm by 0.3 dm has an area of 6 hundredths of a square decimetre, or 0.06 dm².

The calculator provides confirmation of these calculations, showing

$$0.2 \times 0.3 = 0.06$$
$$\text{and } 1.2 \times 2.3 = 2.76$$

The total area of 2.76 dm² is easily identified in Figure 26 : 14 as 1 dm² + 1 dm² + 0.3 dm² + 0.2dm² + 0.2dm² + 0.06dm² .

Working in centimetres provides further confirmation. In Figure 26 : 16, the measurements are shown in centimetres, and the area in square centimetres. The total area is 276 cm².

In the same way that the fact that 10 tens make 1 hundred, or $10 \times 10 = 100$, is a key to the understanding of the place-value system for whole

numbers, so the fact that 1 tenth of 1 tenth is 1 hundredth, or $0.1 \times 0.1 = 0.01$, is a key to the understanding of the place-value system for decimals. Children need a good deal of experience of units which can be broken into tenths, and into tenths of tenths. A square with an area of 1 dm² provides a very convenient unit of this type.

Many children at the primary stage will not reach a full understanding of the calculation of areas in decimals. However, activities such as those suggested above will help them to see that using a calculator to multiply the numbers of units in the length and breadth of a rectangle gives a sensible value for its area. An estimate of the answer should first be made. In the above case,

$$2 < 2.3 < 3$$
$$\text{and } 1 < 1.2 < 2$$

so that area must lie between $2 \times 1 = 2$ dm² and $3 \times 2 = 6$ dm², and is expected to be nearer the lower value.

Older and more able children may also calculate the areas of rectangles with fractional measurements other than tenths. First a rectangle with sides $\frac{1}{2}$–unit and $\frac{1}{3}$–unit could be drawn in the corner of a unit square. Other rectangles of the same size can be drawn to fill the square. It is seen at once that six of six of these rectangles fill the square. So the area of one of the rectangles $\frac{1}{2}$ by $\frac{1}{3}$ is $\frac{1}{6}$ of the unit square (Figure 26 : 17 (i)). It is easier for children to use squared paper for this diagram, choosing a unit length such that 6 small squares fit along the unit side. Children can now readily mark $\frac{1}{2}$ and $\frac{1}{3}$ along the unit sides. The diagram can be completed as before and the result checked by counting the small squares (Figure 26 :17 (ii)).

The rectangle $\frac{1}{2}$ by $\frac{1}{3}$ contains 6 small squares.
The unit square contains 36 small squares.
The rectangle is $\frac{1}{6}$ of the unit square.

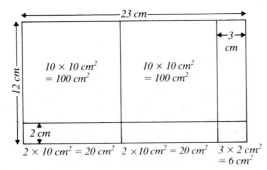

Figure 26 : 16

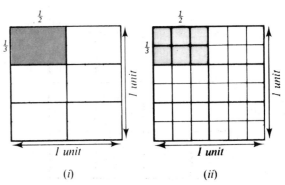

(i)   (ii)

Figure 26 : 17

Children may discover that some of the larger rectangles that they are familiar with, such as a games pitch, a building site, or a cornfield, are measured in *hectares*. They will find that 1 hectare is the area of a square with a 100-metre side.

1 hectare = 10 000 m²

Larger areas are usually stated in hectares and decimals, and can be evaluated in the same way as the other rectangles dealt with in this section; the area will first be found in metre squares and then converted to hectares. Very large areas are measured in square kilometres.

AREAS OF SHAPES RELATED TO RECTANGLES

i) A *square* as a special kind of rectangle, in which the length and breadth are equal, has great interest. It provides the standard units for measuring area. The numbers which connect these units, 100 dm² as 1 m² and the square of 2 dm as 4 dm², recall the numbers found in the diagonal line of the table of multiples. This suggests looking at the other numbers on the diagonal and connecting them with the areas of squares: 4, 16, 25, 36, etc. Placing these squares at a common vertex we see how rapidly the area increases with the side of the square (Figure 26 : 18). If the squares are drawn on squared paper, the strip shaped like a rotated L which must be added to one square to form the next in the sequence can be stated in unit squares. This gives the sequence

$$1 + \ 3 = \ 4 = 2^2$$
$$4 + \ 5 = \ 9 = 3^2$$
$$9 + \ 7 = 16 = 4^2$$
$$16 + \ 9 = 25 = 5^2$$
$$25 + 11 = 36 = 6^2$$
$$36 + 13 = 49 = 7^2$$

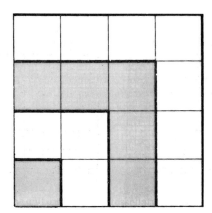

Figure 26 : 18

The pupils will identify the numbers represented by the strips, 3,5,7, ... as the sequence of odd numbers. The areas of the squares can be graphed from the tabulation:

Side of square in cm	1	2	3	4	5 ...
Area in cm²		1	4	9	16	25 ...

The areas of some squares with decimal or fractional sides can then be read from the graph (Figure 26 : 19). The calculator gives confirmation that, for instance, $2 \cdot 5^2 = 6 \cdot 25$, and intermediate points such as these can be used to ensure that the shape of the graph is well drawn.

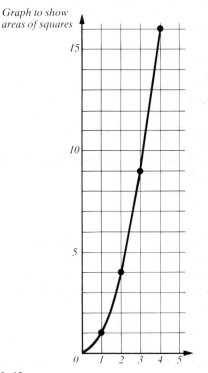

Graph to show areas of squares

Figure 26 : 19

ii) A *triangle* may be one of several types. The one most closely related to the rectangle is the right-angled triangle which is the diagonal half of a rectangle. If such a triangle is rotated about the middle point of its longest side through half a revolution the new and the old positions form a rectangle. Clearly the area of each triangle is half that of the rectangle. Thus every right-angled triangle has a surface area which is

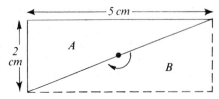

Figure 26 : 20

half that of rectangle whose sides are the same as those that enclose the right angle in the triangle (Figure 26 : 20).

Area of rectangle = (5×2) cm^2
= 10 cm^2
Area of triangle A = $(10 \div 2)$ cm^2
= 5 cm^2

Any triangle with two equal sides has symmetrical halves and is easy to convert into a rectangle by replacing one half and rotating it until the two halves together form a rectangle one of whose sides is half the base of the triangle and the other side is the fold line or altitude (Figure 26 : 21). This can lead to the formula:

Area of a right-angled triangle = (base × height) ÷ 2

From this special case it is easy to move to the general rule which gives the area of any triangle through finding related rectangles.

Any triangle, whatever its shape may be, can be made into two right-angled triangles with a common side. If a scalene triangles, that is, one

Cut along the fold and place triangle A in the reflected position as shown

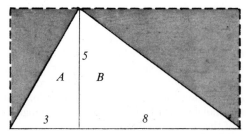

Figure 26 : 21

with unequal sides, is cut out in paper, one of its sides can be folded upon itself so that the fold passes through a vertex. The pupils are familiar with this folding as one which produces a right angle. When the triangle is opened out it is found that the fold is the dividing line between two right-angled triangles each of which is half a rectangle. In fact the two rectangles together form a larger rectangle, and the pattern of areas illustrates neatly the operation of the distributive law. In Figure 26 : 22 the original triangle has a side 11 cm long which is divided by an altitude of 5 cm into two parts, 3 cm and 8 cm long . The use of the two right-angled triangles, A and B, enables us to find the area of the given triangle as follows:

Area of triangle A = $(5 \times 3) \div 2$ cm = $7\frac{1}{2}$ cm^2
Area of triangle B = $(5 \times 8) \div 2$ cm = 20 cm^2
Area of whole triangle = $27\frac{1}{2}$ cm^2

It is not difficult for children to see that the calculation could be shortened by first adding the two parts of the base and multiplying the sum, 11, by $(5 \div 2)$, giving $\frac{55}{2}$, or $27\frac{1}{2}$. This is in fact the use of the distributive law

$$3 \times (5 \div 2) + 8 \times (5 \div 2) = (3 + 8) \times (5 \div 2)$$

The traditional formula for the area of a triangle

$$\frac{1}{2} \times \text{base} \times \text{height},$$

is obtained by realising that divison by 2, or halving, can equally well be done by multiplication by $\frac{1}{2}$. Not many children will come to an understanding of this until the secondary stage, although they may verify on the calculator that, for instance, converting $\frac{1}{2}$ to its decimal form and multiplying, gives

$$\frac{1}{2} \times 55 = 0 \cdot 5 \times 55 = 27 \cdot 5$$
and $55 \div 2 = 27 \cdot 5$

Finally, children might find the area of the triangle in Figure 26 : 23 in the following way:

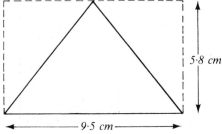

Figure 26 : 22

Figure 26 : 23

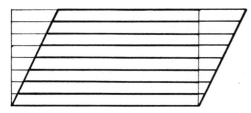

Figure 26 : 24

Area of triangle $= \frac{1}{2}$ (area of rectangle)
$$= \frac{1}{2} (5 \cdot 8 \times 9 \cdot 5) \text{ cm}^2$$
$$= (55 \cdot 1 \div 2) \text{ cm}^2$$
$$= 27 \cdot 55 \text{ cm}^2$$

iii) A *parallelogram* can be obtained from a rectangle by a movement known as a shear. (See Chapter 10 page 128). The base of the rectangle is not moved but each 'layer' is moved to the right (or left) parallel to the base for a given distance beyond the 'layer' below it. A pile of paper or thin pamphlets illustrates the transformation and makes it clear that the amount of surface on a vertical face is unchanged by the transformation. This can be checked by cutting off a triangle from one end of the rectangle and placing it to fit on the other end (Figure 26 : 24). The shape is now a parallelogram but the area is the same as that of the rectangle. The children can then be given a parallelogram and be left to invent a way of finding a rectangle to which it is equivalent in area.

Two possibilities are shown in Figure 26 : 25. The more general arrangement, Figure 26 : 25(*b*), is seen in the translation of any piece made by a line drawn at right angles to the base. When the equivalent rectangle has been found children will measure its height and find the area of the parallelogram. The interest here lies more in the *method* of finding the area of such a shape than in the practical value of the exercise.

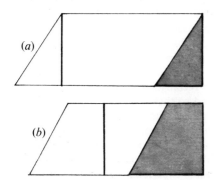

Figure 26 : 25

AREAS OF SHAPES RELATED TO TRIANGLES

In Chapter 12 the regular polygons were studied and these interesting shapes were found to be made up of a number of like triangles, five of one kind for a pentagon, eight of another kind for the octagon, and so on. A group of children could now draw several of these polygons in circles with the same radius and work out ways of finding the area of one triangle of the pentagon, say, and then of the whole polygon. A square and an octagon drawn in equal circles can be compared with regard to the area. A sequence of triangle, hexagon and dedecagon can also be related (Figure 26 : 27).

Problems of this kind where differences are small provide good opportunities for using small units, taking measurements to the nearest $0 \cdot 1$ cm; that is, to the nearest mm. The previous work will have made children aware that a $0 \cdot 1$ cm square has an area of $0 \cdot 01$ cm^2. In other words,

$$1 \text{ mm}^2 = 0 \cdot 01 \text{ cm}^2$$

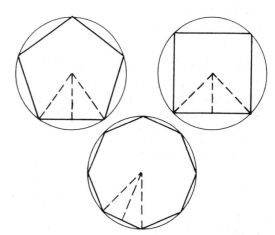

Figure 26 : 26

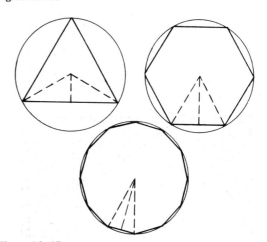

Figure 26 : 27

For convenience in using such small fractions the radius of the circle should not be less than 5 cm.

The usefulness of the multiplication of decimals is apparent in finding areas where tenths of a unit are used in the lengths.

Children may notice that as the number of sides increases a polygon occupies more of the space inside a circle (Figure 26 : 27). They may well then attempt to find the area of the circle itself by counting sqaures.

SURFACES OF THREE-DIMENSIONAL SHAPES

i) The *cube* and its six square faces are well known to children but it sometimes surprises them to find that a 2-cm cube is composed of

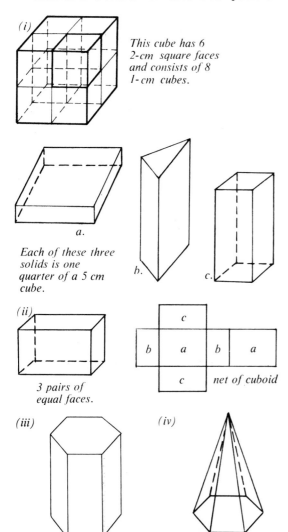

(i)

This cube has 6 2-cm square faces and consists of 8 1-cm cubes.

a.

Each of these three solids is one quarter of a 5 cm cube.

b. *c.*

(ii)

3 pairs of equal faces.

net of cuboid

(iii) *(iv)*

hexagonal prism   hexagonal pyramid

Figure 26 : 28

eight 1-cm cubes whereas it takes twenty four 1-cm squares to cover its surface. The surface area of a sequence of cubes, 1-cm, 2-cm, 3-cm etc., can be tabulated and the graph compared with that of the areas of squares on page 000. An interesting inquiry is to find the surface area of various shapes made by cutting a cube in half. Poleidoblocs include several different-shaped quarters of a cube and the areas of their surfaces can be compared.

ii) The surface area of a *cuboid* has a practical value since this shape is so often used for boxes and rooms. The recognition of congruent faces makes computation easier and may lead to a simple formula. If the net of a box is drawn, the method of finding the area is made clearer. The use of square centimetres in finding the surface area of Cuisenaire rods is practically convenient.

iii) *Prisms* on a triangular, hexagonal or octagonal base give areas of surface which lead up to that of the cylinder.

iv) Covering a *pyramid* may occur in making a spire for a model church, or in making decorative shapes. The importance of the triangle is emphasised. The increasing number of triangles in a sequence of triangular, square, hexagonal and octagonal pyramids bears a relation to the total surface area and may point the way to investigating the cone (Figure 26 : 28).

SUMMARY

In this chapter we have considered the ways of finding the quantity if a plane surface and the units that can be used to measure it. If the region is enclosed within a shape bounded by straight lines it has been shown that subdivisions of the region make it possible to compute the total area in terms of a unit square. Where the boundary is irregular or curved, the device of making an approximate count of squares was adopted.

We have seen that area depends on two properties which may be found in a shape: the number of strips required to cover it and the number of unit shapes that a strip contains. In the case of a rectangular shape the strips are of equal length and so these two properties are the length and breadth of the rectangle. The need to take two properties into account when considering areas is a complication which makes new demands on children's thinking, and they must have considerable experience of practical investigations before they can understand the nature of area.

Area in the National Curriculum

Area makes a very early appearance in the National Curriculum, as children are expected to use non-standard units of area alongside non-standard units of other measures.

- use non-standard measures in length, area, capacity, 'weight' and time; compare objects and events and recognise the need for standard units.

(AT2: Level 2)

Methods of calculating area are developed up to Level 7 and beyond. It is interesting that at Level 4, children are not expected to have progressed beyond finding area and volumes by counting squares and cubes.

- find areas by counting squares, and volumes by counting cubes.

(AT4: Level 4)

- use knowledge and skills in length, area and volume to carry out calculations in plane and solid shapes.
  EXAMPLE: *Calculate lengths, areas and volumes in shapes involving rectangles, triangles, parallelograms, circles, trapezia, cubes, cylinders and other solids of constant cross-sectional area.*

(AT4: Level 7)

27 | OPERATIONS ON DECIMAL FRACTIONS

CHILDREN'S EARLY EXPERIENCE OF FRACTIONS

Early on in children's mathematical work, concrete examples of fractions appear almost as often as concrete examples of natural numbers. On many occasions the language of halves, quarters, thirds and tenths will be needed, and children should be encouraged to use these terms whenever possible.

At first, children can record using halves, quarters and tenths as sub-units, just as they use decimetres as sub-units, so that they will write that the box weighs

500 grams
or half a kilogram.

Similarly, the desk measures

7 decimetres
or 7 tenths of a metre.

The conventional way of writing 1 half as $\frac{1}{2}$, and 1 quarter as $\frac{1}{4}$, will be learnt early, but only when the idea of a fractional part is firmly established need the conventional ways of writing 3 quarters as $\frac{3}{4}$, and 3 tenths as $\frac{3}{10}$ instead of 0·3, be drawn to children's attention.

There is no need at this stage to study equivalences between fractions in any formal way, or to deal with operations on fractions which are written in numerator–denominator form. These will come more easily at a later stage, when a need for them is established by practical experience, and will rest on a sound basis of informal work using fractions such as halves, quarters and fifths (see page 64).

However, the conventional decimal methods of writing

1 tenth as 0·1
and 3 tenths as 0·3

rely only on an extension of the place-value system which children are building up; there is a column for *tenths* on the right of the column for *ones*. In the era of decimal currency, the metric system and the calculator, the emphasis in the early teaching of fractions should be on *tenths* and *hundredths*, on the ways in which they can be written using the place-value system, on the ways in which the

place-value system can be used to calculate with these fractions, and on the application of these fractions in the measuring which children are doing.

EXTENDING DECIMAL NOTATION

Children will not at the primary stage need to use the decimal fractions smaller than one-thousandth, but the teacher should realise that the notational system which uses *place value* enables numbers, however large or small, to be written briefly using only a small number of symbols. We therefore now extend the place-value system of notation (base ten) so that it can be used to write smaller and smaller fractions of a unit.

The extension of place-value notation to include fractions of a unit is immediately clear to the adult reader who is already completely familiar with the place-value notation for natural numbers. Children may, however, first meet the decimal system of notation for fractions before they have a complete grasp of notation for natural numbers; the gradual and practical introduction of decimals, which make use of the place-value system, can do much to help children to understand notation, and so to strengthen their grasp of the number system (Figure 27 : 1).

Thousands	Hundreds	Tens	Ones	Tenths	Hundredths	Thousandths
2	5	7	6	9	4	3

10 thousandths = 1 hundredth

10 hundredths = 1 tenth

10 tenths = 1 one

10 ones = 1 ten

10 tens = 1 hundred

10 hundreds = 1 thousand

Figure 27 : 1

ADDITION AND SUBTRACTION OF DECIMALS

If children know how to add and subtract whole numbers, and particularly how to find the total of a bill in pounds and pence, and how to give change from a sum of money, no new problems arise in addition and subtraction of decimals. For instance, the sum of £1 27 pence and £2 35 pence can be recorded as

$$\begin{array}{r} £1\cdot27 \\ +\ 2\cdot35 \\ \hline 3\cdot62 \end{array}$$

This addition, if it is done mentally, might be shown as

$$£1\cdot27 \xrightarrow{+£2} £3\cdot27 \xrightarrow{+£0\cdot30} £3\cdot57 \xrightarrow{+0\cdot05} £3\cdot62$$

The principle that pence must be added to pence, tenpences to tenpences and pounds to pounds, becomes the principle that hundredths are added to hundredths, tenths are added to tenths, ones are added to ones, and so on. Of course, ten hundredths are changed to one tenth in exactly the same way that ten pence are changed to one tenpence.

Subtraction follows exactly the same principle. If 37 centimetres of ribbon are cut from 1 metre 50 centimetres, the calculation of the remaining length can be shown as

$$\begin{array}{ll} 37 \longrightarrow 50 & 13\ cm \\ 50 \longrightarrow 150 & 100\ cm \\ & \overline{113\ cm} \end{array}$$

or equally well as

$$\begin{array}{ll} 0\cdot37 \longrightarrow 0\cdot40 & 0\cdot03 \\ 0\cdot40 \longrightarrow 0\cdot50 & 0\cdot10 \\ 0\cdot50 \longrightarrow 1\cdot50 & 1\cdot00 \\ & \overline{1\cdot13} \end{array}$$

Another written form is

$$\begin{array}{ccccc} m & dm & cm & & m \\ 1 & 5 & 0 & or & 1\cdot50 \\ - & 3 & 7 & & -0\cdot37 \\ \hline 1 & 1 & 3 & & 1\cdot13 \end{array}$$

Activities such as making boxes, model building, and so on, provide older children with many opportunities for measuring in centimetres and millimetres, and making decimal calculations. The four walls of a model of a building may be made from a continuous strip of card, whose length must be found and measured out. Placing a door in the centre of a wall will give rise to more calculations

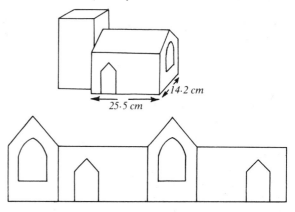

Scale 1 cm to represent 1 metre

25·5 cm

14·2 cm

Total length of walls
= (25·5 + 14·2 + 25·5 + 14·2) cm
= (51·0 + 28·4) cm
= 79·4 cm

$$25\cdot5 \times 2 = 51\cdot0$$
$$14\cdot2 \times 2 = 28\cdot4$$

Figure 27 : 2

using decimal measurements. Figure 27 : 2 shows a few of the calculations used in building a model of a village church.

We see also in this calculation that multiplying a decimal by a whole number presents no problems.

ESTIMATION IN DECIMAL CALCULATION: USE OF THE CALCULATOR

Children will perform many of the calculations they use in their practical activities with a calculator. At an early stage they should be encouraged to acknowledge the fact that the calculator makes mistakes, and to think out ways of detecting and correcting these mistakes. Most calculator mistakes are due to the accidental pressing of wrong keys, and this may easily go unnoticed if children do not form a habit of checking. There are two ways of checking calculator working, and they should both be used:

i) before the calculation is done, an estimate of the expected result should be made;

ii) the calculation can often be repeated on the calculator *by another method*, to check the exact figures.

Estimation involves replacing the exact figures by approximations which are easy enough to be handled mentally. For instance, in the calculations on the model church (Figure 27 : 2), children might replace 25·5 cm by 25 cm, and 14·2 cm by 15 cm. Then 25 + 15 = 40, so the total length of wall should be about 80 cm. If the result produced by the calculator is far from 80 cm, the accuracy of the calculation certainly needs checking.

In the past, the art of estimation has never been a very successful part of the learning of mathematics. This is probably because children have been expected to produce *accurate* answers by written methods, and have spent much time in developing this accuracy. Now the calculator can produce accurate answers, provided that it is correctly used. This makes it possible for there to be more emphasis in mathematics teaching on the art of obtaining *sensible* answers with the aid of a calculator. Estimation and mental calculation play a vital part in knowing whether an answer is sensible, while the drudgery of obtaining accuracy with numbers of several digits can be turned over to the machine.

Another way of checking calculations is to repeat them on the calculator, if possible *doing them another way*. The sum

$$(25 \cdot 5 + 14 \cdot 2 + 25 \cdot 5 + 14 \cdot 2)$$

can be done by addition without any multiplication. Thus different keys are pressed, and any habitual pressing of wrong keys is more likely to be noticed. In other cases, subtraction can be checked by addition, and division by multiplication.

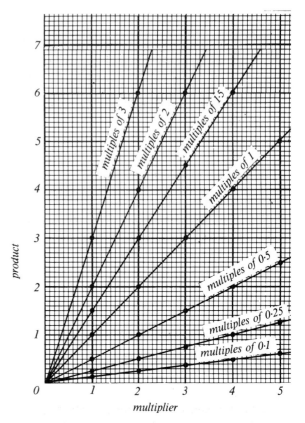

Figure 27 : 3

EXTENDING THE IDEA OF MULTIPLICATION

The multiplication of natural numbers is based on repeated addition of the same number. This idea extends very easily to fractions, and just as children learn to record $5 + 5 + 5 + 5$ more briefly as 4×5, they will find it natural to write $4 \times 0 \cdot 2$ instead of $0 \cdot 2 + 0 \cdot 2 + 0 \cdot 2 + 0 \cdot 2$. Thus we have the idea that repeated addition of decimal fractions is symbolised by the multiplication sign. This is a very natural extension of the previous idea of multiplication. The calculation is carried out in exactly the same way as similar calculations for whole numbers.

$$4 \times 0 \cdot 2 = 4 \times (2 \text{ tenths})$$
$$= 8 \text{ tenths}$$
$$= 0 \cdot 8$$

Children will come to realise that exactly as they can build up tables of multiples of 2, 3, 4, ..., they can also build up multiples of $0 \cdot 1$, $0 \cdot 2$, $0 \cdot 25$, ..., and they will represent these tables by graphs and mapping diagrams. Figure 27 : 3 shows graphs of multiples of $0 \cdot 1$, $0 \cdot 25$ and $0 \cdot 5$, together with multiples of 1, $1 \cdot 5$, 2 and 3. In Figure 27 : 4 we show a mapping diagram for multiples of $0 \cdot 75$. The

calculator can provide reinforcement in building up these multiples:

$1 \times 0 \cdot 75$			$=$	$0 \cdot 75$
$2 \times 0 \cdot 75$	$=$	$0 \cdot 75 + 0 \cdot 75$	$=$	$1 \cdot 5$
$3 \times 0 \cdot 75$	$=$	$1 \cdot 5 + 0 \cdot 75$	$=$	$2 \cdot 25$
$4 \times 0 \cdot 75$	$=$	$2 \cdot 25 + 0 \cdot 75$	$=$	$3 \cdot 0$
$5 \times 0 \cdot 75$	$=$	$3 \cdot 0 + 0 \cdot 75$	$=$	$3 \cdot 75$

The mapping $x \rightarrow x \times 0 \cdot 75$

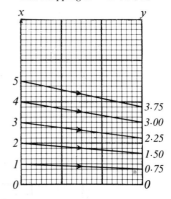

Figure 27 : 4

and so on. In this way, children learn to think of $3 \times 0 \cdot 75$ as an abbreviation for the repeated addition $0 \cdot 75 + 0 \cdot 75 + 0 \cdot 75$. How are they to think of $0 \cdot 75 \times 3$, and where does a need for the writing of $0 \cdot 75 \times 3$ and similar multiplications occur? The idea of repeated addition of threes cannot be used when considering $0 \cdot 75 \times 3$ in the way it was for 4×3, since there is not now a whole number of threes to be added together. But we not only think of 4×3 as 'four threes', but also as '*four times as much as* 3', and the words '... *times as much as* ...' are always symbolised by a multiplication sign; when the number of times may be fractional this can often be abbreviated to 'as much as'.

Now we can see the meaning of a simple decimal multiplication: $0 \cdot 1 \times 2 \cdot 5$. In the same way that

$4 \times 2 \cdot 5$ means '4 *times as much as* $2 \cdot 5$',
so $0 \cdot 1 \times 2 \cdot 5$ means '1 tenth *as much as* $2 \cdot 5$'.

The wording '1 tenth *of* $2 \cdot 5$' conveys the same idea. Thus, to work out $0 \cdot 1 \times 2 \cdot 5$, we need to find 1 tenth of $2 \cdot 5$. At first, children will need to represent this by blocks, as in Figure 27 : 5.

They will soon realise that

1 tenth of 2 units is 2 tenths

and

1 tenth of 5 tenths is 5 hundredths, and may record what they have done as $0 \cdot 1 \times 2 \cdot 5 = 0 \cdot 25$.

Children need to observe the effect of multiplication by $0 \cdot 1$ on each digit of $2 \cdot 5$, noting that 2 units have become 2 tenths, and 5 tenths have become 5 hundreths.

The calculator provides reinforcement and children can observe the effect of multiplying any number by $0 \cdot 1$:

$0 \cdot 1 \times 2$	$= 0 \cdot 2$	(1 tenth of $2 = 2$ tenths)
$0 \cdot 1 \times 20$	$= 2 \cdot$	(1 tenth of 2 tens = 2 ones)
$0 \cdot 1 \times 200$	$= 20 \cdot$	(1 tenth of 2 hundreds $= 2$ tens)
$0 \cdot 1 \times 0 \cdot 2$	$= 0 \cdot 02$	(1 tenth of 2 tenths $= 2$ hundredths)

and so on.

Similarly, multiplication by $0 \cdot 01, 0 \cdot 001, \ldots$ can be explored:

$0 \cdot 01 \times 2$	$= 0 \cdot 02$	(1 hundredth of 2 $= 2$ hundredths)
$0 \cdot 01 \times 20$	$= 0 \cdot 2$	(1 hundredth of 2 tens $= 2$ tenths)
$0 \cdot 01 \times 200$	$= 2 \cdot 0$	(1 hundredth of 2 hundreds $= 2$ ones)
$0 \cdot 01 \times 0 \cdot 2$	$= 0 \cdot 002$	(1 hundredth of 2 tenths $= 2$ thousandths)
$0 \cdot 001 \times 2$	$= 0 \cdot 002$	(1 thousandth of 2 $= 2$ thousandths)
$0 \cdot 001 \times 20$	$= 0 \cdot 02$	(1 thousandth of 2 tens $= 2$ hundredths)

$0 \cdot 1 \times 2 \cdot 5$

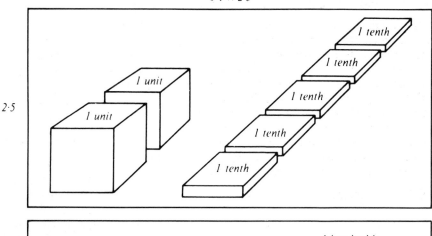

$2 \cdot 5$

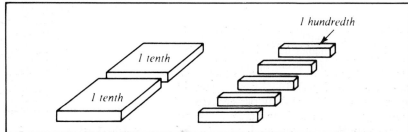

1 tenth of $2 \cdot 5$
$= 0 \cdot 25$

Figure 27 : 5

Multiplication of decimals does not present problems to children who realise that

> tenths of ones are tenths $(0 \cdot 1 \times 1 = 0 \cdot 1)$
> hundredths of ones are hundredths $(0 \cdot 01 \times 1 = 0 \cdot 01)$
> tenths of tenths are hundredths $(0 \cdot 1 \times 0 \cdot 1 = 0 \cdot 01)$

and so on, so that multiplication by

> $\ldots 0 \cdot 01, \, 0 \cdot 1, \, 1, \, 10, \, 100, \ldots$

has the effect of moving the digits of a decimal number, as follows:

$0 \cdot 01 \times$	moves the digits 2 places to the right
$0 \cdot 1 \times$	moves the digits 1 place to the right
$1 \cdot \times$	moves the digits 0 places
$10 \cdot \times$	moves the digits 1 place to the left
$100 \cdot \times$	moves the digits 2 places to the left

This movement is shown in Figure 27 : 6.

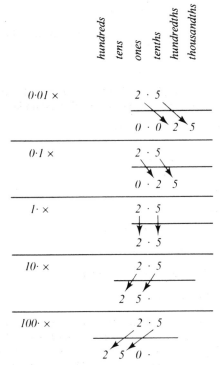

Figure 27 : 6

This property, together with the associative law for multiplication, enables us to multiply decimal numbers easily by other decimals. For instance

$$0 \cdot 2 \times 2 \cdot 5 = (2 \times 0 \cdot 1) \times 2 \cdot 5$$
$$= 2 \times (0 \cdot 1 \times 2 \cdot 5) \text{ by the associative law}$$
$$= 2 \times 0 \cdot 25$$
$$= 0 \cdot 50$$

The effect is the same as if the digits were moved one place to the right and multiplication by 2 carried out.

It now becomes very easy to perform such a multiplication as $1 \cdot 2 \times 2 \cdot 5$.

1	$\times 2 \cdot 5$	$=$	$2 \cdot 5$
$0 \cdot 2$	$\times 2 \cdot 5$	$=$	$0 \cdot 50$
$1 \cdot 2$	$\times 2 \cdot 5$	$=$	$3 \cdot 00$

The calculation is broken up into stages using the distributive law

$$(a + b) \times c = (a \times c) + (b \times c)$$

in exactly the same way that the multiplication of large whole numbers is broken up (*see page 235*). The process is an abbreviation of

$$1 \cdot 2 \times 2 \cdot 5 = (1 \cdot 0 + 0 \cdot 2) \times 2 \cdot 5$$
$$= (1 \cdot 0 \times 2 \cdot 5) + (0 \cdot 2 \times 2 \cdot 5)$$
$$= 2 \cdot 50 + 0 \cdot 50$$
$$= 3 \cdot 00$$

When children perform this calculation on a calculator, they should first estimate the answer as rather more than $1 \times 2 \cdot 5$, so that they expect an answer a little more than $2 \cdot 5$. The ability to estimate the size of an expected answer involves the ability to multiply mentally by a single decimal digit. For instance, $0 \cdot 23 \times 3 \cdot 79$ could be rounded to $0 \cdot 2 \times 4$, and the estimated answer would be $0 \cdot 8$. The calculator gives

$$0 \cdot 23 \times 3 \cdot 79 = 0 \cdot 8717$$

Similarly, $0 \cdot 23 \times 0 \cdot 35$ could be estimated by $0 \cdot 2 \times 0 \cdot 3$; a result rather more than $0 \cdot 06$ would be expected, since tenths of tenths are hundredths. The calculator gives

$$0 \cdot 23 \times 0 \cdot 35 = 0 \cdot 0805$$

DIVISION USING DECIMALS

As soon as children start to use the calculator for division, they find that the answers are not quite as expected; when there is a remainder, the calculator seems to young children to behave very strangely. For example, the calculator shows

> $22 \div 4 = 5 \cdot 5,$

when children are expecting

> $22 \div 4 = 5$ remainder 2

Even more strangely,

> $10 \div 3 = 3 \cdot 3333333,$

$$271 \div 43$$

Calculator shows $271 \div 43 = 6.3023255$

So $271 \div 43 = 6$, with a remainder.

$$6 \times 43 = 258, \qquad 271 - 258 = 13,$$

So remainder $= 13$

$$271 \div 43 = 6 \text{ remainder } 13$$

Figure 27:7

when children expect

$$10 \div 3 = 3 \text{ remainder } 1$$

At first, young children may use the strange display as an indication that there is a remainder; they also need to realise that the part of the display after the decimal point is not the actual remainder. Children can find the actual remainder as shown in Figure 27:7.

When children know the place-value system for tenths and hundredths they are ready to explore why the calculator shows $22 \div 4 = 5.5$.

$$
\begin{array}{rl}
 & 22 \\
4 \times 5 = & 20 \\
\hline
 & 2 \\
4 \times 0.5 = & 2.0 \\
\hline
 & 0 \\
\hline
4 \times 5.5 = & 22
\end{array}
$$

So $22 \div 4 = 5.5$.

Now it becomes possible to do any division such as the following, with or without the calculator, checking the result by multiplication.

$$19 \div 5 = 3.8 \quad \text{and} \quad 5 \times 3.8 = 19$$

The following sequence of keystrokes reinforces the idea of division as inverse multiplication.

Display

	Display
$\boxed{1}\,\boxed{9}$	19
$\boxed{\div}\,\boxed{5}\,\boxed{=}$	3.8
$\boxed{\times}\,\boxed{5}\,\boxed{=}$	19

Examples such as the following are particularly important:

$1 \div 5 = 0.2$; thus 1 fifth $= 0.2$

It follows that

2 fifths $= 2 \times 0.2 = 0.4$
3 fifths $= 3 \times 0.2 = 0.6$
4 fifths $= 4 \times 0.2 = 0.8$

Division also gives

$$2 \div 5 = 0.4$$
$$3 \div 5 = 0.6$$
$$4 \div 5 = 0.8$$

Thus the idea that the fraction 2 fifths means the same as $2 \div 5$ becomes established.

THE DIVISION ASPECT OF FRACTIONS

The major emphasis of the work so far has been on those fractions which can be written in decimal form, and so can be incorporated into the place-value system. We sometimes need to place a fraction which is not made up of tenths, hundredths and thousandths within the place value system. In the case of a fraction such as $\frac{1}{4}$, or 1 quarter, this is easy; one unit has to be divided by 4, and decimal division gives

$$\tfrac{1}{4} = 1 \text{ quarter} = 1 \div 4 = 0.25$$

A decimal equivalent of 3 quarters can now be obtained by multiplication:

$$3 \text{ quarters} = 3 \times 0.25 = 0.75$$

Children will already have met these and similar facts in their practical activities. For example,

$$
\begin{aligned}
\tfrac{1}{2} \text{ metre} &= 50 \text{ centimetres} \\
&= 5 \text{ decimetres} \\
&= 5 \text{ tenths of a metre} \\
&= 0.5 \text{ metres,}
\end{aligned}
$$

leads to the number statement $\frac{1}{2} = 0.5$
Similarly,

25 pence $= 1$ quarter of £1

leads to 1 quarter $= 0.25$,

and 75 pence $= 3$ quarters of £1

leads to 3 quarters $= 0.75$

Another aspect of the fraction 3 quarters is that it is also the result of dividing *three units* by 4. That is, taking $\frac{1}{4}$ of 3 units. Figure 27:8 shows $\frac{1}{4}$ of 3 units and 3 quarters of 1 unit. The reason for the equality of the results is not very easily seen from this diagram, but a rearrangement of the units will make the reason clear. In order to obtain $\frac{1}{4}$ of 3 units, a simple method is to find $\frac{1}{4}$ of *each* unit and combine the results. If 3 cakes are to be shared between 4 people it is usually simplest to give each person $\frac{1}{4}$ of each cake. Figure 27:9 illustrates this, and also shows the application of the same idea to the length shown in Figure 27:8.

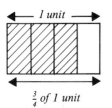

3 units

¼ of 3 units

1 unit

$\frac{3}{4}$ of 1 unit

Figure 27 : 8

(a)   1 quarter of 3 units = 3 ÷ 4

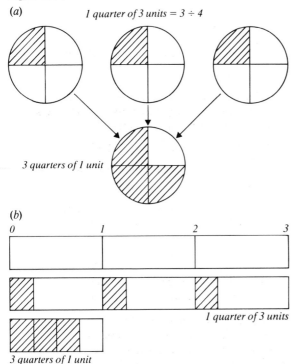

3 quarters of 1 unit

(b)

0   1   2   3

1 quarter of 3 units

3 quarters of 1 unit

Figure 27 : 9

Now the reason for the traditional numerator–denominator form of writing a fraction becomes clear. The symbols $\frac{3}{4}$, or 3/4, mean 3 ÷ 4. In schools, the form $\frac{3}{4}$ is usually used. However, many variants on this notation are in use. Road signs use the method shown in Figure 27 : 10, where no bar is used in the fraction; on a calculator the ÷ key has to be used, so that $\frac{3}{4}$ is entered by the keystrokes

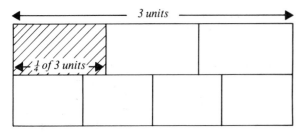

Shelford 1½

Figure 27 : 10

$\boxed{3}\ \boxed{\div}\ \boxed{4}\ \boxed{=}$

The keyboard of a computer a does not have a ÷ sign, but uses the solidus / as a division sign. On the computer, $\frac{3}{4}$ is entered as 3/4. Children should know all these forms, so that they can use the following equivalences:

$$3 \text{ quarters} = 3 \text{ units} \div 4$$
$$= 3 \div 4$$
$$= 3/4$$
$$= \frac{3}{4}$$

In general, the fraction $\frac{m}{n}$ can be visualised as the result of dividing m units into n equal parts, or as one nth of m units.

$$\frac{m}{n} = \frac{1}{n} \text{ of } m = m \div n = m/n$$

Now the fraction 3 quarters can be expressed in decimal form directly, by dividing 3 units by 4. We have

$$3 \text{ quarters} = 3 \div 4 = 0\cdot 75$$

The result, $0\cdot 75$, is either obtained by the calculator or by the written calculation

$$
\begin{array}{ll}
 & 3\cdot 0 \\
4 \times 0\cdot 7 & = 2\cdot 8 \\
\hline
 & 0\cdot 2 \\
4 \times 0\cdot 05 & = 0\cdot 20 \\
\hline
 & 0 \\
\hline
4 \times 0\cdot 75 & = 3
\end{array}
$$

It is important that practical experiences of equivalences between fractions and decimals should run along-side these calculations, and that the link between division and multiplication should be firmly established:

$$\frac{3}{4} \text{ of } £1 = £0\cdot 75 = 75 \text{ pence,}$$
$$\text{and } 4 \times 75 \text{ pence} = £3$$

On many calculators, mishaps can occur when division is checked by multiplication. Many inexpensive calculators give 10 ÷ 3 = 3.333 333 3 and 3·333 333 3 × 3 = 9.999 999 9. This provides children with their first introduction to recurring decimals, and to the fact that the calculator can only hold a finite number of digits (often eight), and so cannot always be completely accurate. In fact, $10 \div 3 = 3 \cdot 333\,333\,333\,\ldots$, but the calculator cannot cope with more than eight digits. It displays $3.333\,333\,3$, and the remaining digits are lost.

More advanced calculators retain two more digits internally than are displayed, and round the result before displaying it. On such a calculator.

$$(10 \div 3) \times 3 = 10$$

A decimal such as $3 \cdot 333\,\ldots$, in which the digits repeat without end, is called a recurring decimal. Many fractions, in their decimal forms, are recurring decimals. For instance,

$$\frac{1}{9} = 0 \cdot 1111\,\ldots \qquad = 0 \cdot \dot{1},$$
$$\frac{1}{7} = 0 \cdot 1428571428\ldots = 0 \cdot \dot{1}4285\dot{7},$$
$$\frac{1}{11} = 0 \cdot 09090\ldots \qquad = 0 \cdot \dot{0}\dot{9}$$

In writing a recurring decimal, a dot is placed over the recurring digit, or if a cycle of digits recurs, over the first and last digits of the cycle or *period*. Children may verify that the length of the recurring period is always less than the denominator of the fraction. No more digits can occur in the period since, when division by a number n is performed, only $(n-1)$ different non-zero remainders are possible. For instance, when we evaluate $1 \div 7$, the only possible remainders at any step of the division are 0, 1, 2, 3, 4, 5, 6. If 0 occurs as a remainder, the decimal terminates. If not, it recurs. In fact,

$$1 \div 7 = 0 \cdot \dot{1}4285\dot{7};$$

all the possible non-zero remainders occur, and the period of the recurring decimal is 6 digits.

It can also be verfied that the decimal equivalent of a fraction only terminates if the denominator of the fraction has 2 or 5 or both 2 and 5 (possibly repeated) as its only fractors. For example

$$\frac{1}{4} = \frac{1}{2 \times 2} = 0 \cdot 25$$
$$\frac{1}{50} = \frac{1}{2 \times 5 \times 5} = 0 \cdot 02$$
$$\frac{1}{125} = \frac{1}{5 \times 5 \times 5} = 0 \cdot 008$$

DIVISION BY POWERS OF TEN

Just as it is extremely important for children to know what happens when a number is multipled by 10, 100, 1000, ... so also it is very important for them to know the pattern of division by 10, 100, 1000, ... This is not a new pattern, because for instance

$$20 \div 10 = 1 \text{ tenth of } 20$$
$$= 0 \cdot 1 \times 20$$
$$= 2$$

Thus division by 10 is the same as finding one-tenth, or multiplying by $0 \cdot 1$. Similarly, division by 100 is the same as finding one-hundredth, or multiplying by $0 \cdot 01$. Patterns such as the following can be built up, using structural apparatus and a calculator.

$$20 \div 10 = 0 \cdot 1 \times 20 = 2$$
$$20 \div 100 = 0 \cdot 01 \times 20 = 0 \cdot 2$$
$$20 \div 1000 = 0 \cdot 001 \times 20 = 0 \cdot 02$$
$$2 \div 10 = 0 \cdot 1 \times 2 = 0 \cdot 2$$
$$2 \div 100 = 0 \cdot 01 \times 2 = 0 \cdot 02$$
$$2 \div 1000 = 0 \cdot 001 \times 2 = 0 \cdot 002$$

and so on. Some children may want to extend this pattern in the other direction, using the calculator; the first result

$$2 \div 1 = 1 \times 2 = 2$$

is obvious, but the next may be a surprise:

$$2 \div 0 \cdot 1 = 20$$

Children who are used to checking division by multiplication, and regarding division as inverse multiplication, will not be surprised:

$$2 \div 0 \cdot 1 = 20 \quad \text{because} \quad 20 \times 0 \cdot 1 = 2$$

The multiplication and division pattern now becomes

$$2 \div 1000 = 0 \cdot 001 \times 2 = 0 \cdot 002$$
$$2 \div 100 = 0 \cdot 01 \times 2 = 0 \cdot 02$$
$$2 \div 10 = 0 \cdot 1 \times 2 = 0 \cdot 2$$
$$2 \div 1 = 1 \times 2 = 2$$
$$2 \div 0 \cdot 1 = 10 \times 2 = 20$$
$$2 \div 0 \cdot 01 = 100 \times 2 = 200$$
$$2 \div 0 \cdot 001 = 1000 \times 2 = 2000$$

Young children inevitably think that multiplication makes a number bigger, and division makes it smaller. This is because their only experience of multipication and division is of natural numbers. They now need to find out that it is only multiplication by a number *greater than 1* which makes the result biger. Multiplication by a number less than 1 makes the result smaller. For instance

$$3 \times 2 \cdot 9 = 8 \cdot 7, \text{ and } 8 \cdot 7 > 2 \cdot 9$$
$$\text{but } 0 \cdot 3 \times 2 \cdot 9 = 0 \cdot 87, \text{ and } 0 \cdot 87 < 2 \cdot 9$$

Similarly, division by a number greater than 1 makes the result smaller:

$$8 \cdot 7 \div 3 = 2 \cdot 9, \text{ and } 2 \cdot 9 < 8 \cdot 7,$$

but division by a number less than 1 makes the result larger:

$$8 \cdot 7 \div 0 \cdot 3 = 29, \quad \text{and} \quad 29 > 8 \cdot 7$$

DIVISION AS INVERSE MULTIPLICATION

As a result of this exploration of decimal division, the idea that division is the inverse operation of multiplication is reinforced. The statement

$$14 \div 2 = 7$$

is merely another way of stating

$$2 \times \square = 14$$

The wording, 'How many 2's in 14? is very helpful as a way of reading $14 \div 2$. In exactly the same way,

$$17 \cdot 75 \div 2 \cdot 5 = 7 \cdot 1$$

is another way of stating

$$2 \cdot 5 \times \square = 17 \cdot 75$$

The symbols $17 \cdot 75 \div 2 \cdot 5$ can be read, 'What must $2 \cdot 5$ be multiplied by to make $17 \cdot 75$?'

The result of a division such as

$$8 \cdot 7 \div 0 \cdot 3 = 29$$

now becomes much less surprising. The missing number in

$$0 \cdot 3 \times \square = 8 \cdot 7$$

must clearly be fairly large; indeed, a simple mental estimate shows that because

$$0 \cdot 3 \times 10 = 3,$$
$$\text{then} \quad 0 \cdot 3 \times 30 = 9$$

For future use, the idea that division is inverse multiplication is the aspect of division which children need to carry forward into their understanding of more advanced mathematics.

Multiplication and division of decimals in the National Curriculum

The National Curriculum does not require children to be able to multiply or divide decimals without a calculator, except for single-digit decimals.

At Level 6, children are expected to convert fractions to decimals:

- convert fractions to decimals and percentages and find one number as a percentage of another.

(AT2: Number, Level 6)

It is not stated that any particular method of calculation is to be used, but probably a calculator is intended, as the maximum level of non-calculator calculation required is at Level 5, when children are expected to:

- understand and use non-calculator methods by which a 3-digit number is multiplied by a 2-digit number and a 3-digit number is divided by a 2-digit number.

(AT2, Level 5)

The statements do not cover the skills required to convert a fraction to a decimal without a calculator. At Level 7, children are expected to understand the ideas on which the multiplication and division of decimals is based, and to make use of their knowledge of multiplication and division in practical problems.

- multiply and divide mentally single-digit multiples of any power of 10, and realise that, with a number less than 1, multiplication has a decreasing effect and division has an increasing effect.
  EXAMPLE: *Work out mentally 80×0.2 and $600 \div 0.2$.*

Solve problems and use multiplication and division with numbers of any size.
EXAMPLE: *Use a calculator to convert inches to centimetres given that there are 0.394 inches to the centimetre.*

(AT2, Level 7)

28 | FURTHER COMPUTING

SPREADSHEETS

During the upper primary years, children are able to explore the mathematical uses of substantial computer software which they have not previously used. *Spreadsheets* are now almost universally used in business, but they have only recently begun to find uses in the classroom. However, they have many mathematical applications; by automating computation, they allow children to concentrate on exploration and problem solving.

A spreadsheet is a computerised rectangular table, which has a number of *cells*, organised in rows and columns, into which numerical or other data can be entered, and calculations carried out (Figure 28 : 1). In most spreadsheet programs the tables of data can be long or short, wide or narrow.

In all spreadsheet programs it is possible to make the values in some cells depend on the values in other cells; in Figure 28 : 2, the spreadsheet has been instructed to make the numbers in the cells of the second column three times the numbers in the corresponding cells of the first column. If changes are made in the first column, the spreadsheet automatically makes changes in the second column, so that the relation between columns is preserved. This property of spreadsheets makes them very useful for exploring questions of the type 'What woud happen if . . .'. Most spreadsheet programs allow tables to be printed out, as in Figure 28 : 2. Spreadsheets also often provide facilities for drawing various types of graphs of numerical data in the spreadsheet. (Figure 28 : 3)

Number	Three times
1	3
2	6
3	9
4	12
5	15
6	18
7	21
8	24
9	27
10	30

Figure 28 : 2

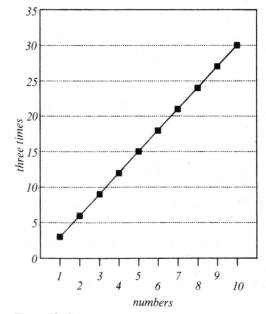

Figure 28 : 3

Not only numbers can be entered in the cells of a spreadsheet; words can also be used, either as headings for the table or as data. Consequently, children who have collected data from a survey sometimes wonder whether it would be better to store it in a spreadsheet or a database. If any of the data is numerical, and if the children wish to make calculations on the numerical data, a spreadsheet is usually the best tool. For example, a class might collect data about their heights and weights, their time for running 60 metres, and their jumping ability. This may lead them to wish to work out

Figure 28 : 1

average heights, weights and speeds for the class. Questions may be asked about whether taller children can run faster or jump higher.

A spreadsheet is an ideal tool for exploring these questions. It is possible to save the table and to print it out at any time. Further rows or columns can be added to the table when they are needed, and new calculations made, as new ideas occur to the children. Figure 28 : 4 shows data for a group of children. The graphs in Figures 28 : 5 and 28 : 6 indicate that there is little correlation between speed of running and ability to make a standing high jump, but there seems to be a slight tendency for taller children to be heavier. These graphs were printed out from the spreadsheet.

Name	B/G	Height cm	Weight kg	St. jump cm	Time 60m sec
Al	B	137	31	198	13·1
Carol	G	140	35	201	13·9
Eddie	B	150	36	213	12·8
Hazel	G	142	30	200	14·1
Jean	G	152	39	220	14·7
Mary	G	143	45	201	14·6
Pete	B	158	40	224	13·2
Roy	B	143	31	198	14·2
Ruth	G	156	45	203	15·5
Sim	B	143	38	204	13·4
Steve	B	147	38	200	12·7
Sue	G	154	30	213	13·5

Figure 28 : 4

Spreadsheets use a co-ordinate system to name each cell. The rows are usually called 1, 2, 3, . . . and the columns A, B, C, ... These names are shown on the screen at the top and left-hand side of the spreadsheet (Figure 28 : 7), but they are not printed when the spreadsheet is printed out. In some spreadsheet programs, the grid lines are

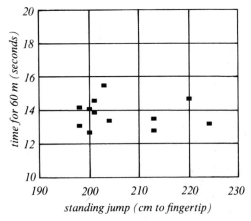

Figure 28 : 5

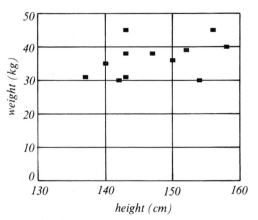

Figure 28 : 6

visible on the screen; in others they are not visible, but pressing the arrow keys moves the cursor from cell to cell. In Figure 28 : 7, the number 10 appears in cell B3. It is usually possible to build a spreadsheet table which is larger than the size of the screen; when this is done, the spreadsheet can be scrolled so that any part of it can be made visible.

	A	B	C	D	E	F	G	H
1								
2								
3		10						
4								
5								
6								
7								
8								
9								
10								
11								
12								
13								
14								

Figure 28 : 7

FORMULAE AND NUMBER PATTERNS

When children have learnt how a spreadsheet works, they will find it a very useful tool for exploring number patterns. When the spreadsheet has been set up to display a particular pattern, children may easily change the starting numbers while keeping the same pattern. At first the teacher may wish to set up the spreadsheet for the children, but they can without difficulty change the starting numbers for themselves, or extend the pattern to larger and larger numbers, and see the effect.

For example, in an investigation of square numbers, a child noticed that the unit digits of square numbers formed a pattern which reversed itself after the square of 5, as follows:

Number	1	2	3	4	5	6	7	8	9	10
Square	1	4	9	16	25	36	49	64	81	100
Units digit	1	4	9	6	5	6	9	4	1	0

The children predicted that the same pattern would occur for the unit digits of the squares of numbers from 11 to 20, and similarly for higher numbers. However, it was not feasible, using a calculator, to verify this prediction for many repetitions of the pattern. Figure 28 : 8 shows a spreadsheet which has been set up to make it easy to verify this pattern as many times as the children wish. The number in cell A3 has been entered directly into the spread-sheet as a starting number; in Figure 28 : 8(a) this number is 1. All the other numbers in the spreadsheet have been automatically calculated from this single number. If the number in cell A3 is changed by typing a new number into that cell, all the other numbers are automatically *recalculated*. In Figure 28 : 8(b), the number in cell A3 has been changed to 21; in (c), the number in cell A3 is 561. Children are able to verify the pattern of the units digits of square numbers for any range of twenty numbers that they choose. Once the spreadsheet has been set up, changing it is merely a matter of retyping the starting numbers; the spreadsheet makes all the recalculations automatically.

How does a spreadsheet know how to calculate the numbers in some cells from the numbers in other cells? Three types of information can be entered into the cells of a spreadsheet; these types of information are *labels, data* and *formulae*. 'Labels' are words, which can be used as the headings of rows or columns of a table. Numbers which are directly entered into the cells of the spreadsheet are 'data'. The number 561 in Figure 28 : 8(c) is an item of data; it has been directly typed in to the cell from the keyboard. 'Formulae' are instructions which tell the computer how to calculate the contents of a cell from the contents of other cells; the use of formulae is a very important feature of spreadsheets.

For example, in Figure 28 : 8, the cell A4 contains the formula A3 + 1, which tells the computer to place in cell A4 the result of adding 1 to the contents of cell A3. On the screen, or in a printout, a formula is not visible in its cell; it can be thought of as sitting behind the cell, and producing the number in the cell. The formula in the cell on which the cursor is placed is usually shown on the screen somewhere in the border of the spreadsheet, so that the user is reminded of the formula in that cell. A formula can be typed in at the keyboard, after giving the computer a specific signal that what follows is a formula, not a label. The procedure for placing formulae in cells is slightly different in different spreadsheet packages; the appropriate manual should be consulted for

(a)

	A	B
	Number	Square
1	Number	Square
2		
3	1	1
4	2	4
5	3	9
6	4	16
7	5	25
8	6	36
9	7	49
10	8	64
11	9	81
12	10	100
13	11	121
14	12	144
15	13	169
16	14	196
17	15	225
18	16	256
19	17	289
20	18	324
21	19	361
22	20	400

(b)

	A	B
1	Number	Square
2		
3	21	441
4	22	484
5	23	529
6	24	576
7	25	625
8	26	676
9	27	729
10	28	784
11	29	841
12	30	900
13	31	961
14	32	1024
15	33	1089
16	34	1156
17	35	1225
18	36	1296
19	37	1369
20	38	1444
21	39	1521
22	40	1600

(c)

	A	B
1	Number	Square
2		
3	561	314721
4	562	315844
5	563	316969
6	564	318096
7	565	319225
8	566	320356
9	567	321489
10	568	322624
11	569	323761
12	570	324900
13	571	326041
14	572	327184
15	573	328329
16	574	329476
17	575	330625
18	576	331776
19	577	332929
20	578	334084
21	579	335241
22	580	336400

Figure 28 : 8

details. To continue the pattern of the calculations shown, the cell A5 contains the formula A4 + 1, A6 contains the formula A5 + 1, and so on for the remaining cells of the A column. A 'copy' command enables the formula in one cell to be easily copied, with appropriate changes, to other cells in a way that preserves the pattern.

In Figure 28 : 8, the cells in the B column follow a different pattern from those in the A column; cell B3 contains the formula A3*A3 (the computer uses * as its multiplication sign), B4 contains A4*A4, and so on.

Figure 28 : 9 shows the formulae in all the cells of the spreadsheet of Figure 28 : 8. It can clearly be seen that only cell A3 contains data; all the other cells (except the headings) contain formulae. Many spreadsheet packages contain facilities to display and print out the formulae in this way, or in a similar way.

	A	B
	Number	Square
1	Number	Square
2		
3	1	A3*A3
4	A3 + 1	A4*A4
5	A4 + 1	A5*A5
6	A5 + 1	A6*A6
7	A6 + 1	A7*A7
8	A7 + 1	A8*A8
9	A8 + 1	A9*A9
10	A9 + 1	A10*A10
11	A10 + 1	A11*A11
12	A11 + 1	A12*A12
13	A12 + 1	A13*A13
14	A13 + 1	A14*A14
15	A14 + 1	A15*A15
16	A15 + 1	A16*A16
17	A16 + 1	A17*A17
18	A17 + 1	A18*A18
19	A18 + 1	A19*A19
20	A19 + 1	A20*A20
21	A20 + 1	A21*A21
22	A21 + 1	A22*A22

Figure 28 : 9

When a data number is changed, the spreadsheet recalculates the numbers in all the cells whose formulae show that they depend on changed cells. In Figure 28 : 8, cell A3 contains data. The data in cell A3 is 1 in Figure 28 : 8 (*a*), 21 in (*b*), and 561 in (*c*). The formulae in all the other cells can be traced back to show that they depend on cell A3, and so the spreadsheet calculates a new set of entries when A3 is changed. This feature makes spreadsheets very useful for exploring number patterns; children can very easily try many examples

of the same pattern.

Spreadsheets can, of course, be saved on disk, and the teacher may sometimes wish to provide a spreadsheet 'template', where children can work with a spreadsheet in which the teacher has already set up some labels, data and formulae. The children then only need to change the data to explore other examples of the pattern. However, the notation in which spreadsheet formulae are written is very similar to the notation of arithmetic, and it leads naturally to algebraic notation. Older primary children should therefore be encouraged to read the formulae in the teacher's spreadsheet templates, and to write simple spreadsheets for themselves.

In Figure 28 : 10, the spreadsheet has been extended to enable children to investigate the patterns in the unit digits of higher powers of numbers. It will be seen that the pattern of the units digits of the sixth powers is the same as the pattern of the squares; looking at the pattern of the fifth powers shows why this is the case.

Number	Square	Cube	Fourth power	Fifth power	Sixth power
1	1	1	1	1	1
2	4	8	16	32	64
3	9	27	81	243	729
4	16	64	256	1024	4096
5	25	125	625	3125	15625
6	36	216	1296	7776	46656
7	49	343	2401	16807	117649
8	64	512	4096	32768	262144
9	81	729	6561	59049	531441
10	100	1000	10000	100000	1000000
11	121	1331	14641	161051	1771561
12	144	1728	20736	248832	2985984
13	169	2197	28561	371293	4826809
14	196	2744	38416	537824	7529536
15	225	3375	50625	759375	11390625
16	256	4096	65536	1048576	16777216
17	289	4913	83521	1419857	24137569
18	324	5832	104976	1889568	34012224
19	361	6859	130321	2476099	47045881
20	400	8000	160000	3200000	64000000

Figure 28 : 10

OTHER USES OF SPREADSHEETS

Spreadsheets are useful whenever the same calculations need to be made on different sets of numbers. For example, children may try to find an arrangement of a set of numbers to make a 3 × 3 magic square. Until a correct arrangement is found, the numbers in the square will constantly need to be changed, and the sums of the rows, columns and diagonals will need to be calculated after each change. Figure 28:11 shows a spreadsheet which has been set up to do the needed calculations. The nine numbers in cells A4 to A6, B4 to B6, and C4 to C6 are the trial numbers for the magic square, and the numbers to the right and below these are the sums of rows, columns and diagonals of the magic square. For example, the 24 in cell D6 is the sum of 7, 8 and 9. Children can change the numbers in the square until they find an arrangement in which the sums of each row, column and diagonal are equal.

	A	B	C	D
1				
2				15
3				
4	1	2	3	6
5	4	5	6	15
6	7	8	9	24
7				
8	12	15	18	15

Figure 28:11

Spreadsheets can often be used to make systematic the solving of problems by 'trial and improvement' methods. A suitable problem is the building of a cubical container with a capacity of half a litre, or 500 millilitres, or 500 cm³. Because the container is a cube, its length, breadth and height are equal; thus a number needs to be found whose cube is 500 (Figure 28:12); that number will give the side of the cube in centimetres.

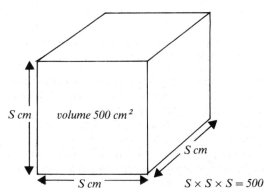

S cm   volume 500 cm²
S cm
S cm $S \times S \times S = 500$

Figure 28:12

Figure 28:13(a) shows a spreadsheet which has been set up to give a first approximation to the side of the cube. It can easily be seen that the length of the side is between 7 cm and 8 cm. In Figure 28:13(b) the spreadsheet is set up to tabulate sides between 7 cm and 7·9 cm, and the corresponding volumes, at intervals of 0·1 cm. It might be thought that this change would require tiresome changes in the formulae in column A, to produce intervals of 0·1 cm instead of 1 cm.

(a)

	A	B	C
1	Side	Volume	Step
2			1
3	1	1	
4	2	8	
5	3	27	
6	4	64	
7	5	125	
8	6	216	
9	7	343	
10	8	512	
11	9	729	
12	10	1000	

(b)

	A	B	C
1	Side	Volume	Step
2			0·1
3	7	343	
4	7·1	357·911	
5	7·2	373·248	
6	7·3	389·017	
7	7·4	405·224	
8	7·5	421·875	
9	7·6	438·976	
10	7·7	456·533	
11	7·8	474·552	
12	7·9	493·039	

(c)

	A	B	C
1	Side	Volume	Step
2			0·01
3	7·9	493·039	
4	7·91	494·9137	
5	7·92	496·7931	
6	7·93	498·6773	
7	7·94	500·5662	
8	7·95	502·4599	
9	7·96	504·3583	
10	7·97	506·2616	
11	7·98	508·1696	
12	7·99	510·0824	

(d)

	A	B	C
1	Side	Volume	Step
2			0·001
3	7·93	498·6773	
4	7·931	498·8659	
5	7·932	499·0547	
6	7·933	499·2434	
7	7·934	499·4323	
8	7·935	499·6211	
9	7·936	499·81	
10	7·937	499·999	
11	7·938	500·188	
12	7·939	500·3771	

Figure 28:13

Certainly, if the formula used in cell A4 is A3 + 1, the formula has to be changed to A3 + 0·1, with similar changes to the formulae in all the other cells in column A. However, cell C2 has been used to make this change of formula unnecessary. Cell C2 contains the *step* between successive entries in column A. In Figure 28 : 13 (*a*) the step is 1, and in Figure 28 : 13 (*b*) the step has been changed to 0·1. The formula used in cell A4 is A3 + C2. To produce Figure 28 : 13 (*b*) from Figure 28 : 13 (*a*), all that is needed is to change the contents of cells A3 and C2. From Figure 28 : 13 (*b*) it is clear that the side of the cube is between 7·9 cm and 8 cm. Figures 28 : 13 (*c*) and (*d*) show the changes in the spreadsheet needed to find the second and third decimal places. It can be seen that the side of the cube is very slightly more than 7·937 cm. Figure 28 : 14 shows the formulae used in all the cells of the spreadsheet.

	A	B	C
1	*Side*	*Volume*	*Step*
2			1
3	1	B3⋆B3⋆B3	
4	B3 + C2	B4⋆B4⋆B4	
5	B4 + C2	B5⋆B5⋆B5	
6	B5 + C2	B6⋆B6⋆B6	
7	B6 + C2	B7⋆B7⋆B7	
8	B7 + C2	B8⋆B8⋆B8	
9	B8 + C2	B9⋆B9⋆B9	
10	B9 + C2	B10⋆B10⋆B10	
11	B10 + C2	B11⋆B11⋆B11	
12	B11 + C2	B12⋆B12⋆B12	

Figure 28 : 14

THE BASIC LANGUAGE

Young children will have used the computer language LOGO to drive the floor turtle or to make drawings on the screen (*see pages 133*). Another programming language which is simple enough for older primary children to use is BASIC. In the early states of learning, LOGO is geometric in nature; BASIC is well adapted for carrying out arithmetic tasks. In some computers used in schools, the BASIC language is built in, and is always accessible. In other computers, BASIC is easily loaded. Children can, at first, use BASIC in direct drive, without writing a program for the computer to execute. In direct drive, each command is executed immediately it has been typed in, as soon as the RETURN key is pressed.

All the facilities of a calculator are built into BASIC, and are released by the command PRINT.

Figure 28 : 15 shows two stages in using the computer as a calculator. A child types in at the keyboard

PRINT 234 + 567

and the computer responds with the answer

801

and the message that it is

READY

to do another calculation.[1]

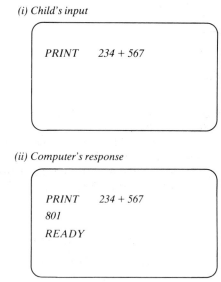

(i) Child's input

(ii) Computer's response

Figure 28 : 15

More complicated calculations and combinations of calculations can also be set up. If children want to verify what happens when a number is multiplied by 10, 100 and 1000, they can ask the computer to print the answers to all three calculations, as shown in Figure 28 : 16, in which it must be remembered that the computer uses a star (*) as a multiplication sign.

Soon children at the upper primary age range will want to take advantage of the computer's most important feature; it can be programmed to perform the same calculation many times over, without the calculation having to be entered separately every time. For example, when the computer is used as a calculator, the multiplication of 137 by 10, 100 and 1000 has to be entered as a new calculation, but a

[1]The detailed layout of the display varies slightly according to the make of computer.

(i) Child's input

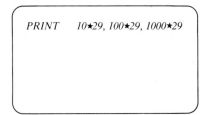

```
PRINT    10*29, 100*29, 1000*29
```

(ii) Computer's response

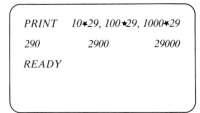

```
PRINT    10*29, 100*29, 1000*29
290         2900         29000
READY
```

Figure 28 : 16

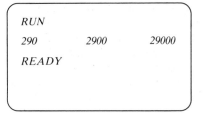

```
RUN
290         2900         29000
READY
```

Figure 28 : 17

program can be constructed to multiply *any number* by 10, 100 and 1000.

In order to do this, children have to learn a few programming ideas, but these are very few and very powerful, and they enable them to use the computer at a simple level to do many things.

FIRST IDEAS OF BASIC PROGRAMMING

In BASIC, the computer distinguishes a *program line* which is entered at the keyboard from a *command* by one simple device: a program line starts with a *line number*. If we type in

10   PRINT 10*29, 100*29, 1000*29

nothing happens immediately. The computer knows we have typed in a program line, because the typing started with the line number 10. The program lines are stored in the computer's memory, to be acted upon at some later time. They are activated by typing

RUN

The computer then looks to see if it has a program in its memory, and carries out the instructions in the program, displaying

290   2900   29000

in exactly the same way as it did when given the similar *command*.

The next idea children need is that a letter can be used to stand for a number, so that the number can

easily be changed. The program

10 LET A = 29
20 PRINT 10*A, 100*A, 1000*A

responds to RUN as shown in Figure 28 : 17.

A further refinement is produced by arranging for the number for which A stands to be fed in during the program run. The command INPUT does this; it stops the run, displays a question mark, and waits for an input. The instruction

INPUT A

waits for the input of a number, gives A that value, and continues. Thus the program

10 INPUT A
20 PRINT 10*A, 100*A, 1000*A

will ask for a number, and print out its multiples by 10, 100 and 1000.

Continuity is achieved by building *loops* into the program. Program lines are carried out in numerical order, unless the program itself contains instructions to do something else. The program below produces the displays shown in Figure 28 : 18. At each loop the program waits for a new number to be typed in.

10 INPUT A
20 PRINT 10*A, 100*A, 1000*A
30 GOTO 10

This program contains an endless loop; the user has to break out from the loop by typing Ctrl-C (holding down the Ctrl key while pressing the C key). Children will later learn better ways than this for arranging an escape from a loop. Programs can be saved on disk, for later use or modification, by using the command SAVE, and the program lines can be listed on the screen by typing LIST. The manual should be consulted for details of these and other 'housekeeping' commands.

If a teacher writes programs for children to use, it will probably be necessary to put further statements into the program, so that the children can understand what the program does. The teacher's final program for multiplying numbers by 10, 100

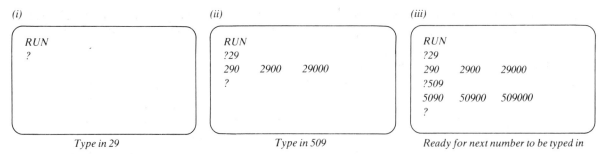

(i)	*(ii)*	*(iii)*
RUN ?	RUN ?29 290 2900 29000 ?	RUN ?29 290 2900 29000 ?509 5090 50900 509000 ?
Type in 29	*Type in 509*	*Ready for next number to be typed in*

Figure 28 : 18

and 1000 is shown in Figure 28 : 19. The words which immediately follow PRINT are written between " and ". This causes them to be displayed as messages on the screen. The screen output of the program is shown in Figure 28 : 20.

> 10 PRINT "THIS PROGRAM MULTIPLIES A
>   NUMBER BY 10, 100, 1000"
> 20 PRINT
> 30 PRINT "REPLY TO '?' BY TYPING IN A
>   NUMBER"
> 40 INPUT A
> 50 PRINT TAB (10), 10$\star$A, 100$\star$A, 1000$\star$A
> 60 GOTO 40

Figure 28 : 19

If children write their own BASIC programs to use themselves, they may not produce such a polished layout; their achievement is in using the computer to explore numbers, and in the mathematical and computing knowledge which they gain from doing this.

The purpose of the above description of the build-up of a program is not to teach programming, but to demonstrate that BASIC programming is simple enough for children to start in the later primary years, provided that a small number of commands only are used. The programs described so far in this chapter used only the commands

PRINT INPUT LET GOTO

and these are sufficient to enable children to write quite a number of arithmetical programs.

Every programmer makes mistakes in programming, and the help of the teacher in 'debugging' children's programs is very important. Children cannot be expected immediately to find out what is wrong with their programs, so that the teacher needs to have acquired this skill before children embark on programming. A program framework is a useful device. Equipped with the framework

> 10 INPUT A
> 20 PRINT _____
> 30 GOTO 10

children can decide what instructions to insert at line 20, and so adapt this program to many situations.

There are two methods of editing a BASIC program. To change line 20, all that is needed is to type in a new line 20, which replaces the previous one. To delete line 20, type 20 and press RETURN. This makes line 20 empty. This method of editing a line by writing a replacement may not, however, be of much help to those children who make frequent typing errors. The alternative way of editing line 20 is to type EDIT 20. Line 20 is then displayed on the screen in editing mode, and insertions or corrections can be made at any point of it. See the manual for details of how to make these corrections. In all cases, pressing RETURN finishes the editing of a line, and places that line in the computer's memory.

Children need to realise that, in BASIC, the computer can only hold in its memory, at any time, one single program. New lines, as they are written, are added to lines already in memory. To get rid of all the lines in memory, type NEW. All the lines in memory are then completely lost, unless the program has previously been stored on disk by using the command SAVE.

```
READY
THIS PROGRAM MULTIPLIES A NUMBER BY 10, 100, 1000

REPLY TO '?' BY TYPING IN A NUMBER

?   29
    290        2900        29000
?   509
    5090       50900       509000
?
```

Figure 28 : 20

FURTHER USES OF BASIC PROGRAMS

If children know a little BASIC, they can often use a BASIC program as an alternative to setting up a spreadsheet, either to explore a number pattern or to solve a problem by trial and improvement. These uses of BASIC programs will be illustrated by two examples; spreadsheets were used for the same two examples earlier in the chapter.

The first example concerns the patterns in the unit digits of the squares, cubes and higher powers of natural numbers. A spreadsheet was set up to print out a list of the squares, cubes and higher powers of numbers, so that children could look at the patterns in the unit digits. A simple BASIC program can be used to do the same task. The following program asks for the input of a starting number, named A; the program then prints out a list of 20 natural numbers, starting with A; it also calculates and prints out the squares of these numbers.

```
10 CLS
20 INPUT A
30 FOR N = A TO A + 19
40 PRINT N, N*N
50 NEXT N
```

Two new BASIC commands have been used in this program. One is the command CLS (an abbreviation for **CL**ear **S**creen) in line 10. This command clears the screen, so that the program starts with no other text on the screen. The other new command is the FOR . . . NEXT loop which repeats line 40 the required 20 times, increasing N by 1 at each repetition.

Children may sometimes wish to send the output from a program to the printer, in order to preserve a permanent copy of it. They may also want to list the program on the printer, so that they can make plans, away from the computer, for changing it or debugging it. The command LLIST sends a listing of the program to the printer. Replacing PRINT in a program by LPRINT sends the output to the printer instead of to the screen.

In the next example, the previous program has been changed, so that it will print the first five powers of a list of numbers, beginning with a starting number A, and ending with a finishing number B. The values of A and B are entered as input at the beginning of the program.

```
10 CLS
20 INPUT A, B
30 FOR N = A TO B
40 PRINT N, N*N, N*N*N, N*N*N*N,
     N*N*N*N*N
50 NEXT N
```

An output from the program is shown in Figure 28 : 21. In this example, A = 1 and B = 20.

1	1	1	1	1
2	4	8	16	32
3	9	27	81	243
4	16	64	256	1024
5	25	125	625	3125
6	36	216	1296	7776
7	49	343	2401	16807
8	64	512	4096	32768
9	81	729	6561	59049
10	100	1000	10000	100000
11	121	1331	14641	161051
12	144	1728	20736	248832
13	169	2197	28561	371293
14	196	2744	38416	537824
15	225	3375	50625	759375
16	256	4096	65536	1048576
17	289	4913	83521	1419857
18	324	5832	104976	1889568
19	361	6859	130321	2476099
20	400	8000	160000	3200000

Figure 28 : 21

Figure 28 : 22 shows the output from the program when A = 30 and B = 40. Unfortunately, BASIC only allows numbers of up to seven digits to be printed in the usual place value notation. BASIC prints larger numbers in *scientific notation* (*see page 223*). Children who have not previously met this notation for large numbers will need to explore it at this stage. Scientific notation does not allow all the digits of a number to be displayed, but only the first seven digits. Scientific notation is therefore not well adapted to studying the unit digits of numbers of more than seven digits.

30	900	27000	810000	$2 \cdot 43E + 07$
31	961	29791	923521	$2 \cdot 862915E + 07$
32	1024	32768	1048576	$3 \cdot 355443E + 07$
33	1089	35937	1185921	$3 \cdot 913539E + 07$
34	1156	39304	1336336	$4 \cdot 543543E + 07$
35	1225	42875	1500625	$5 \cdot 252188E + 07$
36	1296	46656	1679616	$6 \cdot 046618E + 07$
37	1369	50653	1874161	$6 \cdot 934396E + 07$
38	1444	54872	2085136	$7 \cdot 923517E + 07$
39	1521	59319	2313441	$9 \cdot 02242E + 07$
40	1600	64000	2560000	$1 \cdot 024E + 08$

Figure 28 : 22

In fact, spreadsheets suffer from the same limitation as does BASIC, in the size of numbers which they can display in place value notation. The spreadsheet program which was used to print out Figure 28 : 10 allowed eight-digit numbers to be printed out in place value notation, but nine-digit numbers would have been printed out in scientific notation. The teacher should experiment to find out the size of the largest numbers which a particular software package will print out in place value notation. With all software which allows numbers to be used, however, children will need to understand scientific notation when they start to explore number patterns using very large numbers.

In many trial and improvement methods of problem solving, the same calculation has to be repeated at each trial. For example, in finding the side of a cubical box which has a volume of 500 cubic centimetres (*see page 000*), at each trial the length of the side has to be cubed to find the volume of that box. A short BASIC program can be written to automate this calculation. The following program asks for the length of the side as an input, and prints out the volume as the cube of the side. The program then loops back to enable the user to try another value.

```
10 CLS
20 INPUT A
30 PRINT A, A*A*A
40 GOTO 20
```

The program could be improved by printing out explanations on the screen, as the teacher would do in writing the program for children. However, if children write programs such as these for their own use, the value is in the mathematical thinking which goes into devising the structure of the program, and very simple programs are acceptable.

Figure 28 : 23 shows an output from this program. The first value chosen for trial was a side of length 5 centimetres; this was much too small. Successive trials narrowed the length of the side down to a length between 7·9370 centimetres and 7·9371 centimetres.

5	125
6	216
7	343
8	512
7·9	493·039
7·95	502·4599
7·94	500·5662
7·93	498·6772
7·935	499·6211
7·936	499·8101
7·937	499·999
7·938	500·1881
7·9371	500·0179

Figure 28 : 23

Further computing in the National Curriculum

In this chapter we have seen how older primary children can make good use of computer software which easily handles numerical data; attention has particularly been given to spreadsheets and to the BASIC programming language.

Both software packages are mentioned in Attainment Target 3 (algebra).

- Follow instructions to generate sequence.

    EXAMPLE: *Understand the program:*
    10 FOR NUMBER = 1 TO 10
    20 PRINT NUMBER*NUMBER
    30 NEXT NUMBER
    40 END

    (AT3: Level 5)

- Use spreadsheets or other computer facilities to explore number patterns.

    (AT3: Level 6)

However, more important than these specific mentions of computer software is the contribution that computer use can make to children's mathematical understanding; it can thus contribute to children's achievement of other Attainment Targets. For example, children who explore number patterns on the computer are constantly making and testing predictions and statements, and are asking 'What would happen if . . .?' (AT1, Levels 2 to 5). Trial and improvement methods are mentioned in AT 1, Level 6. AT 2, Level 5, and AT 3, Level 6; although the computer is not explicitly mentioned here, we have seen how useful it can be as an aid to trial and improvement.

- Refine estimations by 'trial and improvement' methods.

    (AT2: Level 5)

Both spreadsheets and BASIC use their own adaptations of algebraic notation, and their use can help children to feel comfortable with standard algebraic notation, when they meet it later.

- Understand and use simple formulae or equations expressed in algebraic form.

    (AT3: Level 5)

Surprisingly, scientific notation (standard form) does not appear until Level 8, although children need it if they are to handle very large numbers and very small numbers on the computer.

- Express and use numbers in standard index form, with positive and negative integer powers of 10.

    (AT2: Level 8)

PART 4 | *EXTENDING MATHEMATICS AND ITS USES*

29 VOLUME, MASS AND DENSITY

THE INTERNAL VOLUME OF HOLLOW SHAPES

Measuring the contents of hollow containers such as cups, bottles, hollow cubes and cuboids, by using water or sand or rice, is an easy procedure. These substances can be poured from the container to be measured into a container graduated to show standard measures such as litres or spoonfuls. Fluids can take any shape and thus the units required for measuring capacity do not refer to lengths. For instance, a litre jug need not be of a specified shape. It may not have a uniform cross-section. If the cross-section varies the intervals between graduation marks on the jug will not be equal. The graduation line will not have the regular intervals of a number line. For accurate reading of a graduation it is best to have a container such as a cylinder or a rectangular vessel which will give regular intervals when graduated to show decimal parts (Figure 29 : 1). Children will find that many of the packages that they use or see in shops are either cylindrical or rectangular.

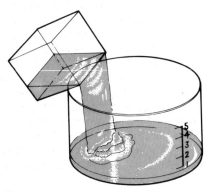

Figure 29 : 1

Of the two forms it is the cuboid which is most commonly used because they can be densely packed. A collection of such rectangular packets will enable children to discover that two packets may differ in length, breadth and height yet have the same capacity. It would be convenient if we could relate the measurements of the packets to their volume and thus avoid the necessity to measure the capacity. We could calculate the volume if we knew just how the volume depends on the measurements of the cuboid. With the experience of finding a unit

for measuring area behind them, children may well recall the use of the unit square and suggest the unit cube for measuring volume.

The next step is to make a hollow unit cube and use it. The 1-cm cube is too small for children to manipulate precisely. A 2-cm cube is possible, but a 5-cm cube can be easily made; 5-cm graph paper is useful in drawing the net of the cube. Figure 29 : 2 shows how the cube can be strengthened by folding the extra squares back to reinforce the faces of the cube.

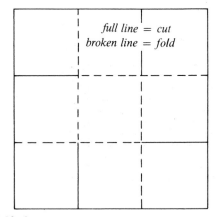

full line = cut
broken line = fold

Figure 29 : 2

The unit cube can be used to graduate a cylinder or cuboid which will serve to measure the internal volume of many containers in terms of the adopted unit cube.

The next step must be to link centimetre cubes to the litre. Children can make a strong 10-cm cube which will hold light cereal or plastic grains. When the cube has been filled its contents can be poured into a litre measure and the children will see that the 10-cm cube holds a litre. A 10-cm cube can be filled from eight of the 5-cm cubes already made but the important question now is: 'How many 1-cm cubes are needed to fill a litre cube?'

BUILDING WITH UNIT CUBES

So far we have been considering the volume of the contents of a container but the idea of volume is wider than capacity. It means the space occupied by a *solid* body as well as the space *inside* a *hollow* body. It is easy to use fluids to measure internal volume. It is more difficult to find units with which to measure the volume of any solid body. Which shapes fit together well so that we can count how many small ones are equivalent to a larger one? Children who are familiar with the cubes and rods of number apparatus will supply the answer. Cubes fit together to makes rows, layers and cuboids or cubes. See page 217. Centimetre cubes can be used to make cuboids whose edges can be stated in centimetres and the volume found by counting the number of 1-cm cubes in each row, in each layer and in the whole cuboid (Figure 29 : 3).

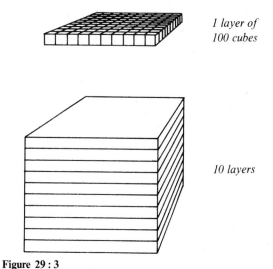

1 layer of 100 cubes

10 layers

Figure 29 : 3

The number of 1-cm cubes in the 10-cm cube already made can now be counted by building up such a cube in solid form with the 10-rods. When children have found that 1000 cm-cubes are equal in volume to 1 litre they can recall the millilitre and realise that 1 millilitre and 1 cm^3 have the same volume. Shapes which have a regular form may now be studied to discover the dependence of their volume on the lengths of their edges, altitudes, and so on. Thus ways of *calculating* the volume of some of the simpler shapes will evolve. The first step is to experiment with forms that can be made from a set of unit cubes so that counting cubes may show equality of volume in objects of different shape. Models of modern architectural forms give excellent examples of solids whose volumes can easily be found and pupils can make interesting designs. If it is possible to acquire some architect's models these will give a variety of forms to investigate. Some recording should be made of the numbers of units in the rows and layers used in any particular construction. Wooden or plastic unit

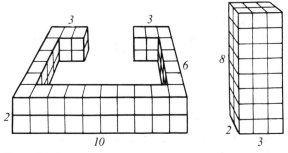

Figure 29 : 4

cubes are also useful in this type of modelling. Each of the models in Figure 29 : 4 contains 48 cubes.

VOLUMES OF RECTANGULAR BLOCKS

The way is now clear for finding the volume of any cuboid by counting the unit cubes it contains. After experience of finding the area of a rectangle by multiplying the numbers of units in its length and breadth, children will readily see that multiplying the numbers of units in the length, breadth and height together will give the number of units of volume in a cuboid. The volume of a variety of interesting packets, boxes, etc., can now be found; that is the amount of space they occupy on a shelf or in a carton. An important aspect of being able to deal with volumes is that many types of goods such as wood, gravel, etc., are sold or distributed in cubic metres. The size of a metre cube often surprises children. A class of 7-year-olds set up a cubic metre in the corner of their classroom with the aid of a vertical metre rod and metre-square sheets of paper. As many children as possible crowded, crouching, into the cube. They were astonished to find that there was room for 14 children. It is interesting, too, for children to measure the space under a table, and similarly to find how many children can be accommodated within it.

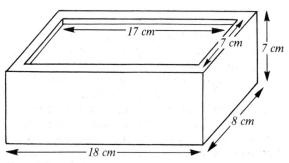

Figure 29 : 5

Another development is to find the internal and the external volume of a box or tank made from fairly thick material (Figure 29 : 5). This makes use of both the total space occupied by the object and its internal capacity. It also shows the volume of the actual material used in making the object. The question of whether a lid is included appears in such problems. It is essential that a real situation should be presented to children for investigation so that verbal ambiguities do not occur and the lengths to be used are measured by the pupils. A description of the procedure followed and a statement of what has been found show the lines of thought which the children have followed.

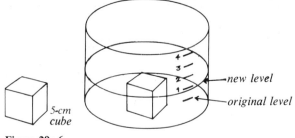

Figure 29 : 6

whose volume has importance should be chosen for measuring; the pupils themselves can produce things whose size they would like to compare, such as heavy balls or tins (Figure 29 : 6).

THE IMMERSION OF SOLIDS IN WATER

Experiment will show that some substances sink and others float. Through experience children become skilled in guessing whether a solid piece of material will float or not. First, we study the effect of immersing objects that sink, such as stone, a lump of lead or a piece of Plasticine. The level of the water rises and, if the container is of a suitable size so that the rise in water level is noticeable, pupils can mark the levels on a strip and compare these levels with their own previously estimated order of size of the objects immersed.

Obviously the solids take up some of the space that was occupied by water. The question arises: 'What happens when the objects are taken back into the air?' They still occupy space and must displace air when they are moved, as we notice when a draught of air is created by a moving object. Children may ask how much space a particular object occupies.

Previous experiences of measuring capacity in cubic centimetres should now tie up with experiments in immersing objects in water. A vessel graduated to show cubic centimetres can be used to record the volume in cubic centimetres which corresponds to the rise in the water level when a particular solid is immersed. Interesting objects

VOLUMES OF SHAPES USED FOR PACKING

Cubes and cuboids are well-known for their property of packing closely together in a cuboid container. Half-cubes also possess this property because they can be combined into cubes. If a diagonal cut is made the cube yields two identical triangular prisms whose volumes we can find because each is half that of the cube. It will be noticed that the prism has a right-angled triangle for its base whose area is half that of the square face of the cube. The height of the prism is the same as that of the cube. It follows that to find the volume of such a prism we can multiply the area of its base by its height (Figure 29 : 7(*a*)).

A cuboid could be halved in the same way and produce triangular prisms with base half the rectangular base of the cuboid. Again we multiply the area of the base by the height to find the volume of the prism (Figure 29 : 7(*b*)).

The base of this prism is a right-angled triangle. It has already been found that *any* triangle can be divided into two right-angled triangles and this fact has been used to find the area of a triangle. We can use such a prism as that in Figure 29 : 8 to find the volume of *any* triangular prism.

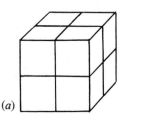
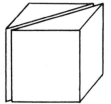
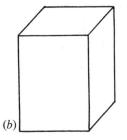
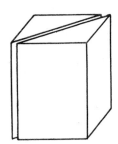

(*a*)   (*b*)

Figure 29 : 7

We need a licence if we own
a television, a car or a gun.
How many of our houses have these?
1. We all have television sets.
2. Only two houses have all three.
3. The majority (that means the greater
number) of us have cars.

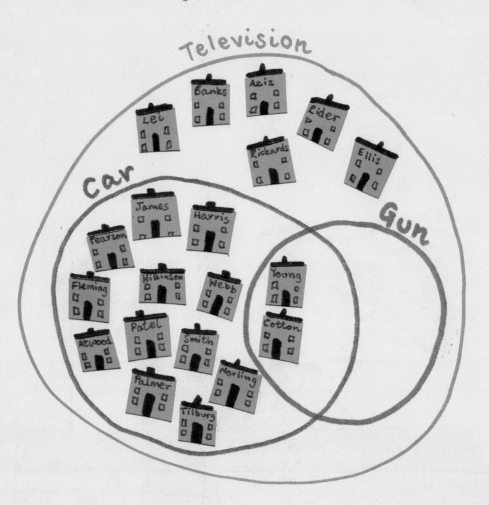

plate 6 : Children's map of the school garden

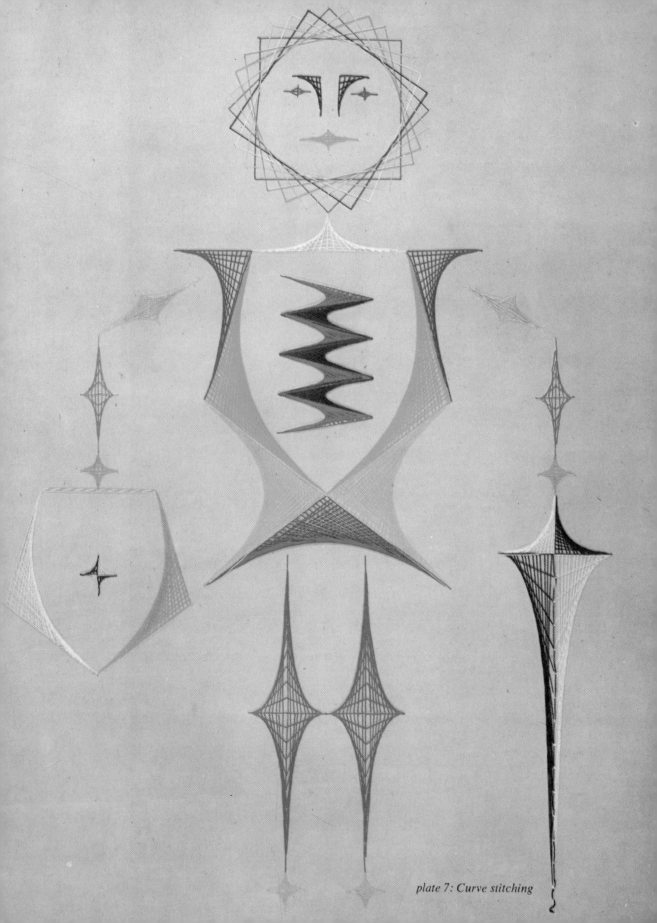

plate 7: Curve stitching

plage 8 :
Tessellations

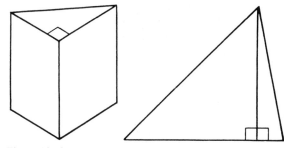

Figure 29 : 8

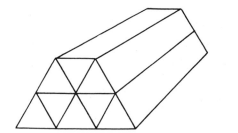

Figure 29 : 9

The triangular prism which is most used in packaging is the one whose base is an equilateral triangle. The containers used for Toblerone chocolate demonstrate that as the rectangular faces are all congruent the prisms can be packed into cartons with great speed, as shown in Figure 29 : 9. The volume of one such prism can be found, for if the prism is cut through an axis of symmetry of the triangular face, two prisms will be produced, each on a base which is a right-angled triangle half the area of the base of the original prism.

Another three-dimensional shape whch can be used to fill a space is a hexagonal prism (Figure 29 : 10). This is also used for packing some kinds of sweets. Since it is composed of six prisms on an equilateral triangle as base its volume can easily be found from the work of the last paragraph. Pupils can experiment with triangular and hexagonal prisms and discover these methods for themselves. They depend very largely on the area properties discussed in Chapter 26. Some pupils will go on to find the volumes of other types of prism and may be able to state a general rule such as, 'To find the volume of a prism multiply the area of the base by the height'.

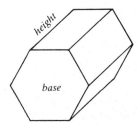

Figure 29 : 10

Many of the shapes in Poleidoblocs can now be studied and their volumes found and compared. Cylinders, cones and pyramids will probably lie beyond children's skill in calculation at this stage but some children may propose using the method of immersion for these solids. Since wood floats in water, they will have to face the problem of making the solids sink. See page 356.

Cuisenaire rods and approximately the Dienes Multibase Arithmetic Blocks are based on the centimetre. The cube found in both sets can profitably be used as a unit to find the volumes of all the other cubes and cuboids. On this foundation of experience of volume, pupils could find in cubic centimetres the internal volume of some tins which have the weight of their contents stated in grams on the labels. They could compare the volumes of equal masses of different substances.

RELATION OF SURFACE AREA TO VOLUME

The comparison of the surface area of a 2-cm cube (24 cm^2) and the number of unit cubes which composed it was mentioned on page 319. We can now take a series of cubes with edges 1 cm, 2 cm, 3 cm, 4 cm, ... and find the surface area and the volume of each, tabulating the results.

The rates at which surface area and volume grow can be seen and graphs of the two sets of numbers can be drawn. But the most interesting feature of the table is the changing relation of surface to volume. The decrease in the ratio of the units of surface area to the units of volume is striking and is important for living creatures. It means that smaller organisms have a larger area of skin in relation to volume. For small warm-blooded creatures this involves a greater loss of heat than for larger creatures. A baby loses heat more rapidly than a full-grown person in the same conditions. Consequently, a baby needs more heat-producing food than an adult to maintain its body temperature. Similarly, a mouse needs more food, in proportion to its size, than an elephant.

If the set of ratios of areas to volumes of the cubes tabulated above is plotted against the corresponding lengths of edges it will be found that the points lie on a curve which can be recognised as having the same shape as the one drawn in Chapter 17, page 218. The product of corresponding pairs of numbers is constant. It can be verified from the table that the product is 6. Pupils may wish to find additional points to show the shape of the curve more clearly (Figure 29 : 12).

Any set of similar solids will show this characteristic relationship and pupils can find

Edge of cube in cm	Surface area in cm²	Volume in cm³	Ratio of number of units of area to units of volume
1	6	1	6:1
2	24	8	3:1
3	54	27	2:1
4	96	64	1·5:1
5	150	125	6:5 or 1·2:1

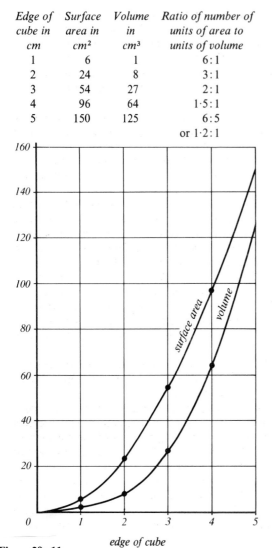

Figure 29 : 11

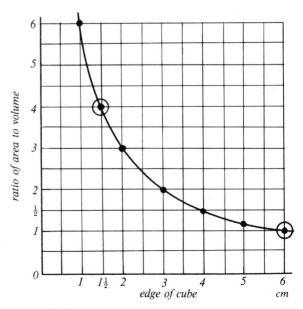

Figure 29 : 12

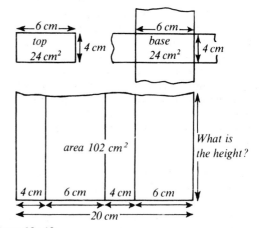

Figure 29 : 13

corresponding sets of ratios for cuboids and possibly other shapes. The growth of crystals illustrates the principle well since crystals maintain their shape as they grow.

On page 351, a variety of shapes was made with the same volume. It is now interesting to compare the volumes of cuboids with the same surface area. Which shape has the greatest volume for a given area of surface? This is a task suited only to the abler pupils. They can make different cuboids with the same amount of surface if they choose the base and then discover what the height must be to give the required surface.

If a 5-cm cube is taken as the first cuboid every other cuboid must have 150 cm² of surface. When we make a cuboid with 150 cm² of surface on a base 6 cm by 4 cm, we first notice that the base and the top together have an area of 48 cm², leaving 102 cm² for the four side faces. But the perimeter of the base is $2 \times (6 + 4)$ cm, i.e. 20 cm. If the area is to be 102 cm² the height of the cuboid must be $(102 \div 20)$ cm, i.e. 5·1 cm. This can be checked as follows. The base of the cuboid is 6 cm by 4 cm.

$$\text{Its surface area} = (2 \times 6 \times 4) + (2 \times 5 \cdot 1 \times 6)$$
$$+ (2 \times 5 \cdot 1 \times 4) \text{ cm}^2$$
$$= 48 + 61 \cdot 2 + 40 \cdot 8 \text{ cm}^2$$
$$= 150 \text{ cm}^2$$
$$\text{Its volume} = 6 \times 4 \times 5 \cdot 1 \text{ cm}^3$$
$$= 122 \cdot 4 \text{ cm}^3$$

This calculation is quite complicated and should be carried out in relation to the actual model being made. Figure 29 : 13 shows two stages in the process of making a paper model.

The following table shows the dimensions and volumes of several possible cuboids and indicates that the cube has the greatest volume for a given surface area.

Dimensions of base (in any given unit)	Height (in same units)	Volume (in cubic units)
2 by 2	2	8
2 by 1	$3\frac{1}{3}$	$6\frac{2}{3}$
3 by 1	$2\frac{1}{4}$	$6\frac{3}{4}$
4 by 1	$1\frac{3}{5}$	$6\frac{2}{5}$
2 by 3	$1\frac{1}{5}$	$7\frac{1}{5}$
2 by 4	$\frac{2}{3}$	$5\frac{1}{3}$

THE RELATION OF MASS TO VOLUME

We now consider the relationship between two quite different properties possessed by objects: mass and volume, which are measured is unrelated units. When surface and volume are compared each is measured in terms of a unit based on a length. If this unit of length is one centimetre then the unit of area is 1 cm^2 and the unit of volume 1 cm^3. Although the properties being compared are different in kind we can usefully think of the *ratio* of the *number* of units involved in an area (or volume) to the *number* of units of length because of the interdependence of the units concerned. In comparing such different properties as mass and volume it is best to think of the relation as a *rate* stating the mass of a specified volume, e.g. grams per cubic centimetre. This rate, mass per unit of volume, is known as the *density* of a substance and is usually studied as part of the science programme. The mathematical aspects should be integrated with that programme.

First we must show that for any particular substance mass increases regularly as volume increases. Weighing 1 cm^3, 2 cm^3, 3 cm^3, ... of a substance we find that mass is doubled, trebled, etc. Any cm^3 of the same substance will therefore have the same mass. Hence if we weigh a volume of 7 cm^3 we can divide the mass by 7 to find the mass per cm^3. Archimedes used this principle in his brilliant solution of the problem: 'Was the king's new crown made of pure gold or had some silver been introduced into it?' He made a crown in pure gold and of the same mass as the one in question. If both crowns were of the same substance they should have the same volume. But how could their volumes be measured? His famous discovery was that immersing the crowns in water would cause the water level to rise the same amount if the volumes were equal. In the event the original crown displaced more water, and so its volume was greater. It therefore contained a substance lighter than gold, producing more volume for an equal mass. Hence the suspicion that the crown contained some silver was confirmed.

In finding the volumes of various objects pupils will have realised again that large objects may be light to handle and small things heavy. If the objects are solid the differences must be due to the substances of which they are made. To investigate this it is necessary to consider objects of the same size but of different materials. A set of 2-cm cubes made from brass, wood, cheese, Plasticine, etc., may be available. For example, a 2-cm cube of brass weighs 60 g approximately, cheese 14 g, wood 7 g. In cases where 1 cm^3 of the substance is not available the volume of the piece used must be found. The mass divided by the number of cm^3 gives the mass per cm^3. For instance, a strip of brass 20 cm by 2·5 cm by 1·3 cm weighs 490 g. The volume of the cuboid is 65 cm^3. The mass per cm^3 is 7·5 g.

When the substance has an irregular shape its volume must be found by the immersion method described on page 352.

Fluids and granular substances or powders have usually to be weighed in a container. This presents the problem of finding the mass of the contents alone. Children should be able to *find* a method of doing this. The container is first weighed empty and then filled with the substance; subtraction gives the mass of the contents. But we need the mass of *1 cm^3* of the liquid. We must therefore either have a measured volume to start with or we must find the volume in the container.

The following examples could be worked out in an ordinary classroom. A small tin of mustard powder is sold full and labelled as containing 113 g of mustard.

The full tin weighs 169 g.
Thus the empty tin weighs 56 g.
Filled with water in weighs 271 g.
The water must weigh 215 g.

Calculation shows that the tin has an internal volume of 216 cm^3. Therefore we can state the mass per cm^3 of

mustard as 113 ÷ 216 = 0·5 g approx.
water as 215 ÷ 216 = 1·0 g approx.

Since a gram is the mass of 1 cubic centimetre of water the density of water is 1 gram per cm^3. It is therefore easy to compare the density of any substance with that of water.

FLOTATION

So far we have experimented with objects which sink when placed in water or whose shape enabled us to calculate their volume. Is it possible to find the density of a body of irregular shape which floats? For example, finding the density of a piece of cork is a problem which demands inventiveness from the children.

The question is whether a floating body can be made to sink so that we find its volume by displacement. Experiments with a variety of materials which float, such as wood, plastics and paraffin wax will help. The flotation of hollow bodies and the children's own ability to float in water will provoke discussion, as will the position in which a piece of ice floats. When a light object is placed so that it floats in the water in a small tank, the level of the water rises. The mass of the floating object can be a compared with the mass of the water which has risen above the original level. The mass of the water displaced may be found by using a displacement can or by an improvised method. It will be found that the mass of water displaced equals the mass of the object. A study of ships and small model boats, observing the variations in their water line according to their load or cargo, will make the principle clear. When a light hollow vessel is floating and water is slowly poured into it the moment will come when it will sink. The levels of the water inside and outside the boat should be noted when it is on the point of sinking. The water that was added should be weighed. Instead of water, sand can be put in and the same procedure followed. The level of the sand at the point of sinking is not the same as that of the water. But the masses should be compared.

Now that a floating hollow body has been made to sink and the equality of mass between the water displaced and the body submerged established, the pupils can consider the problem of finding the volume of *solid* bodies which are *lighter* than water. All that is required is that the body shall have added to it something heavy enough to bring about

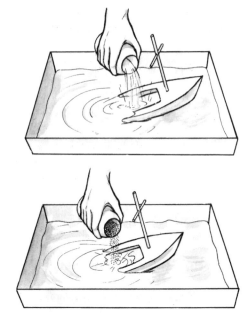

Figure 29 : 14

the sinking. A piece of paraffin wax can be attached, by thin cotton, to a piece of metal. If the volume of the metal is known it can be subtracted from the total volume as recorded by the rise in the water level. The mass of the wax must then be divided by its volume to give its density. The pupils are now in a position to compile a list of the densities of some substances which are lighter than water and of some that are heavier.

CONCLUSION

The work of this chapter has been concerned with measuring important properties of solid bodies, their volumes, masses and densities. The experiments suggested should lead to a fundamental grasp of these properties and their relationships with one another. The range of shapes for which volume can be calculated at this stage is limited, but the procedure of immersion may lead the more enterprising pupils to investigate the volumes of pyramids, cones, cylinders and spheres, which are widely used in tools and mechanisms.

Volume and density in the National Curriculum

Ideas of volume and density occur in Attainment Targets 2 and 4 of the National Curriculum. It is expected that children's idea of volume will develop gradually, over a period of years.

- use non-standard measures in length, area, volume, capacity, 'weight' and time; compare objects and events and recognise the need to use standard units.

(AT2, Level 2)

- find area by counting squares, and volumes by counting cubes, using whole numbers.

(AT4, Level 4)

- use knowledge and skills in length, area and volume to carry out calculations in plane and solid shapes.

(AT4, Level 7)

Density is one of the compound measures that children are expected to be able to use at Level 7.

- understand and use compound measures, e.g. speed, density.

(AT2, Level 7)

In order to work out densities, however, children will need to be able to calculate the volumes of simple objects such as cuboids, or to find volumes by displacement.

30 | INDIRECT MEASUREMENT

INTRODUCTION

During the early years at school children acquire a great deal of experience of measuring distances, and use the measurements they have made in making models and in drawing simple scale plans. Some of the things they would like to measure may, however, be out of their reach. It may be possible to make a model of the classroom, but often children cannot make a model of the school hall (although they can draw a plan of it), because they cannot reach the ceiling of the hall to measure its height. When they study a tree, children will want to know its height, but will not be able to measure this directly. The width of a river cannot be measured directly, nor can the height of a church tower or a factory chimney. But some methods of measuring these distances indirectly are within the understanding of many older children in the primary school, and the problems of making these measurements provide situations where they can use their developing geometrical concepts. The simple instruments which are used can often be made by children, and although the results will not always be very accurate, the principles used will be clear to the children, and will extend their knowledge of the uses of mathematics.

Another quantity which must always be measured by indirect means is time, since the passage of time must always be matched with some regular occurrence, like the swing of a pendulum. The study of various ways of measuring time helps to deepen children's concept of time, and leads to an understanding of the measurement of speed. The indirect measurement of the three quantities of distance, time and speed, and the relation between them, form the theme of this chapter.

USING TRIANGLES TO MEASURE HEIGHTS

Let us suppose that children want to measure the height of a house, or of a wall of the school hall. First they can estimate the height of a door in the wall, or imagine how many times a child's height would fit into the height of the wall, or use the number of storeys in the building to provide clues. Counting the number of courses of bricks may be another possible method, but it becomes very difficult to count layers of bricks at any considerable height. The height of modern multi-storey buildings is often found most easily by measuring the height of one storey and multiplying by the number of storeys. All these methods may fail, however, for instance in finding the height of a tree. All other methods depend basically on the drawing of a triangle from the measurements which can be made at ground level. The simplest situation is shown in Figure 30 : 1. From the measurement of the horizontal distance AC and of the angle BAC, a scale drawing of the triangle ABC can be made, and the scale height of the tree measured from the drawing (Figure 30 : 2). The angle between the horizontal and the line to the top of the tree is the *angle of elevation* of the top of the tree.

Variations on this method of making a scale-drawing of a triangle are often used, but the basic method is simple enough for children to grasp as soon as they understand the ideas of horizontal and vertical and the relation between them, and

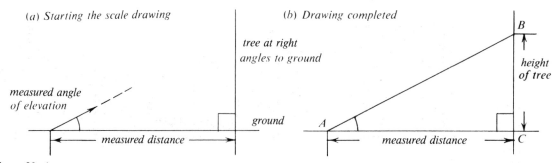

(a) *Starting the scale drawing*

measured angle of elevation

measured distance

(b) *Drawing completed*

tree at right angles to ground

ground

height of tree

measured distance

B

A

C

Figure 30 : 1

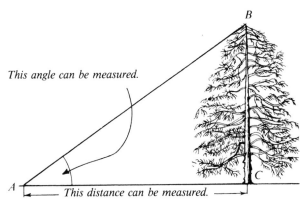

This angle can be measured.

This distance can be measured.

Figure 30 : 2

when they can visualise a line from the ground to the top of the tree, which does not have the physical existence of lines drawn on the ground or on a sheet of paper. All the methods of measuring the angle of elevation *BAC* involve 'sighting' the top of the tree, and measuring the angle between the invisible line *AB* and the horizontal (or sometimes the vertical). Other invisible lines are often used as well, for it is more convenient to measure angles at eye-level than at ground-level. In Figure 30 : 3, which shows the most convenient practical arrangement, all three lines in the triangle *ABC* are invisible, and have to be supplied by children's imagination.

Finding the height of a tree

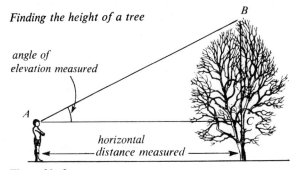

angle of
elevation measured

*horizontal
distance measured*

Figure 30 : 3

The construction and use of the instruments for measuring the angle of elevation of the top of the tree will be described on page 361.

SOME CONCEPTS USED IN THE INDIRECT MEASUREMENT OF DISTANCE

The use of a triangle to measure distances indirectly is conceptually a complex process, but the concepts needed are usually established during the primary years, and the experience provided by this type of measurement helps these concepts to become firmly fixed and operational. Some of these concepts are now discussed and it will be seen that they are closely inter-related.

The idea that a tree or a building with a sloping roof has a 'height' is not immediately obvious. The line whose length must be measured has to be supplied by the imagination, and has to be a vertical line. Figure 30 : 4 shows some objects which have obvious vertical heights, and others whose heights are less obvious. The heights of the door and the wall are measured along lines which have a real physical existence. In the case of the oak tree this line is less obvious, and the height of the leaning tree bears no relation to any physical line *in* the tree. In all these instances the vertical line has to be supplied by the imagination. Children usually learn early to measure each other's height by using a ruler placed horizontally to make a mark on a vertical wall at the right height. They do not always realise the necessity, as opposed to the convenience, of this method, and even older children may sometimes be seen measuring each other's heights by applying a tape-measure to the body, so that the tape-measure is curved and does not lie in a vertical straight line.

This mistake would be expected until children have securely established the ideas of horizontal and vertical, and know that in a particular place the vertical always has the same unchanging direction,

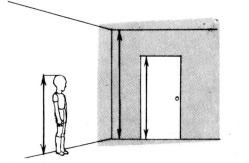

Figure 30 : 4

the direction in which a plumb-line hangs. Piaget has shown that children are not secure in this idea until the stage of concrete operations,[1] and Beard found that only 9 out of a sample of 183 English children aged between 6 and 11 were able to draw correctly the position which they expected a plumb-line to take up within a tilted jam-jar, but 49 of the same sample drew correctly the expected position of the water level in a tilted jam-jar half full of water.[2] Figure 30 : 5 shows typical earlier attempts at these drawings, before the unvarying vertical direction of the plumb-line and the unvarying horizontal level of the water have become clear to the child.

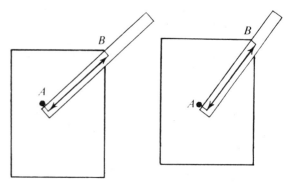

Figure 30 : 6

Figure 30 : 5

Until they have achieved a permanent frame of reference of stable horizontals and verticals, children find it difficult to judge the slope of oblique lines, and to appreciate differences of slope between different lines. Piaget performed an experiment in which he put a dot on a piece of paper, and asked a child, who was provided with tools for measuring, to put a dot in the same position on a similar piece of paper. The two pieces of paper were fixed at opposite corners of a table.[3] Children aged about 7 often measured the distance of the dot from one corner of the paper and transferred this measurement to the other piece of paper, but without understanding the need to keep the direction of the oblique line constant, or realising that it would be better to make two measurements parallel to two edges of the paper (Figure 30 : 6). It is likely that this mistake occurs because only at the stage of concrete operations are children able to relate two aspects of a situation to one another. In this experiment children must take account of both distance and direction, or they must relate the dot to two edges of the paper, if they are to put it in the correct position.

Clearly, the ability to judge and measure the direction of oblique lines is essential to the use of a triangle for indirect measurement. There remains the further difficulty that the oblique line needed (*AB* in Figure 30 : 3) can only be 'seen' by the observer at *A*, and then only by 'sighting' along it. By the age of about 7 many children are able to arrange objects in a line by sighting along the line, and a year or two later they can co-ordinate the viewpoint of the observer who looks along *AB* with the viewpoint of the observer who looks at triangle *ABC* from the side, and so can accept Figure 30 : 3 as a correct picture of what is happening. Piaget says

'. . . it is most significant that co-ordination of the perceptual field reaches its maximum efficiency at about the age of 9, the same at which the concepts of vertical and horizontal finally emerge as potential co-ordinate axes.'[4]

The idea of a 'correct picture' needs examination, however. A 'correct picture' is a scale drawing. This is an idea with which children will already be familiar from making simple plans and models. Most of these scale drawings are rectangular in shape, and they have always been made by measuring lengths. Children may not realise that all the angles of a scale drawing are equal to the angles of the original object, and that they can make a scale drawing of a triangle simply by making the angles of the two triangles equal. Here again, the ability to co-ordinate measurements in two dimensions and to take account of slope is needed.

It must be stressed that the understanding of such mathematical concepts as these comes through action and through experience of situations in which the concepts arise. The fact that a children do not appear to have a very firm grasp of all the

[1]Piaget, J. and Inhelder, B. *The Child's Conception of Space,* Chapter 13.

[2]Beard, R. 'Further Studies in Concept Development', *Educational Review,* 17(**1**), 1964.

[3]Piaget, J. and Inhelder, B. *The Child's Conception of Space,* Chapter 7.

[4]Piaget, J. and Inhelder, B. *The Child's Conception of Space.*

ideas which they need should not always dissuade the teacher from introducing them to new experiences which may be exactly what they need to help the development of some concept. Analysis of the ideas used in a piece of work may also help in the design of preliminary experience, for a piece of work is more likely to succeed if children can start it from a secure basis of previous experience, and are not overwhelmed by a great variety of new ideas and problems which all have to be solved at the same time.

We now turn to the discussion of the practical problem of measuring an angle of elevation such as angle *BAC* of Figure 30 : 3.

INSTRUMENTS FOR MEASURING ANGLES OF ELEVATION

Modern optical instruments for measuring angles, such as the theodolite and sextant, are not usually available to children, and even if they are, simpler and more primitive instruments form a useful introduction to more accurate and complicated equipment. We therefore discuss only simple instruments, most of which can easily be made by children.

The first instruments we describe avoid the problem of actually measuring the angle of

elevation. If one stands near the tree and walks away from it, the angle of elevation of the top of the tree gradually decreases. By moving far enough away from the tree, the triangle *ABC* can be made of any desired shape (Figure 30 : 7). A triangle with two equal sides *AC* and *BC* is particularly simple. A square of cardboard may be cut in half diagonally to give a right-angled triangle with two equal sides. If children sight the top of the tree along the longest side of this triangle (Figure 30 : 8), they are assured that the large triangle *ABC* which they are making has two equal sides, for the half-square *APQ* is of the same shape as triangle *ABC*. It is necessary to ensure that *AQ* is horizontal, and this is most easily done by hanging a plumb-line from the triangle near the edge *PQ* so that another child, standing at the side, can see that *PQ* is vertical. If the distance *AC* is then measured, it will be equal to *BC*.

The child using the half-square has to move until the top of the tree can just be seen along *AP*. This is not always possible. If the tree is not very slender, it is often necessary to get further away from it in order to get a clear view of the top. A half-square is not, however, the only shape of triangle which can be used. Figure 30 : 9 shows the use of a right-angled triangle, one of whose sides is twice the length of the other.

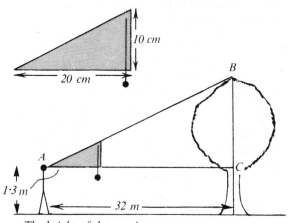

The height of the tree is
16 m + 1·3 m = 17 m to the nearest metre.
Figure 30 : 9

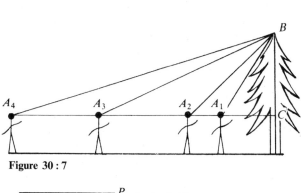

Figure 30 : 7

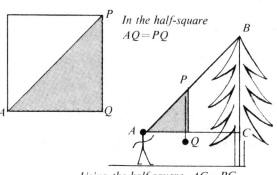

Using the half-square   AC = BC

Figure 30 : 8

In other methods, the angle of elevation *BAC* is actually measured, and the instruments used are devices for sighting across a protractor. A simple Meccano sighting device using a cardboard protractor is shown in Figure 30 : 10(*a*), and the medieval *astrolabe* in Figure 30 : 10(*b*). The astrolabe needed no plumb-line. It was suspended from a ring held in the hand, and the movable

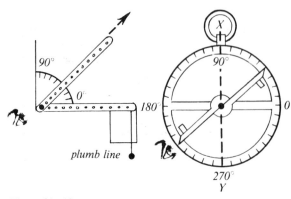

Figure 30 : 10

pointer carrying the sights was symmetrically balanced, so that the instrument would always hang with the line *XY* vertical, whatever the position of the pointer.

A school protractor and a straw can be used to make a simple *clinometer* (Figure 30 : 11). The straw is taped to the protractor, and is used to support a plumb-line consisting of a piece of thread and a small weight. This clinometer is slightly more difficult to use then the previous instruments, as the

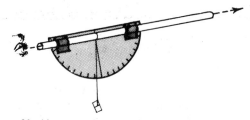

Figure 30 : 11

angle read off from the protractor is not the angle of elevation of the top of the tree, but the angle between the oblique line and the vertical (Figure 30 : 12).

Using the clinometer

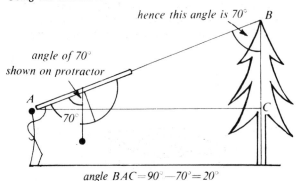

angle BAC = 90° − 70° = 20°

Figure 30 : 12

Simple clinometers are also commercially available. These are easier to use than a clinometer made from a protractor, because their scales record the actual angle of elevation of the treetop.

When the angle of elevation *BAC* of the top of the tree has been measured by one of these methods, the distance *AC* between the observer and the tree is measured, and the diagram can then be drawn to scale. The scale height of the tree is then read off from the scale drawing.

Whatever method of measuring is used, children should be encouraged to estimate the height of the tree, looking at it in proportion to the distance on the ground, so that major errors can be discovered. The degree of accuracy to be expected in the measuring should also be discussed. Taking measurements from a scale drawing may give a spurious feeling of accuracy. In Figure 30 : 13(*a*) angle *A* has been measured with a home-made clinometer, and the distance *AB* with a measuring-tape. We can read off from the drawing that the height *BC* of the building is 13 m to the nearest metre. But if the length *AB* had been measured with an error less than $\frac{1}{4}$ metre, and the angle was correct within 2°, which is unlikely with a home-made clinometer, the height might be anywhere between 11·2 m and 14·2 m, as is shown

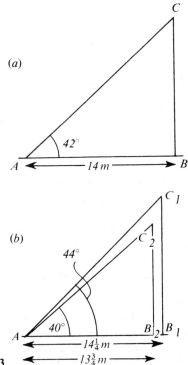

(*a*)

(*b*)

Figure 30 : 13

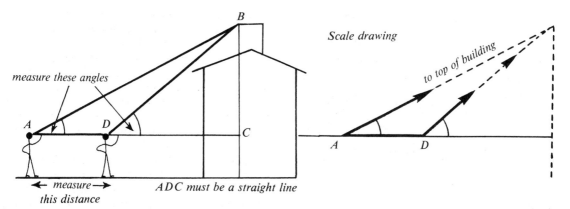

measure these angles

A *D* *C*

← *measure* →
this distance

ADC must be a straight line

Scale drawing

to top of building

A *D*

Figure 30 : 14

in Figure 30 : 13(*b*). It would be better to state that the height is approximately 13 metres.

When the height of a building is to be found, it often happens that it is not possible to measure the distance of the observer from the point vertically below the top of the object. In this case, observations should be taken from two points. Figure 30 : 14 explains the method.

This method was used by armies in the sixteenth century to find the distance and height of a castle. It was known as 'drumhead trigonometry', the required lines being drawn by direct sighting on the vertical side of a drum (Figure 30 : 15).

Drumhead trigonometry

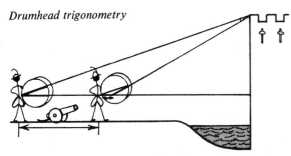

Figure 30 : 15

LINES AND RIGHT ANGLES ON THE GROUND

A natural extension of the use of triangles to measure the vertical heights of inaccessible objects is the use of triangles to measure horizontal distances. This leads to the introduction of simple surveying. In this section, we discuss a few uses of the idea of sighting, which can be used in marking out a football pitch, or any other large-scale construction on the ground.

Children will know by now that pulling a rope or measuring-tape taut gives them a straight line. They should also know how to measure out a straight line whose length is greater than the length of the

Sighting a straight line

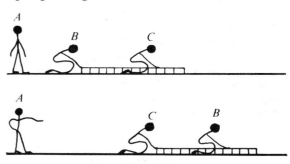

A directs B as he moves forward so as to keep the line straight.

Figure 30 : 16

measuring-tape by using an observer who remains behind when the tape is moved (Figure 30 : 16).

A previously drawn scale-plan, mounted on a horizontal board, can also be used for sighting when the shape to be marked out is a complicated one (Figure 30 : 17).

When heights are being measured, right angles are obtained by using horizontal and vertical lines. Right angles are more difficult to mark out on the ground. Among a variety of methods, the '3, 4, 5 triangle' may be used, or a sighting method. The Romans used a simple device called a *groma*, consisting of two rods fixed at right angles, from

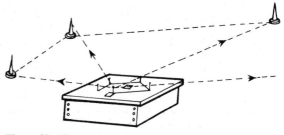

Figure 30 : 17

The groma

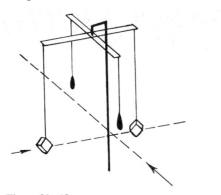

Figure 30 : 18

The sighting-box

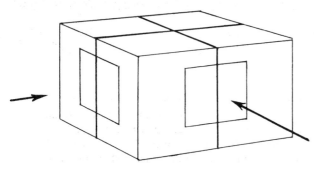

*A window is cut in each side of the box
and vertical threads are used as sights.*

Figure 30 : 19

which plumb-lines were hung (Figure 30 : 18). The
same idea is used in the sighting-box (Figure
30 : 19), and in the simple theodolites now
available, which consist of a clinometer mounted on
a 360° protractor.

THE MEASUREMENT OF TIME

Some distances have to be measured indirectly
because they are inaccessible; periods of time always
have to be measured indirectly. We can never lay a
measuring rod between two events; all we can do is
to find some occurrence which we believe happens
at regular intervals (for example, the recurrence of
the seasons or the swing of a pendulum) and count
how many times this happens between the two
events. And we can never go back and check our
measurements. Time has gone; the same events
cannot be repeated. Because of this, young
children's ideas of time and its measurement
develop slowly. Their growing memory, together

with the important events which provide landmarks
in time, help them to become aware of time in an
increasingly quantitative way.

The ability to read a clock, the recurring pattern
of events in the day, the school week, and the
weekend, the regular recurrences of the new school
year, Guy Fawkes Day, Christmas, spring, Easter,
summer holidays, events such as birthdays, using
the calendar: all these help to provide the necessary
landmarks in time. At first, time is not quantitative;
it is a stream of present and past moments, only
gradually differentiated by the memory and
anticipation of these landmarks. During the first few
years at school, the different scales of measurement
of time, the years, the seasons, months, days, hours
and minutes, need to be co-ordinated and set in
relation to one another. One way of doing this is by
focusing children's attention on ways in which time
can be, and has been, measured. The experience of
humankind's struggle to catch and measure time
can help children in their personal struggle with this
most intangible of all the quantities which we
measure. Children need experience like this as
much as the ability to tell the time, for it focuses
their attention on the passing of time and on the
possibility of comparing intervals of time.

The rhythm of the year is slow, and variations in
the weather cause slight variations in the more
obvious landmarks. Because of these variations,
primitive peoples find it difficult to judge how long
a year is, and young children need to relate
recurring events of nature, the lengthening and
shortening of the days, the waxing and waning of
the moon, the rise and fall of the tides, to the
calendar of months which keeps in step with
nature's year. A graph showing the beginning and
ending of lighting-up time can be constructed over
the period of a year, and will help children to
associate the rhythm of the calendar year with
nature's variations (Figure 30 : 20). New moons,
times of high tide, the first lamb, the first cuckoo,
the beginning of haymaking, and so on, can be
added to this calendar of the year. The Jewish New
Year, Ramadan and the Chinese New Year are
familiar to many children, and will stimulate
discussion of ways in which various peoples
measure time.

With a little experiment, children can discover
the quantity of sand or sugar needed to run through
a funnel in a minute, and so make their own
timers. A candle-clock can be marked at five-minute
intervals, and the principle of the ancient
water-clock demonstrated to show how long cartons
with different-sized holes in them take to sink in a
bucket of water (Figure 30 : 21). The different but
regularly repeating fast and slow rhythms which

The beginning and ending of lighting-up time during the school year

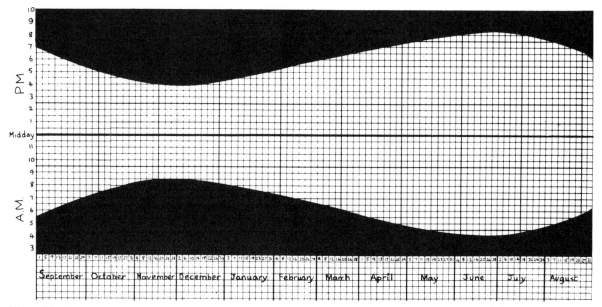

Figure 30 : 20

children meet in music and in movement also help to establish the idea of measurable time. The metronome, with its clear tick and good visual embodiment of this beat, fascinates children, and can be used to establish the idea of a second. A 'seconds pendulum' 1 metre long can be hung beside the metronome, and children will experiment in altering the length of the pendulum to try to make it match an altered beat of the metronome. Later, this experiment will become quantitative.

While children's ideas of a second, a minute and an hour are growing, they will be interested in learning what a minute feels like when they are engaged in various activities. Piaget found that only during the older primary years was the idea of the duration of time firmly established, and separated from the speed at which an activity was performed.[5] Lovell and Slater[6] describe an

experiment invented by Piaget in which two dolls moved simultaneously on parallel courses *AB* and *CD*, where *AB* was longer than *CD*. The doll moving on the longer course *AB* went faster, and took the same time as the other doll. More than half of Lovell's average-to-bright 9-years-olds thought that the first doll had taken a longer time than the second, because it went farther. This number included some children who realised that the two dolls started and stopped at the same times.

Children can measure how far they can walk, run or skip in half a minute or a minute, or they can

[5]Piaget, J. *The Child's Conception of Time* (Routledge and Kegan Paul, 1969).

[6]Lovell, K. and Slater, A. 'The Growth of the Concept of Time: a Comparative Study.' *Journal of Child Psychology and Psychiatry,* **1** (1960), 179-90.

Some home-made clocks

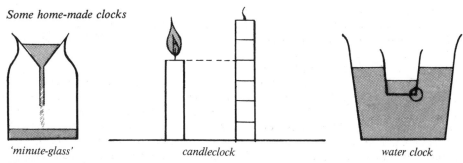

'minute-glass'   candleclock   water clock

Figure 30 : 21

count how many times they can bounce a ball. This repetition of the objective measurement of time alongside their varying activities will help them to establish the objectively of time and to dissociate it from speed. They will also notice how much longer a minute seems if they are sitting still than when they are reading and they will learn to make their own estimates of time by counting seconds. The slow movement of the seconds hand of the clock shown on television gives practice in counting down in seconds to the start of the programme.

Children should also examine the use of the sun as a timekeeper and the movement of the shadows cast by the sun. Young children do not think that a shadow is produced by an object blocking out rays of light, but think of it as something emanating from the object itself, and it is not until around 8 or 9 years of age that they can usually predict the direction of a shadow.[7] When this occurs, however, the apparent movement of the sun during the day can be linked with the movement of the shadow of a stick, and children can construct a horizontal sundial by marking the position of the shadow of a stick on the ground at different times during the day (Figure 30 : 22). A vertical sundial can also be constructed by using a nail in south-facing wall (Figure 30 : 23). Such primitive 'scratch dials' or 'Massdials', a few of which date from Saxon times, can be found on the south walls of some churches. These later developed into magnificent and complicated sundials like the one in Queens' College, Cambridge.

When they use a horizontal sundial, children

Vertical sundials

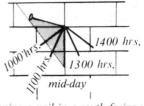

Anglo-Saxon 'Scratch-dial'

using a nail in a south facing wall

Figure 30 : 23

should notice that the shortest shadow is the mid-day one, and that it points due north, so that the sun is due south at mid-day Greenwich Mean Time.

Older children can be introduced to the idea that the apparent movement of the sun is due to the movement of the earth. This involves the idea of relative motion, which many understand when they see it on television or at the cinema. The movement of the camera (or the use of a zoom lens) makes an object seem to move nearer or further away, or to change its position in the picture. Many children can relate this apparent movement of the object to the movement of the camera, and so are beginning to appreciate relative motion. Pictures of the clouds from above, which are seen on television weather maps, enable children to look at the earth from a point of view outside it, which also helps them to imagine the earth moving around the sun. The 'Starship Enterprise' and similar space fiction also makes this idea more accessible.

A simple horizontal sundial

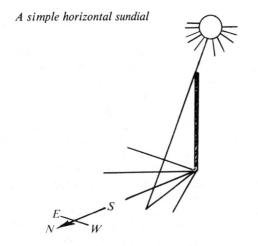

Figure 30 : 22

Hemispherical sundial[8]

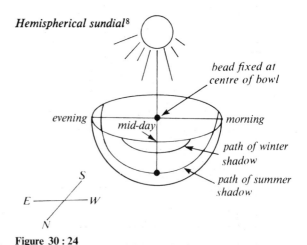

head fixed at centre of bowl

evening *mid-day* *morning*

path of winter shadow

path of summer shadow

Figure 30 : 24

[7]Piaget, J. *The Child's Conception of Physical Causality* (Kegan Paul, 1930), Chapter VIII.

[8]The invention of the hemispherical sundial is ascribed to Berossus, a Babylonian astronomer of the third century BC.

Another useful sundial, which exactly mirrors the apparent movement of the sun across the bowl of the sky, is the hemispherical sundial. A bead is fixed by a wire so that it is at the centre of a hemispherical bowl (Figure 30 : 24), and the path of its shadow during the day can be marked on the inside of the bowl. This sundial can be used to study the variations in the altitude of the sun during the year.

THE CONNECTION BETWEEN DISTANCE AND TIME

Children cannot form *directly* an idea of larger units of distance, such as the *kilometre*. They know the smaller units which they can handle, but a kilometre can only be experienced in terms of movement. The statement that there are 1000 metres in a kilometre means very little in terms of actual experience, for the number is too large.

Children may find it helpful to break the kilometre down into smaller units. It may be possible to mark out 200 metres on the school field, and from this children can discover how long it would take them to walk a kilometre of 5 times 200 metres. Figure 30 : 25 shows a graphical treatment of this problem by two children who took different times to walk 200 metres. This graph can also be used to read off the distance when a child has

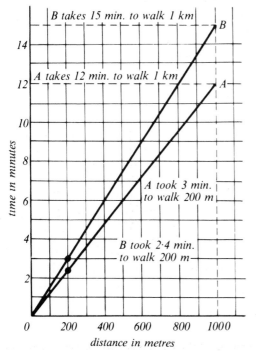

Figure 30 : 25

walked for a certain time. It also demonstrates how inaccuracies are magnified when extrapolation is used. Children can use this knowledge to find places a kilometre from school, or to find how far their homes are from school. This idea of distance must, however, be based on an appreciation of how long it takes to get from one place to the other by some familiar means of transport: walking, bicycle, bus or car.

At this stage, children will also be able to use reference books to find out the history of measures and will be able to compare the traditional British measures which they will still find in books and on signposts and milestones with the metric units.

The adult traveller relies for knowledge of distance on the car's odometer or on a watch and a knowledge of the approximate average speed. Distances like the kilometre and its multiples are too large in relation to the human body for us to measure directly, except by such mechanical means as the odometer, and so the measurement of distance is gradually supplemented in our minds by measurements of speed.

THE MEASUREMENT OF SPEED

The idea that time can be divided into equal units and measured is a sophisticated one; so is the idea that speed can be measured. The clock and the calendar catch the stream of time and make it measurable; the speedometer of a car catches movement and attaches a number to it. The measure of speed — centimetres per second or kilometres per hour — is a compound of the measures of distance and of time, but to young children speed is a property of movement, and does not yet depend on the relationship between a distance and the time taken to cover that distance. Only gradually do they distinguish between being late for school because they started late and being late for school because they dawdled by the way. Before the stage of concrete operations they may think that when two toy cars race, one having a start on the other, that the one which catches up on its opponent has somehow taken longer, although they are sure that both cars started and stopped in the same instant.[9] Time and speed are still personal and not universal, and they are not differentiated from one another. Outside events and their speed seem to influence time. An egg-timer or a stop-clock may be thought to move faster if children walk quickly round the table while watching it than if

[9]Piaget, J. *The Child's Conception of Movement and Speed* (RKP, 1970), Chapter VII.

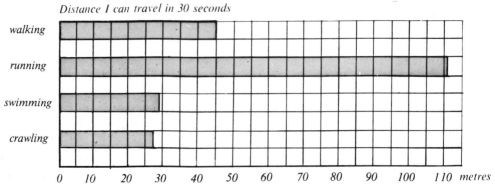

Distance I can travel in 30 seconds

Figure 30 : 26

they move slowly.[10] They certainly cannot yet
co-ordinate the three variables of time, distance and
speed.

But as children's idea of time develops and they
learn to measure it, so their idea of 'faster' becomes
measurable. If they make water-clocks from two
identical cartons with different-sized holes in the
bottom, and one sinks in two minutes while the
other takes four minutes, then the first has sunk
twice as fast as the second. The graph in Figure
30 : 26, which they will make when they are finding
out about the duration of minutes, will lead them
to compare how fast they can travel in different
ways. They will describe their speed as 90 metres in
a minute, or 90 *metres per minute,*and on the basis
of measurements they can make graphs to show
how far they could travel in each of these ways in 1
minute, 2 minutes, 3 minutes, etc. (Figure 30 : 27).

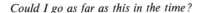

Could I go as far as this in the time?

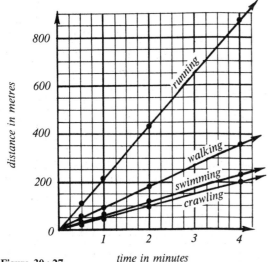

Figure 30 : 27

time in minutes

[10]Piaget, J. *The Child's Conception of Time* (RKP, 1969),
Chapter VIII.

Theoretically, there are two possible ways of
comparing speeds of movement. We can fix the
time during which we move, and measure *how far*
we travel in that time. This is the principle of the
Le Mans 24-hour motor race. Alternatively, we can
fix the distance and measure the length of time it
takes to cover that distance. Almost all other races
are run on this principle, and most comparisons of
speed are made on the basis of a fixed distance.
The train from Cambridge to Liverpool Street takes
less time than the same journey by car, so the train
has a *greater average speed.* A runner who covers
1 kilometre in 2 minutes 20 seconds goes faster
than one who covers 10 kilometres in 28 minutes.
Their average speeds could be expressed in either of
the following ways:

	Method 1	*Method 2*
Shorter-distance	2·33 minutes	0·43 kilometres
runner	per kilometre	per minute
Longer-distance	2·8 minutes	0·36 kilometres
runner	per kilometre	per minute

Method 1 would be preferable if it were not for the
fact that the *faster* runner takes fewer minutes per
kilometre; 2·33 minutes per kilometre is faster than
2·8 minutes per kilometre; the larger number is
attached to the smaller speed. But 0·43 kilometres
per minute is faster than 0·36 kilometres *per
minute*; here the larger number is attached to the
greater speed. So in spite of the fact that speeds are
usually measured over a fixed distance, they are
always stated as if the time had been fixed and the
distance measured.

Children will easily obtain information about the
time it takes to travel a fixed distance. Figure
30 : 28 shows some typical information and a way
of dealing with it graphically. A reference graph
showing travel at some well-known speeds may be
useful for comparison with the children's
information (Figure 30 : 29), and will help to relate

Travelling to town

> *Distance from bus terminus to*
> *city centre 4 kilometres*
> *By bus it takes 15 minutes*
> *By car it takes 8 minutes*
> *By bicycle it takes 18 minutes*
> *On foot it takes 45 minutes*

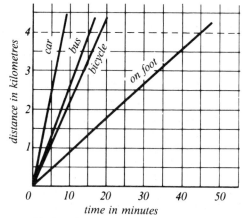

The bicycle goes 4 kilometres in 18 minutes
or 4 ÷ 18 km in 1 minute;
or 0·222222 km in 1 minute.
It goes 60 × 0·222222 km in 60 minutes.
This is 13 kilometres per hour.

Figure 30 : 28

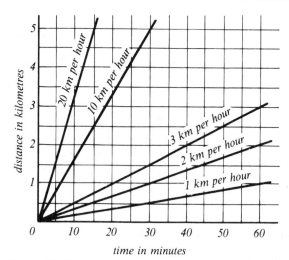

Figure 30 : 29

the steepness of slope of the graph to the speed of travel.

The calculations needed to translate the average speed of the bus or the cyclist into kilometres per hour are well within the range of children who use a calculator; these calculations can be checked graphically by extending Figure 30 : 28 to cover a time of one hour.

Rather than concentrating on calculation, however, it is more important that children should

Journey of the Ost-West Express

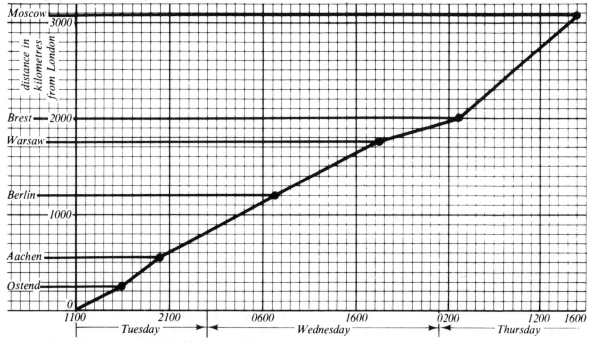

Figure 30 : 30

(a) Baby's actual mass

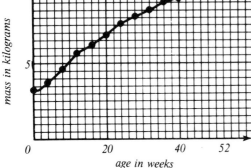

Figure 30 : 31

(b) Increase in baby's mass

understand how to measure speeds, and how to illustrate their measurements graphically. Conventionally, speed graphs are drawn with distances measured vertically and times horizontally, so that the steeper the graph, the faster the speed it represents. Of course, a variable speed will not produce a straight-line graph. Figure 30 : 30 illustrates a journey of the Ost–West Express, and shows the variation in speed over different parts of the line.

Measurements of speed at this stage need not be confined to the speeds of vehicles. The rates at which other things move and grow will give experience of measurement in different units. The rate of growth of a plant, and so the speed of its growing tip, is appropriately measured in centimetres per week or per month. The rate of growth of a baby is more easily measured in terms of mass, and so expressed in kilograms per week. Figure 30 : 31 shows two graphs of a baby's growth; the first shows the actual mass each week and the second the monthly increase in mass, and so approximates to the rate of growth.

The speeds of athletes and swimmers can be worked out from race-winning times, and the speeds of long-distance runners compared with those of sprinters, and with the children's own running speeds. The *Guinness Book of Records* is a useful resource for this work.

Children can also find the speeds of other natural phenomena. The speed of a stream can be found by timing a piece of wood as it is swept downstream. This may lead to a consideration of the rate of flow of the stream in litres per day. The speed of a breeze can be measured by using a home-made anemometer (Figure 30 : 32), and it is even possible to measure the speed of sound with some degree of

The pivot should be as frictionless as possible.

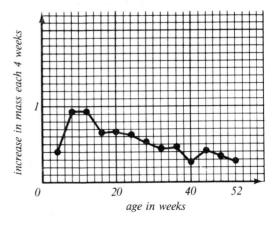

light plastic cups   one cup coloured to help counting

Figure 30 : 32

accuracy. The most primitive method is to measure with a stop-watch the time-lag between seeing the beating of a drum several hundred metres away and hearing the sound. Since sound takes 1 second to travel about 340 metres, this time-lag is measurable at distances of 200 metres, but the accuracy of the result is affected by the fact that stop-watches only register in intervals of one-fifth of a second. Variation in the observer's reaction time also considerably affects the results, so that the method is unreliable. A more sophisticated and accurate method uses an echo from a wall. Children may be able to beat a drum in steady rhythm, beat—echo—beat—echo—beat—echo, so that the time for a number of beats can be measured with the stop-watch and the error in measuring the time the sound takes to travel is reduced.

Such experiments as these link very closely with work in science, and in the field of measurement mathematics and science become nearly indistinguishable.

Time, distance and speed in the National Curriculum

There are few explicit references in the National Curriculum mathematics attainment targets to the work described in this chapter. However, work of this type will certainly strengthen children's understanding of measures, and their ability to estimate. A statement to which the work is related is:

- choose and use appropriate units and instruments; interpret numbers on a range of measuring instruments, with appropriate accuracy.

(AT2: Level 3)

However, this statement is at Level 3, and children should certainly continue to develop the range of measuring instruments which they can use throughout the primary years.

Other related statements are:

- make sensible estimates of a range of measures in relation to everyday objects.

(AT2: Level 4)

- measure and draw angles to the nearest degree.

(AT4: Level 5)

- understand the notion of scale in maps and drawings.

(AT2: Level 5)

- understand and use compound measures, e.g. speed, density.

(AT2: Level 7)

- recognise that measurement is approximate; and choose the degree of accuracy appropriate for a particular purpose.

(AT2: Level 7)

31 | Movement: Force and Momentum

Introduction

At about the age of 9 years children can use their growing command of number, their skill in measuring, and their understanding of movement to explore more fully the working of the multitude of machines which have been invented; machines intended to widen and increase our control over our material surroundings. In Chapter 13 we outlined the kinds of experience that could give children convincing evidence of *how* simple tools and mechanisms work: but the more profound question of *why* they work as they do, what instigates their action, had to be postponed to the stage when children can *infer* an unseen *force* from the kind of movement that they see taking place. Hitherto, they have known that a certain push, pull or lift will produce the movement and they have even taken the pull of the earth for granted. They have not been able, however, to identify the nature of the 'force', nor to measure it, nor to predict its effect. But now they have learned to measure speed and to use this knowledge to calculate distances and times of journeys. They know that a car, train, ship or plane will take them on a certain journey and they can record the distances, times and speeds involved. Yet they understand little of what makes these complicated constructions move along the ground or through water or air.

In this chapter we shall consider the forces that children can identify, measure, analyse and use in their own experience. Thus they can realise that mathematical relationships give us precise insights into the natural forces that operate in the universe, such as gravity and friction, as well as the forces of our human bodies, all of which we can modify and extend through the inventive activities of the human mind.

If children have had ample experience with constructional materials, such as Meccano, and with springs, screws, wooden strips and rods etc., they will have acquired a useful vocabulary and a framework of ideas about the effects of forces and mechanisms. From about 9 years of age children will begin to make deliberate experiments and record results in tabulations and diagrams which will enable them to draw conclusions and may even in simple cases lead to the formulation of laws connecting, for example, the time of swing of a pendulum and the length of its string. We shall now describe and relate together some of the ideas and structures which become evident in such experiences.

Forces

The idea of a force is a fundamental one which develops out of experience of feeling and exerting forces. There are two ways in which we may notice that a force is being exerted. If a person leans on the edge of a table, we do not notice how hard they are pressing until the table suddenly tips; the force the person is exerting causes a movement and we notice it. But the person knows that they are exerting a force before the table tips; they can feel it in their body, and they can feel the force increasing as they press harder. It is the combination of a bodily feeling of exerting a force by pushing, pulling or lifting, and the observation of the results of exerting force in causing something to start moving, stop moving, turn, twist, topple or break, that gives children their first idea of what a force is. It will be helpful to them to add the word 'force' to their vocabulary at this stage.

Some forces, however, are so much part of our environment that we do not easily notice them. The weight of the air around us causes a force on our bodies which we do not notice unless it changes suddenly, but the deep-sea diver is painfully aware of the results of changes of air-pressure if he is brought up too quickly from the depths. The most important of these often unnoticed forces is that of *gravity*, which pulls everything on the earth towards its centre. Young children do not easily think of gravity as a force for two reasons: firstly, all the forces which they themselves exert are *contact forces*; you have to hold an object or make contact with it to push, pull, lift or twist it, but gravity works *at a distance*; a ball does not have to be in contact with the earth for the earth to pull it. Secondly, gravity is always present; it can never be switched off, as can all the forces of pulling, pushing and twisting which we choose to exert. Because gravity is always present and we always have to take account of it, we do not feel its pull as anything out of the ordinary. Children, however, may notice the force of gravity on their bodies in various ways. Children can feel the muscular force needed to hold their arms at right angles to their bodies, and the way in which the arms flop down when the muscles relax. They can feel the force which their legs exert when they jump, and can also feel that they have to exert no force to come down again, for gravity pulls them down. They feel, too, the upward force which the floor exerts to stop them moving as they land.

Familiarity with the behaviour of magnets will also contribute to the idea that forces can act at a distance and can be unseen. Children will notice a pin jumping to meet a magnet, and will be able to feel two bar magnets pulling towards one another as they are held with opposite poles facing each other, and feel them pushing apart if similar poles are facing. This also helps the growth of the idea that a force may be either a push or a pull. As one child said: 'The magnet is half like gravity because it can hold things down . . . . The earth is really better because a magnet can't attract us; but the earth can attract dirt and wood and grass and even a big piece of iron.'[1]

So 'force' will become a familiar idea and children will know that force is present, either by feeling it or by observing its results, long before they begin to measure forces. The effect of a force is to change the speed or direction of motion of the object to which it is applied; that is, to change the *velocity* of the object. It is difficult, however, to make this idea precise until forces and velocities can be measured fairly accurately, and for some time children will only notice the qualitative effects of forces in starting, stopping and turning things, and in making them go faster or slower.[2]

The first step towards the measurement of forces is familiarity with the behaviour of springs and of elastic. A variety of springs of different shapes and sizes and of pieces of elastic of various types should be available for experiment, so that children can discover that all springs need a pulling force to stretch them and a pushing force to compress them, and that the greater the force children exert, the more they can stretch or compress the spring. If a very strong spring can be found and attached to a rail in the playground, children can use it for a tug-of-war (Figure 31 : 1).

length of spring

0 1 2 3 4
number of children pulling spring

Figure 31 : 1

Springs can be stretched by pulling on them in various ways, and children will already have used the method of hanging the spring up and tying something heavy to the lower end of it. It is important that they should come to realise the interchangeability of pulling the end of the spring and of hanging something heavy on the end, so that either

i) the *child* pulls the string and stretches the spring, or

ii) the *earth* pulls the object, and this pulls the string and stretches the spring.

The next step is the realisation that the earth pulls a 'heavier' object harder, and so stretches the spring more. A useful demonstration of this fact may be set up by using a number of identical elastic bands carrying increasing numbers of equal heavy beads (Figure 31 : 2). Children should also find out early that every spring and piece of elastic has an *elastic limit*, and that if it is stretched beyond this limit it will not return to its original length and so will become useless.

At this stage, a spring balance can be seen as a device which measures forces by measuring the stretching of a spring. The 2-kg marking on a spring balance means 'the force with which the earth pulls a 2-kg mass'. Children will use spring balances to measure the force they use to pull a truck, hold up a mass or have a tug-of-war.[3] They will be surprised

[1]Navarra, J. G. *The Development of Scientific Concepts in a Young Child* (Teachers' College, Columbia University, 1955), page 121.

[2]Forces may have other effects; they can change the shape of a rubber ball by denting, or stretch a spring by pulling.

[3]A spring balance for measuring large forces can be constructed by enclosing a strong spring in a cardboard tube with a window. A pointer is attached to the spring and the device graduated by hanging masses from it.

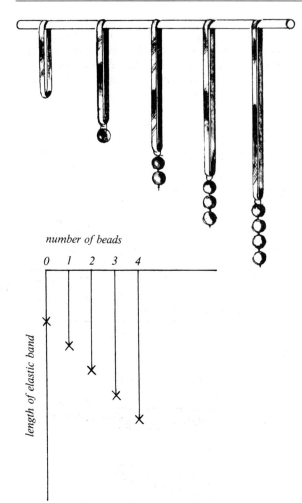

number of beads

0   1   2   3   4

length of elastic band

Figure 31 : 2

on comparing the reading of a spring balance when one child pulls against a fixed bar and when two children pull against each other. Kitchen and bathroom scales should be regarded as devices for measuring force by pushing springs inwards, instead of pulling them out. Children will not only weigh things on these scales, but will experiment with exerting a force to push them in. They will find that on the bathroom scales they can exert a force less than their own weight, by not letting the whole pull of the earth on the body be measured by the scales, but they cannot exert more force than their own weight unless there is something to push themselves against and thus push more strongly on the scales (Figure 31 : 3).

It is also possible to make a device for measuring force by the compression of springs, using upholstery springs and a board (Figure 31 : 4). Such experiences as these will help children to grasp the fact that when they weigh anything, they are measuring the pull of the earth on it.

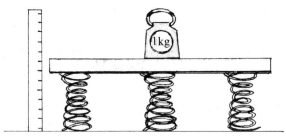

Figure 31 : 4

Figure 31 : 3

MOVING HEAVY MASSES AND DISCOVERING FRICTION

Children take wheels for granted, and cannot realise the enormous step forward in civilisation brought about by the invention of the wheel.[4] The force needed to move a load decreases greatly with the use of wheel, and therefore much heavier loads can be moved. A baby can be pushed in a pram instead of being carried everywhere. Enormous tree-trunks, blocks of stone and steel girders can be transported on wheeled vehicles when they could not be dragged. But because children are surrounded by wheels—on prams, trucks, bicycles, cars, wheelbarrows, rollerskates—they do not fully realise their advantages. Wheels form a fruitful topic for children to investigate further, and as they do so they will acquire many more ideas about force.

Children can use springs to find the force they need to exert to drag a heavy box along the floor. This experiment can be tried on a rough floor and a smooth floor, and the box mounted on a toboggan and on a set of pram wheels (Figure 31 : 5). Alternatively, a smaller scale experiment using a block of wood which can be mounted on Meccano

[4]See Chapter 13, page 152.

wheels or a rollerskate may be easier. This block can also be used to compare the force that is needed to move blocks of different masses, and on surfaces made of different materials. For instance, a piece of rubber tyre may also be used to cover the underside of the block (Figure 31 : 6).

Dragging a block against friction

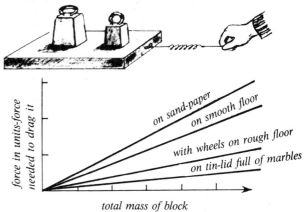

Figure 31 : 6

Dragging and rolling

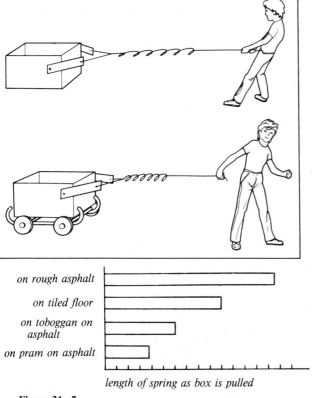

Figure 31 : 7

Children will thus become aware of the force of *friction*, which always tends to prevent motion from taking place. Friction is caused by the interlocking of tiny hillocks and valleys in the two surfaces which are in contact, so that they cannot easily slide over one another. Children can see and feel this if they rub two pieces of glasspaper together, and will feel that there is much less difficulty in *rolling* one piece of glasspaper over another (Figure 31 : 7). Hence wheels considerably reduce the effects of friction, and so reduce the force needed to move an object. There is also, of course, friction where the axle of the wheel rubs against its fixed support. Children may be able to measure the improvement obtained by oiling the contact (Figure 31 : 8), and they should examine a ball-bearing race.

Friction is extremely important in many aspects of everyday life, and is always present to some

	length of spring as box is pulled
on rough asphalt	
on tiled floor	
on toboggan on asphalt	
on pram on asphalt	

Figure 31 : 5

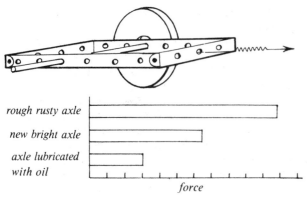

rough rusty axle	
new bright axle	
axle lubricated with oil	
	force

Figure 31 : 8

extent, opposing motion and enabling us to grip things, but also making it necessary to exert force to move a truck along a horizontal surface, to wheel a pram or to drive a car at a steady speed on the flat. Children may, however, examine what happens in the few cases when friction is very nearly absent. The case best known to them is that of sliding on a smooth ice slide. If children get up speed on the slide they find it is impossible to stop or to change direction. A ball rolling on a horizontal table presents a very similar picture; it goes on rolling in the same direction with only a very gradual decrease in its speed. A fairly frictionless trolley can be made by inverting a shallow tinlid over a collection of glass marbles. The marbles replace sliding friction by rolling as the trolley moves over the floor. It is possible to buy or make a 'balloon puck' (Figure 31 : 9). The escaping air from the balloon lifts the puck sufficiently high above a smooth polished table almost to eliminate friction. A more sophisticated version uses the thin cushion of gas between an evaporating block of solid carbon dioxide and the table to create a tiny space between the surfaces so that the puck can glide without

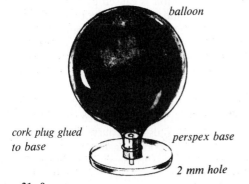

balloon

cork plug glued to base *perspex base*

2 mm hole

Figure 31 : 9

[5]A carbon-dioxide corkscrew can be used instead of the balloon.

friction. The hovercraft uses the same principle, and this can also be seen in operation in some lawnmowers.

From these experiences, children will learn that once a body is in motion on a horizontal surface, if no horizontal forces are acting on it, it will continue to move at the same speed in the same direction as it started. A force is only needed to stop it or to change its speed or its direction. *Force produces change in the speed or direction of motion;*[6] that is, *force produces change of velocity*; force is not needed to keep motion going steadily, except to balance slowing-down forces such as friction. This basic principle, without which it is not possible to understand most of modern physical science, was stated by Sir Isaac Newton in 1687 as, 'Every body continues in its state of rest or of uniform motion in a straight line unless it is compelled to change that state by forces impressed upon it.'[7] Although this is so fundamental a principle, it is difficult for a child, or an adult, to come to the correct conclusion, as friction is so ever-present that we tend to think that force is necessary to keep motion going steadily. A ball which has been thrown horizontally continues at a nearly constant horizontal speed, because there is very little horizontal force to retard it, while the vertical force of gravity makes it gather speed vertically. As Newton said: 'Projectiles persevere in their motions, so far as they are not retarded by the resistance of the air or impelled downwards by the force of gravity.' In ancient times, however, this phenomenon had puzzled men greatly. Aristotle's view has been described as: 'It is the air that plays the part of motor. Shaken by the projectile issuing from the sling of the catapult it flows after it and drives it along.'[8] Piaget found children who passed through a stage of giving the same explanation,[9] and we have ourselves asked an educated adult why, when one starts to slide on ice, one goes on at the same speed, and have obtained the spontaneous answer, 'the air rushes round to the back and pushes you'! What is clearly lacking is sufficient experience of the absence of frictional force to enable a correct conclusion to be drawn. If the idea

[6]This should be taken to include starting or stopping the motion.

[7]Newton's First Law of Motion.

[8]Reymond, A., *Histoire des Sciences Exactes et Naturelles dans l'Antiquité Gréco-Romaine* (Presses Universitaires, Paris. 2nd Ed., 1955).

[9]Piaget, J. *The Child's Conception of Physical Causality* (Kegan Paul, 1930), pages 18–24.

that a force *changes* motion is discovered at this stage, children will have time to absorb the idea into their patterns of thought before, later in their education, they measure these changes and make deductions from them.

MASS AND WEIGHT

It must be emphasised that the *weight* of an object is the force exerted on it by a gravitational field. All weighing machines measure force, either directly by the extension or compression of a spring, or indirectly by balancing the force of gravity on an object in one pan of a balance against the force of gravity on a standard object such as a kilogram in the other pan.

The force exerted by gravity on an object depends on the strength of the gravitational field exerting the force. This field varies slightly from place to place on the earth's surface, but varies much more dramatically as an object such as a spacecraft leaves the earth's gravitational field. Children are now aware, through television, of the phenomenon of *weightlessness* when a spacecraft is outside the influence of a gravitational field. Then things in the spacecraft float because they are not pulled by gravity in any direction. It is correctly said at this stage in a spacecraft's flight that objects are weightless, because weight is the force exerted by gravity.

On the moon, however, there is a gravitational force, which is exerted by the moon. Because the moon is much less massive than the earth, this gravitational force is only about $\frac{1}{6}$ of the gravitational force on the surface of the earth so objects *weigh* only about $\frac{1}{6}$ as much on the moon as they do on the earth. This change of weight would be observed by weighing the same object on a spring balance on the moon, because gravity exerts less force than on earth (Figure 31 : 10(*b*)), but if the object balanced with a kilogram on a balance on earth, it would continue to do so on the moon.

However, a spacecraft, or a human being, does not become less massive as it leaves the earth's gravitational field and become weightless. Another quantity, other than weight, needs to be measured to express this property of massiveness. It is that quantity which remains unchanged as the gravitational field, which produces weight, changes. This quantity is called *mass*. Until recently it has been very difficult for children to form a concept of mass, as they have no experience of mass remaining constant as weight changes by change of gravity. Television and films of space travel have now made it possible for children vicariously to have the experience of weightlessness and of change of weight on approach to the moon or the earth.

The result of this earlier lack of experience is a total confusion in everyday leanguage between mass and weight. We talk about a 'weight of 1 kilogram' when in fact *the kilogram is a unit of mass*, and it would be more correct to talk about a 'mass of 1 kilogram'. Spring balances do in fact *weigh*, because they measure the force of gravity acting on masses, but spring balances are usually calibrated in units of *mass*. When we hang a parcel on a spring balance and read 2 kg, the spring shows an extension which would be produced by the force of gravity acting on a mass of 2 kg. We *deduce* that the mass of the parcel is 2 kg. When we balance the parcel on a pair of scales against a 2-kg mass, the forces of gravity acting on the parcel and the 2-kg mass are equal. We *deduce* that the mass of the parcel is 2 kg.

Since weight is a force, we should expect it to be measured in units of force. The metric unit of force is the *newton*, whose name shows clearly that it depends on Newton's laws of motion. This unit for measuring force depends on the fact that force produces change in velocity. One newton is the force which would produce a change in velocity, or an acceleration, of 1 metre per second in each second if it were applied to a mass of 1 kilogram.

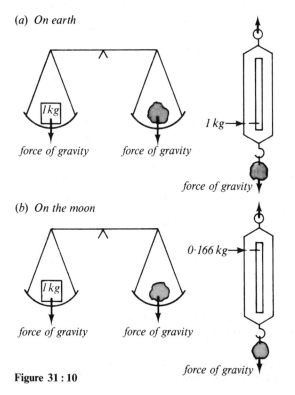

(*a*) On earth

force of gravity   force of gravity

1 kg→

force of gravity

(*b*) On the moon

0·166 kg→

force of gravity   force of gravity

force of gravity

Figure 31 : 10

Now gravity produces an acceleration of about 9·8 metres per second in each second at the earth's surface, and it would take a force of 9·8 newtons to produce an acceleration of 9·8 metres per second per second in a mass of 1 kilogram. Hence a force of 9·8 newtons is equivalent to the force of gravity on 1 kilogram, so that 1 newton is about one tenth of the weight of 1 kilogram.

It is possible to obtain both spring balances and bathroom scales graduated in newtons, and older children should be encouraged to become familiar with this unit of force.

LIFTING HEAVY MASSES

Mechanisms are used to move heavy masses from place to place horizontally with the minimum of effort, but we also need to move masses vertically. Putting a mass on a truck to move it entails lifting it vertically on to the truck. The ancients hauled enormous blocks of stone to a height when they built monuments such as Stonehenge. Nowadays cranes pick up great blocks of stone, rockets take off vertically from a standing start, and lorries struggle up mountain passes with heavy loads. Children already know one device which can help in lifting a heavy object: the lever, and they will want to explore further.

When a person holds a parcel, they have to exert sufficient force to balance the force of gravity which pulls the parcel downwards. It follows from Newton's First Law of Motion that since the parcel is at rest no resultant force can be acting on it, for a force would produce change of motion. But gravity always acts, so as the parcel does not move the force of gravity must be exactly balanced by an

Figure 31 : 12

equal and opposite force exerted by the person's arm. If this force is removed, that is if he lets go, the parcel starts to move and falls to the ground. When the parcel hits the floor and is at rest again, the force of gravity on the parcel is balanced by an upward force exerted by the floor (Figure 31 : 11).

Children can measure the force which the hand provides by holding the parcel up by a string containing a spring balance, or measure the upward force which the floor provides by replacing the floor by the bathroom scales. In either case they are using a spring to measure force. If they now want to lift the parcel vertically up to the first floor they can use a long rope, stand at the top of the stairs, and haul the parcel up the stairwell. The spring balance will tell them that once they have got the parcel moving slowly and steadily, they have to exert a force equal to its weight (Figure 31 : 12). Hauling vertically upwards is awkward, and it is much easier to use the bannisters to change the direction of the force. A little more force has to be used, as friction has to be overcome, but it is more convenient to pull downwards than upwards. Builders often use a single pulley, so that a worker at ground level can haul a bucket to the top of a building (see Chapter 13). Cranes usually use several pulleys. Children should set up simple arrangements of pulley blocks, and discover the effect of the number of strings supporting the load on the force which has to be used to balance it (Figure 31 : 13). They should then, if possible, see and use the pulley blocks which builders actually use.

When a person has to trundle a wheelbarrow up a step he or she uses a plank to change it into an inclined plane. This is not merely because it is less convenient to jolt a loaded barrow up a step than to wheel it up a slope. Children can test this statement by seeing how much less force is needed

upward force
provided by hand

upward
force provided by
floor

force of gravity

force of gravity

No resultant
force on
parcel:
no motion

Figure 31 : 11

Downward force on
parcel: parcel starts
to move downward

No resultant
force on parcel
no motion

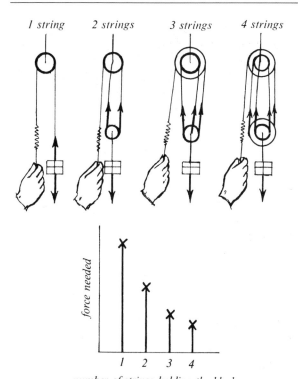

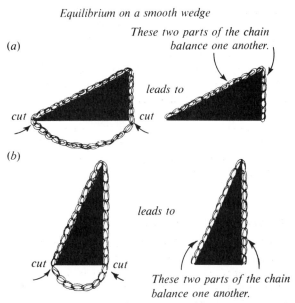

Figure 31 : 13

Equilibrium on a smooth wedge

(a) *These two parts of the chain balance one another.*

leads to

cut — cut

(b)

leads to

cut — cut

These two parts of the chain balance one another.

Figure 31 : 15

to hold a heavy block up on an inclined plane at various angles, compared with the force needed to hold it up vertically (Figure 31 : 14). Both the effect of friction and the effect of the inclined plane enter into this experiment, but the effect of friction can

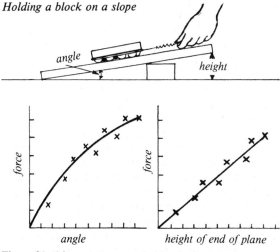

Holding a block on a slope

Figure 31 : 14

[10]Meccano wheels make suitable pulleys. In diagrams of pulley blocks, pulleys in the same sheaf are drawn as if their sizes were different in order to show the path of the string. These pulleys are usually equal in size.

be minimised by polishing the plane and the block or by using a wheeled trolley such as a rollerskate or a set of marbles covered by a tinlid. It may prove more satisfactory to graph the force needed to support the block against the height of the top of the plane, rather than against the angle of the plane. The advantage of the second graph can be seen by repeating the 'thought-experiment' of Stevinus of Bruges (1605), who imagined a loop of uniform flexible heavy chain which would sit in equilibrium on a smooth wedge (Figure 31 : 15). The symmetrically hanging lower part of the loop could clearly be cut away without disturbing the equilibrium.

It was the discovery that the *inclined plane* provided a means of lifting masses easily which first made it possible for people to build such edifices as Stonehenge and the Pyramids. Children will find many more examples of inclined planes, from the mountain path which zigzags up with a shallow gradient rather than taking the shortest route, to the aircraft descending gradually rather than steeply, as it then needs less retarding force to decrease its speed to one suited to landing.

FALLING BODIES

We have to provide a force to lift a heavy mass, but gravity provides a force which will make it fall, as long as we do not balance the force of gravity by an upward force. A parachutist does this by using air resistance to oppose the force of gravity, so that the descent is at a steady and comparatively low speed (Figure 31 : 16).

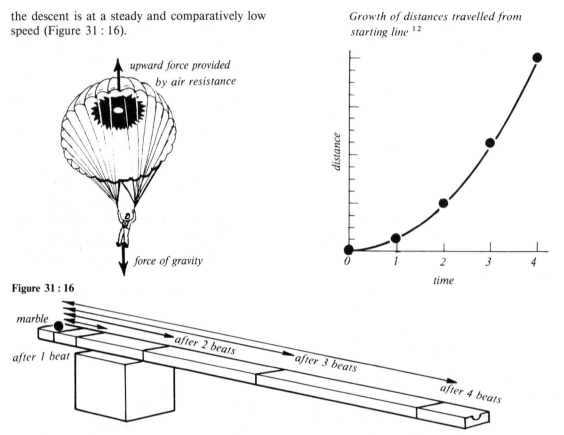

upward force provided by air resistance

force of gravity

Figure 31 : 16

Growth of distances travelled from starting line [12]

distance

time

marble

after 1 beat

after 2 beats

after 3 beats

after 4 beats

Figure 31 : 17

It was thought in ancient times, and children often expect, that a heavier body will fall faster than a lighter one. Galileo was the first to appreciate that if a heavy and a light object are let fall side by side, they will, apart from discrepancies caused by air resistance, continue to fall side by side. Galileo said:

'I who have made the test can assure you that a cannonball weighing one or two hundred pounds, or even more, will not reach the ground by as much as a span ahead of a musket-ball weighing only half a pound, provided both are dropped from a height of 200 cubits.'[11]

The force of gravity makes both bodies increase their speed, or accelerate, but they both accelerate at the same rate. Children will need to drop unequal masses together from a height repeatedly to satisfy themselves of the truth of this. They should also examine the effect of air resistance by dropping a mass attached to a parachute alongside an equal

mass which falls freely. This will help them to attribute slight differences in rate of fall between different objects to air resistance. If a scrap of paper the size of a coin is let fall alongside a coin, the coin will reach the ground first. Air resistance provides an upward force on both objects, but this upward force is more nearly equal to the force of gravity on the paper than that on the coin. But if the paper is placed on top of the coin, so that it is not subject to air resistance, it remains in contact with the coin throughout the fall. Some children may have seen a film of *Apollo 15* astronaut David Scott dropping a feather and a hammer together on the surface of the moon, where there is no air resistance to retard the feather.

The force of gravity produces the same acceleration in all bodies, irrespective of their masses.[13] Since the increase in velocity produced by gravity is so

[12]This graph should be compared with the graphs of Figure 22 : 14 showing the growth of squares.

[13]The value of this acceleration is an increase in velocity of just over 9·8 metres per second in each second, or 9·8 *metres per second per second*. The acceleration varies slightly from place to place on the earth's surface.

[11]Galileo Galilei. *Dialogues Concerning Two New Sciences* (1638). Translated H. Crew and A. de Salvio (Macmillan, 1918, Dover), page 62.

rapid, it is difficult for children to study it quantitatively, but the speeds produced can be reduced by allowing the body to slide down an inclined plane, rather than fall freely. It is now necessary to take precautions to reduce the effect of friction as well as air resistance. A marble rolling down a groove in a plank will produce fairly satisfactory results, and children will find that the distances travelled in increasing times obey the law of growth of squares; that is the graph of distance against time is a parabola (Figure 31 : 17). A metronome or pendulum will be found more convenient for timing than a stop-watch. When Galileo first performed this experiment, he did not have a sufficiently accurate clock, so he allowed water to flow from a large jar with a hole in the bottom into a container, stopping the hole with his finger when the marble had travelled a given distance; he then weighed the water.

The presence of the grooved board constrains the marble to roll down a shallow slope instead of falling vertically. Another type of constraint on a falling mass is produced by tying the mass to the end of a string, so that it must swing as a pendulum, moving through an arc of a circle, instead of falling vertically. Children will have found out earlier that a longer pendulum swings more slowly than a shorter one. Some of them will now be able to make this more precise. By the time that children are approaching the secondary stage, some can suggest various possible explanations of their observations, and design an experiment to check these possibilities. There are several factors which may affect the time of the swing of a pendulum: the mass, the length of the string, the angle through which the pendulum swings, and the vigour of the initial push. Some children will want to investigate why pendulums can be used as reliable timekeepers, and will see the point of varying each factor in turn while the others are kept constant, and will find that it is only the length of the pendulum which affects the time of swing, while the angle of swing, the vigour of the initial push and the mass have no effect.[14] The situation should remain as informal as possible, for if children do not yet think in this way, designing an experiment can only be an artificial exercise from which they do not make the expected deductions. Inhelder and Piaget's work suggests that most children reach this stage only in the secondary school, but it gives no indication of any role which experience of, and familiarity with, the situation involved may play in the development of a child's thinking.

When children have already discovered that unequal masses fall freely under gravity together, it will be no surprise to them to find that pendulums of unequal mass but the same length keep in step with one another. It is more surprising that the angle of swing (provided that it is reasonably small) does not affect the period of swing. It is this property, however, that makes the pendulum useful as a timekeeping device; the same pendulum always takes the same period of time for a swing, even though air resistance makes its swings become shorter and shorter in length (*see page 158*).

When children graph the relation between the period of swing and the length of a pendulum, they can arrange the graph in several ways, each of which gives the appearance of a general trend, but they do not always find it easy to see a numerical

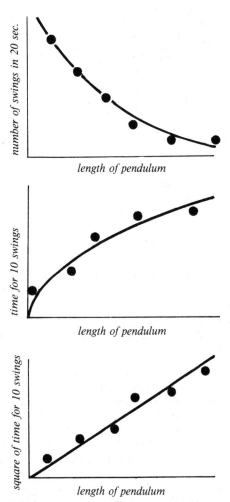

Graphs on the behaviour of a simple pendulum

Figure 31 : 18

[14]Inhelder, B. and Piaget, J. *The Growth of Logical Thinking from Childhood to Adolescence* (Routledge & Kegan Paul, 1958), Chapter 4.

relationship between length and time, even if they have reached the stage of searching for one. Figure 31 : 18 shows various ways of arranging the graph. One of the most fruitful methods is to set up a short pendulum (about 20 cm), whose period is taken as the unit of time, and to try to construct pendulums whose period is twice, three times, and so on, the period of the original pendulum.

A stairwell will soon be needed to accommodate a long enough pendulum, for the law of growth is once again that of the growth of squares. The length of a pendulum is proportional to the square of its period of swing.

ROTATION AND BALANCE

Civilization makes use of forces not only for lifting and carrying, but also for turning: we make a great deal of use of simple turning mechanisms when we turn on taps, open doors, lift the legs of a wheelbarrow from the ground, or ride a bicycle. The use of forces for turning in these situations has been explored in Chapter 13 and by the end of the primary stage many children have discovered the law governing the turning behaviour of forces.

In particular the balance bar (Figure 31 : 19) has become a familiar piece of apparatus. The bar balances if no rings are hung from it. If rings are hung from one side, the force of gravity acting on those rings causes the bar to rotate about the pivot at the centre (*see Chapter 13*). This turning effect can be counteracted by hanging rings on the other side, and children very soon discover that in order to balance the turning effects of the rings on either side of the pivot, the forces on the two sides of the balance need not be equal, but the *product* of the force exerted by gravity and the distance from the pivot must be the same on each side (Figure 31 : 20). Children should realise that they are balancing the *turning effects* of forces; instead of using the force of gravity on different masses the base of the balance bar can be screwed down to a table and the forces exerted upwards, or it can be attached to a wall so that it can be pulled on by

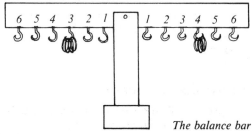

Figure 31 : 19

The balance bar

Using the balance bar

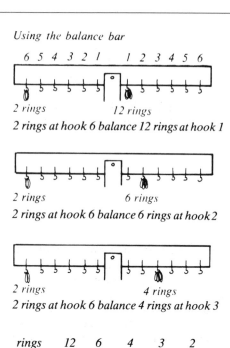

2 rings at hook 6 balance 12 rings at hook 1

2 rings at hook 6 balance 6 rings at hook 2

2 rings at hook 6 balance 4 rings at hook 3

rings	12	6	4	3	2
hook	1	2	3	4	6

Figure 31 : 20

horizontal forces (Figure 31 : 21). Children will very soon need a word for the quantity which measures the turning effect of the force: the *moment of a force about a point* is a measure of the force multiplied by the distance between the line of action of the force and the point. The child in Figure 31 : 21 is exerting a turning moment of 48 units of moment[15] about the pivot with each hand. Using this apparatus, children will find that they need to apply more force if it is not applied at right angles to the bar, and may devise experiments using bent levers (Figure 31 : 22). They will find that when they measure the distance of the line of

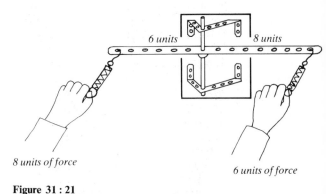

Figure 31 : 21

[15]Moments are measured in units which are a compound of units of force and of length.

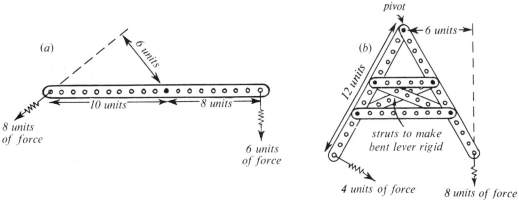

Figure 31 : 22

action of a force from the pivot in order to find its moment about the pivot, they must measure the *perpendicular distance*. In Figure 31 : 22(*a*) the moment of the force on the left of the pivot is 8 × 6 units of moment, not 8 × 10 units of moment.

Children will automatically balance the moments of their own weights about the pivot when they use a seesaw, and they will now be able to find many more examples of occasions when the moments of forces must be balanced. We often make use of the principle of moments by using a small force a long way from the pivot to provide a turning moment rather than a large force near the pivot (Figure 31 : 23).

Children will now be able to use their knowledge of turning moments to make a simple steelyard (Figure 31 : 24). They will also realise the importance, in the simple weighing-balance, of the equality of length of the arms, and will understand that when they weigh on a simple balance, they are balancing the turning moments of the forces of gravity on the two sides of the balance.

Model of a ship's derrick; where is the best place put the tie rope?

A tower crane needs a counterweight: why does the crane not overbalance when it is unloaded?

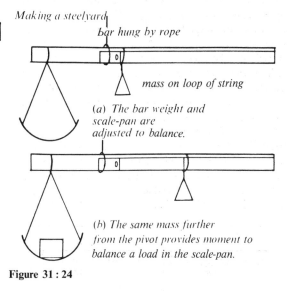

Making a steelyard

(a) The bar weight and scale-pan are adjusted to balance.

(b) The same mass further from the pivot provides moment to balance a load in the scale-pan.

Figure 31 : 24

Measuring the moment exerted by a gate-spring.

Using a claw hammer to get a rusty nail out.

Figure 31 : 23

GEAR WHEELS AND SCREWS

The simplest child's tricycle has its pedals directly attached to the front wheels; so did some penny-farthing bicycles. The enormous size of the

(a) *One revolution of the larger wheel produces two revolutions of the smaller wheel. Both wheels turn in the same direction.*

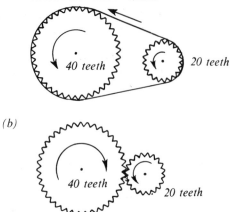

(b)

The wheels turn in opposite directions.

Figure 31 : 25

front wheel enabled the bicycle to move very much further with each revolution of the pedals than did the rider's feet. Children will see that the modern bicycle produces the same effect by the use of chain wheels. They will want to build models and find the relation between the number of teeth in each chain wheel and the rate at which it turns. Similar relations will be found when gear wheels intermesh directly, but the difference in direction of rotation between a chain drive and a drive transmitted by gears will be noticed (Figure 31 : 25). Children may

even reach the stage of building, with Meccano gear wheels, a drive which makes one shaft turn twelve times as fast as another, which could be used to turn the hour hand and minute hand of a clock. For some experiments with gear wheels, corrugated cardboard can be wrapped round the edge of a tin. This shows very well how gears mesh together, but is not of course strong enough to carry a drive.[16]

The key to understanding the relationships between the rates of turning of two gears is the knowledge that a tooth of one wheel always fits an indentation of the other. Figure 31 : 26 illustrates what happens when a gear wheel with 24 teeth meshes with one with 16 teeth.

The purpose of gear wheels and chain wheels is to change the speed of a drive. The screw is another device which alters a drive. It changes a rotational drive, which comes from turning the screw, into a force in the direction of the shaft. A hand turning a screwdriver produces a force enabling the screw to penetrate wood; the rotation of the propeller shaft of a ship or aircraft provides the force which drives the vessel forward. Children will find that the thread of a screw is wrapped continuously round it, and will be able to relate a screw to an inclined plane by wrapping a triangular piece of paper round a pencil (Figure 31 : 27(a)). See Chapter 13. A screw or a bolt is basically a device for lifting a nut up an inclined plane, and children will already know that this can be done more easily when the slope of the plane is small; that is, when the pitch of the screw is small in relation to its circumference. In many cases, such as that of the woodscrew, the nut, which

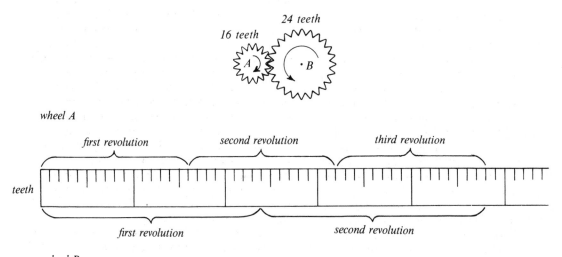

When 48 teeth have engaged, wheel A has made 3 revolutions and wheel B has made 2 revolutions.

Figure 31 : 26

[16]It also leads to work on the relation between the circumference and diameter of a circle, when children try to make a gear wheel to carry a given number of teeth (*see page 454*).

The screw and the inclined plane

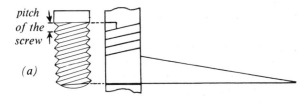

(a) pitch of the screw

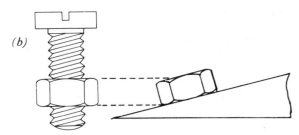

(b)

Figure 31 : 27

is in fact the piece of wood, is fixed. Then the effect of turning the screw is not to lift the nut up the screw, but to drive the screw down into the nut with a forward force which will overcome very considerable resistance from the wood. Similarly, a ship's or aircraft's propeller screws it forward through the water or air.

ACTION AND REACTION

Another basic mechanical principle of which children become aware at this stage, and which they deliberately use, is the one Newton stated as: 'To every action there is always opposed an equal reaction: or the mutal actions of two bodies upon each other are always equal and directed to contrary parts' (in opposite directions).[17] Children push themselves forward away from the side of the swimming pool by trying to push the wall back away from themselves. Their arm movements in swimming force them forward as they pull the water back past themselves. When they run, they obtain the force necessary to push them forward by pushing back against the ground. When they kick a ball, so providing a forward force on it, the ball reacts by pushing the foot back. When they catch a ball, they can feel the ball exerting a force on the hands, and the hands exert an equal and opposite force on the ball which stops it moving. They may

[17]Newton's Third Law of Motion.

try to measure this force by dropping the ball on the bathroom scales, noticing the slight flick of increased force on the scales, and they will see the same principle in operation in reverse on television when they see a rocket lifting itself upward by the downward thrust of the exploding gases from its tail. They may also feel the backward 'kick' of an air-rifle at the fair as the release of air-pressure drives the pellet forward and the rifle back into the shoulder.

FURTHER EXAMPLES

We now enumerate the mechanical principles which we have been using, and apply them to two further types of motion. The principles are:

i) forces produce *change* in the speed or direction of motion of the bodies on which they act; that is, forces produce change of velocity,

ii) forces are either (*a*) *contact forces* such as pushes or pulls, or (*b*) forces which *act at a distance*, i.e. gravity and magnetic forces,

iii) if object *A* exerts a force on object *B*, then object *B* exerts an equal and opposite force on object *A*.

The application of these principles to things which are moving in circles may now be considered. When a conker is whirled round on the end of a piece of string, when a car rounds a bend, or when we are flung violently about by those fairground machines which make use of circular motion, then clearly considerable forces come into play. In order to see how these forces act, we consider first what happens when a movement suddenly stops being circular. A person bowling a cricket ball uses a straight arm to make the ball travel in an arc of a circle. When the bowler releases the ball, and so takes away the force provided by fingers, the ball continues to travel in the direction in which it was moving when it was released. It is then pulled out of this path by the force of gravity. The discus-thrower or the hammer-thrower rotates the missile in a circle inclined at an angle to the horizontal, until it is released to go forward in the direction in which it was travelling when released.

This is expected, for when the force provided by the thrower is removed the only force on the hammer is that of gravity, which pulls it vertically, and does not change the direction of the horizontal motion (Figure 31 : 28). The force which keeps the throwing-hammer moving in a circle before it is

Throwing the hammer

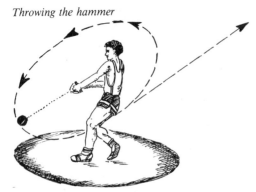

Figure 31 : 28

A sixteenth-century picture of the path of a cannon-ball

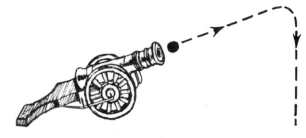

Figure 31 : 29

released is the inward force towards the centre of the circle provided by the wire handle of the hammer. The conker is kept whirling on the end of a string by the force in the string. The moon is kept in its orbit round the earth by the gravitational force of the earth. If this gravitational force were suddenly removed, the moon would not fly directly away from the earth, but would continue in a straight line in the direction in which it was moving at that instant, as does the hammer when the thrower releases it. The rocket which escapes from the earth's gravitational pull behaves in the same way. A train is forced to round a bend by the pressure of the rails which exert an inward force. The passenger who is only loosely attached inside a car rounding a bend sharply tries to go onwards in a straight line until coming into contact with, and being forced into circular motion by, the side of the car which is moving in a circle. An object can only move in a circle *if there is an inward force acting on it which pulls it towards the centre of the circle*, out of the straight-line path which it tries to follow.

The force needed to make an object move in a circle increases as the speed of the motion increases. The motion of a fairground machine which is tame at low speeds becomes much less so as the speed increases and the passenger is subjected to increasing forces from the side of the car to make him move in a circle. When wet clothes are put in a spin-drier, the friction between cloth and water drops is insufficient to provide the force necessary to make the water drops turn in a circle at high speed. So the water moves onwards and escapes from the circular motion through the holes in the basket.

Another type of curved motion which children may want to investigate is that produced by throwing a ball in the air at an angle to the vertical. The curve formed by this path is difficult for children to follow, as the ball moves so quickly, and

the shape of the curve was misunderstood (Figure 31 : 29) until scientific experiment began in the seventeeth century. There are, however, several ways in which the path can be traced. If a hosepipe is held so that a jet of water runs along a wall, the shape of the wet patch shows the shape of the path of the drops of water (Figure 31 : 30). This path can be seen to resemble the parabola or curve of squares.

The shape of a jet of water

Figure 31 : 30

Alternatively the whole process can be slowed down by making it take place on an inclined plane, in the same way that free fall under gravity was slowed down on an inclined plane. If a heavy ball-bearing is rolled obliquely on an inclined plane covered with carbon paper, it will mark out its track on a piece of paper under the carbon; or an inked ball can be used. The shape of the path is that of a parabola (Figure 31 : 31(*a*)).

A further demonstration of this fact is obtained by drawing a parabola on the wall. After a little practice, children will be able to throw a small ball or a rubber gently enough for its path to follow that of the parabola which they have drawn. It is very easy to see why this path is a parabola, for once the

Figure 31 : 31   *(a) Rolling a marble on carbon-paper*   *(b) Throwing a ball alongside a parabola*

The paths of two balls

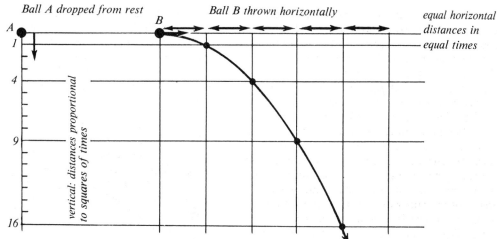

Figure 31 : 32

ball leaves the hand the only force on it (ignoring air resistance) is that of gravity, which pulls it vertically down. There is no horizontal force on the ball, so it continues to travel horizontally at the constant speed with which it left the hand.

Flicking pennies horizontally and from rest

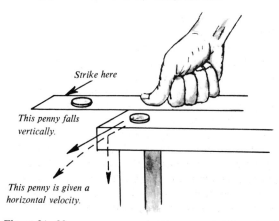

Figure 31 : 33

Vertically, the force of gravity causes the distance the ball has travelled to increase in proportion to the square of the time taken. Figure 31 : 32 shows what happens when two balls are let fall at the same instant, one with no velocity, so that it falls vertically, and the other thrown with a horizontal velocity. Observation of this phenomenon is difficult, but children can see that the two balls keep at the same vertical level as they fall, by flicking two pennies together from the table with an old ruler (Figure 31 : 33).

MOMENTUM

We have been considering the movements of various bodies when influenced by gravity, the force which causes objects to accelerate in a vertical direction downwards. Children should now be well aware that any object, whatever its mass, will experience this acceleration if it is free to move. We now try to compare the movements of bodies of different masses and different velocities. Children can realise that a very heavy lorry, even though moving slowly, could cause considerable damage to anything struck by it. They will also know that a small object such as a bullet can, if given a high speed, penetrate deeply and cause serious harm to anything it hits. In fact it is the *product* of mass and velocity which determines whether two moving objects would make the same impact on a stationary obstacle. This quantity is called *momentum* and is of great importance in studying the effects of a collision between vehicles.

It is not easy to devise experiments to show the difference in momentum of two moving bodies, because collision is likely to cause damage. However, differences in mass and speed can be shown in objects allowed to roll down slopes and the speeds can be kept at safe levels. A small toy truck could be allowed to roll down an inclined board fixed on a horizontal bench. A graduated line of steepest slope is marked on the incline as a guide for the path of the truck and to enable starts to be made by the truck at different levels. At the foot of the incline stands a toy trolley placed so that the descending truck will strike it.

When the truck is released at point A (Figure 31 : 34), gravity causes it to gather speed as it rolls and it will hit the stationary trolley, causing it to move in a continuation of the path of the truck. When it comes to rest its position should be marked. The same procedure can be followed from points B and C; the truck will then have further to fall and so will have gathered more speed before striking the trolley, which is now at its original position at the foot of the incline. The distances which the trolley has moved after each impact will show that the greater the speed of the truck before impact the greater the effect on the trolley.

Now we ask whether a change in the *mass* of the truck would also affect the trolley. A fairly heavy

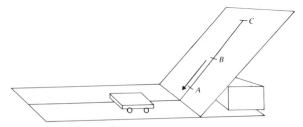

Figure 31 : 34

mass is placed on the truck and the whole procedure is repeated, showing the longer distances travelled by the trolley when struck by the larger mass. Children should now realise that momentum, the product of mass and velocity, is a useful indication of the way a moving object will behave when it collides with something.

So far no *measuring* of momentum has been suggested. Children may themselves wish to experiment with toy trains, measuring their speed in a steady run, using the methods mentioned in Chapter 20. It is easy to find the mass of toy clockwork trains. A gentle series of collisions may then be arranged and the results forecast from the known momentum of each vehicle. Units of momentum are necessarily expressed in the standard units of mass and velocity.

The experiences which we have described in this chapter should be seen as paving the way for more precise mathematical study of the relationship between force and its effect in causing motion. Mathematical relationships are more easily accepted later if they are built on a structure of qualitative experience which is absorbed into children's thinking and which they must take into account when building their framework of scientific concepts.

This chapter forms one of the important links between mathematics and science, although it is often studied as part of the science programme.

32 | CALCULATIONS USING FRACTIONS

INFORMAL IDEAS OF FRACTIONS

In the early years in school, children will have handled many concrete examples of fractions of shapes, numbers lengths, masses, volumes and times. The following examples show some ways in which the language of fractions can be used alongside the language of multiplication and division to describe these situations.

i) Two 500 millilitre jugs fill a litre jug. The smaller jug holds *half* a litre.

ii) In 15 minutes the minute hand of a clock makes a *quarter* of a turn. Four quarter-turns make a complete turn. Four times 15 minutes is an hour; 15 minutes is a *quarter* of an hour.

iii) A bar of chocolate can be broken into eight equal pieces. Each piece is *one eighth* of the bar.

iv) Five 200-gram masses balance a kilogram. A 200-gram mass in *one fifth* of a kilogram.

v) Using Cuisenaire rods, ten white rods are equivalent to an orange rod. The white rod is *one tenth* of the length of the orange rod.

When children fold or cut a square of paper into four equal parts, each part is a quarter of the square. They may become interested in exploring the number of different ways in which they can make quarters of a square. Figure 32 : 1 shows some possibilities, and the variety of these possibilities may be contrasted with the single simple method of dividing a circle into quarters.

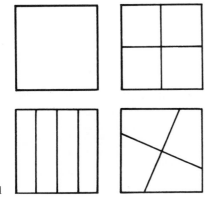

Figure 32 : 1

If fractional language is used consistently in such situations as these, and if children are encouraged to discuss and record their work, a number of ideas about fractions take shape informally in their minds.

The first of these ideas is that a whole or unit has been divided into a number of *equal* parts. This may need emphasising, as children sometimes hear outside school the word 'half' being used merely for a part of a whole, rather than for one of two equal parts. Children also become aware that, in concrete terms, the unit may be anything which can be divided up: a shape, a length, a mass, a time, or a set of things; so they use fractions naturally in some situations and not in others. They cannot talk about a quarter of a child in the same way that they can talk about a quarter of a cake, although they can see the relationship between a set of two children and a set of eight children, and say that there are a quarter as many children in the first set.

These informal experiences make children familiar with

1 half
1 third
1 quarter
1 fifth
1 eighth
and 1 tenth.

They also come across the expression 'three quarters of an hour', and notice that two quarter-hours make half an hour. When throwing dice, they notice that three faces of a die have even numbers on them, so that the chance of throwing an even number is 3 sixths, and this is the same as 1 half.

Until fairly late in the primary school, however, the emphasis in work with fractions should be on the decimal system of recording fractions which is found in work with money and with the metric system, and which is used in calculators. Thus, children come to see decimal fractions as an extended use of the place-value system which deals with parts of a unit. In this chapter, we discuss work with those fractions which are not easily expressed in decimal notation, and find ways in which advantage can be taken of the numerator/denominator way of writing a fraction.

Young children will write in the same way as they speak

'3 quarters'
or '5 sixths'.
Later, as they realise that 3 quarters is not only 3
quarters of 1 unit, but also 3 units divided by 4
(*see page 334*), they learn to use division notation,
and to write

$$3 \text{ quarters} = 3 \div 4 = \tfrac{3}{4} = 3/4$$

Of these notations, $3 \div 4$ is required on the
calculator, which displays $0 \cdot 75$ on entry of the
keystrokes

$$\boxed{3}\ \boxed{\div}\ \boxed{4}\ \boxed{=}$$

A full understanding of the fact that

3 quarters = 7 tenths 5 hundredths
or $\tfrac{3}{4} = 0 \cdot 75$

depends on an understanding of decimal division,
but children meet practical examples of this
equivalence at an early stage, when they find that

$$\tfrac{3}{4} \text{ of } £1 = 75 \text{ pence}$$
and $\tfrac{3}{4}$ of 1 metre = 75 centimetres

Another example of equivalence occurs when
children fold a square into quarters. They should be
encouraged to look at and use not just one quarter
of the square, but to fit together two of the quarters
or three of the quarters, and to notice that when
one quarter of the square has been cut out, three
quarters are left. They will write

2 quarters = 1 half
or $\tfrac{2}{4} = \tfrac{1}{2}$,

and $\qquad 1 - \tfrac{1}{4} = \tfrac{3}{4}$

Thus the idea grows that the same part of a unit
can be described in many different ways. Children
need much experience of equivalence in different
situations and with fractions of varied units if they
are to grasp this idea. Shape provides one
convenient illustration, for circles, squares and
rectangles can easily be divided into halves, quarters
and eighths. Figure 32 : 2 shows some illustrations
of equivalences among fractions of different unit
shapes which are divided into halves, quarters and
eighths. A more sophisticated example than the
others shows that the quarters made by the
diagonals of the rectangle are not the same shape,
although each quarter is made up of two eighths
which are the same shape. Children may at first
refuse to accept that the parts are quarters, since
they cannot be fitted over one another without
further cutting up. In fact, the quarters which are
being formed in this and other examples are
quarters of the *area* of the rectangle. When fractions
of plane shapes are made, it is this area property
which is used.

FRACTIONS OF NUMBERS

A fraction is a part of some divisible unit; in many
examples the unit is a quantity such as a metre, or
a shape such as a rectangle whose area can be
divided into parts. That is, the unit which is
subdivided is a measurable quantity to which a
number can be attached, such as a number of units

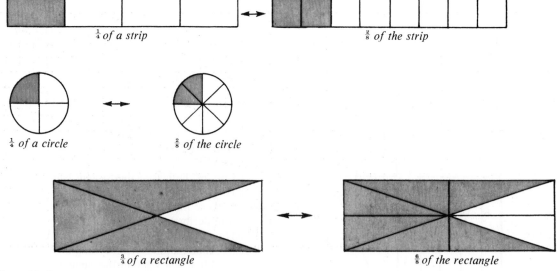

$\tfrac{1}{4}$ *of a strip* $\tfrac{2}{8}$ *of the strip*

$\tfrac{1}{4}$ *of a circle* $\tfrac{2}{8}$ *of the circle*

$\tfrac{3}{4}$ *of a rectangle* $\tfrac{6}{8}$ *of the rectangle*

Figure 32 : 2

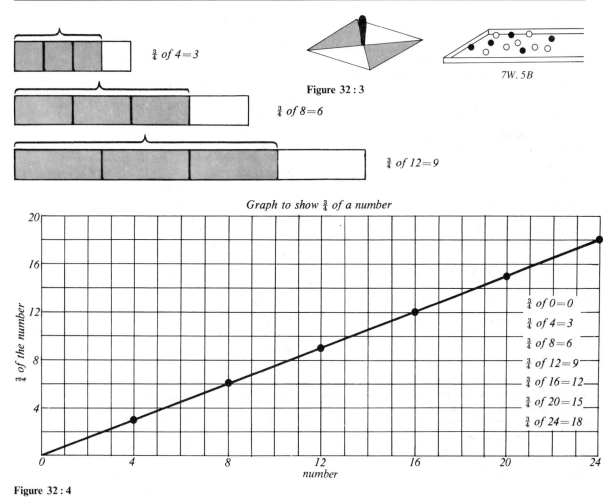

$\frac{3}{4}$ of $4=3$

Figure 32 : 3

$\frac{3}{4}$ of $8=6$

$\frac{3}{4}$ of $12=9$

7W. 5B

Graph to show $\frac{3}{4}$ of a number

$\frac{3}{4}$ of $0=0$
$\frac{3}{4}$ of $4=3$
$\frac{3}{4}$ of $8=6$
$\frac{3}{4}$ of $12=9$
$\frac{3}{4}$ of $16=12$
$\frac{3}{4}$ of $20=15$
$\frac{3}{4}$ of $24=18$

number

Figure 32 : 4

Graph to show fractions of numbers

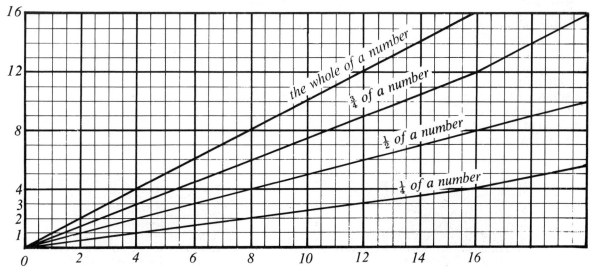

the whole of a number

$\frac{3}{4}$ of a number

$\frac{1}{2}$ of a number

$\frac{1}{4}$ of a number

Figure 32 : 5

of area. The number may be attached to this divisible unit in various ways; we can talk about $\frac{1}{4}$ of *one* metre or $\frac{1}{4}$ of 100 centimetres. Thus $\frac{1}{4}$ of 100 begins to be meaningful. A set of things can also have a number attached to it, the *number of things in the set*. Children will say that a set of 4 bricks contains *half as many* as a set of 8 bricks. Hence $\frac{1}{2}$ of 8 is equal to 4. Similarly, the set of 8 children in the class wearing brown shoes contains a *quarter as many* as the set of 32 children in the class; $\frac{1}{4}$ of 32 is equal to 8. By generalisation from many such situations, a fraction of a *number* takes on meaning for children, so that they will understand and be able to find $\frac{1}{2}$ of 8 and $\frac{1}{4}$ of 32. When they spin a 4-sided spinner, they will expect that it will come down resting on a particular side about $\frac{1}{4}$ of the times. Out of 32 spins, $\frac{1}{4}$ of 32, or 8, are expected to rest on one face (Figure 32 : 3). Similarly, out of a bag of 7 white beads and 5 black beads from which large numbers of draws are made, $\frac{7}{12}$ are expected to give a white bead. Fractions of numbers can also be explored with structural apparatus, and graphs can be drawn, as in Figure 32 : 4.

This graph makes interpolation possible, and children will find that $\frac{3}{4}$ of 10 = $7\frac{1}{2}$. This can be verified in terms of length by folding a piece of paper 10 cm long, or by folding up the first 10 cm of a tape-measure.

The similarity between this graph and the multiplication graphs of Chapter 17 is easily seen. Figure 32 : 5 shows several such graphs drawn on the same axes, and forms a useful preliminary to the linking of 'a fraction of' with multiplication.

ADDITION AND SUBTRACTION OF FRACTIONS

We now turn to other discoveries which children make in their exploration of fractions. From their concrete experiences children not only discover equivalences between fractions, but also find ways in which fractions of quantities can be put together, compared and taken apart, which will lead them to addition and subtraction, multiplication and division of fractional numbers.

The exploration of shapes also gives many instances of the ways in which parts of a unit area combine to make the unit, or to make other fractions of the unit. The simple folding of a unit square into quarters shown in Figure 32 : 6 illustrates not only the equivalence $\frac{1}{2} = \frac{2}{4}$, but also a great variety of other facts, such as the following, which children can find for themselves.

$$\frac{1}{2} + \frac{1}{2} = 1 \qquad 1 - \frac{1}{2} = \frac{1}{2}$$
$$\frac{1}{4} + \frac{3}{4} = 1 \qquad 1 - \frac{3}{4} = \frac{1}{4} \qquad 1 - \frac{1}{4} = \frac{3}{4}$$
$$\frac{1}{4} + \frac{1}{2} = \frac{3}{4} \qquad \frac{3}{4} - \frac{1}{2} = \frac{1}{4} \qquad \frac{3}{4} - \frac{1}{4} = \frac{1}{2}$$
$$\frac{1}{4} + \frac{1}{4} = \frac{1}{2} \qquad \frac{1}{2} - \frac{1}{4} = \frac{1}{4}$$

$$\frac{1}{4} + \frac{1}{4} = 2 \times \frac{1}{4} = \frac{1}{2} \qquad \frac{1}{2} \div 2 = \frac{1}{4}$$
$$\frac{1}{4} + \frac{1}{4} + \frac{1}{4} = 3 \times \frac{1}{4} = \frac{3}{4} \qquad \frac{3}{4} \div 3 = \frac{1}{4}$$
$$\frac{1}{4} + \frac{1}{4} + \frac{1}{4} + \frac{1}{4} = 4 \times \frac{1}{4} = 1 \qquad \frac{1}{2} \text{ of } \frac{1}{2} = \frac{1}{4}$$
$$\frac{1}{3} \text{ of } \frac{3}{4} = \frac{1}{4}$$

All these combinations are illustrated whenever a piece of paper is folded into quarters, and children may be encouraged to see how many mathematical facts they can find in a simple and familiar situation such as this.

Among the most interesting statements which are produced in this way are those, such as $\frac{3}{4} + \frac{1}{8} = \frac{7}{8}$, where the denominators of the fractions are not the same; that is, where the unit has not been divided into the same number of parts each time. The statement $\frac{3}{4} + \frac{1}{8} = \frac{7}{8}$ is only another way of putting $\frac{6}{8} + \frac{1}{8} = \frac{7}{8}$ (Figure 32 : 7), and children soon realise that in order to see the relationship between $\frac{3}{4}$ and $\frac{1}{8}$ they must think of $\frac{3}{4}$ as $\frac{6}{8}$; that is, they must replace $\frac{3}{4}$ by an equivalent fraction which they can handle more easily in a given situation. The fractions $\frac{3}{4}$ and $\frac{1}{8}$ cannot immediately be added, as they are measured in terms of different sub-unit; $\frac{3}{4}$ must be replaced by $\frac{6}{8}$. Now both fractions are measured in eighths, and so they can be added. Even the very simple $1 - \frac{1}{3}$ involves thinking of 1 as $\frac{3}{3}$, so that it can be compared with $\frac{1}{3}$.

If children are encouraged to make their own problems in addition and subtraction, and to solve them practically, they will find that they are using two principles.

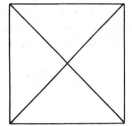

Figure 32 : 6

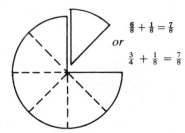

$$\frac{6}{8} + \frac{1}{8} = \frac{7}{8}$$
or
$$\frac{3}{4} + \frac{1}{8} = \frac{7}{8}$$

Figure 32 : 7

i) Only fractions which are measured in terms of the same sub-unit can be added or subtracted immediately; in fact children very rarely need to use any form of apparatus for $\frac{2}{6}+\frac{3}{6}$ or for $\frac{7}{8}-\frac{2}{8}$.

ii) If the fractions which they wish to add or subtract are not measured in terms of the same sub-unit, children can replace them by equivalent fractions which are measured in the same sub-unit. Then the writing of

$$\frac{3}{4}+\frac{1}{8}=\frac{6}{8}+\frac{1}{8} \quad \text{or} \quad 1-\frac{2}{5}=\frac{5}{5}-\frac{2}{5}$$
$$=\frac{7}{8} \qquad\qquad =\frac{3}{5}$$

is a record of an action which the child has performed either physically or mentally.

Finding $\frac{1}{6}+\frac{1}{4}$ is more difficult than $\frac{1}{8}+\frac{1}{4}$, because one fraction is not an immediate subdivision of the other. Here, both quarters and sixths must be replaced by twelfths, obtaining

$$\frac{1}{6}+\frac{1}{4}=\frac{2}{12}+\frac{3}{12}$$
$$=\frac{5}{12}$$

Problems of this type very rarely occur in practical situations, and children will not wish to tackle them until they can generalise enough to ask, 'Can *any* two fractions be added together?' By then they will understand equivalence sufficiently to search for suitable equivalent fractions by which to replace $\frac{1}{6}$ and $\frac{1}{4}$, until they find a pair which can be added because they are measured in the same sub-unit.

SYSTEMATISATION OF THE IDEA OF EQUIVALENCE

The notion that there is more than one way of writing the same number, that $\frac{1}{2}$, $\frac{2}{4}$, $\frac{5}{10}$, and so on, all represent the same fraction of a unit, is an idea which is very similar to that of writing the same natural number using different bases. When children find different ways of writing the same fraction, they can record them on a list of equivalent fractions. Some of those which may be found are

$\frac{1}{2}=\frac{2}{4}$ (quarters of an hour)

   $=\frac{6}{12}$ (divisions of the clock-face)

   $=\frac{4}{8}$ (folding a circle)

   $=0\cdot5$ (half a metre in decimetres)

   $=\frac{5}{10}$ (writing $0\cdot5$ in numerator/denominator form)

   $=\frac{3}{6}$ (even faces on a die)

and $\frac{1}{3}=\frac{20}{60}$ (20 minutes as part of 1 hour).

Similar sets of fractions can be found for $\frac{1}{4}$, $\frac{3}{4}$, $\frac{1}{5}$ and $\frac{1}{10}$ or $0\cdot1$. From examination of the sets of equivalent fractions which have been built up, there will eventually emerge the generalisation that two fractions are *equivalent*, or have the same value, when the numerator and denominator of one fraction are the same multiples of the numerator and denominator of the other. The fraction $\frac{15}{24}$ is equivalent to $\frac{5}{8}$, and the numerical relationship between the two expressions is $15 = 3 \times 5$, $24 = 3 \times 8$. Numerator and denominator have both been multiplied by 3. The sets of equivalences

$$\frac{3}{4}=\frac{6}{8}=\frac{9}{12}=\frac{12}{16}=\frac{15}{20}=\cdots$$

can be written as

$$\frac{3}{4}=\frac{2\times3}{2\times4}=\frac{3\times3}{3\times4}=\frac{4\times3}{4\times4}=\frac{5\times3}{5\times4}=\cdots$$

It must be emphasised that this result is not an arbitrary rule, but a generalisation from a number of real experiences, and that when children need to use equivalent fractions, they must be given experiences from which they can make this generalisation.

Some children will be able to generalise, and to make a statement such as, 'You get an equivalent

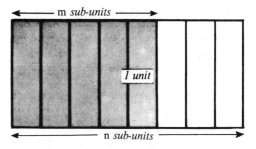

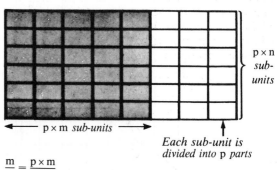

$$\frac{m}{n}=\frac{p\times m}{p\times n}$$

Each sub-unit is divided into p parts

Figure 32 : 8

fraction by multiplying the numerator and denominator of any fraction by the same number.' The next step is to express algebraically the generalisation which has been arrived at in words. This is a more difficult process, not to be expected until the secondary school stage. The algebraic method of stating the generalisation, as

$$\frac{m}{n} = \frac{p \times m}{p \times n},$$

will then be found very satisfactory, as it is less cumbersome than words. Figure 32 : 8 illustrates this generalisation. Here the *area* of a rectangle is used to represent the unit rather than using a length.

When the idea of equivalence has become fully operational children will know that the process of replacing a fraction by an equivalent one is reversible, so that they not only know that $\frac{3}{4}$ is equal to $\frac{9}{12}$, but that $\frac{9}{12}$ can be replaced by the simpler equivalent fraction $\frac{3}{4}$. Thus they can obtain an equivalent fraction by dividing the numerator and denominator by the same number.

THE DIVISION ASPECT OF FRACTIONS

We have used the language of fractions to describe many experiences which children will also describe in other ways. They say 'one third of 6' as an alternative to '6 divided by three' and a further aspect of the idea of a fraction is based on the interchangeability of the language of fractions and of division.

In Figure 32 : 9 the construction of a graph of quarters of numbers is described in two ways. Children can use this graph to find such further

facts as $\frac{1}{4}$ of 9 or $9 \div 4 = 2\frac{1}{4}$. When natural numbers only are used, and the units remain indivisible, the only way of dealing with $9 \div 4$ is to divide eight of the nine units by four, leaving an indivisible remainder of one unit; but when fractions are used the one remaining unit is no longer indivisible, and now $9 \div 4 = 2\frac{1}{4}$. We see that all the following expressions are equal:

$$\tfrac{1}{4} \text{ of } 9 = 9 \div 4 = 9 \times \tfrac{1}{4} = \tfrac{9}{4} = 2\tfrac{1}{4}$$

As children's experience widens, they will find that the fractional method of describing the relationship between two quantities can be used in situations where a multiplication or division relationship cannot so easily be used. The relation between the shaded area and the whole rectangle in Figure 32 : 10 cannot be expressed directly by a single multiplication or division statement.

But fractions can be used to express this relation in two ways:

i) the shaded area $= \frac{5}{6}$ of the rectangle, or

ii) the rectangle $= \frac{6}{5}$ of the shaded area.

The second statement is obtained by thinking of the shaded area, which consists of 5 squares, as the *unit*, and expressing the relationship of the rectangle consisting of 6 squares to the unit of 5 squares.

Figure 32 : 10

Graph of quarters of numbers

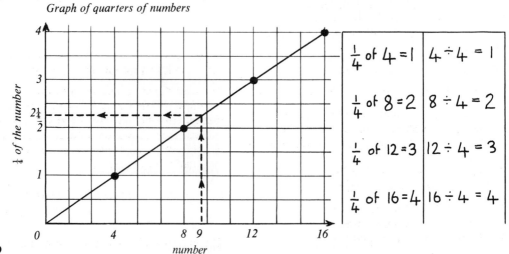

Figure 32 : 9

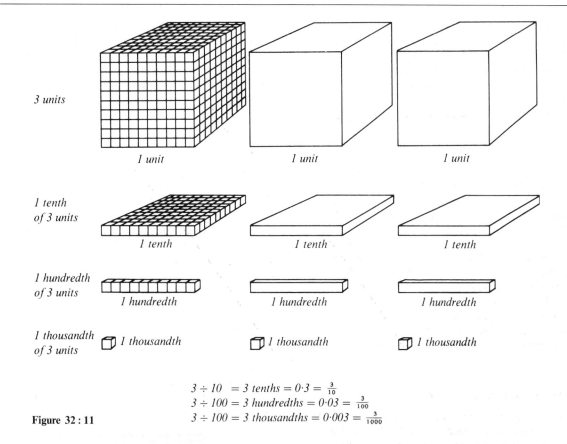

$3 \div 10 \ = 3 \ tenths = 0\cdot3 = \frac{3}{10}$
$3 \div 100 = 3 \ hundredths = 0\cdot03 = \frac{3}{100}$
$3 \div 100 = 3 \ thousandths = 0\cdot003 = \frac{3}{1000}$

Figure 32 : 11

The division of a unit into a number of equal parts can always be expressed in terms of a fraction whose numerator is 1. 'Divide by 6' and 'take $\frac{1}{6}$ of' mean the same. If this were the only idea which a fraction could express, the fraction notation would have very little advantage over the division notation, but 'take $\frac{5}{6}$ of' is a considerable extension of this idea, and it can only be expressed conveniently by using fractional language.

It is particularly important that children should understand how this relationship applies to tenths, so that they think of $0\cdot3$ not only as

i) 3 tenths of one unit, but also

ii) 3 units divided by 10, or one tenth of 3 units.

In Figure 32 : 11, 3 units have been divided by 10, using base ten blocks with the large cube as unit. The diagram also shows the division of 3 units by 100, and by 1000.

The pattern which arises from these divisions by 10, 100, and 1000 is a great importance:

$3 \div \quad 10 = 0\cdot3 \quad$ (3 tenths)
$3 \div \quad 100 = 0\cdot03 \quad$ (3 hundredths)
$3 \div 1000 = 0\cdot003 \quad$ (3 thousandths)

A division such as $\div 4$ can be carried out within the decimal system for any remaining units can always be changed into sub-units, as the following example shows.

$3 \ units \div 4 = 30 \ tenth \div 4$
$\qquad = 7 \ tenths + (2 \ tenths \div 4)$
$\qquad = 7 \ tenths + (20 \ hundredths \div 4)$
$\qquad = 7 \ tenths + 5 \ hundredths$
$\qquad = 0\cdot75$

FRACTIONS OF A FRACTION AND THE MULTIPLICATION OF FRACTIONS

At the secondary stage, when theoretical work with fractions is undertaken, it is necessary to be able to multiply together any two fractional numbers, whether they are written in decimal or fractional notation. We then need to find such products as $\frac{1}{3} \times \frac{2}{5}$, and to generalise

to $\frac{a}{b} \times \frac{c}{d}$. These results are deduced from facts such as

$\frac{2}{3} \times \frac{1}{5} = \frac{1}{3} \ of \ \frac{2}{5}$

The meaning of $\frac{2}{3} \times \frac{1}{5}$ is obtained by recalling that,

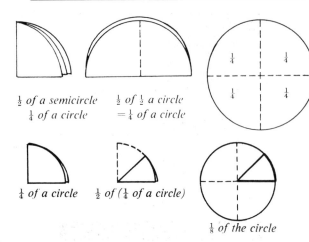

$\frac{1}{2}$ *of a semicircle*
$\frac{1}{4}$ *of a circle*

$\frac{1}{2}$ *of* $\frac{1}{2}$ *a circle*
$=\frac{1}{4}$ *of a circle*

$\frac{1}{4}$ *of a circle*

$\frac{1}{2}$ *of* ($\frac{1}{4}$ *of a circle)*

$\frac{1}{8}$ *of the circle*

Figure 32 : 12

for instance, 2×4 means 'twice 4' and $2 \times \frac{1}{5}$ means *'twice as much as* $\frac{1}{5}$*'*. Also $\frac{2}{3} \times 12$ means *'*$\frac{2}{3}$ *as much as* 12', or '$\frac{2}{3}$ of 12'. Hence, $\frac{2}{3} \times \frac{1}{5}$ may be taken to mean '$\frac{2}{3}$ *as much as* $\frac{1}{5}$*.* or $\frac{2}{3}$ of $\frac{1}{5}$'. This can be found practically by drawing or folding, but children at the primary school age find it difficult to abstract the idea of a fraction of a fraction, although they very often make fractions of a fraction in the course of their work.

When children fold a semicircle in two, they make half of the semicircle, or a quarter of the whole circle (Figure 32 : 12). When they open out the folds they relate the new subdivision to the original unit. Whenever children subdivide a fraction of a unit by folding it again, they make a fraction of a fraction of the original unit. The subdivision of a circle into eight equal parts (Figure 32 : 12) contains many examples of fractions of a fraction.

Children should be encouraged to look for such relationships, but they may find difficulty in expressing them, although the relationship is implicit in the folding.

The difficulty lies in the double role played by the shape obtained at the first fold: it is first of all a fraction of the original unit, and then the unit of the fraction produced by the second fold.

Children have to bear both relationships in mind at the same time. They must be able to move backwards and forwards easily in thought between a unit and its part if they are to relate $\frac{1}{2}$ of a quarter to $\frac{1}{8}$ of the original unit.

However, the teacher will be able, in Figure 32 : 13, to relate the heavily shaded area to the original rectangle and to see that

$$\frac{1}{3} \times \frac{2}{5} = \frac{1}{3} \text{ of } \frac{2}{5}$$
$$= \frac{2}{15}$$

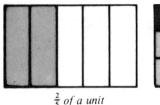

$\frac{2}{5}$ *of a unit*

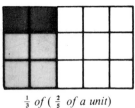

$\frac{1}{3}$ *of (* $\frac{2}{5}$ *of a unit)*

Figure 32 : 13

In general we find that

$$\frac{a}{b} \times \frac{c}{d} = \frac{a}{b} \text{ of } \frac{c}{d} = \frac{a \times c}{b \times d}$$

This is illustrated in Figure 32 : 14.

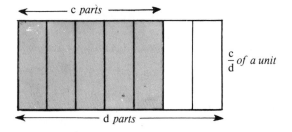

c parts

$\frac{c}{d}$ *of a unit*

d parts

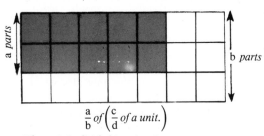

a parts

b parts

$\frac{a}{b}$ *of* $\left(\frac{c}{d} \text{ of a unit.}\right)$

The unit is divided into b × d *parts of which* a × c *are shaded*

$$\frac{a}{b} \times \frac{c}{d} = \frac{a}{b} \text{ of } \frac{c}{d} = \frac{a \times c}{b \times d}$$

Figure 32 : 14

THE GRAPH OF RECIPROCALS

The graph of a set of fractions and their reciprocals (Figure 32 : 15) can now be drawn from the tabulation below.

number	$\frac{1}{2}$	1	$1\frac{1}{4}$	$1\frac{3}{4}$	2	$2\frac{1}{2}$	$2\frac{3}{4}$	3	$3\frac{3}{4}$	$4\frac{1}{2}$
reciprocal	$\frac{2}{1}$	1	$\frac{4}{5}$	$\frac{4}{7}$	$\frac{1}{2}$	$\frac{2}{5}$	$\frac{4}{11}$	$\frac{1}{3}$	$\frac{4}{15}$	$\frac{1}{4}$
number	$4\frac{1}{4}$	$4\frac{1}{2}$	$4\frac{3}{4}$	5						
reciprocal	$\frac{4}{17}$	$\frac{2}{9}$	$\frac{4}{19}$	$\frac{1}{5}$						

Graph of reciprocals

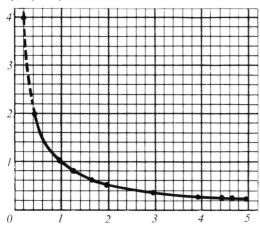

Figure 32 : 15

In marking the points of this graph, it is necessary to express the more inconvenient of these fractions as decimals, using the calculator; for instance, $\frac{4}{19} \approx 0 \cdot 21$.

The shape of the graph which results is similar to the graph of a constant product (see Figure 21 : 24). This suggests a similar relation. In fact, as we know, the product of any number and its reciprocal is 1. The graph of reciprocals shows symmetry among its points. The point $(2, \frac{1}{2})$ can be matched with $(\frac{1}{2}, 2)$. If we write 2 as $\frac{2}{1}$ in fractional form it is very clear that each of the two numbers is the reciprocal of the other.

THE COMMUTATIVE LAW FOR THE MULTIPLICATION OF FRACTIONS

When children first multiply natural numbers, it does not occur to them that multiplication is commutative. To them, 3×4 means $4 + 4 + 4$, and 4×3 means $3 + 3 + 3 + 3$; children do not at first see any reason why the different operations yield the same result. But as their experience widens, they come to understand and take for granted that fact that the result of a multiplication does not depend on the order in which the numbers are handled. That is, they accept the fact that the multiplication of natural numbers is commutative.

We have begun to see that the multiplication of fractions is also commutative; this fact does not, however, follow simply because the multiplication of natural numbers is commutative.

When children first use one of the operations which they will eventually think of as multiplication of fractions, they are finding a *fraction of a fraction*.

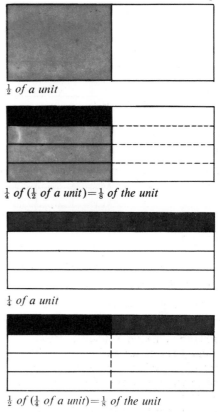

$\frac{1}{2}$ *of a unit*

$\frac{1}{4}$ *of* ($\frac{1}{2}$ *of a unit*)$=\frac{1}{8}$ *of the unit*

$\frac{1}{4}$ *of a unit*

$\frac{1}{2}$ *of* ($\frac{1}{4}$ *of a unit*)$=\frac{1}{8}$ *of the unit*

Figure 32 : 16

Finding $\frac{1}{2}$ of $\frac{3}{4}$ is an entirely different problem from finding $\frac{3}{4}$ of $\frac{1}{2}$. Finding 1 tenth of 1 hundredth is not the same as finding 1 hundredth of 1 tenth. This is exactly parallel to the situation encountered with whole numbers, when ten hundreds do not look like a hundred tens. It is surprising that the results of the two operations are the same, and it is only after some experience of doing both operations that children will expect the results always to be the same.

Figure 32 : 16 illustrates the equality of $\frac{1}{4}$ of $\frac{1}{2}$ and $\frac{1}{2}$ of $\frac{1}{4}$. The result is the same, whether the unit is divided first into 2 parts and then each part divided into 4 parts, or alternatively the unit is divided first into 4 parts and then each part divided into 2 parts. The final result is the division of the unit into 8 parts.

This process can be generalised to show that

$$\frac{a}{b} \times \frac{c}{d} = \frac{c}{d} \times \frac{a}{b} = \frac{(a \times c)}{(b \times d)},$$

as in Figure 32 : 17.

The resulting fraction is the same, irrespective of

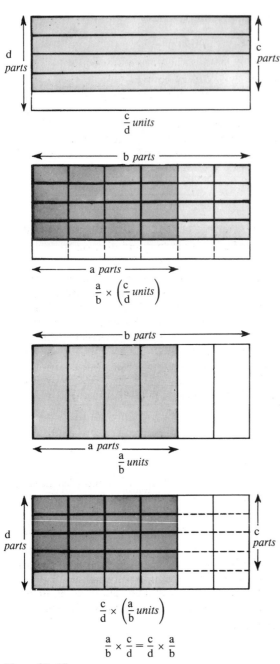

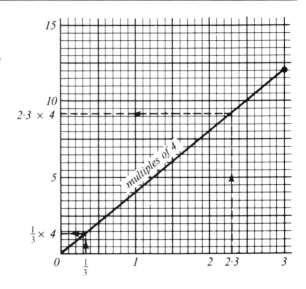

Figure 32 : 18

$$\frac{a}{b} \times \frac{c}{d} = \frac{c}{d} \times \frac{a}{b}$$

The fractions may of course be written in decimal form, so that for instance

$$1 \cdot 2 \times 3 \cdot 5 = 3 \cdot 5 \times 1 \cdot 2$$

With understanding of the commutative law of multiplication comes the unification in children's minds of two separate processes, the multiplication of natural numbers and the multiplication of fractions, making one united whole – the multiplication of numbers. It is now clear that among the multiples of a number such as 4 there are not only 2×4, 3×4, 4×4, and so on, but fractional multiples such as $\frac{1}{3} \times 4$ and $2 \cdot 3 \times 4$, and that there exists an indefinite number of such fractional multiples (Figure 32 : 18). It is also plain that not only whole numbers have multiples. The multiples of 2, 3, 4 . . . are only a few specimens among the set of multiples of all numbers, which include multiples of $\frac{1}{2}$, $0 \cdot 6$, $4 \cdot 3$, and so on. These multiples may be whole numbers, such as $2 \times 4 \cdot 3$, or they may be fractional multiples, $1 \cdot 7 \times 4 \cdot 3$ or $\frac{1}{2} \times 4 \cdot 3$ (Figure 32 : 19).

Just as children can replace 4×3 by 3×4 if they wish, using the commutative law for multiplication, so also they can now replace $0 \cdot 7 \times 6$ by $6 \times 0 \cdot 7$ or $4 \cdot 3 \times 1 \cdot 7$ by $1 \cdot 7 \times 4 \cdot 3$, using the commutative law for multiplication, if they find one operation more convenient than the other. At this stage, also, the reading of $\frac{3}{4} \times \frac{1}{3}$ as '$\frac{3}{4}$ multiplied by $\frac{1}{3}$' becomes natural, for no longer is the order of the factors of any importance.

Figure 32 : 17

whether a fraction $\frac{c}{d}$ is first made, and then a part $\frac{a}{b}$ of that fraction taken, or a fraction $\frac{a}{b}$ is first made, and then a part $\frac{c}{d}$ of that fraction is then taken. In either case, the unit has been divided into $(b \times d)$ parts, and $(a \times c)$ of them have been taken.

The operation of multiplying two fractions hence satisfies the *commutative law for multiplication of fractions*:

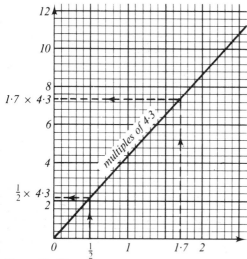

Figure 32 : 19

DIVISION BY A FRACTION: MULTIPLICATION BY THE RECIPROCAL

Children meet the division of a fraction into a number of equal parts, that is, the division of a fraction by a whole number, early in their exploration of fractions, and they will describe what they have done in folding up the semicircle of Figure 32 : 20 into 4 equal parts as

$$\tfrac{1}{2} \div 4 \;=\; \tfrac{1}{8}$$
$$\text{or } \tfrac{1}{4} \text{ of } \tfrac{1}{2} \;=\; \tfrac{1}{8}$$

This can also be written

$$\tfrac{1}{4} \times \tfrac{1}{2} \;=\; \tfrac{1}{8},$$

or using the commutativity of multiplication

$$\tfrac{1}{2} \times \tfrac{1}{4} \;=\; \tfrac{1}{8}$$

On the calculator, the division of $0 \cdot 5$ by 4 is entered

$$\boxed{0.5}\ \boxed{\div}\ \boxed{4}\ \boxed{=},$$

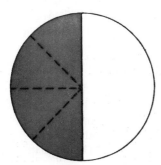

Figure 32 : 20

while the multiplication $0 \cdot 5 \times \tfrac{1}{4}$ can be entered as

$$\boxed{0 \cdot 5}\ \boxed{\times}\ \boxed{1}\ \boxed{\div}\ \boxed{4}\ \boxed{=},$$

because $\tfrac{1}{4}$ is $1 \div 4$. Alternatively, $\tfrac{1}{4}$ can be converted to a decimal first by entering $\boxed{1}\ \boxed{\div}\ \boxed{4}\ \boxed{=}$, to obtain $0 \cdot 25$, and then multiplying by $0 \cdot 5$. Thus, the idea grows that division by 4 and multiplication by its reciprocal, $\tfrac{1}{4}$ or $0 \cdot 25$, are equivalent. Children find many instances of such equivalences; for instance, if a coin is tossed 50 times, the expected number of heads is

$$\tfrac{1}{2} \text{ of } 50$$
$$\text{or } 50 \div 2$$

The first form, $\tfrac{1}{2}$ of 50, can also be written $\tfrac{1}{2} \times 50$ or $50 \times \tfrac{1}{2}$. Multiplication by $\tfrac{1}{2}$ and division by 2 produce the same result.

Later, the need to record division by a decimal or fraction, as well as a whole number, arises. 'How many $1 \cdot 5$ cm lengths of ribbon can be cut from 15 cm?' gives $15 \div 1 \cdot 5 = 10$ as an alternative form to $1 \cdot 5 \times \square = 15$. This is exactly parallel to the recording of, 'How many 3 cm lengths can be cut from 15 cm?' by using $15 \div 3 = 5$ instead of $3 \times \square = 15$. If fraction notation is used instead of decimal notation for $1\tfrac{1}{2}$, the recording is

$$15 \div 1\tfrac{1}{2} =$$

instead of

$$1\tfrac{1}{2} \times \square = 15$$

Another situation which can be recorded in terms of division by a fraction is, 'How many half centimetres in ten centimetres?', which leads to $10 \div \tfrac{1}{2} = 20$, as an alternative to $\tfrac{1}{2} \times \square = 10$. Again, we notice that the reciprocal of $\tfrac{1}{2}$ is 2, and $10 \times 2 = 20$. Division by $\tfrac{1}{2}$ yields the same result as multiplication by its reciprocal, 2.

Thus, division by a number and multiplication by its inverse or reciprocal are always equivalent:

$$\boxed{m} = 10 \times 0 \cdot 4$$

and

$$\boxed{m} = 10 \div 2 \cdot 5$$

are equivalent to each other, and $10 \div 2 \cdot 5$ can be read as, 'What must $2 \cdot 5$ be multiplied by to equal 10?'

At this stage, $3\tfrac{1}{3} \div 1\tfrac{1}{2}$ can be read as, 'What must $1\tfrac{1}{2}$ be multiplied by to equal $3\tfrac{1}{3}$?' This question leads to the usual written method of dividing one fraction by another. A number can easily be constructed which, when multiplied by $1\tfrac{1}{2}$, yields $3\tfrac{1}{3}$.

We need to find, in fractional form, the missing number in

$$\square \times \tfrac{3}{2} = \tfrac{10}{3}$$

The reciprocal of $\tfrac{3}{2}$ is $\tfrac{2}{3}$, and

$$\tfrac{3}{2} \times \tfrac{2}{3} = 1$$

Thus, since $\square \times \tfrac{3}{2}$ is equal to $\tfrac{10}{3}$, it is also the case that

$$\square \times \tfrac{3}{2} \times \tfrac{2}{3} \text{ is equal to } \tfrac{10}{3} \times \tfrac{2}{3}, \text{ or}$$

$$\square \times \tfrac{3}{2} \times \tfrac{2}{3} = \tfrac{10}{3} \times \tfrac{2}{3}$$

This is the same as

$$\square \times 1 = \tfrac{10}{3} \times \tfrac{2}{3}$$

or $\qquad \square = \tfrac{10}{3} \times \tfrac{2}{3}$

Hence the number by which $\tfrac{3}{2}$ must be multiplied to give $\tfrac{10}{3}$ is $\tfrac{10}{3} \times \tfrac{2}{3}$. This statement can be written as

$$\tfrac{10}{3} \div \tfrac{3}{2} = \tfrac{10}{3} \times \tfrac{2}{3}$$

We now see the emergence of the usual written method of dividing by a fraction, which is multiplication by its reciprocal. This has often been described as, 'Turn the second fraction upside down and multiply', but children cannot understand this method until they understand the abstract process of reasoning which has been described above, which is unlikely to be the case until fairly late in the secondary school. There is no need for this process to be taught at an earlier stage; if there is a need for $3\tfrac{1}{3} \div 1\tfrac{1}{2}$ to be evaluated earlier for some practical purpose, decimal notation can be used, so that

$$3 \cdot 3333333 \div 1 \cdot 5 = 2 \cdot 2222222$$

is obtained on the calculator, and the result can then be rounded to an appropriate number of decimal places.

THE DISTRIBUTIVE LAW FOR FRACTIONS

In Chapter 19 we saw the importance of the *distributive law*

$$a \times (b + c) = (a \times b) \div (a \times c)$$

in the multiplication of natural numbers. This law is also often used to simplify the multiplication of decimal numbers. A further example of the use of the distributive law is that children who wish to find the total length of 8 paper strips each $2\tfrac{1}{2}$ cm long will find 8 twos and 8 halves and add the results. They are using

$$8 \times (2 + \tfrac{1}{2}) = (8 \times 2) + (8 \times \tfrac{1}{2})$$

We use the distributive law in the multiplication of fractions as naturally as in the multiplication of natural numbers. If a, b and c are any natural numbers or fractions,

$$a \times (b + c) = (a \times b) + (a \times c)$$

When we find the areas of rectangles, the lengths of whose sides are given in decimal form, much use is made of the distributive law.

PERCENTAGES AND COMPARISONS

A very convenient way of talking about and writing fractions, especially when fractions are to be compared, is to express them as percentages. Examples should be simple and within the children's range. The statement, '63% of the vehicles which passed the school gates between 10·30 a.m. and 10·45 a.m. were private cars', means that 63 hundredths of these vehicles were private cars. 'Per cent' means 'out of 100', and 63% means 63 hundredths. It is most unlikely that exactly 100 cars passed the gate during the given quarter of an hour, but expressing the proportion of private cars as a percentage enables comparison to be made with different times of day, when different numbers of vehicles pass. The chief use of percentages is for comparison. Of the two statements:

i) On road A, 46 vehicles out of 79 were cars, but on road B, 83 vehicles out of 123 were cars', and

ii) On road A, 58% of vehicles were cars, but on road B, 67% of vehicles were cars',

the second is easier to grasp, and enables comparisons to be made between the proportion of cars travelling on the two roads.

Also, the parts of 100 are much more familiar than parts of other numbers. The statement '26% of the children in this class have birthdays in the autumn term' conveys the proportion more easily than does '8 out of the 31 children in this class have birthdays in the autumn term', as well as making comparisons with other classes and with national statistics easier.

There are two methods which children can use to convert the fraction $\tfrac{8}{31}$ of the class into a percentage. We need to know how many *hundredths* are equivalent to $\tfrac{8}{31}$. In other words, $\tfrac{8}{31}$ needs to be converted to a decimal. The calculator enables this to be done very easily:

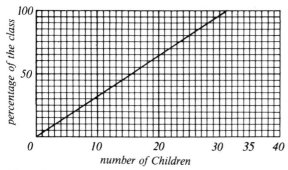

Figure 32 : 21

$$\frac{8}{31} = 8 \div 31$$
$$= 0 \cdot 258. \ldots$$
$$= 26 \text{ hundredths to the nearest hundredth}$$
$$= 26\%$$

Alternatively, a conversion graph may be drawn, to convert parts out of 31 to parts out of 100. This is particularly useful if several pieces of information about the 31 children in the class are to be expressed as percentages. Figure 32 : 21 shows the conversion graph for a class of 31 children.

When children need to compare probabilities, these can be expressed as percentages. For instance, the chance of throwing a 6 on a 6-faced die is $\frac{1}{6}$, while the chance of throwing an 18, 19 or 20 on a 20-faced die is $\frac{3}{20}$. These fractions can be turned into decimals or percentages for comparison:

$$\frac{1}{6} = 0 \cdot 1666. \ldots$$
$$\approx 17 \text{ hundredths}$$
$$\approx 17\%,$$
$$\text{and } \frac{3}{20} = 0 \cdot 15$$
$$= 15 \text{ hundredths}$$
$$= 15\%$$

Thus, the first event is more likely, although the probabilities are so close that children are unlikely to detect the difference in throwing the two dice.

APPROXIMATION AND ACCURACY IN COUNTING AND MEASURING

A major use of fractions and percentages is in thinking about the degree of accuracy in counting and measuring. Children discover, as their experience of counting and measuring grows, that often when they count a set and always when they measure a quantity, these tasks can only be done approximately.

Several difficulties arise when a set is to be counted. The numbers of things in the set may be very large, making counting difficult. The number of grains of rice in a particular $\frac{1}{2}$ –kilogram bag of rice is a definite number which could be counted. It would be easier to approximate to this number by weighing out 50 grams of rice, counting the grains in it, and multiplying by 10. Anyway, 'Exactly how many grains of rice are there in $\frac{1}{2}$ kg?' is a nonsensical question. Often, it is only sensible to state an approximate number in a set.

Again, in practical situations it may be difficult to decide exactly what objects belong to the set we wish to count, or to make the members of the set stand still for long enough to be counted. Even when young children count simple sets like the set of pets they have at home, arbitrary decisions may have to be taken on such problems as, 'Should I count my sister's pony?' The set of people who attend an open-air political rally cannot in practical terms be counted although the set of those who attend at least part of the rally is well defined. There are passers-by who drift in and out, and many other practical barriers to forming more than a rough estimate. If the plants in an area are sampled by throwing a quadrat and counting the number of plants of a species within it, it may be difficult to decide whether a plant is inside the quadrat or not. Hence, in many cases the count of a set can only be regarded as approximate.

In any form of measurement, accuracy is inevitably limited by the skill of the measurer and the accuracy of the measuring instruments used. When children measure the length of a postcard, we expect them to obtain a measurement which is correct to the nearest millimetre; but when they measure the length of a room they do not use a measuring-tape marked in millimetres, and if they did it would be false to pretend that the length of the room could be measured with this degree of accuracy. Unevenness in the skirting board, slight crookedness or stretch in the measuring-tape, or inequalities in the floor surface would account for considerably more than this, and in any case it would never be necessary to give the length of a room with greater accuracy than to the nearest centimetre, if that.

It is often not sensible to give measurements to more than a certain degree of accuracy. If a person's mass is 62·5 kg at the moment of weighing, at a different time of the same day their mass may well be 62·2 kg. The AA book gives distances 'by the shortest practicable route using classified roads'. How often can this information be revised to take account of one-way streets, diversions, road rebuilding, or other variations? However, approximate information is sufficient for planning the journey.

Children will enjoy using a calculator to work out how many days they have been alive, but they will realise that, even if they know the time of their birth, it is not sensible to work out exactly how many minutes they have been alive, as the time changes while they do the calculation. Measurement can only ever be approximate, in this or in any other case. The statement, 'I have drawn a line exactly 10 cm long' is never true. It means, 'I cannot, with the naked eye, using my rather thick pencil and mass-produced ruler, see a difference in length between my line and the length of 10 cm shown by this ruler, the markings on which are not much more than 0·2 mm thick.'

The teacher should work for an understanding of approximation from the beginning. When children measure a pencil, they may say it is 'about 8 cm long', '8 cm and a bit long', or 'between 8 and 9 cm long'. Any of these is a more correct statement than just '8 cm long'. The idea that a measurement is *between* two limits is helpful in several ways. When a package is weighed on a balance, its mass may be more that 200 grams but less than 300 grams. With the scales available, children cannot obtain greater accuracy than this. A jug may hold more than $\frac{1}{4}$ litre but less than $\frac{1}{2}$ litre; the fact that its capacity is between $\frac{1}{4}$ litre and $\frac{1}{2}$ litre will help children to put $\frac{1}{4}$ and $\frac{1}{2}$ in order of size, as the weighing experience helps them to put 200 and 300 in order, and to see the need for numbers between 200 and 300. Such experiences help in building up a picture of the number line.

As children grow older, they progress in such an activity as measuring a pencil through using descriptions such as these:

i) between 13 cm and 14 cm,

ii) between 13 cm and $13\frac{1}{2}$ cm,

iii) nearer to $13\frac{1}{2}$ cm than to 13 cm,

iv) $13\frac{1}{2}$ cm, to the nearest half centimetre,

v) between 13·0 and 13·5 cm,

vi) 13·3 cm, to the nearest millimetre.

By this stage they should be querying the value of the last measurement. During the initial writing of this paragraph, the pencil used shrank in length from approximately 13·3 cm to 13·1 cm.

We now list some ways which will help children at different stages to describe approximate counts and measurements.

i) 230 tickets for the school concert were sold; the number of people at the concert ≤ 230.

ii) 13·0 cm < length of pencil < 13·5 cm.

iii) The corridor is 55 ± 0·05 m long.

iv) The population of the British Isles was 55 347 000 (to the nearest thousand).

Percentages and fractions can be used to enable us to look at the accuracy of counts and measurements. When the population of the British Isles was counted as 55 347 000 to the nearest thousand, this tells us that the error was estimated to be less than 500, one way or the other. An eeror of 500 in 55 347 000 is

$$\frac{500}{55\,347\,000} = 0\cdot000\,009$$
$$= 0\cdot0009\%$$

This is enormously impressive accuracy, far exceeding that obtained in most measurements.

Children can use the same idea to compare their skill at estimating different quantities:

an error of 5 cm in a length of 79 cm
$= \frac{5}{79}$ error.

Now $\frac{5}{79} = 0\cdot0632\ldots$
≈ 6 hundredths
$\approx 6\%$,

so the error in this estimate was 6%.

Children may investigate whether they find it more difficult to estimate masses, times or volumes, or how much worse they are at estimating long distances than short distances.

CALCULATION SKILLS: WHAT IS NEEDED?

When children have gained a complete idea of notation, and are able to use the place-value system for whole numbers and decimals, it is time to consider what degree of skill they need to attain in systematic computation. Skill in computation is not an end in itself, since computation is always needed for some purpose, and so for finding the answer to something we need to know. The first essential, therefore, is knowledge of which operation needs to be performed in a particular situation. Once this knowledge is gained, it is then important that children have available the computational skills they need for their purposes. These skills are three types:

i) skills in mental computation,

ii) the skilled use of a calculator,

iii) skill in computation using pencil and paper, without a calculator.

The question of an appropriate balance between the second and third types of skill has still not been completely resolved. We need to find a balance which will equip children with the understanding and facility they need for the future, without clinging to archaic methods which neither promote understanding nor provide necessary skills.

It is certain that long and heavy calculations need no longer be performed by pencil-and-paper methods. The use of calculators whenever a large amount of arithmetic has to be done is now universal, in shops, offices, industry and science, and is growing rapidly in schools. Our guide to the standard of arithmetical performance, as distinct from mathematical understanding, should be what will be needed in everyday life and in the child's future mathematical and scientific work. Many of the calculations needed in everyday life are performed mentally, so that accuracy in mental calculation with small numbers is certainly necessary. This means that the addition bonds up to $9 + 9$, and the multiplication tables up to 9×9, should be accurately known. Children should have considerable facility in the use of these facts in mental addition and subtraction, particularly of money, together with simple multiplication and division, so that bills and change can be checked, tickets bought for a family, or a restaurant bill shared between a group.

For calculator use, there are four major skills:

i) translating from the problem to the needed calculation;

ii) estimating the size of answer to be expected from the calculation, so that errors of translation or of calculation can be detected;

iii) checking the calculation on the calculator, so that wrong keystrokes can be detected;

iv) recording the calculations, including intermediate results, so that these can be checked and errors detected.

These skills are based on understanding what the processes of addition, subtraction, multiplication and division are used for, so that translation from problem to calculation can be correctly made.

A skill whose importance is greatly increased by the use of calculators is that of *estimation*. Finding the area of a rectangle 17 cm by 23 cm should be approximated by a mental estimate of $20 \times 20 = 400$. When a probability of $\frac{7}{12}$ is to be converted into a decimal, an answer rather more than $0 \cdot 5$ is to be expected.

Every opportunity should be taken from the beginning to develop the habit of estimation in counting, measuring and calculation. Not only does the habit of estimation reveal errors in calculation,

but is also indicates children's understanding of the ideas of number and measurement. A 6-year-old who said to a visitor to his class, 'Go away: you're too tall', and then returned to say with astonishment, 'You must be two metres tall', showed considerable insight in the estimate; but infants who guess an adult's age with estimates between 18 and 80 show their lack of grasp of the idea of age in adults.

An estimate should be made as a matter of course when children measure: a tape-measure may become twisted and be read from the wrong end; children using a measuring-tape may forget how many times they have stretched it out; children often read the wrong angle from a protractor. A sensible use of the habit of estimation will often detect errors of this type.

Similarly, in calculation, an estimate of the size of answers to be expected, however rough, will often reveal slips. For instance, the average height of a group of children must certainly be between the greatest and least heights. Every piece of mathematical information should be checked constantly by the criterion, 'Is this sensible?'

Some teachers may still ask how far it is necessary for children at the primary stage to become skilful at pencil-and-paper computation now that calculators are a part of everyone's equipment. It is certainly useless for children to be able to perform addition, subtraction, multiplication and division of numbers, money or measures if they do not understand the meaning of these operations, or when each one is called for. This understanding does not come through mechanical practice in performing the operations, but through setting them in real situations where their meaning can be grasped.

The results of calculations should be examined to see if they are reasonable: the average speed of a train journey can be compared with the speed of other forms of transport, the height of a house found with a clinometer can be very roughly checked by estimating the height of its rooms, and so on. Such inspection will often detect gross arithmetical errors. Children should also check subtraction by addition and division by multiplication. Important calculations should be performed independently by more than one person, or in more than one way. These precautions are particularly important when children are not doing sums from a textbook, but are making calculations on data they have themselves obtained. The relevance of the work to the children's interest does not in itself ensure accuracy, and much good work has been spoilt by a slip in the early stages.

Children who are working together on a project should be encouraged to do the calculations independently, checking each other at every stage.

The solution of any mathematical problem has two stages: finding out how to solve it, and solving it. When children invent their own problems or solve problems suggested by practical situations, rather than working through a set of sums in a text-book, their justification for faith in the correctness of their results can no longer be agreement with the answer-book. Something much more convincing and personal is now called for. A group of children can maintain that a result they have obtained is correct only if they are convinced (and can convince others) of the rightness of their method, if they have all obtained the same result, which is a sensible one, and if they have as far as possible checked their calculations. Individual children working by themselves can do most of this, particularly if it is possible for them to do the calculations in more than one way; but the teacher will probably have to investigate their methods of solving a problem in some detail, since errors of understanding are more likely to go undetected when children work alone.

Fractions, percentages and estimation in the National Curriculum

Children are not expected to do much calculation with fractions and percentages in the National Curriculum until the higher levels. Until Level 4, they are only required to use simple everyday fractions and percentages.

- understand the meaning of 'a half' and 'a quarter'.

(AT2: Level 2)

- recognise and understand simple fractions in everyday use.

(AT2: Level 4)

- recognise and understand simple percentages.

(AT2: Level 4)

The ability to calculate with fractions and percentages is expected from Level 5.

- calculate fractions and percentages of quantities using a calculator where necessary.

(AT2: Level 5)

- work out fractional and percentage changes.

(AT2: Level 6)

- convert fractions to decimals and percentages and find one number as a percentage of another.

(AT2: Level 6)

However, children are not expected to make formal calculations with fractions until Level 8, which takes this type of exercise well outside the range of the primary school.

- calculate with fractions.

(AT2: Level 8)

Estimation and approximation play an important part in the National Curriculum. The work ranges through making sensible estimates of quantities, rounding numbers, and using estimation to verify that calculations give results of the right size. Some of the statements are:

- estimate and approximate to check the validity of addition and subtraction calculations.

(AT2: Level 4)

- make sensible estimates of a range of measures in relation to everyday objects.

(AT2: Level 4)

- use estimation and approximation to check that answers to multiplication and division problems involving whole numbers are of the right order.

(AT2: Level 6)

33 | EXTENDING THE NUMBER SYSTEM AND ITS NOTATION

THE SIGNLESS RATIONAL NUMBERS

As children learn to handle decimals and fractions with confidence, and come to understand their addition, subtraction, multiplication and division, they cease to distinguish sharply between the natural numbers and the fractional numbers, for natural numbers and fractional numbers behave very similarly. They also think of the decimal and fractional ways of writing a fractional number as interchangeable; $0 \cdot 25$ and $\frac{1}{4}$ are symbols for the same number. Every fractional number can be written in many ways; $\frac{1}{2} = \frac{2}{4} = \frac{5}{10} = 0 \cdot 5 = \ldots$, but every whole number can also be written in many ways:

$$3 = \frac{3}{1} = \frac{6}{2} = \frac{30}{10} = 3 \cdot 0 = \ldots,$$

so the behaviour of fractional numbers and whole numbers is similar in this respect. Both natural numbers and fractional numbers have their appointed places on the number line (Figure 33 : 1).

For convenience, in Figure 33 : 1, the points corresponding to halves, thirds, quarters . . . are shown on separate lines, but it is then possible to visualise all these lines on top of one another to form a single number line. On this line, *any* fraction will correspond to a definite point on the line.

The point of the number line which is made to correspond to the fraction $\frac{1}{2}$ in the second line of Figure 33 : 1 also corresponds to the fraction $\frac{2}{4}$, the fraction $\frac{3}{6}$, and so on. But $\frac{1}{2} = \frac{2}{4} = \frac{3}{6} = \frac{4}{8} = 0 \cdot 5 \ldots$, and $\frac{1}{2}, \frac{2}{4}, \frac{3}{6}, \ldots$ are different names for the same fraction. Hence every possible fraction has a unique point on the number line corresponding to it.

The natural numbers can be placed in an *order* of increasingly magnitude: 0, 1, 2, 3, 4, . . . which

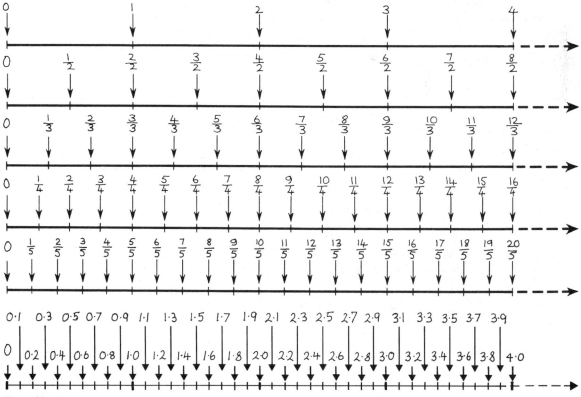

Figure 33 : 1

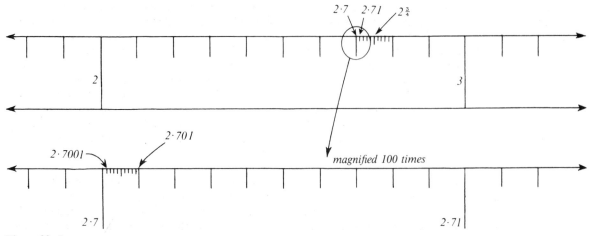

Figure 33 : 2

corresponds to their position in order on the number line. Putting the fractional numbers in order of magnitude is a slightly more complicated problem. There is a *next natural number* (in order of magnitude) after, say, 3; but there is not a *next fraction* (in order of magnitude) after, say, 2·7. There is a multitude of different fractions which are all a little larger than 2·7, each with its representative point on the number line. Among these fractions are 2·8, 2·75, 2·71, 2·701, 2·7001, 2·70001 and a whole host of others (Figure 33 : 2). It will be seen that we can never find a *closest* or *next* fraction to 2·7; there is always another which is closer to 2·7 than the last fraction we thought of.[1]

It is, however, always possible to decide which of two fractions is the greater. The fraction $2\frac{3}{4}$ is greater than 2·7, since $2\frac{3}{4} = 2·75$. In this ordering of positions on the number line the whole numbers have their places among the fractions, and so are not distinguished from the fractional numbers in a child's mind. After some years of experience many children can think in terms of, and operate with, the set of numbers consisting of the natural

numbers and the fractional numbers written in either decimal or fractional form.

This set of numbers is the set of *signless rational numbers*.[2] 'Rational' signifies that the number can be expressed as a *ratio*; the signless rational numbers include not only fractions such as $\frac{2}{5}$, which is the ratio of 2 units to 5 units, but also 3, which is the ratio of 3 units to 1 unit. All signless rational numbers can be written in a fractional form, such as $\frac{3}{1}$ or $\frac{5}{2}$. A signless rational number written in decimal form can easily be transformed into fractional form, for 0.37 is $\frac{37}{100}$, and 2·701 is $\frac{2701}{1000}$. In general, *a signless rational number is a number which can be expressed in the form* $\frac{p}{q}$, *where p and q are natural numbers, and q is not zero.*[3] Many of the numbers which children use at the primary school stage are signless rational numbers, although many other types of number exist.

The set of signless rational numbers has one great advantage as a mathematical tool over the set of natural numbers. This advantage can be expressed either practically or theoretically. The practical usefulness of the rational numbers is that they make measurement possible to any desired degree of accuracy. A metre is not a sufficiently small unit of measurement to measure the length of a book; the smaller unit of the centimetre is necessary.

[1] If 3 is regarded as a *fraction* rather than as a natural number there is not a next fraction after it, in order of magnitude. We can find many fractions which are a little larger than 3, such as 3·1, 3·01, 3·001,... but it is impossible to find a fraction which comes *next* after 3 on the number line.

[2] We shall discuss the set of *directed* rational numbers later. The directed rational numbers include numbers such as ($-\frac{2}{3}$) and ($^+3$).

The present set of numbers has been described as the set of *signless* rational numbers in order that the two sets may be distinguished.

[3] It is impossible for a fraction to have zero as a denominator. The symbols $\frac{1}{0}$, $\frac{2}{0}$, etc., have no meaning, for the denominator of a fraction shows the number of sub-units into which a unit has been divided. Also, a division such as $2 \div 0$ is impossible, for there is not a multiple of 0 which is equal to 2. The numerator of a fraction may, however, be zero, and $\frac{0}{1} = \frac{0}{2} = \frac{0}{3} = \ldots$ are fractional representations of 0.

A centimetre is not a small enough unit to measure the thickness of a page. Two courses of action are possible: a smaller unit such as micrometre could be used, and the thickness of the page described by a natural number of the smaller units, for instance 70 micrometres. Secondly, fractions of a centimetre could be used and the thickness of the page described in thousandths of a centimetre. The second system is more flexible and can be adapted, without the invention of new units, to stating the thickness of a human hair. The fact that a unit can be divided into smaller and smaller parts, and these parts described by rational numbers, makes the use of the set of signless rational numbers indispensable for all measurement.

This same advantage which the signless rational numbers have over the natural numbers can be described theoretically as: the set of signless rational numbers is *closed for division* (except for division by zero). We recall that the set of natural numbers is not closed for division (*see page 162*) since although some divisions of natural numbers, such as $12 \div 4$, have answers which are natural numbers, there are many natural numbers such as 12 and 5 which cannot be divided exactly to give a result which is a natural number. That is, there is no natural number n such that $5 \times n = 12$, so that $12 \div 5 = n$ has no solution within the set of natural numbers. But if we work in the set of signless rational numbers, not only can the rational number 12 be divided by the rational number 5 to give the rational number $\frac{12}{5}$, or $2\frac{2}{5}$, but *any* pair of rational numbers can be divided to give a result which is a rational number (unless the second one is zero). For instance,

$$\frac{3}{5} \div 2\frac{1}{2} = \frac{3}{5} \div \frac{5}{2}$$
$$= \frac{3}{5} \times \frac{2}{5}, \text{ since } \frac{2}{5} \text{ is the reciprocal of } \frac{5}{2}$$
$$= \frac{6}{25}$$

This complete freedom to perform division (except by zero), as well as addition and multiplication, of *any* rational numbers, is a considerable theoretical advantage. Among the natural numbers the only operations which can be performed with complete freedom, and with certainty that the result will be a natural number, are addition and multiplication.[4] The link between the theoretical and practical aspects of this improvement is that the rational numbers allow one to state the result of dividing 1 unit of measurement into, say, 10 equal parts, that is, to perform $1 \div 10$, which was not possible in the set of natural numbers.

The problem of subtraction has, however, not been solved among these signless rational numbers. There are many pairs of natural numbers whose subtraction cannot be performed within the set of natural numbers, such as $3 - 7$. But there are also many pairs of signless rational numbers, such as $3 - 7$, $2\frac{1}{2} - 3\frac{1}{3}$, or $0 - 2 \cdot 3$, whose subtraction cannot be performed within the set of signless rational numbers. The set of signless rational numbers, like the set of natural numbers, is *not closed for subtraction*.

The set of directed numbers provides a set of numbers which is closed for subtraction. Before discusssing these numbers, however, we notice that the laws of behaviour of the natural numbers, which we listed in Chapter 19 (*see page 237*) are exactly paralleled, with one exception, by laws for the behaviour of the signless rational numbers. Since all methods of performing arithmetical calculations depend on these laws, it follows that the arithmetical methods which can be used when calculating with natural numbers have exact parallels in calculation with signless rational numbers. On pages 408–409, we list the laws for the behaviour of natural numbers which were stated in Chapter 19, alongside the corresponding laws for the signless rational numbers.[5]

It will be seen that the only difference in behaviour between the natural numbers and the signless rational numbers is in Law 6, which expresses the nearest we can get to closure for division. We have not yet, however, obtained a set of numbers which is closed for subtraction. We now try to find a set of numbers which will have as much as possible of the structure of the signless rational numbers, but will have the additional property of being closed for subtraction.

---

[4]The set of natural numbers is *closed for addition and multiplication (see page 162).*

[5]The numbering of the laws corresponds to that of Chapter 19, page 237. Law 4, the distributive law, occurs among the multiplication laws on page 409.

Laws for Addition and Subtraction

Natural numbers

1 *Closure for addition*
The set of natural numbers is closed for addition; that is, the sum of any pair of natural numbers is a natural number.

2 *The commutative law for addition*
For any natural numbers a and b,

$$a + b = b + a$$

3 *The associative law for addition*
For any natural numbers a, b and c,

$$(a + b) + c = a + (b + c)$$

5 *The identity for addition*
The natural number 0 is the identity for addition. For any natural number n,

$$n + 0 = 0 + n = n$$

6 *Subtraction*
Subtraction is the inverse operation of addition.

$$a - b = x$$

means

$$b + x = a$$

The set of natural numbers is *not closed for subtraction*; many equations such as

$$7 + x = 3$$

have no solutions in the set of natural numbers.

Signless rational numbers

1 *Closure for addition*
The set of signless rational numbers is closed for addition; that is, the sum of any pair of signless rational numbers is a signless rational number.

2 *The commutative law for addition*
For any signless rational numbers $\frac{p}{q}$ and $\frac{r}{s}$,

$$\frac{p}{q} + \frac{r}{s} = \frac{r}{s} + \frac{p}{q}$$

3 *The associative law for addition*
For any signless rational numbers $\frac{p}{q}$, $\frac{r}{s}$ and $\frac{t}{u}$,

$$\left(\frac{p}{q} + \frac{r}{s}\right) + \frac{t}{u} = \frac{p}{q} + \left(\frac{r}{s} + \frac{t}{u}\right)$$

5 *The identity for addition*
The signless rational number 0 is the identity for addition. For any signless rational number $\frac{p}{q}$,

$$\frac{p}{q} + 0 = 0 + \frac{p}{q} = \frac{p}{q}$$

6 *Subtraction*
Subtraction is the inverse operation of addition.

$$\frac{p}{q} - \frac{r}{s} = x$$

means

$$\frac{r}{s} + x = \frac{p}{q}$$

The set of signless rational numbers is *not closed for subtraction*; many equations such as

$$3\frac{1}{2} + x = 2\frac{1}{2}$$

have no solutions in the set of signless rational numbers.

Laws for Multiplication and Division

1′ *Closure for multiplication*
The set of natural numbers is closed for multiplication; that is, the product of any pair of natural numbers is a natural number.

1′ *Closure for multiplication*
The set of signless rational numbers is closed for multiplication; that is, the product of any pair of signless rational numbers is a signless rational number.

2′ *The commutative law for multiplication*
For any natural numbers a and b,

$$a \times b = b \times a$$

2′ *The commutative law for multiplication*
For any signless rational numbers $\dfrac{p}{q}$ and $\dfrac{r}{s}$,

$$\frac{p}{q} \times \frac{r}{s} = \frac{r}{s} \times \frac{p}{q}$$

3′ *The associative law for multiplication*
For any natural numbers, a, b and c

$$(a \times b) \times c = a \times (b \times c)$$

3′ *The associative law for multiplication*
For any signless rational numbers $\dfrac{p}{q}$, $\dfrac{r}{s}$ and $\dfrac{t}{u}$

$$\left(\frac{p}{q} \times \frac{r}{s}\right) \times \frac{t}{u} = \frac{p}{q} \times \left(\frac{r}{s} \times \frac{t}{u}\right)$$

4′ *The distributive law*
For any natural numbers, a, b and c

$$a \times (b + c) = (a \times b) + (a \times c)$$

and

$$(a + b) \times c = (a \times c) + (b \times c)$$

4′ *The distributive law*
For any signless rational numbers $\dfrac{p}{q}$, $\dfrac{r}{s}$ and $\dfrac{t}{u}$,

$$\frac{p}{q} \times \left(\frac{r}{s} + \frac{t}{u}\right) = \left(\frac{p}{q} \times \frac{r}{s}\right) + \left(\frac{p}{q} \times \frac{t}{u}\right), \text{ and}$$

$$\left(\frac{p}{q} + \frac{r}{s}\right) \times \frac{t}{u} = \left(\frac{p}{q} \times \frac{t}{u}\right) + \left(\frac{r}{s} \times \frac{t}{u}\right)$$

5′ *The identity for multiplication*
The natural number 1 is the identity for multiplication; for any natural number n

$$n \times 1 = 1 \times n = n$$

5′ *The identity for multiplication*
The signless rational number 1 is the identity for multiplication; for any signless rational number $\dfrac{p}{q}$,

$$\frac{p}{q} \times 1 = 1 \times \frac{p}{q} = \frac{p}{q}$$

6′ *Division*
Division is the inverse operation of multiplication;

$$a \div b = x$$

means

$$b \times x = a$$

The set of natural numbers is not closed for division; many equations such as

$$7 \times x = 3$$

have no solution in the set of natural numbers.

6′ *Division*
Division is the inverse operation of multiplication;

$$\frac{p}{q} \div \frac{r}{s} = x$$

means

$$\frac{r}{s} \times x = \frac{p}{q}$$

The set of signless rational numbers is closed for division, except by zero. Every equation such as

$$7 \times x = 3 \quad \text{or}$$

$$\frac{2}{3} \times x = \frac{4}{5}$$

has a solution in the set of signless rational numbers. The only such equations without solutions are of the type

$$0 \times x = 3$$

Hence $3 \div 0$, and other divisions by zero, are not possible.

THE DIRECTED NUMBERS

The directed rational numbers will provide the structure we are seeking. Directed numbers were introduced in Chapter 24, where it was seen that directed numbers are one-dimensional vectors.

An essential property of directed numbers is their method of addition, which consists of successively performing the movements of the two vectors to be added (Figure 33 : 3).

Figure 33 : 4 shows the number line of directed rational numbers. We have seen that the directed rational numbers behave rather similarly, as far as addition is concerned, to the signless rational numbers which have been used previously. By saying that two sets of numbers 'behave rather similarly' we mean that they obey rather similar arithmetical laws.

We now examine the arithmetical laws which describe the behaviour of directed rational numbers, and notice any arithmetical advantages and disadvantages which the directed rational numbers have over the previous set of numbers we have used.

Two laws which directed numbers obey for addition have already been described:

i) the set of directed numbers is *closed for addition*; that is, *any two* directed numbers can be added together to give a result which is also a directed number,

Addition of vectors

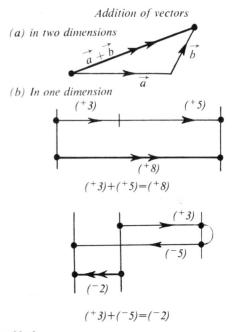

(a) in two dimensions

(b) In one dimension

$(^+3)+(^+5)=(^+8)$

$(^+3)+(^-5)=(^-2)$

Figure 33 : 3

ii) *the addition of directed numbers is commutative;* that is, the order in which directed numbers are added makes no difference to the final result.

$$a + b = b + a$$

Part of the number line

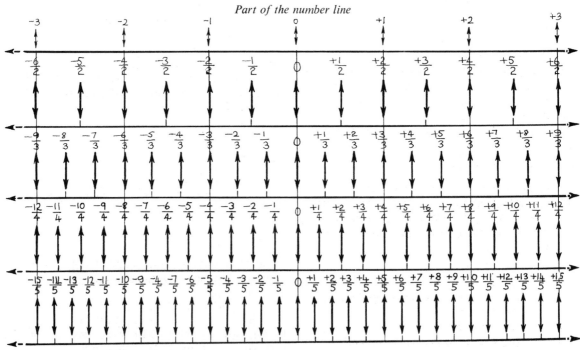

Figure 33 : 4

(i) $[(^+10)+(^+7)]+(^-9)=(^+17)+(^-9)=(^+8)$

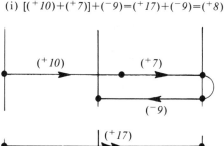

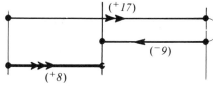

(ii) $(^+10)+[(^+7)+(^-9)]=(^+10)+(^-2)=(^+8)$

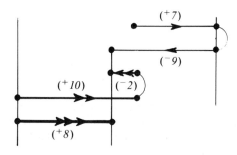

The final vector is the same, irrespective of the order in which the addition was performed.

Figure 33 : 5

These two laws are the same as the first two addition laws for natural numbers and for the signless rational numbers. We now examine the other laws for addition. Figure 33 : 5 illustrates the fact that directed numbers are *associative for addition*; that is, for any directed numbers a, b and c,

$(a + b) + c = a + (b + c)$

The importance of the associative law for addition of natural numbers and signless rational numbers is its use in rearranging and regrouping addition when dealing with large numbers. For example:

$27 + 9 = (20 + 7) + 9$
$= 20 + (7 + 9)$
[regrouping to take ones together]
$= 20 + (10 + 6)$
$= (20 + 10) + 6$
[regrouping to take tens together]
$= 36$

The same associative law is true for directed numbers, and so we can deal equally freely with directed numbers when adding them. Children may well prefer, when working out $(^+27) + (^-9)$, to argue

$$[(^+20) + (^+7)] + (^-9) = (^+20) + [(^+7) + (^-9)]$$
$$= (^+20) + (^-2)$$
$$= (^+18)$$

The next addition law is the existence of an *identity for addition* (*see page 237*). Zero performs the function of an identity for addition, since for any directed number a,

$a + 0 = 0 + a = a$

For instance, $(^-3) + 0 = 0 + (^-3) = (^-3)$.

SUBTRACTION OF DIRECTED NUMBERS

We now consider the subtraction of directed numbers. The subtraction of natural numbers is *inverse addition*; $9 - 3$ asks us to find the missing number in

$3 + \Box = 9$

The same idea applies to directed numbers. The subtraction of directed numbers is also done as addition with a missing number (*see page 174*). The subtraction

$(^+5) - (^-2)$

asks us to find the missing number in

$(^-2) + \Box = (^+5);$

the missing number is $(^+7)$.

We saw earlier (page 174) that every subtraction of directed numbers can be performed by addition. Instead of

$(^-9) - (^+3) = (^-12),$

we can do

$(^-9) + (^-3) = (^-12)$

with the same result. This is no coincidence, for if

$x = (^-9) - (^+3)$

then $(^+3) + x = (^-9)$.

Now if we add the opposite of $(^+3)$, which is $(^-3)$, to both sides of the equation, we obtain

$$(^+3) + (^-3) + x = (^-9) + (^-3)$$
or $\qquad x = (^-9) + (^-3).$
But also $\qquad x = (^-9) - (^+3),$
so $\qquad (^-9) - (^+3) = (^-9) + (^-3).$

Similarly, the subtraction of any directed number can always be performed by *addition of its opposite*.

CLOSURE OF THE SET OF DIRECTED NUMBERS FOR SUBTRACTION

One of the most important properties of directed numbers is that they are *closed for subtraction*. Given any directed number, there is always a directed number which can be added to it to make any other directed number; if a lift is at floor ($^+3$), there is a movement which will take it to floor ($^-2$), and similarly for any other example (*see page 172*).

Here at last, in the directed rational numbers, we find a set of numbers which has the complete list of properties for addition for which we have been searching. The directed rational numbers have members which correspond to the natural numbers and fractions; their addition obeys all the laws which we expect, and these numbers have the additional property of being closed for subtraction.

We complete our study of the addition and subtraction of directed numbers by stating the laws which they obey, and then go on to discuss multiplication and division of directed rational numbers.

Laws for addition and subtraction of directed rational numbers

1 Closure for addition
The set of directed rational numbers is closed for addition; that is, the sum of any two directed rational numbers is a directed rational number.

2 The commutative law for addition
For any directed rational numbers a and b,

$$a + b = b + a$$

3 The associative law for addition
For any directed rational numbers a, b and c,

$$(a + b) + c = a + (b + c)$$

4 The identity for addition
The directed rational number 0 is the identity for addition. For any directed rational number a,

$$a + 0 = 0 + a = a$$

5 Subtraction
Subtraction is the inverse operation of addition;

$$a - b = \boxed{x}$$

means

$$b + \boxed{x} = a$$

The set of directed rational numbers is *closed for subtraction*; every equation $b + x = a$ has a solution which is a directed rational number.

MULTIPLICATION OF DIRECTED NUMBERS

The multiplication of directed numbers may occur in children's graphical work. When children find a parabola, either as the path of a ball thrown in the air (*see page 387*), or by curve-stitching (*see page 482*), or by cutting a section of a cone (*see page 469*), the parabola is seen to be a symmetrical curve. But when a parabola is drawn as a curve of squares (Figure 33 : 6 (*b*)), only half of the curve is obtained. Children may suggest extending the horizontal axis backwards, and putting in the squares of negative numbers, in an effort to find the other half of the parabola. Calculators are also able to multiply directed numbers. This will lead to an attempt to attach a meaning to $(^-2) \times (^-2)$, $(^-3) \times (^-3)$, and so on.

We shall first give an account of the multiplication of directed numbers at an adult level, one which demands a type of thinking outside the range of primary school children. We do this in order to show how the multiplication of directed numbers *must* behave, before going on to suggest a

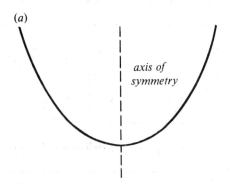

(*a*)

axis of symmetry

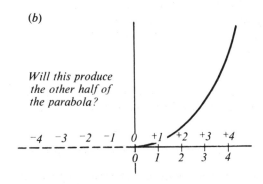

(*b*)

Will this produce the other half of the parabola?

Figure 33 : 6

simpler method which begs some questions, but by which children may be convinced of its likelihood.

We have already seen that there is an isomorphism between the positive directed numbers and the signless numbers (*see page 171*); this correspondence holds for addition:

$$(^+3) + (^+2) = (^+5)$$

corresponds to ↕   ↕   ↕

$$3 + 2 = 5$$

It is important, if we are to continue to use the positive directed numbers and the signless numbers interchangeably, that the same correspondence should also hold for multiplication. We must have

$$(^+3) \times (^+2) = (^+6)$$

corresponds to ↕   ↕   ↕

$$3 \times 2 = 6$$

It is also necessary, as the directed numbers are used as a generalisation of the signless numbers, that the multiplication of directed numbers should obey the same laws as the multiplication of signless numbers. Therefore the multiplication of directed numbers must be *closed*,[6] *commutative, associative,* and *distributive.* We now examine the results of these requirements.

Let b be any directed number, positive, negative or zero; it will have an opposite $(-b)$, such that

$$b + (-b) = 0 \quad \dots\dots\dots\dots\dots\dots\dots\dots(1)$$

Let a be any other directed number, and multiply both sides of equation (1) by a:

$$a \times [b + (-b)] = a \times 0$$

We now make the further requirement that $a \times 0 = 0$. Hence

$$a \times [b + (-b)] = 0$$

We now use the distributive law to expand the left-hand side:

$$(a \times b) + a \times (-b) = 0 \quad \dots\dots\dots\dots\dots\dots(2)$$

But the directed numbers are to be closed for multiplication, so $(a \times b)$, or ab, is also a directed number, and therefore has an opposite, which we call $(-ab)$, such that

$$ab + (-ab) = 0 \quad \dots\dots\dots\dots\dots\dots\dots\dots(3)$$

Comparing equation (2) with equation (3), we see that $a \times (-b)$ is also the opposite of ab.

Hence $a \times (-b) = (-ab)$

In words, the number a *multiplied by the opposite of*

[6]That is, it must be possible to multiply *any* two directed numbers together and obtain a directed number.

b *is equal to the opposite of* (ab). This relationship completely fixes the behaviour of the multiplication of directed numbers.

Consider, for instance, $(^+4) \times (^-3)$. Now $(^-3)$ is the opposite of $(^+3)$. Hence $(^+4) \times (^-3)$ is equal to the opposite of $(^+4) \times (^+3) = (^+12)$, to preserve the correspondence with $4 \times 3 = 12$. Hence, in symbols, the argument becomes

$$(^+4) \times (^-3) = -[(^+4) \times (^+3)]$$
$$= -[^+12]$$
$$= (^-12),$$

and similarly $(^-4) \times (^+3) = (^-12)$. Now consider $(^-4) \times (^-3)$. We repeat the same argument:

$$(^-4) \times (^-3) = -[(^-4) \times (^+3)]$$
$$= -[^-12]$$
$$= (^+12)$$

Summarising these four results, we see that it is a necessary consequence of the structure which we have required of the multiplication of directed numbers, that

$$(^+4) \times (^+3) = (^+12),$$
$$(^+4) \times (^-3) = (^-12),$$
$$(^-4) \times (^+3) = (^-12),$$
$$(^-4) \times (^-3) = (^+12),$$

In general $a \times (-b) = -ab,$
$$(-a) \times b = -ab,$$
$$(-a) \times (-b) = ab$$

It is now possible to complete the graph of squares, for $(^-1)^2 = (^-1) \times (^-1) = (^+1)$,
$(^-2)^2 = (^-2) \times (^-2) = (^+4)$, and so on.
The other half of the parabola appears, and completes the expected pattern (Figure 33 : 7).

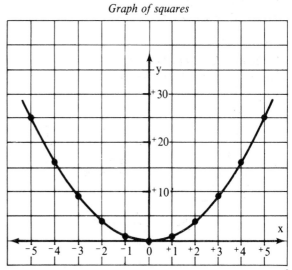

Graph of squares

Figure 33 : 7

Building up a multiplication table for the integers

a) *The multiplication table for natural numbers*

×	0	1	2	3	4	..	..
0	0	0	0	0	0	..	..
1	0	1	2	3	4	..	..
2	0	2	4	6	8	..	..
3	0	3	6	9	12	..	..
4	0	4	8	12	16	..	..
..	..	..	..	..	..	..	..
..	..	..	..	..	..	..	..

Figure 33 : 8(a)

b) *The framework of a multiplication table for the integers*

×	..	−4	−3	−2	−1	0	+1	+2	+3	+4	..
·											
−1											
−2											
−3											
−4											
0											
+1											
+2											
+3											
+4											
·											

Figure 33 : 8(b)

c) *The correspondence between (a) and (b) fills in part of the table for integers*

X	−4	−3	−2	−1	0	+1	+2	+3	+4
					⋮				
−4					0				
−3					0				
−2					0				
−1					0				
0	·· 0	0	0	0	0	0	0	0	0
+1					0	+1	+2	+3	+4
+2					0	+2	+4	+6	+8
+3					0	+3	+6	+9	+12
+4					0	+4	+8	+12	+16
⋮					⋮	⋮	⋮	⋮	⋮

Figure 33 : 8(c)

Next stages in building the multiplication table for the integers

×	−4	−3	−2	−1	0	+1	+2	+3	+4
−4					0				
−3					0				
−2					0				
−1					0				
0	0	0	0	0	0	0	0	0	0
+1	−4	−3	−2	−1	0	+1	+2	+3	+4
+2	−8	−6	−4	−2	0	+2	+4	+6	+8
+3	−12	−9	−6	−3	0	+3	+6	+9	+12
+4	−16	−12	−8	−4	0	+4	+8	+12	+16

Figure 33 : 9(a)

×	··	−4	−3	−2	−1	0	+1	+2	+3	+4	··
·	·	·	·	·	·	·	·	·	·	·	·
−4						0	−4	−8	−12	−16	··
−3						0	−3	−6	−9	−12	··
−2						0	−2	−4	−6	−8	··
−1						0	−1	−2	−3	−4	··
0	··	0	0	0	0	0	0	0	0	0	··
+1	··	−4	−3	−2	−1	0	+1	+2	+3	+4	··
+2	··	−8	−6	−4	−2	0	+2	+4	+6	+8	··
+3	··	−12	−9	−6	−3	0	+3	+6	+9	+12	··
+4	··	−16	−12	−8	−4	0	+4	+8	+12	+16	··
·	·	·	·	·	·	·	·	·	·	·	·

Figure 33 : 9(b)

The finished multiplication table for the integers

X	−4	−3	−2	−1	0	+1	+2	+3	+4
−4	+16	+12	+8	+4	0	−4	−8	−12	−16
−3	+12	+9	+6	+3	0	−3	−6	−9	−12
−2	+8	+6	+4	+2	0	−2	−4	−6	−8
−1	+4	+3	+2	+1	0	−1	−2	−3	−4
0	0	0	0	0	0	0	0	0	0
+1	−4	−3	−2	−1	0	+1	+2	+3	+4
+2	−8	−6	−4	−2	0	+2	+4	+6	+8
+3	−12	−9	−6	−3	0	+3	+6	+9	+12
+4	−16	−12	−8	−4	0	+4	+8	+12	+16

Increase of (+ 1) at each entry → +1
Increase of (+ 2) at each entry → +2
Increase of (+ 3) at each entry → +3
Increase of (+ 4) at each entry → +4

Figure 33 : 10

We should stress that this account of the multiplication of directed numbers is an abstract argument from stated assumptions, and represents a type of thinking which does not develop until well on in adolescence. It is therefore unsuitable for primary school children.

There are various ways in which children can be introduced to the multiplication of directed numbers. One of the simplest, at this stage, is an attempt to adapt the multiplication table with which children are so familiar, so that it will contain positive and negative directed integers. The correspondence between the natural numbers and the positive and zero integers must be preserved, so that for instance $(^+3) \times (^+2) = (^+6)$ corresponds to $3 \times 2 = 6$. Figure 33 : 8 shows that first stages in building up this table. The problem of filling in the other three quarters of the table remains. The rows marked in Figure 33 : 8 (c) can be completed by counting downwards along the directed number line (Figure 33 : 9) (a), and the oppposite quarter filled in by relying on the expectation that multiplication will be commutative; that is, we expect that $(^+1) \times (^-4) = (^-4) \times (^+1)$ (Figure 33 : 9 (b)).

The pattern of the three completed quarters of the table now shows very clearly how the last corner should be filled in to complete the pattern (Figure 33 : 10).

This appeal to the continuing pattern of the multiplication table is an informal embodiment of the principles used in the more formal argument: the need for the laws of multiplication to be satisfied, and the correspondence between the positive integers and the natural numbers.

Children will now be able to use their knowledge of the multiplication of integers to complete the graph of squares, and so to obtain the missing part of the parabola.

COMPLETION OF THE STRUCTURE OF DIRECTED NUMBERS

The last part of the previous section may have given the impression that we have only set up a method of multiplying directed *whole* numbers. This is not the case. The reader will have noticed that the proof of 'a *multiplied by the opposite of* b *is equal to the opposite of* (ab)' is valid for *any* directed numbers a and b. For instance the result can be applied to:

$$(^+\tfrac{2}{3}) \times (^-\tfrac{4}{5}) = -[(^+\tfrac{2}{3}) \times (^+\tfrac{4}{5})]$$
$$= -[^+\tfrac{8}{15}]$$
$$= (^-\tfrac{8}{15})$$

Thus we have constructed a multiplication which is valid for *any* positive, negative or zero rational numbers. In fact, *the set of directed rational numbers is closed for multiplication*. This multiplication was constructed so that it would obey the commutative, associative and distributive laws. We are therefore well advanced in obtaining a multiplication of directed rational numbers which obeys all the laws asked of an arithmetical operation.

There is also an identity for multiplication; the rational number $(^+1)$ has the property which distinguishes an identity: its product with any rational number a is the same rational number:

$$(^+1) \times a = a \times (^+1) = a$$

The reciprocal of a signless rational number a is the signless rational number whose product with a is 1. The reciprocal of $\frac{2}{3}$ is $\frac{3}{2}$, since $\frac{2}{3} \times \frac{3}{2} = 1$, and the reciprocal of $\frac{3}{2}$ is $\frac{2}{3}$. Every signless rational number except 0 has a reciprocal.

Similarly, every directed rational number except 0 has a reciprocal. The reciprocal of $(^+\tfrac{2}{3})$ is $(^+\tfrac{3}{2})$, since $(^+\tfrac{2}{3}) \times (^+\tfrac{3}{2}) = (^+1)$; and the reciprocal of $(^-\tfrac{2}{3})$ is $(^-\tfrac{3}{2})$, since $(^-\tfrac{2}{3}) \times (^-\tfrac{3}{2}) = (^+1)$. The rational number 0 has no reciprocal, for there is no rational number x such that

$$0 \times x = (^+1)$$

In order to complete the structure of the directed rational numbers we now only need to consider the *division* of one rational number by another. As usual, we define division as inverse multiplication; $(^+\tfrac{2}{3}) \div (^-\tfrac{1}{2})$ means, 'What must $(^-\tfrac{1}{2})$ be multiplied by to give $(^+\tfrac{2}{3})$?'; or, 'solve the equation

$$(^-\tfrac{1}{2}) \times \boxed{x} = (^+\tfrac{2}{3})\text{'}$$

This equation is solved by multiplying both sides of it by the reciporocal of $(^-\tfrac{1}{2})$, which is $(^-2)$, since $(^-2) \times (^-\tfrac{1}{2}) = (^+1)$.
Hence

$$(^-2) \times (^-\tfrac{1}{2}) \times \boxed{x} = (^-2) \times (^+\tfrac{2}{3}),$$
$$\text{and } \boxed{x} = (^-\tfrac{4}{3})$$

Clearly, almost all such equations can be solved. The only exceptions are of the form

$$0 \times \boxed{x} = (^-\tfrac{2}{3})$$

There is no rational number which multiplied by 0 gives $(^-\tfrac{2}{3})$, and so the equation cannot be solved. In other words, the division $(^-\tfrac{2}{3}) \div 0$ cannot be performed, but all divisions other than by 0 are possible. To perform the division $a \div b$ where a and b are rational numbers, we have to solve the equation

$$b \times \boxed{x} = a$$

This can be done by multiplying both sides of it by the reciprocal of b (unless $b = 0$).

Hence the set of directed rational numbers shares the property of the signless rational numbers, of being *closed for division*, EXCEPT FOR DIVISION BY ZERO. We have now completed our aim of constructing a set of numbers among which it is completely possible to do arithmetic. Any pair of directed rational numbers can be added, subtracted, multiplied or divided (except for division by zero), and the result is still a directed rational number. Moreover, the directed rational numbers contain a subset isomorphic with the natural numbers, with which we can count any number of things; they contain another subset isomorphic with the signless rational numbers with which we can measure any length to any degree of accuracy we like, and with the directed rationals themselves we can measure quantities such a time and temperatue where an arbitrary starting-point is needed. The search for arithmetical completeness which began from the natural numbers has now come to a (temporary) end with the directed rational numbers.

Mathematicians call a set of numbers which is closed for addition, subtraction, multiplication and division (except for division by zero) a *field*. The *field of directed rational numbers* is the first field which children use. It is not, however, the last. If they continue their mathematical education, they will soon need to operate in more extensive fields than the field of rational numbers. The *field of real numbers* and *the field of complex numbers* have the same basic structure as the field of rational numbers, but they contain other numbers, such as $\sqrt{(^+2)}$ and $\sqrt{(^-1)}$, which do not belong to the field of rational numbers. The importance of the field structure is that the laws for the behaviour of a field which children have learnt from the field of rational numbers – the closure, associative, commutative, distributive, and identity laws, together with the existence of inverses – also hold in every other field. All methods of arithmetical and algebraic procedure depend on these laws, and so the methods and structure learnt at this early stage are continued through all further extensions of the number system of mathematics.

We now state the complete set of laws for the field of directed rational numbers. The reader will contrast the completeness of this structure with the incompleteness revealed by the laws of behaviour of

natural numbers (*see page 237*) and signless rational numbers (*see page 408*).

In the statements of these laws we use a single letter, such as a, to represent a positive, negative or zero directed rational number. For instance, a may stand for $(^+3)$, $(^-\frac{2}{3})$, 0, or any other rational number.

The Field of Directed Rational Numbers

Laws for addition and subtraction

1 *Closure for addition*
The set of directed rational numbers is closed for addition; that is, the sum of any pair of directed rational numbers is a directed rational number.

2 *The commutative law for addition*
For any directed rational numbers a and b,

$$a + b = b + a$$

3 *The associative law for addition*
For any directed rational numbers a, b and c,

$$(a + b) + c = a + (b + c)$$

4 *The identity for addition*
The directed rational number 0 is the identity for addition. For any directed rational number a,

$$a + 0 = 0 + a = a$$

5 *Subtraction*
Subtraction is the inverse operation of addition;

$$a - b = \boxed{x}$$
means
$$b + \boxed{x} = a$$

The set of directed rational numbers is *closed for subtraction*; every equation such as

$$(^-3) + \boxed{x} = (^+\tfrac{2}{3})$$

has a solution in the set of directed rational numbers.

Laws for multiplication and division

1' *Closure for multiplication*
The set of directed rational numbers is closed for multiplication; that is, the product of any pair of directed rational numbers is a directed rational number.

2' *The commutative law for multiplication*
For any directed rational numbers a and b,

$$a \times b = b \times a$$

3′ *The associative law for multiplication*
For any directed rational numbers a, b and c,

$$(a \times b) \times c = a \times (b \times c)$$

4′ *The distributive laws*
For any direct rational numbers, a, b and c

$$a \times (b + c) = (a \times b) + (a \times c)$$

and

$$(a + b) \times c = (a \times c) + (b \times c)$$

5′ *The identity for multiplication*
The directed rational number $(^+1)$ is the identity for multiplication. For any directed rational number a,

$$a \times (^+1) = (^+1) \times a = a$$

6′ *Division*
Division is the inverse operation of multiplication;

$$a \div b = \boxed{x}$$

means

$$b \times \boxed{x} = a$$

The set of directed rational numbers is closed for divison, *except by zero*. Every equation such as

$$(^-3) \times \boxed{x} = (^+\tfrac{2}{3})$$

has a solution in the set of directed rational numbers. The only equations without solutions are of the type

$$0 \times \boxed{x} = (^-\tfrac{2}{3})$$

Hence $(^-\tfrac{2}{3}) \div 0$ and other divisions by zero are not possible.

GENERALISATION AND EXTENSION OF THE IDEA OF NUMBER

We have now generalised and extended the concept of number so that children who started by exploring the behaviour of a few (small) whole numbers grow into people who have within their grasp a complete set of positive and negative rational numbers, with which they can measure in either direction to any degree of accuracy, however large or small the quantity or number they are measuring. This development will probably take one or other of the paths shown in Figure 33 : 11 as children's idea of number extends and becomes more general. The relation between the various sets of numbers is also symbolised in the Venn diagram of Figure 33 : 12; where each new set of numbers contains the previous one as a subset. The natural numbers form

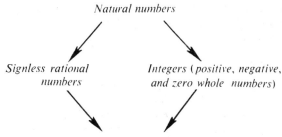

Figure 33 : 11

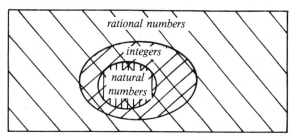

Figure 33 : 12

a subset of the integers, and the integers are a subset of the rational numbers.[7]

It is not to be expected that children will completely and explicitly understand this structure of sets of numbers until late in their secondary school career. Teachers should, however, realise their part in helping children to extend their number system, and should know that each extension of the number system is designed to solve a problem. The integers solve the problem of subtraction, and the rational numbers solved (almost completely) the problem of division. Nor is this the end of the road. The operation of square root demands the use of more extensive sets of numbers than the rational numbers, but for most other purposes in the primary school the set of rational numbers is sufficient, and numbers such as $\sqrt{2}$ and π, which are not rational, can be approximated by rational numbers.

NEGATIVE INDICES

We have used index notation earlier to abbreviate the writing of powers of a number. We now consider how this notation can be extended to express those numbers, smaller than one, which are used to head the columns of the decimal system containing numbers smaller than one. These labels

[7]In more advanced work, the set of integers has a subset which is *isomorphic* to the set of natural numbers.

for columns follow the pattern

Thousands Hundreds Tens Ones Tenths Hundredths Thousandths

or

$10^3 \quad 10^2 \quad 10^1 \quad 10^0 \quad ? \quad ? \quad ?$

The progression of the indices needs negative numbers to continue it. The powers

$10^3 \quad 10^2 \quad 10^1 \quad 10^0$

are followed by

$10^{-1} \quad 10^{-2} \quad 10^{-3}$

and so on, and it is natural to use the symbols

10^{-1} for one-tenth
10^{-2} for one-hundredth
10^{-3} for one-thousandth,

and so on.

Thus we have

$$10^3 = 10 \times 10 \times 10 = 1 \text{ thousand}$$
$$10^2 = 10 \times 10 \qquad = 1 \text{ hundred}$$
$$10^1 = 10 \qquad\qquad\qquad = 1 \text{ ten}$$
$$10^0 = 1 \qquad\qquad\qquad = 1 \text{ one}$$
$$10^{-1} = \frac{1}{10} \qquad\qquad\qquad = 1 \text{ tenth}$$
$$10^{-2} = \frac{1}{100} = \frac{1}{10 \times 10} = \frac{1}{10^2} \qquad = 1 \text{ hundredth}$$
$$10^{-3} = \frac{1}{1000} = \frac{1}{10 \times 10 \times 10} = \frac{1}{10^3} = 1 \text{ thousandth}$$

and so on. We have set up a one-to-one correspondence between the integers on the number line and the labels of the columns in positional notation (Figure 33 : 13).

These symbols are used not only as headings for columns in the notational system, but as convenient symbols for $\frac{1}{10}$, $\frac{1}{100}$, etc. We notice that 10^3 represents one thousand and 10^{-3} represents one thousandth, and so on. This makes the notation particularly convenient to handle.

Negative powers of other numbers can of course be defined and used similarly. In base five

$$5^3 = 5 \times 5 \times 5$$
$$5^2 = 5 \times 5$$
$$5^1 = 5$$
$$5^0 = 1$$
$$5^{-1} = \frac{1}{5}$$
$$5^{-2} = \frac{1}{5 \times 5} = \frac{1}{5^2}$$
$$5^{-3} = \frac{1}{5 \times 5 \times 5} = \frac{1}{5^3}$$

The index notation can thus be used to label the columns when we express a number, large or small, using any base.

Not only can indices, positive and negative, be used to express powers of numbers but indices can also be used in connection with *units* of measures. Thus, in the metric system the symbol for a square centimetre is cm^2 and the symbol for a cubic centimetre is cm^3. The volume of a rectangular block 3 cm by 3 cm by 5 cm is

$$3 \times 4 \times 5 \text{ cm}^3,$$

or 60 cm³

If the block is made of solid iron and has a mass of 735 grams, symbolised by 735 g, then the density of the block is given by

$$\text{density} = \frac{735g}{60cm^3} = 12 \cdot 25 \text{ g/cm}^3$$
$$= 12 \cdot 25 \text{ g cm}^{-3}$$

Thus the symbols for metric units and their powers can be manipulated just as the symbols for powers of numbers are manipulated. A speed of 10 metres per second is symbolised either by

10 m/s,

using the solidus / to indicate division, or by

10 m s⁻¹,

using m s⁻¹ to indicate that a distance in metres is divided by a time in hours.

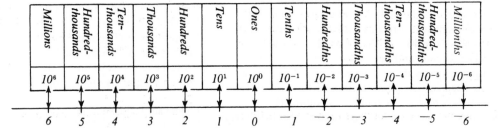

Millions	Hundred-thousands	Ten-thousands	Thousands	Hundreds	Tens	Ones	Tenths	Hundredths	Thousandths	Ten-thousandths	Hundred-thousandths	Millionths
10^6	10^5	10^4	10^3	10^2	10^1	10^0	10^{-1}	10^{-2}	10^{-3}	10^{-4}	10^{-5}	10^{-6}
6	5	4	3	2	1	0	⁻1	⁻2	⁻3	⁻4	⁻5	⁻6

Figure 33 : 13

Very large and very small quantities

Modern science often relies on the measurement of very large quantities such as the distances between stars, and very small quantities such as distances in the atom. Children will read and ask about these measurements. The conventional units of measurement are too large or too small, and scientists use new units for their purposes. Sometimes they give these units new names such as the light-year, the distance which light travels in a year, which is approximately 9 468 000 000 000 km. Often, however, they adapt more usual units by multiplying or dividing the unit by a thousand or a million. We see this happening in a simple case when we say that the distance of the earth from the sun is 149 million kilometres. The unit is a million kilometres.

We can write 149 million kilometres as 149×10^6 km, since 10^6 is a million (*see page 226*). This indicates clearly that the unit of measurement is 10^6 km, or one million km. Similarly

$$1 \text{ light-year} = 9\ 468\ 000\ 000\ 000 \text{ km}$$
$$= 9468 \times 10^9 \text{ km}$$

since $1\ 000\ 000\ 000 = 10^9$. The unit is 10^9 km. This distance could also be written as $9 \cdot 468 \times 10^{12}$ km, using a unit of 10^{12} km or a million million km, which has been sub-divided into thousandths.

When an exceedingly small unit is needed for measuring the wavelength of light the Ångstrom unit, which is one hundred-millionth of a centimetre, can be used. Visible light of different colours has wavelengths ranging between 4000 and 7500 Ångstroms. The fraction one hundred-million is 10^{-8}; hence an Ångstrom unit, which is one hundred-millionth of a centimetre, or $\frac{1}{100\ 000\ 000}$ cm, is written 10^{-8} cm. We can now write the wavelength of violet light, 4000 Ångstroms, as 4000×10^{-8} cm. It can also be written as 400×10^{-7} cm, or 40×10^{-6} cm, or 4×10^{-5} cm.

Scientific notation

Scientific calculators and computers have the capability of dealing with numbers expressed in *scientific notation*. This is a slight modification of the notation used in the last section. We saw that 1 light-year can be written as

9468×10^9 km
or $9 \cdot 468 \times 10^{12}$ km

The second of these forms is known as scientific notation; the power of 10 is chosen in such a way that the other part of the number, known as the *mantissa*, lies between 1 and $9 \cdot 999 \ldots$. Similarly, in scientific notation,

4000 Ångstroms $= 4 \times 10^{-5}$ cm

Scientific notation is of great use when the numbers being used are too large or too small for the capacity of the calculator. On a simple calculator, the entry

$40\ 000 \times 8\ 000\ 000 =$

causes an error message to be displayed; the result

320 000 000 000,

contains too many digits for the size of the calculator display. A scientific calculator, however, changes the answer into scientific notation, and displays it as

$3 \cdot 2 \times 10^{11}$

Neither calculator nor computer has the capability of display 10^{11} as it stands, and each uses it own code for the display. The calculator displays

$3 \cdot 2 \quad 11$,

using two digits after a space to display the power of ten. A computer, which can display alphabetic characters, prints

$3 \cdot 2 \text{ E} + 11$
for $3 \cdot 2 \times 10^{11}$,

using E (standing for *exponent*) before the power, and explicitly displaying a + sign for 10^{11}. The result of

$0 \cdot 000\ 04 \times 0 \cdot 000\ 000\ 8$

is displayed as

$3 \cdot 2 \text{ E} - 11$,

standing for $3 \cdot 2 \times 10^{-11}$.

Activities using indices

Children will investigate powers of other numbers as well as ten. Power of two form a convenient starting-point for experiment, as they are obtained by continual doubling; each power of two is twice the previous power:

$2^1 = 2$
$2^2 = 2 \times 2 = 4$
$2^3 = 2 \times (2 \times 2) = 8$
$2^4 = 2 \times (2 \times 2 \times 2) = 16$, and so on.

420 .

Powers of 2 using Cuisenaire rods

$2^0 = 1$
$2^1 = 2$
$2^2 = 4$
$2^3 = 8$
$2^4 = 16$
$2^5 = 32$

Figure 33 : 14

With very little labour the table can be built up for some distance:

2^{-5}	2^{-4}	2^{-3}	2^{-2}	2^{-1}	2^0	2^1	2^2	2^3	2^4	2^5
$\frac{1}{32}$	$\frac{1}{16}$	$\frac{1}{8}$	$\frac{1}{4}$	$\frac{1}{2}$	1	2	4	8	16	32

2^6	2^7	2^8	2^9	2^{10}	2^{11}	2^{12}	2^{13}
64	128	256	512	1024	2048	4096	8192

If children make powers of two by using Cuisenaire rods (Figure 33 : 14), they will notice that the first few members of the set of powers of 2 form one of the 'colour families'. A graphical representation of the powers of 2 is more practicable, since the vertical scale can be reduced to more manageable proportions, but it should be remembered that increasing the power of 2 by one will always result in doubling the height of the graph (Figure 33 : 15). Graphing powers of 2 will help children to realise the extremely rapid growth of powers of ten, where graphing is almost impossible since an increase of 1 in the index increases the height of the graph tenfold.

Children can be encouraged to try the effect of multiplying and dividing numbers which they have chosen from among those listed in the table of powers of 2. Some children will search for a reason underlying their results.

For example, $16 \times 128 = 2048$, which also appears in the table of powers of 2. In fact

$$2^4 \times 2^7 = 2^{11}$$

In reverse,

$$2048 \div 128 = 16 \quad \text{or} \quad 2^{11} \div 2^7 = 2^4$$

Powers of 10 can be explored in the same way. This is a valuable exploration, because it strengthens children's understanding of place value. For instance,

ten $\times$ (1 hundred) = 1 thousand

can be written

$$10 \times 100 = 1000,$$
$$\text{or } 10^1 \times 10^2 = 10^3$$
and (1 hundred) $\times$ (1 million) = 1 hundred million
is $100 \times 1\ 000\ 000 = 100\ 000\ 000$
$$\text{or } 10^2 \times 10^6 = 10^8$$

More difficult is

(1 hundredth) of (1 thousand) = ten
$$\text{or } 0.01 \times 1000 = 10$$
$$\text{or } 10^{-2} \times 10^3 = 10^1$$

The *index laws for multiplication and division*

$$a^m \times a^n = a^{m+n} \quad and \quad a^m \div a^n = a^{m-n}$$

will not be explicitly stated at this stage but this numerical experience will pave the way for the theoretical study of indices and many children can reach the stage of stating as a result of their experiences that, 'to multiply the numbers, you add the indices'.

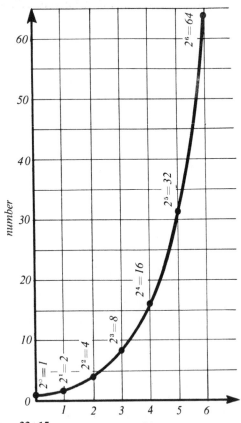

Figure 33 : 15   *power of 2*

Extensions of the number system in the National Curriculum

By Level 6 of the National Curriculum, children are expected to know and be able to use the directed number system. These words are not explicitly used, but the use of negative numbers and decimals indicates that directed rational numbers are expected. Negative numbers appear at Level 3, and a full understanding of decimals is achieved by Level 6.

- recognise negative whole numbers in familiar contexts, e.g. a temperature scale, a number line, a calculator display.

(AT2, Level 3)

- order decimals and appreciate place values.

(AT2, Level 6)

Of course, children at this stage are not expected to carry out a formal treatment of the structure of numbers, such as that provided in this chapter for the teacher. However, children are expected to realise by Level 8 that positive and negative decimals can be added, subtracted, multiplied and divided.

- solve problems and use multiplication and division with numbers of any size.

(AT2, Level 7)

- substitute negative numbers into formulae involving addition, subtraction, multiplication and division.

(AT2, Level 8)

The use of index notation is expected at Level 5, but the full use of scientific notation, which the National Curriculum calls 'standard index form', is not required until Level 8.

- use index notation to express powers of whole numbers.

(AT2, Level 5)

- express and use numbers in standard index form, with positive and negative integer powers of 10.

(AT2, Level 8)

34 | *POSITION*

POSITION RELATIVE TO THE OBSERVER

In response to objects around them, babies make movements with their bodies. They reach out towards objects; they follow moving objects with their eyes; when they become mobile they move towards things they want. In all these situations, they relate the positions of objects to themselves. Two factors are involved: direction and distance. A young child may look, reach or walk in the right direction, but the object may be too far away. Gradually, children acquire the ability to assess both distance and direction with fair accuracy; they now save themselves ineffective effort, and they begin to notice the effects of moving. When the child or the object moves, the scene changes, and things are no longer in the same relationship. Children become less egocentric and more able to see how one thing is positioned relative to another (Figure 34 : 1).

Figure 34 : 1

THE RELATIVE POSITION OF TWO OBJECTS

When children can understand and use language they show that they are aware of some position

relationships. They will know that the cat is *under* the table, that the book is *on* the shelf, that David is *next* to Peter, and so on. From this stage there is a rapid growth in the variety of ways in which children can answer the question, 'Where is . . .?' Yet until they have some understanding of number and distance they cannot give a precise answer. They may *remember* the exact position in which a toy was placed in regard to another object but they do not yet have the mental imagery or the concepts with which to describe it.

POSITION IN AN ORDER OR SEQUENCE

Before the skill of counting is acquired children will be able to place a toy, such as a car or a doll, in a particular place in a sequence; it may be a sequence of size, colour, shape or type but it follows some rule or pattern. From this kind of experience the idea of number develops and children learn to count. Now they can specify a position in an order. They use ordinal numbers to say, for example, that their book is on the third shelf, or that Ann is fourth in the line. The form of speech may not be quite correct; children may say that Ann is number four in the line, but their recognition of the use of number to describe position in a sequence is evident.

POSITION AS GIVEN BY DISTANCE ALONG A LINE

The first measurements of length will almost certainly be along a straight edge. The distance being measured is the length of a line along which the measuring unit can be placed. At this stage children are not yet thinking about how far one *end* of the line is from the other *end*; they are not therefore considering the *position* of one end relative to the other. This latter idea emerges as children measure the distance of one object from another; for instance, the distance from the door to a picture, or from one corner to the tree. They may have actually to set out or to imagine the line which must be measured in order to find the distance. They will *state a position* as 5 m along a wall, 4 decimetres above the table, 6 cm beyond the mark, and so on. They are now answering the question, 'How far?' or, 'Where?' and not the question, 'How long?' This is an important stage and should not be forgotten when measuring becomes a strong interest.

ONE MEASUREMENT MAY BE INSUFFICIENT TO FIX A POSITION

In the instances quoted there is another object to which a position can be related. If the thing to be located is on a line or in a certain sequence of things in a plane it is easy to define its position by a single measurement along the line or by one ordinal number to give the place in the sequence. When an object is not on a known fixed line or in a sequence, as, for example, a pylon in a meadow, then more than one measurement is required to describe its position in the plane. The need to define such a position will usually arise in an attempt to map an area near the school or to make a model of a real or an imagined scene in which certain landmarks are to be accurately placed. Children will experiment to find out how the precise spot can be fixed. The kinds of measurements which are necessary to define such a position become familiar during the upper primary years.

USING TWO DISTANCES TO FIX A POSITION

Awareness of the need for *two* pieces of information to tell us where a thing is in a plane comes through such experiences as describing the exact position of a child's own classroom tray as in the third row up and the fourth along from the left; the book is on the second shelf and third from the right-hand end; on a map which is covered with a square grid the home town is in row *p* and column *F*. When children can readily use this kind of two-fold

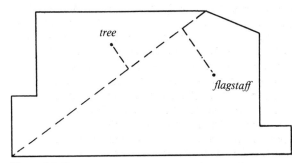

Figure 34 : 2

statement they have established the idea of *co-ordinates* to fix a point in a plane. They can use two lines, such as the edge of the floor and the vertical edge of a wall, as a frame of reference and can state the position of any point in the plane by its distances from the two reference lines. Later on, they will put in reference lines, or axes, wherever is most convenient for the task in hand. For example, they may put a line diagonally across the playground and measure the distances of a flagstaff from the corner measured along this diagonal line and perpendicular to it (Figure 34 : 2).

Plans, maps and charts, such as those associated with buried treasure, all call for an understanding of the use of a pair of numbers to define a position, either to enable the observer to record it on a map or to pass on the information to another person. Figure 34 : 3(b) shows the general case where a point is shown by the number pair (*a*, *b*).

(*a*)

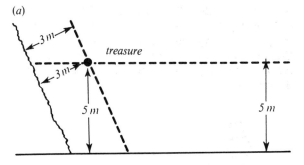

(*b*)

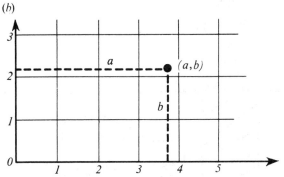

Figure 34 : 3

USING A VECTOR TO FIX A POSITION

It is not always possible or convenient to measure the two distances of a point from lines of reference. Children already know that to reach a place by the shortest path they must move in a certain direction and for a certain distance. The position of the place can therefore be represented by a vector from the starting-point. For example, the pylon in the

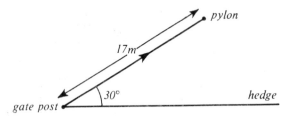

Figure 34 : 4

meadow can be shown on a plan if the direction
and distance from a gatepost can be found. For this
purpose a base line through the starting-point must
be chosen, say the hedge running from the gatepost.
The angle between this base line and the direction
of the pylon must be recorded. This angle need not,
however, be measured if a plane table is used for
recording it, as described in Chapter 30. Once more
a pair of numbers is required to fix the position.
The vector we use has both *direction*, given by the
angle with the base line, and *length*, given by the
distance from the gatepost to the pylon. In Figure
34 : 4 the position shown could be written (17 m,
30°). The starting-point and the base line must be
defined and the distance and angle given. It is often
possible to use a North–South line as a base line,
and to give a position as (17 m, N 60° E); the
bearing of the point is N 60° E.

Using two angles to fix a position

We have now seen two ways of fixing a position in
a plane. First, choosing two axes of reference we
can measure two distances; secondly, we can choose
a base line with an end-point and then measure the
angle with the base line and the distance from the
end-point. There is a third way. We may choose a
base line with both end-points marked. We can then
measure the angles made at the end-points by the
base line and the lines pointing to the object to be
fixed. The two given end-points provide enough
information for us to complete the fixing of the
position because we can find the distance between
them if their sites are known. In Figure 34 : 5, *A*

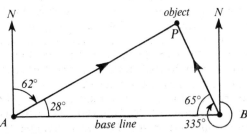

Figure 34 : 5

and *B* are given points, trees or gateposts. They are
found to be 9 metres apart. The angles which the
sighting lines *AP* and *BP* make with *AB* are
measured. If the angles are 28° and 65° the
position of *P* is as shown.

Position in three dimensions

Children at the upper primary stage are often
keenly interested in space and the objects in it, both
the astronomical bodies and the human-made
satellites and spacecraft. They want to know
something about the ways in which position in
three-dimensional space can be defined. Many of
the techniques are too difficult for primary
programmes but a foundation of basic methods can
be laid. The first step may be to extend the use of
co-ordinates to include fixing a point above a plane.
Children may wish to show position relative to
ground level. For example, a child's desk may be on
the third floor, at a given distance from an outside
wall and at a certain distance from an adjacent
wall. The position can be stated in terms of three
distances as shown in Figure 34 : 6. The position is
represented by the three co-ordinates (4, 5, 10).

A rectangular room provides a good
three-dimensional framework: the two walls and
floor which meet at one corner of the room form
the three planes of reference. The positions of
various objects in the room, such as the lower tip of
an overhead light, can be stated using co-ordinates.
Any structure which is based on cuboids can also
have points, such as the vertices and the
intersections of diagonals, described by reference to
three planes which meet at a vertex.

The positions so far considered have either been
in a plane or have been related to planes as in the

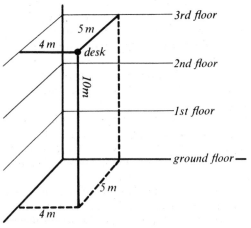

Figure 34 : 6

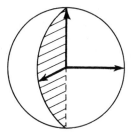

Figure 34 : 7

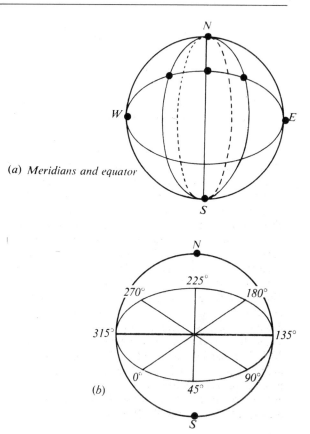

(a) *Meridians and equator*

(b)

Figure 34 : 8

paragraph above, where the walls and floor served as reference planes. Portions of the earth's surface can only be treated as planes if they are very small. The navigation of a ship or aircraft, or the control of a satellite, must take account of the spherical shape of the earth. This makes it necessary to be able to state any position on a sphere, and for this purpose to have some reference points and lines. Although for some mathematical purposes it is useful to think of the earth's surface as a sphere which can be related to three reference planes through its centre, this approach is not the most practical for tracking changes of position on the surface. Navigators prefer to use latitude and longitude. It is clear, therefore, that geography and mathematics should go hand in hand in dealing with the ways of stating precisely where an object is either on the surface of the earth or in orbit round it.

LONGITUDE

As the earth rotates during the day the sun appears to be overhead at a succession of places in a path from East to West. Noon therefore occurs later at places West of an observer. Children may become aware of a difference of time which depends on this East-to-West relationship by their interest in the timing of live television programmes from other parts of the world. Longitude measures these East-to-West differences in position and can be understood more easily than latitude, the significance of which is not at first apparent to children. We shall therefore begin by considering longitude.

A large globe showing the countries of the world, the poles and the equator gives meaning to this work. A plain black sphere on which the position of points can be marked is equally important. Pupils should be able to make the skeleton of a sphere by taking four equal circles of cane or wire, such as are used for Christmas decorations, and fastening them together at the ends of a common diameter (Figure 34 : 8). They should be symmetrically placed so that

another equal circle representing an equator is divided into eight equal arcs. The North and South poles are represented by the common points of the four circles, each of which is made up of two *meridians*, or two semicircles each containing all points that have the same noon. Every point on the surface of a sphere lies on a meridian: a wire circle of the same radius as the other circles could be placed so as to pass through any such point and the two poles. This circle would show the meridian through the point. If this meridian could be named we should be able to state one fact about the position of the point, namely that it lies on a particular meridian.

We can see that any meridian could be transformed into another by rotating about the N–S axis. The meridians could therefore be given a rotation or angle measure from any fixed meridian chosen as the zero. By tradition the Greenwich meridian is universally taken as the zero or starting position. The meridians in the skeleton structure, starting from the zero, mark rotations of 45°, 90°, 135°, 180°, 225°, 270°, 315° and 360°, completing one revolution from the Greenwich meridian. If diameters of cane or wire are placed across the equator these angles can be identified as shown in Figure 34 : 8(*b*).

In practice the angles are recorded from 0° to 180° East of Greenwich and 0° to 180° West of Greenwich. These angles state the longitude of any point on a particular meridian.

The meridian opposite Greenwich is 180° East or West according to the direction in which it is approached. This creates a strange situation in regard to naming time on the two sides of this meridian. Places to the East of Greenwich have their noon earlier than Greenwich; places to the West have a later noon. Consequently travelling to the East one finds the local time becoming increasingly later than Greenwich time. Thus, people in England hear the end of the day's cricket live on the radio from Australia in the early morning. Eventually, as one approaches the 180° East meridian, local time is approaching the midnight which has yet to come to Greenwich where it is noon, local time. If the date is April 24th at Greenwich, the time at 180° East is midnight of April 24/25th. A traveller moving West from Greenwich finds local time earlier than Greenwich, so that American sporting events which take place in the afternoon are seen live on British television in the late evening. Eventually, when we reach 180° West, local time is the midnight *before* Greenwich noon, and so it is midnight on April 23/24th. Therefore the same moment of time has a different date on the two sides of the 180° meridian, which is known as the *date line*.

The time relative to Greenwich at places on any particular meridian can now be worked out readily. Since one daily revolution of the earth through 360° takes 24 × 60 minutes it is clear that a rotation of 1° takes 4 minutes. A place with longitude 18° *East* will be 18 × 4, or 72 minutes *later* than Greenwich; the sun was overhead there 1 hour 12 minutes earlier than at Greenwich. A place 18° *West* of Greenwich will have time 1 hour 12 minutes *earlier* than Greenwich; the sun will not be overhead until 1·20 p.m. Greenwich Mean Time. The time at important cities such as Delhi, New York, Moscow, Singapore, Sydney, Peking can now be found with the use of a map which gives longitude.

For convenience there are agreed time belts covering approximately 15° of longitude throughout which the same time is kept officially. The time in the neighbouring belt to the East will be one hour later, and the belt to the West one hour earlier. If children become especially interested in the recording of time a wide field of investigation is open to them, both contemporary and historical.

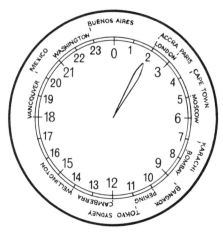

Figure 34 : 9

A world clock shows the times kept at the most important cities (Figure 34 : 9) and some digital watches can be easily adjusted to show the time at any longitude.

LATITUDE

The position of a point on a sphere is only partly given by its longitude. To give it precisely we must know where on its meridian the point lies. The skeleton of the sphere can show this. As an example we will take a point on one of the wire meridians as shown in Figure 34 : 10. A wire or stretched string joining the point to the centre of the sphere shows the angle of rotation from the point on the same meridian which lies on the equator. If this angle is 42° we say that the point is 42° North. In Figure 34 : 10, *B* is 64° South.

Thus the position of a point on a sphere is given by two angles, one indicating the longitude East or West of Greenwich, the other the *latitude* North or South of the equator.

If cane or wire circles smaller than the equator of the model can be provided they can be placed on the spherical skeleton or on a globe so that all points on each circle have the same latitude. If the circles are of a size to be placed at intervals of 15°

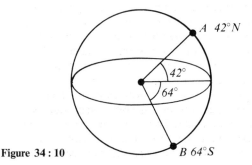

Figure 34 : 10

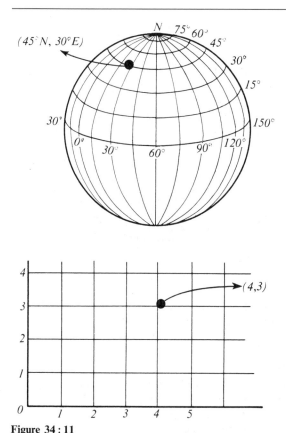

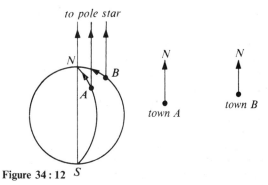

Figure 34 : 12

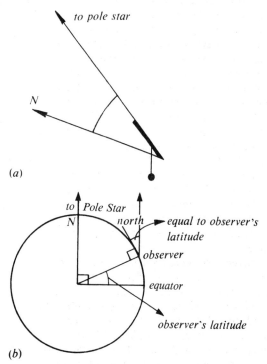

(4,3)

Figure 34 : 11

of latitude it will be seen that the meridians and these parallels of latitude cover the sphere with a grid which the pupils can compare and contrast with the square grid which they knows so well can cover a plane. Figure 34 : 11 shows both grids.

NORTH POLE AND POLE STAR

In the northern hemisphere the magnetic North is not far from the pole, and the line of the meridian through any point is given fairly closely by North shown on the compass. At two towns A and B which are only a few hundred km apart, a map shows the North direction by two parallel lines. On the earth's surface the meridians of which these North-pointing lines are parts actually meet at the pole. This apparent contradiction puzzles children and they need to realize for themselves that a small portion of the earth's surface can be taken as flat and the difference of the two North directions as negligible (Figure 34 : 12).

The diference between a near view and a view from a very great distance is also brought out by studying the pole star. This star is in line with the earth's axis but so far away that, seen from any point in the northern hemisphere, it appears to be

on a line parallel to the earth's axis. Thus it is always seen in a northerly direction as demonstrated in Figure 34 : 12.

Pupils can be encouraged to find the angle between the line pointing to the pole star and the horizontal line pointing North at the observer's position. This can be done by using the clinometer described in Chapter 30. If children find the angle at the beginning and the end of a two- to three-hour interval they will discover that the position of the pole star is unchanged, although other stars are in a different position relative to the pole star.

Some children may notice that this angle is the same as the latitude of their own position. Figure 34 : 13(b) shows the right angles which make the equality of these angles clear.

Figure 34 : 13

GREAT CIRCLES

The equator and the circles on which the meridians lie all have the same radius, which is equal to the radius of the sphere. The parallels of latitude (except the equator) have a smaller radius. It is interesting for children to realise that any number of circles can be drawn on the surface of a sphere through any two points on it. If a set of wire circles of different sizes are placed so as to have two points in common (Figure 34 : 14), pupils will see how many and different are the possible circular paths from one point to the other.

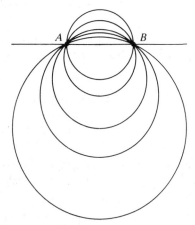

Figure 34 : 14

If such a set of circles of different radii are drawn through two points on a *plane* the different lengths of the arcs between *A* and *B* are seen at once to depend on the radii. The greater the radius of the circle the shorter the arc between *A* and *B*. Similarly, on a sphere the shortest path between two points will be along the circle with the greatest radius; this circle has the same radius as the sphere itself. Such a circle is called a *great circle* (Figure 34 : 15). The equator is a great circle; a meridian is half a great circle.

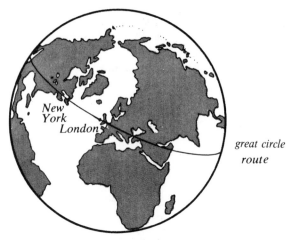

Figure 34 : 16

If a ship or an aircraft wishes to take the shortest route it will follow a great circle route. If several wire circles of different radii are placed to join, say, London and New York on a globe, the position of the great circle will probably surprise the pupils (Figure 34 : 16).

The calculation of a great circle distance between two places on the earth is, in general, too difficult for primary school children but if the points happen to lie on a meridian or on the equator some children may be able to find the difference of longitude or latitude and thus calculate the length of the great circle arc. In every case a piece of fine string can be stretched as tightly as possible between the two points on the globe and then measured to give an approximate globe distance. This must then be converted to the true distance, reckoning the earth's radius as about 6371 km. This method can check the calculation of the distance in the case of two points on a meridian. Figure 34 : 17 shows two such points: *A* with latitude 65°N, and *B* with latitude 28°N.

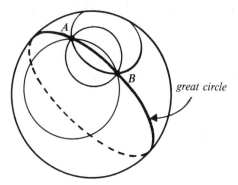

Figure 34 : 15

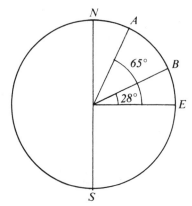

Figure 34 : 17

Difference in latitude $= 65° - 28°$
$$= 37°$$
Circumference of great circle
$= 2 \times \pi \times 6371$ km
$= 40030$ km, using the calculator.

Length of arc AB

$= \frac{37}{360} \times 40030$ km

$= 4114$ km

The position of A can now be stated as approximately 4100 km North of B.

CHANGE OF POSITION

Movement means change of position. Plotting the position of a ship or aircraft on a map gives vital information to its navigator. The accuracy of navigation depends on the instruments available to provide the information. The history of the development of such instruments to give more extensive and more accurate information makes interesting reading for older and abler pupils in primary schools.

Children can also collect information and charts to help them to study the movements of satellites, space probes, and so on. In this way they learn about circular and elliptical orbits. We consider these curves in Chapter 33.

Position and location in the National Curriculum

The development of children's ideas of position and location are dealt with in Attainment Target 4 (shape and space). At Level 1, simple descriptions of location are expected:

- use common words, such as 'on', 'inside', 'above', 'under', 'behind', 'next to', to describe a position.

(AT4: Level 1)

The eight points of the compass are mentioned at Level 3:

- understand and use compass bearings and the terms 'clockwise' and 'anticlockwise'.

(AT4: Level 3)

By Level 4, children are expected not only to give the position of a point by means of its co-ordinates, but also by using distance and angle:

- specify location by means of co-ordinates in the first quadrant and by means of angle and distance.

(AT4: Level 4)

Bearings appear at Level 6, and co-ordinates in three dimensions at Level 7.

- understand and use bearings to define directions.

(AT4: Level 6)

- use co-ordinates to locate position in 3-D.

(AT4: Level 7)

Latitude and longitude are not mentioned in National Curriculum mathematics, but they will be of interest to children who wish to understand their use to give location in an atlas, or who become interested in the climatic features of countries in different latitudes.

35 | SCALE, RATE AND RATIO

EARLY EXPERIENCES OF RATIO

We can trace the beginning of the idea of ratio in very early experiences in childhood. Objects are recognised as having the same shape even though their sizes differ. An object such as a toy will be seen as the same object although when it is further away from a child it appears to be smaller. Seen at a greater distance the height of the toy will appear to be reduced but if all the lengths show a similar reduction the thing is readily identified by a child. With further experience children come to recognise an object even when its shape seems different because the thing has been rotated or raised or lowered. Yet the easiest and most memorable recognition occurs when only size is changed and the appearance of shape is unaltered. This is shown in Figure 35 : 1.

Enlargement, as by projection of a slide on to a screen, or reduction in size, as in a picture, reinforces children's awareness of similarity of shape. Later on, the observation of shadows will show that many shadows are distortions of the silhouette of the original object. A child's own shadow may be a very elongated shape when the sun is low in the sky, or a very short shape if it is cast by a high light close at hand. Occasionally a shadow is an enlarged version of the original, as when a hand is placed in the beam of light from a projector (Figure 35 : 2).

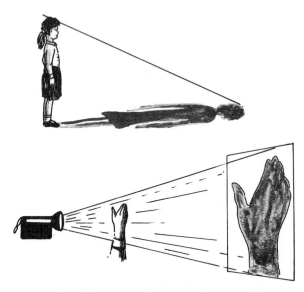

Figure 35 : 2

Children's delight in miniature versions of everyday objects is very marked during the early years at school. The range of such toys is vast. The demand for precision in the miniatures increases rapidly and shows clearly the children's recognition of the correspondences that should exist between the parts of an object and its model.

Even before school days objects like jugs, model cars, shoes, jerseys, which are made in sets of different sizes are described by a child as 'the same only larger (or smaller)'. But any discrepancy in the size of corresponding parts in two somewhat similar objects is noticed. For example, in Figure 35 : 3(*a*) the spout is 'too long'; in Figure 35 : 3(*b*) the lorries have the 'wrong trailer'.

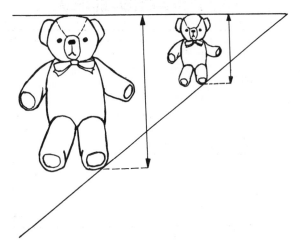

Figure 35 : 1

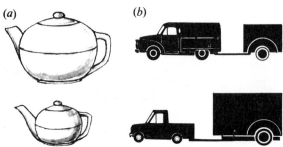

Figure 35 : 3

Such observations show that children are becoming aware of equality of ratios of length but only in an intuitive way. As yet there is nothing numerical or precisely quantitative in their perceptions.

THE RATIO OF LENGTHS

The classification of blocks of various shapes which are made in two different sizes, such as Logiblocs, will lead to closer observation of lengths: the sides of the 'big' squares and the 'little' squares make pairs like the sides of the 'big' triangles and the 'little' triangles, or the sides of the 'big' rectangles and the 'little' rectangles.

Construction of models with two sets of structural apparatus based on different unit lengths, such as Stern rods and Cuisenaire rods, will bring out the fact that one model is a smaller version of the other. The idea of scale is emerging.

When children have built a staircase with each of these sets of rods they will associate a number with each rod in terms of the unit cube of its set. They will then be able to describe the structures in Figure 35 : 4 using the number names of the rods. The lengths of the rods in the two models can be compared. Any two rods of the one shape are then seen to have the same relationship as the corresponding pair in the other shape; for instance, a six-rod and an eight-rod always have the same relationship, whatever their size. The ratio of the lengths of these two rods is always 6 : 8, whatever the actual sizes of the rods.

To children, the relation is between 6 and 8 seen as unmeasured lengths of a pair of rods in the same set. To the teacher another relationship, that between pairs of corresponding rods, one from each set, is also apparent and is seen in terms of the scale used in constructing the rods. In the Cuisenaire set the unit cube has an edge of 1 cm; in the Stern set the unit is 1·9 cm. The ratio of the edges is thus 1·9 cm to 1 cm. This ratio can be expressed as a ratio of numbers as 1·9 to 1 (Figure 35.5). Such a numerical statement becomes possible to children only after experience with measures and numbers.

Although children see intuitively that the relation between a pair of rods from one set is the same as for the corresponding pair from another set, when they have one pair only they compare one with another at first in terms of 'bigger than', 'smaller than'. The staircase of rods shows each rod as 'one more than' the next smaller one, when unit cubes are used to make up the differences; or children will say that the two-rod needs a four-rod to match a given six-rod. They are not yet thinking in terms of how many two-rods would make a six-rod. In fact it is only when more than one pair of rods are seen to have the same relationship, though different in size, that the notion of ratio emerges as a way of comparing each pair. It is then usually stated as 'twice, 3 times, 5 times . . . as long'; this implies that the ratio is 2 : 1, 3 : 1, 5 : 1. The inverse statement, half as long, which comes very readily, can be extended at this stage and 'one third, one fifth . . . as long' can be used. In this fractional statement, the numbers, one and three, or one and five, contain

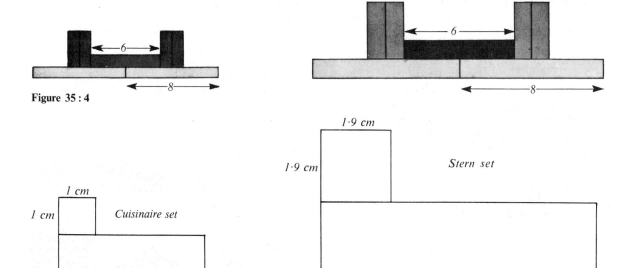

Figure 35 : 4

Figure 35 : 5

one → *three times*   *one third* → *one*

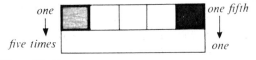

one → *five times*   *one fifth* → *one*

Figure 35 : 6

the idea of the ratio 1 : 3 or 1 : 5, though children are not yet able to think in this abstract way (Figure 35 : 6).

A particularly simple ratio of sizes is found if children build the same model with Multilink cubes, which are 2-cm cubes, and with Centicubes, which are 1-cm cubes (Figure 35 : 7).

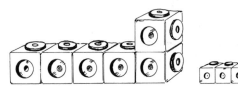

Figure 35 : 7

The ratio of every pair of lengths in the two models is 2 : 1. If the total length of each model is measured, the larger is 10 cm long, and the smaller is 5 cm long. Thus

10 : 5 = 2 : 1

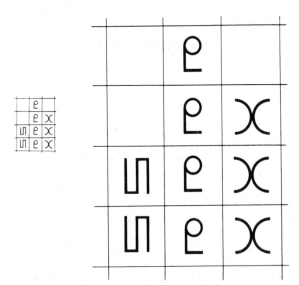

Figure 35 : 8

Another type of experience which helps the growth of the ratio concept is given when a class records several sets by using a block graph on 2-cm squared paper and individual children make copies on $\frac{1}{2}$ –cm squared paper. At first they will not know the lengths of the sides of the squares but they will recognise the identity of pattern in the two grids and can judge whether the smaller copy of the large block graph 'looks the same'. Children may also discover that four of the small squares would fit along the edge of a large square. Again there is an initiutive awareness of scale (Figure 35 : 8).

FRACTIONS AS RATIOS

A fraction expresses a relationship between two quantities, which is a ratio, For example, the fraction $\frac{5}{6}$ represents any of the relationships shown in Figure 35 : 9, and many others as well. In each case, we can either say that the first quantity is $\frac{5}{6}$ of the second, or that the ratio of the two quantities is 5 : 6.

Figure 35 : 10 shows a block graph of halves of numbers. Such graphs and their corresponding line graphs have already been used in several ways. From the ratio point of view, the aspect to be emphasised is that the height of each shaded block bears the same relation to the height of its corresponding outline block; its height is always half

The fraction $\frac{5}{6}$ or the ratio 5 : 6

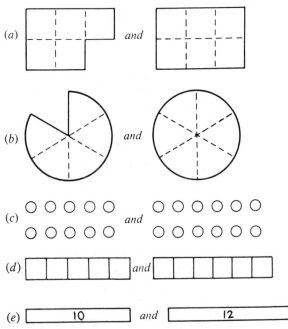

(a) ... and ...

(b) ... and ...

(c) ... and ...

(d) ... and ...

(e) 10 and 12

Figure 35 : 9

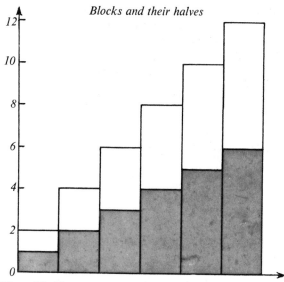

Figure 35 : 10

that of the outline block. Hence the relation of a shaded block to its outline block is always expressed by the ratio 1 : 2, and the ratio of an outline block to its shaded block is 2 : 1. But, for instance, the last pair of blocks shown on the graph are of heights 6 units and 12 units, so that here the ratio is 6 : 12. The ratio 6 : 12 is equivalent to the ratio 1 : 2. This can be written in fraction form as $\frac{6}{12} = \frac{1}{2}$. Each column of the graph is a different embodiment of the ratio 1 : 2, and successive columns of the graph illustrate the equivalent ratios or fractions

$$\frac{1}{2} = \frac{2}{4} = \frac{3}{6} = \frac{4}{8} = \frac{5}{10} = \frac{6}{12}$$

Comparison of length based on

difference	*ratio*
	For these rods:
$6 - 4 = 2$	crimson rod $= \frac{2}{3}$ of (dark-green rod)
$4 + 2 = 6$	dark-green rod $= \frac{3}{2}$ of (crimson rod)
	crimson rod : dark-green rod $= 2 : 3$
	$\dfrac{crimson\ rod}{dark\text{-}green\ rod} = \dfrac{2}{3}$
	dark-green rod : crimson rod $= 3 : 2$
	$\dfrac{dark\text{-}green\ rod}{crimson\ rod} = \dfrac{3}{2}$

Figure 35 : 11

A real understanding that the ratio of the heights in each column is 1 : 2 often does not seem to develop until fairly late. This is possibly because children are asked so often to make comparisons between quantities in terms of the *difference* between them, rather than in terms of their *ratio*. Both methods of comparison are valid and useful in different circumstances. Two sets of comparisons between the crimson and dark-green Cuisenaire rods are shown in Figure 35 : 11, those based on the ideas of sum and difference, and those based on the ideas of fraction and ratio.

PROBABILITY AND RATIO

When children try to compare the chances of drawing a white bead out of bags containing different numbers of white and black bleads (*see page 244*), at first they find it difficult to believe that they have the same chance of getting a white bead out of a bag containing

1 white and 3 black

beads as they do out of a bag containing

2 white and 6 black

beads, although the ratios of white to black in both bags are the same. However, two bags each containing 1W, 3B can be put together without affecting the chances. Thus the idea grows that the ratio

white : black = 1 : 3

is the same for both bags. This is sometimes described by saying that the odds are *3 to 1 against* getting a white bead. However, the *probability* of getting a white bead is $\frac{1}{4}$, for when we measure the probability we look at the ratio of the number of white beads to the *total* number of beads.

CORRESPONDENCES AND RATES

Ideas about rates and ratios may develop from experience of the correspondences to be found between the members of two sets. One-to-one and one-to-many correspondences have been studied in earlier chapters. It is in the consideration of one-to-many correspondences that special cases occur which children notice when they are building up tables of multiples. If three children make between them nine models of animals they may make different numbers of animals: Ann may make a dog and a horse; Sue may make a cat, a mouse

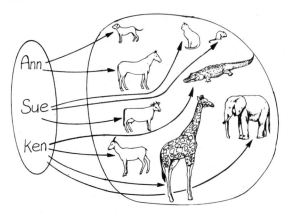

Figure 35 : 12

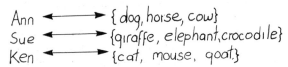

Figure 35 : 13

and a cow; Ken may contribute a giraffe, an
elephant, a crocodile and a goat. Figure 35 : 12
shows these correspondences. But if each child
makes 3 animals then we have the special case
when the three subsets, Ann's animals, Sue's
animals, and Ken's animals, each contain the same
number. Figure 35 : 13 shows this correspondence.
We can say that the *rate* of production is 3 animals
per child. If this rate is the same for other children
in the class they can tabulate the animals that will
be made by different numbers of children, counting
the animals in threes.

    children 1 2 3   4   5
    animals   3 6 9   12   15

Children may say that there are 3 times as many
animals as there are children, or that when twice as
many children are at work they make twice as
many animals. They are seeing relationships
between *numbers* of children and of animals but
they are not yet ready to think of the abstract idea
of ratio as a special kind of relationship between
two numbers.

   At this stage children can see the three-to-one
correspondence of animals to children; they can
understand the rate of production as 3 animals per
child but they could be confused if they were asked
to think of the relationship of the numbers
themselves apart from their meaning in stating the
rate at which the animals are made. As we shall see
in succeeding paragraphs, two *quantities of the same*

kind, e.g. two lengths, can be compared by a ratio;
two *numbers* can be related by a ratio, e.g. 2 : 1.
But sets of *different kinds* of things or quantities
measured in *different units* lead to examples of
correspondences that can be connected by a rate but
cannot be compared in terms of the ratio of pairs
of members. Obviously a wide experience of
correspondences and rates prepares for the more
abstract study of ratio. Later on, children will solve
many problems from seeing the equality of such
ratios as 2 children to 3 children and 6 animals to
9 animals, and the equality of rates such as 6
animals to 2 children and 9 animals to 3 children.

MULTIPLICATION AND RATIO

The extension of experiences such as those
described in the last paragraph, which lead on to
the notion of ratios of numbers, will produce sets of
multiples (see Chapter 17). The tabulation of the
multiples of 3 suggests a correspondence between
the natural numbers and their multiples. Any
member of a set of numbers can be transformed
into a multiple of 3, and we can relate each number
to a multiple and vice versa. The *operation* which
transforms the number is multiplication by 3. The
relation between the multiple and the corresponding
starting number is the ratio 3 : 1 (Figure 35 : 14).

number	1	2	3	4	5	6	7
multiple	3	6	9	12	15	18	21

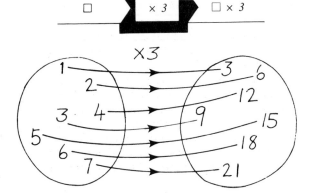

Figure 35 : 14

   A mapping diagram illustrates the transformation
and can lead on to an awareness of the ratio. If the
lines joining corresponding points on the two
number lines are continued they will all pass

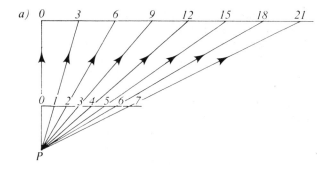

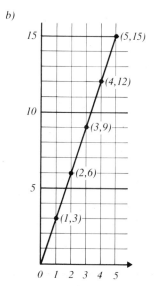

Figure 35 : 15

GRAPH OF MULTIPLES

The line graph of the multiples of any number is also the representation of number pairs which have the same ratio. For example, the multiples of 2 are shown by the line $y = 2x$. This equation can be written $\dfrac{y}{x} = 2$, and the ratio $y : x$ is equal to the ratio $2 : 1$. Therefore the point (x, y) represents the ratio $y : x$, i.e. the ratio of the *second number to the first* in the pair of co-ordinates. The graph of the multiples of 2 shown in Figure 35 : 16 contains the points $(\frac{1}{2}, 1)$, $(1, 2)$, $(1\frac{1}{2}, 3)$, $(2, 4)$, $(3, 6)$, each representing a number and the corresponding multiple of 2. Hence the ratios represented by the points are $1 : \frac{1}{2}$, $2 : 1$, $3 : 1\frac{1}{2}$, $4 : 2$, $6 : 3$. These ratios are all equal, since the triangles we have made using the lines of the graph paper are all the same shape, or *similar*.

The point P (3, 6) is the vertex of a triangle with sides 3 units and 6 units. Each point on the line OP is the vertex of one of the similar triangles. Thus the straight line in the graph is the image of all pairs of numbers which are in the ratio $2 : 1$.

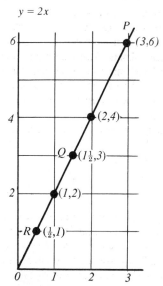

Figure 35 : 16

through the same point, P. A light placed at P would project the points 0, 1, 2, 3, . . . on the starting number line into the points 0, 3, 6, 9, . . . on the number line of multiples (Figure 35 : 15 (*a*)). It can be seen that the ratio of the corresponding line segments is $3 : 1$.

The pairs of corresponding numbers in this diagram can be written as ordered pairs: (1, 3), (2, 6), (3, 9), . . . (7, 21). This arrangement emphasises the relation between each pair: the *second number is 3 times the first*, or their ratio is $3 : 1$. At this stage the close connection between multiplication and the ratio of a pair of numbers is clear:

$3 : 1 = 6 : 2 = 9 : 3 . . . = 21 : 7$.

The inverse ratios are also equal, i.e.

$1 : 3 = 2 : 6 = 3 : 9 = . . . = 7 : 21$.

The graph of multiples of 3 (Figure 35 : 15 (*b*)) shows the same ordered pairs in another way. The ratio of the vertical to the horizontal co-ordinates of any point on this graph is always $3 : 1$.

MEASUREMENT AND SCALE

In earlier sections of this book we have seen how important for children's understanding of space is the growth of their ability to represent both individual objects and their relative positions by drawing pictures and maps.

Children's first representational drawings are pictorial and they are satisfied if in certain respects the drawing looks like the thing they see. It must show certain features which they have associated with the object, but its dimensions may not be proportional to those of the original. Eventually the idea of scale emerges, so that a model or plan can be an accurate representation of the original.

When a tabulation is made to show scale lengths and actual lengths in related pairs children will discover the relationship between the pairs of numbers. For example if 1 cm represents 4 metres the tabulation will show *numbers* which are in the ratio 4 : 1.

Actual length in *metres*

1 2 3 4 5 6 7 8 9 10

Scale length in *centimetres*

$\frac{1}{4}$ $\frac{1}{2}$ $\frac{3}{4}$ 1 $1\frac{1}{4}$ $1\frac{1}{2}$ $1\frac{3}{4}$ 2 $2\frac{1}{4}$ $2\frac{1}{2}$

The ratio of the *number* of metres in the actual length to the *number* of centimetres in the corresponding scale length is 4 : 1; this is quite

different from the ratio of the *lengths*, 400 : 1, which can be seen when both lengths are expressed in terms of the same unit.

When a scale drawing is made as a representation of any shape the ratio of scale length to actual length is the same for every pair of corresponding lengths. For example, if a scale of 1 cm to 5 metres is chosen to make a plan of a rectangular plot 15 m by 25 m, each actual length is 500 times the scale length; for example, 15 m is 500 times 3 cm; 25 m is 500 times 5 cm. The perimeter, 80 m, is 500 times the perimeter of the plan which is 16 cm. When the ratio of the scale length to the actual length, in this instance 1 : 500, is expressed as a fraction, $\frac{1}{500}$, it is known as the *representative fraction* of the plan or map. Many of the maps that pupils read and use have the representative fraction stated.

Ordnance Survey maps use representative fractions such as $\frac{1}{25\,000}$; the ratio of scale length to true length is 1 : 25 000. Thus, a scale length of 2 cm represents a true length of $2 \times 25\,000$ cm, or 500 m. Children can calculate the representative fractions for maps drawn on other scales; e.g. the scale of 1 cm to 1 kilometre leads to a representative fraction $\frac{1}{100\,000}$ or a ratio of 1 : 100 000.

Figure 35 : 17 shows part of two Ordnance Survey maps of the same area. They are the old 1 inch to 1 mile map, whose scale is 1 : 63 360, and the 1 : 25 000 map. Each length on the larger map is approximately $2\frac{1}{2}$ times the corresponding length on the smaller-scale map. Each length on the smaller map is $\frac{2}{5}$ of the corresponding length on the larger-scale map. Every pair of corresponding distances, such as *ab* and *AB*, or *bc* and *BC*, or the distances representing the same road on the two maps, is an embodiment of the fraction, or ratio, $\frac{2}{5}$. This may be shown on a graph which represents the fraction (Figure 35 : 18). The longer of each pair of

Figure 35 : 17

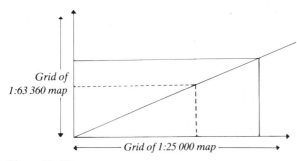

Figure 35 : 18

corresponding lines is plotted horizontally, and the shorter one vertically, so that each vertical line is $\frac{2}{5}$ of its corresponding horizontal line. It is not necessary to measure the distances on the two maps. They can be transferred directly to the graph by using a piece of cotton.

This graph could be described either as a graph of the fraction or ratio $\frac{2}{5}$, or as a graph which shows $\frac{2}{5}$ of different lengths. After their earlier experience of multiplication graphs, and of graphs showing fractions of numbers, children will expect it to be a straight-line graph.

More accurate work with the calculator shows that the ratio of distances on the two maps, which is 63 360 : 25 000, is 2·53. However, a ratio of 2·5 or $2\frac{1}{2}$ is a good enough approximation for practical purposes.

If a graph obtained in this way by plotting corresponding distances on two maps is not a straight line, the ratio of these distances is not constant, and one map is a distortion of the other. It is possible to test whether two toys of different sizes or two models of the same thing are similar in shape, by drawing a graph of their corresponding measurements. Figure 35 : 19 shows an examination of corresponding measurements of two out of a set of carved wooden elephants. Two children of different ages, or an adult and a child, can do the same with their own measurements.

A set of several similar geometrical shapes can also be used to give a set of examples of the same

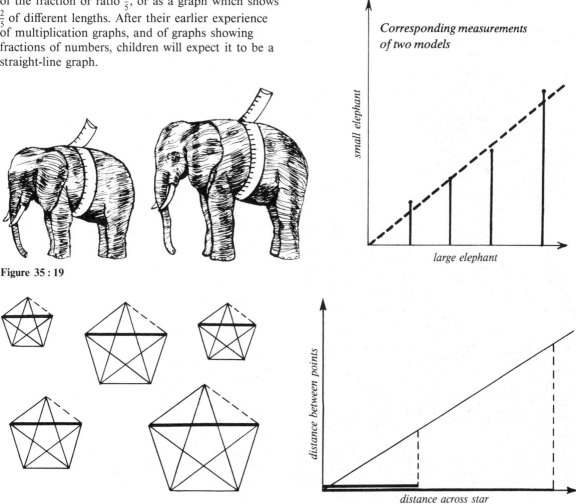

Figure 35 : 19

Figure 35 : 20

ratio. If children make five-pointed stars of different sizes, for instance, they may show the distance across each star and the distance between the points of the star on a graph (Figure 35 : 20). Here a different ratio is plotted; for the elephants, we took the ratio of small elephant : large elephant, using different measurements. For the stars, we have plotted the ratio of two measurements

distance between points : distance across star,

using different stars.

In all these activities, children are developing the habit of looking for a relationship or ratio between two quantities, and of seeing the same ratio expressed in many forms; the ratio of 3 cm to 4 cm is the same as the ratio of 6 cm to 8 cm, or of 9 cm to 12 cm, and all these representations of the same ratio can be expressed by the set of equivalent fractions $\frac{3}{4} = \frac{6}{8} = \frac{9}{12} \ldots$.

RATIO OF QUANTITIES

Drawing plans and maps leads naturally to a comparison of lengths in terms of ratio, but other quantities frequently need to be compared or transformed by the use of ratio. For example, substances are often mixed by mass, as in cooking. To preserve the properties of the mixture the ingredients must remain in *proportion* if the total quantity is changed, i.e. the ratio of the masses of any pair of ingredients must be maintained.

If a recipe gives 100 grams of lard to $\frac{1}{2}$ kilogram of flour it is stating a *rate* in units which are thought to be convenient. A rate of 200 grams of lard to 1 kilogram of flour is the same rate, since the ratio of old mass to new mass is 2 : 1 for both lard and flour. For $\frac{3}{4}$ kg of flour a ratio of new mass to old mass of $1\frac{1}{2} : 1$ or 3 : 2 must be used to find the required masses of the other ingredients; so it will need $\frac{3}{2} \times 100$ grams, or 150 grams of lard. Thus we find that ratios are necessary in using a constant rate.

The ratio of the *quantities* in the recipe will only be seen, however, if the masses are stated in the same units; 100 grams of lard to 500 grams of flour. The ratio of the quantities is 1 : 5 by mass and this relation enables us to say at once that 750 grams of flour require $\frac{750}{5}$ grams (or 150 grams) of lard. The ratio of the actual quantities is independent of the units used and therefore holds for all units.

The same principles apply to other measurable quantities: the ratio of any two quantities of the same kind can be stated numerically if they are expressed in the same units. For example, $\frac{1}{2}$ hour per day is equivalent to $\frac{1}{2}$ hour in every 24 hours, a ratio of 1 : 48. A rate of discount of 5 pence in £1 can be expressed in fivepences to give a ratio of 1 : 20.

A suitable diagrammatic way of representing certain ratios is by drawing pie-charts. The ratio of parts to whole is shown by the ratio of the angles at the centre of the circle to one complete revolution. For example, if a discount of 10 per cent is allowed, and £1 is represented by an angle of 360° at the centre of the circle, the discount will be represented by $\frac{1}{10}$ of 360°, i.e. 36°. The area of the sector of the circle formed by this angle will bear the same ratio, 1 : 10, to the area of the whole circle. If a set of 24 children is making a survey of individual preferences for the subjects of the curriculum, a pie-chart will show plainly the ratios of the number who do and the number who do not prefer mathematics to the total number in the set. Figure 35 : 21(*a*) illustrates the ratio 9 : 24 for those who *do*, and 15 : 24 for those who *do not*. At the same time it demonstrates the ratio of do's to don'ts as 9 : 15. The angles at the centre of the circle are

$$\frac{9}{24} \text{ of } 360° \quad \text{and} \quad \frac{15}{24} \text{ of } 360°,$$
$$\text{or } 135° \quad \text{and} \quad 225°.$$

A pie-chart can also be used to display several ratios. For example, in Figure 35 : 21(*b*) the ratios are 8 : 24, 6 : 24, 4 : 24, 3 : 24, 2 : 24, represented by sectors which can be compared by means of the angles at the centre. The shaded residue is found to have an angle of 15° which represents a ratio of 15° : 360° or 1 : 24. The chief value of a pie-chart lies in the visual imagery of parts in relation to one another and to the whole.

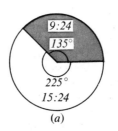

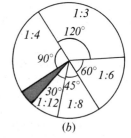

(*a*)

(*b*)

Figure 35 : 21

RATE AND RATIO FOR QUANTITIES OF DIFFERENT KINDS

We have examined the way in which quantities of the same kind can be compared: by a rate if they are measured in different units, by a ratio if they are measured in the same units. If a rate is to be maintained, when one quantity is changed in a certain ratio, say 2 : 1, the other quantity must be changed in the same ratio. For example, if the price of goods is reduced at the rate of ten pence in the pound the price of an article which costs 300 pence must be reduced by an amount whose ratio to £1 is 10 : 100 or 1 : 10. The reduction will be $\frac{1}{10} \times 300$ pence, or 30 pence.

It frequently happens that we must compare two different *kinds* of quantity, e.g. *distance* travelled and *time* taken for a journey. If the rate connecting them is constant, say 40 km/h, then if the distance is altered in a certain ratio the time taken will be altered in the same ratio. For a distance of 56 km the original time of 1 hour for 40 km must be changed in the ratio 56 : 40, or 14 : 10. The time will be $\frac{14}{10} \times 1$ hour, that is 1 hr 24 min. If 3 things cost 18 pence the cost of 5 things at this rate will be $\frac{5}{3} \times 18$ pence, which is 5×6 pence, or 30 pence.

This ratio connection between a pair of quantities of one kind and the corresponding pair of another kind gives us a fundamental method of solving problems concerning two quantities changing at a constant rate.

PERCENTAGES

The comparison of ratios is carried out in their fractional form; 2 : 3 can be compared with 10 : 17 if we find out whether $\frac{2}{3}$ is greater or less than $\frac{10}{17}$. This can be done by converting the fractions to decimals. Dividing 2 by 3 to the third decimal place we obtain $0 \cdot 667 : 1$ as an equivalent form of the ratio 2 : 3, correct to 3 decimal places. Dividing 10 by 17 gives the decimal form for 10 : 17; the ratio 10 : 17 becomes $0 \cdot 588 : 1$. This procedure is a general one, suited to every ratio stated as a number pair. However, the decimal form is not as simple as one that can be stated in integers. It is therefore standard practice to make 100 the second number of the ratio, so that 1 : 2 is written as 50 : 100 or 50 per cent. This means, in fact, working in hundredths, 1 : 2 is $\frac{50}{100}$ or $0 \cdot 50$. Since the second decimal place gives hundredths we see that $0 \cdot 50$ can be read immediately as $\frac{50}{100}$ or 50%.

Returning to $\frac{2}{3}$ and $\frac{10}{17}$, we can now look at the hundredths place in each decimal expression and read $0 \cdot 667 : 1$ as $66 \cdot 7\%$ and $0 \cdot 588$ as $58 \cdot 8\%$.

There is also a graphical way of converting a ratio to a percentage. We know that equal ratios can be represented by a straight-line graph. In Figure 35 : 22 we see a line which represents ratios equal to 4 : 5. One of these ratios is 8 : 10. Another

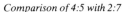
Comparison of 4:5 with 2:7

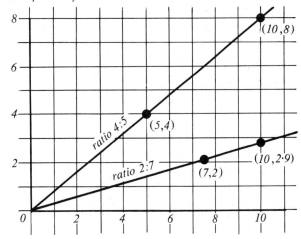

Figure 35 : 22

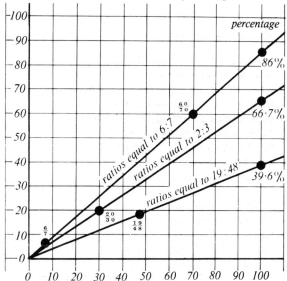

Figure 35 : 23

line shows the ratio 2 : 7; it also shows an equal ratio $2 \cdot 9 : 10$. We can thus compare 4 : 5 with 2 : 7 by using the ratios 8 : 10 and $2 \cdot 9 : 10$. This idea is extended to percentages by finding equal ratios with 100 as the right-hand number (Figure 35 : 23). Notice also the use of $\frac{20}{30}$ as well as $\frac{2}{3}$ to give greater accuracy in drawing the graph.

GEOMETRICAL REPRESENTATION OF RATIO

On page 435 we saw that ratios can be shown in mapping diagrams. Figure 35 : 24 shows not only

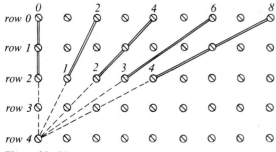

Figure 35 : 24

placed at equal intervals from 0 to 4. We can see at once the distance at which the elastic band *AE* crosses each of these rows. The ratios of the corresponding pairs of sides of the triangles can therefore be found as in the following table.

Side of triangle	Vertical side	Horizontal side	Ratio of vertical to horizontal side
AE	4	2	$4 : 2$
BE	3	$1\frac{1}{2}$	$3 : 1\frac{1}{2}$
CE	2	1	$2 : 1$
DE	1	$\frac{1}{2}$	$1 : \frac{1}{2}$

The ratios are all equal to $2 : 1$. We see that in a set of similar triangles *the ratio of a pair of sides in one triangle* is equal to the ratio of the *corresponding pair* in any of the other triangles.

The relationship between the sides of two similar triangles can be stated in a different way. In Figure 35 : 25 we can compare the horizontal side of the largest triangle with the horizontal side of the smallest triangle. The ratio is $2 : \frac{1}{2}$, or $4 : 1$. If we now compare the vertical sides of these two triangles the ratio is seen at once to be $4 : 1$. We can also compare the sloping sides, *AE* and *DE*; these are also in the ratio $4 : 1$. It can be said that in a set of similar triangles the *ratio of a side of one* of them to *the corresponding side of another* triangle in the set is the same for each of the sides.

the number relation in terms of length: it also brings out the geometrical pattern that equal ratios form when they are presented on a pair of parallel lines. A practical way of demonstrating this is through the use of elastic bands on a nail-board or geoboard. The diagram shows the bands placed round nails to relate 2, 4, 6, 8, ... to 1, 2, 3, 4, ... The distances in rows 0 and 2 are in the ratio $2 : 1$.

Children can discover from this experiment that all the bands can be stretched along their length to pass round the same nail, as in the figure. They can also notice where the bands cross the lines of nails in row 1 and row 3. The distances between the bands at row 1 are $1\frac{1}{2}$ times the interval between adjacent nails. In row 3 the distances are a half of the interval. The ratio of the distance in row 1 to the distance in row 2 is $1\frac{1}{2}$ to 1. For row 3 and row 2 the ratio is $\frac{1}{2} : 1$.

Again, a pattern of triangles is suggested and the parallel lines crossing them are clearly defined by the rows of nails.

If we look carefully at the set of triangles made by the two elastic bands on the left (Figure 35 : 25) we see that there is a set of *similar* triangles with a common vertex, *E*, in row 4. The rows of nails are

GEAR RATIOS

Children who ride bicycles or make working Meccano models are familiar with ways in which two geared wheels can be connected so that when one turns the other also turns. The rates of rotation will be different unless the wheels are of the same size. The teeth of the wheels must fit either on to a chain, or into one another; therefore the rate of rotation of one compared with the other depends on the number of teeth in the respective rims of the wheels. The gear ratio is the ratio of the rates of rotation.

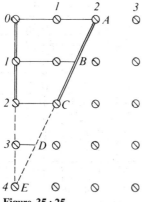

Figure 35 : 25

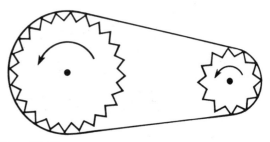

Figure 35 : 26

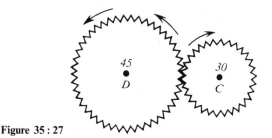

Figure 35 : 27

For example, the chain wheels of a bicycle may have 24 and 12 teeth respectively (Figure 35 : 26). The wheel turned by the pedals has 24 teeth; the small wheel which is attached to one of the bicycle wheels has 12 teeth; the chain passes round both toothed wheels, making them turn in the same direction, and moving with them. For one rotation of the pedal wheel the small wheel makes two rotations, its 12 teeth having been in contact with the chain twice because the pedal wheel has 24 teeth. The ratio of the number of rotations of the small wheel to those of the larger wheel is 24 : 12 or 2 : 1.

In some bicycles the numbers of teeth are 45 and 18; the ratio is 45 : 18 or 5 : 2 or 2·5 : 1. It will be seen that the ratio of numbers of rotations is also 2·5:1 since the smaller gear wheel makes $2\frac{1}{2}$ rotations to each complete rotation of the pedal wheel.

If two gear wheels are meshed together, as in Figure 35 : 27, they will turn in opposite directions, but the gear ratio will still depend on the numbers of teeth on each wheel. When the wheels have 45 and 30 teeth respectively the ratio is 3 : 2.

When more than two gears are used to make a mechanical system the ratios can be combined. For example, wheel E can be geared to C as in Figure 35 : 28. The gear ratio of D to E is 75 : 45, or 5 : 3.

D makes $\frac{5}{3}$ revolutions to each revolution of E

C makes $\frac{3}{2}$ revolutions to each revolution of D

Thus C makes $\frac{3}{2} \times \frac{5}{3}$ revolutions, or $\frac{5}{2}$ revolutions, to each revolution of E. This can be checked by comparing E directly with C. The gear ratio is 75 : 30, or 5 : 2 (Figure 35 : 28).

One of the purposes of the middle wheel is to make the third wheel turn in the same direction as the first wheel. Since two meshed wheels rotate in opposite directions, C rotates in the same direction as E, whereas if C and E were directly meshed together they would rotate in opposite directions.

The combination of gears leads to the multiplication of ratios and can furnish an example of a procedure for multiplying one fraction by another.

GROWTH WITH CHANGING RATIOS

When a rate of growth is constant we know that a graph of the changing quantities is a straight line. The perimeter of a square increases uniformly with equal increases in the length of a side: the ratio of the perimeters of two squares is equal to the ratio of the lengths of their sides. If the squares have sides of length 3 units and 5 units respectively their perimeters are 12 units and 20 units. The ratio 20 : 12 = 5 : 3 = 1·67 : 1.

Length of side, l units	1	2	3	4	5
Area of square, A sq. units	1	4	9	16	25
Ratio A:l	1 : 1	2 : 1	3 : 1	4 : 1	5 : 1
Differences in A for unit differences in l	3	5	7	9	

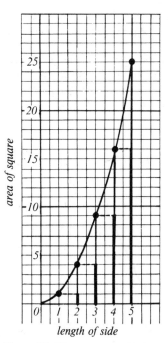

Figure 35 : 29

area of square

length of side

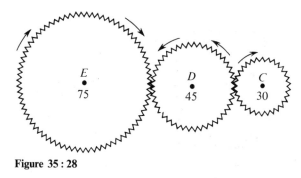

Figure 35 : 28

Squares with sides 3 units and 5 units long have areas of 9 square units and 25 square units respectively; the ratio of areas is $25:9$ or $2\cdot78:1$, whereas the ratio of sides is $5:3$ or $1\cdot67:1$.

The ratio of the perimeter of a square to its sides is constant and equal increases in length of the side produce equal increases in the perimeter. The graph of the area of the square (Figure $35:29$) shows that the ratio of the number of units of area in the square to the number of units of length in its side

Enlargement of square and rectangle

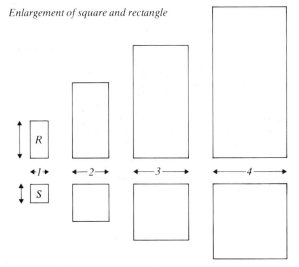

Figure 35 : 30

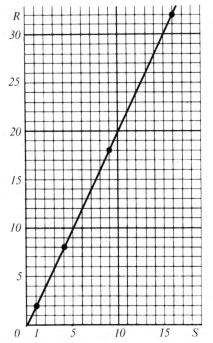

Figure 35 : 31

is not constant and equal increases in the length of the side do not produce equal increases in the area.

We saw in Chapter 22 that the pattern of growth of any set of similar figures is the same as the pattern of growth of squares. This suggests comparing the area of two different sets of similar figures. For example, successive enlargements of a 1 by 2 unit rectangle and a square (Figure $35:30$) give the following tabulation:

Length of short side	1	2	3	4
Area of rectangle, R	2	8	18	32
Area of square on short side, S	1	4	9	16
Ratio of areas, R:S	2:1	8:4	18:9	32:16

The ratio of the area of each rectangle to the area of the corresponding square is constant and the graph of the two sets of areas shows the relation $R = 2S$, or $R : S = 2 : 1$ (Figure $35:31$).

NUMBERS PROPORTIONAL TO SQUARE NUMBERS

The equation $y = x^2$ states the relation between numbers and their squares, but measurement or experiment sometimes produces a set of numbers which increase rapidly like the squares but are not square numbers. It is possible that they are proportional to squares but we need to find a way to check whether this is so. It is not easy to decide by looking at a graph whether it is of similar form to $y = x^2$. The form of graph which is easy to check is of course the straight line. We know, too, that the straight line represents pairs of numbers whose ratio is the same. We use this to find a method of comparing a set of experimental results with the square numbers.

Suppose that a set of similar triangles have been measured, and their areas found. The first triangle has a base of 1 cm, and a height of $\frac{1}{2}$ cm. Its area is $0\cdot25$ cm². The other triangles form a sequence with bases $1\frac{1}{2}$, 2, $2\frac{1}{2}$, 3, ... cm (Figure $35:32$). Their areas (to 2 decimal places) are shown in the diagram, together with the areas of corresponding squares. The points of the graph are seen to lie on a line. The ratio of the area of a triangle to that of the square on the same base must therefore be constant. The graph shows us that this ratio is 1 to 4. We can then describe the relation by a formula as $y = \frac{1}{4} \times x^2$, where the base of the triangle is x units and its area is y square units.

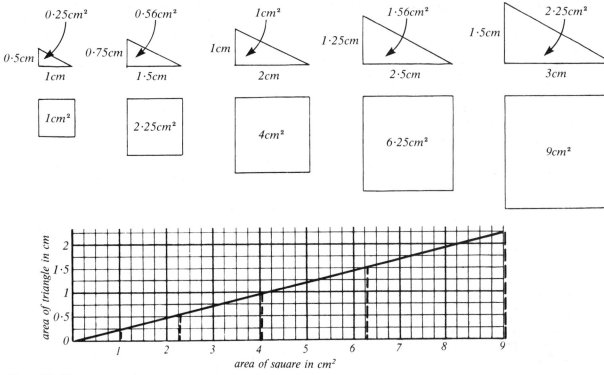

Figure 35 : 32

INVERSE RATIOS

In some investigations, such as timing a journey for different average speeds, it is found that as one sequence of numbers increases, the other decreases; as average speed increases the time for the journey grows less. Since the distance travelled, d, is equal to the product of the average speed, s, and the time taken, t

$$d = s \times t$$

$$t = \frac{d}{s}$$

For a particular journey of 120 kilometres,

$$t = \frac{120}{s}$$

$$= 120 \times \frac{1}{s}$$

Thus, t is a multiple of the reciprocal of s. The graph of t against s has the characteristic shape of the hyperbola or curve of reciprocals (*see page 397*); it is shown in Figure 35 : 33 (a).

When the results of an experiment show a similar pattern, with a sequence of decreasing numbers corresponding with an increasing sequence, the procedure of graphing the inverse, as in Figure

(a)

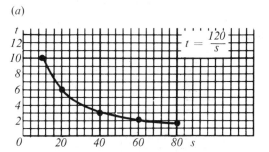

(b)

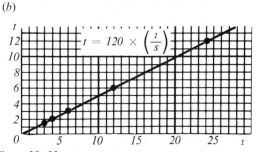

Figure 35 : 33

35 : 33 (b), may reveal the actual relation in the form $r = K \times \left(\frac{1}{t}\right)$ where r is the dependent variable, t is the independent variable and K is a constant which can be found from the graph.

The importance of ratio

The development of the idea of ratio has been shown to grow from a wide experience of similar shapes, of quantities which are related by a constant rule of correspondence, and of sets of numbers of which one is a transform of the other by a multiplication operation. The correspondences found in these three kinds of experience have a particular pattern in a mapping diagram or a graph. The use of a straight-line graph to illustrate a constant ratio has been extended to show that other relations can be illustrated by straight-line graphs; for instance, variation with the square or with the inverse can be shown.

Rate, ratio and scale in the National Curriculum

References to ratio occur in Attainment Target 2 (number) of the National Curriculum. A *unitary ratio* is a ratio whose first number is 1.

- use unitary ratios.
  EXAMPLE: *Use a ratio of 1 : 50 for drawing a plan of the classroom.*

  (AT2: Level 5)

- calculate, using ratios in a variety of situations.
  EXAMPLE: *Enlarge a design in a given ratio.*

  (AT2: Level 6)

Scale drawing is also found in AT 2.

- understand the notion of scale in maps and drawings.

  (AT2: Level 5)

The idea of *rate*, and the idea that a straight-line graph represents a constant rate, underlies one of the statements in AT 3 (algebra):

- draw and interpret the graphs of linear functions.
  EXAMPLE: *Use travel graphs to solve distance/time problems.*

  (AT3: Level 7)

36 | *FAMILIAR SHAPES: NEW NUMBERS*

SQUARE AND CIRCLE

Among the shapes best known to children are certainly the square and circle. Yet when we draw the diagonal of a square or try to find out how far a wheel of given diameter would move along a path in one revolution we find that we cannot give a precise answer within our decimal number system. We must investigate further. Our enquiry will involve shapes which have already been discovered by such simple methods as folding a square or circle, such shapes as the rectangle, triangle, hexagon, and octagon. Additional shapes can be found by making loosely hinged frameworks, say a square and hexagon, and changing their angles to produce a parallelogram, rhombus, etc.

A good method of studying these shapes and the measurements of their sides, angles, diagonals, etc. is by trying to make tessellations with them. Children already know well that a square can be tessellated to make the familiar graph paper. They have also made a variety of patterns with circles which show that inevitably there are spaces between closely placed circles; they will not tessellate.

TESSELLATIONS AND LATTICE POINTS

Early experiences of simple tessellations are described in Chapter 12. We now extend this study in order to reach an understanding of spatial relationships which will enable us to see the need for new numbers and also the ways in which we can use them. (See Chapter 38) We look first at a tessellation of squares (Figure 36 : 1(*a*)) and notice that all vertices lie on two sets of parallel lines at right angles to one another. The vertices form the *lattice points* of the tessellation. It is evident that these lattice points could also be joined by diagonals of the squares and thus four new tessellations could be made, as shown in Figure

36 : 1(*b*), (*c*), (*d*) and (*e*). These are all tessellations of parallelograms but they are not all fundamentally different; (*c*) can be produced from (*b*) by rotation through a right angle, and (*e*) from (*d*); (*d*) is the reflection of (*b*) in a vertical axis. The five tessellations have the property that the basic tile or *period tile* of each tessellation has *the same area*, which is equal to one square of the original tessellation. In Figure 36 : 1 a period tile of each tessellation is shaded and divided into two triangles which are half-squares, showing that each period tile has the area of the square. The period tile is so called because it repeats itself after a period.

Figure 36 : 2 shows this principle in use in another tessellation, one of the brick patterns. The use of squared paper will help children to see that, in Figure 36 : 2, tiles of each tessellation have the same area.

Tessellations made from a brick pattern.

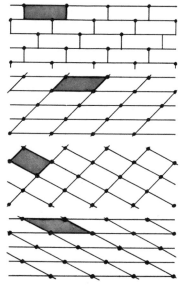

Figure 36 : 2

Five tessellations with the same lattice points

(*a*) 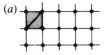 (*b*) 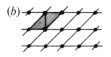 (*c*)  (*d*)  (*e*)

Figure 36 : 1

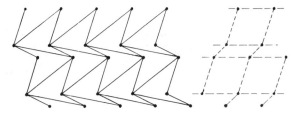

Figure 36 : 3

Figure 36 : 3 is a tessellation of equal tiles, but the obvious marking of vertices shown in this diagram does not yield a grid of lattice points which can be tessellated with *equal* parallelograms. The difficulty lies in the fact that the period tile of Figure 36 : 3 is not one quadrilateral, but two. A period tile is a tile from which the whole tessellation can be built up by *translations only*, without rotation. The whole tessellation can be built up by translations only if a two-quadrilateral tile is used, whereas if we use a one-quadrilateral tile, we have to rotate it as well as translating it. Once the period tile has been picked out, lattice points can be found by marking one vertex of each tile (Figure 36 : 4). New tessellations of parallelograms can be made by joining these lattice points. Each tile of the new tessellation has an area equal to that of the period tile.

Original tessellations showing period tile and translation vectors

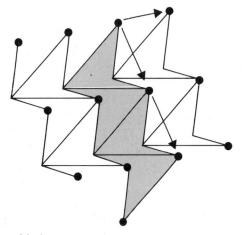

Figure 36 : 4

Figure 36 : 5 shows a period tile and lattice points of the parquet-floor pattern.

We next consider the tessellation obtained by drawing all the diagonals of a tessellation of squares (Figure 36 : 6(a)). This has the property that it is also a tessellation of squares, but since more lattice points are used, these squares are not equal in area to the original squares, but are half their area. The second tessellation can also be produced by using

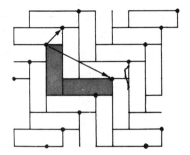

Figure 36 : 5

all the lattice points of a brick pattern, if the bricks are made up of two squares (Figure 36 : 6(b) and (c)). The right-angled isosceles triangle plays an important part in both the square tessellations. If the two tessellations are superimposed, each right-angled isosceles triangle is bordered by three squares (Figure 36 : 7); two of these squares are small and one large.

We see that the larger square, the square on the hypotenuse[1] of the isosceles right-angled triangle, is equal in area to the sum of the two smaller squares.

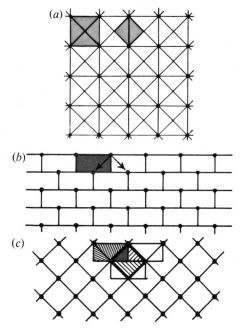

Figure 36 : 6

It is thought that this special case of Pythagoras' Theorem may have been discovered by observation of this very common tile pattern. *Pythagoras' Theorem* states that *the area of the square on the hypotenuse of any right-angled triangle is equal to the sum of the areas of the squares on the other two sides.*

[1]The *hypotenuse* is the longest side of a right-angled triangle. It is always situated opposite the right-angle.

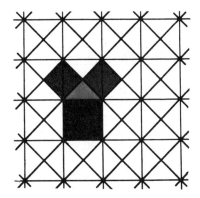

Figure 36 : 7

THE SQUARES ON THE SIDES OF A
RIGHT-ANGLED TRIANGLE

Children can very easily experiment on squared
paper with squares on the hypotenuse of various
right-angled triangles. There is no difficulty in
drawing these squares. If children start with a
right-angled triangle whose sides are of length 2
units and 5 units (Figure 36 : 8(*a*)), its hypotenuse is
a vector $\overrightarrow{AB}$ which is the sum of vectors of 5 units
to the right and 2 units upwards, that is, a vector
$\begin{pmatrix} +5 \\ +2 \end{pmatrix}$. The next side of the square is obtained by
counting from *B* 5 units up and 2 units to the left;
that is, by drawing from *B* a vector $\begin{pmatrix} -2 \\ +5 \end{pmatrix}$ (Figure
36 : 8(*b*)), and so on all round the square (Figure
36 : 8(*c*)). Nor is there any difficulty in finding the
area of this square, because it can easily be related
to the squares of the original squared paper. This
can be done by the subtraction method suggested by
Figure 36 : 8(*c*)), taking the area of the four
right-angled triangles from that of the large square
and finding what remains. Perhaps a simpler
method is to divide up the square on the
hypotenuse into parts whose area can be found.

Triangle sides 1 and 2 units

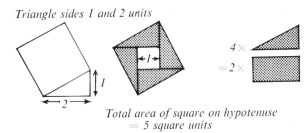

Total area of square on hypotenuse
= 5 square units

Triangle sides 1 and 3 units

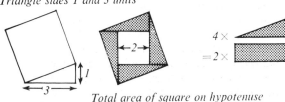

Figure 36 : 9

Total area of square on hypotenuse
= (2×3)+4 square units
= 10 square units

Shorter sides of right-angled triangle		Area of square on hypotenuse	Length of hypotenuse (by measuring)
1 unit	*1 unit*	*2 sq units*	*1·5 units*
1	*2*	*5*	*2·2* ↙
1	*3*	*10*	*3·1*
2	*3*	*13*	*3·7*
1	*4*		
2	*4*		
3	*4*	*25*	*5·0*

Figure 36 : 10

Figure 36 : 9 illustrates this for two different
triangles. Children should tabulate their findings, as
in Figure 36 : 10. Some children may notice that
the area of the square on the hypotenuse is equal to

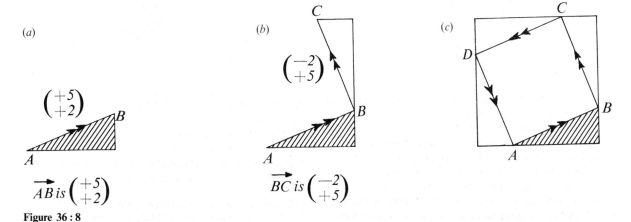

Figure 36 : 8

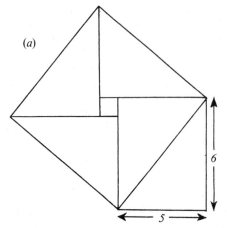

(a)

Area of square on hypotenuse = 61 square units.
Length of hypotenuse = √61 units ≈ 7·8 units.

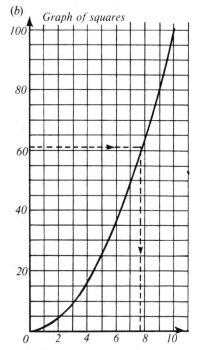

(b)

Figure 36 : 11

graph has been used to find the square root of 61. Results obtained in this way will have about the same degree of accuracy as those obtained by measurement. Children will probably realise that although the length of the hypotenuse of the triangle in Figure 36 : 11 is *approximately* 7·8 units, the area of the square on it is exactly 61 square units. They did not have to approximate at all in finding the area of the square; the four triangles in it make two rectangles each of area 30 square units, and there is exactly one square unit in the middle.

The calculator enables a better approximation of the hypotenuse to be made. If the calculator has a square root key $\boxed{\sqrt{\ }}$, it tells us that

$$\sqrt{61} = 7 \cdot 8102$$

If not, numerical exploration by a trial and improvement method is easy:

$$7 \cdot 8^2 = 60 \cdot 84$$
$$\text{and } 7 \cdot 9^2 = 62 \cdot 41$$

The hypotenuse must only be slightly more than 7·8; the calculator tells us that

$$7 \cdot 81^2 = 60 \cdot 9961,$$

which is very close to 61. Thus, 7·81 is an excellent approximation to $\sqrt{61}$.

The last triangle given in the table of Figure 36 : 10 differs from the others. The area of the square on its hypotenuse is a perfect square, and so the hypotenuse is a whole number of units. This triangle, the 3, 4, 5 triangle, is the simplest of a number of right-angled triangles whose sides are all whole numbers of units. The 3, 4, 5 triangle has been known as a right-angled triangle since very early times. It is thought that the surveyors of

Using a 3, 4, 5 triangle to make a right angle

Figure 36 : 12

the sum of the areas of the squares on the other two sides.

They will probably also measure the length of the hypotenuse of the triangles they have drawn, as shown in Figure 36 : 10, and will want to check the accuracy of their measurements by squaring the results. The first measurement shown in the table is too great, as $(1 \cdot 5)^2 = 2 \cdot 25$; the second is too small, as $(2 \cdot 2)^2 = 4 \cdot 85$, but 2·3 would be too large, as $(2 \cdot 3)^2 = 5 \cdot 29$. Use may also be made of the graph of squares, as shown in Figure 36 : 11, where the ancient Egypt used 3, 4, 5 triangles for marking out right angles, and the same method, which only needs a rope or measuring-tape, is still useful for marking out right angles on the ground (Figure 36 : 12).

TESSELLATIONS USING TWO SQUARES

In general, the squares on the two shorter sides of a right-angled triangle are of different sizes. We now explore the consequences of trying to make a

A tessellation of two squares

(*a*) **Squares on two sides of a right-angled triangle**

(*b*) *Use these two squares to make a tessellation*

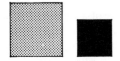

(*c*) *Starting the tessellation*

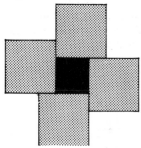

(*d*) *Building more of the tessellation. A period tile and some lattice points are shown.*

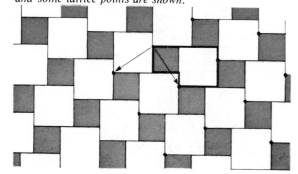

Figure 36 : 13

tessellation with squares of two different sizes (Figure 36 : 13 and plate 8). The smaller of the squares can be surrounded by larger ones (Figure 36 : 13(*c*)), and it is then a simple matter to continue the tessellation (Figure 36 : 13(*d*)). The period tile consists of a large and a small square. Lattice points have been marked at the top left-hand corner of the period tiles, and the vectors of translations needed to build up the tessellation from its period tile are shown. These vectors are at right angles, so the lattice points can be joined to make a new tessellation of squares, each of area equal to the period tile (Figure 36 : 14).

Tessellation of squares using the same lattice-points.

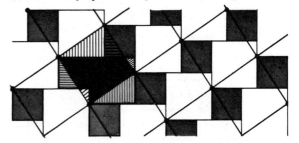

Figure 36 : 14

We notice that the pattern now contains many of the original right-angled triangles, together with the squares on all three of their sides (Figure 36 : 15). The square on the hypotenuse of the right-angled

Tessellation of 1^2 and 4^2 squares.

(*a*)

(*b*)

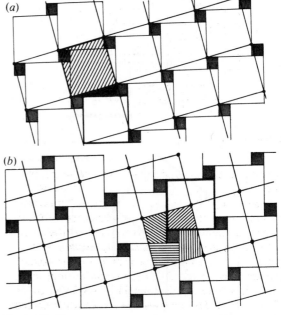

Figure 36 : 15

triangle is equal in area to the period tile of the tessellation, which is the sum of the two smaller squares. That is, the square on the hypotenuse of the right-angled triangle is equal in area to the sum of the squares on the other two sides.

Experiments on squared paper will convince children that they can make a tessellation with two squares of any sizes, and by marking lattice points they will always obtain a new tessellation of squares on the hypotenuse. Figure 36 : 15 shows a tessellation of 1^2 and 4^2 squares.

An interesting and symmetrical variation in the pattern is obtained by taking lattice points at the centre of each larger square (Figure 36 : 15(b)). In

this arrangement, the larger square of the original tessellation is divided into four equal parts by the lines of the new tessellation. Conversely, the square of the new tessellation is made up of the four quarters of the original larger square together with the original smaller square. This tessellation forms the basis of the demonstration of Pythagoras' Theorem known as *Perigal's Dissection* (Figure 36 : 16). Here the larger original square is dissected into four quarters which fit, together with the original smaller square, on to the square on the hypotenuse of the right-angled triangle. Other choices of lattice point in the tessellation give rise to other demonstrations of Pythagoras' Theorem by dissection.

The lattice points of Figure 36 : 15(a) give the dissection shown, for a different triangle, in Figure 36 : 17.

MORE ABOUT PYTHAGORAS' THEOREM

At this stage, children will think of Pythagoras' Theorem entirely as a statement about equality and rearrangement of *areas*. They can rearrange the two squares on the shorter sides of a right-angled triangle to make up the square on the hypotenuse. Another very simple demonstration of this fact is suggested by Figure 36 : 8(c), which shows the

Perigal's Dissection for Pythagoras' Theorem
(a) Part of the tessellation   (b) Perigal's dissection.

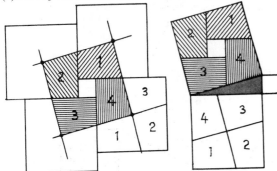

Figure 36 : 16

Another dissection for Pythagoras' Theorem.
(a) Part of the tessellation

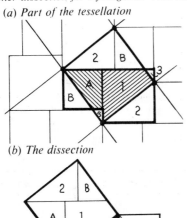

(b) The dissection

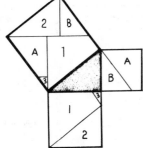

Figure 36 : 17

Jigsaw for Pythagoras' Theorem.
(a) Four triangles and square on hypotenuse.

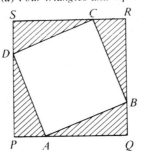

(b) Four triangles and squares on other two sides.

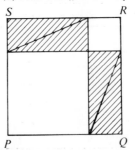

Figure 36 : 18

drawing of the square on the hypotenuse. The large square *PQRS* (Figure 36 : 18(*a*)) is made up of four right-angled triangles and the square on the hypotenuse *ABCD*. It is a simple matter to rearrange the four right-angled triangles within square *PQRS* so that the remaining space consists of the squares on the other two sides of the right-angled triangle (Figure 36 : 18(*b*)). Children can make this demonstration into a jigsaw, to fit inside a square hole *PQRS* cut from a piece of card.

We can now find *exactly* the area of the square on the hypotenuse of any right-angled triangle if the lengths of the other two sides are known. For instance in Figure 36 : 18, the triangle has shorter sides of lengths 5 units and 2 units.
Hence: area of square on hypotenuse

$= (5^2 + 2^2)$ square units

$= (25 + 4)$ square units

$= 29$ square units

In order to find the length of the side of this square, we have to find the number whose square is 29, that is to find the *square root* of 29. This may be done directly on the calculator, or from the graph of squares, and it is found that

$$5 \cdot 4^2 = 29 \cdot 16$$

so that $5 \cdot 4$ is a reasonable approximation to $\sqrt{29}$.

Children will be fascinated by the 3, 4, 5 triangle, where the area of the square on the hypotenuse is $(3^2 + 4^2)$ square units, or 25 square units, and is a perfect square. The length of the side of the square on the hypotenuse is therefore an exact whole number of units, so that this triangle is extremely convenient to deal with. Children may wish to find

Right-angled triangles with integral sides

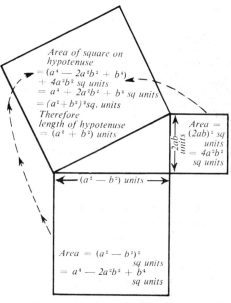

A search for right-angled triangles with integral sides

Area of square on one shorter side.

+1	4	9	16	25	36	49	64	81	100	121	144	169	196	225
1	2	5	10	17	26	37	50	65	82	101	122	145	170	192	224
4		8	13	20	29	45	53	68	85	104	125	148	173	200	229
9			18	[25]	34	45	58	73	90	109	130	153	178	205	234
16				32	41	52	65	80	97	116	137	160	185	212	241
25					50	61	74	89	106	124	145	[169]	194	221	250
36						72	85	[100]	117	136	157	180	205	232	261
49							98	113	130	149	170	193	218	248	274
64								128	145	164	185	208	233	260	[289]
81									162	181	212	[225]	250	277	306
100										200	231	244	269	296	325
121											242	265	290	317	346
144												288	313	340	360
169													338	365	394
196														392	421
225															450

Area of square on other shorter side.

Figure 36 : 19

Sides are of length $a^2 - b^2$, $2ab$, $a^2 + b^2$ units. If a and b are natural numbers the triangle will have integral sides.

Figure 36 : 21

Right-angled triangles with integral sides.

Squares on shorter sides		Square on hypotenuse	Lengths of sides	Remarks
9	16	25	3, 4, 5	
25	144	169	5, 12, 13	
36	64	100	6, 8, 10	Twice 3, 4, 5
64	225	289	8, 15, 17	
81	144	225	9, 12, 15	Three times 3, 4, 5

Figure 36 : 20

out whether there are any other right-angled triangles whose sides are all exact whole numbers of units. Figure 36 : 19 shows a systematic search for more such triangles. Possible areas of squares on the two shorter sides of the triangle have been tabulated, together with their sums. Those sums which are also perfect squares are marked. Four new right-angled triangles whose sides are integers have so far emerged from this search. Figure 36 : 20 tabulates them. It will be seen that right-angled triangles with integral sides are rare, but that a few can be found. In fact, an infinite number exist.

sides of Triangle

a	b	$a^2 - b^2$	$2ab$	$a^2 + b^2$
2	1	**3**	**4**	**5**
3	1	8	6	10
3	2	**5**	**12**	**13**
4	1	**15**	**8**	**17**
4	2	12	16	20
4	3	7	**24**	**25**
5	1	24	10	26
5	2	**21**	**20**	**29**
5	3	16	30	34
5	4	**9**	**40**	**41**
6	1	**35**	**12**	**37**
6	2	32	24	40
6	3	27	36	45
6	4	20	48	52
6	5	**11**	**60**	**61**
.	.	.	.	.

Triangles in which the sides do not have a common factor are printed in bold type.

Figure 36 : 22

The teacher will be interested in a formula which gives all right-angled triangles with integral sides. This formula, with a list of the first 15 such triangles, is given in Figures 36 : 21 and 36 : 22. These triangles whose sides are not multiples of the sides of a previous triangle are printed in heavy type.

THE GROWTH OF SIMILAR FIGURES

In Chapter 35 we discussed the idea of *similarity*, and saw that a child can recognise that when objects are of the same shape, all their corresponding measurements behave in the same way. Some of the names of geometrical shapes always belong to shapes which are similar, others do not. All squares are similar and differ only in size, but not all rectangles are similar. All cubes are similar, but not all cuboids. All equilateral triangles are similar, but not all isosceles triangles. The list can be prolonged indefinitely (Figure 36 : 23). Among the most important examples where every figure with the same name has the same shape are the regular polygons and the regular polyhedra. All regular hexagons are of the same shape, so are all regular octahedra. Another important example is the circle; all circles are of the same shape.

If a set of shapes is similar, all their measurements behave in the same way. If children draw a graph of the perimeters of different squares (Figure 36 : 24), the graph will be a straight line, and is identical with the graph of the four times table. The perimeter of every square is four times the length of its side.

Similarly, if a graph of the lengths of the diagonals of different squares is drawn (Figure 36 :25), it will again be a straight line, although the relationship cannot be stated using whole numbers. The diagonal of the square will be seen from the graph to be slightly less than $1\frac{1}{2}$ times the length of the side. In fact, we know from Pythagoras' Theorem that the diagonal of the square is $\sqrt{2}$ times the length of the side, or approximately $1 \cdot 41$ times the length of the side.

Children can make graphs to show the corresponding measurements of other similar shapes. The perimeters of regular hexagons, and the lengths of straw used in making the edges of different sized cubes are easily shown on graphs.

When we examine the growth of similar shapes, we find that the perimeters are always the same multiple of the lengths of their sides. This multiple varies according to the shape, but is a constant for each shape (Figure 36 : 26).

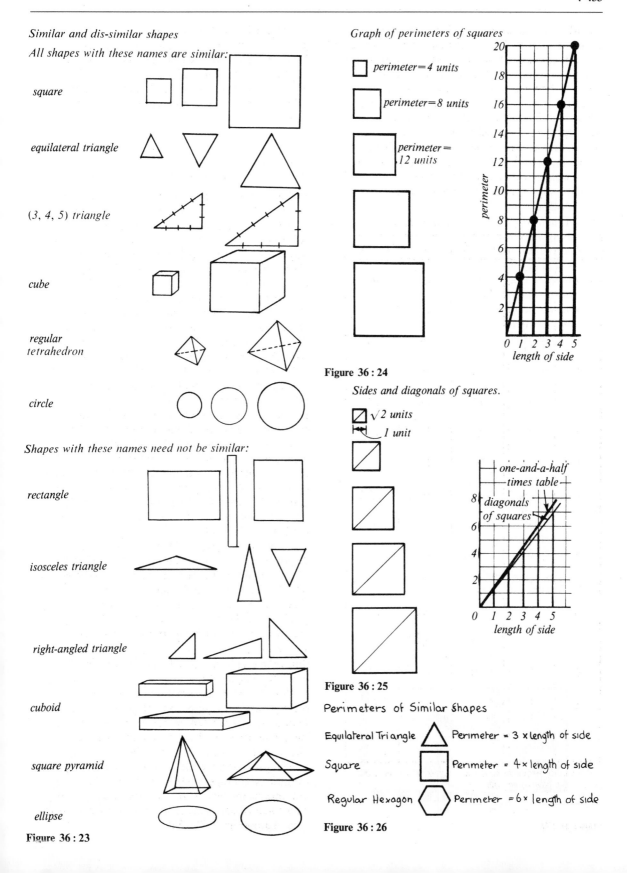

Similar and dis-similar shapes

All shapes with these names are similar:

square

equilateral triangle

(3, 4, 5) triangle

cube

regular tetrahedron

circle

Shapes with these names need not be similar:

rectangle

isosceles triangle

right-angled triangle

cuboid

square pyramid

ellipse

Figure 36 : 23

Graph of perimeters of squares

perimeter=4 units

perimeter=8 units

perimeter = 12 units

perimeter
length of side

Figure 36 : 24

Sides and diagonals of squares.

$\sqrt{2}$ units

1 unit

one-and-a-half times table

diagonals of squares

length of side

Figure 36 : 25

Perimeters of Similar Shapes

Equilateral Triangle   Perimeter = 3 × length of side

Square   Perimeter = 4 × length of side

Regular Hexagon   Perimeter = 6 × length of side

Figure 36 : 26

We turn now to consider circles, the simplest set of similar figures with curved sides, and examine the relationship of the perimeter of a circle to its other measurements.

CIRCLES

By the middle years of schooling children have used circles for several years in their building and pattern-making. They know that wheels are circular in shape so that the axle of the wheel is always the same distance from the ground; that is, they know that all *radii* of a circle are equal. They know that a circle is symmetrical about every *diameter*, and they can find the centre of a circular piece of paper by folding it. They have used a trundle wheel, whose *circumference* is a metre, for measuring distances. They have cut circles into *sectors* which are fractions of the whole circle. They have learnt to draw an equilateral triangle by using compasses to make *arcs* of equal radius. They have probably

Talking about circles, and using them

(a)

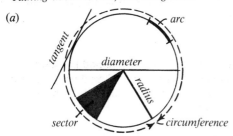

(b) *Drawing an equilateral triangle*

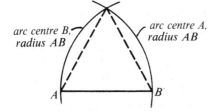

arc centre B,
radius AB

arc centre A,
radius AB

(c) *Measuring the diameter of a tin*

Figure 36 : 27

measured the diameter of a tin or ball by putting it between two books which just touch, or are *tangents* to it (Figure 36 : 27). By now, their questions are more concerned with the measurement of circles. They may ask how should we make a trundle wheel to measure $\frac{1}{2}$ metre: what diameter should it be? Is the cog-wheel with 40 teeth twice the diameter of the cog-wheel with 20 teeth? Which is the better buy, two small round tins of coffee, or one large one? How many times does a bicycle wheel go round in a kilometre? Do the tyres of a Mini wear out faster than those of a car with bigger wheels?

Children who have seen that the perimeters of similar regular polygons are a constant multiple of the length of their sides will expect a similar relation to be true for circles. All circles are similar, so the perimeter, or circumference, of any circle will be the same multiple of its diameter. The only remaining question is, what multiple of the diameter is the circumference? It is easy to see that the circumference of a circle must be more than 3 times its diameter, and less than 4 times its diameter. Figure 36 : 28 shows a regular hexagon drawn within a circle, and a square surrounding the circle. The hexagon has a smaller perimeter, and the square a larger perimeter, than the circle. Hence the circumference of a circle is between three and four times its diameter. A more accurate value can be obtained by measuring the circumferences and diameters of various circular objects, and drawing a graph of the results (Figure 36 : 29). Lines showing $3 \times$ (diameter) and $4 \times$ (diameter) can be drawn on the same graph for comparison. Many tins and other circular objects of a variety of sizes should be measured. A simple way of measuring the circumference of a tin is to wrap a piece of paper tightly round it and to prick with a pin through two layers of paper. The paper can then be opened out and the distance between pinholes either measured

Approximations to the circumference of a circle

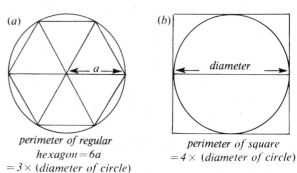

(a)

perimeter of regular
hexagon $= 6a$
$= 3 \times$ (diameter of circle)

(b)

perimeter of square
$= 4 \times$ (diameter of circle)

Figure 36 : 28

*Graph of diameters and
circumferences of circles*

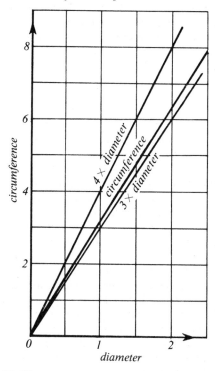

Figure 36 : 29

or transferred directly to the graph. Children are likely to conclude from their graphs that the circumference of a circle is about $3\frac{1}{4}$ times its diameter.

The actual value of the multiple of the diameter of a circle which gives the circumference is known as π; hence

circumference of circle = $\pi \times$ (diameter)

or

$$\frac{\text{circumference}}{\text{diameter}} = \pi$$

The value of π, which is $3\cdot141592653\ldots$, has been evaluated with an increasing degree of accuracy over the centuries. The ancient Jews used 3 as an approximation.[2] Archimedes proved that the value of π was between $3\frac{1}{7}$ and $3\frac{10}{71}$; Roman surveyors often used $3\frac{1}{8}$ instead of the closer approximation $3\frac{1}{7}$, as this made calculation rather easier. The advent of the electronic computer has now made it possible to calculate π to any number of decimal

[2]The description of the work of Hiram the worker in brass in the furnishing of Solomon's Temple contains the words: 'And he made a molten sea, ten cubits from the one brim to the other: it was round all about, . . . and a line of thirty cubits did compass it round about.' (I Kings 7 : 23)

places, and more than 10 000 places are known. Children sometimes think that $3\frac{1}{7}$ is the exact value of π. In fact

$$3\frac{1}{7} = 3\cdot142857\ldots$$

and

$$\pi = 3\cdot141592\ldots,$$

so that $3\frac{1}{7}$ is an approximation to π which is only correct to 2 decimal places. The decimal approximation $3\cdot14$ is, however, quite sufficient for practical purposes, and children should be encouraged to use a decimal approximation to π, in their working, particularly when using a calculator.

The teacher will notice that we have used a graphical method of estimating π. Another method is to measure the diameter and circumference of a circle, divide circumference by diameter, repeat several times and average the results. Children may ask how the value of π can be calculated with great accuracy. Archimedes and many other later calculators did it by drawing regular polygons inside and around the circle, and calculating their perimeters. Archimedes used polygons with 96 sides to arrive at

$$3\frac{10}{71} < \pi < 3\frac{1}{7}$$

Since about 1700AD this method has been superseded by calculations based on variations on the formula obtained by methods of higher mathematics:

$$\pi = 4(1 - \tfrac{1}{3} + \tfrac{1}{5} - \tfrac{1}{7} + \tfrac{1}{9} - \tfrac{1}{11} + \ldots)$$

AREAS OF SIMILAR SHAPES

We now consider the behaviour of the areas of similar shapes. We have already drawn a graph of the growth of the areas of squares (*see page 275*) and have examined the behaviour of square numbers. Equilateral triangles and similar rectangles obey the same law of growth as squares. Figure 36 : 30 shows a graph of the growth of the areas of equilateral triangles. The same method of examining the growth of area can be used for any shape which will cover a plane area without leaving gaps. In Figure 36 : 31 we use this method to study the growth of similar rectangles, scalene triangles and regular hexagons.

It therefore seems quite likely that if we have any two similar shapes, and if the linear measurements of one are n times the linear measurements of the other, then their areas will be connected by the relation

Growth of the areas of equilateral triangles

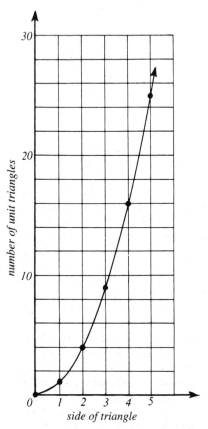

Side = 1 unit
Area = 1 unit triangle

Side = 2 units
Area = 4 unit triangles

Side = 3 units
Area = 9 unit triangles

Side = 4 units
Area = 16 unit triangles

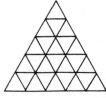
Side = 5 units
Area = 25 unit triangles

Figure 36 : 30

(area of shape of side n units)
$$= n^2 \times (\text{area of shape of side 1 unit})$$

From the tessellation of Figure 36 : 31(*b*), this relation is true for triangles. It follows from this that it will be true for any shape with straight sides, since any such shape can be divided up into triangles (Figure 36 : 32). Hence, if we know the area of a basic shape, we can find the areas of all figures which are similar to it. The square is of course particularly easy, as we usually take the unit of area to be a square of side 1 unit. In Chapter 26

(*a*) *Rectangles*

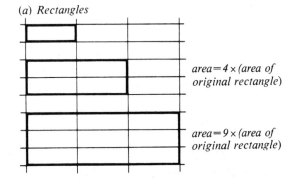

area = 4 × (area of original rectangle)

area = 9 × (area of original rectangle)

(*b*) *Triangles*

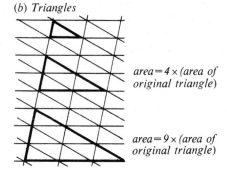

area = 4 × (area of original triangle)

area = 9 × (area of original triangle)

(*c*) *Regular hexagons*

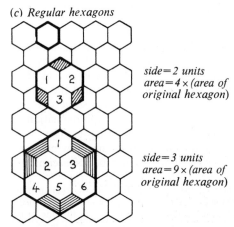

side = 2 units
area = 4 × (area of original hexagon)

side = 3 units
area = 9 × (area of original hexagon)

Figure 36 : 31

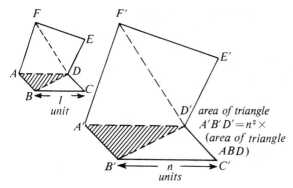

area of triangle
$A'B'D' = n^2 \times$
(area of triangle ABD)

Hence *(area of shape A'B'C'...) =*
$n^2 \times$ *(area of shape ABC...)*

Figure 36 : 32

we saw how the areas of rectangles and triangles can be found, by finding the number of unit squares which will cover a rectangle, and by using the fact that a triangle is half of a rectangle.

THE AREA OF A CIRCLE

We now turn to the problem of finding the area of a circle. Circles cannot be used to make tessellations without leaving gaps, so this method of finding the area is unsuitable. But the area of a circle is clearly less than the area of the square which contains it (Figure 36 : 33(a)), and so is less than the area of the square on its diameter, or if the square on the diameter is subdivided, the area of the circle is less than 4 × (area of square on the radius).

Another approximation to the area of a circle is obtained by drawing a square inside the circle (Figure 36 : 34). It will be seen that four quarters of this square together make up twice the square on the radius, and so

2 × (square on the radius) < area of circle

and

area of a circle < 4 × (square on the radius)

A circle and the containing square

(a) *area of circle*
< area of square
on diameter

(b) *area of circle*
< 4 × (square
on radius)

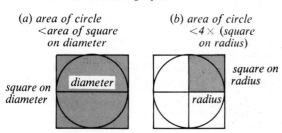

Figure 36 : 33

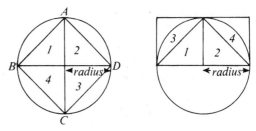

Figure 36 : 34

It is certainly to be expected that the area of a circle will be a constant multiple of the square on the radius, since all circles are similar shapes. Figure 36 : 35 shows similar regular polygons with a large number of sides inscribed in two circles of radius 1 unit and r units. The previous result on the area of similar shapes with straight sides is then used. Hence we expect that the area of a circle will be a constant multiple of the square on the radius, and that this constant multiple will be between 2 and 4. A dissection and rearrangement of the circle, suggested by the regular polygons in Figure 36 : 35, enables a better result to be obtained.

The circle is cut into many equal sectors, which can be arranged into the shape shown in Figure 36 : 36(b). This shape is very nearly a rectangle. Its length is half the perimeter of the polygon inscribed in the circle, and its breadth is nearly equal to the radius of the circle. If we use a polygon with a very large number of sides, half the perimeter of the polygon becomes more and more nearly equal to

Similar polygons inscribed in circles

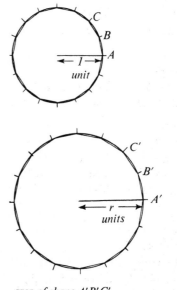

area of shape A'B'C' ...
Figure 36 : 35 $= r^2 \times$ *(area of shape ABC...)*

458 .

Dissection of a circle to find its area

(a)

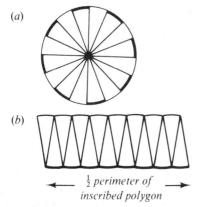

(b)

← ½ perimeter of →
inscribed polygon

Figure 36 : 36

half the circumference of the circle. In the end, if the number of sides of the polygon is increased indefinitely, the area of the circle has been rearranged in the form of a rectangle whose length is *half the circumference of the circle*, and whose breadth is the *radius* (Figure 36 : 37).

This seems a very suitable formula for the area of a circle for children to use at this stage, as it reminds them of the thought-process used in

The area of a circle

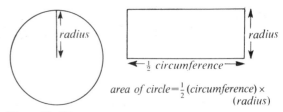

area of circle = ½ (*circumference*) × (*radius*)

Figure 36 : 37

obtaining the result. We may, however, rearrange the result slightly. The circumference of a circle is $\pi \times$ (diameter). But the radius is half of the diameter, so

$$\frac{1}{2} \text{ circumference} = \frac{1}{2} (\pi \times \text{diameter})$$
$$= \pi \times (\frac{1}{2} \text{ diameter})$$
$$= \pi \times \text{radius}$$

The result now takes the form demonstrated in Figure 36 : 38.

We see that the area of a circle is a constant multiple of the square of the radius, and that the value of the constant multiple is π. We can write the usual formula:

$$\text{area of circle} = \pi r^2$$

The area of a circle

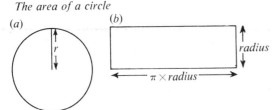 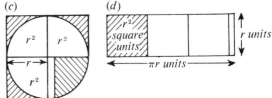

Figure 36 : 38

Further study of shape in the National Curriculum

The study of shape appears in Attainment Target 4 of the National Curriculum. At Level 6, children are expected to be familiar with tessellations, and with those properties of shapes which can be linked with tessellations. The study of Pythagoras' Theorem occurs at Level 7.

- know and use angle and symmetry properties of quadrilaterals and other polygons.
  EXAMPLE: *Use transformations and symmetry properties to produce tessellations.*
  (AT4: Level 6)
- understand and apply Pythagoras' theorem.
  (AT4: Level 7)

Calculations concerning similar shapes do not occur until Level 8, although children will

recognise whether shapes are similar at an earlier stage than this.

- understand and use mathematical similarity; know that angles remain unchanged and corresponding sides are in the same ratio.
  (AT4: Level 8)

The use of formulae for areas and volumes also occurs in AT 4.

- use knowledge and skills in length, area and volume to carry out calculations in plane and solid shapes.
  EXAMPLE: *Calculate lengths, areas and volumes in shapes involving rectangles, triangles, parallelograms, circles, trapezia, cubes, cuboids, cylinders and other solids of constant cross-sectional area.*
  (AT4: Level 7)

37 | RATIONAL AND IRRATIONAL NUMBERS

THE NUMBER LINE OF RATIONAL NUMBERS

The idea of the number line has now reached the stage where we can picture all the positive and negative integers as being represented by a set of equally spaced points on a line. All the rational numbers also have their appropriate places on the number line. It will be remembered that each rational number corresponds to a set of equivalent fractions. For instance,

$$^+(\tfrac{3}{5}) = {}^+(\tfrac{6}{10}) = {}^+0 \cdot 6 = {}^+(\tfrac{9}{15}) = \ldots$$

and all these equivalent fractions correspond to the same point on the number line. This representation of a set of fractions which are written differently, but which have the same value, by the same point on the number line helps to strengthen the idea of a rational number. A rational number is a number which is represented by a set of equivalent fractions, and which corresponds to a single point on the number line (Figure 37:1).

The rational number points are extremely closely packed on the number line. Between the points representing 0 and $^+1$ on the number line there are points representing the rational numbers $^+0 \cdot 1$, $^+0 \cdot 2, \ldots, {}^+0 \cdot 9$, points representing $^+0 \cdot 01$, $^+0 \cdot 02$, $\ldots, {}^+0 \cdot 99$, points representing $^+0 \cdot 001$, $^+0 \cdot 002$, $\ldots, {}^+0 \cdot 999$, and so on, using ever smaller intervals on the line. As children realise how they can use the decimal system to represent ever smaller fractions, they will think that the number line contains ever more and more points representing rational numbers (Figure 37:2). Here we have used successive subdivisions of each unit into tenths to

The number line of positive and negative rational numbers

Figure 37 : 1

Filling up the number line with more closely packed rational numbers
(a) Tenths

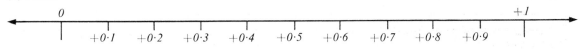

(b) Hundredths

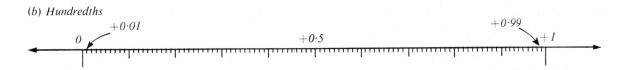

(c) Thousandths (enlarged)

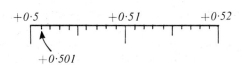

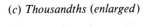

(d) Ten-thousandths, etc.

Figure 37 : 2

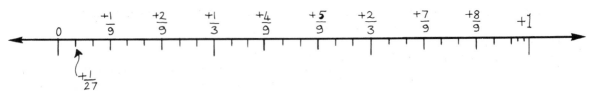

Figure 37 : 3

yield more and more rational number points on the number line. Any number of subdivisions of the unit will do equally well. In Figure 37 : 3 we use subdivisions of the unit into thirds, ninths, etc., to give rational number points. Most of these rational numbers are different from those marked in Figure 37 : 2, since $\frac{1}{3}$ cannot be exactly written as a terminating decimal fraction and recurs as $0\cdot333\ldots = 0\cdot\dot{3}$. We could carry out the same process of marking in rational number points with any subdivision of the unit, and so we eventually build up a mental picture of a number line on which *every* rational number has its place. The rational numbers on this number line are extremely close-packed. Every interval, however small, on the number line contains an infinity of rational numbers, for it we take a tiny interval such as that between $^-1\cdot000002$ and $^-1\cdot000001$, we could make in this interval continually repeated subdivisions similar to those shown in Figure 37 : 2; each of the points obtained would have a fractional representation and so would correspond to a rational number.

It is a surprising fact that when *all* the possible subdivisions of each unit of the number line, and so all the rational numbers, have been put in, there are still points of the number line which have not been covered. In spite of the density of packing of the rational number points, there are in fact many other points on the number line with no number alloted to them. Children will meet these *irrational numbers*[1] first when instead of measuring the diagonal of a square, they use Pythagoras' Theorem to work out its length, and so have to find a value for $\sqrt{2}$. The full significance of irrational numbers

[1]See page 447 and 452.

will not, however, be appreciated until later.[2]

We can very easily see that $\sqrt{2}$ does not fall on any of the *decimal* subdivisions of the number line. For if we try to find better and better decimal approximations to $\sqrt{2}$ using a calculator,

$1\cdot4 < \sqrt{2} < 1\cdot5$, since $1\cdot4^2 = 1\cdot96$ and $1\cdot5^2 = 2\cdot25$;
$1\cdot41 < \sqrt{2} < 1\cdot42$, since $1\cdot41^2 = 1\cdot9881$ and $1\cdot42^2 = 2\cdot0364$;
$1\cdot414 < \sqrt{2} < 1\cdot415$, since $1\cdot414^2 = 1\cdot999396$ and $1\cdot415^2 = 2\cdot002225$
$1\cdot4142 < \sqrt{2} < 1\cdot4143$, since $1\cdot4142^2 = 1\cdot9999616\ldots$ and $1\cdot4143^2 = 2 = 0002444\ldots$,

and so on. It will be seen that this process could be continued indefinitely. The limitations of a calculator, which can only hold a comparatively small number of decimal places, make themselves felt; but the first few places, and a knowledge of the structure of multiplication, make it clear that the process does not terminate. If, for instance, it was thought that

$$1\cdot41419^2 = 2 \text{ exactly,}$$

then performing a tiny part of the multiplication process whose beginning is shown,

$$\begin{array}{r} 1\cdot41419 \\ \times\,1\cdot41419 \end{array}$$

$0\cdot00009 \times 1\cdot41419 = \ldots\ldots 71$
$0\cdot0001\ \times 1\cdot41419 = \ldots\ldots 9$

[2]A *rational number* can be written as a fraction or ratio; an *irrational number* has a place on the number line, but cannot be so written.

Fixing the position of $\sqrt{2}$ on the number line

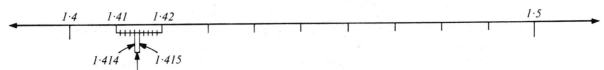

The position of $\sqrt{2}$ lies within a series of segments of ever-decreasing length.
Figure 37 : 4

would give immediate conviction that the last digit of the product is 1. The process of approaching more and more nearly the value of $\sqrt{2}$ by putting it within smaller and smaller decimal subdivisions of a unit (Figure 37 : 4) would eventually fix a point on the number line corresponding to $\sqrt{2}$, although an *exact* decimal for $\sqrt{2}$ cannot be found.

This point representing $\sqrt{2}$ is not one of the exact *decimal* points on the number line, but, on the other hand, neither is

$$\tfrac{1}{3} = 0\cdot 33333\ldots = 0\cdot\dot{3}$$

or

$$\tfrac{1}{7} = 0\cdot 1428571428571\ldots = 0\cdot\dot{1}4285\dot{7}$$

To show that $\sqrt{2}$ is not a rational number we must show that the point representing $\sqrt{2}$ is not a result of *any* subdivision of a unit of the number line into equal parts. The proof of this famous result is ascribed to the followers of Pythagoras, who found it as disturbing as do people today whose previous acquaintance with numbers has only included whole numbers and fractions. The Pythagoreans even attempted to suppress their discovery for a time because it undermined the foundations of their beliefs.

Children will not understand the very abstract nature of the following argument until they are well into the stage of formal operations but it is of value to the teacher in showing that irrational numbers are needed if we are to handle square roots. Children's questions are likely to be of the type, 'Surely the decimal for $\sqrt{2}$ must end sometime?' and, 'If you wrote the numbers to another base, would $\sqrt{2}$ end then?'

The Pythagoreans proved their result by supposing that $\sqrt{2}$ did fall on a rational subdivision of the unit in some base, and showed that this led to a contradiction. If $\sqrt{2}$ were in fact a rational

number it could be written as a fraction:

$$\sqrt{2} = \frac{p}{q},$$

where p and q are *integers*, and where the fraction has been cancelled down to its lowest terms. Then, by squaring both sides

$$2 = \frac{p^2}{q^2}$$

and so $2q^2 = p^2$.

Now if we factorise p and q into their prime factors, however many factors p has, each of these factors occurs *twice* in p^2. Hence p^2 has an even number of prime factors. So has q^2, by a similar argument. But this means that $2q^2$ must have an *odd* number of prime factors, and so cannot be equal to p^2, which has an even number of prime factors. The only thing which can have gone wrong with this argument, which leads to such a disastrous conclusion, is the original assumption that $\sqrt{2}$ could be written as a fraction $\frac{p}{q}$. But every rational number can be written as a fraction in its lowest terms, and so $\sqrt{2}$ cannot be a rational number. Hence $\sqrt{2}$ is represented by a point on the number line which is left uncovered by *all* rational subdivisions of the units of the number line.

IRRATIONAL NUMBERS AND REAL NUMBERS

In the same way that we have shown that $\sqrt{2}$ is not a rational number, it can be shown that $\sqrt{3}$, $\sqrt{5}$, $\sqrt{6}$, $\sqrt{7}$, ... are irrational numbers. Children who have met Pythagoras' Theorem will find these numbers of interest because, although they cannot calculate exact values for them, they can use a calculator to approximate to them, or obtain an approximation by scale drawing, or read their

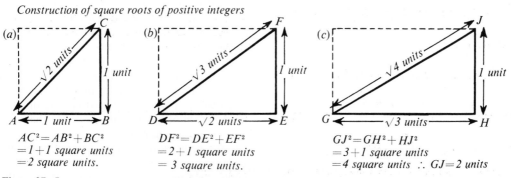

Construction of square roots of positive integers

(a) $AC^2 = AB^2 + BC^2$
$= 1 + 1$ square units
$= 2$ square units.

(b) $DF^2 = DE^2 + EF^2$
$= 2 + 1$ square units
$= 3$ square units.

(c) $GJ^2 = GH^2 + HJ^2$
$= 3 + 1$ square units
$= 4$ square units $\therefore GJ = 2$ units

Figure 37 : 5

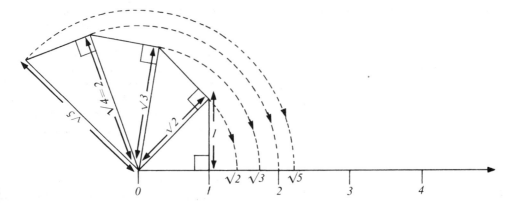

Figure 37 : 6

approximate values from the graph of squares, and so they can mark them in on the number line.

A simple way of drawing lengths of $\sqrt{2}$ units, $\sqrt{3}$ units, etc., is shown in Figure 37 : 5. The diagonal of a square whose length is 1 unit is $\sqrt{2}$ units. This starts the construction, which is continued by using the length last constructed. The accuracy of the construction can be checked each time the square on the diagonal is a perfect square. Figure 37 : 6 shows another way of arranging this construction, and transfers the lengths to the number line.

The only square roots of rational numbers which are themselves rational numbers are those such as $\sqrt{4}$ and $\sqrt{\frac{9}{25}}$ which are square roots of perfect squares. All other square roots, such as $\sqrt{10}$, $\sqrt{\frac{8}{25}}$, $\sqrt{0\cdot001}$ are irrational numbers; so are most cube roots, fourth roots, and so on. Many other numbers which are not roots of rational numbers are also irrational. An example of these is π, which is equal to $3\cdot1415926535\ldots$ Although it was known in ancient times that $\sqrt{2}$ was an irrational number, it was a much more difficult matter to prove that π was irrational, and this problem was not solved until almost 1800AD.

In fact, all numbers which, when written in decimal form, neither terminate nor recur are irrational. Conversely, all rational numbers when written as decimals either terminate or recur. It is easy to see that a terminating decimal is a rational number. For example, $1\cdot8731 = \frac{18731}{10000}$, which is a rational number. But it is not quite so obvious that a recurring decimal such as $3\cdot054054054\ldots$ is a rational number. But if

$$n = 3\cdot0\dot{5}\dot{4} = 3\cdot054054054054\ldots$$

then

$$1000n = 3054\cdot054054054\ldots$$

But

$$n = \quad 3\cdot054054054\ldots$$

If we subtract these two expressions, the recurring part of the decimal is removed, and

$$999n = 3051$$

Hence $n = \frac{3051}{999}$,

and this is a rational number.

Similarly, we can find a fraction corresponding to any recurring decimal. Therefore, a terminating or recurring decimal is a rational number. A decimal which neither terminates nor recurs, but which has an infinite number of decimal places without continuous cyclic repetition of the digits, represents an irrational number.

Although the rational numbers are so densely packed on the number line, there are very many spaces between them which are occupied by irrational numbers. In fact, it can be shown that rational numbers are only thinly scattered on the number line compared with the great profusion of the irrational numbers.

In practical problems, irrational numbers are always handled by means of rational approximations to them, which will give a numerical result to any desired degree of accuracy. In theory, however, it is desirable to use a number system which contains both the rational and the irrational numbers. The number system used in much of more advanced mathematics is the *real number system*. The set of real numbers is the set of rational numbers together with the set of irrational numbers. *Every* real number is represented by a point on the number line, and *every* point on the number line represents a real number. The number line of rational numbers which we have previously used has the fundamental disadvantage of having gaps in it, but the *real number line* is complete.

In the primary school children will probably be convinced that every point on the number line represents a number, but for many children the

Interpolation from the graph of squares

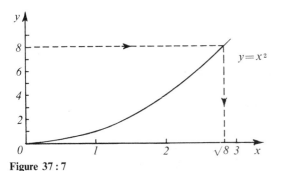

Figure 37 : 7

distinction between rational and irrational numbers will be postponed to the secondary school stage. In fact, children are intuitively aware of the real number line and its completeness long before they understand irrational numbers. Much of this intuitive awareness comes from graphical work. When children interpolate a value such as $\sqrt{8}$ from the graph of squares (Figure 37 : 7), they expect that the point which they obtain on the horizontal axis will correspond to a number which is the value of $\sqrt{8}$. It does not occur to them that there is no *rational* number whose square is exactly 8; what they do is to find the best decimal approximation they can to the real number whose square is 8.

Similarly, when a particular calculator which has a square root function gives

$$\sqrt{8} = 2 \cdot 828\,427\,1,$$

children become intuitively aware that this is only an approximation, and is the best approximation this calculator can give on its 8-digit display. Some caution is needed here, as some calculators confirm the rounding of square roots by rounding squares. The sequence of keystrokes below then produces the displays shown:

		display
8	√x	2·828 427 1
	x²	8

However, $(2 \cdot 828\,427\,1)^2$ certainly cannot be exactly 8, as the square of any number ending in 1 itself ends in 1.

We thus see that the *real number line* is essential for the treatment of square roots, but we can only expect an informal intuitive handling of it at this stage. In the rest of this chapter we discuss some more situations in which children may meet $\sqrt{2}$ and other well-known irrational numbers.

REDUCTION, ENLARGEMENT AND $\sqrt{2}$

Children often make booklets or folders for their work by folding a large piece of paper as many times as they need. This process is also used in making books. A number of pages are printed on the same sheet of paper, and the sheet is then folded so that the pages come in the right order. Figure 37 : 8 shows a way in which children, and printers, often fold their paper to make smaller pages. This process can be continued to make more, smaller, pages. The fold is always made so as to halve the longer side of the rectangle. The shape of the page which results is not always the same shape as the sheet from which it was folded. The quarter of a sheet, or quarto page, is the same shape as the original sheet (Figure 37 : 9(a)), and the octavo page

Folding a sheet of paper for a booklet

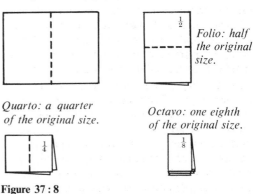

Quarto: a quarter of the original size.

Octavo: one eighth of the original size.

Figure 37 : 8

The sheet of paper opened out.

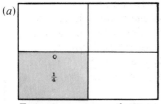

Four quarto pages, the same shape as the sheet.

Figure 37 : 9

(b) Eight octavo pages, the same shape as the folio.

The folding continued. $\frac{1}{32}$ of the sheet is the same shape as $\frac{1}{8}$ and $\frac{1}{2}$ of the sheet.

is the same shape as the folio (Figure 37 : 9(*b*)). It is rare for the folio and octavo to be the same shape as the sheet and the quarto. This book is of size 246 mm × 189 mm before trimming. Each page has been folded from a sheet 1008 mm × 768 mm. Hence 32 pages of the book (16 pages printed on each sides) were folded and cut to make one 32-page section from a single sheet.

Children can check whether two rectangles are the same shape by putting one on top of the other (Figure 37 : 10).

Finding out whether rectangles are similar

(*a*)

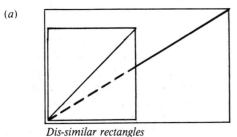

Dis-similar rectangles

(*b*)

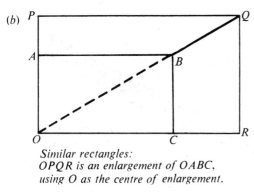

Similar rectangles:
OPQR is an enlargement of OABC,
using O as the centre of enlargement.

Figure 37 : 10

Figure 37 : 11 shows the shapes of a half, quarter, eighth, etc., of a rectangular sheet of paper. The shapes made by $\frac{1}{2}, \frac{1}{8}, \frac{1}{32}, \ldots$ of a sheet are similar to each other, and the shapes made by 1, $\frac{1}{4}, \frac{1}{16}, \frac{1}{64}, \ldots$ of a sheet are similar to each other. Often the two sequences of fractional parts folded in this way are not the same shape as each other. Children may try to find a sheet of paper whose half is the same shape as the original sheet, in which case all the pages folded from it will be the same shape as the sheet. They will find that the length of the sheet is rather less than $1\frac{1}{2}$ times the breadth. Sheets of paper in metric sizes, A0, A1, A2,... have this property that half a sheet is the same shape as the whole sheet (Figure 37 : 12). Children are very familiar with folding an A4 sheet of paper in half to make A5 sheets.

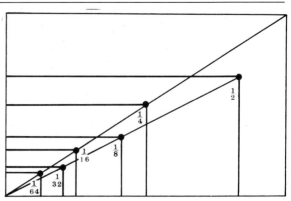

Figure 37 : 11

Systems of proportion based on similar rectangles have often been used by architects. For example, the columns on the façade of the Erechtheion at Athens divide the rectangular façade into smaller rectangles. The proportions are such that a rectangle whose sides are next-door-but-one columns is

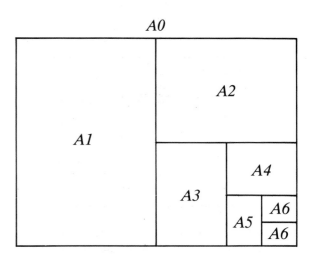

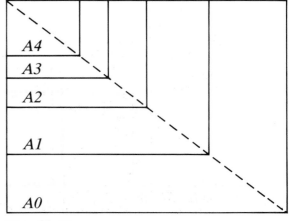

Figure 37 : 12

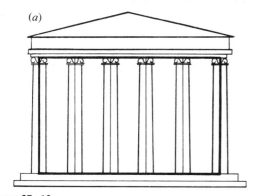

Figure 37 : 13

Another test for similar rectangles

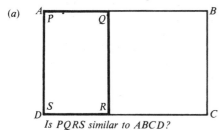

(a)

Is PQRS similar to ABCD?

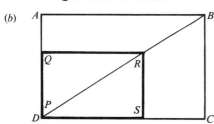

(b)

Rotate PQRS through a right angle and test for similarity.

(c)

Return PQRS to its original position. Diagonal PR is now at right angles to diagonal BD.

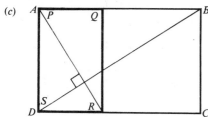

(d)

Similar rectangles in the Erechtheion can be picked out by their diagonals.

Figure 37 : 14

(b)

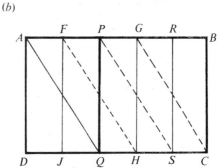

The four small rectangles APQD, FGHJ, PRSQ, GBCH, are all similar to ABCD.

similar to the whole façade (Figure 37 : 13). In Figure 37 : 13(b) these four small rectangles have been picked out by drawing a diagonal of each one. This makes it very easy to see whether rectangles such as ABCD and PQRS (Figure 37 : 14) are similar.

Constructing a rectangle whose halves are the same shape as the whole rectangle

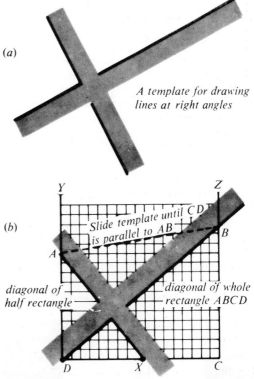

(a)

A template for drawing lines at right angles

(b)

Draw DC, DY, CZ. Put in pins at A and X, so that DX=½DC. Slide template about, touching pins, until AB is parallel to DC

Figure 37 : 15

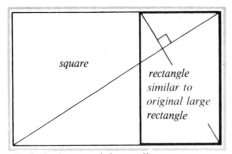

Both the large and the small rectangles are golden rectangles.

Figure 37 : 16

Two rulers rigidly fixed at right angles, or a cardboard or Meccano template for drawing two lines at right angles now makes it easy to construct on squared paper a rectangle whose halves are the same shape as the original (Figure 37 : 15). When the sides of this rectangle are measured, it will be found that the longer side is about 1·4 times the length of the shorter side. In fact, the longer side is $\sqrt{2}$ times the shorter side. A few children may be able to see algebraically that this must be so (Figure 37 : 16).

THE GOLDEN RECTANGLE

There is another shape of rectangle which has many interesting properties. This is the so-called *golden rectangle*, the ratio of whose sides, the *golden ratio*, has often been thought to form the basis for an ideal system of proportion. This ratio seems to appear both in shapes and among numbers, and to be approximated to both by nature and by artists and architects.

We can find the golden rectangle by folding a piece of paper. Children know well the method of folding a square piece of paper from a rectangular one (Figure 37 : 17). The rectangular piece of paper left over (shaded in Figure 37 : 17(*b*)) is usually a different shape from the original piece. It may happen, however, that the piece left over is the

Folding a rectangle to make a square

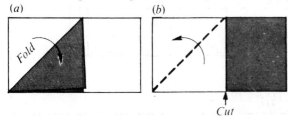

(*a*) (*b*)

Fold

Cut

Figure 37 : 17

Ratio of sides when half-rectangle is similar to whole

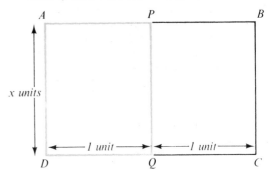

If ABCD is similar to APQD, then $\dfrac{AD}{AB} = \dfrac{AP}{AD}$

hence $\dfrac{x}{2} = \dfrac{1}{x}$

and $x^2 = 2$

Figure 37 : 18

same shape as the original piece (Figure 37 : 18). The shape of such a rectangle is called the *golden rectangle*. Its proportions have often been thought to be particularly pleasing to the eye. The shape of a postcard or of a catalogue card the sides of which are in the ratio 5 : 3 is a fairly good approximation

Constructing a Golden Rectangle

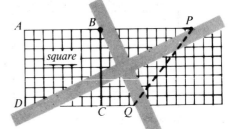

Draw square ABCD. Put in pins at B and D. Slide template until PQ is parallel to AD.

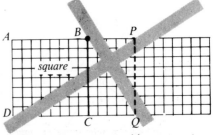

APQD and BPQC are now golden rectangles

Figure 37 : 19

to a golden rectangle. A sheet of foolscap paper is even better, as here the sides are in the ratio 13 : 8. Children who have used a right-angle template for the construction of the rectangle shown in Figure 37 : 15 will be able to construct a golden rectangle by a similar method (Figure 37 : 19).

When the sides of the golden rectangle are measured it will be found that they are in about the ratio $1 \cdot 62 : 1$ (Figure 37 : 20). This ratio, which Leonardo da Vinci called 'the divine proportion', was renamed in the nineteenth century the *golden ratio*. It is an irrational number, the first few digits of whose decimal expansion are $1 \cdot 61803398 \ldots$ It is often denoted by the Greek letter ϕ.

A property of the golden rectangle is that the ratio of the larger to the smaller part of AP (Figure 37 : 21) is equal to the golden ration ϕ. This is because $AB = AD$ and so the golden ratio $\frac{AP}{AD}$ is equal to $\frac{AP}{AB}$. Also the golden ratio $\frac{PQ}{BP}$ is equal to $\frac{AB}{BP}$, since $PQ = AB$. But all golden ratios are equal, so $\frac{AP}{AB} = \frac{AB}{BP}$. In words, *the ratio of the whole of AP to its larger part is equal to the ratio of the larger the smaller part.* The line AP is said to be divided in *golden section*.

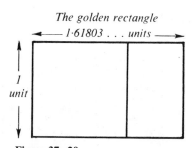

The golden rectangle

Figure 37 : 20

Golden ratios in the golden rectangle

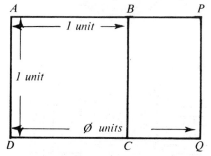

Rectangle APQD is similar to PQCB.

Hence $\frac{AP}{AD} = \frac{PQ}{BP} = $ *golden ratio and so* $\frac{\phi}{1} = \frac{1}{\phi - 1}$

Figure 37 : 21

Construction of a golden rectangle with ruler and compasses

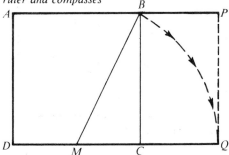

(i) *Construct square ABCD*
(ii) *Find M, mid point of CD.*
(iii) *With centre M, radius MB, draw an arc.*
(iv) *Complete the golden rectangle ADQP.*

Figure 37 : 22

The Greeks knew a very simple geometrical construction for a golden rectangle (Figure 37 : 22), and a very similar method enables a line to be divided in golden section.

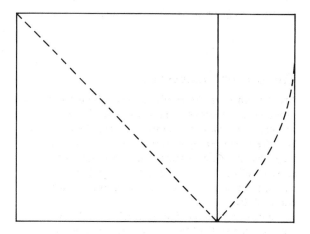

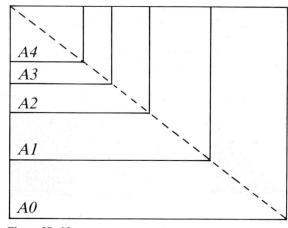

Figure 37 : 23

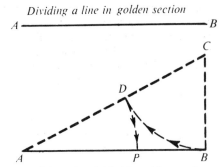

Dividing a line in golden section

(i) *Line AB is to be divided in golden section.*

(ii) *Draw $BC = \frac{1}{2} AB$, perpendicular to AB.*

(iii) *Centre C, radius CB, draw an arc.*

(iv) *Centre A, radius AD, draw an arc.*

P then divides AB in golden section.[3]

Figure 37 : 24

Children will not at this stage be able to prove the correctness of the construction, but they will be able to verify by measurement that it does in fact give a golden rectangle.

This construction can be compared with the similar construction for $\sqrt{2}$, which gives the shape of the metric paper sizes (Figure 37 : 23).

Much of the interest of the construction for dividing a line in golden section (Figure 37 : 24), has sprung from the occurrence of golden section in art, and in such shapes as the regular pentagon.

Another interesting property of the golden rectangle is its link with the *equiangular spiral* found in nature in the shells of *Nautilus* and in

[3]By Pythagoras' Theorem, if $AB = 2$ units, $AP = (\sqrt{5} - 1)$ units and

$$\frac{AB}{AP} = \frac{2}{\sqrt{5} - 1} = \frac{2(\sqrt{5} + 1)}{(\sqrt{5} - 1)(\sqrt{5} + 1)} = \frac{2(\sqrt{5} + 1)}{4} = \frac{\sqrt{5} + 1}{2} = \phi.$$

[4]See D'Arcy Thompson, *On Growth and Form* and Weyl, H., *Symmetry.*

snail-shells.[4] When a square is cut from a golden rectangle, a golden rectangle remains, from which another square can be cut. If this process is continued, rotating the rectangle through a right angle each time (Figure 37 : 25), corresponding points of the golden rectangles lie on an equiangular spiral. This spiral rotates for ever about the point of intersection of diagonals of all the golden rectangles in the diagram. This centre point is the *pole* of the spiral.

The spiral formed in this way is known as the *equiangular* spiral because it always cuts the radius from the pole at the same angle (Figure 37 : 26). D'Arcy Thompson likens the equiangular spiral to the result of rolling up a cone, so that the section of the curled-up trunk of an elephant roughly resembles an equiangular spiral, as does the section of a curled growing animal like *Nautilus.*

Equiangular spirals.

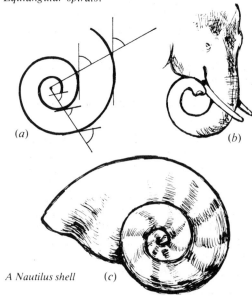

(a)

(b)

A Nautilus shell (c)

Figure 37 : 26

The equiangular spiral made from a golden rectangle

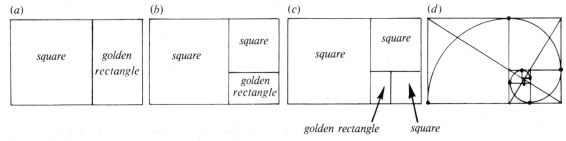

(a) square | golden rectangle

(b) square | square | golden rectangle

(c) square | square | golden rectangle | square

(d)

golden rectangle *square*

Figure 37 : 25

THE FIBONACCI SEQUENCE AND THE GOLDEN RECTANGLE

Children make up sequences of numbers by many methods, and enjoy continuing these sequences and finding out how they behave. The following sequences can be made from the numbers 1, 2, 3, 4, 5,. . .

i) 1, 4, 9, 16, 25, . . . by squaring each natural number,

ii) 2, 4, 6, 8, 10, . . . by doubling each natural number,

iii) 7, 10, 13, 16, . . . by multiplying each natural number by 3 and adding 4.

Another way of making sequences which follow regular patterns is to take a number, perform some arithmetical operation on it, and repeat this operation to form a sequence. For instance,

i) 7, 10, 13, 16, . . .; start with 7, add 3, add 3 to the result, etc. This sequence is the same as the previous one but the method of construction is different.

ii) 1, 2, 4, 8, 16, 32, . . .; start with 1, double it, double the result, etc.

iii) 2, 4, 16, 256, . . .; start with 2, square it, square the result, etc.[5]

Yet another way of building up a sequence by using the terms already obtained to generate the next term is shown in the *Fibonacci sequence*. Such sequences are named after the greatest of medieval mathematicians, Leonardo of Pisa, nicknamed Fibonacci (*c.* 1170–1250 AD), who discovered the best known of them. Each term of a Fibonacci sequence is built up as the sum of the *two* previous terms, For instance, starting with 0 and 1, we have

$$0, 1, 0 + 1 = 1, 1 + 1 = 2, 1 + 2 = 3, 2 + 3 = 5, 3 + 5 = 8,. . .$$

that is

$$0, 1, 1, 2, 3, 5, 8, 13, 21, 34, . . .$$

The reader will notice that two of the

---

[5] The numbers obtained by adding 1 to each member of this sequence are called the *Fermat numbers*. They are

$$3, 5, 17, 257, 65537,. . .$$

Fermat (*c.* 1608–65 AD) conjectured that all these numbers were prime. But it is now known that the next Fermat number is 641×6700417, and that many later Fermat numbers are composite. No further prime Fermat numbers have been found.

---

approximations which we have used to the golden rectangle, 5 by 8 and 8 by 13, appear as pairs of successive terms of this sequence. In fact, every pair of successive terms of the Fibonacci sequence gives an increasingly better approximation to the proportions of the golden rectangle. The first few of these rectangles are:

Rectangle
1 by 1   2 by 1   3 by 2   5 by 3   8 by 5
13 by 8   21 by 13   34 by 21   55 by 34   89 by 55

Ratio of sides
$\frac{1}{1} = 1$ $\frac{2}{1} = 2$ $\frac{3}{2} = 1·5$ $\frac{5}{3} = 1·6666$ $\frac{8}{5} = 1·6$
$\frac{13}{8} = 1·625$ $\frac{21}{13} = 1·6153$ $\frac{34}{21} = 1·6190$
$\frac{55}{34} = 1·6176 . . .$ $\frac{89}{55} = 1·6181 . . .$

We see that the ratio of the sides becomes closer and closer to the golden ratio.

A sequence of rectangles which approximate more and more closely to a golden rectangle can be built up using the Fibonacci sequence by a method which is the reverse of Figure 37 : 25. In Figure 37 : 25 a golden rectangle was cut down into squares; now we use squares to build up more and more nearly golden rectangles (Figure 37 : 27).

It is not necessary to start with the numbers 0 and 1 to generate a Fibonacci sequence. Any two natural numbers will do. For instance 5 and 1 give the sequence

$$5, 1, 6, 7, 13, 20, 33, 53, 86, 139, . . .$$

It is possible to show that the ratio of successive terms of *any* Fibonacci sequence approaches the golden ratio. Hence, good approximations to a golden rectangle can be made by the whirling square method from *any* rectangle.

It has often been thought that a golden rectangle has more pleasing proportions than other rectangles, or that a line divided in golden section was more aesthetically pleasing than when divided elsewhere. Leonardo da Vinci used the golden section when drawing a face; the lines in Turner's 'Battersea Bridge' are placed so as to divide the picture in golden section, and the modern painter Mondrian uses the golden section to organise some of his compositions of line and colour. The architect le Corbusier was much struck by the fact that 144 appears in the Fibonacci sequence

$$0, 1, 1, 2, 3, 5, 8, 13, 21, 34, 55, 89, 144, 233,$$
. . .

and that 144 half-inches is the height of a six-foot man. He founded his Modular scales of proportion

Building a nearly golden rectangle

(*The whirling square method*)

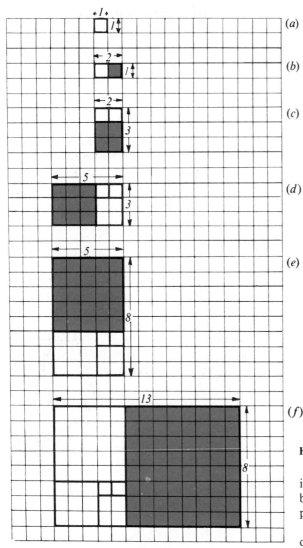

(a)

(b)

(c)

(d)

(e)

(f)

Start with a 1 by 1 square (the terms 1, 1 of the Fibonacci series).
Put another 1 by 1 square on to one side of it, giving a 2 by 1 rectangle (we have now used the terms 1, 1, 2 of the Fibonacci series). Put a square on the longer side, giving a 3 by 2 rectangle (1, 1, 2, 3 have been used). Continue to add 'whirling squares' to the rectangle. This step gives a 5 by 3 rectangle. At each stage, the length of the new rectangle is equal to the sum of the length and breadth of the last rectangle.

Figure 37 : 27

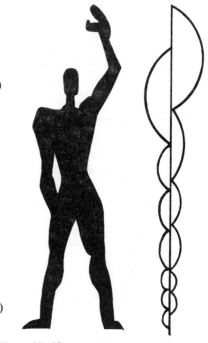

Figure 37 : 28

in architecture on various Fibonacci sequences, believing that he was relating architectural proportions to the human body.

In nature, numbers in the Fibonacci sequence often occur.[6] The Greek interest in the golden section seems, however, to have derived partly from the fact that it occurs in the regular pentagon, and therefore in the regular dodecahedron and icosahedron.

THE REGULAR PENTAGON AND THE GOLDEN SECTION

The Greek geometers directed much of their attention to the problem of making constructions with ruler and compasses, a protractor not being

[6]See Land, F. *The Language of Mathematics*, Chapter 13.

used. A regular pentagon is easy to construct if a protractor is allowed; otherwise, a method of construction is not immediately obvious. We now show how the golden section makes another appearance in the regular pentagon, and so makes it possible to construct a regular pentagon without using a protractor.

A regular pentagon is made up of three isosceles triangles, one of which is acute-angled, while the other two are congruent and are obtuse-angled. The angles of these isosceles triangles are easily found (Figure 37 : 29). We have seen earlier that drawing diagonals of a regular pentagon produces a smaller regular pentagon inside it (*see page 148*). As these diagonals are drawn, many further triangles are drawn inside the original pentagon, but they are all of one of the two shapes shown in Figure 37 : 29. Figure 37 : 30 shows some of these triangles, which are of different sizes, but are all of one or other of the two fundamental shapes. This is because the angles of the two triangles are such that a triangle

More isosceles triangles in the regular pentagon.

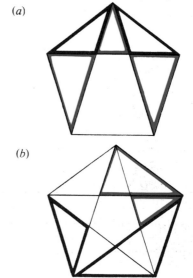

Figure 37 : 30

The isosceles triangles in a regular pentagon.

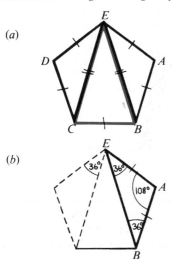

Each angle of the regular pentagon is 108°.
Hence the other angles of △ ABE are each 36°.

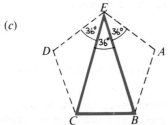

angle BEC = 36°
Hence the other angles of △ BCE are each 72°.

Figure 37 : 29

Combinations of isosceles triangles in the regular pentagon

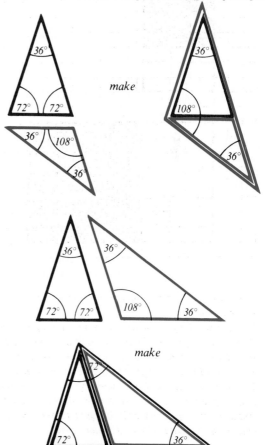

Figure 37 : 31

Golden sections in these isosceles triangles

Constructing a regular pentagon

(a)

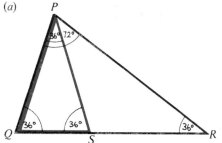

Triangles *RPQ* and *PQS* are similar.

$$\frac{Longer\ side\ of\ RPQ}{Shorter\ side\ of\ RPQ} = \frac{Longer\ side\ of\ PQS}{Shorter\ side\ of\ PQS}$$

$\frac{QR}{PQ} = \frac{PQ}{QS}$. But $PQ = PS = SR$ and so $\frac{QR}{SR} = \frac{SR}{QS}$.

Hence *QR* is divided in golden section.

(b)

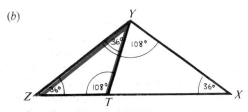

Triangles *YXZ* and *TYZ* are similar, hence, as before

$\frac{XZ}{XT} = \frac{XT}{TZ}$ and *XZ* is divided in golden section.

Figure 37 : 32

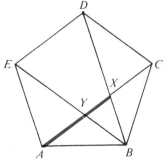

AXB is to be an isosceles triangle. First draw AX of the length required for AB, and divide it in golden section at Y. Now we need AY = YB = XC, and AB = AX.

Figure 37 : 33

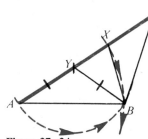

When the position of B has been found, BX and BY are produced, and the pentagon completed.

Figure 37 : 34

It is now easy to see how to construct a regular pentagon by using the division of a line in golden section (Figure 37 : 34).

of each shape (of the right sizes) can be put together to make either isosceles triangle, as shown in Figure 37 : 31.

These larger isosceles triangles each have the further property that a side is divided in golden section. Figure 37 : 32(a) shows this for the acute-angled triangle, and Figure 37 : 32(b) for the obtuse-angled triangle. Hence all the diagonals of the regular pentagon are divided in golden section. In fact, each diagonal contains four golden sections (Figure 37 : 33).

Rational and irrational numbers in the National Curriculum

Little of the work described in this chapter appears explicitly in the National Curriculum. At Level 9, pupils are expected to know about the existence of irrational numbers. Very able pupils are expected to reach this level before the age of 16.

- distinguish between rational and irrational numbers.
  EXAMPLE: Know that $\sqrt{2}$ and π are irrational. Know the significance of recurring and non-recurring decimals in this context.

(AT2, Level 9)

However, able pupils should start to build up the experience which leads to a knowledge of irrational numbers several years before this, and some of the activities in this chapter can provide that experience.

38 | MORE ABOUT SHAPES AND CURVES

THE RANGE OF INTERESTING SHAPES

In the past the number of three-dimensional shapes studied in the majority of primary schools has been very limited. Models of the *regular* solids have sometimes been made (see Chapter 25), but there has been little investigation of their properties, such as is suggested in Chapter 25. The interest and practical value of some other shapes, such as those related to the circle, including the sphere, cylinder and cone, are undoubtedly great. Equally general has been the neglect of important curves, and many children have left school knowing nothing about any curve except the circle. In this book such curves as the parabola and the hyperbola have already appeared several times, generally as the form of a graph illustrating the relation between two sets of numbers. For instance, the parabola was seen to be the graph of the square numbers (*see page 413*) and the hyperbola appeared as the graph obtained by mapping a set of numbers into their inverses (*see page 397*). We now investigate some of the three-dimensional shapes which are interesting not only for their own properties and modes of construction but also because they give rise to curves with many practical uses. Other curves will be studied for their pleasing form, their usefulness, or for the ingenuity of their construction. Children can find many of these curves in buildings, in machines, or in decorative designs; others not mentioned here may well be noticed and investigated. As children make or draw these various forms they come to realise that their shape and other mathematical properties depend on the methods used in their construction. In some cases a property can be expressed by pupils themselves in an algebraic formula.

Figure 38 : 1

from a sheet of paper. If a disc is rotated very quickly about a diameter, it produces the illusion of a sphere. A plane cuts a sphere in a circle wherever the cut is made. This suggests another method of making an approximation to a spherical surface. We can build up a series of discs on a rod as axis. If a sphere is cut in half in any direction the cut surface has for its boundary the largest circle that can be drawn on a sphere, a 'great circle' (see Chapter 34). The disc of which this great circle is a boundary will be the largest disc required for our construction. Discs can be arranged symmetrically to indicate the hemispheres. Figure 38 : 1 shows the arrangement. The problem is where to put a particular disc on the axis. We can mark the ends of the axis (calling them the North pole and the South pole) and fit the equatorial disc midway between them. We now have to fit pairs of equal discs in their correct places, knowing that the rim of a disc must lie on the surface of the sphere. Children will experiment to find where the position *seems* to be right but they can be encouraged to draw the section through the north and south poles and then attempt to find an accurate way of placing the discs.

THE SPHERE

The symmetry of a spherical ball is so well known to children that they may take it for granted and nor be aware of some of the properties and problems associated with the sphere.

It is possible to produce a good approximation to a sphere by rolling clay or dough round and round but it is *not* possible to make a spherical surface

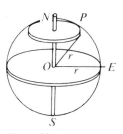

Figure 38 : 2

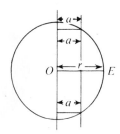

Figure 38 : 3

 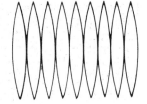

Figure 38 : 4

If a parallel to the axis is drawn at a distance from it equal to the radius *a* of the disc it will cut the circle at the two points where the rims of the equal discs must be. The perpendiculars from these points to the axis give the positions of the centres of the discs. The positions of other discs can, of course, be found in the same way (Figures 38 : 2 and 38 : 3).

Since a spherical surface cannot be opened out to lie flat, the area of the surface cannot easily be found. The method of making a soft ball by sewing together pieces of material shaped like the outer surface of sections of an orange suggests a way of finding a fair approximation to the surface area. If the sections are thin enough they lie almost flat and can be placed on squared paper so that a count can be made of the squares covered by one section. If this number is multiplied by the number of sections in the whole surface we have a rough figure for the area. It can be compared with the surface area of a cube into which the sphere would just fit. A ball about 10 cm in diameter is convenient for this experiment. The area is then about 315 square centimetres (Figure 38 : 4). Children will learn later that the surface of a sphere of radius *r* has area $4\pi r^2$.

The volume of a sphere can be found by immersion as described in Chapter 29, page 350. If the volumes of a set of spheres can be compared with the volumes of a set of cubes with edges equal to the radii of the spheres a correspondence may be found. A graph will show the ratio of the volume of sphere to cube. Since the formula for the volume of a sphere of radius *r* is $\frac{4}{3}\pi r^3$ an approximate value for the ratio of the volume of a sphere of radius *r*

to that of the cube whose edge is *r* units is 4 : 1. This enables a teacher to judge whether children made a reasonably good attempt.

The cube with edge equal to the diameter of the sphere has a volume about twice that of the sphere (Figure 38 : 5).

THE CYLINDER

The simplicity of a cylindrical shape, with its uniform circular cross-section, makes it easy to construct and very serviceable in daily life, both as a container and as a means of conveying fluids and gases. Children will probably have met the method of making a hollow cylinder by joining opposite edges of a rectangular sheet of paper. They will also know that steadily rolling a lump of Plasticine or stiff dough will produce a reasonable approximation to a solid cylinder. A sharp knife will cut across this cylinder without deforming it. The shapes of cut surfaces can be studied. Children will expect the section at right angles to the axis to be a circle but many of them will have noticed the form of an oblique section. A slanting cut will have one diameter equal to the diameter of the cylinder; the diameter perpendicular to this will be elongated, as can be seen in Figure 38 : 6. The cuts can be traced on paper and compared. The elongated shape is an ellipse; we shall consider the properties of this shape more fully later.

A spherical surface contains no straight lines, but a cylinder can have straight lines drawn upon its

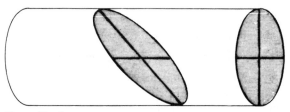

Figure 38 : 6

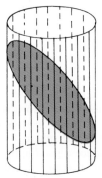

Figure 38 : 7

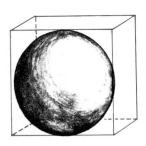

Figure 38 : 5 ⟵ 2r ⟶

surface parallel to its axis. This adds greatly to the strength of a cylindrical object. If rods of equal length are fitted into holes equally spaced round the rim of a circular base, as in basketry, a cylindrical framework will be produced. If several ellipses are made by elongating the circular shape of the base they will be found to fit into the framework in the position of oblique cuts of the solid cylinder (as shown in Figure 38 : 6 and 38 : 7).

Since a hollow cylinder can be made from a rectangular sheet of paper the area of its surface must be equal to that of the rectangle. The circumference of the cylinder was produced by bending the rectangle so that two opposite sides became circles. The other pair of sides were joined to make a straight line lying in the surface and showing its height or altitude (Figure 38 : 8).

The area of the rectangle from which a cylinder is made is found by multiplying the circumference of the cylinder by its height. The method described in Chapter 36, page 454, shows how to measure the diameter of a solid cylinder and then to find its circumference. The numbers obtained will involve decimals and the calculator is useful.

The circumference of a cylinder can be measured directly by placing a tape-measure tightly round it.

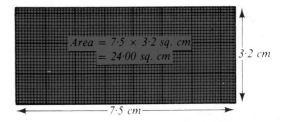

Figure 38 : 9

For example, if the circumference is 7·5 cm and the height 3·2 cm, the area of the surface is 7·5 × 3·2 square centimetres. Figure 38 : 9 shows the rectangle drawn on squared paper. The small squares are hundredths of a sq cm; the number of small squares in the rectangle, 2400, can be checked from the diagram. Such experience is invaluable in connection with work on decimals.

The volume of a cylinder may be found practically by the methods given in Chapter 29, page 352. A method of calculating the volume, by multiplying the area of the circular base by the height of the cylinder, may occur to a few pupils but for others it is best left to a later stage.

The ellipse

The ellipse will be familiar to children as a possible shadow cast by a circle, as the shape of a pool of light when a circular beam shines on a sloping plane surface, as the slanting cut across a cylinder, as the orbit followed by some spacecraft as well as by planets, and so on. Yet many children have no explicit knowledge of this curve. It is an interesting as well as important curve and can profitably be studied in primary schools in conjunction with the circle.

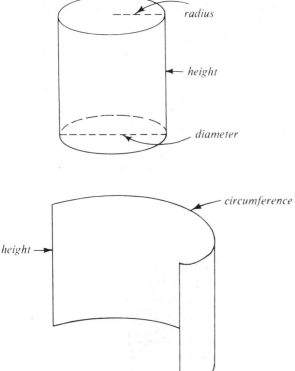

Figure 38 : 8

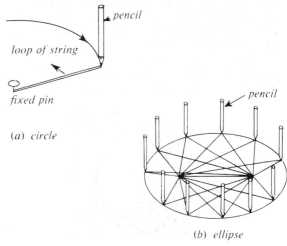

Figure 38 : 10

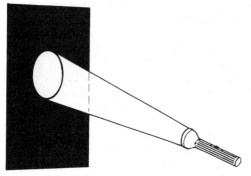

Figure 38 : 11

The circle, as children know from using compasses, is a set of points which are at the same distance from a given point, the centre. It can be drawn by moving a pencil in a loop of string which passes round a fixed pin. A different curve will be drawn if the loop of string passes round *two* fixed pins. Children can find what kind of path the pencil now follows (Figure 38 : 10). By moving the position of the fixed pins, putting them closer or further apart, they can find a variety of different shapes, all with an oval form and two axes of symmetry, one of which is longer than the other. Curves that look like these can be made from casting a variety of shadows from a disc or by projecting a circle of light on to various plane surfaces (Figure 38 : 11). Children can investigate these ways of constructing what looks like an ellipse and find out whether in fact they are ellipses or other types of oval.

distances increased in ratio 3 : 2

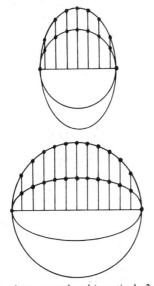

Figure 38 : 12 *distances reduced in ratio 1 : 2*

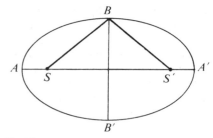

Figure 38 : 13

The shadow cast by a disc is like the slanting cut of a cylinder which was seen to be an elongation of a circular section. We can construct such an elongation by increasing the distances of points on a circle from one of its diameters in the same ratio, say 3 : 2 (Figure 38 : 12). A curve of the same kind is made by reducing the distances, say in the ratio 1 : 2.

This construction shows very clearly the correspondence between an original point on the circle and its image point after the transformation.

Do these curves have the same form as those made by a string and two pins? If we look carefully at a curve made with string and pins, we see that AA' is the same length as the length of string between the pins in which the pencil is placed (Figure 38 : 13). When the pencil point is at A this becomes clear because the length of string is then $SA + AS'$. The lenght AS' is equal to $A'S$, so the length of the string is $SA + A'S = AA'$.

If the pencil point is at B or B' the midpoint of the loop is at this point. Thus the length of BS or BS' is half the length of AA'.

Now we can take one of the elongated circles and test whether it can be made by the pins and string method. Draw the diameters AA' and BB'. Take a piece of string equal in length to AA' and fix its midpoint at B. Where the two ends of the string reach AA' are the points S, S'. If pins are placed at S and S' and the ends of the string fixed to them, the pencil will trace out an ellipse. This should fit one of the curves made by cutting a cylinder. Thus we have found experimentally that these curves are ellipses. Figure 38 : 14 shows the procedure. The

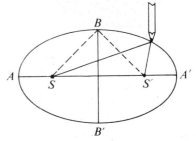

Figure 38 : 14

ellipse is seen as a set of points which have the common property that the sum of their distances from two fixed points is a constant length.

Some pupils will be interested in collecting information about elliptical orbits and drawing some of them to scale. They can also read something of the history of the discovery of the elliptical orbits of planets.

THE CONE

Funnels and certain containers (like ones which hold ice creams, sweets, etc.) are approximately conical. The shape is easy to make if a rectangular sheet of paper is twisted diagonally and neatly trimmed. This shows that if we cut a hollow cone from the vertex to the base by a straight cut we can lay it out flat. We see the two-dimensional shape from which the surface of a cone could be made (Figure 38 : 15).

This proves to be the sector of a circle, the radius of which is the slant height of the cone. If we have several paper discs of the same size, such as filter papers, we can take various fractions of the circle,

such as $\frac{1}{2}$, $\frac{1}{4}$ and $\frac{3}{4}$, and find out what shapes of cone can be made from them. Figure 38 : 16 shows two examples.

Following such constructional work children may try to find the area of the surface of a given conical shape. They know that the surface is part of a circle with radius equal to the slant height of the cone. Suppose this measures 6 cm and a circle, A, with radius 6 cm is drawn. What fraction of the circle would make the cone? The diameter of the base of the cone can be found; suppose it is 8 cm. A circle, B, with radius 4 cm can be drawn to represent the base. Then a part of circle A must be cut out so that its arc equals the circumference of circle B. Figure 38 : 17 shows the two circles and the required sector of A. The calculation is as follows:

The circumference of a circle = $\pi \times$ (diameter)
$$\text{Circumference of } A = 12 \times \pi \text{ cm}$$
$$\text{Circumference of } B = 8 \times \pi \text{ cm}$$
Ratio of circumference B to circumference A
$$= 8 : 12$$
$$= 2 : 3$$

Thus $\frac{2}{3}$ is the fraction of circle A which must be cut as a sector to make a cone with circle B as base. This means that the area of the surface of the cone is $\frac{2}{3}$ of the area of circle A. Hence, area of curved surface

$$= \tfrac{2}{3} \text{ of } \pi \times 6^2 \text{ cm}^2$$
$$= \tfrac{2}{3} \times 36\pi \text{ cm}^2$$
$$= 24\pi \text{ cm}^2$$

Figure 38 : 15

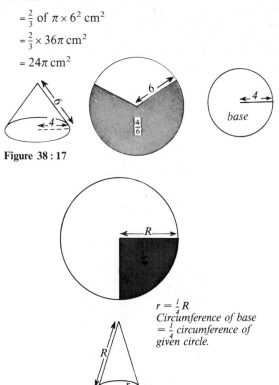

Figure 38 : 17

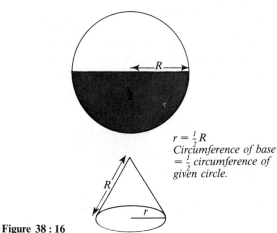

$r = \frac{1}{2}R$
Circumference of base
= $\frac{1}{2}$ circumference of
given circle.

$r = \frac{1}{4}R$
Circumference of base
= $\frac{1}{4}$ circumference of
given circle.

Figure 38 : 16

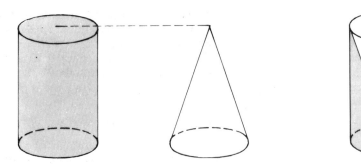

Figure 38 : 18

The area is therefore approximately 75 cm².

A model of the cone could now be made. A sector which is $\frac{2}{3}$ of a circle has an angle at the centre which is $\frac{2}{3}$ of 360°, i.e. 240°. Such a sector can be cut out and the cone constructed from it.

Children may find a cone and a cylinder which have the same base and height. Such a pair occurs in Poleidoblocs. If asked about the relation between the volume of the two solids most children will guess that the cone has half the volume of the cylinder. This can be investigated by immersing the two solids to find their respective volumes. Several cones and cylinders should be examined and it becomes apparent that the volume of the cylinder is three times the volume of the corresponding cone. This can be further checked by comparing the capacity of a hollow cylinder with that of the corresponding cone. It is fairly easy to make such a pair from thin stiff card and then to fill the cylinder from the cone using a fine but light cereal as a filling. It will take three fillings of the cone to fill the cylinder (Figure 38 : 18).

SECTIONS OF A CONE: THE HYPERBOLA

In comparison with the sphere and the cylinder the cone can be cut across in an interesting variety of ways which are well worth examining. A fairly true circular cone can be modelled in Plasticine or dough and can be cut to give a good indication of the shapes of the sections. For more accurate investigations it is better to buy a set of sections made of plastic or wood. Initial discovery from children's own models is more memorable than copying or measuring the ready made. If a solid cone is being examined it is a good idea to make a paper cover to fit it so that a section of a hollow cone can be traced.

The most obvious cut to make is along a plane of symmetry through the vertex. This produces a triangular surface from the solid cone and a pair of intersecting lines from a hollow cone. Circular and elliptical sections of the cone are easy to find (Figure 38 : 19).

A plane parallel to the plane of symmetry will be perpendicular to the base and will make a cut which has a curved edge. Some children will find it interesting to try to identify this curve. If the cut face is traced on paper it can be placed against the cut made by the parallel plane of symmetry. In Figure 38 : 20 we show the result in the case of a cone whose vertical angle is a right angle. This curve may remind children of the curve of inverses, which they have drawn earlier. In fact the curve is a hyperbola, like the curve of inverses.

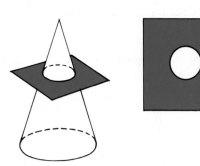
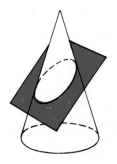
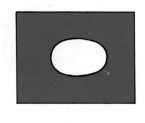

Figure 38 : 19

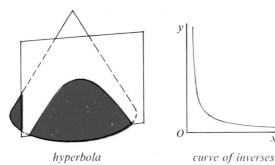

hyperbola   *curve of inverses*

Figure 38 : 20

THE PARABOLA

The other section of a cone which recalls a curve familiar to the pupils is made by a plane parallel to the slant height of the cone. If this is traced on paper and cut out, children will find by folding that it is symmetrical and that it is similar in shape to the curve of squares. We can test whether it is in fact this curve by the following method. Place the half of the cut-out shape on squared or lined paper as shown in Figure 38 : 21. Draw in the two axes and graduate the horizontal axis. The tabulation for the curve of squares gives the following number pairs for points on the graph: (1, 1), (2, 4), (3, 9), (4, 16), ... Find the point on the curve which corresponds to 1 on the x axis. If the curve is a curve of squares the value of y for this point will be 1. Take this length as unit on the y-axis and use it to graduate the y-axis. We can now examine the curve to see whether the points (2, 4), (3, 9), and so on, do in fact lie on it. If so, it is indeed the curve of squares, or the parabola. When children have verified that this is so they can look again at the set

of shapes that are derived from the cone and notice their variety. At the secondary school stage they will study them once more and see that in spite of their differing forms they have common properties which can be expressed algebraically.

CYCLOIDS: ROLLING WHEELS

A. A wheel which rolls along a straight line

As a wheel rolls along a path its movement at any instant is a rotaton about the point of contact with the ground. As the wheel continues to turn and travels along a line on the ground each point on the rim follows its own path which children can trace. A point on the rim can be clearly marked and the wheel then rolled along a line without slipping. If a sheet of paper or card is placed behind the wheel a number of positions of the point can be marked upon the sheet. Pupils usually begin with the point in a special position; for instance, they may start with it in contact with the ground. Clearly when it comes back to its original position it will then repeat the kind of path it has already traced. This may be the children's first experience of a curve which repeats itself (Figure 38 : 22).

A geared wheel on a toothed strip shows the form of the curve very well and enables the pupils to see the position of the point in relation to the distance travelled along the strip because the number of teeth can be counted. Figure 38 : 23 shows the path of one tooth as the wheel turns.[1]

The name of the curve which the point traces out, the *cycloid*, is easily remembered by children because of its association with the bicycle, but when they discuss its shape they may say that it is part of

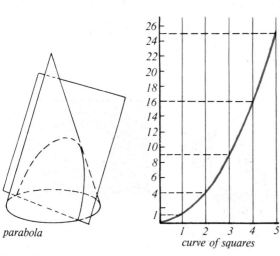

parabola

Figure 38 : 21

curve of squares

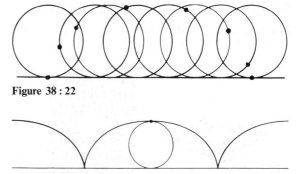

Figure 38 : 22

Figure 38 : 23

[1]Suitable materials for these experiments are provided in the game called Spirograph.

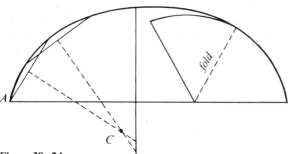

Figure 38 : 24

Figure 38 : 25

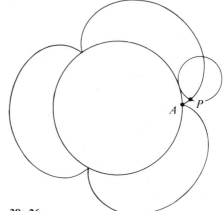

Figure 38 : 26

a circle. This statement should be tested. A circle has the property that any part of it can be cut out and fitted exactly over any other part. We therefore cut out one unit of the cycloid and find whether any part of it can be fitted exactly on another part. The parts of a cycloid do not quite fit. Alternatively, the bisectors of two chords could be drawn (or folded) as in Figure 38 : 24. If the curve were a circle the point of intersection of the chords, C would be the centre of the circle. When compasses are used to draw a circle with centre C, through A, it will be found to lie within the arc of the cycloid. Yet the nearness to the shape of a circle is very striking.

B. A wheel which rolls on the outside of a circle

In playing with equal discs a child may discover that six of them can be packed around one of them, as Figure 38 : 25 illustrates. The lines joining the centres show why this is so. The pupils may follow this up by asking what happens when a circle is rolled round the outside of an equal circle. To prevent the circles slipping this can be shown by moving a geared wheel round an equal one and marking the path of a particular tooth.

Figure 38 : 26 shows enough points to give the essential shape of curve. A point where the direction of the curve suddenly changes, known as a cusp, is found in all curves drawn in this way. The curves are called *epicycloids*. If a circle with radius one third of that of a fixed circle is rolled round the outside three cusps are produced, as Figure 38 : 26 illustrates; its name is the three-cusped epicycloid. A cusp occurs each time the rolling circle completes a revolution. Pupils may find this shape in the stone tracery of a church window. They can make other designs by taking the radius of the rolling circle to be some other fraction of the fixed one. A single-cusped epicycloid is also called a *cardioid* (Figure 38 : 27).

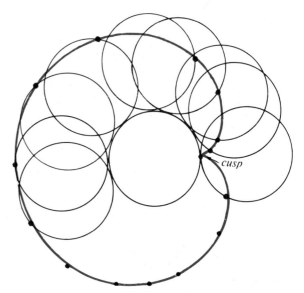

Figure 38 : 27

C. A wheel which rolls on the inside of a circle

After discovering epicycloids children may experiment with the path that would be traced out by a point on the circumference of a wheel on the

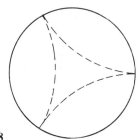

Figure 38 : 28

inner side of the rim of another wheel. If the wheel were of the same size it is obvious that the inner wheel would simply rotate about its centre and each point on its rim would be carried with it in a circle. If, however, the inner wheel has a radius which is a fraction of the radius of the outer wheel, say $\frac{1}{2}$, $\frac{1}{3}$, or $\frac{1}{4}$, it would make 2, 3, or 4 rotations before regaining its original position. A point on the rim would thus have 2, 3, or 4 points of contact with the outer wheel. Its path will have 2, 3, or 4 cusps. These curves are known as *hypocycloids*. Figure 38 : 28 shows the three-cusped hypocycloid formed when the radii of the two wheels are in the ratio 1 : 3. The two-cusped hypocycloid is a segment of a straight line. The hypocycloids have pleasing shapes and are widely used in decorative designs.

WAVE CURVES

A curve of great importance in the world of science is the one which records vibrations. Children often see it on television and in books about scientific phenomena such as sound waves. When a child holds the end of a rope and gives it a rhythmic up and down movement the rope has a rippling movement which shows waves (Figure 38 : 29).

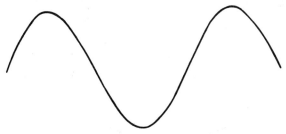

Figure 38 : 29

To make a drawing of a wave curve we first study the movement of a point on the circumference of a circle which is rotated steadily about its centre. We look at the height of the point above or below a diameter *AB*, and notice that the height increases very rapidly at first and then more slowly as the point approaches the highest position, *C* (Figure

38 : 30). As the point moves beyond *C* the height decreases at first slowly and then more rapidly until the point is again on the diameter, this time at *B*. The pattern of heights is symmetrical about the axis *OC*.

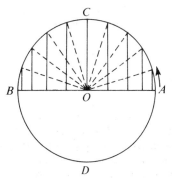

Figure 38 : 30

When the point moves on below the diameter it will show the same pattern of change in the distances from the diameter but they will all now be in the opposite direction, that is, from the diameter downwards. The lower half of the diagram in Figure 38 : 31 is the reflection of the upper half. We can make a graph to represent the heights as they change during a complete revolution and we shall expect to find in it evidence of the symmetries which we have just noticed. The *x*-axis must be graduated to show the fractions of a revolution through which the radius has turned. It is helpful if this axis is drawn in line with the diameter of the circle as in Figure 38 : 32. The distances can then be marked off directly from the circle. Four points on the graph correspond to *A*, *B*, *C*, *D*, (Figure 38 : 30). *A*, the starting-point, will give the origin. At *B*, after a rotation of 90°, the height is equal to the radius of the circle. At *C* the height is again zero. At *D*, the end of the diameter through *C*, the height is negative and is equal to the radius. For other points on the graph we transfer the heights from the circle to the graph.

When the points are joined by the best-fitting curve we find a shape like one part of the wave curve in Figure 38 : 29. If the rotation round the

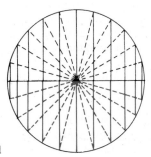

Figure 38 : 31

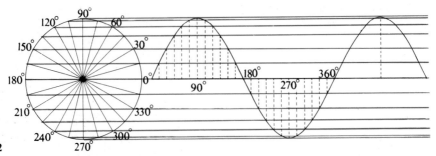

Figure 38 : 32

circle is continued the pattern of the distances will be repeated and the graph shows repetitions of the curve already drawn.

Teachers may realise that this graph is the *sine curve*, the sine of the angle between the *x*-axis and a rotating arm *OP* being the ratio of the height to the radius (Figure 38 : 33).

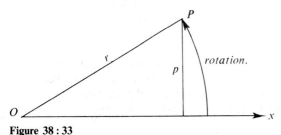

Figure 38 : 33

It will be noticed that the wave curve is a graph of the relation between the rotation of a point on a circle and the distance of the point from a diameter, whereas the curves that we have previously discussed were the actual paths traced by a point moving under given conditions.

ENVELOPES

The curves that we have considered so far are *sets of points* which satisfy certain conditions. Some have been found as the intersection of a plane with a three-dimensional shape such as the cylinder or cone. Others have been obtained as the path of a point moving in a defined way as in the case of the cycloids. The wave curve appeared as the graph of a relation between distance and rotation. Curves can also be formed when a *set of lines* is constructed so as to satisfy certain conditions. The lines may be ruled in a specified way, or they may be stitched according to certain instructions, or they may consist of a set of folds of a sheet of paper made in a particular way.

A stitched pattern which is fairly well known is that obtained by joining points on two intersecting lines (rays from *O*, say) graduated on the same

scale, successive marked points on one ray in a sequence *from O* being joined to successive marked points on the other ray in a sequence *towards O* (Figure 38 : 34). If the stitches (or ruled lines) are sufficiently close together they appear to mark out a curve which can be sketched in with some confidence. Such a curve is said to be the *envelope* of the line which satisfies the given conditions. Sometimes an envelope is immediately recognisable by pupils. For example, the lines which join pairs of points the same distance apart on a circle give rise to a circle concentric to the given one. Other envelopes are not readily identified but further investigation may lead to recognition. For instance, the stitched curve of Figure 38 : 34 may be cut out, and folded about its axis of symmetry. If may then suggest the curve of squares; this idea can be checked by the method described on page 479. It should then be evidence that the envelope is in fact a parabola.

Another curve which can be identified after a closer examination is obtained from folding a circle. A filter paper, say, can be successively folded so that the circumference of the part folded over passes through a certain point, *P*, inside the circle. The fold can be marked in pencil or ink to make it easy to see. Each fold should be undone before

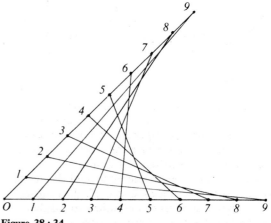

Figure 38 : 34

making the next one. When a fairly large number of folds has been made the envelope looks like an ellipse and can in fact be shown to be one by the method given on page 475.

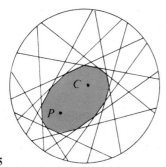

Figure 38 : 35

An interesting link with tables of multiples is found in the following method of producing a curve as an envelope. Pupils may recognise the shape of the curve if they have already carried out the experiment described on page 480. A circular disc can be graduated to show 36 divisions. This can be done by using either a protractor or a sheet of polar graph paper, marking at intervals of 10° the numbers from 1 to 36. The table of fours gives the number pairs (1, 4), (2, 8), (3, 12), ... and the two numbers in any pair correspond to two points on the circumference which are joined by a line (Figure 38 : 36).

The joins are made as shown in Figure 38 : 36.

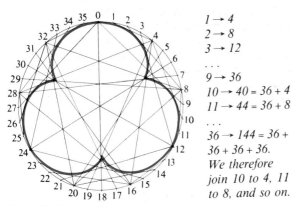

$$1 \rightarrow 4$$
$$2 \rightarrow 8$$
$$3 \rightarrow 12$$
. . .
$$9 \rightarrow 36$$
$$10 \rightarrow 40 = 36 + 4$$
$$11 \rightarrow 44 = 36 + 8$$
. . .
$$36 \rightarrow 144 = 36 + 36 + 36 + 36.$$
We therefore join 10 to 4, 11 to 8, and so on.

Figure 38 : 36

This construction is a difficult task and the resulting curve is not alwas easy to see. But three cusps can be distinguished and also three points on the circumference equidistant from two cusps. The curve can then be sketched in and may be recognised as the three-cusped epicycloid. If a circle with diameter 7·5 cm is used, a marked two-pence piece (diameter 2·5 cm) can be rolled round the inside and the form of the curve verified as an

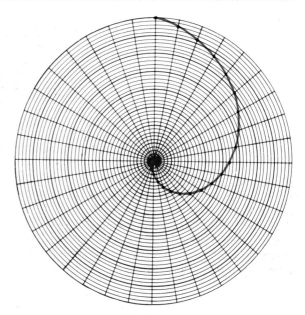

Figure 38 : 37

epicycloid. By taking other tables of multiples epicycloids with more cusps can be drawn. The table of twos produces the single-cusped heart-shaped cardioid (Figure 38 : 26).

SPIRALS

There are several kinds of spiral that children meet in daily life. Some of them are curves in a plane like those we have already studied. Others, such as the spring, are three dimensional. A plane spiral, drawn on a sheet of paper, can be cut along the length of the curve; it will then open into a three-dimensional curve which is sufficiently attractive to be used as a Christmas decoration. The construction of spirals gives children much pleasure and supplies a number of mathematical experiences.

The easiest plane spiral to draw is the one which joins points marked on a rotating arm so that the distance from the centre of rotation increases regularly as the arm rotates (Figure 38 : 37). Children can draw a set of concentric circles or use polar graph paper. They next draw the position of the arm after rotations of 10°, 20°, 30°, ... 360°. If the concentric circles have radii which increase by equal amounts the points on the arm will occur

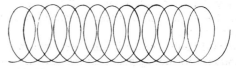

Figure 38 : 38

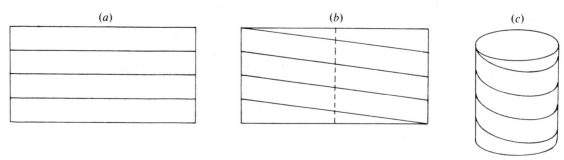

(a)   (b)   (c)

Figure 38 : 39

at the intersections with successive circles, as can be seen in the diagram. This is the spiral of Archimedes who, in the third century BC, published a paper about spirals which is still in existence.[2]

The three-dimensional spiral, or helix, which is easiest to construct is drawn on the surface of a cylinder. It is the form we find in the common spring with which pupils are already very familiar from earlier work (see Chapter 31). They will know that the distance between adjacent turns of the helix is constant and will be able to use this fact to invent a way of drawing on a rectangle a pattern which will make a spiral when the rectangle is bent round to form a cylinder (Figure 38 : 39). It will be seen that lines drawn parallel to a side of a

rectangle will make rings if the rectangle is suitably bent to form a cylinder. This may suggest to the pupils the drawing shown in Figure 38 : 39(b). If the diameter and pitch of a given spring are measured it is possible to construct the rectangle which would enclose the spring, to draw the slant lines upon it which represent the turns of the helix and thus to find its length.

Some helices are obviously not cylindrical because their diameter is not constant. This can be seen in many types of screw. Pupils can examine such helices and try to find ways of making them. They should be able to discover that helices can be drawn on the surface of a cone, and perhaps invent methods for drawing them.

[2]If this spiral is reflected about a line through the origin a very attractive shape results.

39 | *Some Mathematical Structures*

More advanced classification

By the middle years of schooling, many children will be able to take their earlier work in classifying things into sets to a more advanced stage. Further work on classification can unite and fit into a structure many facts which children have known earlier. It can also lead towards the discovery of some very general mathematical ideas which will be studied in more detail at the secondary school stage.

We start our further work on classification by looking systematically at the properties of some shapes which will already be well known to children. Earlier, children will have collected shapes and sorted them into sets using various methods of classification, and will have recorded the results in diagram form. Some of these classifications will have been combined, as in the classification of the set of Poleidoblocs shown in Figure 39 : 1.

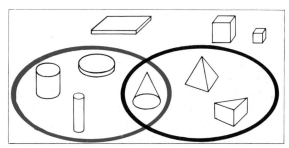

Figure 39 : 1

By now, however, children will be able to invent shapes to classify, and for instance, they will cut out as many paper triangles of different shapes and sizes as possible before starting to classify them. Several different classifications are then possible, and these can easily be combined. Some possibilities are:

Some classifications of triangles

(a) Classification by number of axes of symmetry

Triangles with no axis of symmetry	Triangles with only one axis of symmetry	Triangles with exactly two axes of symmetry	Triangles with three axes of symmetry

universal set = {all triangles}

Triangles with one or more axes of symmetry are isosceles.
Triangles with three axes of symmetry are equilateral.

(b) Classification by number of axes of symmetry and by type of angle

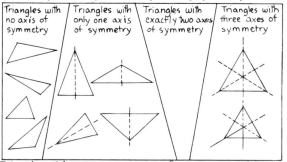

Figure 39 : 2

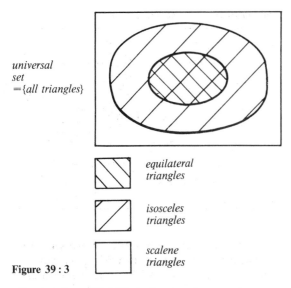

universal
set
= {all triangles}

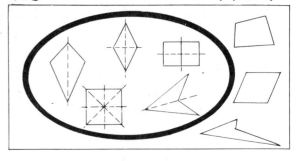

Classification of quadrilaterals by symmetry
(a) Quadrilaterals with at least one axis of symmetry

equilateral
triangles

isosceles
triangles

scalene
triangles

Figure 39 : 3

i) triangles with 0, 1, 2, 3 axes of symmetry,

ii) acute-angled, right-angled, obtuse-angled triangles,

iii) triangles with three, two or no equal sides.

Carroll diagrams for some of these classifications are shown in Figure 39 : 2. They may lead children to formulate, and to answer, such questions as, 'Why can't you have a triangle with exactly two axes of symmetry?' and, 'Is an equilateral triangle isosceles?' By asking and answering such questions, some children will begin to realise the need for carefully defining the words they are using, and they will also begin to reason about properties of the shapes they are using. The distinction between 'at least one axis of symmetry' and 'exactly one axis of symmetry' becomes very clear. The world 'isosceles' is normally used of triangles with at least one axis of symmetry, so that Figure 39 : 3 shows that the class of equilateral triangles is included within the class of isosceles triangles.

Children will also classify quadrilaterals by symmetry, making use of the fact that a quadrilateral may have a centre of symmetry as well as one or two axes of symmetry. Figure 39 : 4 shows stages in one such possible classification.

Some children will now formulate, as a result of this classification, the statement, 'if a quadrilateral has a centre of symmetry and an axis of symmetry, it must have at least two axes of symmetry.' A few children may go on to convince themselves by argument that the statement must be true.

In this work, we notice a considerable progression in abstraction. At the stage of concrete operations, children could handle the classification of a set of objects which they had in front of them. Now they

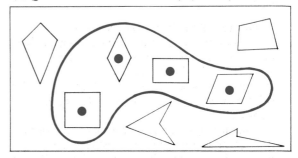

(b) Quadrilaterals with a centre of symmetry

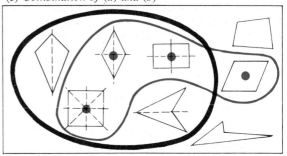

(c) Combination of (a) and (b)

Figure 39 : 4

are beginning to be able to imagine the class of *all* possible quadrilaterals, and to make classifications and definitions of subsets of this complete class of quadrilaterals. At this stage the models or drawings which children make are only specimens representing a selection of all possible quadrilaterals. They are reaching towards the adolescent and adult method of logical thinking, the stage of *formal operations*. Here abstraction becomes much easier, for as Piaget says, '*possibility* no longer appears merely as an extension of an empirical situation or of actions actually performed. Instead, it is reality that is now secondary to *possibility*.'[1] It appears

[1]Inhelder, B. and Piaget, J. *The Growth of Logical Thinking from Childhood to Adolescence* (Basic Books, 1958) page 251.

Definition and classification of quadrilaterals

(a) *kites*

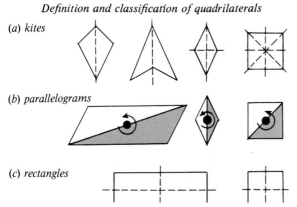

(b) *parallelograms*

(c) *rectangles*

(d) *universal set = {quadrilaterals}*

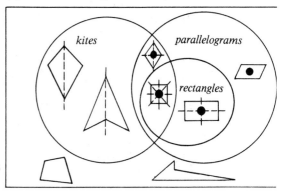

Figure 39 : 5

possible to children when they are assembling information that there may be a quadrilateral with a centre of symmetry but only one axis of symmetry. In reality this cannot happen, but children are now able to explore all the possibilities which may appear in the abstract class of all quadrilaterals.

Children might also start from such questions as 'Is a square a rectangle?' to investigate the relationships between all the types of quadrilaterals they know. Kites, parallelograms and rectangles are helpful subsets of the set of all quadrilaterals with which to start a classification. Such working definitions as the following may be evolved:

i) a *kite* is a quadrilateral with at least one axis of symmetry;

ii) a *parallelogram* is a quadrilateral with a centre of symmetry;

iii) a *rectangle* is a quadrilateral both of whose medians[2] are axes of symmetry.[3]

Figure 39 : 5 illustrates these definitions, together with a Venn diagram of the classification. It will be noticed that a kite which is also a parallelogram is a rhombus, and a kite which is a rectangle is a square.

THE CARTESIAN PRODUCT OF TWO SETS

The systematic exploration of a situation where two properties are dealt with can be greatly helped by

[2]A *median* of a quadrilateral is a line joining midpoints of opposite sides.

[3]Other definitions are possible; for instance, a rectangle is a parallelogram one of whose medians is an axis of symmetry.

the idea of the *Cartesian product* of two sets. If a girl has three jumpers and two skirts, she can combine these in six possible ways, as shown in Figure 39 : 6. Children will often experiment haphazardly before they discover a systematic way of producing all possible combinations by holding one member of the pair constant while all possibilities are explored for the other member. The possible outfits can be written:

(red jumper, black skirt),
(blue jumper, black skirt), etc.

We shall say that the Cartesian product of the two sets

$J = \{$red jumper, blue jumper, green jumper$\}$

and

$S = \{$black skirt, white skirt$\}$

is the set of the six possible outfits, or ordered pairs of jumper and skirt;

Six outfits from three jumpers and two skirts

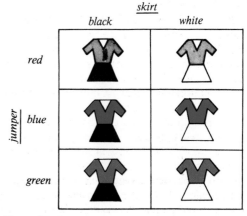

Figure 39 : 6

C = {(red jumper, black skirt), (red jumper, white skirt),

(blue jumper, black skirt), (blue jumper, white skirt),

(green jumper, black skirt), (green jumper, white skirt)}

That is, it is the set of the six possible *ordered pairs* whose first member belongs to the first set, and whose second member belongs to the second set. We can write the Cartesian product of J and S as $C = J \times S$.[4]

The process of forming all possible ordered pairs whose first member is chosen from one set and the second member from another is a common one in mathematics. For example, when two dice, one with black spots and the other with blue spots, are tossed together, all the possible ways in which they can fall are shown in Figure 39 : 7, which displays the Cartesian product of

A = {1, 2, 3, 4, 5, 6}

with

B = {1, 2, 3, 4, 5, 6}

Score on blue die

(1,1)	(2,1)	(3,1)	(4,1)	(5,1)	(6,1)
(1,2)	(2,2)	(3,2)	(4,2)	(5,2)	(6,2)
(1,3)	(2,3)	(3,3)	(4,3)	(5,3)	(6,3)
(1,4)	(2,4)	(3,4)	(4,4)	(5,4)	(6,4)
(1,5)	(2,5)	(3,5)	(4,5)	(5,5)	(6,5)
(1,6)	(2,6)	(3,6)	(4,6)	(5,6)	(6,6)

Score on black die

total score = 7   total score = 12

Figure 39 : 7

It can be seen that out of the 36 possible ways in which the pair of dice can fall, the score of 12 occurs only as (6,6), but the score of 7 can be made up in six ways:

(1,6), (2,5), (3,4), (4,3), (5,2), (6,7).

Thus, the probability of getting a score of 12 is $\frac{1}{36}$, while the probability of scoring 7 is $\frac{6}{36}$ or $\frac{1}{6}$. We are six times as likely to score 7 as to score 12.

Thus, the systematic exploration of all possibilities, on which probability depends, is simplified by the notion of the Cartesian product. In general, the Cartesian product $A \times P$ of two sets $A = \{a, b, \ldots\}$ and $P = \{p, q, r, \ldots\}$ is defined to be the set of all possible ordered pairs whose first member belongs to A, and whose second member belongs to P.

$A \times P = \{(a,p),\ (a,q),\ (a,r),\ \ldots\ (b,p),\ (b,q),\ (b,r),\ \ldots\}$

Another example which children can explore is the set of meals containing a main course and a sweet which they can make up from a given menu. They may also fill in a table such as that in Figure 39 : 8, where not all the possibilities which the idea of Cartesian product suggests can actually happen. When the classfication is examined, it seems that the properties 'two pairs of opposite sides parallel' and 'two pairs of opposite sides equal' are equivalent, as one property cannot happen without the other.

The idea of the Cartesian product of two sets is also seen at work in the labelling of the points of a graph by their co-ordinates. We have seen that the points of a line can be labelled by one co-ordinate which is a real number (Figure 39 : 9(a)). To label a point in a plane, we set up a pair of axes and describe the point by its distances from each of the axes, using the convention that the x-distance is always named before the y-distance (Figure 39 : 9(b)). That is, we need an *ordered* pair of real

Classification of Quadrilaterals by Properties of Opposite Sides

	Two pairs of opposite sides equal.	Only one pair of opposite sides equal.	Opposite sides unequal
Two pairs of opposite sides parallel.	Parallelogram		
Only one pair of opposite sides parallel.		Isosceles trapezium	trapezium.
No sides parallel.			

Figure 39 : 8

[4]This is read '*J* cross *S*'.

Labelling a point by co-ordinates

(*a*) *Any point on a line needs one real number to label it.*

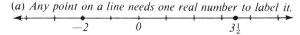

(*b*) *Any point in a plane needs an ordered pair of real numbers to label it.*

Figure 39 : 9

numbers as a label. The point (4,3) is not the same as the point (3,4). All possible points in the plane could be labelled by using all possible ordered pairs

of real numbers, and so the labelling of points in the plane is produced by the Cartesian product of the set R of real numbers with itself. That is, the set of labels is the set $R \times R$.

Ordered pairs of real numbers are not only used in labelling a plane. When we perform the arithmetical operation of addition or subtraction, we have selected an ordered pair of numbers to combine by the operation. The symbols $6 + 8$ tell us to perform the operation of addition on the ordered pair of numbers (6,8), and the symbols $5 - 3$ ask for the operation of subtraction to be performed on the ordered pair (5,3). Since addition is commutative, it gives the same result to perform the operation of addition on the ordered pairs (6,8) and (8,6). The results of the operation of subtraction on (5,3) and on (3,5) are, however, different. It is therefore

Arithmetical operations on ordered pairs of numbers

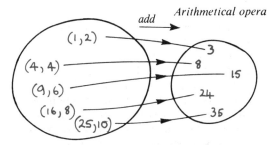

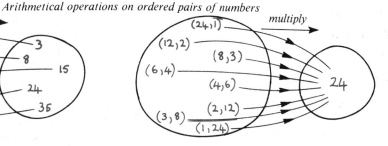

Figure 39 : 10

Graphs of arithmetical operations

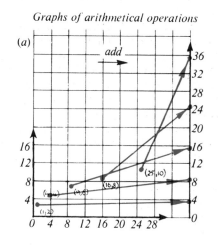

(*c*) *The set of ordered pairs of natural numbers (x, y) such that $x + y = 7$.*

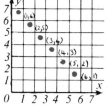

Figure 39 : 11

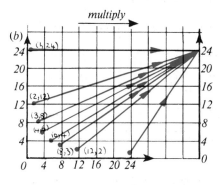

(*d*) *The set of ordered pairs of real numbers (x,y) such that $x + y = 7$.*

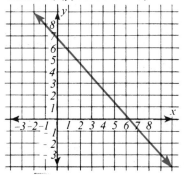

necessary to keep in mind the distinction of order between (a, b) and (b, a). Children may record their results using this idea, as in Figure 39 : 10, or they may use points on graph paper to represent ordered pairs of numbers, as in Figure 39 : 11.

RELATIONS

Figures 39 : 11(c) and (d) illustrate subsets of the plane R × R. In this example we are particularly interested in the ordered pairs marked in the graph because the members, x and y, of each pair have the property that their sum is 7. Any subset of a Cartesian product is called a *relation*. That is, a relation is a set of ordered pairs, whose first members are drawn from a set X, and second members from a set Y. The two members of each ordered pair are related together by the fact of our interest in them, and we are not interested in other ordered pairs which also belong to the Cartesian product X × Y. Usually a relation is not a random collection of ordered pairs; we are interested in these particular ordered pairs because their members are related in some significant way. For instance, having earlier made the complete set of outfits consisting of a jumper and skirt, a girl may then pick out a subset of outfits in which the

jumper goes well with the skirt. This might be:

(red jumper, black skirt)

and

(green jumper, white skirt)

The relation could also be described in words as 'goes well with', and illustrated in the relation diagram of Figure 39 : 12.

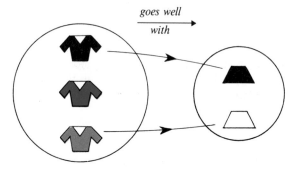

Figure 39 : 12

In other words, to form the Cartesian product of two sets X and Y, we make all possible ordered pairings of a member x of set X with a member y of set Y. A relation from the set X to the set Y is a

(a) *The Cartesian product X × Y*

	20	21	22	23	24	25	26	27	28	29	30
1	(1,20)	(1,21)	(1,22)	(1,23)	(1,24)	(1,25)	(1,26)	(1,27)	(1,28)	(1,29)	(1,30)
2	(2,20)	(2,21)	(2,22)	(2,23)	(2,24)	(2,25)	(2,26)	(2,27)	(2,28)	(2,29)	(2,30)
3	(3,20)	(3,21)	(3,22)	(3,23)	(3,24)	(3,25)	(3,26)	(3,27)	(3,28)	(3,29)	(3,30)
4											
5				etc.							
6											
7											
8											
9											
10											

(b) *A relation from X to Y*

	20	21	22	23	24	25	26	27	28	29	30
1	(1,20)	(1,21)	(1,22)	(1,23)	(1,24)	(1,25)	(1,26)	(1,27)	(1,28)	(1,29)	(1,30)
2	(2,20)		(2,22)		(2,24)		(2,26)		(2,28)		(2,30)
3		(3,21)			(3,24)			(3,27)			(3,30)
4	(4,20)				(4,24)				(4,28)		
5	(5,20)					(5,25)					(5,30)
6					(6,24)						(6,30)
7		(7,21)							(7,28)		
8					(8,24)						
9								(9,27)			
10	(10,20)										(10,30)

Figure 39 : 13

sub-collection of these ordered pairs; the relation can also be thought of as the rule which enables us to pick out a subset of the ordered pairs. Figure 39 : 13(*a*) shows the Cartesian product of the two sets

$$X = \{1, 2, 3, \ldots 9, 10\}$$

and

$$Y = \{20, 21, 22, \ldots 29, 30\}$$

and Figure 39 : 13(*b*) shows a subset of this Cartesian product, which is a relation from set X to set Y.

This relation could be described in words as '*is a factor of*'. The pair (x, y) belongs to the relation if x is a factor of y. Some other ways of illustrating this relation are given in Figure 39 : 14.

The sets X and Y which are connected by a relation need not be sets of numbers. Figure 39 : 15 shows the relation 'has his birthday in the month' from a set of children to the set of months in the year.

Every relation is from some *starting set X* to some *finishing set Y*. These two sets may in fact be the same set, as in Figure 39 : 16, where their relation 'was the father of' has the set of Tudor kings and queens as both its starting and finishing set. The starting set may, however, have some members, such as Mary among the Tudors, which are not first members of pairs; the finishing set may likewise have members, such as Henry VII, which are not second members of pairs. The set of *actual* first members of the ordered pairs of the relation is called the *domain* of the relation, and the set of

The relation 'is a factor of'

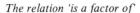

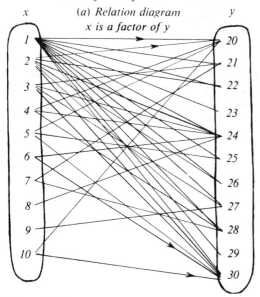

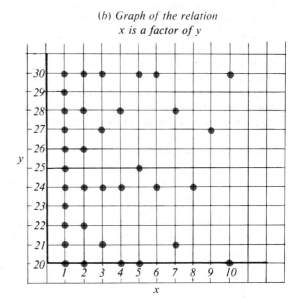

Figure 39 : 14

The relation 'has his birthday in the month'

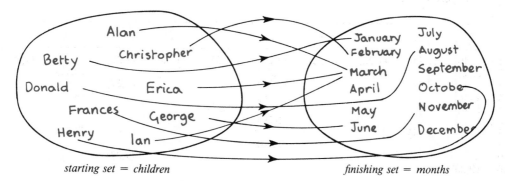

starting set = children   finishing set = months

Figure 39 : 15

The relation 'was the father of' on the Tudor Kings and Queens

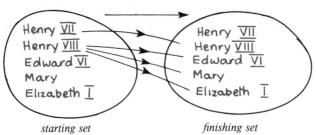

starting set finishing set

Figure 39 : 16

Domain and range of 'was the father of' on the set of Tudors

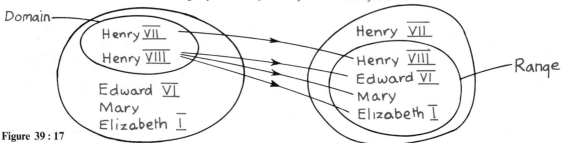

Figure 39 : 17

actual second members is the *range* of the relation (Figure 39 : 17).

From Figure 39 : 18 we see that altering the domain of a relation can make a considerable

difference to its appearance. The actual domain of a relation is usually more important than a starting set, some of whose members may play no part in the relation.

The relation 'the square of x is y'

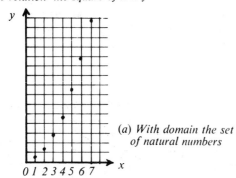

(a) With domain the set of natural numbers

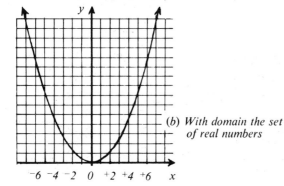

(b) With domain the set of real numbers

Figure 39 : 18

(a) The relation 'was the father of' on the Tudors

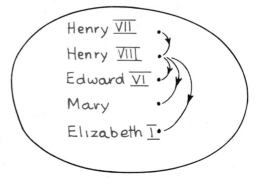

(b) The relation 'is older than' on a set of children

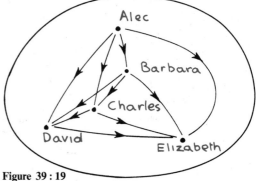

Figure 39 : 19

If the starting set and the finishing set of a relation are the same, it may be possible to draw a diagram of the relation without drawing the same set twice. Figure 39 : 19 shows two such diagrams.

THE IMPORTANCE OF THE IDEA OF A RELATION

As we look over the topics which have been discussed earlier in this book, it will be seen that the idea of a relation provides a common structure underlying many of the topics.

In the early development from sets to number, the relation of *one-to-one correspondence* between two sets is fundamental to the development of cardinal number (*see pages 54–55*) (Figure 39 : 20(*a*)). Ordinal number grows from the operation of putting the members of a set into an order (*see pages 92–94*). Order is a relation from the set to itself. If four children stand in a line in the order Alan, Betty, Carol, Donald, then Alan comes before Betty, Carol and Donald, Betty comes before Carol and Donald, and Carol comes before Donald. Donald does not come before anybody (Figure 39 : 20(*b*)). That is, ordinal number depends on the relation 'comes before', or its inverse, 'follows'.

Ordering of objects according to their length or their mass depends on the relations 'is longer than' or 'is heavier than'.

When the operations of addition, subtraction, multiplication and division are performed on pairs of numbers, these operations can also be thought of as relations. The starting set of the relation of subtraction is the set of ordered pairs of numbers, and the finishing set is the set of numbers (Figure 39 : 20(*c*)). When children take a traffic census, they

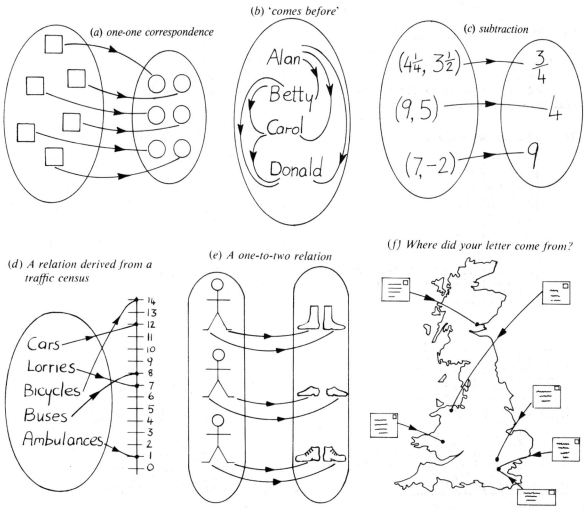

(a) one-one correspondence

(b) 'comes before'

(c) subtraction

(d) A relation derived from a traffic census

(e) A one-to-two relation

(f) Where did your letter come from?

Figure 39 : 20

(a) *day of week on which birthday falls this year*

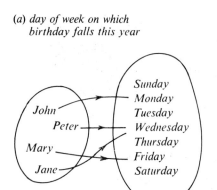

(b) *square*

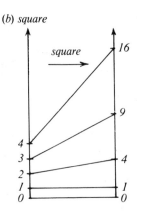

(c) *average*

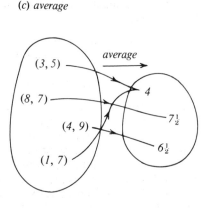

Figure 39 : 21

set up a relation from the set of types of vehicle to the set of natural numbers (Figure 39 : 20(d)). *One-to-many* relations like the ones in Figure 39 : 20(e) lead to multiplication, and in reverse, many-to-one relations produce division.

Children will compare these numerical relations to such non-numerical relations as 'is the sister of', 'lives in the same road as', 'is the teacher of', or the relation of a letter to the distance it has travelled or the place it came from (Figure 39 : 20(f)).

The examples of relations which we have so far taken have not been drawn from the spatial side of mathematics. Two particular types of relation, however, underlie most of the children's geometrical work, as well as emerging again and again throughout mathematics. These are *functions* or *mappings* and *equivalence relations*.

FUNCTIONS OR MAPPINGS

Among the many relations we have described, there are some which have the property that

corresponding to each member of the domain there is exactly one member of the range. That is, only one arrow leaves each member of the domain. These relations are called *functions* or *mappings*. They are rather simpler than other relations, since there is never a choice of routes from any member of the domain. Some functions are shown in Figure 39 : 21, and it will be recognised that, among the relations shown in Figure 39 : 20, (a), (c), (d) and (f) are functions. We see that functions are one-to-one or many-to-one relations.

Almost all the graphs which children draw are graphs of functions, for, corresponding to any value or number along the horizontal axis, there is just one value which is plotted on the vertical axis. The birthday graph (Figure 39 : 22(a)) is a graph of a function from the set of months in the year to the set of numbers. The graph of any multiplication table is also the graph of a function, as in Figure 39 : 22(b), where a number such as ($^+$3) is mapped by the 'ten times' function on to the number ($^+$30). A general number x is mapped by the 'ten times' function on to $10x$. We write $x \rightarrow 10x$.

(a) *The function*
'The number of children whose birthdays fall in the month ——— *is* ———'

(b) *The 'ten times' function,* $x \rightarrow 10x$

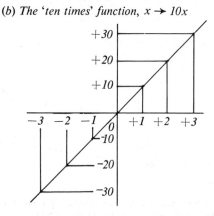

Figure 39 : 22

Many other simple relations are functions. Examples are

{children in the school} →
              {mothers of children in the school},
{children in the school} →
              {classes to which they belong}

In all maps and pictures, each point in the real world is mapped on to a single point of the map or picture. Usually several points of the real world are mapped on to the same point of the map, as, for instance, a town will be represented by a point on a map. All these mappings are many-to-one correspondences or functions. A photograph in which the camera has moved and created a blur represents a relation but not a function from the world to the photograph, since any point in the real world is represented by several points in the photograph.

All the transformations which we perform in geometry are mappings or functions.[5] When children make a repeating pattern by sliding one unit of the pattern along to make the next unit, they are mapping all the points of one pattern unit on to corresponding points of the next pattern unit (Figure 39 : 23). This mapping is a *translation*. It has the properties that every shape is mapped on to a congruent shape, and that every line in the shape is parallel to the line which is its map.

Other mappings which children use in making patterns are *rotation* and *reflection*. When a shape is rotated about a centre, every point of the shape is mapped on to a different point, except the centre of rotation, which is mapped on to itself (Figure 39 : 24). The centre of rotation is a fixed point of the mapping. Children may ask whether it is possible to have a mapping with more than one fixed point, and they will explore *reflection, enlargement, shear* and *rotation about a line in three dimensions* to see whether they have fixed points.

Reflection (in two dimensions) is a very simple mapping in which every point on the axis of

The mapping of translation

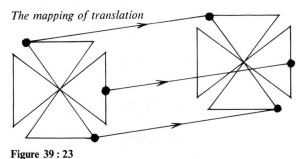

Figure 39 : 23

[5]The word mapping is more commonly used in spatial contexts, and function in numerical contexts.

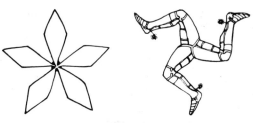

Figure 39 : 24

The mapping of reflections in a line

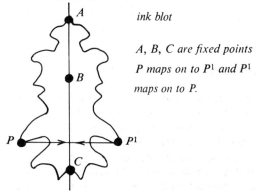

ink blot

A, B, C are fixed points
P maps on to P¹ and P¹
maps on to P.

Figure 39 : 25

reflection is a fixed point, and every other point is mapped on to a point equidistant from the axis and on the other side of the axis of reflection (Figure 39 : 25).

EQUIVALENCE RELATIONS

Another type of relation which occurs frequently in mathematics in the primary school and in everyday life is the *equivalence relation*. Some examples of equivalence relations which children deal with are

'goes to the same school as',
'lives in the same house as',
'belongs to the same family as',
'is the same height as',
'is of the same nationality as'

These are all equivalence relations concerning sets of people. Some more conventionally mathematical equivalence relations are

'is just the same shape as', for shapes,
'is parallel to', for lines,
'leaves the same remainder when divided by 2 as', for natural numbers,
'is equivalent to', for fractions,
'can be put into one-to-one correspondence with', for sets.

Clearly a great variety of apparently rather dissimilar situations can be thought of as containing

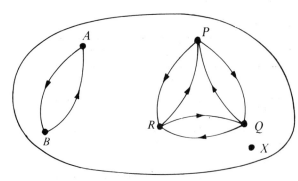

Figure 39 : 26

equivalence relations. We look for the common element in all these situations.

First, an equivalence relation is a relation in which the starting set and the finishing set are the same. The relation 'goes to the same school as' has the set of children who go to school as both its starting set and finishing set. It can therefore be represented by the type of relation diagram shown in Figure 39 : 19, where none of the arrows leaves the starting set. Figure 39 : 26 shows the relation 'goes to the same school as' for a set of children who travel to school on the same bus. A pair of children (A, B) belong to this relation if *A goes to the same school as B.* clearly, if A goes to the same school as B, then B goes to the same school as A. The ordered pairs (A, B) and (B, A) both belong to the relation. If *whenever* a pair (x, y) belongs to a relation, the pair (y, x) also belongs to it, we say that the relation is *symmetric*, (Figure 39 : 27(a)).

Also, among the trio of children P, Q and R, if P goes to the same school as Q and Q goes to the same school as R, then certainly P goes to the same school as R. The relation is *transitive.* A relation is said to be transitive if *whenever* the pairs (x, y) and (y, z) belong to the relation, the pair (x, z) *also* belongs to the relation (Figure 39 : 27(b)).

Child X is the only boy from his school who travels on this bus. He does, however, belong to a pair in the relation. He goes to the same school as himself! X goes to the same school as X, so the pair (X, X) belongs to the relation. We say that a relation is *reflexive* if *all* pairs of the form (x, x) belong to it (Figure 39 : 27(c)).

In Figure 39 : 27(d), arrows have been added to the diagram of Figure 39 : 26 to show that this relation is reflexive as well as symmetric and transitive. If a relation is reflexive, symmetric and transitive it is called an *equivalence relation.* This idea is useful because the three conditions of reflexivity, symmetry and transitivity together put the members of the domain into closed subsets in which all the members of a subset are related to each other, but not to anything outside that subset. In the case we have discussed, the subsets are the sets of children who go to the same school. The children at any one school are all related to one another and to themselves in this way, but not to the children who go to another school. Figure 39 : 28 tabulates a number of equivalence relations, the domain of each relation, and the subsets or *equivalence classes* into which the domain is partitioned.

Symmetric, transitive and reflexive relations

(a) symmetric

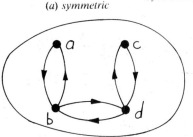

symmetric, but not transitive or reflexive

(b) transitive

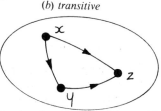

This relation on the set {x, y, z} is transitive but not symmetric or reflexive.

(c) reflexive

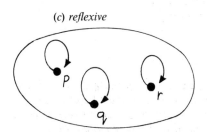

(d) reflexive, symmetric and transitive relation

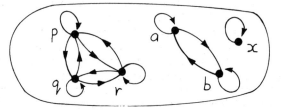

Figure 39 : 27

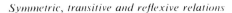

Some equivalence relations

Domain	Equivalence relation	Equivalence classes in the domain
{ Children over 5 }	'goes to the same school as'	schools
{ People }	'belongs to the same family as'	families
{ People }	'is of the same nationality as'	nations
{ Polygons }	'has the same number of sides as'	triangles, quadrilaterals, pentagons, hexagons, ...etc.
{ Natural Numbers }	'leaves the same remainder on division by 2 as'	odd numbers even numbers
{ Fractions }	'corresponds to the same point on the number line as'	sets of equivalent fractions or rational numbers
{ Sets }	'can be put into one—one correspondence with'	sets having the same cardinal number
{ Lines }	'is parallel to'	sets of parallel lines, that is, lines in the same direction

Figure 39 : 28

Clearly, whenever children do any partitioning of a set into subsets, they are using an equivalence relation, which may only be vaguely grasped, but is certainly there. Things go into the same subset because they 'have the same colour as', or 'are the same shape as', or 'are made of the same material as' other things.

MAPPINGS AND OPERATIONS

We have seen that the operations of arithmetic can also be regarded as examples of relations. These relations are mappings or functions. In an arithmetical operation such as addition or subtraction, we take *two* members of a set of numbers, perform the operation, and we may then arrive at a member of the same or another set of numbers. In Figure 39 : 29 are shown all the possible addition operations performed on the set of numbers $A = \{1, 2, 3, 4\}$. The domain of this mapping is the set of all possible ordered pairs of numbers chosen from the set A. That is, the domain is the set $A \times A$. The range of the mapping is the set $\{2, 3, 4, 5, 6, 7, 8\}$. Earlier, this situation was described by saying that the set $\{1, 2, 3, 4\}$ was not closed for addition. For a set of numbers X to be closed for an operation, we now see that if the

The addition mapping on the set $\{1, 2, 3, 4\}$

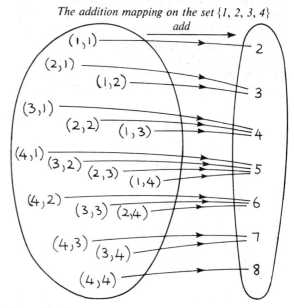

Figure 39 : 29

operation is regarded as a mapping of $X \times X$ into some finishing set Y, then Y must be the same set as X. Figure 39 : 30 shows one of the rare cases in which a *finite* set of numbers is closed for an arithmetical operation.

The multiplication mapping on the set {0,1}

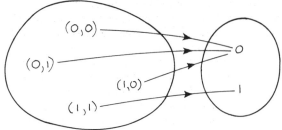

Figure 39 : 30

GROUPS

In earlier chapters we have seen how important is the property of closure for an operation in the growth of the number system of mathematics. The set of natural numbers is closed for addition and multiplication, but not for subtraction or division (*see page 162*). The set of positive, negative and zero integers (*see pages 171–173*) is closed not only for addition and multiplication but also for subtraction. It is not, however, closed for division (*see pages 415–416*). The set of directed rational numbers (*see page 416*), however, is as near to being a completely closed set of numbers for the four arithmetical operations as it is possible to obtain. It is closed for addition, subtraction, multiplication, and for all divisions except division by zero.

Children may enjoy, as a curiosity, the *clock arithmetics* or *modular arithmetics*, some of which have similar properties of closure for the four

arithmetical operations with the more familiar set of directed rational numbers, but which can be very easily handled, as, unlike the arithmetic of ordinary numbers, a clock arithmetic only uses a finite set of numbers.

We consider the ordinary clock-face with its hour hand, and perform addition and subtraction of hours in the day. The time 3 hours after 8 o'clock is 11 o'clock, so we say $8 + 3 = 11$. The time 7 hours after 8 o'clock is 3 o'clock, so we say $8 + 7 = 3$. By this method, any two clock numbers can be added, or similarly subtracted. For example, 11 hours before 8 o'clock it was 9 o'clock, so $8 - 11 = 9$. This is the inverse operation of $9 + 11 = 8$. Hence a complete addition table can be made for the clock, and can also be use for doing any clock subtraction (Figure 39 : 31).

The set of numbers {1, 2, 3, ... 11, 12}, as used on the clock, shares many of the properties of the integers. In particular, 12 is the identity for addition, as for instance $12 + 8 = 8$, $12 + 11 = 11$, and so on. Also, every equation such as $8 + \boxed{x} = 3$ has a solution, and so every subtraction can be performed. Negative numbers are not needed in order to make subtraction possible. The clock arithmetic is closed for subtraction.

Multiplication can also be performed on the clock. Since for instance $8 + 8 = 4$, we can write $2 \times 8 = 4$. This leads to the multiplication table shown in Figure 39 : 32.

We see that a variety of situations occur in division. To find $11 \div 7$, the equation $7 \times \boxed{x} = 11$ must be solved. Reading along the seventh row of the table, $x = 5$, and so $11 \div 7 = 5$. However, $11 \div 8$

Addition and subtraction on the clock

(a)

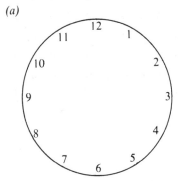

Since 8+7=3. it follows that 3—7=8. The set of clock numbers is closed for addition and subtraction.

Figure 39 : 31

(b)

+	1	2	3	4	5	6	7	8	9	10	11	12
1	2	3	4	5	6	7	8	9	10	11	12	1
2	3	4	5	6	7	8	9	10	11	12	1	2
3	4	5	6	7	8	9	10	11	12	1	2	3
4	5	6	7	8	9	10	11	12	1	2	3	4
5	6	7	8	9	10	11	12	1	2	3	4	5
6	7	8	9	10	11	12	1	2	3	4	5	6
7	8	9	10	11	12	1	2	3	4	5	6	7
8	9	10	11	12	1	2	3	4	5	6	7	8
9	10	11	12	1	2	3	4	5	6	7	8	9
10	11	12	1	2	3	4	5	6	7	8	9	10
11	12	1	2	3	4	5	6	7	8	9	10	11
12	1	2	3	4	5	6	7	8	9	10	11	12

The clock multiplication table

×	1	2	3	4	5	6	7	8	9	10	11	12
1	1	2	3	4	5	6	7	8	9	10	11	12
2	2	4	6	8	10	12	2	4	6	8	10	12
3	3	6	9	12	3	6	9	12	3	6	9	12
4	4	8	12	4	8	12	4	8	12	4	8	12
5	5	10	3	8	1	6	11	4	9	2	7	12
6	6	12	6	12	6	12	6	12	6	12	6	12
7	7	2	9	4	11	6	1	8	3	10	5	12
8	8	4	12	8	4	12	8	4	12	8	4	12
9	9	6	3	12	9	6	3	12	9	6	3	12
10	10	8	6	4	2	12	10	8	6	4	2	12
11	11	10	9	8	7	6	5	4	3	2	1	12
12	12	12	12	12	12	12	12	12	12	12	12	12

Figure 39 : 32

does not exist, as the equation $8 \times \boxed{x} = 11$ has no solution in the table. One the other hand, $12 \div 8$ is equal to 3 or 6 or 9 or 12, since $8 \times 3 = 12$, $8 \times 6 = 12$, $8 \times 9 = 12$ and $8 \times 12 = 12$. The clock arithmetic is certainly not closed for division.

Children who are interested in looking for number patterns will enjoy making up a variety of clock arithmetics, by imagining clock-faces in which the hour hand makes a complete turn not every twelve hours, but say every ten hours or every three hours. The behaviour of these clocks is shown in Figure 39 : 33, together with an important variation in the clock-face which will now be described.

In the arithmetic of the twelve-hour clock-face, the number 12 plays exactly the same part as 0 plays in the arithmetic of integers; for instance, $12 + 8 = 8$ (clock arithmetic) but $0 + 8 = 8$ (arithmetic of integers); and $12 \times 8 = 12$ (clock arithmetic) whereas $0 \times 8 = 0$ (arithmetic of integers). The parallel between clock arithmetic and ordinary arithmetic is considerably strengthened by re-labelling the 12 of the twelve-hour clock-face 0. Similarly, on a ten-hour clock-face, 10 can be re-labelled 0, and on a three-hour clock-face 3 can be re-labelled 0 (Figure 39 : 33).

The reader will notice that the arithmetic of the ten-hour clock-face is also found in the operation of the digit of a car odometer. Similarly, the arithmetic of the three-hour clock-face is the arithmetic of one column only of the integers written to base three.

The arithmetic of a clock is known as *modular*

The ten-hour and three-hour clocks

(a) The ten-hour clock

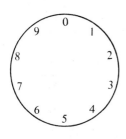

+	0	1	2	3	4	5	6	7	8	9
0	0	1	2	3	4	5	6	7	8	9
1	1	2	3	4	5	6	7	8	9	0
2	2	3	4	5	6	7	8	9	0	1
3	3	4	5	6	7	8	9	0	1	2
4	4	5	6	7	8	9	0	1	2	3
5	5	6	7	8	9	0	1	2	3	4
6	6	7	8	9	0	1	2	3	4	5
7	7	8	9	0	1	2	3	4	5	6
8	8	9	0	1	2	3	4	5	6	7
9	9	0	1	2	3	4	5	6	7	8

×	0	1	2	3	4	5	6	7	8	9
0	0	0	0	0	0	0	0	0	0	0
1	0	1	2	3	4	5	6	7	8	9
2	0	2	4	6	8	0	2	4	6	8
3	0	3	6	9	2	5	8	1	4	7
4	0	4	8	2	6	0	4	8	2	6
5	0	5	0	5	0	5	0	5	0	5
6	0	6	2	8	4	0	6	2	8	4
7	0	7	4	1	8	5	2	9	6	3
8	0	8	6	4	2	0	8	6	4	2
9	0	9	8	7	6	5	4	3	2	1

(b) The three-hour clock

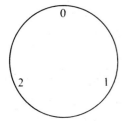

+	0	1	2
0	0	1	2
1	1	2	0
2	2	0	1

×	0	1	2
0	0	0	0
1	0	1	2
2	0	2	1

Figure 39 : 33

arithmetic, whose modulus is the number of hours on the clock. For example, the arithmetic of the three-hour clock is *arithmetic modulo three*. If the reader experiments with multiplication and division in different modular arithmetics, it will be found that division contains fewer irregularities if the modulus is a prime number than otherwise. If zero is omitted from the set of numbers considered, a prime modular arithmetic is closed for division.

All the modular arithmetics are 'better behaved', in the sense that there are fewer irregularities, for addition and subtraction than there are for multiplication and division. The 'well-behaved' parts of modular arithmetic, together with sets of numbers such as the integers and the rationals which are closed for an arithmetical operation and for its inverse operation, all these form examples of a fundamental mathematical structure called a *group*.

Group do not appear only in arithmetic, but they also underlie the transformations of a plane or of space which form the basis of much geometry. Piaget also finds the structure of a group in the type of thinking which is characteristic of the adolescent and adult stage of formal operations.

A *group* is a set S, which may be a set of numbers or of other things such as geometrical transformations, together with an operation mapping $S \times S$ into S, such that the operations is 'well-behaved' and can be performed with complete freedom. The requirements for complete freedom in performing the operation are stated below.[6] The sign ∗ is used to denote an operation which may be addition or multiplication of numbers, or the combination of two transformations, or some other operation.[7]

A set S which has the four properties stated below is a *group*:[8]

1 Closure
The set must be closed for the operation; that is, the combination of any pair of members of the set

S must also be a member of the set.

2 The associative law
For any members a, b and c of the set S
$$(a*b)*c = a*(b*c).$$

3 The identity for the operation
There is a member, say i, of the set S which is an identity for the operation; that is, i is such that
$$a*i = i*a = a$$
for any member a of the set S.

4 The inverse operation
The inverse of the operation can always be performed; that is, every equation of the form $b * \boxed{x} = a$ has a single solution belonging to the set S.

It is easy for the reader to check that the set of directed rational numbers form a group for the operation of addition. If page 416 is compared with the definition of a group, replacing + by ∗ and 'directed rational number' by 'member of the set S', it will be seen that all the requirements for a group are satisfied by the directed rational numbers of the operation of addition. Other groups of numbers which we have met in this book are tabulated in Figure 39 : 34.

Some groups of numbers

Set	Operation
Integers	Addition
Signless rational numbers without zero	Multiplication
Directed rational numbers	Addition
Directed rational numbers without zero	Multiplication
Arithmetic of any clock	Addition
Arithmetic of a clock of prime modulus	Multiplication

Figure 39 : 34

---

[6]This is not a minimum set of requirements. The reader may realise that the third requirements is a special case of the fourth.

[7]An example of a similar set of laws, not quite the same as those for a group, but which applies to a set neither of numbers nor transformations is given by Piaget's statement of a child's ability to combine logical operations at the stage of concrete operations (*see pages 48–51*).

[8]These laws should be compared with the laws of behaviour of the natural numbers, signless rationals, integers and directed rationals stated on pages 228, 398, 407.

Children of primary school age should not be expected to appreciate the abstract idea of a group. In order for this idea to be meaningful, examples of structures which are in fact groups must be well known, and children must have reached a stage where they can appreciate the underlying similarity of a variety of apparently different structures which are themselves abstract. Clearly, a majority of children do not reach this stage until fairly late in the secondary school. If, however, teachers are aware of the underlying structure, and know that the children will later study this structure, they will be able to handle the sets of numbers which children are using in a way which is helpful for later work. For instance, some upper juniors may well be able to understand, particularly by using clock arithmetics, what the closure of a set of numbers for an operation means. They may also see the likeness between the role of 0 in addition and of 1 in multiplication.

It is also desirable that teachers should not, when using mathematical language, use *group* as a synonym for *set*. In colloquial language, 'a group of children', is a meaningful phrase. Mathematically, a group is a *set with an operation* which combines pairs of members of the set, and which obeys the laws stated earlier. Hence, a group is a much more complicated structure than a set, and a set of children does not have the structure of a group.

GROUPS OF TRANSFORMATIONS

We said earlier that not only can numbers form groups, but that there also exist groups of transformations which underlie a good deal of geometrical work. A simple example of a geometrical transformation is a *translation*. A two-dimensional shape is translated in its plane when it is slid along without rotation (Figure 39 : 35). Every point of the shape undergoes an equal parallel movement, and the movement of each point can be represented by a vector. All these vectors are parallel and of the same length. The whole translation can therefore be described by a single vector, which shows what happens to *any* point when it is translated.

It is very easy to see that vectors form a group

The vector of a translation

(a)

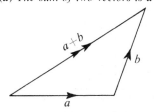

(b)

Every point of the shape makes an equal parallel movement.

Figure 39 : 35

The vector of the translation. If applied to any point of the shape, it translates the point to its new position.

The group structure of vector addition

(a) *The sum of two vectors is a vector*   (b) *Vector addition is associative*

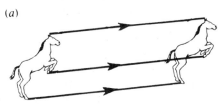

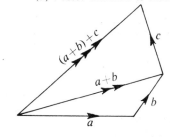

$(a+b)+c=a+(b+c)$

(c) *The zero vector*

For any vector a, $a+O=a$

Figure 39 : 36

(d) *The equation $a+x=b$ always has a solution.*

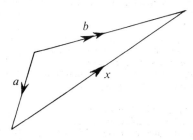

The group structure of translations

(a) *The combination of two translations is a translation*

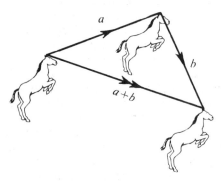

(b) *Translation is an associative operation*

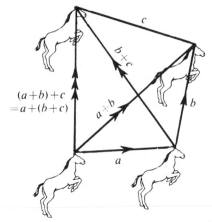

$(a+b)+c$
$=a+(b+c)$

(c) *The zero translation (no motion)*

(d) *Equations can be solved: $a+x=b$*

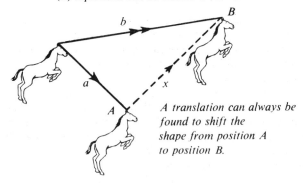

A translation can always be found to shift the shape from position A to position B.

Figure 39 : 37

for the operation of *vector addition* or of following one movement by another. The laws which vectors obey were described in Chapters 14 and 34. Figure 39 : 36 recalls these properties of vectors and shows that they form a group for the operation of vector addition.

As vectors form a group for the operation of addition or of following one vector by another, it is natural to say that the *translations* which these vectors represent form a group for the operation of *following one translation by another*. It is clear that the movements of one translation followed by another translation could be effected by a single translation (Figure 39 : 37 (a)), and that similarly the other group properties are true of translation (Figure 39 : 37).

The other sets of transformations which we have used can be studied in the same way. It will be found, for example, that reflections do not form a group, because the combination of two reflections is not a reflection, but a translation or a rotation. Thus the set of reflections is not closed for the operation of combination. A large part of geometry

may be unified at the secondary school age by the study of groups of transformations.[9]

THE DEVELOPMENT OF FORMAL OPERATIONS

In this chapter we have seen a change in the type of thinking which is necessary for the understanding of the mathematical structures used. These structures are more abstract than earlier ones. Previously, we have abstracted ideas such as 'natural number', 'triangle', or 'multiplication' from direct experiences of the physical world. Now we are beginning to generalise from these abstractions, to see that a set may be a set of things of any sort, but that all sets behave in similar ways, to find that relations of very different sorts may have a property in common, and that arithmetical operations are examples drawn from a wider set of operations. Children will only be able to handle this later stage in abstraction when they have moved out of the

[9]See, for example, Max Jeger, *Transformation Geometry*.

stage of concrete operations into the formal operations of adolescence. The progression towards more abstract thinking will happen first in situations with which children are most familiar, where they can see the common structure in different situations which they know well. When they meet something new and unfamiliar there is often a reversion to earlier ways of thinking. The movement towards more formal thinking will already be starting for some children in the middle years of schooling.

The chief characteristic of this type of adolescent and adult thinking which Piaget calls *formal thinking* or *formal operations* is that adolescents can now think out all the possibilities inherent in a situation (and often enjoy this new power). They then experiment to find out which of these possibilities actually occurs. Scientists make much use of this type of thought. When faced with a new situation, they will often make a hypothesis in the light of their experience, draw deductions from the hypothesis, and then experiment to find out whether the practical results of these deductions do in fact exist. The experiment is a verification, or otherwise, of the hypothesis which was formed before the experiment took place.

Before adolescence we do not see many examples of this characteristic adult way of thinking, although children do make hypotheses earlier. Piaget says, however, that these earlier hypotheses 'do no more than outline plans for possible actions; they do not consist of imagining what the real situation would be if this or that hypothetical condition were fulfilled, as they do in the case of the adolescent.'[10]

Some children, therefore, by the end of this stage, will need to be given work of a more challenging type, in which they can try to envisage all the possibilities inherent in a situation, begin to make deductions, and so experiment in this new way of thinking which they are beginning to reach. It must be recognised, however, that a large number of children do not begin to develop in this way until well after they reach the secondary school. They should not be expected to think in a way for which they are not yet ready, for this leads to a deadening of the simple practical mathematical thinking which they have achieved earlier.

It is interesting to notice that Piaget sees logical and mathematical laws at work in the types of combination of operations of thought which children can manage at the stage of concrete operations. These laws are parallel to the laws of closure, associativity and identity which we have

seen in the structure of a group. Piaget does not, however, find the complete group structure in thinking until the stage of formal operations. Then, the subject's ability to handle mentally the combination of logical propositions, their negations, reciprocals and correlatives is seen by Piaget to be parallel to the behaviour of a particular group containing four members.[11] An analysis of adolescent thinking is beyond the scope of this book, as is a detailed description of the more complex and abstract structures which mathematics builds on the foundations laid in the primary school.

We have tried to show that from the beginning of children's encounter with the world, they are finding examples of mathematical ideas and structures. Gradually these ideas are clarified, made more precise and more abstract, and combined with one another into more general and inclusive systems. This development is paralleled and bounded by the children's mental development and by their ability to use more abstract ideas and complex relationships. However, all mathematics starts for children from encounters with the world, and with the exploration of its behaviour. Abstraction and generalisation are late stages in a process which starts with handling, doing and talking. This process cannot be completed, and children cannot grow to full mathematical maturity, unless both aspects, the real and the abstract, have been explored and knitted into one whole.

Mathematical structures in the National Curriculum

Vectors appear at the later stages of the National Curriculum.

- understand and use vector notation, including its use in describing translations.

  (AT4: Level 8)

- understand and use the laws of addition and subtraction of vectors.

  (AT4: Level 9)

The other structures discussed in this chapter are not explicitly mentioned in the National Curriculum. However, these structures implicitly underlie all the children's work in mathematics, from their first sorting and counting activities onwards. The formal detailed study of the structures is likely to be postponed for specialist work in late adolescence.

---

[10]Inhelder and Piaget; *The Growth of Logical Thinking from Childhood to Adolescene*, page 251

[11]See Piaget, J. *Logic and Psychology* and Flavell, J. H. *The Developmental Psychology of Jean Piaget.*

SAMPLE SCHEME OF DEVELOPMENT

Sets and Structures	Numbers & Number Operations	Algebraic Ideas	Shape and Space
Making collections of objects; likeness and difference; another and another. Making sets. Matching sets Classification according to shape, colour, size, purpose, etc. Comparison of sets; arranging in rows, columns; more, fewer, as many as 1, 2, 3	Recognition of one, two, none, more, many, few, some, all Recognition of three, four. Ordering one to four Matching number names 1 to 4. Ordinal numbers first to fourth 3	Sequences, repeating patterns 2, 3	Spatial 'play'; building with 3-D shapes; cubes, cuboids, Poleidoblocs, et[c] Patterns with tiles. Rectangles, triangles, squares, discs. Free construction Names of shapes; classification. Observatio[n] of natural and man-mad[e] shapes 4,
One-to-one correspondence. Equivalence of sets. The number property of sets. The empty set Classification by two properties, AND, OR, NOT Partition and combination of sets. Intersection of sets. Multiplication of sets. Sets of numbers 4	The sequence of number names. Zero as the starting point. Numbers 5 to 10, 11 to 20. Ten as the counting set Operations of addition and subtraction using coins, cubes, spoonfuls, lengths etc. Addition patterns Extending the range of numbers to 100 Introduction of the electronic calculator 6, 8, 9	Making a sequence of sets 4	Symmetry through folding. Horizontal, vertical, sloping. The ide[a] of an angle; rotation. Logo Translation, reflection, rotation. Fractions of a revolution 5, 11, 1
Transformation of a set of numbers by adding or subtracting a number from each Number notation; grouping 6, 8	Mental and written procedures for addition and subtraction. The commutative law for addition Second grouping; square layers. Coinage; hundreds. Extension to larger numbers First use of decimal fractions Use of the calculator 9, 14	Exploring and using number patterns in addition and subtraction facts to 10 Understand the use of a symbol to stand for an unknown number 6, 9, 11	Position on a line. Properties of disc and circle. Pattern making with bas[ic] shapes and transformations Practical approach to enlargement and shear

Numbers in the sections refer to relevant chapters

Measures	Handling Data	Movement and Mechanisms
Pouring fluids, sand, etc. Invariance of quantity under change of shape	Sort a set of objects, describing the criteria used	Children arranging themselves in rows, columns, rings.
Containers of different shapes with same quantity	Representative and symbolic drawings	Drawing straight lines and curves in pictures showing movement. Constancy of object when moving
Use of words; big, little, long, short, heavy, light, slow, fast, tall	The sorting tree	Turning left and right. Using seesaw, swing, mass handling on string
Matching and ordering quantities; length, capacity, weight	4	
2, 5, 7		1, 5

Using a small quantity repeatedly to match a larger quantity	Recording with diagrams	Balance bar; experiments in balancing different masses
Comparison of two lengths. Comparison of two masses on balance bar or spring	Venn diagrams; Carroll diagrams	The lever. The spring and the Jack-in-the-box; stretch and compression
Graduated strip. Informal units; handspans, longer, heavier	3, 4, 21	Compasses for drawing a circle, the wheel; rolling a cylinder
Pendulum; slower, faster		Movements on the number line
Recognising time on a clockface		10, 13
5, 7		

Conventional units of measure for length, mass, capacity. Use of tape-measure, metre rod, trundle wheel. Distances. Spoonfuls, pints, litres	Recognise possible outcomes of random events	Wheel and axle. Pulley; gear; pistons and pumps; use of a cylinder
Flow-charts; clock-face; digital watch, sundial, pendulum	Interpret relevant data which has been collected	Spring, screw. Use of the pendulum
Addition and subtraction of money and 2-unit measures. Thermometer reading	7, 11, 17, 20, 21, 28	Linkages
		Vectors
7		10, 13, 14

B The Middle Years

Sets and Structures	Numbers & Number Operations	Algebraic Ideas	Shape and Space
Number sequences; iteration Open sentences 14, 17	Characteristic patterns of numbers shown in shapes and arrangements Thousands, thousandths Iteration of the counting set 17, 18	Develop strategies to perform mental calculations using number patterns and equivalent forms of 2-digit numbers 9	Folding rectangles, squares, triangles, circles to show ½, ¼, ⅓, etc. Building with cubes and cuboids to show 1000 cube and ¹⁄₁₀₀₀ 16, 18
The commutative law for multiplication Notation in various bases Place value; index notation 17, 18	The multiplication tables and their patterns; arrangements of products in rectangular arrays Expressing numbers in other bases 17, 18	Use doubling and halfing, addition and subtraction, FORWARD and BACKWARD (in Logo), etc. as inverse operations Simple function machines Number sequences, open sentences 9, 11, 14	Building with cubes in various bases, e.g. two and five 18
The two-number structure for fractions; notation The distributive law 18, 19	Sharing and grouping; division. Division as the inverse of multiplication and as a fraction; ratio Multiplication of larger numbers. Written division outside the tables Use of the calculator 17, 19	Create shapes using turtle geometry in an appropriate computer language Laws of Arithmetic for natural numbers 11, 14, 19	First ideas of scale; accuracy. The first map. Representative fraction The use of drawing instruments Parallel lines Enlargement and reduction of patterns 23
The number line; isomorphism Zero; special properties of 0 and 1 Fractions and directed numbers Fractions as part of a divisible unit; and as division and multiplication 14, 24	Fractions; decimal notation for fractions. Multiplication and division of decimals Division aspect of fractions The calculator and estimations Division by powers of ten Addition and subtraction of directed numbers 14, 15, 24, 27	Notation for directed numbers Vectors 14, 15	The idea of an angle; rotation Tessellations; regular polygons Polyhedra; regular solids. Euler's formula Spheres, cylinders, cones 12, 25

Numbers in the sections refer to relevant chapters

Measures	Handling Data	Movement and Mechanisms
Measuring perimeters; fractions, e.g. ½ metre, ¼ kg, Tenths and metric system. Main units, kg and g; km, m, cm	Construct and interpret bar charts, pictograms, etc. Simple databases	Forces; friction; mass and weight Falling bodies
16	3, 4, 6, 9, 11, 15	31
Addition and subtraction of heights, distances, masses, capacity, temperature in 2-unit measures and decimals Time and the 24-hour clock	Place events in order of 'likeliness' and use appropriate words to identify the choice Understand the idea of 'evens'	Momentum
16	20	31
Making maps from necessary measurements Enlarging patterns	Construct a survey	Gear ratios Gear wheels and screws
23	4, 6	35
asurement of angles periences of covering a surface. ndard units of area; cm², hectare. a of a rectangle and related shapes. faces of 3-D shapes. ernal volumes of hollow shapes. ume of rectangular blocks. ation of surface area to volume and mass to volume	Card database	Epicycloids and hypocycloids
12, 29, 30	32	38

C The Later Years

Sets and Structures	Numbers & Number Operations	Algebraic Ideas	Shape and Space
Calculation of average; mean, median; spread Tabulation of pairs Cartesian product Constant ratio 21, 39	Calculator for average by division of total. Guessed average, excess and defect; true average Factors, multiples, primes. Composite numbers. Square, rectangular, triangular numbers. Magic squares 21, 22	Conventions of co-ordinate representation of points in the first quadrant 21	Patterns of shapes and patterns in numbers Cubes, tetrahedra, pyramids built up with shapes 21
Commutative law for multiplication of fractions and the distributive law Approximations; accuracy Systematization of operations on numbers and measures 32	Fractions; equivalence, addition, subtraction. Reciprocals. Multiplication of fractions; distributive law. Division as multiplication by the reciprocal Percentages; comparisons 32	Follow instruction to generate a sequence Understand and use co-ordinates in all four quadrants 21, 28	The ratio of lengths. Fractions as ratios, enlargements, $\sqrt{2}$ 35, 37
Signless rational numbers and directed numbers Structures of directed numbers 33	Multiplication of directed numbers. Negative indices Using a computer 11, 28, 33	Understand and use such terms as 'prime', 'cube', 'square root' and 'cube root' Understand patterns in number through spatial arrangement Understand and use simple formulae or equations expressed in algebraic form 22, 28	Position on a line. Position in a plane given by 2 distances, or a vector, or 2 angles 3-D; longitude and line; latitude; great circles; N and S poles
Rational and irrational numbers Cartesian product; relations, their importance; mappings or functions; equivalence relations Groups, Formal operations 37, 39	Rate, ratio, inverse ratio 35	Draw and interpret simple mappings in context. Fibonacci sequence. Structures of directed numbers. Multiplication of negative numbers. Negative indices. Draw and interpret graphs of linear functions. 21, 31, 33, 35, 37	Lattice points; tessellations using two squares; Pythagoras The golden rectangle; regular pentagon; golde section Sphere, cylinder; cone and its sections; ellipse parabola, hyperbola. Cycloids, rolling wheels Wave curves, envelope: spirals 36, 37,

Numbers in the sections refer to relevant chapters

Measures	*Handling Data*	*Movement and Mechanisms*
Tabulating measurements; average and spread 21	List all the possible outcomes of an event 20	Folding and building with unit shapes
Approximation in measurement 32	Understand the probability scale from 0 to 1 Calculate and understand mean, median, mode and range of a set of results Pie charts 21, 22, 35	Records of distances run, hopped, etc. in given times Comparisons 16
Very large and very small quantities Flow charts Longitude; great circles, World time; navigation; latitude 11, 28, 33, 34	Insert and interrogate data in a computer database Construct and interpret frequency diagrams with suitable class intervals Construct and interpret conversion graphs 11, 21, 28, 32	Measuring sites for map-making involving larger units 23
Areas of similar shapes Area of a circle 36	Distinguish between theoretical and experimental probability Understand that if each of *n* events is equally likely, the probability of one occurring is *1/n* 20, 39	Immersion of solids in water. Flotation Vectors; addition and subtraction; movements Folding and knotting regular polygons; rigidity of polygons and polyhedra Distance, time and speed 12, 14, 15, 24, 25, 29, 30

INDEX